Radio Stars

io Stars

*An Illustrated Biographical
Dictionary of 953 Performers,
1920 through 1960*

by

THOMAS A. DELONG

McFarland & Company, Inc., Publishers

Jefferson, North Carolina, and London

British Library Cataloguing-in-Publication data are available

Library of Congress Cataloguing-in-Publication Data

DeLong, Thomas A.
    Radio stars : an illustrated biographical dictionary of 953
performers, 1920 through 1960 / by Thomas A. DeLong.
       p.   cm.
    Includes bibliographical references and index. ∞
    ISBN 0-7864-0149-0149-0 (library binding : 50# alk. paper)
    1. Radio broadcasters — United States — Biography — Dictionaries.
I. Title.
PN1991.4.A2D46   1996
791.44′028′092273 — dc20
[B]   96-24424
                                             CIP

Manufactured in the United States of America

McFarland & Company, Inc., Publishers
  Box 611, Jefferson, North Carolina 28640

To Ward Byron
1906 – 1996

Radio and television
writer-producer-director,
friend and mentor

Acknowledgments

Research for this volume includes some 500 interviews of broadcasters for earlier books and articles, encompassing a writing period of more than 25 years. Many performers helped specifically with biographical information and photographs, and for their contribution, I am most grateful. They are George Ansbro, Mason Adams, Arthur Anderson, Mario Braggiotti, Vanessa Brown, Jackson Beck, Tommy Bartlett, Joan Banks, Vivian Block, Conrad Binyon, Ralph Bell, Gaylord Carter, Gwen Davies, Gloria DeMarco, Jean Dickenson, Rosemary DeCamp, Larry Dobkin, Win Elliot, Herb Ellis, Florence Freeman, Barbara Fuller, Jack Grimes, Page Gilman, Art Gilmore, Paula Heminghaus, Cy Harrice, Ed Herlihy, Larry Haines, Gene Hamilton, Hildegarde, John Milton Kennedy, Joseph Kahn, Louise King, Durward Kirby, Jackie Kelt, Peg Lynch, Rita Lloyd, Peggy Joan Moylan, Jan Miner, Audrey Marsh, Shirley Mitchell, Tyler McVey, Norma Jean Nilsson, George Petrie, Genevieve Rowe, Rosa Rio, Jack Smith, Arnold Stang, Stefan Schnabel, Arthur Tracy, Les Tremayne, Sybil Trent and Miriam Wolfe.

Family, coworkers, friends and fans of various performers provided invaluable information. They are Tim Hollis and The National Lum & Abner Society, Daniel Clemson of The Mills Brothers Society, Sally Bennett and The Big Band Hall of Fame, Helen Chappell, Amy E. Jordan, George W. Engelhardt, Charles Kitchell, Charles Bulotti, Inez E. Cline, Jim Harmon, Leo Walker, Ward Bryon, Anthony Diflorio, Evelyn Kleinsorge, Burla Love, Northcutt Ely, William J. Ryan, Constance A. Gardner, Mary Anna Waterman, Marilyn Hannon, Stuart Warner, John Guedel, Charlotte P. Berch, John Rayburn, John T. Setina, Maureen T. Hillpot, Bill Szturma, Mrs. Henry Levine, Fred Edmiston, James Pegolotti, Paul Trietsch, Jr., Robert White, Bill M. F. Johnson, Wanda Gropher, Doug McClelland, Tony Toran, Michael Stevenson, Betty Cannon Renzulli, Shirley Morabito, John Matson, Sue Chadwick, Charles Higham, Ted Theodore, Peter Mintun, Charles Laughlin, Rita Morley, Jess L. Hoaglin, Celia Thomas, Doris Hewes, Rodney Steiner, Miles Kreuger, Jack French, Robert Walsh, Jay A. Fulton, Michael Fulton and Robert D. Campbell. All in all, there has been a multitude of people who acknowledged questions and inquiries, and helped fill in biographical gaps.

Scores of libraries and organizations delved into their records and archives, contributing an array of facts: Field Museum of Natural History, Chicago; University of Texas Alumni Office; Garland-Montgomery Regional Library, Hot Springs, AR; Scottsdale (AZ) Public Library; Dartmouth College Library; Case Western Reserve University; Alumni Association of The City College of New York; City of Clearwater (FL) Public Library System; Roanoke College Archives; Ithaca College Publications; Metropolitan Opera Association Archives; University of Iowa Division of Alumni Services; Phi Sigma Kappa International Headquarters, Indianapolis; Indiana University Alumni Association; Edison National Historic Site, West Orange, NJ; Howard Lanin Productions, New York; Williams College Society of Alumni; Larchmont (NY) Avenue Church; Gospel Spreading Church,

Washington, DC; Stanford University Libraries; Alumni Records, University of Wisconsin; Putnam County (NY) Historical Society; First Congregational Church, Redwood City, CA; Berkshire Athenaeum, Pittsfield, MA; Society of Alumni Records, The College of Wooster; Office of Alumni Programs, Franklin & Marshall College; Norwalk (CT) Public Library; Alumni Association, Pomona College; Museum of Broadcast Communications, Chicago; Wellesley College Alumnae Association; Alumni/Development Information Services, Ohio State University; Miriam Coffin Canaday Library, Bryan Mawr College; American Federation of Television and Radio Artists (AFTRA) Los Angeles Local; Gilbert Hart Library, Wallingford, CT; Alumni Relations, The Curtis Institute of Music; Department of Alumni Relations, Rutgers University; San Mateo (CA) Public Library; Brooks Memorial Library, Brattleboro, VT; Sunset Publishing Corporation, Menlo Park, CA; Archives Room, Harrow School, Middlesex, UK; News & Information Service, University of Wisconsin; Galesburg (IL) Public Library; The Lambs, New York; Information Center, Syracuse University; Stanford University Magazine; Atlanta-Fulton (GA) Public Library; Cherry Hill (NJ) Free Public Library; Alumni Relations Office, Northwestern University; American Federation of Musicians Local 47 and 802; University of Kansas Alumni Association; Office of Alumni Records, Princeton University; Alumni Relations, Lenoir-Rhyne College; True Light Middle School of Hong Kong; Scottsdale (AZ) Public Library; Pequot Library, Southport, CT; Fairfield (CT) Public Library; Office of Alumni Relations, Carnegie-Mellon University; Lawrence (MA) Public Library; Public Library of Charlotte & Mecklenburg County (NC); Pontotoc County (OK) Historical & Genealogic Society; Fairfield University Library; Jersey City (NJ) Public Library; College of Journalism and Mass Communication, University of Georgia; Margaret Herrick Library, Academy of Motion Pictures Arts and Sciences.

Most significantly, this biographical compilation has drawn upon the resources of outstanding archives and the expertise of those staff individuals who work diligently to document and preserve the annals and artifacts of radio. They are the Museum of Television and Radio (Ken Mueller, Brian Quinn, Jonathan Rosenthal), SPERDVAC—The Society to Preserve and Encourage Radio Drama, Variety and Comedy (Larry Gassman, Barbara Watkins), Pacific Pioneer Broadcasters (Jeanne Brown, Margo Ewing, Ron Wolfe, Martin Halperin), Broadcast Pioneers Library (Catherine Heinz, Mike Mashon), Friends of Old-Time Radio (Jay Hickerson), Museum of Broadcast Communications (Mike Cervone), and the Library of the Performing Arts at Lincoln Center.

Jeff Hearn's data searches in Washington furnished vital statistics and direction. For providing numerous illustrations, I thank Brandon Stoddard of ABC Productions and Peter Murray of Capital Cities/ABC, Inc.

And I applaud Steve Jelf for providing many vintage portraits from his extraordinary collection.

Final stages in the composition and collation of the manuscript were expedited by Elizabeth De-Long. I am specially grateful for the abiding and perspicacious contributions of my wife Katharine in the page-by-page progress of each biography.

Contents

Introduction

How many voices give "life" to radio? During a comparatively brief period of country-wide network broadcasting, an impressive array of actors, singers, commentators, comedians, announcers, emcees, newscasters, preachers and various other artists and journeymen, individually and collectively, shaped and characterized the content of the "live" airwaves. Whether a Jack Benny, an Edward R. Murrow, an Orson Welles or a Jane Froman, each gave a solid measure of his or her talent to the microphone during the period 1920 (the year Westinghouse started commercial broadcasting) to the early 1960s (when soap operas ended on radio). Comedians came chiefly from vaudeville; newscasters, mainly from print journalism. Announcers, to a degree, came from the concert hall; singers, in large numbers, from recording studios; actors, notably from stock companies, and bandleaders, often from ballrooms. Day after day, week after week, they became familiar voices and welcome guests in the homes of millions of Americans. Their number — easily 1,500 or so — entertained and informed, inspired and aroused.

As radio reached out into more and more homes, broadcasters assumed a greater and greater role in the cultural and social fabric of the land. To a lesser degree, a number influenced the economic and political currents of the country. Many contributed in ways clearly defined; others had a less certain impact. Consequently, in telling of their lives on the air, an informal history of the performing arts and programming on radio has unfolded. Has it not been said that past events can be related best through life stories and memoirs?

Because of a scholarly as well as a nostalgic interest in vintage radio — and particularly in its extant air checks and transcriptions — these broadcasters are being rediscovered and re-enjoyed, and in many instances, reappreciated. A narrative summary of their individual radio days (and nights) and accomplishments and credits within the framework of their overall career seemed overdue. This dictionary of biography seeks to fill this void and hopes to stand as a companion volume to the already published works on that era's specific radio programs and series.

A Note About Listings and Format

This compendium gathers biographies of over 950 individuals who headlined or significantly contributed to prime-time and daytime programs. Some were stars; many stood as featured players or sidekicks. Others created characters who brought the very woof and warp of radio to a listener. A few stood as radio personalities whose initial success had been achieved in fields quite removed from the microphone. While recognizing the enjoyment provided by Broadway and Hollywood actors and actresses on a recurrent basis, sports and literary figures from guest appearances, and big and less-than-big bands and their vocalists on remotes and standbys, these performers are profiled on their own if they were part of a noteworthy series, be it sustaining or commercial, summer replacement or half-season tryout. Throughout this volume, I have stressed the unusual or unique contributions to radio by an individual. Moreover, where pertinent, I have touched upon the ways radio shaped careers and achievements, and in a few cases, impacted a life apart from the microphone. A sizable number of broadcasters, of course, made a successful transition to the video screen, and I have noted their work there and in films and on stage. Nonetheless, dozens of airborne personalities ended their career in the wake of Uncle Miltie, Lucy and Howdy Doody.

Individual program credits in most instances are a representative selection of a performer's work and not inclusive. Moreover, they are only series on which a performer or personality appeared on a regular ongoing basis. The dates given do not necessarily represent a full year; they could be as brief as one day in the month of December or January. Where applicable I have included an individual's sobriquet, a catchphrase and the title of his theme song. The nature of show business has been to subtract from one's age. Where there is a discrepancy in a date of birth, I have usually opted for the earlier date, after due consideration of the reliability of a particular source. I occasionally make note of conflicting sources. The abbreviation "c" (for *circa*) is used to approximate a year. I generally abbreviate the four major networks: NBC (National Broadcasting Company), CBS (Columbia Broadcasting System), MBS (Mutual Broadcasting System), ABC (American Broadcasting Company). The Blue Network was the forerunner of ABC from 1926 to the mid–1940s.

Biography has been called "the impossible craft." In this rarely-definitive realm, dates, places and broadcast credits can be elusive. And even well-founded anecdotes, too, are sometimes fanciful and embellished. Where there are omissions and inaccuracies, I turn to the more knowledgeable reader for clarification and information.

Thomas A. DeLong
Southport, Connecticut
Summer 1996

The Performers

1. ABBOTT, Bud (comedian; b. Oct. 2, 1900, Asbury Park, NJ; d. April 24, 1974, Woodland Hills, CA). *Kate Smith Show* (1938); *Chase & Sanborn Hour* (1941–42); *Abbott & Costello Show* (1942–49).

The straight man of the classic comedy team of Abbott and Costello who lifted buffoonery to a high state in the 1940s. They attracted a mass audience for their burlesque-honed slapstick and pratfalls — routines that worked best on screen but nevertheless transferred to the air well enough for the duo to place in the upper ratings of comedy shows.

Tall and thin, Abbott was the insulting wise guy who lorded over the short, fat and inept Lou Costello. They first meshed as a team in 1931 and played touring circuits until Kate Smith's scout saw them at Loew's State in New York and invited them to a guest spot. Broadway and movies beckoned, as did radio and, later, television. Offstage, the two comics often argued, usually over inconsequential matters. However, their partnership endured until 1957. The split, however, was amicable. Abbott continued with occasional solo appearances, and after the death of Costello, revived some of the old acts on stage with Candy Candido doing the Costello role.

When Abbott and Costello first made the big time, theatre critic Brooks Atkinson welcomed the new young pair as reassurance of "the future of low comedy."

2. ACE, Goodman (comedian, writer; b. Jan. 15, 1899, Kansas City, MO; d. March 25, 1982, New York, NY).

ACE, Jane (comedienne; b. Oct. 12, 1905, Kansas City, MO; d. Nov. 11, 1974, New York, NY). *Easy Aces* (1930–45); *Jane Ace, Disc Jockey* (1951–52).

Seeking to supplement his newspaper salary in Kansas City, Goodman did extra work as *The Movie Man*, a film reviewer for KMBC. As he finished his 15 minute stint one day in 1929, he faced a frantic station manager who told him to keep talking because the performer for the next segment had not shown up. He and his wife Jane Sherwood Ace, who happened to be at the studio, ad libbed a conversation about a bridge game of the previous evening. The filler was so good

that the Aces were hired to do two programs a week and paid $40. In 1931 the show moved to Chicago for the sponsor, Lavoris mouthwash.

The CBS series was best known for the malapropisms, or "Jane-isms," Goodman wrote ("Time wounds all heels," "You get up at the crank of dawn," "He's a ragged individualist," "Home wasn't built in a day"). The carefully fashioned scripts drew appreciative reviews and audiences for 15 years. Goodman then switched to writing for the shows of others — Milton Berle, Perry Como, Danny Kaye, Tallulah Bankhead and Bob Newhart — and became the highest paid writer in early television. He also had a regular column in *The Saturday Review* for many years. In the early 1950s the Aces returned to the air in the roles of DJ (Jane) and her "permanent guest star" (Goodman).

3. ACUFF, Roy (singer [The King of Country Music]; b. Sept. 15, 1903, Maynardsville, TN; d. Nov. 23, 1992, Nashville, TN). *Grand Ole Opry* (1938–58).

A regular of the *Opry* for some 50 years, Acuff was country music's first superstar. He went on the Nashville program with his Smokey Mountain Boys in the late 1930s. The group brought down the house with his "Great Speckled Bird" and was heard for the

Roy Acuff

first time throughout the country via WSM's 50,000 watts. He had been playing fiddle and singing at a Knoxville station but the WROL transmitter range was only about 50 miles. One of the first to use a strong country voice at a mike, Acuff was backed by a traditional mountain string band. He was *Opry's* emcee along with Whitey Ford in 1945–46 and guest emcee in 1957–58.

In 1942 he formed Acuff-Rose Publishing Company to handle his own music, and it became an important promoter of country music throughout the United States. He was the first living person elected to the Country Music Hall of Fame (1962), and is recognized as a major influence and model for contemporary country singers. During breaks at the *Opry*, he entertained by doing yo-yo tricks and balancing his fiddle upright on the bridge of his nose.

4. ADAMS, Franklin Pierce (panelist; b. Nov. 15, 1881, Chicago, IL; d. March 24, 1960, New York, NY). *Information Please* (1938–48, 1950).

A panelist on the very first broadcast of *Information Please*, and continuing weekly for over a decade, F.P.A. wrote the widely enjoyed column "The Conning Tower" that ran in New York newspapers for 35 years. Adams was regarded as the father of the illustrious Round Table at the Algonquin Hotel and first encouraged Dorothy Parker, Deems Taylor, George S. Kaufman and others by publishing their work in his erudite column. Noted for his urbanity and high wit, the deadpan, innocent-sounding Adams seldom missed on any questions connected with Shakespeare.

Most of his comments were unexpected and irreverent. His biographer Sally Ashley wrote of him in 1986: "He often captured ideas nobody listening dared express, even though they agreed. His was a special kind of exhibitionism. He didn't display himself in any vulgar sense but loved to show himself as an oddity, a crochety observer and commentator." He was once described as a cigar-smoking, pool-playing little gargoyle with a long neck, big nose and bushy mustache — who had a wonderful time each week in one of quizdom's hot seats. He attempted to emcee a series of his own on the spelling and usage of words (*The Word Game*). Dead air, pauses and slurred words characterized this bland and shortlived CBS program.

Adams had quit the University of Michigan to sell insurance before he landed a job as a cub reporter in Chicago. During World War I, F.P.A. served overseas, and worked on the *Stars & Stripes*. Fond of light verse, he published several books of poetry and short prose sketches.

5. ADAMS, Mason (actor; b. Feb. 26, 1919, New York, NY). *Pepper Young's Family* (1945–59); *Road of Life* (1946–47); *Big Town* (1948–51).

Actor in one of the best scripted soaps, *Pepper Young's Family*, Adams reluctantly took over the lead

Mason Adams (courtesy of Mason Adams)

role as newspaper editor Pepper Young in 1945 and continued to the last broadcast 14 years later. At the time he had just been discharged from the Army and signed for the play *Dear Ruth* in Chicago. Radio paid more so he found a replacement for the stage role. The serial proved so popular that for a time it was broadcast twice a day on both CBS and NBC simultaneously.

Adams also picked up ongoing parts as Clifton Wadsworth on *Road of Life* and cab driver Harry the Hack on *Big Town*. Ford, US Steel and American Tobacco cast him in their dramatic presentations. His voice was heard on many commercials. He returned to the newsroom in the 1970s as managing editor Charles Hume on television's popular *Lou Grant* and enjoyed wide recognition and acclaim.

His career in radio began in the early 1940s by dint of constantly auditioning for anyone who would listen. His first professional job was in an NBC wartime drama directed by Anton Leader. He acted on stage in community theatre, college and stock. His initial Broadway show was Saroyan's *Go Away Old Man*, directed by George Abbott, with a cast that included such radio actors as Richard Widmark and Ed Begley.

"For all the years I did it, radio acting provided me with great pleasure and a comfortable living, even as it allowed me to pursue my major objective: work in the theatre," Adams has said. "To paraphrase Webster about Dartmouth: 'Radio acting is a small talent, but there are those who love it.' I was one of those. And thought it could never compare in its challenges and demands to first-rate work in theatre, film or television, its variety, spontaneity and quick-silvery quality provided those of us who were lucky enough to do it well with much joy."

6. ADAMS, William P. (actor, announcer; b. May 9, 1887, Tiffin, OH; d. Sept. 29, 1972, New York, NY). *Collier's Hour* (1927–32); *March of Time* (1931–38); *Cavalcade of America* (1935–38); *Let's Pretend* (1943–54).

Originator of characters, Uncle Henry for *Collier's Hour* and Uncle Bill for *Let's Pretend*. A legit actor, he performed *Hamlet* with John Barrymore on Broadway. His first radio role was in a Shakespearean play in 1924. Adams appeared in the first broadcast of *Uncle Tom's Cabin*, aired over WGBS, Gimbel's New York station. On Election Day 1932 he impersonated Franklin D. Roosevelt and continued that assignment often on dramatized news segments of *March of Time*, and periodically played Lincoln on *Cavalcade of America* and *Eternal Light*.

In 1943 Adams became narrator-spokesman for the Cream of Wheat–sponsored run of *Let's Pretend*. His kindly demeanor and resonant voice brought charm and believability to that series' stories (and cereal commercials). This Cincinnati College of Music graduate was at ease as an announcer on musical features (*Saturday Night Serenade*) or player on soaps (*Pepper Young's Family*). He once recalled his role as a physician on *Ma Perkins*. "When I came into the scene everybody was cured almost instantly. But this was very bad for me. It meant I worked only one or two episodes."

7. ALBANESE, Licia (singer; b. July 22, 1913, Bari, Italy). *Treasure Hour of Song* (1942–47).

Soon after joining the Met, this operatic soprano branched out into radio with a series over Mutual called *Treasure Hour of Song*. From her broadcasts of prima donna arias and current pop tunes, she developed a devoted following. The rich, polished voice of Albanese, combined with a superb technique, made her a favorite of conductors, such as Toscanini who featured her with the NBC Symphony on presentations of *La Boheme* and *La Traviata*, both in 1946 and with Jan Peerce.

She made her formal debut in the role of Madama Butterfly in Palma, Italy, in 1935 and made records of *Boheme* with Beniamino Gigli. He recommended her to Met manager Edward Johnson. Before leaving Italy she sang at the inauguration of the Vatican City radio station. From the stage of the Met, Albanese sang on a record number of Saturday afternoon broadcasts. In 1948 she starred in the opening night performance of *Otello* in the first telecast from that house. Her vocal

Licia Albanese

engagements continued into the 1980s. By then, she was teaching master classes for singers, and through her Puccini Foundation, helping in the education of young musicians.

8. ALBANI, OLGA (singer; b. Aug. 13, 1905, Barcelona, Spain; d. June 3, 1940, Tucson, AZ). *Coca-Cola Hour* (1931); *Silken Strings* (1934).

Concert-program soprano who left the air because of illness at age 30 in 1935. She studied music in Milan and New York where she won a leading role in *New Moon*. When the show closed she was signed by NBC in 1929. She substituted for Jessica Dragonette on *Cities Service Concert* during her summer breaks in 1932 and 1934, and sang with opera companies in New York and Chicago. Her recordings for Victor were chiefly popular tunes in Spanish. She did, however, wax "Why Do I Love You?" for the first multi-disc album of a Broadway musical (*Show Boat*) in 1932.

She was often billed as Countess Albani; the title came from her first marriage to Spanish Count Arturo Albani.

9. ALBERT, Eddie (actor; b. April 22, 1908, Rock Island, IL). *The Honeymooners* (1934–37); *Rain and Sunshine* (1937–38); *Eddie Albert Show* (1947, 1949–50).

Light comedy and musicals brought the amiable actor centerstage. *The Honeymooners*, a daily show for Olson Rugs at NBC, featured Eddie and Grace Bradt in vocal duets. Earlier he had figured in a song-dance-and-patter act on a Minneapolis station. Broadway leads in *Room Service* and *Brother Rat* led to dramatic nice-guy film roles in *Smash-Up* and *Carrie*. In 1942 he joined the Navy and saw action in the South Pacific. In 1949 he returned to the stage as leading man in Irving Berlin's *Miss Liberty* for 308 performances. With actress-wife Margo, they were guests on variety and dramatic programs, and headliners on the nightclub circuit.

10. ALEXANDER, A. L. (Albert) (moderator; b. April 26, 1906, Winthrop, MA; d. Feb. 24, 1967, New York, NY). *Goodwill Court/Court of Human Relations* (1933–38); *Alexander's Mediation Board* (1943–51).

Originator and moderator of a program that discussed domestic problems and their solution. Actual individuals came before his microphone with their personal troubles; about 70 percent were willing to substitute the point of view of a panel for their own judgment. The sessions began over WMCA in the early 1930s, then were aired by CBS and NBC on as many as 66 stations. Its chief sponsor was *True Story* magazine. The panel gave free advice on each show but the legal profession took issue. The New York County Lawyers Association recommended to the Appellate Court that any attorneys on the panel not give legal advice to a "publicity medium." Hence, the Court forbade lawyers airing cases over the air.

Alexander revamped his program into a Board of Arbitration for WHN in 1939, and then into a Mediation Board with a panel of educators and social workers. Mutual and Serutan picked it up.

Alexander unknowingly prepared for his broadcast career from a background as a divinity student, actor and police reporter. He became a cub announcer in 1926, doing newscasts from the city room of the New York *World*. At WMCA in 1929 he slipped a portable transmitter on his back and did *Street Forum*, a man-in-the-street remote. His *Court of Human Relations* was carried on NBC television in the 1950s where Alexander continued to possess a "propensity for slinging verbiage in large doses" as he helped settle conflicts by "complainants." In 1940 he compiled an anthology, *Poems That Touch the Heart*; it sold over 250,000 copies, chiefly to his troubled listeners.

11. ALEXANDER, Ben (actor; b. May 26, 1911, Goldfield, NV; d. July 3 (?), 1969, Hollywood, CA). *Chase & Sanborn Hour* (1940–41); *It Happened in the Service* (1942–43); *Heart's Desire* (1946–48); *The Great Gildersleeve* (1946–47); *Dragnet* (1952–57).

Actor, emcee and announcer, he had been a child star from age three when he played in a Cecil B. DeMille film. Roles in *All Quiet on the Western Front* and the Penrod and Sam series were largely forgotten when he played Bashful Ben Waterford on *The Great Gildersleeve*, or assisted on *Queen for a Day*. It took the part of rotund police officer Frank Smith on *Dragnet* to bring lasting recognition, more so when the Jack Webb series branched into television in the early 1950s.

Educated at Stanford, he pictured himself as a

Ben Alexander (courtesy of Photofest)

broadcast executive but radio acting paid much more. Nonetheless, his business pursuits made him wealthy, chiefly from investments in service stations, auto agencies and mortuaries years before Sgt. Joe Friday made him his right-hand man.

12. ALEXANDER, Jeff (conductor; b. July 2, 1910; d. Dec. 23, 1989, Whidbey Island, WA). *Amos 'n' Andy* (1943–48); *Light Up Time* (1949–50); *Tums Hollywood Theatre* (1951–52).

Well-esteemed orchestra leader and arranger, chiefly for *Amos 'n' Andy* and *Hollywood Star Playhouse*. Besides directing musicians, he led a chorus backing Gordon MacRae on *Texaco Star Theatre* in the late 1940s. A founder of the Screen Composers of America, he contributed incidental music to films and television's *Columbo* and *Wagon Train*.

13. ALEXANDER, Joan (actress); b. 1916, St. Paul, MN). *Against the Storm* (1941–42); *Bright Horizon* (1943–44); *David Harum* (1950–51).

Versatile and busy actress with roles on many soaps and thrillers. Well cast as Lois Lane on *Superman* and Della Street on *Perry Mason*, she played ongoing characters on *Lone Journey*, *Light of the World* and *This Is Nora Drake*. Alexander had reached radio in 1940 after modeling jobs and stage roles (Theatre Guild's *Merrily We Roll Along*). On her first audition, she picked up a part, then six more in a row.

She studied acting in Europe with director-coach Benno Schneider, and toured leading cities just as Hitler's troops went on the march. "I even got to Casablanca before Roosevelt and Humphrey Bogart put it on the map." During early television's attachment to panel shows, she competed on *To Tell the Truth* and *Name's the Same.*

14. ALEY, Albert (actor; b. April 25, 1919, New York, NY; d. Jan. 1, 1986, Seattle, WA). *Let's Pretend* (1934–52); *Hop Harrigan* (1944–46).

Mainstay of *Let's Pretend* where as a child actor he often played a young prince or romantic adventurer. He occasionally directed the program while still a teenager. His other CBS acting jobs included co-lead as Teddy on *Sunday Morning at Aunt Susan's.* Aley turned to script writing in the 1940s, for *Don Winslow of the Navy* and *Superstition.* He took over the acting role of wartime flyer Hop Harrigan and was made its chief writer, too. Although he continued to act into the early '50s, he considered writing as his career, and prepared scripts for *Mark Trail,* an outdoorsman saga. In 1952 he added *Tom Corbett, Space Cadet,* a series he helped to produce on both radio and TV. Eventually his credits included *Barnaby Jones, Quincy* and *Ironsides,* and Disney's *Ugly Dachshund.*

Aley's parents once owned a photography studio, and there young Albert began as a child model. His fees paid tuition at New York's Professional Children's School.

15. ALLEN, Fred (comedian; b. May 31, 1894, Cambridge, MA; d. March 17, 1956, New York, N.Y.). *Linit Bath Club* (1932–33); *Fred Allen Show* (1934–40, 1945–49); *Texaco Star Theatre* (1940–45); *The Big Show* (1951–52).

One of the country's greatest natural humorists. A vaudeville circuit juggler and Broadway revue per-

Fred Allen

former before his entry into radio, he also wrote much of the material used on his broadcasts. His sing-song style and nasal delivery were instantly recognized by 20 million listeners at his peak.

Allen's brilliant wit contributed to a variety show on which he and his wife and partner Portland Hoffa presided week after week for 17 years, beginning on October 23, 1932. A humorous highlight was the stroll among the inhabitants of Allen's Alley — Senator Claghorn, Titus Moody, Ajax Cassidy, Mrs. Nussbaum — who offered offbeat opinions to a question based on some happening from the headlines that week. Allen frequently appeared as One Long Pan, a take-off of the Charlie Chan type of detective.

Allen made guest appearances on the *Collier's Hour, Bond Bread Program* and *Bits of Theatre* as a warmup for his *Linit Bath Club Revue* on CBS. Following a four-month run on *Salad Bowl Revue,* he began his long-running *Town Hall Tonight* series for Bristol-Myers at NBC in 1934. It switched to CBS and sponsorship by Texaco in the fall of 1940. Known as a cynical and cantankerous genius among his broadcast contemporaries, he once said about radio: "I don't hold with furniture that talks."

In the late '30s Allen and Jack Benny staged a running feud on their programs — a battle of wits that delighted fans of both stars. In 1946 he judged a "I can't stand Jack Benny" contest on Benny's program, although in fact they were good friends. On the air, Fred also mocked network executives. Eventually, in 1947 a NBC vice president ordered all jokes deriding network officials to be deleted from his script. Allen refused, and was cut off the air on the next show as he led into the planned satire. There was dead air for 25 seconds. Other comedians reminded listeners of the Allen cut-off — and were similarly shut down. They joined a general revolt over being silenced. Vaudeville midgets, hired by Allen, picketed NBC studios with signs saying the network was unfair to little people. NBC surrendered; comics could ridicule the Radio City establishment.

In addition to many guest appearances on Jack Benny's show, Allen often brought his comic gift as a panelist to *Information Please* and as a "contestant" to *The Quiz Kids.* In 1948 he and Tallulah Bankhead did a classic take-off on "Mr. & Mrs." morning radio shows. (Two years later they revived it on *The Big Show* where Allen became permanent writer and comedian.) He made numerous appearances on the *Henry Morgan Show* and once narrated "Peter and the Wolf" on *The Telephone Hour.*

His career slumped badly when a ratings-poor ABC mounted a big prime-time giveaway, *Stop the Music!,* opposite Allen's Alley. Competing against a mountain of merchandise as prizes to at-home listeners (waiting to be called) he dropped from the Top Ten to No. 38 in merely a few weeks. Although he fought back during the 1948–49 season with a clever parody over the folly of quiz contests and even purchased insurance for those listeners who dialed in his show and might have been phoned by ABC quizmaster Bert Parks, and lost a jackpot, Allen found himself on the ropes and without his own show.

In 1950 he made his debut in television but it proved an ill-matched medium for his topical subjects and sharp ad libs. His best TV moments came later as a regular member of the *What's My Line?* panel. In 1954 he wrote a book, *Treadmill to Oblivion,* believing that all a radio comedian had to show for years of work and aggravation was "the echo of forgotten laughter."

16. ALLEN, Gracie (comedienne; [signature song: "Love Nest"]; b. July 26, 1906, San Francisco, CA; d. Aug. 27, 1964, Hollywood, CA). *Burns and Allen* (1932–50).

The secret of Gracie's humor was her ability to deliver the most incredible lines with absolute sincerity, as part of the comedy team of Burns and Allen. An example of her wacky, offhand remarks: "My uncle eats concrete. Mother asked him to stay for dinner, but he said he was going to eat up the street." George Burns was in vaudeville in 1923 when he made Gracie his comedy partner. She, too, had been on stage since her school days and was a member of an Irish repertoire company. At first, Burns gave her the straight lines and himself all the jokes. But audiences laughed harder when it was reversed. By the time they married in 1926, George had become the straight man.

Their husband-and-wife routines took them to England where in 1930 they broadcast for 15 weeks over the BBC. Their U.S. program began at CBS in February 1932, balancing comedy with the music of Guy Lombardo. One of the most successful gimmicks was a search by Gracie for an imaginary lost brother. She popped up on so many shows seeking the brother that NBC put an end to the gag. In 1940 she ran for President of the United States—a candidate of the Surprise Party. When Paul Whiteman supplied their music in the early '40s, the program's writers concocted a running gag that had Gracie taking piano lessons with the notion of playing in a symphony hall. The plot soon had her planning for the big debut. It was actually broadcast from Carnegie Hall as a wartime fundraiser for the Red Cross. Her concert piece was called *Piano Concerto for Index Finger.* It opened with an octave, the last note a clinker, and was repeated over and over until Gracie conquered the full scale. Gracie immortalized the piece on screen in MGM's *Two Girls and a Sailor.*

The onstage Gracie was poised and steady but the real Gracie was shy and somewhat self-conscious. "Applause meant nothing to her," Burns said. "There was a curtain between her and the audience." The audiences for Burns and Allen grew even larger and more zealous when the show, on CBS, moved to TV screens in 1950. Gracie retired after eight seasons to concentrate on being a homemaker and gardener.

17. ALLEN, Ida Bailey (host; b. c1885, Danielson, CT; d. July 16, 1973, Norwalk, CT).

Prolific cookbook author and homemaking writer with frequent network programs. Allen told listeners her favorite recipes and household hints at CBS (for Beechnut, Durkee, Hormel) from 1929 to 1932. NBC aired her Best Foods series in the mid-1930s. She founded the National Radio Homemakers Club at WHN. Her *Modern Cookbook* was the best known of her many recipe volumes. She wrote for *Family Circle, Ladies' Home Journal, Parade* and King Features' "Let's Eat."

18. ALLEN, Mel (sportscaster, announcer [catchphrase: "How about that!"]; b. Feb. 14, 1913, Birmingham, AL; d. June 16, 1996, Greenwich, CT). *Army Hour* (1944); *Chesterfield Supper Club* (1946–47); *White Owl Sports Smoker* (1947–48).

A baseball enthusiast since boyhood and a sports colum-

George Burns and Gracie Allen

Mel Allen (courtesy of Steve Jelf)

nist in college, he first broadcast a contest between his alma mater, the University of Alabama, and Tulane. CBS heard the gridiron coverage and signed him as an announcer in New York where he handled news and disc jockey programs. Major league baseball was added in 1939; he teamed with J.C. Flippen for the Yankees games and with Joe Bolton for those of the Giants.

During his stint as a staff sergeant, he worked as an announcer on the *Army Hour* from Ft. Benning. Upon his release, Allen remained The Voice of The Yankees for 20 years. His on-the-nose play-by-play accounts set a sportscasting standard, and led to "Mel Allen Day" at Yankee Stadium in 1950 and many industry awards. They included the first Ford C. Frick Award for broadcasting excellence. He handled numerous sports roundups, kickoff festivities, games of the week, and all-American awards dinners.

Among his early non-sports chores was announcer of Ralph Edwards' *Truth or Consequences.*

19. ALLEN, Steve (comedian b. Dec. 26, 1921, New York, NY). *Steve Allen Show* (1950).

A decade of Pacific Coast radio honed his skillful handling of comedy, music and interviews. A personable ad-libber and excellent pianist, Allen did not reach national audiences until the summer of 1950 when CBS decided to air his midnight disc jockey session at KNX. At its conclusion, he came to New York to begin a TV series five days a week, and was considered a new video discovery. On a fast career track, it led to the outstanding *Tonight Show* and top-rated prime-time variety series. Together with frequent panel and game show appearances, Allen was one of the most visible and engagingly funny men ever to go on television.

While in high school, he decided on radio as an career and went on as an amateur actor. His professional chores began in 1942 as an announcer for KOY Phoenix. Los Angeles stations, KFAC and KMTR, gave him announcing jobs, and Mutual, for its Western lineup, comedy exposure on *Smile Time*. In 1947 he joined KNX as a DJ six nights a week.

A prolific composer and writer, Allen has managed to meld his many interests and diverse talents for the enjoyment of a broad spectrum of listener-viewers and readers.

20. ALLISON, Fran (actress, singer; b. Nov. 20, 1907, La Porte City, IA; d. June 13, 1989, Sherman Oaks, CA). *The Breakfast Club* (1938–50); *National Barn Dance* (1940–41); *Meet the Meeks* (1947–49); *Kukla, Fran and Ollie* (1952–53).

A school teacher before becoming a staff singer on a Waterloo, Iowa, station, she went to Chicago in 1937, and was hired by NBC. As gossipy Aunt Fanny on Don McNeill's *Breakfast Club,* she became an early morning personality. This warmhearted country character was also well received on the Chicago-based *National Farm and Home Hour, Uncle Ezra* and *National Barn Dance.* But her early TV show *Kukla, Fran and Ollie* with hand puppeteer Burr Tillstom helped establish the new medium in many homes. One of the most imaginative and spontaneous programs of video, it brought her widespread popularity and acclaim among both children and adults. It also aired on radio for one season.

21. ALLMAN, Elvia (actress; b. Sept. 19, 1904, Concord, NC; d. March 6, 1992, Santa Monica, CA). *Bob Hope Show* (1939–41); *Al Pearce and His Gang* (1942–43); *Life of Riley* (1945–46); *Burns and Allen* (1946–49); *Fibber McGee and Molly* (1949–50).

Cobina of the husband-hunting Brenda (Blanche Stewart) and Cobina on Bob Hope's Pepsodent show. The comic duo was based on highly touted New York glamour-girl debutantes Brenda Frazier and Cobina Wright, Jr. Her characterization led to ongoing parts with Abbott and Costello (Mrs. Niles), Jimmy Durante (Mrs. Vandeveer), *Life of Riley* (Honey Bee Gillis) and *Mr. & Mrs. Blandings* (Maude).

Her first radio engagements at KHJ Los Angeles in 1930 entailed the reciting of poems and monologues on *Uncle John's Children Hour.* A singer and dancer in vaudeville, Allman joined Fred Allen's *Town Hall Tonight* in 1937. When her radio work ended in the 1950s, she became part of the television cast of *Beverly Hillbillies* and *Petticoat Junction.*

22. AMECHE, Don (actor; b. May 31, 1908, Kenosha , WI; d. Dec. 6, 1993, Scottsdale, AZ). *First*

Don Ameche (courtesy of Steve Jelf.)

Nighter (1932–37); *Grand Hotel* (1933–36); *Charlie McCarthy Show* (1937–39, 1942–45, 1948); *The Drene Show* (1946–47); *Don Ameche's Real Life Stories* (1958).

His sonorous voice over NBC Chicago scored high with audiences of the dramatic playhouse, *First Nighter.* He had auditioned at the urging of actress Bernadine Flynn, with whom he had worked at the University of Wisconsin. Hollywood recognized this handsome actor's possibilities, and Fox cast him in a dozen starring roles (including the lead in *The Story of Alexander Graham Bell,* a biography of the telephone inventor). But his gratitude and affection for radio remained strong. Ameche emceed the *Chase & Sanborn Hour* with Bergen and McCarthy for a half-dozen seasons. He teamed with Dorothy Lamour, Jimmy Durante and Frances Langford — the latter in sharp connubial sketches about marriage called "The Bickersons."

In 1950 he moved to New York and starred in several Broadway musicals and on TV series and specials. His movie fame was rekindled at age 75 and led to his Oscar-winning performance in *Cocoon.*

23. AMECHE, Jim (actor, announcer; b. Aug. 6, 1915, Kenosha, WI; d. Feb. 4, 1983, Tucson, AZ). *Jack Armstrong— The All American Boy* (1933–37); *Grand Hotel* (1937–38); *Rinso-Spry Vaudeville Theatre* (1941–42); *Grand Marquee* (1946–47); *Silver Eagle, Mountie* (1951–55).

Ameche's older brother Don was already an established actor when Jim heard about auditions for a new serial called *Jack Armstrong.* Don called 18-year-old Jim in Kenosha, and he won the part as the all-

American boy. While the fame of the clean-living hero spread, Ameche's identity was kept secret. "Nobody ever knew I was on the show. There was an unwritten law against revealing who played Jack." He was paid $59.50 a week for the five-day-a-week Chicago broadcast. It was the best-known character Ameche ever played, although he spent the rest of his life as an actor, emcee, announcer, disc jockey and TV commercial performer.

Jim resembled Don in mannerisms and appearance. Their voices were very similar, and both had dark, wavy hair and a quick, pleasant smile. Jim replaced Don as the lead on *Grand Hotel,* and he worked on the West Coast in *Hollywood Open House* from 1938–41, before moving to New York for *Big Sister* and *Here's to Romance.*

24. AMSTERDAM, Morey (comedian; b. Dec. 14, 1912, Chicago, IL). *Stop Me If You've Heard This One* (1947–48); *Morey Amsterdam Show* (1948–49).

A fast-humor man, he usually played second banana to headliners but often had the last punch line. He began with the *Al Pearce Gang* in the mid-30s. Then came a stint as comedy writer for Fanny Brice, Milton Berle, Rudy Vallee and others. He appeared as a joke-topping panelist on *Stop Me If You've Heard This One* while continuing to write material. When television came into homes, he hosted several late-night programs. *The Dick Van Dyke Show* and game shows brought him a new generation of fans.

He studied the cello, but as a comic used it chiefly as a prop. His father was first violinist with the Chicago Opera and later concertmaster of the San Francisco Symphony. Morey composed several popular hits, including the calypso-styled "Rum and Coca-Cola."

25. ANDERSON, Arthur (actor; b. Aug. 29, 1922, Staten Island, NY). *Let's Pretend* (1936–54); *Aunt Jenny's Real Life Stories* (1938–41); *Lawyer Tucker* (1947); *Mr. Jolly's Hotel for Pets* (1955–56).

Leading character-parts actor in the fairy tale fantasies of *Let's Pretend* from age 14 to 32. Program creator-director Nila Mack utilized his talents to play a variety of voice-changing roles — from old men to talking crows — and became his mentor for the Saturday morning children's series and other CBS shows (*American School of the Air, The March of Games*). Anderson's only break as a weekly Let's Pretender came when the Army drafted him in 1943 for three-year stint in a "distinctly non-starring role."

He first came to radio through a children's community playhouse and started appearing regularly in 1934 on *Uncle Nick Kenny's Radio Kindergarten* at WMCA. He did two-minute sketches, doing all the voices, plus dog barks. Arthur turned professional in 1935 on NBC's *Tony and Gus.* He appeared at the mike with Helen Hayes in "Bambi" and Orson Welles' *Mercury Theatre on the Air.* In Welles' land-

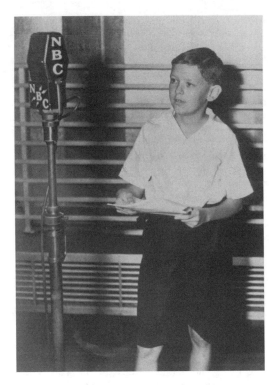

Arthur Anderson (courtesy of Arthur Anderson)

mark modern dress production of *Julius Caesar* on Broadway in 1937, Anderson played Lucius. During the run of that play, he once interrupted a performance when he inadvertently set off the sprinkler system backstage and flooded the set.

In the 1950s Anderson returned to the theatre with *The Doctor's Dilemma,* directed by ex-Pretender Sidney Lumet. He worked in television (*Omnibus*) and films (*The Group, Zelig*). He also did commercials, including the voice of Lucky Charms Leprechaun for 29 years.

Above all, Anderson retained an enduring affection for radio. His incisively-told account of the program closely linked to his life and career was published as *Let's Pretend: A History of Radio's Best Loved Children's Show by a Longtime Cast Member.* "Acting on radio," he says,"allowed me to use my talents without worrying about the limitations of age or physical appearance. The magic of drama (and comedy) in radio's Golden Age consisted of three things: the creativity of the writers, the art of the performers, and the imagination of the listeners."

26. ANDERSON, Eddie "Rochester" (comedian [catchphrase: "What's that, Boss?"]; b. Sept. 18, 1905, Oakland, CA; d. Feb. 28, 1977, Los Angeles, CA). *Jack Benny Program* (1937–55).

The best known and most popular character on the Benny show. As Rochester, the valet, he never failed to pick up laughs with lines from his unforgetable gravel voice. It was described variously as "rasping, wheezing and scratchy." He regularly turned the verbal tables on the pretentious, penny-pinching Benny, his boss. Anderson started the role in 1937 in a skit in which he played a Pullman porter for a trip the Benny troupe was making from New York to Los Angeles. He had answered an open call, and proved so popular that Benny's scriptwriters had to develop a storyline in which Jack hired Rochester away from the railroad and made him a permanent part of the Benny household. Many listeners believed that he was an actual emloyee playing himself.

Anderson had begun his career at 14, appearing in an all-black revue with his parents who were circus aerialists. He and his brother formed a vaudeville team until Anderson secured movie parts. Later, he parlayed Rochester into a series of screen roles, including several with Benny, and won acclaim for his portrayal of Little Joe in *Cabin in the Sky.*

27. ANDRE, Pierre (announcer; b. c1900; d. July 21, 1962, Evanston, IL). *Little Orphan Annie* (1931–40).

Mainstay at WGN Chicago from 1930 to 1962. Andre handled such Midwest-based programs as *Helen Trent, Betty and Bob, Backstage Wife* and *Captain Midnight.* He became closely identified with *Little Orphan Annie* through his attention-getting introduction: "Who's that little chatterbox? . . . " and persuasive reminders to try Ovaltine, an instant coca mix that you added to milk.

His early dance band remotes from the Blackhawk Restaurant were called "The Midnight Flyer." In the 1920s Andre had worked at KSTP St. Paul.

28. ANDREWS SISTERS (singers).

ANDREWS, LaVerne (b. July 6, 1915, Minneapolis, MN; d. May 8, 1967, Los Angeles, CA).

ANDREWS, Maxene (b. Jan. 3, 1918, Minneapolis, MN; d. Oct. 21, 1995, Hyannis, MA).

ANDREWS, Patty (b. Feb. 16, 1920, Minneapolis, MN). *Honolulu Bound* (1939); *Glenn Miller Orchestra* (1940–42); *Andrews Sisters Revue* (1944–46).

This peppy trio brought to the 1940s what the Boswell Sisters had introduced in the 1930s: close, smooth harmony fed into a microphone for listeners at a phonograph or radio. Their "Bei Mir Bist du Schoen" was one of the biggest hits of 1937. The following year the Sisters were heard on two series for Wrigley: *Double Everything* and *Just Entertainment;* the latter was aired Monday to Friday from 7 to 7:15 p.m. Beginning in January 1940 Glenn Miller featured them often on his CBS Chesterfield programs. They made guest appearances on the all-star *Treasury Hour* and *Command Performance,* and with Abbott and Costello with whom they co-starred in several films, and Bing Crosby, their co-harmonizer on best-selling discs.

George Ansbro (courtesy of George Ansbro)

Andrews Sisters: Maxene, Patty, LaVerne (courtesy of Capital Cities/ABC)

Nash Kelvinator sponsored their programs in the mid-40s. By the end of that decade their off-stage harmony was not quite as smooth as the vocalizing center-stage, and several times they dissolved the act, over family squabbles, then reunited. In 1956 they were back together, in part, they said because the public never wanted them to break up.

Veterans of the vaudeville circuit in the Midwest, Patty, Maxene and LaVerne first sang their way to success in nightclubs and on such vintage recordings as "Rum and Coca-Cola," "Victory Polka" and "Chattanooga Choo Choo."

29. ANSBRO, George (announcer; b. Jan. 14, 1915, Brooklyn, NY). *Mrs. Wiggs of the Cabbage Patch* (1936–38); *Omar The Swingmaker* (1937–40); *Young Widder Brown* (1938–56); *Waltz Time* (1939–48); *Pick-A-Date* (1949–50); *Manhattan Maharajah* (1951).

His deep, resonant voice was heard for more than 55 years over network radio and television, as announcer, narrator, product spokesman, newscaster, disc jockey and sometime actor. For 18 consecutive years he announced *Young Widder Brown* ("If I had ever said 'Young Widow Brown', I'd have been off the air the next day for sure!"). Ansbro was kept on the NBC soap under the terms of the 1942 split of the Red and Blue Networks — the last announcer to have dual NBC-ABC affiliation.

First brought to radio as a boy soprano, he had tagged along with a friend who performed on Milton

Cross's children hour, *Coast-to-Coast on a Bus*, at WJZ. An audition won a spot on the show. But not until 1931 did he work regularly in the industry. This self-taught staff announcer began as an NBC page and guide, and in his off-hours, trekked without pay to WAAT Jersey City to gain experience in announcing. For the annual NBC pages' talent showcase, "The Brass Button Revue," he made an impression as emcee. A year later, in May 1934, 19-year-old Ansbro was promoted to junior announcer.

Along with many soaps, he handled music programs (*Sunday Serenade*), newscasts (Lowell Thomas), game shows (*Go for the House*), dramatic series (*Mr. Keen, Tracer of Lost Persons*) and band remotes (Dorsey Brothers). In July 1952 he embarked on the maiden voyage of S.S. *United States* to broadcast live every day with Ed and Pegeen Fitzgerald and an array of celebrities bound for Europe. His weekly ABC series entitled *FBI Washington*, consisting of discussions with various department heads, ran for 25 years. Shortly after its sign-off in December 1989, Ansbro retired as the oldest employee of any network in terms of service (59 years).

30. ANTHONY, John J. (moderator [catchphrase: "Don't touch the microphone!"]; b. Sept. 1, 1902, New York, NY*; d. July 16, 1970, San Francisco, CA). *Good Will Hour* (1937–c1946); *John J. Anthony Hour* (1951–53).

Considered an authority on marriage, divorce and marital relations, this brusque-mannered, self-trained psychologist made a living out of other people's misery. His Marital Relations Institute started in 1927,

Some sources give 1896 and 1898.

and by 1935 he had made public a number of reports and surveys that purportedly led to improved divorce laws. Repeatedly, he was warned by the Bar Association and American Medical Association to stay out of their lines of work.

A high school dropout, he began to give speedy solutions to personal problems of studio guests locally on WMCA in 1937. NBC-Blue and Ironized Yeast Co. picked up his *Hour,* and with its unintended pathetic comedy, it surpassed in audience ratings rival advice-givers. His "Mr. Agony" sessions were satirized through the years by radio and television performers. Proceeds from books and lectures on marital problems augmented his estimated weekly paycheck of $3,000. In 1941 he briefly narrated *A Helping Hand,* a dramatized daytime guide to better human relations.

Anthony claimed his interest in marriage as a moral and legal institution stemmed from a first marriage alimony court battle and jail sentence. His real name was Lester Kroll.

31. ANTOINE, Josephine (singer; b. Oct. 27, 1908, Boulder, CO; d. Oct. 30, 1971, Jamestown, NY). *Contented Hour* (1942–45).

Leading soprano at Met Opera and NBC. Winner of the 1929 Atwater Kent radio competition, she used her prize for a year's study at a conservatory, and after more preparation at Juilliard made her professional bow as a soloist in Handel's "Messiah" at Carnegie Hall. NBC provided role experience on Chase & Sanborn's *Series of Grand Opera,* translated into English in condensed form, and on Palmolive's *Beauty Box Theatre.* In January 1936 Antoine made a Met debut as Philene in *Mignon,* and the following season was heard twice on the coveted Saturday matinee broadcasts in that well-suited coloratura role. Guest appearances for Kraft, RCA, Firestone and Westinghouse segued into a long run with Carnation's *Contented Hour.*

Antoine was raised in Colorado. One of her last broadcasts as soloist saluted NBC's 25th anniversary in Denver in December 1949. By then she had left the Met and was headed for the teaching of singing. At her death she was professor of voice at the University of Rochester.

32. ANTONINI, Alfredo (conductor; b. May 31, 1901, Alessandra, Italy; d. Nov. 3, 1983, Clearwater, FL). *La Rosa Concerts* (1939–40); *Treasure Hour of Song* (1942–47).

Conductor of the CBS Symphony for radio and television for some 30 years, he studied organ, composition and choral work at the Royal Conservatory of Music in Milan. After graduation, he headed for New York. He joined CBS in 1941, but also conducted over Mutual. His Stradivari Orchestra series aired pleasant and relaxing light concert pieces. In 1947 he conducted the radio premiere of Menotti's opera *The Medium* with the original Broadway cast.

He later served as chairman of the Music Department, St. John's University, Brooklyn.

33. ARCHER, John (actor; b. May 8, 1915, Lincoln, NE). *Gateway to Hollywood* (1939); *The Shadow* (1944–45).

Launched as a Hollywood talent quest discovery, he already was into pictures when *Gateway to Hollywood's* Summer Playhouse first signed him. The program cast him in a 13-week mini-series based on his debut film *Career.* When his movie work stalled, he looked to Radio City. "When I was under contract to 20th Century Fox, I noticed all the young actors who were getting all the good parts were out of New York," Archer observed. "Of course, everyone wanted to be in the theatre at that time but you had to start in radio because that was where the bread and butter were."

In 1944 he became *The Shadow* and appeared on Broadway. Parts on *Gangbusters* and *FBI in Peace and War* carried him back to Hollywood for roles in *Destination Moon* and *White Heat,* and later on TV's *Lassie* and *Batman.*

Archer studied at USC after Hollywood High School, and once worked as an aerial cinematographer.

34. ARDEN, Eve (actess; b. April 30, 1912, Mill Valley, CA; d. Nov. 12, 1990, Beverly Hills, CA). *Sealtest Village Store* (1945–48); *Our Miss Brooks* (1948–57).

Wisecracking actress-comedienne who carved out a special career niche as the sharp-tongued but warm-hearted English school teacher Miss Brooks. Her superb comic timing was widely praised and admired. A series with Jack Haley and Jack Carson for Sealtest established her as a radio attraction.

Arden made the most of her lines in *Stage Door, Mildred Pierce* and over 100 other movies, becoming typecast in roles characterized by caustic humor. She intermittently appeared on Broadway, beginning with the 1934 *Ziegfeld Follies.* While continuing on radio, *Our Miss Brooks* moved to CBS television in 1952 and earned her an Emmy award in 1953.

35. ARDEN, Victor (conductor, pianist; b. March 8, 1893, Wenona, IL; d. July 31, 1962, New York, NY). *Chase & Sandborn Hour* (1929–30); *Waves of Melody* (1931–32); *American Album of Familiar Music* (1931–51); *Manhattan Merry-Go-Round* (1941–49); *America the Free* (1941–42); *American Melody Hour* (1942–48).

Part of the innovative and popular piano team of Ohman & Arden in the 1920s and early '30s, Vic Arden began radio work with partner Phil Ohman for Roxy's broadcasts from the Capitol Theatre, New York. The duo's engaging piano pyrotechnics contributed to the success of such '20s Gershwin shows as *Lady Be Good, Tip Toes, Oh Kay* and *Funny Face.* Their interpretations were copied by many other piano players through their broadcasts, recordings and piano rolls. By 1932 they had been identified with no less than 16 important commercial series on the air.

The team broke up in 1933. Arden, whose real name was Lewis J. Fuiles, turned to conducting NBC staff musicians on that net's high-rated *Manhattan Merry-Go-Round* and *Waltz Time* (although Abe Lyman's orchestra was credited). Arden joined with pianist Phil Wall to form Arden & Arden, featured on *American Album*.

36. ARMBRUSTER, Robert (conductor; b. Oct. 9, 1897, Philadelphia, PA). *Cookoo Hour* (1932); *Chase & Sanborn Hour* (1937–41); *Cavalcade of America* (1945–47); *Adventures of Sam Spade* (1950–51); *Dangerous Assignment* (1950–52); *Two in the Balcony* (1954–55).

An adaptable, scholarly conductor for Nelson Eddy and Gladys Swarthout, as well as Bergen & McCarthy and Judy Canova. His assignments — they included musical background and bridges — kept him in studios from 1929 to 1955. They ranged from *Natural Bridge Program* to *Eternal Light,* a quarter-century later. Armbruster started out at a piano at WJZ, Newark while he was with Aeolian, a major piano roll producer.

His debut as a pianist at age eight was with the Philadelphia Orchestra. In 1917 he played at a White House diplomatic dinner, just before joining the U.S. Navy.

He moved to Hollywood for radio and film work in the early 1940s, and conducted the NBC Hollywood Orchestra on many specials for the Red Cross, CARE, U.S. Treasury and Girl and Boy Scouts. He handled *Kraft Music Hall* for summer series in the late '40s, and for its last full season, 1950–51.

37. ARMEN, Kay (singer; b. c1920, Chicago, IL). *Rambling in Rhythm* (1943–44); *Stop the Music!* (1948–51); *Pet Milk Show* (1948–49); *Bob Crosby Show* (1949–50).

Armen once analyzed her musical attributes: an untrained natural voice with perfect pitch and a steel-trap memory for words and music. It all paid off on radio, first in Chicago where she worked as a movie house ticketseller and as an occasional ballroom vocalist. In 1943 WSM Nashville added her to staff for popular tunes, traditional songs and hymns, for a total of 12 programs a week. Her Saturday night series with Beasley Smith's orchestra was fed into NBC. In January 1944 the newly organized ABC hired her at $75 a week for similar duty. That month she appeared, by command of network musical director Paul Whiteman, on his *Philco Hall of Fame,* singing selections from *Carousel.*

On *Stop the Music!* she garnered her largest audience but suffered the frustrating experience of not being able to finish the song or sing its title. Armen toured with Whiteman's orchestra, cut many discs, and appeared in MGM's *Hit the Deck.*

Kay Armen

38. ARNALL, Curtis (actor; b, Oct. 1, 1898, Cheyenne, WY*; d. Sept. 22, 1964, Washington, DC). *Buck Rogers in the 25th Century* (1932–36); *Red Davis* (1934–36); *Pepper Young's Family* (1936–42).

Acting occupied 15 or so years of his many-faceted life. Local theatre and repertory work — including roles in Mabel Talliaferro's company in Honolulu and at the Pasadena Playhouse — opened studio doors to the lead as Buck Rogers opposite Adele Ronson as Wilma. Arnall also played Red Davis and initiated the role of Pepper Young. From 1932 to 1942 he enjoyed running parts on *Just Plain Bill, One Man's Family,* and other serials. Before and after radio, he pursued jobs as a cowpuncher, broker, telegrapher and fisherman, and during World War II, Coast Guardsman.

39. ARNOLD, Eddy (singer [Tennessee Plowboy]; b. May 15, 1918, Henderson, TN). *Checkerboard Square* (1947–50); *Eddy Arnold Show* (1953).

Arnold brought traditional rustic melodies into the mainstream and gave them a contemporary spin, resulting in a new kind of music called "country pop." A best-selling Victor recording artist and regular guest on *Grand Ole Opry,* the likeable, expressive baritone became both a country music and pop superstar. Arnold began playing a guitar and singing on local stations in Jackson, Tennessee and St. Louis. In 1940 he joined Pee Wee King's western band, a group that appeared often on *Opry.* He left King to become a single and was kept on at WSM. His noontime program for Ralston Purina aired over some 300 Mutual stations in the late 1940s. Guest spots included *Chesterfield Supper Club* and *The $64 Question.* As his

Other sources give Denver and 1904, 1907.

Edward Arnold (courtesy of Capital Cities/ABC)

audience widened, he made his television bow on Milton Berle's show, presented a country and western program at Carnegie Hall, collaborated on "Just a Little Lovin'" and headlined at El Rancho Vegas in Las Vegas. In 1966 he was elected to the Country Music Hall of Fame and named the year's most popular singer on coin machines.

40. ARNOLD, Edward (actor; b. Feb. 18, 1890, New York, NY; d. April 26, 1956, Encino, CA). *Mr. President* (1947–53).

Numerous film roles as business tycoon and financial nabob led to inspired casting on radio as *Mr. President,* a series of stories about denizens of The White House. His statesman-like bearing and voice carried this program to a long run over ABC. On screen the heavy-set veteran actor portrayed such notables as Diamond Jim Brady, King Louis XIII and Daniel Webster but never a U.S. President. His career spanned a half-century, from a stock company in Trenton in 1905 to a film role in Paris a month before his death. In 1939 he spoke on several "I am an American" Day programs under the auspices of the citizenship foundation that he helped to establish in Hollywood on the eve of World War II.

41. ARQUETTE, Cliff (comedian, actor [catchphrase: "That ain't the way I heered it."]; b. Dec. 28, 1905, Toledo, OH; d. Sept. 23, 1974, Los Angeles, CA). *The Fred Astaire Show* (1937); *Hollywood Mardi Gras* (1937–38); *Fibber McGee and Molly* (1949–53, 1955–56); *Mr. and Mrs. Blandings* (1951).

An amusement park musician and vaudeville comedian, Arquette found his vehicle to real success — radio — in 1936. He did his first network show with Astaire and Charles Butterworth. On *Fibber McGee and Molly,* he had various oldtimer roles, including the hardware store clerk. His sly-witted, folksy Charley

Weaver grew out of that character. He starred on *Glamour Manor,* a daytime situation comedy of the mid-40s and played Thaddeus Cornfelder on *Myrt and Marge* in Chicago. A regular on television, especially as a sidekick of Dave Willock and Jack Paar, he spun countless yarns about the folks back home.

42. ARTHUR, Jack (singer, emcee; b. June 21, 1900, Brooklyn, NY; d. Oct. 1, 1980). *Echoes of New York* (1936–37, 1940–41); *Family Time* (1943); *Jack Arthur Show* (1951–53).

Baritone in musical comedy and radio. At WOR he sang 15-minute interludes and handled the quiz *Press Time.* On Consolidated Edison's *Echoes,* he initially portrayed Henry Hudson, Jr., one of the emcees. He appeared as vocalist, emcee or narrator on *Melody Treasure Hunt, Grand Central Station, The Song is Ended, Clipper Tim* and *Star Spangled Theatre.* From 1940 to 1942 he sang the theme song for *Lincoln Highway.* His own show ran on WEAF in the mid-40s, and later was revamped into children's program for the network.

Brooklyn-raised and Juilliard-trained, Arthur had roles in *The Desert Song* and 1932 edition of *Ziegfeld Follies.* On the 1936 run of *Ziegfeld Follies of the Air,* he played the role of Daddy to Fanny Brice's Baby Snooks, a character she had just introduced. In the mid-30s at NBC he performed with the name Johnny Hart.

43. ASTAIRE, Fred (dancer, actor; b. May 10, 1899, Omaha, NE; d. June 22, 1987, Los Angeles, CA). *Fred Astaire Show* (1936–37).

While creating triumphful film musicals with dancing partner Ginger Rogers, Astaire broke away from RKO sound stages to tap and sing on radio for a season. Packard Motor Car sponsored his variety show with Johnny Green's orchestra, comedian Charles Butterworth and singers Allan Jones and Anne Jameson. The "nimble feet of Fred Astaire" were actually heard. NBC created a section of "dance floor" for him to perform on during the full-hour program. It was put to good use, especially with the presentation of specialty numbers, such as "Bojangles of Harlem." His rather shy way of speaking endeared him to listeners as much as his smooth, easy style of singing and tap dancing. In spite of *Radio Guide's* award to Astaire for outstanding work on the air and similar media accolades, the premier popular music dancer declined offers to continue the show.

Astaire with his sister Adele had first broadcast with Rudy Vallee in 1931 during the duo's last big hit together, *The Band Wagon.* As a single, he made a half-dozen appearances on *Your Hit Parade* in 1935, chiefly presenting the outstanding film score of Irving Berlin's *Top Hat.* After 1944 he agreed to very few guest spots. A notable exception was a version of his wartime picture *The Sky's the Limit* on *NBC Theatre* in 1949.

Fred Astaire

44. ATKINS, Chet (guitarist; b. June 20, 1924, Luttrell, TX). *Boone County Neighbors* (1945–46); *Grand Ole Opry* (1946–52, 1957–58).

Multi-style guitar player, featured on jazz and symphony programs as well as country platforms. He played with Bill Carlisle, Red Foley and the Carter Sisters, and became top session guitarist for RCA in Nashville in the late 1940s while appearing on *Opry*. Atkins took charge of RCA's new studio there and became A&R manager in 1960, and later vice president. He helped create the new Nashville Sound that attracted many artists to that city.

He started out as a fiddler on WNOX Knoxville at 18. In 1973 Atkins was elected to the Country Music Hall of Fame.

45. AUTRY, Gene (singer, actor [signature song: "Back in the Saddle Again"]; b. Sept. 29, 1907, Tioga, TX). *National Barn Dance* (1930–34); *Melody Ranch* (1940–57).

Dressed in a striking powder-blue suit with a ten-gallon hat to match, the world's most famous singing cowboy, circa 1940, was worshipped by most kids and plenty of grownups. Crowds flocked to his movies and rodeo shows, as much as they did to his broadcasts. Born to the saddle, he worked as a cowpuncher on his father's ranch; his preacher-grandfather corralled him for choir practice each week. As a youngster he toured with a small medicine show. Later he was telegraph operator in Oklahoma, and would pass the time by strumming his guitar and singing. One day a stranger walked in to send a telegram, listened and told him that he had a real voice and should pursue a career. He signed the telegram: "Will Rogers."

Encouraged by Rogers' remarks, he got a job at KVOO Tulsa in 1929, becoming "The Oklahoma Yodeling Cowboy." NBC brought him to Chicago for *National Barn Dance* where he met Smiley Burnette who became his partner in radio and films. His records for Vocalion ("That Silver-haired Daddy of Mine") sold well, and in 1934 he was cast in his first movie, *The Phantom Empire*. His success in that serial brought a contract to star in musical westerns, a new genre. He began his own weekly radio program *Melody Ranch* for Wrigley Chewing Gum. When Autry joined the Army Air Corps in 1942, he was sworn in on one of his broadcasts. As a flight officer he served 27 months over-

Gene Autry

seas. The Sunday show returned true to form at war's end, and later moved with Gene's horse Champion onto TV screens. He introduced scores of cowboy ballads, but his biggest hit proved to be a Christmas song, the perennially popular "Rudolph, the Red-Nosed Reindeer."

46. AVERBACK, Hy (announcer, actor; b. 1920, Minneapolis, MN). *Sealtest Village Store* (1947–48); *Bob Hope Show* (1948–49); *Take It or Leave It* (1949–50).

While still in high school, Hy picked up work at KMPC Los Angeles as an announcer-writer. During World War II he met Jack Paar overseas, and later announced his 1947 summer show and *Take It or Leave It*. The job as emcee for bandleader Les Brown opened the door to announcer-actor chores on the *Bob Hope Show*. In 1949 he added *Hollywood Calling* as announcer-assistant emcee. Many character roles followed. They included film parts in *The Benny Goodman Story* and *Frances*. Hy also moved into television as a producer and director (*Burke's Law, Real McCoys*).

47. AYRES, Mitchell (bandleader [signature song: "You Go to My Head"]; b. Dec. 24, 1910, Milwaukee, WI; d. Sept. 5, 1969, Las Vegas, NV). *The Dunninger Show* (1945); *Chesterfield Supper Club* (1948–50).

His danceable "Fashions in Music" orchestra was a cooperative whose road travels totaled 25,000 miles during its first three years in the mid-30s. The ten-piece outfit was featured on Andy Russell's show and in several movies. Ayres disbanded his group in 1948 to become musical director for Columbia Records and for Perry Como on NBC radio and television. His catchy Bluebird disc, "Down By The O-HI-O," featured band vocalist Mary Ann Mercer.

48. BABBITT, Harry (singer; b. Nov. 3, 1913, St. Louis, MO). *Kay Kyser's Surprise Party* (1937); *Kollege of Musical Knowledge* (1938–44, 1946–48).

Lead vocalist for Kay Kyser and his musical quiz sessions. Babbitt had his own orchestra in the early 1930s but gave it up to travel as emcee in theatres and night clubs. While singing on sustaining programs in St. Louis, he caught the ear of Kyser. Babbitt joined his organization in February 1937 at Chicago's Blackhawk Restaurant. Babbitt was helpful in establishing the Kollege, and with Kay made seven films and recorded many hit songs, including "I Got Spurs That Jingle, Jangle, Jingle" and "Praise the Lord and Pass the Ammunition." In 1944 he joined the Navy; he returned two years later as featured soloist (and for the comic role of Harry Hookenlooper).

Babbitt left the Kollege to do a CBS early morning program from Hollywood. Known as *The Second Cup of Coffee Club,* it became a popular show on the West Coast, and left him time to enter Los Angeles television, and host *Glamour Girl* for NBC. In the

1980s Babbitt reorganized the Kay Kyser orchestra under his direction for concert tours and steamship cruises.

49. BACKUS, Jim (actor; b. Feb. 25, 1913, Cleveland, OH; d. July 3, 1989, Santa Monica, CA). *Gaslight Gayeties* (1945); *Alan Young Show* (1946–47, 1949); *Bob Burns Show* (1946–47); *Jim Backus Show* (1947–48, 1957); *Penny Singleton Show* (1950).

Free-lance performer on scores of programs in the late 1930s, beginning with *Columbia Workshop* and *Kate Smith Hour.* "I decided to try radio as a source of livelihood because I liked to eat regularly," said the American Academy of Dramatic Arts graduate after several years of struggling in summer stock and New York productions. In 1945 he began to land ongoing character parts, such as Victor Cavendish on *Gaslight Gayeties.* A year later he became a regular scene-stealer as Hubert Updyke III, a comical snob, first with Eddie Cantor, then for Alan Young and Judy Canova. Various roles with Bob Burns and on *The Drene Show* made Backus one of the busiest new actors of the 1946–47 season.

In 1949 he originated the booming voice of the nearsighted cartoon character, Mr. Magoo, for moviegoers. On TV he won wide popularity as ultra-rich Thurston Howell on *Gilligan's Island.* And for the screen he played James Dean's ineffectual father in *Rebel Without a Cause.*

50. BAER, Parley (actor; b. 1914, Salt Lake City, UT). *The Truitts* (1950–51); *Honest Harold* (1950–51); *Tales of the Texas Rangers* (1951–52); *Gunsmoke* (1952–61).

Character actor who originated Chester in *Gunsmoke* opposite William Conrad as Marshal Matt Dillon. "Much of the show was ad lib," he noted in a 1963 interview. He often played sheriffs, doctors, landlords, hired hands and manservants. Baer made many appearances as a cast member on *The Railroad Hour* and *Lux Radio Theatre* from 1953–55. On television he supported Ozzie Nelson as Darby, the next-door neighbor, and Andy Griffith as Mayor Stoner. His 60 films included *The Young Lions* and *Gypsy.*

A sixth-generation performer, Baer enjoyed a long association with circuses as a ringmaster, producer and publicist. He did his first radio work in 1933 on KSL Salt Lake City. His first network show was *The Whistler.*

51. BAILEY, Jack (emcee; b. Sep. 15, 1907, Hampton, IA; d. Feb. 1, 1980, Santa Monica, CA). *Queen for a Day* (1945–56); *Truth or Consequences* (1955–56).

During its long reign of tears, *Queen for a Day* packed in a surfeit of human misery. Host Jack Bailey led a daily parade of hard-luck homemakers with sad stories, each hoping to be crowned Queen and receive a windfall of gifts. It also gave women all over

Jack Bailey (courtesy of Capital Cities/ABC)

America a vicarious thrill from hearing an average housewife have her wish come true.

Before crowning more than 5,000 women on radio and television from 1945 to 1964, Bailey worked as a fair barker, jazz band musician and tent show director. His first venture into radio at San Diego in 1938 proved unsuccessful. He tried again as a disc jockey for Don Lee, then went on the network with *Potluck Party* and *Meet the Missus*. Bailey once was the voice of Goofy in Donald Duck cartoons, circa 1940.

52. BAILEY, Mildred (singer, [Rockin' Chair Lady] [signature song: "Rockin' Chair"]; b. Feb. 27, 1907, Tekoa, WA; d. Dec. 12, 1951, Poughkeepsie,

Mildred Bailey

NY). *Old Gold Program* (1929–30); *Camel Caravan* (1939–40); *Mildred Bailey Show* (1944–45).

An emotion-charged jazz singer who influenced many vocalists with her unsurpassed phrasing and timing. Sister of Al Rinker of Whiteman's Rhythm Boys, she caught the ear of that orchestra leader at an informal house party in Los Angeles in 1929. On his payroll she became the first female vocalist of stature in the early big band era. She sang on his many broadcasts and on her own 15-minute spot, thrice weekly, in 1932.

Bailey married Whiteman xylophone player Red Norvo, a frequent co-performer and accompanist. They became known as Mr. & Mrs. Swing, but were divorced in the 1940s. Her high register voice handled a variety of material with Benny Goodman, Louis Armstrong and Jack Teagarden.

53. BAIRD, Eugenie (singer; b. c1924; d. June 12, 1988, Brewster, NY). *Kraft Music Hall* (1944–45); *Forever Tops* (1946); *Sing It Again* (1949–50).

Featured vocalist on bandstands and primetime. In the early 1940s she began singing with Tony Pastor ("The Mem'ry of This Dance"), then Glen Gray ("My Heart Tells Me"). Crosby spotlighted her on his Kraft series and Whiteman on his ABC *Forever Tops* and in concerts. She made guest apperances with Alec Templeton and on *Your Hit Parade*. Baird joined Robert Q. Lewis's show and the money-laden musical quiz *Sing It Again* at CBS in 1949. She later specialized as singer of commercial jingles.

54. BAKER, Art (announcer, emcee; b. Jan. 7, 1898, New York, NY; d. Aug. 26, 1966, Los Angeles, CA). *The Grouch Club* (1939); *People Are Funny* (1942–43); *Dinah Shore Show* (1953–55).

The relatively forgotten host who first introduced the stunt-filled series on human nature called *People Are Funny*. A better-suited, dynamic emcee Art Linkletter co-assisted. Producer John Guedel had had Baker on the series' local Los Angeles forerunner, *Pull Over, Neighbor*. NBC favored Baker but Guedel opted for the other Art who had worked up most of the stunts himself. When dropped, Baker threatened to sue; the dispute was settled out of court. He moved on as emcee of the Pacific Coast program, *A Song Is Born,* and on television, *You Asked for It.*

A music student and gospel singer, Art joined the Army, going overseas where he led soldiers in World War I song fests. In the 1920s he sang in a barbershop quartet and evangelistic choir. To make a living, he lectured at Forest Lawn Cemetery on its stained-glass window depicting "The Last Supper" and then became announcer for its program *Tapestries of Life.* By 1937 his "voice of sincerity" aired over *Hollywood in Person,* and *Art Baker's Notebook.*

55. BAKER, Kenny (singer; b. Sept. 30, 1912, Monrovia, CA; d. Aug. 10, 1985, Solvang, CA). *Jack*

Kenny Baker

Phil Baker

Benny Program (1935–39); *Texaco Star Theatre* (1940–43); *Blue Ribbon Town* (1943–44); *Glamour Manor* (1945–47); *Kenny Baker Show* (1954).

Boyish tenor Kenny Baker was the vocalist and fall guy on two of radio comedy's top programs: Jack Benny's and Fred Allen's. In 1930 his mother persuaded him to enter the Long Beach district Atwater Kent Radio audition; he finished second. His first radio job was a 15-minute sustainer on KFOX Long Beach for 20 weeks. In 1935, while a movie studio "ghost" singer and choirister, he entered a national radio contest conducted by Eddy Duchin and Texaco and out of some 1,500 soloists was selected. With this exposure came an engagement at the famed Cocoanut Grove, a movie offer, and a contract with Benny. As the timid foil for his boss's caustic wit he was well cast. But in the same overshadowing rut with Fred Allen, then Groucho Marx, he quit the air for concert work and the Broadway musical *One Touch of Venus*.

He recreated his favorite movie role as Nanki Poo in a 1949 *Railroad Hour* broadcast of *The Mikado*. Baker ended his career with a 15-minute weekday music-drama program for Mutual which emphasized spiritual aspects of man's life — an area that the deeply religious, family-oriented singer had long nurtured. Baker once remarked that the lean years were very few but the "struggle came afterwards," referring to his efforts to prove himself a legitimate concert singer.

56. BAKER, Phil (comedian, emcee; b. Aug. 24, 1896, Philadelphia, PA; d. Dec. 1, 1963, Copenhagen, Denmark). *Honolulu Bound* (1938–39); *Take It or Leave It* (1941–47, 1951).

December 28, 1941, for Phil Baker, changed the course of his show business career. That Sunday he took over the $64 Question quiz program, already well established and high in audience ratings. This garrulous comic and accordian player proved to be the ideal quizmaster of contestants randomly selected from the studio audience. Easy-going and generous, he often gave them broad hints spiced with humor. By 1945 the show was the most popular American radio quiz, especially among servicemen who flocked to his broadcasts.

A talented accordianist in the citadels of vaudeville, he began in radio in 1933 with his own NBC evening series, *The Armour Jester*. Baker was the first radio performer to introduce the heckling stooge with his "Beetle and Bottle" routine. ("Bottle" was the impeccable British butler; "Beetle," the haunting stooge, whose voice came through a loudspeaker, was not seen by the studio audience.) In 1940 Baker, tired of the show, left the air until he replaced Bob Hawk on the $64 game. He took a break from that series in the late 1940s, appearing as emcee of a short-lived giveaway called *Everybody Wins*.

At 14 he ran away to Boston and there won first prize in a theatre amateur contest. Five years later his partner in an accordian-violin act was Ben Bernie. In the 1920s Baker played in musical revues (*Greenwich Village Follies*) and in the '30s in musical comedy (*Crazy Quilt*). His accordian was always close at hand. As a quizmaster he used it to "play the question" when a contestant chose the musical category.

57. BALL, Lucille (actress; b. Aug. 6, 1911, Celoron, NY; d. April 26, 1989, Los Angeles, CA). *My Favorite Husband* (1948–51).

Her domestic comedy series for CBS radio proved

to be the foundation of her phenomenally successful *I Love Lucy* on television a few years later. She undertook the program in order that she and bandleaderhusband Desi Arnaz might work together. The Cuban entertainer had spent most of his time on the road; it was estimated that in the first eleven years of their marriage they were apart a total of eight years because of Desi's tour schedules. However, actor Lee Bowman, not Desi, in the role of a conservative banker, was given the co-starring role, chiefly because of Desi's difficulty with the English language and their inter-ethnic marriage.

Lucy's first series won wide applause. *Radio Best* magazine called it "adult intelligent radio that manages to amuse the folks at home, as well as spellbound customers in the studio audience — and always manages to do it in good taste."

In 1950 Lucy and Desi formed a corporation, Desilu, to insure that they would work as a comedy team in television, a medium overtaking radio. They tested their theory on a nation-wide vaudeville tour. Encouraged by audience response, they focused their efforts on a revamped TV version of *My Favorite Husband*. The irresistibly funny doings of the Ricardo family bowed over CBS as a filmed show in October 1951. Through continual re-runs Lucy and Desi have never left video screens around the world. (*I Love Lucy* briefly aired on radio in the early 1950s.)

A model and chorus girl, Lucille Ball had learned the picture business from the ground floor, going from an extra and bit player on to a major star and production executive and studio owner. An early breakthrough, after many undistinguished films, Rodgers and Hart's *Too Many Girls* showcased her musical talent and introduced her to fellow cast member Desi in 1940, the year they married. Dramatic parts in *The Big Street* and *The Dark Corner* proved she could act. Comedy roles in *Easy to Wed* and *Fancy Pants* made it clear she could handle farce. Her seemingly boundless energy and twinkling natural timing found its most comfortable niche in television. Her marriage broke up in 1960, but Lucy continued her raucous comedy as a single on some 500 subsequent shows well into the mid-80s.

In the 1930s, to escape from the rut of B pictures, the flame-haired, husky-voiced comedienne made an early foray onto the air as a regular on Jack Haley and Phil Baker programs. From 1939 on, her guest shots were numerous and diverse, from Horace Heidt and Bing Crosby to *Lincoln Highway* and *Screen Guild Players*.

58. BAMPTON, Rose (singer; b. Nov. 28, 1909, Cleveland, OH). *Songs You Love to Hear* (1934–35); *Palmolive Beauty Box Theatre* (1935); *Vacation Serenade* (1944).

A Met contralto with a determination to sing soprano roles, she made the transition to a full range of two and a half octaves in 1937. Making her debut as the lower-range Laura in *La Gioconda* in 1932, she studied diligently and rebuilt her voice to produce higher notes for Leonora in *Il Trovatore*. While studying voice at Curtis Institute, she sang with other students over a Philadelphia station and later made a notable impression in the American premiere of Schoenberg's *Gure-Lieder* by Leopold Stokowski and the Philadelphia Orchestra.

A tall, regal-looking presence, she established herself firmly as a leading dramatic soprano, enhanced by depth of musicianship. Her eloquent and opulent voice brought her many opportunities to broadcast on *RCA Magic Key, Show Boat, Palmolive Beauty Box Theatre, Kraft Music Hall* and *Voice of Firestone* (including several programs with her husband, conductor Wilfred Pelletier). In December 1944 the American-trained singer joined Toscanini for a two-part NBC Symphony airing of Beethoven's *Fidelio* with Jan Peerce and Eleanor Steber — a broadcast described by critic Vigil Thomson as "animated, swiftly paced and graceful."

Opera commentator Milton Cross once tried to describe Bampton in her bare midrift Aida costume during a Saturday Met broadcast. Her husband tuned in. When she came home from the performance, he told her about Cross's thorough wardrobe analysis. "By the time he got through, Rose, the only thing left to talk about was your belly button."

In the 1950s she began the teaching of voice and served as a faculty member at Manhattan School of Music, North Carolina School of the Arts and Juilliard.

59. BANKHEAD, Tallulah (actress; b. Jan. 31, 1902, Huntsville, AL; d. Dec. 12, 1968, New York, NY). *Johnny Presents* (1942); *The Big Show* (1950–52).

The self-indulgent, good-humored mistress of ceremonies of network radio's last major, all-star program. Produced to keep broadcast advertisers and listeners in the NBC fold, *The Big Show* hired the bombastic and unpredictable Tallulah. Her famous name and distinctive deep voice drew a large audience. Surrounded by great comics — Jimmy Durante, Groucho Marx, Fred Allen — and fine singers — Ethel Merman, Jane Powell, Frankie Laine — plus conductor Meredith Willson and announcer Ed Herlihy, the legendary actress gave exhilarating breadth to the airwaves, and for her efforts received a Variety Showmanship Award. A major audience attraction, the show took over the large Center Theatre next to Radio City. After two seasons, there were 30,000 unfulfilled requests for seats.

Born into a political family of Senators and Congressmen, she grew up among the powerful and accomplished, and her success, in her words, stemmed from "not giving a damn." She once said "I'm the foe of moderation, the champion of excess."

Her stage triumphs in New York and London — *The Little Foxes, The Skin of Our Teeth, Private Lives* —

Tallulah Bankhead

left little space for any extended radio series. But Tallulah had her choice of guest shots and vied with the best: Eddie Cantor, Hildegarde, Charlie McCarthy, Bob Hope, The Quiz Kids. A tenacious rehearser, she appeared also in scenes from her plays, dramatic skits and monologues. With Fred Allen, she once did a hilarious take off on Mr. and Mrs. radio couples that became a classic sketch. For Hitchcock, she created a memorable film role in the wartime saga, *Lifeboat.*

60. BANKS, Joan (actress; b. Oct. 30, 1918, New York, NY). *Mary and Bob's True Stories* (1938–39); *Portia Faces Life* (1941–43); *A Woman of America* (1944–45); *Today's Children* (1947–50).

Key cast member of leading New York-based soaps of the 1940s. Some roles lasted for years (Camilla, *Young Widder Brown;* Peggy, *The O'Neills;* Joan, *Valiant Lady*); others for a month or so (Eleanor, *This Day is Ours;* Nora, *Bringing Up Father;* Mildred, *Joyce Jordan, M.D.*). There were many evening dramas that sought her talents: *Manhattan at Midnight, Hollywood Star Theatre, The Saint, Man Called X.* She met actor, and future husband, Frank Lovejoy on a 1941 program. When his career led to Hollywood, she appeared on his series *Nightbeat* and the syndicated *Maisie* with Ann Sothern for whom she later played the girlfriend on TV's *Private Secretary.*

Banks entered radio straight from Hunter College. She started out as a stooge for Stoopnagle and Budd.

61. BARBER, Red (sportscaster [The Old Redhead] [catchphrase: "Oh-ho Doctor!"]; b. Feb. 17, 1908, Columbus, MS; d. Oct. 22, 1992, Tallahas-

see, FL). *Schaefer Star Revue* (1945–46).

With colorful language and a crisp, conversational delivery, Barber was hailed as the greatest baseball broadcaster of his day. He began his play-by-play career with the Cincinnati Reds in 1934 and ended it with the Yankees in 1966. But he was most closely identified with the Brooklyn Dodgers (1939–53) at Ebbets Field. Barber broke into radio over the University of Florida, Gainesville, campus station. He eventually dropped out of school to become its director and chief announcer. At age 26 he took his place behind a mike in Cincinnati to broadcast the first major league game he had ever seen! On May 24, 1935 he broadcast baseball's first night game. In 1961 as a Yankee announcer he called Roger Maris's 61st home run.

In the 1980s he became a fixture on National Public Radio, providing weekly informed commentary on whatever crossed his mind. He and Mel Allen were the first broadcasters honored by the National Baseball Hall of Fame (1978). In the mid-40s he appeared four times as a guest expert on *Information Please.*

62. BARCLAY, John (singer, actor; b. May 12, 1892, Bletchingly, Surrey, England; d. Nov. 21, 1978). *Palmolive Beauty Box Theatre* (1934–35); *Road of Life* (1943); *Guiding Light* (1944–c47).

British performer equally versed as a vocal soloist or dramatic lead. With experience in oratorio and symphonic works, Barclay came to the United States in 1921 to play roles in a string of Gilbert & Sullivan operettas on Broadway. He preserved his commanding characterization of the Mikado on film in the 1939 movie version with Kenny Baker. Beginning in 1934 he emceed and co-starred (often with Gladys Swarthout) on broadcast condensations of "Dearest Enemy," "The Pink Lady," "Babes in Toyland," "New Moon" and dozens of musical evergreens.

Barclay turned to acting, appearing on soap operas and prime-time dramas, and on tour with Lunt and Fontanne. During 1947–48 he narrated "The Pickwick Papers" and played Sergeant Cuff in "The Moonstone," both on *World's Great Novels.* In the 1950s he returned to England.

Educated at Harrow and Cambridge, Barclay enlisted at the outset of World War I and saw action in France during 1916, rising to a captain. He then studied voice with Jean de Reszk in Paris. In 1929 he sang with the Philadelphia Opera Company and taught briefly at Curtis Institute. CBS soon utilized his talent for its grand opera quartet and *School of the Air.*

63. BARLOW, Howard (conductor; b. May 1, 1892, Plain City, OH; d. Jan. 31, 1972, Bethel, CT). *March of Time* (1931–43); *Voice of Firestone* (1943–57); *Harvest of Stars* (1945–46).

The newly formed Columbia network signed up Barlow as one of its first staff conductors in 1927. He had served as founder-conductor of the American National Orchestra and conductor-music director of the Neighborhood Playhouse, New York. At CBS he was responsible for much of its serious music presence, and as leader of the network's important Columbia Symphony Orchestra. For several seasons CBS commissioned musicians to write compositions utilizing "new musical materials in the form of instrumental effects made possible through the microphone — effects which are entirely useless in the concert hall." The commission guaranteed a performance, a cash stipend and any help the network could provide the awardees in learning the radio musical technique. Among the composers commissioned in 1937–38 were Roy Harris, Aaron Copland, Howard Hanson and Robert Russell Bennett.

Following two years as conductor of the Baltimore Symphony and a brief stint as guest conductor of the New York Philharmonic, Barlow returned to radio as director for the long-established *Voice of Firestone,*

Howard Barlow

a first-rate music program. The series initiated one of the earliest and best-received simulcasts when NBC aired the prestigious Monday concert on radio and TV. It won *Musical America* magazine's 1948 award for outstanding musical program with featured artists.

Howard Barlow attended Reed College and Columbia University, and in the years before World War I conducted choral groups and arranged choral works for music publishers. He sharpened his talent for orchestral conducting at the MacDowell Colony and its Federation of American Music Clubs festival in 1919.

64. BARRETT, Pat (actor; b. Sept. 27, 1887, Holden, MO; d. March 25, 1959, Harvard, IL). *National Barn Dance* (1934–39); *Uncle Ezra* (1934–41).

He created the high-voiced character Ezra Waters, owner and operator of a mythical five-watt radio station EZRA. This homespun philosopher appeared on *Uncle Ezra* and *National Barn Dance.* Born of a theatrical family, Barrett had a long vaudeville career before radio. He frequently played opposite Nora Cunneen, his wife, and was an occasional guest and fill-in emcee on *Barn Dance* in the mid-40s. When Barrett lost his sight, he retired to a working farm in northern Illinois.

65. BARRY, Jack (emcee, announcer; b. March 20, 1918, Lindenhurst, NY; d. May 2, 1984, New York, NY). *Juvenile Jury* (1946–53); *Joe DiMaggio Show* (1950).

His partnership with producer Dan Enright began at WOR and led to *Juvenile Jury* with Barry as host. He presided over a batch of youngsters from 7 to 14 years of age who discussed ordinary issues in their lives. This lively, amusing series took Barry-Enright into early television where they introduced *Life Begins at 80* and *Winky Dink and You,* and a lucrative lineup of game shows, including *Concentration* and *Tic Tac Dough.*

Barry was emcee of *Twenty-One* which fed answers to contestants and coached them on how to perform. The scandal led him into exile for a dozen years. He returned in the 1970s as host of the daytime game *The Joker's Wild,* again with Enright.

Barry began his career at WTTM Trenton, then moved to WOR. He was announcer for *Uncle Don* (Carney) and his children's show in the early 1940s. Ownership of an FM station in California provided the base for his reestablishment as a game show producer-emcee.

66. BARRYMORE, John (actor [The Great Profile]; b. Feb. 15, 1882, Philadelphia, PA; d. May 29, 1942, Hollywood, CA). *Streamlined Shakespeare* (1937); *Rudy Vallee Show* (1940–42).

An outstanding American actor who confined his last years chiefly to radio. The butt of comedy on Rudy Vallee's program, he got many laughs, often at the expense of his brilliant career as a Shakespearean actor and part of a famous theatre family. The excess of ill-temperate living had brought deep lines and sallowness to his matinee-idol face but his magnificent voice remained strong and recognizable.

A personal favorite of Vallee, who had featured him as early as 1935, Barrymore was readily accommodated at the mike. Suffering the after-affects of heavy drinking at many broadcasts, Barrymore was given large-type script pages and kept his balance by gripping a waist-level stanchion. His performances usually measured up to his past grand eloquence. He periodically delighted audiences with an off-the-cuff quip.

Barrymore, a struggling cartoonist, had turned to acting out of desperation in 1903. It proved to be his destiny. He rose to the heights of his profession as *Hamlet.* Motion picture roles in the silent features *Don Juan, Moby Dick* and *Beau Brummel* broadened his stature. His sound pictures — *Grand Hotel, Topaz, Twentieth Century* — won widespread critical and popular acclaim; his flamboyant spirit and rakish escapades made tabloid headlines and good box office.

Apart from Vallee's Sealtest series, Barrymore only performed in a summer run of condensed Shakespeare plays. He made occasional guest appearances and spoke on a special tribute to sister Ethel Barrymore's 40th anniversary as a star on February 4, 1941, as did their brother Lionel. Ethel, who appeared in dramatizations of her many plays on *Famous Actors Guild* in the 1936–37 season, also had been brought to radio by Vallee, for scenes from *Twelve-Pound Look, White-oaks* and *The Ghost of Yankee Doodle.*

67. BARRYMORE, Lionel (actor; b. April 28, 1878, Philadelphia, PA; d. Nov. 15, 1954, Van Nuys, CA). *Good News of 1938/ 1939* (1938–39); *Mayor of the Town* (1942–49); *Hallmark Playhouse* (1952–54).

By age 60 a hip injury and arthritis confined him to a wheelchair. His movie roles, written around his disability, however, continued; his radio work accelerated. The part as Mayor of rural Springdale proved inspired radio casting. His voice carried endearing ingredients of guffness and warmth in this human interest drama called *Mayor of the Town.*

Barrymore's annual interpretation of Ebenezer Scrooge in Dickens' *Christmas Carol* was Yuletide tra-

dition. He first read the work in 1938 on *Good News* and continued the offering each December for 17 years. A frequent guest on Rudy Vallee's Sealtest program in the early 1940s, he aired many appeals for war loan drives, the March of Dimes, Army recruiting and U.S. Treasury Bond programs.

A member of a famous family of the stage, he entered the profession at 15 in his grandmother's (Mrs. John Drew) production of *The Rivals.* He appeared in many plays along with early films in New York. His 1918 role in *The Copperhead* measured up to the theatrical clan's standards already set by his sister Ethel Barrymore and brother John. In 1931 he won an Academy Award for his performance in *A Free Soul,* and became a mainstay at MGM. He also achieved recognition for his artistic and musical achievements.

68. BARTLETT, Tommy (emcee; b. July 11, 1914, Milwaukee, WI). *Welcome Travelers* (1947–54).

As a youngster, Bartlett became enamored of people speaking over the air without any wires. His crystal set picked up Milwaukee stations and on good nights the powerful KDKA. A high school dropout, he claims to have started as an announcer at WISN Milwaukee before his 15th birthday in 1929. By age 19 he was a mainstay at WBBM Chicago where he handled the regional series, *Meet the Misses* and *The Misses Goes to Market.*

As host of ABC's *Welcome Travelers,* he reached his

Tommy Bartlett (courtesy of Capital Cities/ABC)

largest audience. Daily interviews of visitors at the College Inn of the Hotel Sherman paralleled the format of *Vox Pop.* There usually were questions relating to the state from which the traveler hailed and to a particular problem or dilemma facing an out-of-towner in Chicago. Bartlett was considered among the most able and least offensive emcee in the area of human-interest stories.

When he did a radio pickup from the Chicago Railroad Fair in 1950, his booth was next to the promoters of Florida's Cypress Gardens water skiing show. He soon organized a ski show in the Midwest. It grew into an annual summer attraction called Tommy Bartlett's Ski, Sky and Stage Show & Robot World & Exploratory at the Wisconsin Dells.

69. BARTON, Eileen (singer [signature song: "If I Knew You Were Comin' I'd've Baked a Cake"]; b. Nov. 24, 1927, Brooklyn, NY). *Frank Sinatra Show* (1944–45); *Teentimers Show* (1945); *Eileen Barton Show* (1945–46).

At 17 Barton sang opposite Frank Sinatra on his CBS show. The slim, 5-foot 3-inch bobbysoxer often wore loafers with copper pennies stuck in the flaps to show she was a Sinatra fan. (Silver pennies meant that you were for Crosby.) By August 1945 she had her own NBC program for teens every Saturday morning where she sang, acted and emceed.

Daughter of music publisher Ben Barton, she bowed on stage at age three, singing "Ain't Misbehavin'." She joined Ted Healy and his gang, then played on Horn and Hardart *Children's Hour.* At seven she was singing 18 songs a week over WMCA and making appearances with Vallee and Cantor. She had a long run on *Community Sing* with Berle, and appeared as guest on *Your Hit Parade* in the early '50s.

70. BARUCH, Andre (announcer, disc jockey; b. Aug. 20, 1906, Paris, France; d. Sept. 15, 1991, Beverly Hills, CA). *Your Hit Parade* (1935–53); *Kate Smith Program* (1937–40); *Jack Benny Show* (1946–47).

Closely identified with *Your Hit Parade* and sponsor Lucky Strike cigarettes, he brought a distinctive attention-getting manner to introduce songs and singers. Trained as a pianist, he entered the wrong audition line at CBS and was handed a list of foreign composers' names to read. It started his career as announcer in 1932. Remembered for stints on NBC's *American Album of Familiar Music* as well as *Myrt and Marge* and *The FBI in Peace and War,* he did many band remotes, baseball games and newsreel voiceovers.

With his wife, the singer Bea Wain, they launched *Mr. & Mrs. Music,* an early DJ show on WMCA New York. In the 1970s they had a radio talk show on WPBR Palm Beach. They later produced a nationally syndicated radio series of *Your Hit Parade* for a new generation of listeners and remained active at big band and broadcast industry events. A major in the

Andre Baruch

U.S. Army Signal Corps, Baruch was involved with the Armed Forces Radio Service in North Africa during World War II.

71. BAUER, Charita (actress; b. Dec. 20, 1923, Newark, NJ; d. Feb. 28, 1985, New York, NY). *The Aldrich Family* (1941–53); *Lora Lawton* (1944); *Guiding Light* (1950–56).

Dramatic actress in numerous daytime serials from the age of 17. From *David Harum* to *Guiding Light,* she remained popular for over 40 years as a key character on radio and television soaps. Charita came to the role of the matriarch, Bert Bauer, on *Guiding Light* first on radio in 1950, and enjoyed a very rewarding 34-year run in that part. For four years after the TV premiere of the program she continued to perform in both versions.

A photographer's model as a young child, she began broadcasting with *Let's Pretend* in the 1930s. Beginning in 1941 for a dozen years, she played the role of Mary Aldrich, Henry's sister, on *The Aldrich Family.* Bauer was periodically heard on *Front Page Farrell, Stella Dallas* and *Johnny Presents.*

72. BAUKHAGE, Hilmar Robert (H.R.) (commentator [catchphrase: "Baukhage talking."]; b. Jan. 7, 1889, La Salle, IL; d. Jan. 31, 1976, Washington, DC). *Four Star News* (1939); *News and Comment* (1942–50).

Writer and news commentator. Educated at the University of Chicago and at European universities prior to World War I service, Baukhage hit his stride on radio as war again broke out in Europe. One of his most famous broadcasts was made for NBC from The White House on December 7, 1941. He arrived at the same time as Steve Early, Roosevelt's press secretary. Early agreed to install a microphone in the newsroom for the first time, and Baukhage broadcast the news of the Japanese attack on Pearl Harbor that afternoon.

In 1942 he began a daytime news and commentary series for the Blue Network.

73. BAUR, Franklyn (singer; b. 1903, Brooklyn, NY; d. Feb. 24, 1950, Brooklyn, NY). *Palmolive Hour* (1927–28); *Voice of Firestone* (1928–31).

Tenor heard in the earliest network period. Brooklyn church soloist at 19, he became part of the Shannon Four, forerunner of The Revelers. They recorded for Victor and sang on the air with pianist-arranger Frank Black who built the quartet into a major vocal attraction. Baur appeared in *Ziegfeld Follies of 1927* and waxed many popular tunes as a freelancer. After a season on the *Palmolive Hour,* he left The Revelers, who replaced him with James Melton.

Firestone inaugurated its prestigious Monday concert series with Baur and Vaughn DeLeath. In 1930 or so his sponsor requested that he sing for a special industry meeting. But he refused unless the company paid an extra stipend in addition to his large weekly broadcast fee. Not long after, Firestone dropped Baur and he was shunned by other potential sponsors. In 1931 he left radio to study voice in France. A recital debut at Town Hall followed two years later, but it did little for a fast-fading career.

74. BEASLEY, Irene (emcee, singer; b. Jan. 28, 1904, Whitehaven, TN; d. Jan. 7, 1980, Ardsley, NY). *Old Dutch Girl* (1930–32); *Good Neighbors* (1943–46); *Grand Slam* (1943–53).

Originator and emcee of CBS' *Grand Slam,* a daytime musical quiz whereby listeners sent in song questions for studio contestants to answer. Both won merchandise as prizes. Mail entries averaged about 10,000 a week, spurred chiefly by Beasley's enthusiastic appeals and even-handed emcee manner.

A teacher in rural Mississippi, she sold records in a phonograph shop and sang the latest songs in a five-and-ten after school sessions and during vacations. She launched her radio career in Memphis with Art Gilham in 1928, then spent a year in theatres, studios and clubs in Chicago. Beasley wrote most of her own material, including original music, and in 1930 broadcast the *Old Dutch Girl* series, a personality program. In 1938 CBS signed her to develop, sing and announce *R.F.D. #1,* an institutional one-woman program designed for service to the rural housewife. She handled similar assignments on *Good Neighbors,* originally held by Frank Crumit and Julia Sanderson. She also pioneered the idea of singing commercials, and handled many for Proctor & Gamble.

Beasley retired from radio in the mid-50s, then worked in the realty business.

Irene Beasley

75. BEATTY, Morgan (newscaster; b. Sept. 6, 1902, Little Rock, AR; d. July 4, 1975, St. John's, Antigua). *News of the World* (1946–67).

Newspaper reporter and Associated Press chief, Beatty covered Europe on the eve of World War II. Joining NBC in 1941, he went to London as a war correspondent for two years. After serving as the network's Washington newsman, he took over as editor in chief and commentator of NBC's *News of the World.* From 1969 to 1975 he was the news analysis voice of AP NewsBreak, a tape service syndicated to stations. Beatty wrote and taped five commentaries weekly.

At the outset of the war, he compiled the first comprehensive map of the European Western front. His information was so complete that War Department strategists used the map for reference purposes.

76. BECK, Jackson (actor, announcer; b. July 23, 1912, New York, NY). *Myrt and Marge* (1937); *Believe It or Not* (1938); *Joe and Ethel Turp* (1942–43); *Brownstone Theatre* (1945); *Joe DiMaggio Show* (1950).

By age 31 Beck had performed on virtually every radio outlet in metropolitan New York. Announcer and narrator as well as actor, he began at WINS and WHN in the early 1930s. Initially, he also produced programs. Making the rounds of ad agencies week after week paid off. He picked up *Death Valley Days* and *Easy Aces* at NBC. Many assignments on serials and dramatic shows followed. He is especially remembered for the indelible opening line, "It's a bird . . . it's a plane . . . it's Superman," for Mutual's *Superman.* His endearingly husky voice led to the delivery of countless commercials, and associations with products from spark plugs to roach killers — long after most of his contemporaries had left the air. He was a voice — usually villainous — in more than 200 cartoons. He served AFTRA as a national board member and vice president.

After high school Beck worked as a detective-elevator operator in a department store where his ear picked up many accents from customers with roots in Italy, Greece, Russia and other far-off locales. The experience proved invaluable for radio. "Actors learned to 'play' a mike," he once remarked. "If I was doing a deep voice, for example, I would move close; if I was doing a high voice, I moved away. You had to know where the mike's magnetic field was and how to use it."

77. BECKER, Bob (commentator; b. Oct. 27, 1890, Terryville, SD; d. Aug. 10, 1962). *Fireside Chats About Dogs/Pet Parade* (1934–36, 1938–45).

Dog authority and sports writer. Red Heart Dog Food sponsored his canine series on NBC for ten years. A dogbreeder, he emphasized the training of household pets. Not long after Becker joined the *Chicago Tribune* in 1921 as an outdoor editor, he had gone on the air at WGN.

A graduate of Beloit College, he became a field naturalist with the Field Museum of Natural History in Chicago in 1912. Just before World War I service, he made several expeditions to South and Central America to collect species of birds and mammals. Becker wrote books on fishing and birds as well as *The Dog Book.* He also worked as managing editor of *Outdoorsman.*

78. BEEMER, Brace (actor [catchphrase: "Hi-yo, Silver, away."]; b. c1902, Mt. Carmel, IL; d. Feb. 28, 1965, Lake Orion, MI). *The Lone Ranger* (1941–54); *Challenge of the Yukon* (1941, 1953–54).

Most famous of all who played the role of *The Lone Ranger.* Beemer broadcast the Western serial for 13 years from WXYZ Detroit for the Blue-ABC network. Earlier, he had been its narrator and Sergeant Preston on *Challenge of the Yukon.* He took over as the Lone Ranger when Earle Graser was killed in an automobile accident in 1941. The program had started in 1933 with future film director-producer George Seaton in the role.

Beemer began his radio career in Indianapolis in 1922 and joined WXYZ in 1932. He played the masked rider until its last live episode in September 1954. In all, there were 2,958 half-hour programs. The lead character's distinctive voice proved to be a handicap. Beemer was unable to get back in radio because sponsors believed that his voice was identified too closely with the Lone Ranger.

An adventurous boy, Brace somehow enlisted in the Army in World War I, then suffered wounds while serving in France with the famed Rainbow Division. He was barely 14.

79. BEGLEY, Ed (actor; b. March 25, 1901, Hartford, CT; d. April 28, 1970, Hollywood, CA). *Adventures of Charlie Chan* (1944–47); *Richard Diamond, Private Detective* (1949–50).

A versatile and hardworking performer with more than 12,000 radio programs to his credit. In the 1940s he was detective Charlie Chan, while, at the same time, appearing in two serials, and in plays (*All My Sons*) and films (*Boomerang*). He capped his career with an Oscar in 1963 for his portrayal of a Southern political boss in *Sweet Bird of Youth.*

Following World War I Navy service and work as a jack-of-all trades, he was hired as announcer at WTIC Hartford in 1931. Nine years later he tried his luck in New York, and radio work came easy. His deep sonorous voice was well suited to the microphone. On screen he usually played villains and callous, hard-driving characters. In a lighter vein, he had periodic spots on *Fibber McGee and Molly, Aldrich Family, Father Knows Best,* and once played Santa Claus on *Chesterfield Supper Club.* His son, Ed, Jr., became a film actor.

80. BELCHER, Jerry (interviewer; b. Nov. 7, 1895, Austin, TX; d. June 1962). *Vox Pop* (1935–36); *Our Neighbors* (1937–38).

A station engineer-manager, Belcher helped to bring to radio *Sidewalk Interviews* at KTRH Houston in 1932 and worked as co-emcee with Parks Johnson.

Ed Begley (courtesy of Photofest)

Picked up by NBC, this *Vox Pop* series — called the newest and most novel stunt on the air in 1935 — scored high. In the wake of its success, Belcher developed a drinking problem and as a result missed broadcasts. At the same time, he publicly claimed ownership of the program, leading Johnson to file a suit to establish proprietorship. Belcher admitted in a pre-trial examination that he had no stake in *Vox Pop*. His misrepresentation and unreliability cost him his coveted job. He later worked as host of wandering vox pop-type programs, including *Interesting Neighbors* from WGY Schenectady.

A graduate of the University of Texas and a war veteran, Belcher wrote for farm magazines and city newspapers in the 1920s. While at KTRH he was Uncle Jerry to the children of the Southwest with readings of the Sunday comics.

81. BELL, Ralph (actor; b. c1916, New York, NY). *Valiant Lady* (1941–43); *This Is Nora Drake* (1948–59); *Five Star Matinee* (1957–58).

His deep portentous voice brought recurring roles as "heavies" in *Gangbusters, The FBI in Peace and War, Mr. District Attorney* and *Ellery Queen*. Soaps, beginning at Mutual, provided ongoing parts, notably as Arthur Drake, long-lost father of Nora Drake, Detective Mitchell on *Backstage Wife* and Charlie Gleason of *The Strange Romance of Evelyn Winters*. Bell worked on numerous *Eternal Light* dramas, *Falcon* mysteries and *Dimension X* stories.

A graduate of the University of Michigan, he appeared on Broadway in *What a Life, Native Son, The Crucible* and *View from the Bridge,* and with the Lincoln Center Repertory and Bucks County Playhouse. He became a familiar voice on TV commercials and as a cast member of *Pueblo, Wanted — Dead or Alive* and *Law and Order* into the 1990s.

82. BELL, Shirley (actress; b. Feb. 21, 1921, Chicago, IL). *Little Orphan Annie* (1931–40); *Arnold Grimm's Daughter* (1939).

Child actress in Chicago where she made her first appearance at WGN in 1927. Bell played Annie in the juvenile adventure serial from its beginning for Ovaltine. The sponsor paid the ten-year-old performer $50 a week. By the time the comic strip spinoff began to fade, her salary had risen to about $150. When the stage musical *Annie* took the country by storm in the 1970s, the media re-discovered Bell, the wife of a Chicago banker. By then her only work before a microphone was as a dedicated volunteer who recorded textbooks for the blind.

83. BENADERAT, Bea (actress; b. April 4, 1906, New York, NY; d. Oct. 13, 1968, Los Angeles, CA). *Tommy Riggs and Betty Lou* (1942–43); *Great Gildersleeve* (1943–49); *Fibber McGee and Molly* (1945–51); *Jack Benny Program* (1945–55); *A Day in the Life of Dennis Day* (1946–51).

Ralph Bell (courtesy of Ralph Bell)

A supporting player in various character roles for many comedians. She was well cast as Gertrude, a switchboard operator on *Jack Benny*. In 1947 Bea took various parts for *Burns and Allen,* and for their TV series played next-door neighbor Blanche Morton. Major roles on *Petticoat Junction* and *The Flintstones* (the voice of Betty Rubble) were highlights of the last years of her career.

Bea first appeared on radio at 12 singing in a children's production of *The Beggar's Opera* in San Francisco. Not long after, KGO hired her as a singer. "Little voices were in demand then because radio didn't have the knowhow yet for projection and sound," she said in 1966. Beginning on network in 1936 with the likes of Orson Welles, she periodically appeared on the *Red Skelton Show, Halls of Ivy* and *Railroad Hour*. Her first husband was announcer Jim Bannon.

84. BENCHLEY, Robert (comedian; b. Sept. 15, 1889, Worcester, MA; d. Nov. 21, 1945, New York, NY). *Buick Program* (1932–34); *Melody and Madness* (1938–39).

Writer-humorist. As president of the Harvard *Lampoon* while in college, he first nurtured his literary talent. A writer of humorous essays, skits and books, he worked as managing editor of *Vanity Fair* and dramatic critic of *The New Yorker*. Benchley branched out as a whimsical actor-comedian in musical revues and vaudeville, and an engaging after-dinner speaker and wit. He also created dozens of memorable movie shorts, including *How to Sleep,* a 1935 Oscar winner, and played supporting roles in such features as *I Married a Witch* and *The Sky's the Limit*.

Benchley began a 15-minute, twice-weekly radio series for Buick Motors at CBS in December 1932; a second program for Old Gold cigarettes ran in the late '30s. He was also a sought-after guest for *RCA Magic Key, Chase & Sanborn Hour* and *Duffy's Tavern.* One of his last appearances brought him to Hildegarde's *Raleigh Room.*

85. BENDIX, William (actor; b. Jan. 14, 1906, New York, NY; d. Dec. 14, 1964, Los Angeles, CA). *The Life of Riley* (1944–51).

He started out without any advantages, but was lucky and successful as an actor, and to borrow the title of his popular comedy drama lived "the life of Riley." For many long and lean years, Bendix struggled on the fringes of his profession — cabaret jobs, Federal Theatre projects, summer stock — until the Theatre Guild cast him in *The Time of Your Life,* his first real break. He then gained film parts, good-guy and bad-guy characterizations.

His lovable Chester Riley was a radio favorite that brightened the ABC and NBC weekend lineup. He said that Riley was the most difficult role for him to play. "You've always got to strive for laughs as a bumbler." When the happy but often harassed Riley appraised events in the fictional plot as an ex-Brooklynite working in an aircraft plant in California, he would groan: "What a revoltin' development dis is."

The series moved to television but the heavy-set, moon-faced Bendix was prevented from doing the role because of contract limitations. Jackie Gleason did it but the show did not do well. The onetime Bronx bat boy soon stepped back into the part as Riley, and regained for the comedy its original popularity.

His guest spots ranged from comedy sketches with Rudy Vallee and Bob Hope to dramatic leads on *Cavalcade of America* and *Screen Guild Players* (where he recreated his starring role in *The Babe Ruth Story*).

86. BENNY, Jack (comedian [signature song: "Love in Bloom"]; [catchphrase: "Now cut that out."]; b. Feb. 14, 1894, Chicago, IL; d. Dec. 26, 1974, Beverly Hills, CA). *Jack Benny Program* (1932–55); *Truth or Consequences* (1947–48).

His radio character stood as a national institution. Jack Benny, in the words of *New York Times* critic John J. O'Connor, "was perhaps the most enduring and astonishingly shrewd creation of radio. For anyone growing up in the nineteen thirties and forties, Sunday night at 7 o'clock meant Jack Benny and 'the gang'. . . . The brilliantly calculated Benny persona, offering magnanimous displays of the hilariously petty, was being fixed securely in the public's affection."

Few if any star-caliber performers are more closely identified with the days of radio than this top-rated funny man. An earnest, hard-working entertainer, he prepared long and studiously for his well-scripted broadcasts. His peerless punch-line timing was a paragon to be studied by every actor. His deadpan

silence between lines generated some of his greatest and longest audience laughs (namely, the demand of a hold-up thug: "Your money or your life" and Benny's response: "I'm thinking.") His double takes were the envy of his profession.

Benny's character was a tight-wad and show-off who was often deflated by the program's sure-footed cast: Phil Harris, the orchestra leader; Eddie Anderson as the valet Rochester; Mary Livingstone, his girl; Don Wilson, the announcer; and Mel Blanc, a performer of many voices in supporting roles. This readily recognized Benny family became welcome visitors each week; their keen-witted dialogue stimulated the imaginations of listeners who conjured up settings and contexts. Benny and his gang, in the process, became real friends.

He came to radio as a guest on Ed Sullivan's show in March 1932, and two months later had his own program for Canada Dry on NBC. A veteran of vaudeville — including a coveted booking as emcee at the Palace — Benny was always among the top ten programs. His national character developed unusual longevity, outlasting cohort Fred Allen with whom he had a good-natured on-the-air feud. His position in show business was such that he was picked as a *Truth or Consequences* mystery celebrity, "The Walking Man," in their audience-participation sweepstakes.

In 1948 Benny took his show to CBS as part of a multi-million-dollar capital gains package deal. That network kept him on radio until the mid-50s. But

Jack Benny

by then he had settled well into television, although critics in 1950 initially noted his program had little visual appeal. For many it contrasted with the magic of radio listening when Benny could create an imaginative show of an inestimable appeal.

A sought-after guest on radio and television, Benny often played his violin for laughs. He could, indeed, handle the instrument very well, and his benefit concerts in symphony halls on behalf of good causes yielded millions of dollars during the last 15 years of his life.

87. BENSON, Court (actor; b. Nov. 4, 1914, Vancouver, Canada; d. Feb. 5, 1995, Mount Kisco, NY). *Tennessee Jed* (1946–47); *Gang Busters* (1946–48).

Character actor-announcer. From 1946 to 1959 Benson was intermittently heard on more than 14 soap operas, ranging from *Backstage Wife* and *Big Sister* to *Young Widder Brown* and *Wendy Warren*. He was narrator-announcer of *Tennessee Jed,* a juvenile adventure serial, and narrator for *Gang Busters*. For *Lux Radio Theatre* over CBC, he cut in to speak the intro, sign-off and commercials because Lever Brothers marketed different products in Canada. His prime-time work included *The Falcon, Big Town* and *Suspense*.

He performed on *The CBS Mystery Theatre* when this series revived radio in the 1970s. In comparing the long-rehearsed *Cavalcade of America* with the short run-throughs of the Mystery Theatre, he stated: "Experienced radio actors have a very special talent in that they are able to develop a character instantly although never having seen the script beforehand."

For television, Benson had running parts on *Guiding Light, Edge of Night* and *The Doctors*. His film credits in the United States and England include *No, My Darling Daughter, Guns of August* and *Bananas,* as well as many industrial and educational shorts.

Courtney Benson graduated from law school at the University of Toronto. He began broadcasting hockey games for Imperial Oil over CBC in 1937 and went on to perform in dramatic offerings. He had first spoke at a mike at age 16 in Calgary, playing an Indian. Benson served as a captain in the Canadian infantry in Europe from 1941 to 1945. He and his actress-wife Grace Matthews cracked New York radio in 1946.

88. BENZELL, Mimi (singer; b. April 6, 1924, Bridgeport, CT; d. Dec. 23, 1970, Manhasset, NY). *Jack Pearl and Mimi Benzell* (1951).

Lyric coloratura at the Met for four seasons, beginning in 1945 as Queen of the Night in *The Magic Flute*. Because that house would not permit her to accept a supper club engagement of two weeks in New York in 1949, she rejected her contract renewal that year. With a background in theatre — Benzell had played *Rosalinda* on Broadway — she turned to radio and television. Appearances on *The Railroad Hour* were NBC highlights. But not until 1961 did her career approach the level of her Met success some 15

Court Benson (courtesy of Michael Stevenson)

years earlier. She assumed a starring role in *Milk and Honey,* a long-running Broadway musical in which she appeared opposite another former Met and radio singer, Robert Weede.

In the mid-60s Benzell returned to radio with a daily two-hour WNBC talk show called *Lunch with Mimi,* and described by a critic as "diffuse, freewheeling and sporadically interesting."

89. BERCH, Jack (singer [signature song: "I'm a-whistlin'"]; b. Aug. 26, 1907, Sigel, IL; d. Dec. 10, 1992, Jamaica, NY). *The Kitchen Pirate* (1935–36); *The Sweetheart Serenader* (1939–41); *Jack Berch Show* (1945–52).

Daytime singer with program of light music and informal chatter. When housewives tired of listening to the tribulations of their soap opera characters, they turned for relief to the songs of Berch. His shows ran on all four networks with musical backup ranging from Mark Warnow's orchestra to Charles Magnante's trio. His opened his program with a flirtatious whistle, followed by his self-written theme song. Berch occasionally read poetry and through his "Heart-to-Heart Hookup" regularly sang a number dedicated to a listener, usually a shut-in or someone in distress. Beginning in 1946, Prudential Insurance Company sponsored the baritone's daily 15-minute segments.

Berch's first job was selling coffee door to door. He would arrive at doorsteps singing. One particular housewife was the spouse of the station manager of WKBN Youngstown, Ohio. She got him his first audition.

90. BERG, Gertrude (actress [catchphrase: "Yoo Hoo, Mrs. Bloom."]; b. Oct. 3, 1899, New York, NY; d. Sept. 14, 1966, New York, NY). *The Goldbergs* (1929–34, 1937–45, 1949–50); *House of Glass* (1935, 1953–54).

Berg wrote and directed the sketches in which she starred as Molly Goldberg, starting as an NBC sustainer in 1929. She prepared the scripts based on episodes from her own life as a folksy, warmhearted Jewish housewife, mother and neighbor. Her instinctive showmanship carried her fictional family in the Bronx to long-lasting acclaim, and into early television, plus a re-creation, *Molly and Me,* in a film and as a Broadway play. The series was equally popular with Jewish and non-Jewish audiences, and promoted inter-faith understanding. Pepsodent was sponsor of the program from 1931 to 1934. CBS revived it three years later. In 1941 NBC began airing it, too, giving the Goldbergs simultaneous exposure on both networks.

In 1959 Berg returned to Broadway in *Majority of One* with her well-established hausfrau role, garnering audience and critical praise and winning a Tony award.

91. BERGEN, Edgar (comedian; b. Feb. 16, 1903, Chicago, IL; d. Sept. 30, 1978, Las Vegas, NV). *Fleischmann Hour* (1936–37); *Charlie McCarthy Show* (1937–56).

Ventriloquist Bergen demonstrated to skeptics that his art could succeed on radio. His vaudeville act auditioned for stations and network talent scouts but the answer was always the same, "It's ridiculous." When an agent for Rudy Vallee saw mild-mannered voice thrower Bergen and his outspoken alter ego Charlie McCarthy perform in the Rainbow Room at Radio City, he invited them to make a guest appearance on the *Fleischmann Hour.* An unexpected surprise hit, they returned week after week for four months until bringing their own show to the Sunday NBC comedy lineup.

"Inflections of the voice, so important to a ventriloquist," Bergen explained, "are faithfully registered by the microphone. Voice shading, impossible in the theatre, is easy on the air." Hollywood-based Bergen and his irrepressible, smart-aleck dummy concentrated on radio ($10,000 a week) and films ($150,000 a picture). "Born" July 18, 1920 in Chicago, McCarthy acquired a personality so formidable that people forgot he was not human. There were countless incidents in which people handed objects to Charlie without realizing that he could not hold anything in his curled wooden fingers. When Eleanor Roosevelt was first introduced to Bergen and McCarthy, she impulsively extended her hand to Charlie. And in 1950 he was the honor guest on an unusual two-part *This Is Your Life.*

92. BERLE, Milton (comedian; [signature song: "Near You"]; b. July 12, 1908, New York, NY). *Three-Ring Time* (1941); *Milton Berle Show* (1943–45, 1947–48); *Let Yourself Go* (1945).

Edgar Bergen & Charlie McCarthy (courtesy of Steve Jelf)

Radio occupied much of his time before television claimed him as its king of comedy — and Uncle Miltie — in the late 1940s via his *Texaco Star Theatre.* Beginning in 1913 or so, Berle went on to do it all in show business — silent motion pictures, vaudeville, legitimate stage, Hollywood films, nightclubs and broadcasting. His brash, rat-a-tat joke-telling never took him to the top ranks of radio comedy yet provided many humorous segments, especially on *Fleischmann Hour, Stop Me If You've Heard This One* and *Three-Ring Time.* For two months in 1949 he played "Laughing Boy" in a *Truth or Consequences* mystery voice contest.

In 1948 NBC turned to him for a video variety hour. With a weekly vaudeville stage format, he almost singlehandedly launched the medium, and sold millions of sets to new viewers. Few retrospectives of early TV or roasts of fellow comics are complete without the irrepressible Milton centerstage.

93. BERNARD, Al (singer; [The Boy from Dixie]; b. Nov. 23, 1888, New Orleans, LA;

d. March 6, 1949, New York, NY). *Dutch Masters Minstrels* (1929–30); *Molle Merry Minstrels* (1934–35).

Performer in minstrel shows and vaudeville before his radio bow in 1923. A singer of comic and novelty songs, Bernard recorded frequently and made one of the first talking-singing film shorts. He harmonized with Billy Beard in radio's *Raybestos Twins* from 1928–30. Among the 125 songs he wrote were "Blue-eyed Sally" and "Let Me Be the First to Kiss You Good Morning."

94. BERNER, Sara (actress; b. Jan. 12, 1912, Albany, NY). *Nitwit Court* (1944); *Jack Benny Program* (1945–55); *The Fabulous Dr. Tweedy* (1946–47); *Sara's Private Caper* (1950).

Zesty supporting player on the comedy-variety shows of Fanny Brice, Bill Bendix, Rudy Vallee, Amos 'n' Andy, Charlotte Greenwood and many more. Her longest-running parts were as Jack Benny's girl friend Gladys and as telephone operator Mabel. Among her roles with Eddie Cantor was an impersonation of Hildegarde. NBC and General Mills tried to star-build Sara by a summer intro of *Sara's Private Caper*—she played a typist and file clerk — but the series lasted eight weeks, as did an earlier co-starring format called *Nitwit Court*.

Before reaching the networks, she did "anything and everything" as a parttimer and fill-in at WCAU Philadelphia. While a salesgirl in New York, she enjoyed national exposure through Major Bowes' *Original Amateur Hour*.

95. BERNIE, Ben (bandleader [The Old Maestro] [catchphrase: "Yowsah, Yowsah."]; b. May 30, 1891, Bayonne, NJ; d. Oct. 20, 1943, Beverly Hills, CA). *Ben Bernie Orchestra* (1931–40); *Musical Mock Trial* (1940); *Ben Bernie Musical Quiz* (1940–41).

Bernie's orchestra was chosen to play on the very first NBC network broadcast on November 15, 1926. His segment was a remote pickup from New York's Hotel Roosevelt. Three years earlier he had been one of the first jazz bands to broadcast over network; it consisted of stations in New York and Philadelphia. He was also the first radio bandleader to use a theme song ("My Buddy").

A violinist in a large family that loved music, he studied at New York College of Music and Columbia University. But a concert career was beyond his reach so he played in vaudeville, later teaming up with accordionist-comedian Phil Baker. Bernie's dance band had long runs in major hotels, with much late night exposure over the air. His sentimental signature songs "It's a Lonesome Old Town" and "Au Revoir, Pleasant Dreams" were trademarks of his broadcasts that always included Bernie's corny gags and droll kidding with his musicians, his audience, his sponsors and himself. At one time or another his bandstand "lads" included singers Billy Hillpot, Scrappy Lambert, Dinah Shore and Rudy Vallee, saxophonist Dick Stabile, and pianist Oscar Levant.

96. BESTOR, Don (bandleader [signature song: "Teach Me to Smile"]; b. Sept. 23, 1889, Longford, SD*; d. Jan. 13, 1970, Metamora, IL). *Nestle Program* (1933–34); *Jack Benny Program* (1934–36).

Music director for Jack Benny, he wrote the musical commercial, J-E-L-L-O, which was heard often on the comedian's program. He led the Benson Orchestra of Chicago in the 1920s but his later aggregation did not gain much stature among big bands of the '30s. His compositions, including "Doodle Doo Doo," were catchy but fleetingly popular. He also wrote "Contented," the theme for *The Contented Hour*. A pianist, Bestor served as music director for WHN New York from 1942–46.

A charter member of Music Corporation of America, he went on radio at KDKA, playing very early remotes from the William Penn Hotel in 1922. Bestor claimed his biggest mistake was leaving the Benny show for nightclub and theatre jobs in the East, and

One source gives Madison, WI.

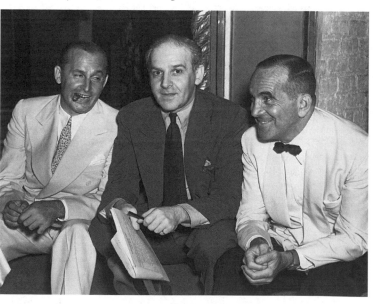

Ben Bernie, Walter Winchell, Al Jolson

not rejoining him later. Instead, Bestor recommended a bandleader named Phil Harris.

97. BIGGS, E. Power (organist; b. March 29, 1906, Westcliff, England; d. March 10, 1977, Boston, MA). *Organ Program* (1942–58).

Foremost recitalist of serious organ music. Biggs contributed to the renaissance of the instrument in its classical mode, and often denounced the encroachment of electronic organs in churches and concert halls. His Sunday recitals over CBS reached many listeners, persuading them of the brilliance and dignity of the organ. For his broadcasts he performed the works of Bach, Mozart and other Old Masters. Nevertheless, he commissioned pieces from such contemporary writers as Roy Harris, Walter Piston, Howard Hanson and Benjamin Britten. His numerous recordings similarly focused wide attention on this ancient instrument.

Born in England where he studied organ, harmony and counterpoint at the Royal Academy of Music, Biggs came to the United States in 1929. He made his New York debut at the Wanamaker Auditorium three years later. He spent most of his career as a church organist in Brookline and Cambridge, Massachusetts, and taught at the Longy School of Music. Biggs was also the official organist of the Boston Symphony.

98. BINYON, Conrad (actor; b. Jan. 30, 1931, Hollywood, CA). *One Man's Family* (1939–50); *Mayor of the Town* (1942–48); *Life of Riley* (1943–44).

His recurring role as young Hank of *One Man's Family*—his radio bow—ran for a dozen years. He played Butch opposite Lionel Barrymore and Junior with William Bendix on *Mayor of the Town* and *Life of Riley,* respectively, and such youngsters as Tad and Kip in adventure segments on Smilin' Ed McConnell's *Buster Brown Gang.*

"I never had any thought about the microphone other than having to 'play to it' so that my dialogue would be heard by the engineer mixing the program," Binyon observed. "I had no formal training for radio. In early childhood, I appeared in showcase children's plays on stage. And that was all."

Radio was his second area of acting, films being the first. At six months of age, a director on Hollywood Boulevard spotted Conrad in a stroller pushed by his mother. An extra and bit player, he appeared in Our Gang scenes, and as his career continued worked with Cary Grant, Joseph Cotton, Elizabeth Taylor and Alan Ladd. He played the key role as an orphan in the band of kids who find shelter and food as guerrillas and slow Nazi advances in a Russian village in the 1943 wartime feature *The Boy from Stalingrad.*

Interested in flying, he got his pilot's license at 17 and joined the Air National Guard. His unit was called up for active duty when the Korean War heated up. His entry into the military led to a 20-year service career and ended his acting days.

E. Power Biggs

99. BIVENS, Bill (announcer; b. March 24, 1915, Wadesboro, NC; d. Jan. 15, 1984, Charlotte, NC). *Fred Waring Show* (1942–49); *Vox Pop* (1943–44).

Announcer-writer, chiefly with Fred Waring. For CBS Bivens worked in Washington and at its network-owned WBT Charlotte, before settling in New York in 1941. He evolved into a "personality" while with Waring; at one point he read baseball scores on

Conrad Binyon (courtesy of Conrad Binyon)

Fred's *Pleasure Time*. He also announced Harry James' musical series and subbed for Arthur Godfrey.

Bivens got his first radio job at WRBU Gastonia at age 12. He worked as chief announcer at WFBC Greenville, South Carolina before going to CBS in 1933. In the 1960s he returned to WBT.

100. BLACK, Frank (conductor; b. Nov. 28, 1894, Philadelphia, PA; d. Nov. 1967, Atlanta, GA). *RCA Radiotrons* (1927–29); *Palmolive Hour* (1927–31); *Jack Benny Program* (1933–34); *RCA Magic Key* (1935–39); *NBC String Symphony* (1936); *Cities Service Concert* (1938–44); *Harvest of Stars* (1946–50).

As music director of NBC, he had his pick of concert programs and contributed his conducting and arranging talents to numerous series and special broadcasts. A pianist, theatre music director and piano roll company executive, he came into contact with the vocal quartet, The Revelers, during a recording session. The group's nationwide fame helped boost Black as a conductor. He frequently led the NBC Symphony and Symphony of the Air.

In 1928 he was named NBC general music director. In that capacity a day's work consisted of: reading and passing on new scores, auditioning artists, consulting with staff conductors and musicians, purchasing musical instruments, making musical arrangements for his programs, rehearsing his orchestra, confering with executives. He often made symphonic arrangements of Tin Pan Alley tunes and simplified versions of classic symphonic works. When network music shows ended, so did his all-consuming career. His last appearance as conductor was for Jane Pickens in the early 1950s.

101. BLAINE, Joan (actress; b. April 22, c1900, Fort Dodge, IA; d. April 19, 1949, New York, NY). *Silken Strings* (1933); *A Tale of Today* (1936–39); *Valiant Lady* (1938–c1944).

Blaine originated the part of Mary Marlin in 1934 and Joan Barrett (*Valiant Lady*) in 1938, both in Chicago where many soaps and serials burst forth. She attended Northwestern University, received a law degree, then put aside her practice to serve an apprenticeship with the Chicago Theatre Guild. A singer and harpist, she toured the country before becoming established in radio and on stage. A native of Fort Dodge, Iowa, she was a descendant

of James G. Blaine, late-19th century Secretary of State and Presidential contender.

For six years she was voted the most popular daytime actress in audience polls — and considered the best dressed by many.

102. BLANC, Mel (actor; b. May 30, 1908, San Francisco, CA; d. July 10, 1989, Los Angeles, CA). *Jack Benny Program* (1939–40, 1944–55); *Abbott and Costello Show* (1943–46); *Maxwell House Coffee Time* (1945–46); *Judy Canova Show* (1945–53).

The voice of some 400 characters, including the cartoon world's Bugs Bunny, Daffy Duck, Tweety Pie and the Road Runner. He had studied music, and with his wife Estelle, won contracts to appear on daily radio programs at KEX Portland in the mid-1930s. The sponsors could not afford to hire additional actors, so Blanc used his multi-voiced talent to create a one-man repertory company.

In Los Angeles he began a job in a Warner Brothers cartoon workshop where Porky Pig emerged along with Bugs and his line "What's up, doc?" Radio activities continued. In the Jack Benny show he was Carmichael, the irascible polar bear; Monsieur Le Blanc, the violin teacher; Sy, the Mexican gardener; and Benny's old Maxwell car. His colorful characterizations and sound effects surfaced on numerous comedy shows, including Burns and Allen (as the wistful postman), Abbott and Costello (as Bugs) and Judy Canova (as Pedro and Paw).

Blanc formed his own company to produce and market commercials and fillers for radio and tele-

Frank Black, Sigmund Romberg, Vivienne Segal

Mel Blanc (courtesy of Steve Jelf)

vision. A number of announcements were public service-oriented for the American Cancer Society and State of California. He also composed two of the most memorable cartoon character songs: "The Woody Woodpecker Song" and "I Tawt I Taw a Puddy Tat."

103. BLOCH, Ray (conductor; [signature song: "Music in My Fingers"]; b. Aug. 3, 1902, Alsace-Lorraine, France; d. March 29, 1982, Miami, FL). *Johnny Presents* (1940–42, 1944–46); *Milton Berle Show* (1947–48); *Hollywood Opera House* (1947–48).

Omnipresent musical director on scores of CBS and NBC programs, beginning in 1930. His musicians were heard on *Gay Nineties Revue, Milton Berle Show, Crime Doctor* and *Phillip Morris Playhouse.*

A pianist with small combos and dance band leader in the '20s, he provided music for a number of quiz shows in the peak years of audience games: *Quick as a Flash, Take It or Leave It, Sing It Again* and *Songs for Sale.* Bloch picked up a measure of fame working with Ed Sullivan and Jackie Gleason in early television. He served on the original board of governors of the Academy of Radio and Television Arts & Sciences.

104. BLOCK, Martin (announcer, disc jockey [signature song "Make-Believe Ballroom"]; b. 1903, Los Angeles, CA; d. Sept. 19, 1967, Englewood, NJ). *Chesterfield Supper Club* (1944–50); *Make-Believe Ballroom* (1954–60).

Disc jockey with his enormously successful and widely copied *Make-Believe Ballroom,* a fixture at WNEW for 20 years, beginning in 1934. This local program was so popular that the station built a small-scale ballroom for Block, complete with crystal chandelier, red-velvet chair and black linoleum on the floor. All it lacked was the "revolving stage" for the big

bands he presented via recordings. He once estimated he had played 365,000 records in his late morning and late afternoon shows. Sponsors paid over $10 million to buy time. His mellifluous, persuasive voice reputedly sold $750-million worth of products. Block's on-the-air tools were once analyzed as follows: (1) his voice, which "seems to spell S-E-X to every listening housewife" (said *Collier's*) and (2) his psychology of salesmanship.

Block also worked as a network announcer for Kay Kyser and *Pepper Young's Family.* For Chesterfield he was both an emcee and commercial announcer on the Monday-through-Friday *Supper Club.*

His first radio job was with an outlet in Tijuana, Mexico, where he delivered spiels for clothing and food. In 1934 WNEW hired him for $20 a week. His *Ballroom* originated during the trial of Bruno Hauptmann for the kidnapping of Lindbergh's son. The station had a commentator in the courtroom and Block was expected to fill in the time between his spots. He spun records between trial bulletins, and soon had a sponsor and a set format. Block was influential in promoting records of many artists and ran semi-annual band popularity contests.

In 1954 he signed with ABC at $250,000 a year to spin discs for some 23 hours locally and on the network each week. "It's that old Block magic, only now there's more of it, at a new time, new spot on your dial," ABC declared in full-page ads.

105. BLOCK, Vivian (actress; b. Sept. 10, 1920, Brooklyn, NY). *Let's Pretend* (1934–44); *Wilderness Road* (1936); *March of the Games* (1938–39).

Early radio child performer. Vivian appeared before age eight on NBC's *Coast-to-Coast on a Bus,* then gradually moved into the CBS cast of two Nila Mack productions, *Sunday Morning at Aunt Susan's* and *Let's Pretend.* She played Ann, a member of the pioneering Weston family who were trailblazers with Daniel Boone (Ray Collins) on *Wilderness Road.* A singer as well as an actress, this Professional Children's School graduate ventured into primetime with *Show Boat* and *The Aldrich Family.* Her ability to create baby cries paid off with jobs on *The Life and Loves of Dr. Susan.* She also appeared in the premiere of Aaron Copland's opera *Second Hurricane.* At one time as a teenager Vivian drew over $300 a week from all her assignments.

In 1942 she married a dentist in Connecticut and soon retired.

106. BOND, Ford (announcer; b. Oct. 23, 1904, Louisville, KY; d. Aug. 15, 1962, St. Croix, VI). *Collier's Hour* (1929–31); *Cities Service Concert* (1930–44); *Manhattan Merry-Go-Round* (1932–49); *Highways in Melody* (1944–48); *Cities Service Band of America* (1948–56).

Bond entered radio as a singer. In 1922 he accepted a job as a vocalist and program director at WHAS Louisville. In 1929 he left WHAS to be

Ford Bond

general program executive for NBC's program department in New York. A spokesman for Cities Service from 1930 to the late '50s — the longest sponsor-announcer association in the history of radio — Bond could have easily passed for a high-level corporate leader. In fact, he later became a resort developer and builder. In the 1940s he served as a consultant for radio to Gov. Thomas E. Dewey's campaigns for governor and president, and later radio and TV director in New York State for Eisenhower in the 1952 presidential race. He was married to soprano Lois Bennett.

107. BONIME, Josef (conductor; b. Feb. 26, 1891, Vilna, Poland; d. Nov. 8, 1959, Westport, CT). *Death Valley Days* (1930–c1942); *Five Star Theatre* (1932–33); *Echoes of New York* (1939–41).

Popular and classical music conductor. He directed aggregations for *Columbia School of the Air, Let's Dance* and *Dr. Christian,* and led the CBS Symphony. His music for the Wild West adventure series *Death Valley Days* included the bugle call refrain leading into a brief summary of the next episode. Bonime appeared in Vitaphone shorts and worked as musical counsel to McCann-Erickson ad agency.

Prior to radio he toured as accompanist to violinists Mischa Elman and Eugene Ysaye. His first broadcast was in 1925 at WJZ as director of a small ensemble. He studied piano and composition at Juilliard, and later joined its faculty.

108. BOOTH, Shirley (actress; b. Aug. 30, 1907, New York, NY; d. Oct. 16, 1992, North Chatham, MA). *Duffy's Tavern* (1941–43).

Her best radio role, the wisecracking Miss Duffy on *Duffy's Tavern,* typlified her flair for playing captivating characters in a comic milieu. Booth was married (1929–42) to Ed Gardner, the Archie of *Duffy's Tavern* and the program's creator. Her dramatic performance in *Come Back, Little Sheba* on stage and screen won both a Tony and an Oscar. As TV's perky busybody *Hazel* she received more awards (two Emmys). Her first radio appearance in a dramatic role — Amanda in *The Glass Menagerie* — was on *The Theatre Guild on the Air* in 1953.

109. BORGE, Victor (comedian, pianist; b. Jan. 3, 1909, Copenhagen, Denmark). *Kraft Music Hall* (1941–43); *Victor Borge Show* (1945–47).

His Comedy in Music productions grew from U.S. radio employment after fleeing Nazi-occupied Denmark. An introduction to Rudy Vallee led to a stint as warm-up performer for his studio audience. The pianist did his punctuation number whereby periods, commas, semicolons, and so on became assorted sound effects as he read a love story from a book. "I do not wish to claim that it paralyzed the studio audience," Borge wrote in a 1957 *Saturday Evening Post* series, "but the results were sensational for me, and marked the starting point of my American career." Crosby's scouts signed him when Vallee in-

Shirley Booth

dicated that his show had no room for more cast members.

A week later Borge made a somewhat nervous debut on *Kraft Music Hall*. It made him famous overnight, and led to 54 appearances on that show over the next 14 months. In the meantime, Vallee, losing a major discovery, viewed him as an ingrate; nevertheless, he collected an agent's fee from Borge for several years. A jovial and likeable personality, Borge inaugurated his own show in 1945, a summer fill-in for *Fibber McGee and Molly*. A year later it regrouped as a series with Benny Goodman. He was a frequent guest on *Chamber Music Society of Lower Basin Street* and *Chesterfield Supper Club*.

110. BOSWELL, Connee (singer; b. Dec. 3, 1907, New Orleans, LA; d. Oct. 11, 1976, New York, NY). *Music That Satisfies* (1932–33); *You Said It* (1938); *Kraft Music Hall* (1940–42); *Camel Caravan* (1942); *Chesterfield Supper Club* (1944–45).

When in the mid-1930s Martha and Vet Boswell decided to get married, the close harmony Boswell Sisters broke up, and Connee struck out on her own. Despite being crippled by polio (a disability compounded by an accidental fall while a child) and confined to a wheelchair, she became one of the busiest singing stars on radio. During the 1937–38 season she made 16 guest appearances — more than most network performers during the course of a year. Her frequent work with Bing Crosby endeared her to

swing music fans with a penchant for New Orleans style of vocalizing.

The Boswell Sisters first broadcast over a network on *California Melodies* from CBS in Los Angeles, although they had already sung over a local New Orleans station before touring the midwest. By mid-1931 they had their own Columbia show two nights a week and were soon featured in Paramount's *The Big Broadcast of 1932*.

111. BOURDON, Rosario (conductor; b. March 6, 1885, Longuereil, Quebec, Canada; d. April 24, 1961, New York, NY). *Cities Service Concert* (1927–38); *Great Personalities* (1931–32).

As musical director for the Victor label, he appeared on radio as early as 1925. He chiefly conducted semi-classical and popular works for Cities Service and its soprano Jessica Dragonette, and led broadly appealing concerts of light opera in Carnegie Hall and of the Naumburg Orchestra on the Mall in Central Park.

A cellist, he had studied at Quebec Academy of Music and concertized in Europe. Bourdon made the first successful cello records, played with the Philadelphia Orchestra early in the Stokowski period, and was associated with Victor Herbert.

112. BOWER, Roger (announcer, emcee; b. 1903, New York, NY; d. May 17, 1979, Sharon, CT). *Can You Top This?* (1940–51, 1953–54); *Stop Me If You've Heard This One* (1947–48).

Producer-director, moderator and scorekeeper on the joke-swapping *Can You Top This?* that began as a WOR sustainer. An afterpiece of the game was a

Victor Borge

Boswell Sisters: Vet, Martha, Connie

"clowntable" discussion on the origin of certain gags and types of humor. Bower hosted a similar session in the late 1940s on which he read listener's jokes. If one of the three panelists had heard the joke, he yelled "Stop" and picked up Bower's narration to the punchline.

At WOR from 1928–52, Bower directed *The Witch's Tale,* one of the earliest horror shows, and produced and directed *The Crime Club,* a weekly whodonit. He also announced the first Macy's Thanksgiving Day Parade. Bower broke into radio at WMCA in 1927.

113. BOWES, Major Edward (emcee [catchphrase: "All right, all right,"]; b. June 14, 1874, San Francisco, CA; d. June 13, 1946, Rumson, NJ). *Capitol Family* (1925–41); *Original Amateur Hour* (1934–45).

His amateur show was voted the most popular radio program in 1935, and reputedly reached 20 million listeners a week and paid Bowes one million dollars a year. Thousands of performers applied each week for a place on his stage, and of these a few hundred were invited to try out, and 15 selected for his *Hour.* Tens of thousands of listeners telephoned, telegraphed and wrote in their choice for the best amateur. From the winners and runnersup, he organized troupes to tour the country's theatres. Copycat amateur shows sprung up on all the networks and over regional stations, and at local theatres. Countless organizations throughout the country mounted their own small-scale version of the phenomenally successful and long popular series.

Director of the Capitol Theatre, the Major started his program as a sideline in 1934 when trying to build up Loew's New York Station WHN. *Variety* took note: "For showmanship, deft handling, color and human interest appeal it's one of the slickest things yet effected by any of the New York stations . . . If Major Bowes thinks a tyro's efforts have passed the indulgence point the latter is abruptly halted by the ringing of a gong. The gong idea here is a species of substitute for the hook of the old vaude house days. Talent that Major Bowes parades before his mike is of a highly varied assortment and well balanced."

The proceedings stemmed from Bowes' older program *Capitol Family,* a Sunday morning roundup of his stage show regulars and generally little known guest performers. The "gang" had been organized by "Roxy" Rothafel in 1922 to advertise the Capitol. When that showman departed for the new Roxy Theatre, Bowes assembled his own group.

Actually CBS was the first network to broadcast a contest called *National Amateur Night* with Ray Perkins. By March 1935 NBC grabbed Bowes and his *Hour* from WHN, and provided a major sponsor, Chase & Sanborn. Not too long after, CBS and Chrysler Motors with more money and accommodations added the ruddy-faced showman to its lineup.

Bowes acquired a multi-million-dollar fortune from his gong ringing, along with hundreds of keys to U.S. cities, and numerous police and fire chief badges — and not to overlook the lasting gratitude of thousands of successful radio troupers.

114. BOYD, William (actor; b. June 5, 1898, Hendrysburg, OH*; d. Sept. 12, 1972, South Laguna Beach, CA). *Hopalong Cassidy* (1950–52).

Cowboy star who parlayed his Western films and TV shows into a multi-million-dollar marketing enterprise. His *Hopalong Cassidy* series rode the media trail from theatre screen to home screen, and lastly to radio receivers.

Paramount had first cast the 37-year-old silent screen has-been (*Volga Boatmen, King of Kings*) as the lead in the bottom-of-the-bill oaters in 1935. By 1948 — the year television began to take off as home entertainment — straight-shooting Boyd had made 66 pictures. He acquired all rights to his character and his horse Topper. On TV his Hoppy B Westerns immediately captured the interest and admiration of youngsters. Preaching a code of conduct of honesty, kindness, loyalty and ambition, Boyd became an idol of millions of children and a favorite of their parents. He proceeded to turn out 106 video shows over the next five years. During that period Mutual and General Mills brought the series to radio in a half-hour

Other sources indicate 1895.

Edward Bowes

William Boyd

cowboy thriller heard Sundays over 517 outlets; CBS later picked it up for the second season.

Boyd's broadcast royalties were secondary to his merchandising revenues from comic books, lunchboxes, candy bars, shirts and bicycles. All told there were over 2,000 Hopalong Cassidy products. Boyd retired in 1953 to a quiet and well-cushioned seclusion in Palm Desert.

115. BRACKEN, Eddie (comedian, actor; b. Feb. 7, 1920, Astoria, NY). *The Aldrich Family* (1939–40); *Eddie Bracken Show* (1945–47).

Stage actor in the Aldrich Family story *What a Life*, Bracken had an auspicious start on radio as Dizzy, Henry Aldrich's dopey pal. He followed through with broad comedy shots on *Chase & Sanborn Hour* and *Kraft Music Hall* while making *Life with Henry, The Fleet's In, Caught in the Draft* and a string of outstanding Paramount comedies; several were opposite Betty Hutton and Veronica Lake. His broadcast ac-

tivities were peripheral, although based upon his dithery screen persona and aired with the solid sponsorship of Standard Brands and Texaco in the mid-40s.

A tried-and-true performer, starting from his days in *Our Gang* comedies, Bracken in 1949 returned to Broadway where earlier he had gotten good notices in *Brother Rat* and *Too Many Girls*. He had more success taking over lead roles in established hits (*Seven Year Itch*) than with original productions (*Shinbone Alley*). A stalwart of summer stock, he worked best before a theatre audience in roles that utilized his facial expressions and physical tomfoolery.

116. BRADLEY, Joe "Curley" (actor, singer; b. Sept. 18, 1910, Coalgate, OK; d. June 3, 1985, Long Beach, CA). *Headin' South* (1935–36); *Tom Mix* (1936–42, 1944–50); *The Singing Marshal* (1950–53).

Bradley first played Tom Mix's singing sidekick Pecos Williams; in 1944 he took over the lead. A rider in rodeos and a stuntman in silent pictures, he had worked with the real Tom Mix and doubled for John Gilbert in singing and riding segments of *West of Broadway*. Born and raised on a ranch, Curley taught himself the guitar and banjo, and in the process picked up a store of western songs. He teamed up with Ken (Shorty) Carson and Jack Ross as the Ranch Boys trio for films and radio. *Variety* wrote (1949) that he had a "good range and timber somewhat similar to Gene Autry." His Chicago credits include *Breakfast Club* (as substitute host), *Club Matinee* (with Garry Moore), and *This Amazing America* (for Greyhound Bus Lines).

In May 1938 Curley and the Ranch Boys as a publicity stunt rode from Hollywood to Chicago on horseback—a three-month, 2,875-mile trip ending in a triumphant appearance on *National Barn Dance*.

117. BRADLEY, Oscar (conductor; b. c1892, London, England; d. Aug. 31, 1948, Norwalk, CT). *Gulf Headliners* (1934); *Passing Parade* (1938–39); *We, the People* (1942–48).

Musical director for Ziegfeld and other Broadway shows until the early 1930s. Turning to radio with a contract from Gulf Oil, he made his debut on the Will Rogers program, playing music in the East while the humorist broadcast from the West Coast. He conducted for Phil Baker, Frank Parker, and Stoopnagle and Budd. At CBS he began directing the orchestra for *We, the People*. Six years later, on the eve of a broadcast, he died suddenly. His wife stepped in to conduct without any announcement to the public. The Oscar Bradley Orchestra continued under her direction and supervision until 1951 on *People* and from 1951 to 1953 on *Counterspy*.

Classically trained in England, Bradley conducted the London Symphony and Covent Garden Opera Orchestra before coming to America in 1924. From the pit, he handled the scores of vintage musicals, including *The Student Prince, Whoopee,* and *Show Boat*.

118. BRADLEY, Truman (announcer; b. Feb. 8, 1905, Sheldon, MO; d. July 28, 1974, Los Angeles, CA). *Easy Aces* (1932); *Red Skelton & Co.* (1941–42); *Drene Show* (1945–46).

Chicago announcer in the 1930s, he played the original Brad on *Easy Aces*. Bradley was part of the *Prudential Family Hour, Burns and Allen,* and *Ford Sunday Evening Hour*. He appeared in minor roles in films, and was host of the TV series *Science Fiction Theatre*. He got his start at KMTR Hollywood in 1929.

119. BRAGGIOTTI, Mario (pianist, composer [signature song: "Frere Jacques"]; b. Nov. 29, 1905, Florence, Italy; d. May 18, 1996, West Palm Beach, FL). *Fray & Braggiotti* (1934–37).

Mario Braggiotti (courtesy of Mario Braggiotti)

The duo piano team of Jacques Fray and Mario Braggiotti satisfied the varied tastes of a widespread audience. Their programs comprised music drawn from the pop standards, concert repertoire and jazz field, along with spritely caricatures in the style of the masters on "Yankee Doodle" and other well-known tunes. Mario, a conservatory student in Paris in the 1920s, met Jacques at the Bull on the Roof Cafe which featured two-piano jazz. They first won public acclaim for their unique arrangement of Ravel's "Bolero." Their keyboard artistry brought them into the 1928 London production of George Gershwin's *Funny Face* with Fred and Adele Astaire.

After a trailblazing Carnegie Hall concert in 1931 with Maurice Chevalier, with whom they had toured in Europe, Bill Paley put them on radio. They did a weekly segment as well as guest spots with Kate Smith, Bing Crosby, Rudy Vallee and Ed Wynn. Mario did all the transcriptions with distinctive counterpoint and harmony changes, and often wrote original piano and orchestral numbers for *Ford Hour* and *Radio City Music Hall on the Air*. Their records were considered the most creative of the two-piano repertoire. In the mid-30s Mario also led a dance orchestra that broadcast over Mutual and NBC. World War II broke up the duo. Braggiotti joined the Psychological Warfare Branch of the Army and became program director of Italian Occupational Radio. As a soloist, he later played concert programs and added a satirical "Music is Fun" series, while continuing to compose ballet music, songs, show scores and piano pieces.

120. BREEN, May Singhi (singer [The Ukulele Lady]; b. Feb. 24, 1895, New York, NY; d. Dec. 19, 1970, Neptune, NJ).

With her husband, the composer-arranger Peter De Rose, at a piano, she played the ukulele and sang on pre-network radio beginning at WJZ in November 1923. NBC welcomed their act, "Sweethearts of the Air," and gave it air time into the 1940s. May helped to popularize the ukulele and the use of ukulele arrangements on sheet music. The couple once caused a controversy in the Musicians Union when the question arose as to whether the ukulele could be classed as a musical instrument. The matter threatened to curtail the duo's radio career, until the union ruled in their favor.

A writer of songs, May had organized a group, the Syncopaters, with several other young women, and they sang on radio as early as 1922.

121. BRENEMAN, Tom (emcee; b. June 18, 1902, Waynesboro, PA; d. April 28, 1948, Encino, CA). *My Secret Ambition* (1937–38); *What's on Your Mind?* (1940); *Breakfast at Sardi's/in Hollywood* (1941–48).

Radio friend of middle-aged and elderly women who made him their idol in the 1940s. His *Breakfast in Hollywood* aired from a restaurant bearing his name at Sunset and Vine, and attracted large crowds eager to pay the $1.50 admission to be part of his daily

Tom Breneman, Paul Whiteman (courtesy of Capital Cities/ABC)

quizmaster on CBS's *Answer Auction* at KNX.

122. BRICE, Fanny (singer, comedian [catchphrase: "Da-a-addy"]; b. Oct. 29, 1891, New York, NY; d. May 29, 1951, Los Angeles, CA). *Baby Snooks* (1937–51).

A headliner of song and comedy in vaudeville and seven *Ziegfeld Follies* (1910 to 1936), she was better known to later audiences as the originator of an incorrigible brat called Baby Snooks, a terrifying female counterpart of Peck's Bad Boy. Her radio career began in 1933 as a singer with George Olsen's orchestra, although she had done guest appearances as early as 1927. She first played Snooks in *Sweet and Low* and in the 1936 *Follies,* and brought it to radio as part of an all-star comedy show for Sterling Products. Brice performed as Snooks thereafter on *Good News of 1938* and its successor shows including *Maxwell House Coffee Time* and *Baby Snooks Show.* She periodically appeared as a guest in her Snooks role on *Double or Nothing, The Big Show,* and *Screen Guild Players* (when "Daddy" Hanley Stafford told the story of Pinocchio). Her role as an eternal nuisance was so successful that by 1946 she was earning $6,000 a week and living in an 18-room Hollywood home.

Brice collapsed and died just hours before her May 29, 1951 broadcast was scheduled. NBC transmitted a 30-minute musical memorial to her on her time. She had planned to retire at the end of that season because she was "tired of fighting to stay on top," at a time when most of her radio contemporaries had successfully moved into television comedy. That's something a 60-year-old Baby Snooks could not have carried off.

morning show. It began as *Breakfast at Sardi's* but moved when that eatery proved unable to accommodate Breneman's fans. Tom circulated among the audience of 600 with folksy chatter, interviews and high jinks, with no rehearsal or "planted" persons to come up with off-hand wisecracks. The oldest lady always received an orchid and a kiss from Tom, who never failed to kid around with women's hats. His own personality dominated the proceedings, which inspired a full-length film built around this top ABC daytime show. Breneman died suddenly from a heart condition just hours before a broadcast in April 1948. Garry Moore, then Jack McElroy, took over. But without Breneman at the mike the 186-station hookup lost its appeal and folded a year later.

A song-and-dance man in vaudeville, he settled in radio with *Laugh Club of the Air* in 1929. Not a success, he became a station manager and part-time performer in Los Angeles. His cheerful personality mixed best with audience participation, and by 1940 he was

123. BROEKMAN, David (conductor; b. May 13, 1902, Leiden, The Netherlands; d. April 1, 1958, New York, NY). *Mobil Magazine* (1935–36); *Texaco Star Theatre* (1938–40).

Radio music producer, conductor and composer. He was associated with a number of CBS programs

David Broekman

before serving as director of music for the U.S. Treasury Department. The post included recordings and appearances at War Bond programs, namely *Let's All Back the Attack.*

Coming to New York in 1924, after studying at the Royal Conservatory and conducting the Royal Opera at The Hague, he started his American career with the Philharmonic. He was musical director at motion picture studios from 1928 to 1934. A composer of suites, operas and symphonies, he led Pop concerts at Carnegie Hall, conducted for TV variety shows, served as a quiz panelist and wrote an autobiographical novel.

124. BROKENSHIRE, Norman (announcer [catch phrase: "How do you do, ladies and gentlemen. How DO you Do."]; b. June 10, 1898, Murcheson, Ontario, Canada; d. May 4, 1965, Hauppauge, NY). *Music That Satisfies* (1932–34); *The Theatre Guild on the Air* (1945–c1958).

One of the original "Four Horsemen"— pioneer personality announcers of old WJZ New York. He first won attention as the "Play Boy" of the Reading Railroad Revelers and the Pennsylvania Railroad series. The son of a Methodist minister, he came to the United States in 1918 and joined an artillery unit of the American Army. Following the Armistice he became a secretary for the YMCA and fundraiser for Near East relief. While visiting New York in 1924, he answered an ad for "a college man with knowledge of musical terminology." He and three others were chosen from 400 applicants as announcers for WJZ. "Even for those crude 'mikes' my voice was perfect," he later boasted. "I could vary the tone, the speed, the expression; the engineer's needle would scarcely waver."

From WJZ's sister station WRC Washington, he broadcast the first Inaugural ceremonies (1925) to be put on the air. Brief interludes with WPG Atlantic City (where he broadcast its first beauty contest) and WCAU Philadelphia led to CBS.

Brokenshire's confident approach and ad-lib skills carried him to professional heights, and his voice became known to millions. A dashing man with a trim mustache, he served as announcer for *Music That Satisfies,* Eddie Cantor and Major Bowes' *Original Amateur Hour.* In 1932 he was named "King of the Announcers." At one point his name was so closely associated with Chesterfield Cigarettes that other sponsors would not use him.

"Broke's" career was soon interrupted because of an out-of-control drinking problem that made it difficult to find work. He applied for a Depression-era job as a day laborer with the Works Progress Administration. By the mid-1940s he was on a comeback with *The Theatre Guild on the Air,* Elsa Maxwell's daily series, and as an NBC disc jockey. In 1950 Brokenshire said: "Radio has become part of our lives that we'll never give up. It will be with us as long as people feel the need for pleasant music and the sound of a warm, friendly voice."

125. BROWN, Bob (announcer; b. Dec. 7, 1904, New York, NY). *Vic and Sade* (1932–44); *Quicksilver* (1939–40); *This Amazing America* (1940).

Chicago announcer-host. He joined the NBC staff there in 1932, handling soap operas, dramatic series, children's features and game shows. Brown was the Auctioneer on *Auction Quiz* (1941) and covered special events and parades. He hosted *Science Circus* on early Chicago television.

Brown studied at Cincinnati College of Music and first appeared at the microphone in 1925 as the result of an audition on WGR Buffalo. At WLW from 1928 to 1932, he became in charge of the announcing staff, wrote plays and handled production. He was a member of evangelist Billy Sunday's choir at age eight.

126. BROWN, Cecil (newscaster; b. Sept. 14, 1907, New Brighton, PA; d. Oct. 25, 1987, Los Angeles, CA). *CBS European News* (1939–40); *Sizing Up the News* (1944–45).

Controversial correspondent with a brief, highly charged affiliation with CBS. While with International News Service in Europe in 1939 he switched to radio journalism and joined CBS in Rome. In 1941 he was expelled from Italy by the government of Mussolini for a hostile attitude toward the Fascist regime. In December of that year, Brown was aboard the British battle cruiser *Repulse* when she and the battleship *Prince of Wales* were sunk by the Japanese off Malaya. After being rescued by a destroyer, he broadcast an eyewitness account of the sinking. For his news reporting in 1941, he received a Peabody award.

His subsequent broadcasts from Singapore brought

him into conflict over censorship by the British, who called his commentary detrimental to public morale and barred him from the air. Brown quit CBS in 1943 after a dispute with network executives. He moved to Mutual where he enjoyed a 13-year association, highlighted by a morning news segment. From 1958 to 1962 he served as bureau chief for NBC in Tokyo and later taught English at California State Polytechnic University and served as director of news and public affairs at KCET-TV Los Angeles.

127. BROWN, John (actor; b. April 4, 1904, Hull, England; d. May 16, 1957, West Hollywood, CA). *Life of Riley* (1945–51); *Duffy's Tavern* (1946–49); *A Day in the Life of Dennis Day* (1946–48).

A sought-after straight man and stooge for nearly every top comic. As somber-voiced Digger O'Dell, the friendly undertaker, Brown was an eagerly anticipated character on *Life of Riley.* He had actually worked as a clerk in a mortuary in New York while trying to break into radio. At age 20 he auditioned for Cantor and picked up a one-shot broadcast role. Fred Allen soon added him to his Mighty Art Players. In the 1940s, he popped up on *Maisie, Ozzie and Harriet* (as neighbor Will Thornberry), *A Date with Judy* and *Charlie McCarthy.* In 1941 he worked seven weekly shows, beginning on *The Shadow* on Sunday to *Lincoln Highway* on Saturday. Brown calculated that he had been on 10,000 live broadcasts and 5,000 ETs.

128. BROWN, Les (bandleader [Les Brown and the Band of Renown] [signature song: *"Dance of the Blue Devils"/"Leap Frog"*]; b. March 14, 1912, Reinerton, PA). *Fitch Bandwagon* (1944); *Bob Hope Show* (1947–58).

Veteran big-band maestro who readily moved his brisk, well-focused sound from radio to television shows. He successfully made the transition as a musical aggregation for Bob Hope's many variety series. Brown's conducting career started at Duke University with the Duke Blue Devils, for which he also played clarinet and saxophone. His own band came into play with one nighters in 1938; the turning point proved to be a four-month run at Mike Todd's Theatre-Cafe in Chicago and airtime over NBC remotes. A similar engagement at the Blackhawk and pickups via WGN built up his name. With his vocalist Doris Day, he struck gold with "Sentimental Journey," a hit recording of 1945.

Les made guest appearances on *Fitch Bandwagon* before conducting the show's entire summer run in 1944. As his recordings gained in sales, he was spotlighted on *Teentimers Club.* Hope heard his discs and signed him for the weekly Pepsodent show in 1947. Subsequent sponsors renewed his services throughout the 1950s. Brown traveled with Hope on overseas tours to military bases, including far-off outposts for his traditional Christmas specials before audiences of American servicemen. For 20 years Les remained a fa-

vorite aggregation for all-star Parade of Bands broadcasts. In 1953 he received *Downbeat* magazine's award as the Best Dance Band of the Year.

129. BROWN, Vanessa (actress, panelist; b. March 24, 1928, Vienna, Austria). *Quiz Kids* (1942–44).

Although she made only eight or so appearances as a *Quiz Kid,* she became one of its most illustrious alumni. While in Chicago as an understudy in the national company of *Watch on the Rhine,* 14-year-old Vanessa, then known as Smylla Brind, was chosen as a show business panelist. The increasingly popular and very attractive actress occasionally joined the panel in Chicago or New York, when her acting schedule allowed. "It was one situation when you didn't have to hide the fact you were bright. I enjoyed the friendly atmosphere, too." Her specialty was language and literature.

Important roles in over 20 films and as the Broadway lead in *The Seven Year Itch* followed. She made dramatic appearances on *Lux Radio Theatre, Skippy Hollywood Theatre* and *Theatre Guild on the Air.* Her outstanding performance as Carol Kennicott in *Main Street* was aired twice on *NBC University Theatre* in the late 1940s. Television game panelist and sitcom and soap opera roles were added. She was a correspondent for The Voice of America for over six years. Her multifaceted, well-researched career guidance seminars and audio tapes, "What Do You Want to be Tomorrow," stemmed in part from her positive experiences as a teenage performer and *Quiz Kid.*

Vanessa Brown (courtesy of Vanessa Brown)

130. BRUCE, Carol (singer; b. Nov. 15, 1919, Great Neck, NY). *Ben Bernie Orchestra* (1940–41); *Carton of Cheer* (1944–45).

Featured band vocalist with Ben Bernie and his Bromo-Seltzer series. As a single, Bruce made guest appearances on *Colgate Sports Newsreel, Raleigh Room, Schaefer Revue* and *The Dunninger Show* and with Al Jolson. There were movie roles in the 1940s with Abbott and Costello (*Keep 'em Flying*) but her rise to star status proved elusive. On stage, however, in the 1946 revival of *Show Boat,* Bruce in the role of Julie was acclaimed a worthy successor to Helen Morgan. She followed up as a lead in *Along Fifth Avenue.*

Her earliest work was on *The Children's Hour* and Larry Clinton's bandstand. A breakthrough was a role in Irving Berlin's *Louisiana Purchase* in 1940. Comparing the stage and radio that year, she said: "On the stage you can sell your personality, but on the radio you realize that whether you are pretty or not makes no difference. You've got to get over with your voice alone and it's got to be right the first time."

131. BRUCE, Nigel (actor; b. Feb. 4, 1895, Ensenada, Mexico; d. Oct. 8, 1953, Santa Monica, CA). *Sherlock Holmes* (1939–47).

English performer, best known for his role as Dr. Watson in the Sherlock Holmes series. Bruce played in some 70 films, 16 of which were in the low-budget detective mysteries with Basil Rathbone as Sherlock. His humorous inflection in delivering lines as the bumbling, bewildered crony endeared him to

Basil Rathbone, Nigel Bruce (courtesy of Capital Cities/ABC)

audiences. His 1932 Broadway hit, *Springtime for Henry,* led to radio and films (*Rebecca, The Corn is Green*).

On a tribute to the visiting King and Queen of England in 1939, Bruce sang "Three Little Fishes," the then-rage in novelty tunes.

132. BRYAN, Arthur Q. (actor; b. May 8, 1899, Brooklyn, NY; d. Nov. 30, 1959, Hollywood, CA). *Grouch Club* (1939–40); *Fibber McGee and Molly* (1943–56); *The Great Gildersleeve* (1944–54); *Adventures of Archie Andrews* (1947–49).

Long-standing comic roles as Doc Gamble (Fibber McGee) and Floyd the barber (Gildersleeve) assured Bryan a place in the hall of fame of beloved supporting characters. Quick-witted and jovial, he traded lines with Red Skelton, Milton Berle, Jimmy Durante and Jack Pearl. His dramatic parts ranged from the Angel in "It's a Wonderful Life" (*NBC Theatre*) to the Sheriff of Okmulgee in "The Hatpin Case" (*Richard Diamond, Private Detective*).

Bryan took up radio in the mid-1920s, and at WCAU turned to announcing, writing and producing as well as acting.

133. BRYAN, George (announcer; b. June 9, 1910, New York, NY; d. June 27, 1969, Stamford, CT). *National Amateur Hour* (1936); *Helen Hayes Theatre* (1940–41); *Arthur Godfrey's Talent Scouts* (1946–55).

CBS staff announcer for 28 years, beginning in 1940. At age 26 he won a contest for novice announcers; first prize was 20 weeks as announcer on the *National Amateur Hour.* Bryan gained more experience at WGAR and WKBW in Buffalo. Returning to New York, he handled many Columbia programs: *Road of Life, Armstrong Theatre of Today, We, the People.* He served in the U.S. Air Force, then joined Godfrey's *Talent Scouts* and *CBS Weekly News Review.*

"The real difference between radio announcing and train-calling in a railroad station," he pointed out, "is a capacity for interpretation. If you don't feel what you're saying, nobody else will, either."

134. BUNCE, Alan (actor; b. June 28, 1908, Westfield, NJ; d. April 27, 1965, New York, NY). *Young Doctor Malone* (1939–43); *Home of the Brave* (1941); *Ethel and Albert* (1944–50).

Immensely appealing in his portrayal of Albert on radio and later television, he appeared on that humorous two-character situation comedy with Peg Lynch, *Ethel and Albert*'s writer. He was a well-established actor in plays when he entered radio in 1933 and was the original Dr. Jerry Malone. He had ongoing roles on *Hello Peggy, David Harum* and *Joyce Jordan.* Bunce appeared in some 35 Broadway and stock productions, including *Sunrise at Campobello* (as a genial and amusing Gov. Alfred E. Smith) and *Dream Child* (written by his father-in-law J. C. Nugent and co-starring his wife Ruth Nugent).

135. BURDETT, Winston (newscaster; b. Dec. 12, 1913, Buffalo, NY; d. May 19, 1993, Rome, Italy). *CBS World News Round Up* (1951–56).

A protege of Edward R. Murrow, he covered key World War II events as a freelance reporter, beginning in 1939 in Stockholm. They included the invasion of Southern France, fighting in North Africa and the surrender of German forces in Italy. In 1943 he became a CBS News staff correspondent. After the war, he was posted in Rome, then served a four-year stint as a network anchorman and news correspondent at the UN. He returned in 1956 to Rome, his base until his retirement in 1978. A onetime reporter for the *Brooklyn Daily Eagle,* he won an Overseas Press Club Award in 1959 for his coverage of the death of Pope Pius XII and the elections and installation of his successor.

136. BURKE, Billie (comedienne; b. Aug. 6, 1886, Washington, DC; d. May 14, 1970, Los Angeles, CA). *Billie Burke Show* (1944–46); *The Gay Mrs. Featherstone* (1945); *Chicken Every Sunday* (1949).

When her husband, the master showman Flo Ziegfeld died broke in 1932, she was forced to accelerate her career in pictures. Her roles as the fluttery, slightly neurotic hostess or giddy matron charmed moviegoers in such well received films as *Dinner at Eight, Father of the Bride* and *Bachelor Daughter.* The friendly witch in *The Wizard of Oz,* shot in the still-novel Technicolor process, revealed she had retained much of the great beauty that at the turn of the century had brought her wide acclaim on and off the stage.

Over the air Burke became a favorite of Rudy Vallee and Bob Hope, and appeared on the *Sealtest Village Store* with Edward Everett Horton during the summer of 1944. Her own comedy show ran Saturday mornings over CBS. A brief series as Dora Featherstone, a well-meaning mother-in-law, followed, as did cast assignments with Eddie Cantor in 1948.

The daughter of a singing circus clown in British music halls, she grew up abroad and made her acting bow in a Charles Frohman London play in 1903. The red-haired, blue-eyed ingenue stole the show with her rendition of "The Canoe Song." She told these and other stories in her books *With a Feather on My Nose* and *With Powder on My Nose.*

137. BURNS, Bob (comedian [signature song: "The Arkansas Traveler"]; b. Oct. 2, 1896, Van Buren, AR; d. Feb. 2, 1956, Encino, CA). *Kraft Music Hall* (1936–41); *Arkansas Traveler* (1941–43); *Bob Burns Show* (1943–47).

Radio discovered Burns, plodding along as a middle-aged, struggling vaudeville trouper. In his drawling, Arkansas fashion he told tall tales of his country kin during guest appearances for Rudy Vallee in 1935.

Bing Crosby's *Kraft Music Hall* offered a contract and brought him to Hollywood. Along with the playing of his bazooka — a crude "musical" instrument made of a whiskey funnel and an iron gas pipe — he entertained with his Ozark hillbilly tales.

CBS and Campbell Soup launched his own top-billed *Arkansas Traveler* series in 1941; NBC and Lever Bros. picked it up two years later. At one time called the new Will Rogers, Burns was a well-educated civil engineer who ventured into show business in a modest way. He began by playing a mandolin with his hometown concert band.

138. BURNS, George (comedian [signature song: "Love Nest"]; b. Jan. 20, 1896, New York, NY; d. March 9, 1996, Beverly Hills, CA). *Burns and Allen* (1932–50).

A vaudeville entertainer at age 14, he later teamed with Gracie Allen, who played the serious foil. But after she received the biggest laughs during their early routines, she became the comic and Burns became the straight man. They married in 1926 and made their radio bow over BBC London while touring Europe. Their own series, beginning on CBS for General Cigar, pleased listeners for nearly two decades before moving into television in 1950.

George was in complete charge of the radio scripts, and worked with three writers. The program focused on their day-to-day life as husband and wife. From 1945–49, their show was called *Maxwell House Coffee Time.* They often saluted the Armed Forces and boosted bond drives on various "victory parade" broadcasts.

When Gracie retired in 1958, cigar-toting Burns appeared chiefly as a single, building a new career in nightclubs, theatres and films, even through recordings. The author of comedy and autobiographical books, including the best-selling *Gracie: A Love Story,* he won an Oscar for the 1975 film *The Sunshine Boys.*

139. BURR, Henry (singer; b. Jan. 15, 1882, St. Stephen, New Brunswick, Canada; d. April 6, 1941, Chicago, IL). *National Barn Dance* (1936–41); *Uncle Ezra* (1938–39).

Old-time ballad singer on discs and radio. His first job was as a tenor soloist in a church. With Edison he pioneered in the experimental stages of phonograph recording. Burr sang on one of the first cylindrical waxings. He was also credited with making the first transcontinental broadcast. He performed from New York, and telephone wires carried his voice to guests at a dinner in California. The listeners wore head phones. Later, in Denver he sang into a microphone improvised from a wooden bowl containing an inverted telephone transmitter. The broadcast was heard as far West as San Francisco.

In the mid-30s he joined *National Barn Dance,* and was heard singing such vintage ballads as "In the Shade of the Old Apple Tree" and "Just a Baby's Prayer at Twilight."

Parks Johnson, Jimmy Durante, Ray Bolger, Wally Butterworth

140. BUSHMAN, Francis X. (actor; b. Jan. 10, 1883, Norfolk, VA*; d. Aug. 23, 1966, Pacific Palisades, CA). *Betty and Bob* (1938–39); *Those We Love* (1942–45); *Adventures of Nero Wolfe* (1945–46).

Silent screen matinee idol. Rejected by his fans once they learned he was married and had five children and later by the "talkies," he successfully pursued radio assignments. His longest-running role as New England lawyer John Marshall, on *Those We Love,* introduced him to a new generation, as did the lead in *Nero Wolfe.* Guest appearances on *Rin Tin Tin Thrillers, Fitch Bandwagon, Railroad Hour* and *Rexall Summer Theatre* continued into the 1950s.

His first radio work began in 1931 at CBS Chicago where he did *First Nighter.* Bushman's career had started as a bicycle racer, wrestler and sculptor's model, then led to stock and repertory. In 1911 he entered films for Essanay. They totalled 423 by 1940. A highly photogenic leading man in early pictures, he set the standard for the romantic male image on screen. His roles included the 1925 version of *Ben Hur* and a villain in the *Batman* TV series.

141. BUTTERWORTH, Wally (emcee; b. Oct. 25, 1901, Wallingford, PA; d. March 10, 1962). *Molle Merry Minstrels* (1934–35); *Vox Pop* (1936–42); *Take a Card* (1943).

A skillful inquisitor for voice-of-the-people type interviews with *Vox Pop* co-emcee Parks Johnson. Butterworth, a baritone turned announcer, traveled widely

Another source gives 1885 and Baltimore.

with the show as war clouds mobilized the homefront in 1940. The stress of "live," generally unrehearsed remotes led to heavy drinking. No longer on his toes for such quick-thinking, ad-lib segments (when wartime security was paramount), he was dropped by the producers in 1942. Butterworth reappeared at Mutual on *Take A Card,* a bland quiz with questions and prizes corresponding to face values of playing cards. By 1948 he was on *The Crack O'Dawn Farm and Home Hour* with Tom Page at NBC.

While selling radios in Philadelphia, he took voice lessons. In 1928 he applied at NBC for staff singer but was given the job of announcing its call letters and directing *The National Farm and Home Hour* in Chicago. In 1949 he aired *Voices That Live,* a presentation of rare recordings from his own large collection.

142. BUTTRAM, Pat (actor; b. June 19, 1915, Addison, AL; d. Jan. 8, 1994, Los Angeles, CA). *National Barn Dance* (1940–46); *Saturday Night Roundup* (1946–47).

Comic sidekick on country and western shows. He came into prominence on WLS's *Barn Dance.* Buttram had traveled to the Chicago World's Fair in 1933 and was interviewed in the audience of the Saturday night hoedown. Everything he said got laughs, and he was quickly brought to the program as a frequent guest. In 1940 the Alabama-born "sage of Winston County" became a regular and replaced emcee Joe Kelly at one point during the war when Joe was on War Bond tours. Miles Labs also teamed him with Roy Rogers. But as croaky-voiced partner of Gene Autry in the 1950s, Buttram helped keep the peace out West. The two had met on the *Barn Dance.* As Mr. Haney on TV's *Green Acres,* the onetime theology student extended his career into the 1970s.

His first local radio work stemmed from a performance in a college play at Birmingham Southern College. He once portrayed Chicken Snyder on the Phil Harris–Alice Faye *Fitch Bandwagon.*

143. CADMAN, S. Parkes (preacher; b. Dec. 18, 1864, Wellington, Shropshire, England; d. July 12, 1936, Plattsburg, NY). *National Radio Pulpit* (1923–36).

First minister of the air. Identified with pre-network nondenominational religious services over WEAF beginning in the 1920s, Dr. Cadman delivered more than

500 sermons to listeners. He was regarded as the foremost Congregational minister in America and served the Central Church, Brooklyn, for 35 years.

Outspoken at the microphone and among his fellow clergymen, he advocated world peace, League of Nations membership and child labor laws, and condemned loyalty oaths, Hitlerism and company unions — at times when the consensus of opinion was decidedly against his positions. A worker in English mines as a boy, he began reading books on theology in his spare time, and graduated from college as a candidate for the Methodist ministry before coming to the United States in 1890.

144. CALLOWAY, Cab (band leader [signature song: "Minnie The Moocher"]; b. Dec. 25, 1907, Rochester, NY; d. Nov. 18, 1994, Hosckessin, DE). *Quizzical* (1941–42).

Versatile big-band pied piper. Calloway got his start playing drums in Chicago. With his own band, he became the rage of Harlem at the Cotton Club where stations picked up his "Heigh-de-ho" jazz. He sang and often danced a bit as he led. On screen Calloway showmanship came across in *The Big Broadcast of 1932.*

His parody of Kay Kyser's *Kollege of Musical Knowledge* was the first network quiz with a black cast and black contestants. *Quizzical* first aired from WOR then went on the Blue network as a road show. Cab played a jive-talking Professor Calloway, moderator and quizmaster. Popular with audiences, the spirited musical question-and-answer game, however, attracted

Cab Calloway (courtesy of Steve Jelf)

no sponsors. "It was all right if we came on as entertainers on a white show, but we couldn't have a show of our own," Cab wrote in his autobiographical *Minnie the Moocher and Me.*

145. CALMER, Ned (news analyst; b. July 16, 1907, Chicago, IL; d. March 9, 1986, New York, NY). *World News Roundup* (1940–67).

Newsman with a direct, terse style. He was hired as night editor by CBS in 1940. Working abroad and in the United States, he was part of Edward R. Murrow's wartime radio news team. In 1943 he succeeded Bob Trout and Warren Sweeney on the 11 p.m. newscast. When he started in that assignment, he sounded nervous, hesitant and stiff, according to *Variety.* "His very lack of super-personality is impressive," that journal concluded. He left CBS in 1967 to write full-time. He was the author of a dozen titles, including *The Anchorman,* a book on the influence of television. Calmer attended the University of Virginia and worked for seven years as foreign correspondent in Paris for the New York *Herald Tribune* and *Chicago Tribune.*

146. CANDIDO, Candy (comedian; b. c1905, New Orleans, LA). *Sealtest Village Store* (1947); *Jimmy Durante Show* (1947–50).

Support comic and character actor. Known as the man with three voices, from very high to extremely low and middle range, he dubbed sounds and voices for Disney animated features and Popeye cartoons. Candido appeared on NBC's *What's Your Idea?* in 1941 and later backed Durante. Music, too, provided steady jobs. A bassist, he worked with Ted Fio Rito and Russ Columbo, accompanied by Gene Austin, and periodically fronted his own combo. His musical and comic capers surfaced on screen in Dick Powell's *20 Million Sweethearts* and the Astaire-Rogers *Roberta.*

147. CANOVA, Judy (comedian, singer [signature song: "Go to Sleepy, Little Baby"]; b. Nov. 20, 1916, Stark, FL; d. Aug. 5, 1983, Hollywood, CA). *Paul Whiteman's Musical Varieties* (1936–37); *Charlie McCarthy Show* (1938); *Judy Canova Show* (1943–53).

With brother Zeke and sister Annie, young Judy Canova acquired a handful of hillbilly songs during a family vacation in the North Carolina mountains. They later organized a trio and tried it out on New York radio stations, which didn't fancy their "crazy noises." But the Village Barn in Greenwich Village hired them for a run that extended to some 22 months. An appearance in *Ziegfeld Follies of 1936* led to Rudy Vallee and Paul Whiteman radio shows.

Judy in the role of a likeable country bumpkin starred on her own NBC program for a decade and in a handful of low-budget screen comedies; she always managed to sing a song or two ranging from comic hillbilly ditties to grand opera. Judy with Zeke wrote

Judy Canova, William Bendix, Frank Sinatra, Kay Kyser, Ralph Edwards

cheering section. From then on, Cantor never lacked a studio audience for his weekly series nor dropped out of the popularity polls. But he was often criticized for mugging before such audiences to the annoyance of living-room listeners.

He began as a Bowery amateur night performer and Coney Island singing waiter. By 1920 the wide-eyed comic was clowning, singing and dancing in *Ziegfeld Follies* with W. C. Fields and Will Rogers. He played in the tailor-made *Kid Boots* for several years on Broadway. His greatest success *Whoopee* led to a string of films for Samuel Goldwyn.

Cantor surrounded himself with an engaging and colorful radio cast: announcer Harry Von Zell, comic Bert "Mad Russian" Gordon and bandleader "Cookie" Fairchild. He was always interested in helping new talent; his discoveries included Deanna Durbin, Bobby Breen, Dinah Shore and Eddie Fisher. He enjoyed guest spots, frequently visiting Burns and Allen, Jack Benny, Dinah Shore, Hildegarde and

the music to her theme song, with words by Harry and Henry Tobias.

148. CANTOR, Charles (actor; b. Sept. 4, 1898, Worchester, MA; d. Sept. 11, 1966, Hollywood, CA). *Grand Central Station* (1937–38); *Terry and the Pirates* (1938–39); *Duffy's Tavern* (1944–51).

A character regularly heard with Eddie Cantor, Fred Allen, William Bendix, Alan Young and Tommy Riggs, and most often on *Duffy's Tavern* as Finnegan. Dramatic parts on *Johnny Presents* and *Grand Central Station* were also frequent. In 1939 over Mutual he played Mr. Stowaway in skits which contained geographical clues for *Guess Where*.

Cantor began in vaudeville as a blackface comedian and dialectician. His first radio appearance was on a Brooklyn station with a banjo player.

149. CANTOR, Eddie (singer, comedian [Banjo Eyes]; [signature song: "One Hour with You"]; b. Jan. 31, 1892, New York, NY; d. Oct. 10, 1964, Beverly Hills, CA). *Chase & Sanborn Hour* (1931–34); *Eddie Cantor Show* (1935–39, 1946–49, 1951–54); *Time to Smile* (1940–46); *Take It or Leave It* (1949–50).

One of the very first major Broadway stars to go before a microphone — the date was February 10, 1922 at WDY Roselle Park, New Jersey. Four years later he was a guest on *Eveready Hour,* and by 1931 had his own program at CBS. He, along with Ed Wynn, insisted on a studio audience for laughter and applause as was their modus operandi in vaudeville and musical comedy. Most shows had barred spectators and spontaneous "noise" until Cantor convinced NBC and Standard Brands that no comic should be without a

Eddie Cantor

Bill Stern. With Tallulah Bankhead, he performed his "Maxie the Taxi" sketch on *The Big Show*—a routine that transferred easily to his television shows in the 1950s. For his last radio series, spun records and reminisced.

President of the American Federation of Radio Artists and Screen Actors Guild, Cantor was long active in behalf of his profession and with appeals for many charitable and humanitarian endeavors. His March of Dimes campaigns to aid polio research and treatment received wide radio exposure. He wrote the autobiographical *Take My Life* (1959) and an earlier work *My Life Is in Your Hands*.

150. CAREY, MacDonald (actor; b. March 15, 1913, Sioux City, IA; d. March 21, 1994, Beverly Hills, CA). *Woman in White* (1938–39); *Stella Dallas* (1940–41); *Jason and the Golden Fleece* (1952–54).

His first major radio role and his last television lead were both as physicians: Dr. Lee Markham, a neurologist on *Woman in White,* and Dr. Tom Horton, hospital chief of staff on *Days of Our Lives.* In the 25 years separating the two, the Emmy-winning actor played a gamut of dramatic parts on radio, screen and stage. In 1941 he appeared on Broadway opposite Gertrude Lawrence in *Lady in the Dark.* That led to Alfred Hitchcock's *Shadow of a Doubt* in which he played a detective on the trail of a murderer. He maintained his ties to radio while working in films and early television. The earnest, down-to-earth Carey said that he had not especially liked soap operas when he did them on radio, but found both security and money a higher priority. *First Nighter* and *Young Hickory* were his earliest series.

Educated at the Universities of Iowa and Wisconsin, he toured the country with the Globe Players, a group that offered capsule versions of Shakespeare's plays. Apart from his interpretations of Hamlet and Brutus, Carey's engaging role as Jason, owner of a New Orleans bar and a bayou boat called the "Golden Fleece," entertained adventure-story listeners in the early 1950s. His autobiography *Days of My Life* described his show business successes amid personal disappointments and tragedies.

151. CARLE, Frankie (bandleader, pianist [signature song: "Sunrise Serenade"]; b. March 25, 1903, Providence, RI). *Pot o' Gold* (1939–41); *Treasure Chest* (1940–44); *Chesterfield Supper Club* (1947).

A star attraction on Horace Heidt's bandstand. Carle had a five-year contract to perform a piano solo on every Heidt show. During that time the two became partners, and Carle received equal billing as coleader. "He was instrumental in exploiting my ability over the airwaves, introducing my compositions, and helped me reach the top," Carle said of his mentor. "And when the time arrived Heidt helped me organize my own orchestra."

A top-selling piano soloist for Columbia Records while with Heidt, Carle on his own picked up the lucrative Old Gold program on CBS, and hotel and theatre bookings. Carle earned $100,000 that first year. His theme song, "Sunrise Serenade," written while he was with Heidt, added significantly to his total record sales of over 20 million discs. He believed in playing music straight in a strictly melodic vein; his own compositions "Oh, What It Seemed To Be" and "Falling Leaves" reflect this feeling. His daughter Marjorie Hughes sang with the Carle band in the 1940s.

152. CARLEY, Rachel (singer; [Radio's French Girl]; b. May 24, 1912, Brussels, Belgium). *Manhattan Merry-Go-Round* (1934–41).

European import for popular songs, often done in French. Although born in Belgium, she stressed her Parisian background (and at one point claimed Paris as her birthplace). Main attraction at the Follies Bergere and Opera Comique, Carley came to America to appear in Earl Carroll's *Vanities* in the early 1930s. She bowed on the air with Rudy Vallee, and in 1934 began a 5½-year run on the Hummerts' *Merry-Go-Round.*

Her sense of showmanship, striking figure and pleasing soprano range took her into U.S. theatres and supper clubs. She sang on the *Met Opera Auditions of the Air* in 1941 but her career soon waned.

153. CARLIN, Phillips (announcer; b. June 30, 1894, New York, NY; d. Aug. 27, 1971, New York, NY). *Palmolive Hour* (1927–31).

His announcing of major broadcasts in collaboration with Graham McNamee won them the appellation of "Twin Announcers," due to the marked similarity of their voices. With sports broadcasts, Carlin did the "color" and McNamee the play-by-play description. He made his debut from WEAF in 1923, and was on the air every weekday from 4 to 10 p.m., with an hour off for dinner. His programs included the *Goodrich* and *Atwater Kent Hour.* He was made program director for WEAF in 1925, then for NBC. Later Carlin was vice president in charge of programs until moving to the Blue Network when it became a separate entity in 1942. He was an executive with Mutual two years later. He is credited with the idea and popularization of the NBC chimes.

154. CARLON, Fran (actress; b. April 2, 1913, Indianapolis, IN; d. Oct. 4, 1993, New York, NY). *Today's Children* (1933–37); *Story of Mary Marlin* (1937–43); *Big Town* (1943–52).

As reporter Lorelei Kilbourne on the thriller drama *Big Town* (with Ed Pawley as Steve Wilson), she had her best prime-time role. Such soaps as *Portia Faces Life* (as Portia) filled her daytime schedule. She had entered radio doing commercials on *Amos 'n' Andy.*

Because she appeared in so many ill-fated Broadway plays, she was happy to have radio to insure steady employment. Trained at the Goodman Theatre

Edward Pawley, Fran Carlon (courtesy of Weist-Barron School of Television Commercial Acting)

in Chicago, Fran finally did enjoy a long run in the 1958 hit *Sunrise at Campobello.*

155. CARNEY, Don (host [catchphrase: "Hello, girls and boys, this is your Uncle Don."]; b. Aug. 19, 1889, St. Joseph, MI; d. Jan. 14, 1954, Miami, FL). *Uncle Don* (1928–47); *Friendship Village* (1932); *Dog Chats* (1933–34).

Don Carney

After a brief stint as WMCA announcer, Carney joined WOR in 1928, and almost immediately became the happy-go-lucky idol of youngsters. *Radio Guide* soon hailed him as "saint, oracle and pal to 300,000 children" in the New York metropolitan area. Uncle Don remained a regional pied piper, Monday through Saturday at 5 p.m., bringing stories of all sorts, simple songs, hokey jokes, birthday announcements and behavioral do's and dont's. Then, on Sunday mornings he read comic strips from a New York newspaper. In 1947 he switched to a DJ show for kids.

By then he had made over 8,000 broadcasts and delivered in a nasal monotone an estimated 13,000,000 words. At his peak his annual earnings exceeded $90,000 — proof of his magic among children.

Under his real name, Howard Rice, he appeared as Mayor Luke Higgins on *Main Street Sketches,* and played on *Romance Isle* and *Cabin Door.* Post-Uncle Don, he broadcast for five years at WKAT Miami. Carney always insisted that he never called his young audience "bastards" in an off-the-cuff, on-the-air remark.

156. CARPENTER, Kenneth (announcer; b. Aug. 21, 1900, Avon, IL; d. Oct. 19, 1984, Santa Monica, CA). *Kraft Music Hall* (1936–49); *Packard Mardi Gras* (1937–38); *One Man's Family* (c1940–49); *Charlie McCarthy Show* (1945–48).

Announcer-personality best remembered for working with Bing Crosby. He arrived in Hollywood in 1929, joining KFI. His West Coast assignments included *Lux Radio Theatre, Halls of Ivy* and *Truth or Consequences,* as well as special Hollywood galas. He handled many sports events, notably the Santa Anita Handicaps and Rose Bowl football games.

157. CARROLL, Gene (comedian [signature song: "Hello, Hello, Hello"]; b. April 18, 1898, Chicago, IL; d. March 5, 1972, Boca Raton, FL). *Quaker Early Birds* (1930–32); *Gene and Glenn* (1933–41); *National Barn Dance* (1938).

Comedy music partner with Glenn Rowell. The team created characters Jake and Lena. A voice imitator, Gene played both Lena, a boarding house owner, and Jake, the handyman. Their routine began at WTAM with songs and patter, and plugged into the NBC net. After several seasons from Los Angeles and Chicago, they broadcast from WTIC Hartford. When Glenn left the act, Gene went on as a character actor, chiefly as Lena the maid on *Fibber McGee and Molly.*

From 1948 to 1972, he was host of a weekly WEWS-TV show in Cleveland.

158. CARSON, Jack (comedian, actor; b. Oct. 27, 1910, Carmen, Manitoba, Canada; d. Jan. 2, 1963, Encino, CA). *Jack Carson Show* (1943–47, 1948–49); *New Sealtest Village Store* (1947–48).

Radio, and later television, augmented an active filmmaking schedule for this master of double take and pained expression. The vaudeville and stock com-

Jack Carson

pany veteran regarded himself as an actor rather than a comedian. But comedy proved his forte over the air on *Kraft Music Hall, Dinah Shore's Open House* and his own series (with Arthur Treacher and Eve Arden), and in such '40s pictures as *The Male Animal, Arsenic and Old Lace* and *Two Guys from Milwaukee.* One of his best roles was as a hard-hearted press agent in *A Star is Born* with Judy Garland. His four wives included early *Hit Parade* singer Kay St. Germain and actress Lola Albright.

159. CARTER, Boake (news commentator [catchphrase: "Cheerio"]; b. April 12, 1899, Baku, Russia; d. Nov. 16, 1944, Hollywood, CA).

In 1930 he made his debut at WPEN as a news commentator in Philadelphia, and soon entered into a contract with Columbia's local outlet, WCAU. A newspaper reporter there and a roving correspondent for *London Daily Mail,* he got his real start during the Lindbergh kidnapping story. In 1932 Philco gave him a nightly newscast at CBS. Twice, the public voted him the outstanding news commentator of radio.

Readily identifiable because of his British accent, the Cambridge-educated journalist also wrote a syndicated column, and was the center of controversies when he criticized many facets of the Roosevelt Administration and the British Empire. One of his books summed it up: *I Talk As I Like.* Early in World War II he began a new series for Mutual, where he seemed more compatible with its open-ended talk features.

160. CARTER, Gaylord (organist; b. Aug. 3, 1905, Wiesbaden, Germany). *Amos 'n' Andy* (1936–42); *Breakfast in Hollywood* (1953–54).

West Coast theatre and radio organist. When or-

gan accompaniment and solos fell victim to "talkies," he went into radio. His longest association was with *Amos 'n' Andy* and their "Perfect Song" signature — ending when he joined the Navy and worked as an officer in the recreational area for the duration. On Christmas Eve 1945 he accompanied the Navy Children's Chorus on Bob Hope's Christmas Party over NBC. Carter contributed music to *Hollywood Hotel* and *Breakfast in Hollywood,* and provided themes and background for dramatic series. "At its best," he believed, "the music should be felt but not noticed."

Born of American parents — both music teachers — in Germany, Gaylord moved from Wichita to Los Angeles in 1922. He soon got a job playing piano accompaniment for films and continued the work while at UCLA. In 1926 Harold Lloyd recommended him to the manager of the Million Dollar Theatre in downtown Los Angeles, and he started on its pipe organ on his 21st birthday. Following long engagements at Warner's Hollywood and other houses, he went to Seattle for the Paramount chain in 1932. With the movement to preserve vintage theatres and organs a generation later, Carter was rediscovered in the 1970s as Southern California's pre-eminent silent film organist.

161. CARTER, John (singer; b. 1911, Brooklyn, NY; d. July 22, 1988, New York, NY). *Charlie Mc-Carthy Show* (1938).

Two months after succeeding Nelson Eddy as the vocal soloist on the Bergen & McCarthy program, Carter, a lyric tenor, won the 1938 *Met Opera Auditions of the Air* (along with still-unknown baritone Leonard Warren). Other finalists were Felix Knight, Phil Duey, Margaret Codd and Kathleen Kersting. There were stories that one of the judges virtually rigged Carter's victory to keep a promise to Chase & Sanborn that their new singer would make front-page news through the contest.

Described as "a fresh, young voice of thoroughly pleasing quality," Carter never really measured up to Met standards. Not until December 1939 did its audience hear him — as the Italian singer in *Der Rosenkavalier.* The war interrupted a more or less promising concert career. While chief specialist, U.S. Navy, however, he did sing to good advantage regularly on *Meet Your Navy* and *Hymn Hour* with the Great Lakes Choir in Chicago. "During the day I trained 'boots' to make war and at night, I trained them to make music." Before ending four years in uniform, he served on a submarine in the South Pacific. In March 1946 he resumed his professional work as a guest on *Voice of Firestone.* But few assignments at the mike or Met came his way.

Carter began as a dancer in vaudeville. He switched to singing which came naturally to him, and began serious voice lessons at 24.

162. CASE, Nelson (announcer; b. Feb. 3, 1910, Long Beach, CA; d. March 24, 1976, Doylestown, PA).

Lombardoland (1934–35); *Hour of Charm* (1936–39); *New Carnation Contented Hour* (1946–48); *NBC Symphony* (1953–54).

In 1925 Case made his first appearance as a pianist at KFON Long Beach. He soon formed his own orchestra for the station, and at 17 became an announcer and singer for KGER Long Beach. He interrupted his broadcast activities to attend William and Mary College in the East. He returned as NBC staff announcer in San Francisco in 1931, and worked on *Wheatenaville.* Moving to New York in 1934, Case became well known as the voice introducing Lowell Thomas's nightly newscasts on CBS for seven years. Other assignments included *Marriage Club,* a CBS audience-participation quiz, and big-band airings of Wayne King and Ray Noble.

163. CAVALLARO, Carmen (bandleader [The Poet of the Piano] [signature song: "My Sentimental Heart"]; b. May 6, 1913, New York, NY; d. Oct. 12, 1989, Columbus, OH). *The Schaeffer Revue* (1945–47); *Tums Tune Time* (1948); *Duet in Rhythm* (1956).

Centered around his stylish, flashy piano leads, his orchestra enjoyed long engagements with remotes from New York's Hotel Astor and Biltmore. The classically trained musician started his eight-piece orchestra in 1939, after playing with Abe Lyman, Rudy Vallee and society bandleaders. Cavallaro made the guest circuit, most often on *Fitch Bandwagon, Kraft Music Hall* and *New Carnation Contented Hour.* His own show, *The Schaeffer Revue,* enjoyed nearly a two-year run.

A major artist on the Decca label, he did the piano

Winifred Cecil

sound track for the movie *The Eddy Duchin Story* in 1956. By then, he was featured as a trio and a single attraction.

164. CECIL, Winifred (singer; b. Aug. 31, 1907, Staten Island, NY; d. Sept. 13, 1985, New York, NY). *Show Boat* (1935–36).

What might have been a long and full radio career for this accomplished soprano was sidetracked by vocal studies and operatic appearances in Europe, marriage to a wealthy Italian baron, and wartime perils and crippling injuries. She returned to the United States in 1949, after the death of her husband. Cecil resumed her career with recitals but with little success. Moreover, networks had already begun dropping the musical programs that she might have headlined a few years earlier.

Her brightest broadcast moments came as "Virginia Lee" on *Show Boat* opposite Lanny Ross, and not long after her Town Hall debut in 1933. In her later years she conducted Joy in Singing, a series of public master classes and recitals for promising young singers.

165. CHAMLEE, Mario (singer; b. May 29, 1892, Los Angeles, CA; d. Nov. 13, 1966, Hollywood, CA). *Arco Birthday Party* (1930); *Swift Garden Party* (1934–35); *Tony and Gus* (1935).

Opera tenor noted for his style and diction. His mastery of Italian led to leads in Puccini operas when they were first released to radio in 1928 and sponsored by American Radiator Company. Many guest appearances ran the gamut from *Show Boat* and *Kraft Music Hall* to *RCA Magic Key* and *Your Hit Parade.*

Chamlee became the first serious singer to perform as a radio character in humorous dialect. As Tony, he played an impetuous Italian with operatic aspirations. Gus was the actor George Frame Brown, who had created *Real Folks,* a rural serial.

Chamlee's early singing — in the University of California Glee Club — helped set his goal as a Met Opera tenor. He changed his name — Cholmondeley — to Chamlee which caused him to be taken for an Italian. He and his wife, opera singer Ruth Miller, later taught singing and stage performing in southern California.

166. CHANDLER, Jeff (actor; b. Dec. 15, 1918, Brooklyn, NY; d. June 17, 1961, Culver City, CA). *Michael Shayne, Detective* (1946–47); *Our Miss Brooks* (1948–57).

The role of high school teacher and boyfriend of *Our Miss Brooks* — Eve Arden — was his break. It led to a Universal movie contract and a key part as the Indian, Cochise, in the James Stewart Western *Broken Arrow.* Chandler had settled on acting while a stock company stagehand on Long Island. He picked up jobs on radio after four years of Army duty. Discovered by Dick Powell, Chandler was given a chance on screen in *Johnny O'Clock.* The radio lead as Michael Shayne

Jeff Chandler, Edward Arnold (courtesy of Capital Cities/ABC)

helped to hone his talents as a rugged leading man. For *Screen Directors' Playhouse* in 1950–51, he starred in *Lifeboat, Hired Wife, Only Yesterday* and *Broken Arrow*.

167. CHAPPELL, Ernest (announcer; b. June 10, 1903, Syracuse, NY; d. July 4, 1983, North Palm Beach, FL). *The Song of Your Life* (1940–41); *The Fabulous Dr. Tweedy* (1946–47); *Quiet, Please* (1947–48); *The Big Story* (1947–55).

Commercial announcer for American Tobacco Co.'s Pall Mall brand for 17 years, and its spokesman on *The Big Story*, a series based on true-life stories of investigative reporters. His deep reassuring voice set the scene for *Quiet, Please*, an imaginative mystery offering that he helped to produce; *That They Might Live*, a wartime drama; and *George Jessel's Jamboree*, a variety show. He served as announcer for Edward R. Murrow's wartime newscasts, supervised production of Orson Welles' *Campbell Playhouse* and coached Eleanor Roosevelt for her regular broadcast commentary. At the 1939 New York World's Fair, he was host of the first beauty contest on television, a medium for which he later provided intros and voiceovers for Walter Cronkite's *Eyewitness to History* and CBS coverage of Presidential events.

Graduating from Syracuse University in 1925 with the hope of a singing career, "Chappy" joined local station WFBL that year as on-the-air staff and program director. Two years later he managed the Blue network affiliate WHAM Rochester for Stromberg-Carlson Telephone Manufacturing Co. That led to assignments for Bill Paley and CBS as program and production manager and for the four-station Buffalo Broadcasting Corporation as program vice president. In 1930 Chappell became production manager of Judson Radio Program and its *Atwater Kent, True Story* and Puccini opera programs.

Chappell's voice was once described as one that "begins as a rumble down deep and proceeds to roll in pleasant waves over you like a velvet-covered steamroller."

168. CHONG, Peter Goo (actor; b. Dec. 2, 1898, Miu, China*; d. Jan. 15, 1985, Peking, China).

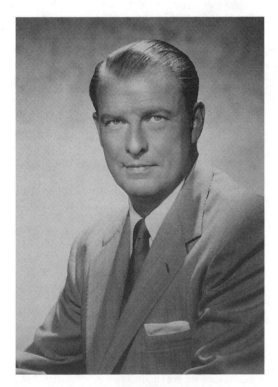

Ernest Chappell (courtesy of Helen G. Chappell)

*Early professional bios list Jersey City as his birthplace.

Peter Chong, left

Collier's Hour (1929); *March of Time* (1934); *Eddie Cantor Show* (1935); *This Day Is Ours* (1938–39).

Oriental character-comedy actor. One of the first ongoing Chinese actors in radio, he had appeared on Broadway in *Twelve Miles Out, Hit the Deck* and *Fast Life* in the 1920s and combined stage work with broadcasting into the 1940s. He once played Charlie Chan on a January 1933 broadcast of *Five Star Theatre*— the only native Chinese to portray the Oriental detective.

His film roles included the Japanese ambassador in *Mission to Moscow* and Ingrid Bergman's house servant in *The Inn of the Sixth Happiness*. A musician, Chong composed and arranged under the name Koh-nie Kuh. While studying for a doctoral degree at NYU, he researched the ancient Chinese whole-tone scale system and discovered the ancient Greek tonal system, which, for some 300 years, musicologists had failed to solve.

169. CLAIRE, Helen (actress; b. Oct. 18, 1911, Union Springs, AL; d. Jan. 12, 1974, Birmingham, AL). *The O'Neills* (1936–41); *Echoes of New York* (1939–40); *Backstage Wife* (1945–46).

Listeners may not have connected her name to her voice but the omnipresent Helen Claire was recognized as a microphone mainstay, be it a comedy hour sketch, a prison drama episode or a soap opera cliffhanger. She appeared with Rudy Vallee and Ethel Barrymore, and on *Death Valley Days, Stella Dallas* and *Counterspy.* On *Great Plays* she recreated the role of Cindy Lou, first played in her long-running 1938 Broadway hit *Kiss the Boys Goodbye.*

As Sally in *The O'Neills* Claire had the distinction of being the only heroine to die on the air in childbirth, this being the device used to write her out of the series when she was about to go into a play. The

play apparently had a short run, so she began appearing again on the soap, sometimes in a flashback and sometimes as a ghost.

Active on Broadway and on the road, she was also a commentator on women's news and fashions for Fox Movietone News from 1937 to 1949.

170. CLAIRE, Marion (singer; b. Feb. 25, 1904, Chicago, IL; d. Feb. 24, 1988, Ft. Lauderdale, FL). *Chicago Theatre of the Air* (1940–47).

Soprano Marion Claire performed opera in Milan and Berlin in the 1920s, then returned to Chicago where she sang lyric roles with its Civic Opera. Earlier, she had been a concert violinist, appearing with the Chicago Symphony at age ten. On WGN-Mutual's *Chicago Theatre of the Air,* she appeared with such guest artists as Thomas L. Thomas, Richard Tucker and Thomas Hayward, chiefly in operettas. An acting cast spoke their dialogue; Betty Winkler usually acted for Claire. Her husband, Henry Weber, conducted. The productions were sponsored by *Chicago Tribune* publisher Col. Robert M. McCormick who at the start of each broadcast spoke on political issues from a conservative (and controversial) stance.

Claire retired as lead singer in 1947 but continued as production supervisor until the final season in 1955. She saw that at each broadcast an elaborate souvenir program was distributed to the large studio audience — a rare frill for most series. Her association with WGN also included director of its FM programs from 1947 to 1953.

171. CLANEY, Howard (announcer; b. April 17, 1898, Pittsburgh, PA; d. April 1980, Charlotte, NC). *American Album of Familiar Music* (c1932–38, 1942–49); *NBC Symphony* (1937–38); *Borden Special Edition* (1938).

Between his New York acting days in *Cyrano, Liliom* and *Juno and the Paycock* in the 1920s and his latter years there as a painter and watercolorist with numerous one-man shows at art galleries, Claney pursued a career as an announcer. He began at WEAF at 195 Broadway and later was a mainstay at Radio City where he was a favorite of the prolific producer of soaps and musical features Frank Hummert. Leading advertisers sought him for their programs with Lawrence Tibbett, Paul Whiteman, Jack Benny and Walter Damrosch. In 1938 he took an extended vacation to study painting abroad. That year's European crisis triggered his return to a mike for on-the-spot news and commentary from London via shortwave. In 1942 NBC welcomed him back to the fold and to several of his old programs, including *Waltz Time.*

NBC Artists Service once described Claney as "clear-voiced, an expert in selling psychology, and blessed with an air personality which strikes a note of genuine sincerity into his excellent delivery."

172. CLAPPER, Raymond (commentator; b. May 30, 1892, LaCygne, KS; d. Feb. 1, 1944, Enivetak, Marshall Islands, No. Pacific).

Columnist and news analyst, gaining a highly respected, national reputation as a political commentator in the 1930s. Based in Washington as United Press syndicated writer for many years, he raised the standards of unbiased reporting and sound craftsmanship in both journalism and broadcasting. Mutual and White Owl Cigars brought him to the air in 1942 with 15 minutes of news commentary, two nights a week. As war gripped the country, he de-emphasized politics to focus his commentaries more upon the human side of the war. In 1943 he visited the Mediterranean theatre and was aboard one of the U.S. planes in the first bombing of Rome. Early the following year Clapper left for a first-hand view of the Pacific war zone. The plane in which he was a passenger was engaged in covering the invasion of the Marshall Islands. It collided with another plane over the Coral Sea, and both crashed in a lagoon. There were no survivors.

Clapper grew up in Kansas City where he sold newspapers on street corners and served as an apprentice printer. He entered the University of Kansas in 1913 and three years later went to work for the Kansas City *Star.* In 1933 he wrote *Racketeering in Washington,* a slightly jaundiced, irreverent look at lawmakers and their many extravagances and wasteful agendas at a time when millions of Americans were out of work. On the eve of World War II NBC broadcast the first of his common sense, plain language reports.

173. CLARK, Buddy (singer; b. July 26, 1911, Dorchester, MA; d. Oct. 1, 1949, Los Angeles, CA). *Your Hit Parade* (1936–37); *New Carnation Contented Hour* (1946–49).

A natural flair for singing brought Clark (born Samuel Goldberg) to the attention of I. J. Fox furriers who sponsored him on Boston radio in the early 1930s. He appeared with Ben Bernie, Vincent Lopez and Wayne King. His network debut was with Benny Goodman on *Let's Dance.* He freelanced voice dubbing for films and recordings, often without credit.

On staff at CBS he sang many 15-minute segments. A pleasant, sweet-sounding singer with mannerisms of delivery parallel to Crosby, Clark achieved his greatest popularity shortly before his death in the late '40s. A private plane emergency landing in a Los Angeles residential area resulted in fatal injuries. His last radio appearance was a four-network hookup to promote the Community Chest of America, with Dinah Shore.

174. CLARK, Lon (actor; b. Jan. 12, 1911, Frost, MN). *Nick Carter, Master Detective* (1943–45); *Backstage Wife* (1946).

Dauntless hero Nick Carter on Mutual's long-running, well-received detective series. Clark came to New York radio in 1941 and picked up roles in *Against the Storm* and *Right to Happiness* at NBC. During World War II he played in many morale-building dramatic shows: *Words at War, Labor for Victory, Workhorses with Wings.* He played David Markham on *Backstage Wife* and Andy Hoyt on *Pepper Young's Family.* In 1947 the New York *Journal-American* engaged him to read its weekly comics to children. As late as 1958 he handled roles on the science fiction series *Exploring Tomorrow.*

Lon studied at Minneapolis Music School where he conducted his own orchestra. He once sang with the Cincinnati Summer Opera Company.

175. CLOONEY, Rosemary (singer; b. May 23, 1928, Maysville, KY). *Rosemary Clooney Show* (1953–55).

An alumna of WLW and its *On the Sunny Side,*

Buddy Clark

Rosemary Clooney

Rosemary and younger sister Betty Clooney toured for three years with Tony Pastor's orchestra, which regularly broadcast from Philadelphia from 1946–48. Betty quit but Rosemary continued as a soloist. Her easygoing, forthright style attracted the record industry. Columbia initially signed her for $50 per disc but not until 1951 did "Come On-a My House," a peppy adaptation of an Armenian folk song, catch fire. Guest spots on *The Big Show, Your Hit Parade* and *Sunday Serenade* led to her own show of popular and folk tunes. A TV version premiered in the mid-50s. A frequent performer with Bob Hope, she ended the decade with a CBS midday radio series with Bing Crosby. They continued to work together, most effectively in personal appearances, into the 1970s.

176. COBB, Irvin S. (humorist; b. June 23, 1876, Paducah, NY; d. March 10, 1944, New York, NY). *The Gulf Show* (1933); *Paducah Plantation* (1936–37).

Writer-lecturer in the characteristically American tradition of Mark Twain and Will Rogers. Cobb, a reporter and managing editor at the turn of the century, broke into the high ranks of New York journalism with well-executed newsworthy stories. His fictional Judge Priest tales made him famous and transferred well to films; he appeared in several.

Cobb's jestful humor first reached listeners from the *Eveready Hour* in 1927. By late 1930 he was a frequent speaker at the microphone for sponsors Cola-Cola and Armour. Gulf Oil put him on the Colum-

bia network on Wednesdays and Fridays in 1933, and at the same time offered Will Rogers over NBC on Sundays. *Paducah Plantation,* set at a mythical Kentucky plantation, included a regular cast: Hall Johnson Choir, Clarence Muse, and the Four Blackbirds Quartet. His radio activity was ended by illness in 1939. His last major endeavor was the autobiographical work, *Exit Laughing.*

177. COLE, Nat "King" (singer; b. March 17, 1919, Montgomery, AL*; d. Feb. 15, 1965, Santa Monica, CA). *King Cole Trio Time* (1946–48).

A night club pianist in a trio (guitar and double bass), Cole did his first singing in 1940 when an inebriated customer insisted that he sing "Sweet Lorraine." His caressing, jazz-flavored phrasing and soft, precise tonality, mesmerized his audience. He evolved into a soloist who occasionally played the piano, although his trio remained an inherent part of his performances. His recordings for Capitol began in 1943; his first disc was his own composition "Straighten Up and Fly Right," a big hit. Sales on his records often topped the 1,000,000 mark. The 1948 ballad "Nature Boy" proved a sensation with a half-million copies sold within a month. Nat and its composer were featured on *We, the People* in an early simulcast.

Very few black artists managed more than token guest appearances. Cole broke the barrier with his own 15-minute show in the mid-1940s. It began as a summer replacement for Bing Crosby and continued into the NBC fall lineup as a late Saturday afternoon segment with Wildroot as sponsor. Both Nat and his trio received numerous musical awards during this period. Guest spots on television were frequent, and in 1956 NBC gave him a weekly slot. It expanded into a well-packaged half-hour series with Nelson Riddle's orchestra and guest artists. But it failed to attract a sponsor because of the fear of a Southern boycott, and was dropped in mid-season 1957–58. Nat summed it up: "Madison Avenue is afraid of the dark." His personal appearances were vastly more rewarding. In 1956 he signed a $500,000 contract for yearly bookings in Las Vegas through 1959. It was the largest single contract in the history of show business up to that time.

178. COLLINGWOOD, Charles (newscaster; b. June 4, 1917, Three Rivers, MI; d. Oct. 3, 1985, New York, NY).

A Rhodes Scholar, he covered World War II for CBS as part of Edward R. Murrow's reporting staff in London. His assignments included the Allied invasions of North Africa and Europe. He became CBS News's first UN correspondent in the 1940s, then the network's White House correspondent. A 1942 Peabody Award winner, distinguished-looking Colling-

The U.S. Postal Service 1994 stamp honoring Cole incorrectly inscribed his birth date as 1917.

wood moved easily onto the video screen as a co-anchorman for coverage of many events and as a host-narrator of the series *Chronicle* and *Adventure.*

179. COLLINS, Dorothy (singer; b. Nov. 18, 1926, Windsor, Ontario, Canada; d. July 21, 1994, Watervliet, NY). *Your Hit Parade* (1949–57).

Vocalist with girl-next-door image on the weekly *Hit Parade.* Collins started out in the series as singer of the commercial jingles for Lucky Strike cigarettes ("Be Happy, Go Lucky"). A protege of its conductor (and her future husband) Raymond Scott, she advanced to the show's female lead and

Ted Collins, Kate Smith

through its simulcasts became a favorite pop artist of the '50s. At one point in 1951 she sang first-place "Too Young" on 17 consecutive Saturdays.

Her earliest work was on a children's program at WJBK Detroit in 1938. At age 16 she was advised by Scott to study singing in Chicago, and soon appeared with Scott and his Quintet. In 1949 when she suddenly took over the *Hit Parade* from his brother, conductor Mark Warnow, Collins stayed on the road and led the Quintet. She did the introductions as well as the vocals. It proved to be useful training for the forthright cigarette commercials that would bring her much success as a spokesperson-singer.

After *Your Hit Parade* she appeared on TV's *Candid Camera* and in the 1971 musical *Follies,* singing one of the show's big songs, "Losing My Mind" and receiving a Tony nomination for her performance.

180. COLLINS, Ray (actor; b. Dec. 10, 1889, Sacramento, CA; d. July 11, 1965, Santa Monica, CA). *Cavalcade of America* (1936–41); *Grand Central Station* (1937–38); *Mercury Theatre of the Air* (1938).

Journeyman-like vaudeville, stock and Broadway actor, he tallied some 900 stage roles by the mid-1940s. He began in radio with *March of Time* in 1933 and became part of Orson Welles' troupe. On "War of the Worlds" he was subdued by Martian invaders. The CBS serial *County Seat* provided a role of some depth — a Will Rogersesque Doc Will Hackett. In 1939 Collins appeared on Norman Corwin's adaptation of "John Brown's Body."

His film bow came in Welles' *Citizen Kane,* and some 75 films followed. On television, beginning in 1956 for nine seasons, he played police officer Lt. Tragg on *Perry Mason.*

181. COLLINS, Ted (announcer, host; b. Oct. 12, 1900, New York, NY; d. May 27, 1964, Lake Placid, NY). *Kate Smith Speaks* (1938–57).

Highly successful, longtime manager of Kate Smith. Collins made her one of America's best known singers. He discovered her doing jazzy songs and fat girl comedy in a Broadway musical, and asked her to do some recordings for Columbia where he was a manager. His counsel and strategy led to radio, beginning with a 15-minute spot on CBS in 1931. They formed a verbal 50-50 partnership that generated over a million dollars a year into the 1950s.

In addition to Kate's variety show, Collins produced a non-singing noonday series for her homey philosophy and casual chatter. He entered the program as announcer and co-host (often reading news bulletins). Collins assumed a more prominent role in her television programs with "Cracker Barrel" spot interviews of famous guests. Over the years, many persons thought of Ted and Kate as husband and wife. Deluged with mail about it, they got up a form letter spelling out the marital status of each: Smith was not married. Collins was, although in later years separated from his wife.

182. COLLYER, Clayton "Bud" (actor, announcer; b. June 18, 1908, New York, NY; d. Sept. 8, 1969, Greenwich, CT). *Superman* (1940–51); *The Man I Married* (1940–41); *Truth or Consequences* (1943–45); *Break the Bank* (1945–51, 1953–55); *Three for the Money* (1948).

From a theatrical family, he turned to the legal profession, and after graduation from Williams College and Fordham University worked as a law clerk. When acting parts in plays and on radio offered more

Bud Collyer (courtesy of Capital Cities/ABC)

remuneration than practicing law, he decided on show business. He portrayed *Superman* over Mutual but could be heard on numerous other programs as an announcer (*Raleigh Room, Schaefer Revue*) and actor (*Terry and the Pirates, Mary Marlin*). "Those were great days, because you weren't seen," he noted years later. "You could appear on as many as 25 to 30 shows a week and grab off $6,000 to $7,000 a year — big dough at that time."

His first job was as a singer at CBS for $85 a week in 1936. This proved a far cry from his ultimate duties as a well-disposed quizmaster-emcee of *On Your Mark,* and on TV's *Beat the Clock* and *To Tell the Truth.* Collyer served as president of the American Federation of Television and Radio Artists.

183. COLMAN, Ronald (actor; b. Feb. 9, 1891, Richmond, Surrey, England; d. May 19, 1958, Santa Barbara, CA). *The Halls of Ivy* (1949–52).

His debonair charm and gentlemanly poise brought him decades of screen popularity. He played an array of parts, from a philosophical diplomat to an elegant thief. In 1950 Colman tied in second place with Laurence Olivier as "best actor of the half-century" in a poll of film workers conducted by *Daily Variety* (Chaplin won first place). He received an Oscar for *A Double Life* in 1948, although his own personal favorite roles were *Beau Geste* and Sidney Carlton in *A Tale of Two Cities.* His radio role as president of a small American college won him acclaim in the later phase of his career. *The Halls of Ivy* starred Colman and his wife, British actress Benita Hume, as Vicky

Hall. The NBC program moved into television but ran only briefly.

Much in demand for special radio tributes and dramatized appeals during World War II, he spoke for Greek War Relief, Bundles for Britain, United China Relief, American Red Cross, War Loan Drives and blood donor campaigns. In December 1945 the Colmans began the first of many appearances on Jack Benny's program.

184. COLONNA, Jerry (comedian [catchphrase: "Greetings, Gate"]; b. Oct. 17, 1904, Boston, MA; d. Nov. 21, 1986, Woodland Hills, CA). *Bob Hope Show* (1938–48).

Zany sidekick of Bob Hope, beginning with the first Pepsodent program on through the frontline GI shows. His facial appearance — bush mustache and rolling goggle eyes — and lines like "Who's Yehudi?" — received plenty of laughs and were part and parcel of Hope's scripts. His distinctive raucous vocal caricatures of "Mandalay," "Sonny Boy" and "I Came to Say Goodby," concealed the fact that he was a proficient singer.

Colonna, a trombonist, became a CBS musician in New York in the 1930s. He developed a reputation for breaking up rehearsals with his wild contortions, and was given a chance at comedy by Fred Allen and Walter O'Keefe. His radio spots and film appearances were frequent and usually hilarious. He returned often to Hope's broadcasts in the early 1950s. Although he suffered a severe stroke in the mid-60s he was able to go to Vietnam for Hope's annual Christmas show in 1969.

185. COLTON, Kingsley (actor; b. Feb. 15, 1924, New York, NY*). *Let's Pretend* (1937–51); *Valiant Lady* (1938–39); *My Son and I* (1939–40).

From 1937, the year of his radio bow on *Let's Pretend,* through 1939, this juvenile performer chalked up 16 commercial shows and 10 sustaining programs. A straightforward, dependable actor, he did modeling and appeared in film shorts prior to radio. He played Buddy, Betty Garde's young boy, on *My Son and I.* He worked periodically on *Kate Smith Hour, March of Time* and *Town Hall Tonight.*

After serving for three years in the US Army Signal Corps Intelligence, he completed Columbia University and switched from acting to the business side of TV advertising.

186. COLUMBO, Russ (singer, bandleader [signature song: "You Call It Madness But I Call It Love"]; b. Jan. 14, 1908, Camden, NJ; d. Sept. 2, 1934, Los Angeles, CA). *Russ Columbo Program* (1931–32).

A performer with the vocal ease of Crosby and the Latin good looks of Valentino, Columbo stood on the cusp of a major career when an accidental discharge

An early bio lists 1927.

from an antique pistol ended his life. Trained as a violinist, he began to mix singing with his playing at Los Angeles hotels. He organized his own orchestra, then opened his own club.

His manager, the songwriter Con Conrad, brought him to New York for broadcasts at NBC in the summer of 1931. Introduced as the "Romeo of the Air," he sang on several short-lived 15-minute series, with Don Voorhees orchestra, and for Listerine into early 1932. That year he was backed by his own orchestra, organized and often led by Benny Goodman. He also appeared with Jimmie Fidler. But more effort went into his work with Victor Records. Columbo supplemented these activities with personal appearances in vaudeville and at the Waldorf-Astoria Hotel. His own compositions—"Prisoner of Love" and "You Call It Madness, But I Call It Love"—epitomized the romantic ballad during the reign of the crooner. In 1933 he left broadcasting to devote himself chiefly to films but was preparing to return to NBC at the time of his fatal mishap.

Perry Como

187. COMBS, George H., Jr. (commentator; b. May 3, 1898, Lee's Summit, MO; d. Nov. 29, 1977, West Palm Beach, FL).

Outspoken news analyst and talk show moderator. Beginning as a lawyer and assistant prosecutor in Kansas City, Combs ran for Congress in 1926 and defeated his Republican incumbent-opponent. Labeled "the baby Congressman," he was one of the youngest ever to serve in the House. He attracted radio executives by his assertiveness and flair for public speaking. By 1938 and settled in New York, he emceed WHN's *Now You Decide,* a series whereby audience members gave their decision on court cases. Broadcasts for MBS accelerated during World War II. At one point he aired his programs from the stage of New York's Roxy Theatre. "Combs is in there pitching with those crisp words that are certain to make a listener reflect on the what-goes around the globe," *Variety* once noted.

ABC also featured his politically liberal commentary as did WMCA. In the early 1950s, although serving as special assistant in the Office of Price Stabilization, he broadcast some 20 hours a week on *Spotlight, New York* at WJZ. Combs founded Radio News International, a news gathering agency.

188. COMO, Perry (singer [signature song: "Dream Along With Me"]; b. May 18, 1913, Canonsburg, PA). *Beat the Band* (1940–41); *Perry Como Program* (1943–44); *Chesterfield Supper Club* (1944–50).

A pleasant enough vocalist with the band of Ted Weems from 1936 to 1942, Como could be tuned in periodically but he was hardly a household name. Weems regularly gave him a vocal number as part of the music for *Fibber McGee and Molly* in 1936–37, but it was this bandleader's musical quiz *Beat the Band* on NBC that helped bring him to more mainstream listeners. He might have continued longer with that aggregation if the war had not caused the band to break up.

On his own in 1943, he began a late afternoon sustaining series and signed a RCA Victor contract, the beginning of 27 Gold records. As singing emcee of *Chesterfield Supper Club,* he moved into the lofty, well-deserved company of Crosby and Sinatra. His easygoing manner and subdued, intimate voice built a loyal following for this onetime teenage barber from Pennsylvania.

189. COMPTON, Walter (quizmaster, announcer [catchphrase: "Thank you and thirty."*]; b. Oct. 9, 1912, Charleston, SC; d. Dec. 9, 1959, Washington, DC). *Double or Nothing* (1940–44).

Compton (real name: Walter Knobeloch) broke into radio in 1936 at WCSC Charleston after a year

His signoff produced many letters inquiring what he meant by "thirty," a newsman's way of signifying the end of a story.

or so as Instructor in Dramatics and Director of Publicity at Roanoke College, his alma mater. He spent time writing and selling scripts, directing, newscasting and announcing on WCSC, WIS Columbia and WFBC Greenville, all in his home state. In 1937 he set out for Washington and landed a job doing daily newscasts and special events for WOL, and also became Mutual's White House announcer.

Compton had the idea for *Double or Nothing* and brought it to life at WOL, then moved it to Mutual. As emcee, he did a commendable job with a quiz format. A close counterpart of *Take It or Leave It*, the series led to an injunction by WOL against the $64 network show, which bowed six months after *Double or Nothing*. The case, however, was dismissed in Federal court.

After World War II, Compton entered television as a news commentator and general manager of WAAM Baltimore and WTTS Washington, but by 1957 had returned to radio as a Mutual commentator-newscaster. He was a charter member of the Radio-Television Correspondents Association.

190. CONNER, Nadine (singer; b. Feb. 20, 1914, Compton, CA). *Show Boat* (1937); *The Songshop* (1938); *Salute to Youth* (1943–45); *Kraft Music Hall* (1947).

She made a highly praised Met debut as Pamina in *The Magic Flute* in 1941 and immediately took her place as an integral member of that house. But radio provided the foundation for this fragile-looking lyric soprano "of even scale and purity of tone." While studying at the University of Southern California, she

sang over radio with a student group in 1933 and soon worked as a staff singer with station KHL Los Angeles. That led to conductor David Broekman's *California Melodies* and vocal assignments with Al Jolson and Bing Crosby.

As a result of her popularity she was booked to make concert and opera appearances, and Nelson Eddy selected her to co-star on his *Open House* series. In 1937 Conner joined Lanny Ross on *Show Boat* as a cast member for six months. A frequent guest artist on *The Railroad Hour* and *Voice of Firestone* in the early '50s, she ended a 20-year Met career in 1960, opting to spend more time with her California-based husband and children.

191. CONRAD, William (actor; b. Sept. 27, 1920, Louisville, KY; d. Feb. 11, 1994, No. Hollywood, CA). *Gunsmoke* (1952–61); *Jason and the Golden Fleece* (1952–53).

The deep, authoritative voice of Marshall Matt Dillon on the adult western *Gunsmoke* on CBS. For several years the network had wanted to develop such an authentic, honest-sounding series. Conrad, who was averaging 10 to 15 shows a week, specialized in drama with roles on *The Whistler, Romance, Lux Radio Theatre,* and *Suspense.* He was also the opening signature voice on *Escape* in the distinctive mode of Orson Welles.

The heavy-set Conrad got his first paying job at age 17 at KMPC Beverly Hills. "I was fascinated with radio and used to hang around with a dear friend who was an announcer," he said in a 1969 interview. "He'd let me do a commercial every now and then."

Nadine Conner

William Conrad (courtesy of Steve Jelf)

During World War II he worked for the Armed Forces Radio Service. After *Gunsmoke,* he filled the TV screen in titles roles in *Jake and the Fat Man, Cannon* and *Nero Wolfe.* His films included *The Killers* and *Sorry, Wrong Number.*

192. CONREID, Hans (actor; b. April 15, 1915, Baltimore, MD; d. Jan. 5, 1982, Burbank, CA). *Alan Young Show* (1946–47); *Burns and Allen* (1947–49); *Judy Canova Show* (1947–53); *My Friend Irma* (1947–54).

On his first radio assignment, Conreid once recalled: "I had the part of a Swiss guardsman. I had nine lines, and my tenth was a death rattle. My fee was $5." A successful freelancer, he portrayed the full spectrum of character roles and comic parts. He set out as a serious actor in Shakespearean roles while attending Columbia University, moving on to radio as a member of Orson Welles' Mercury Theatre and Arch Oboler's presentations.

During World War II, he was cast as menacing Nazi officials in films, but managed to break away for light air roles with Bob Burns and Jimmy Durante. He was at his best in *My Friend Irma* as Professor Kropotkin using one of his exotic East European accents. Television often utilized his articulate wit and sardonic demeanor as a game show panelist.

193. CONTE, John (emcee, singer; b. Sept. 15, 1915, Palmer, MA). *Screen Guild Theatre* (1938–39); *Maxwell House Coffee Time* (1941–45); *Teentimers Club* (1946); *John Conte Show* (1952–53).

All-round radio personality with assignments as emcee, singer, announcer and actor. A baritone, Conte was first heard over KHJ in 1936, then nationally on *Screen Guild Theatre.* He joined *Coffee Time* as announcer and became host in early 1945 but was soon inducted into the Army. A year later Conte was back as a singing emcee and starting to appear in Broadway musicals, including Rodgers & Hammerstein's *Allegro.* He also acted in a 1949 summer radio series called *My Good Wife.*

Early television utilized him as emcee of the daytime drama series *Matinee Theatre,* and as singer on *Show of Shows.* In the 1960s he switched to the management side of television with ownership of a Palm Springs TV station.

In 1944 while filming Abbott and Costello's *Lost in a Harem,* he met, then married, co-star Marilyn Maxwell.

194. CONTINO, Dick (accordionist [signature song: "Lady of Spain"]; b. Jan. 17, 1930, Fresno, CA). *Horace Heidt Youth Opportunity Hour* (1947–49).

A talent-show amateur who won Heidt's Grand National Final competition. Contino, an ex-student at Fresno State, entered the contest in December 1947, proved an instant sensation, and went undefeated for 13 consecutive weeks. He gained the quarterfinals,

Dick Contino

then appeared periodically until his winning of the $5,000 grand prize a year later. He was responsible for a brief accordion craze across the country with his bellow-shaking, lively versions of "Lady of Spain" and "Bumble Boogie." The 18-year-old musician was tied to an exclusive contract with Heidt but brought suit to break away.

Contino formed his own troupe, playing to capacity audiences in major cities. In 1951, when his draft board gave notice of induction, he vanished. Ultimately, he was fined and sentenced to six months in a federal penitentiary for draft evasion. Subsequently, he served in the Army for two years in Korea. The episode dampened his career opportunities for years and brought financial and drinking problems. *The NBC Bandstand* was one of the few series that featured the onetime, all-American boy in the 1950s, and TV exposure was equally spotty.

195. CONWAY, Tom (actor; b. Sept. 15, 1904, St. Petersburg, Russia; d. April 22, 1967, Culver City, CA). *Sherlock Holmes* (1946–47); *The Saint* (1951).

Hero-detective in various film and radio series. A featured player in scores of movies (*Mr. & Mrs. North, Lady Be Good*), Conway inherited the role of the Falcon from his brother, actor George Sanders, who had been in the detective series and had grown tired of it. RKO Pictures killed off Sanders in 1942's *The Falcon's Brother,* and his work as a sleuth was picked up by Conway as his fictional sibling in a half-dozen Falcon films.

On radio Conway starred as Sherlock Holmes and as the sleuth known as *The Saint* (Simon Templar), and in early television as Inspector Mark Saber. In contrast to his brother, he sported a pencil-thin mustache throughout his career.

196. COOK, Joe (comedian; b. 1887, Chicago, IL; d. May 16, 1959, Staatsburg, NY). *House Party* (1934); *Shell Chateau* (1937).

His wide range of comedy, chiefly aimed at the eye, never transferred well to radio. A vaudeville and Broadway star, Cook pitched knives, shot clay targets, walked a slack wire, juggled balls and roped stooges in three editions of Earl Carroll's *Vanities*. But without such horseplay, his spoken lines at the mike often failed to register with listeners.

In the late 1920s the *Eveready Hour* featured him, and from 1931 to 1939 Vallee regularly welcomed him to the *Fleischmann Hour*. His own series for Colgate, Goodrich and Shell struggled with 26-week runs. Cook fared much better on stage in *Rain or Shine* and *Fine and Dandy*. Because of ill health, he retired in 1942.

197. COOK, Phil (comedian, host [catchphrase: "Okay, Colonel"]; b. Sept. 27, 1893, Coldwater, MI; d. Sept. 18, 1958, Morristown, NJ). *The Radio Chief* (1925–c29); *Quaker Oaks Man* (1930–c33); *Morning Almanac* (1937–41).

Three decades in radio demonstrated his versatility as a comedian, writer, singer, actor, composer and guitarist. As the *Quaker Oats Man,* he sometimes impersonated as many as 13 characters on his one-man

Phil Cook

show. He made his debut as *The Radio Chef* at WOR soon after being asked to sing some of his own tunes in an impromptu program. His various credits in a long succession of shows include: *Klein Serenading Shoemaker, Buck and Wing, Flit Soldiers, Physical Culture Shoe Prince, Cotton and Morpheus* and *Cabin Door.* His last program was the local morning feature *Cook's Kitchen* on WCBS, from 1941–52, on which he sang the weather and the news ("I see by the papers . . . "). For years he conducted an annual drive on his show to obtain books and magazines for shut-ins and hospital patients in metropolitan New York.

198. COOPER, Jerry (singer; b. April 3, 1909, Bay Minette, AL*). *Krueger's Musical Toast* (1935–37); *Hollywood Hotel* (1937–38).

A romantic baritone whose voice bore an uncanny similarity to Bing Crosby's. In 1937 *Hollywood Hotel* spot lighted his talent. Wrote *Variety:* "He has an attractive ether personality and is a stronger singing bet than Fred MacMurray, whom he replaces. Lazy style is pleasant." Cooper had come up the ranks as a CBS Artists Bureau hopeful, singing first on *Tea at the Ritz.* He later headlined NBC's *Vocal Varieties* for Tums from Cincinnati.

Originally a trombone player in New Orleans, he found vocalizing easier. He sang in night clubs and on WWL while working day jobs as a fight manager and bank clerk. Encouraged by bandleader Roger Wolfe Kahn to try New York radio, he signed with Columbia. He recorded with Emil Coleman and Eddy Duchin, and on ETs as Jack Randolph. His Broadway musical bow, Ed Wynn's *Boys and Girls Together,* led to a handful of second-feature films. In the 1940s at WOR and on *Hollywood Open House,* he continued to put "the glamour of the South into his songs."

199. COPELAND, Royal (commentator; b. Nov. 7, 1868, Dexter, MI; d. June 17, 1938, Washington, DC). *Health Talk* (1928–32); *Fleischmann Hour* (1933–34).

Advocate of good personal health and individual well-being through a syndicated Hearst column and an NBC discussion series. His 15-minute talks first aired five times a week, then in 1929 moved to Saturdays for Ceresota Flour. Standard Brands once featured him every other week on Vallee's show. The broad response to his health topics encouraged the presentation of programs focusing on etiquette, child hygiene, psychology and good speech.

A physician, he taught at the University of Michigan where he received his M.D. Copeland combined medicine with politics, serving from 1901–03 as the Republican Mayor of Ann Arbor. He became Dean of New York Homeopathic College, and soon switched allegiance to the Democratic Party. With the backing of Gov. Al Smith, he won election to the U.S. Senate

Another source gives 1907 in New Orleans.

in 1922 and was twice re-elected. Throughout many Congressional sessions, Senator Copeland pushed for the enactment of a new and more stringent Pure Food and Drug Bill. Legislation passed in 1938, a week after his death from overwork and exhaustion.

200. CORRELL, Charles (comedian [signature song: "The Perfect Song"]; b. Feb. 3, 1890, Peoria, IL; d. Sept. 26, 1972, Chicago, IL). *Sam 'n' Henry* (1926–28); *Amos 'n' Andy* (1928–60).

The deep-voiced Andy of the team whose comic serial in Negro dialect was the most popular program of the late 1920s and early '30s. The duo — Amos was played by Freeman Gosden — became a part of Americana. Broadcasting 15 minutes five days a week, this collaboration developed the show's characters and prepared most of the scripts in a situation comedy centered around the day-to-day running of the one-cab Fresh-Air Taxi Company. Andy Brown was an easily discouraged, rather lazy, fellow who was readily taken in by the good-hearted, resourceful Amos and his somewhat unscrupulous pal Kingfish.

Actor-authors Correll and Gosden met in Durham, North Carolina in 1919 when they joined the same theatrical company. Their personalities and goals immediately meshed in a professional relationship and warm friendship. They worked out a song and chatter act, a genre that radio would soon favor. Their radio bow took place in New Orleans over an experimental transmitter. By late 1925 WEBH Chicago aired the duo on a regular basis. But at WGN they developed their breakthrough characters, Sam 'n' Henry. When WMAQ offered more money in 1928, they moved there but were required to find a new name for their blackface act. They chose *Amos 'n' Andy*. In November 1929 they went coast to coast on NBC for Pepsodent toothpaste.

Correll and Gosden missed only one show in all their years on the air. In 1931 they were snowed in and unable to reach the studio in time. On a special hookup in 1934 they carried on a two-way conversation between Amos in London and Andy in San Francisco. In 1943 the program began weekly broadcasts; it eventually totaled over 5,000 episodes. It moved to television in the 1950s without its creators. But times had changed. There were complaints that

the racially stereotyped characters, now played by a black cast, were no longer in good taste. The series was dropped. Meanwhile in 1954, the originators had reverted to a daily semi-variety radio show with recorded songs.

201. COSTELLO, Lou (comedian [catchphrase: "I'm a ba-a-ad boy."]; b. March 6, 1908, Paterson, NJ; d. March 3, 1959, Beverly Hills, CA). *Kate Smith Show* (1938); *Chase & Sanborn Hour* (1941–42); *Abbott and Costello Show* (1942–49).

The good-natured dimwit and fall guy of the comic team of Abbott and Costello. The two met in a Brooklyn burlesque theatre in the early 1930s and by the end of the decade were well on their way to international stardom. Their first break came in 1938, when they appeared with Kate Smith for five months. That led to the revue *Streets of Paris* on Broadway, a 1940 summer series for Bristol Myers, and top-grossing films at Universal.

Their old-fashioned knock-about style and tough street-wise dialogue won over audiences of all ages. The fast-talking, sharpshooting Bud Abbott mixed well with Costello's overgrown kid antics. Their enduring routine, "Who's on First?" was a highlight on radio and in personal appearances. They once subbed as visiting professors for Kay Kyser in a riotous version of the *Kollege of Musical Knowledge*. Their transcribed series for ABC in 1947 was one of the earliest prime-time multi-sponsor co-op programs. After several seasons in television, the duo broke up in 1957.

Bud Abbott & Lou Costello (courtesy of Capital Cities/ABC)

202. COTSWORTH, Staats (actor; b. Feb. 17, 1908, Oak Park, IL; d. April 9, 1979, New York, NY). *Lorenzo Jones* (1943–45); *Casey, Crime Photographer* (1943–55); *Front Page Farrell* (1945–54).

An established Shakespearean and repertory actor, accomplished painter and skilled photographer. He was a familiar voice as Casey to CBS listeners. His crime photographer adventures solved murders, prevented holdups, cracked dope rings and sent scoundrels to jail—and saved Ann, a woman reporter, from assorted fates. His other dramatic series included *Stella Dallas, Mr. & Mrs. North, When a Girl Marries* and *Marriage for Two.* In 1946 he was described as the busiest actor in radio; in 12 years he had made 7,500 broadcasts. A typical day ran from an 8:30 a.m. rehearsal on *Lone Journey* to a midnight repeat of *Mr. and Mrs. North.* He appeared on DuPont's prestigious *Cavalcade of America* (1948–53) as historical figures George Washington, Sylvanus Thayer and Charles Pinckney.

203. COTT, Ted (announcer, emcee; b. Jan. 1, 1917, Poughkeepsie, NY; d. June 12, 1973, New York, NY). *So You Think You Know Music?* (1939–41); *Music You Want* (1941–43).

Cott began announcing at a Brooklyn station at 16, and later joined city-owned WNYC in that capacity and as dramatic director at $1,800 a year. He left for WNEW, after nine years with the Municipal station, when the civil service commission pronounced him unqualified. His new job brought an increase to $140 a week. It soon led to Major Bowes' *Original Amateur Hour* and a reputed $18,000 a year.

While at WNEW he originated an education quiz among four contestants on classical music and composers. *So You Think You Know Music?* surprised everyone by becoming so popular that CBS picked it up. The glib and ingratiating Cott was backed by music critic Leonard Liebling as judge of the answers. When the program moved to NBC as a portion of *Schaefer Revue,* the musical portion regularly featured popular tunes played by the Allen Roth orchestra and sung by tenor Felix Knight.

Cott also delved into psychology when he produced *So You Think You Know People,* an audience-participation show. He aired Leopold Stokowski as a classical music disc jockey, also at WNEW. In 1950 he was named general manager of NBC local radio and television stations. He later held the same title at WABD, the DuMont TV channel in New York.

204. COTTEN, Joseph (actor; b. May 15, 1905, Petersburg, VA; d. Feb. 6, 1994, Los Angeles, CA). *Mercury Theatre on the Air* (1938–39).

An early associate of Orson Welles, he slowly built a career as a solidly dependable and highly attractive actor. With New York stage work limited in the 1930s, Cotten toiled as an assistant production manager and gradually moved into radio. *The Goldbergs* and *Cavalcade of America* provided much-needed experience and income. In 1935 he met 20-year-old Welles who cast him in Federal Theatre offerings of *Doctor Faustus* and *Julius Caesar,* the latter in modern dress. His mentor's Mercury Theatre brought important leads at the mike in dramatization of classics from literature and his first film *Citizen Kane.* Katharine Hepburn chose him as co-star in *The Philadelphia Story* on Broadway in 1939. Critics praised his romantic characterizations both in plays (*Sabrina Fair*) and films (*Love Letters*).

He made impressive appearances on *Hollywood Players* and *Screen Directors' Playhouse.* Cotten had his own anthology series on mid-50s television.

205. COUGHLIN, Charles (preacher [The Radio Priest]; b. Oct. 25, 1891, Hamilton, Canada; d. Oct. 27, 1979, Bloomfield Hills, MI).

From his parish, the Shrine of the Little Flower, in Royal Oak, Michigan, Father Coughlin gradually built up a Depression-era audience for his fiery, politically laced sermons through radio. In time he commanded a weekly following of 40 million people. The broadcasts began in 1926 when he went to WJR Detroit each Sunday to explain Catholicism to the heavily biased com-

Charles Coughlin (courtesy of Photofest)

munity. By 1929 stations in Chicago and Cincinnati were carrying his program and thousands of listeners were sending in contributions, most in sums no larger than a dollar. Coughlin built a new church with a seven-story tower with the weekly donations. Soon he turned from religious subjects to political and economic topics — the evils of capitalism, Communism, labor unions, Jewish bankers.

By 1932 his talks were carried every Sunday at 3 p.m. on an 18-station CBS hookup. He climbed on the Roosevelt New Deal bandwagon that year but in 1936 he formed his own Union Party with Congressman William Lemke of North Dakota as its Presidential candidate (who received about a million votes as FDR won by a landslide over Republican Alf Landon). When CBS censors insisted on checking his sermons in advance, he set up his own network of stations. Shortly after the United States entered World War II, Coughlin, under church pressure, was forced to stop his program, which had become divisive and extremely controversial.

206. COWAN, Thomas J. (announcer; b. 1884, Newark, NJ; d. Nov. 11, 1969, West Orange, NJ).

Chief announcer of the country's first city-owned and noncommercial station, New York's WNYC, from its beginning in 1925 to his retirement in 1961. He was with Westinghouse when the company inaugurated broadcasting in the New York area with the opening of WJZ Newark, October 1, 1921. Letters from listeners came as far away as Illinois. Cowan did the first play-by-play account of a World Series in 1921 (NY Giants and NY Yankees). But Newark *Call* sports editor Sandy Hunt at the Polo Grounds actually phoned in a basic description of the contest and Cowan relayed it. Cowan also covered the 1924 Democratic National Convention in Madison Square Garden.

At WJZ he identified himself with a set of initials — ACN. A stood for announcer, C for Cowan, N for Newark (later New York). The custom continued with each new announcer until 1925, and seemingly developed an insatiable curiosity about the nameless voices behind various initials.

207. CRAWFORD, Jesse (organist [Poet of the Organ]; b. Dec. 2, 1895, Woodland, CA; d. May 28, 1962, Sherman Oaks, CA). *Paramount Publix Hour* (1930–31).

Crawford made the pipe organ effective in areas of modern music as it had been for several centuries in the rendition of sacred and classical music. Through his commanding performances in theatres, by radio and on discs, he established the vogue for popular melodies played as organ solos. His "organolgues" of varied moods and texture had a strong effect on listeners, and drew large audiences to movie palaces in Los Angeles and Chicago. From 1926 to 1932 he performed at the new Paramount Theatre on New York's Times Square. Starting in 1929, he broadcast on CBS

and NBC, often with his wife Helen at a twin console. He provided background music for *Counterspy.*

Largely self-taught, Crawford played piano in a moving picture house in Spokane at 18 and soon discovered the powerful allure of the theatre pipe organ. He later studied arranging with Joseph Schillinger (who also taught his mathematical approach to music to Rosa Rio, Glenn Miller, Paul Lavalle, Joseph Kahn and George Gershwin).

208. CRENNA, Richard (actor; b. Nov. 30, 1927, Los Angeles, CA). *A Date with Judy* (1946–50); *Our Miss Brooks* (1948–57); *Burns and Allen* (1949–50); *The Great Gildersleeve* (1949–54).

Growing up in the neighborhood of CBS and NBC in Hollywood, he would go behind the CBS fence and steal old radio scripts they had thrown away. "It was my favorite reading for years," he remembered. A leading young performer of the 1940s and '50s, he played two memorable adenoidal adolescents: Oogie Pringle, Judy's boyfriend on *A Date with Judy* and Walter Denton, the high school student with the changing voice on *Our Miss Brooks* (a role he carried into television). He matured a bit as Bronco Thompson, Marjorie's fiance on *Great Gildersleeve.*

Crenna survived the fiercely competitive world of the juvenile actor to carve out a long and solid career in films (*Wait Until Dark, The Sand Pebbles*) and television (*The Real McCoys, Slattery's People*). He added Broadway to his achievements with a role in *A Hole in the Head* in 1957 as well as credits as a TV director and producer.

At age eleven Crenna had started as a kid who did everything on *Boy Scout Jamboree* at KFI Los Angeles. The station gave him twenty-five cents a week, plus one dollar for transportation and lunch.

209. CROOKS, Richard (singer; b. June 26, 1900, Trenton, NJ; d. Oct. 1, 1972, Portola Valley, CA). *Voice of Firestone* (1932–44).

An unusually sweet, yet virile, tenor voice. His radio appearances made him renowned throughout the country. On his programs, he stressed the lighter side of his repertoire. Crooks had the ability to sing any kind of music with exquisite taste, "reinforced," noted critic Harold Schonberg, "with impeccable phrasing and musical dignity." He made a triumphant Met bow in 1933 as Des Grieux in *Manon,* and pursued a full operatic and concert schedule along with weekly broadcasts on *Voice of Firestone.* About singing over radio he once observed: "It's the loneliest feeling in the world, to have no audience to sing to, to be completely unaware whether you're giving your best."

Crooks kept a promise to himself to retire when he felt that his voice was no longer what it should be, and he withdrew to private life in the 1940s. In his later years he sang from time to time in a church near his California home, rekindling memories of his start as a boy soprano in a church choir in New Jersey.

Bing Crosby, Irving Aaronson (courtesy of Big Band Hall of Fame)

210. CROSBY, Bing (singer; [signature song: "When the Blue of the Night Meets the Gold of the Day"]; b. May 2, 1904, Tacoma, WA*; d. Oct. 14, 1977, Madrid, Spain). *Meet the Artist* (1931–32); *Music That Satisfies* (1933); *Woodbury Program* (1934–35); *Kraft Music Hall* (1935–46); *Philco Radio Time* (1946–49).

Bing considered himself a "very lucky guy" who liked to sing and was well paid for it. His nonchalance and easy manner gave the impression that he barely tried for the estimated $1,000,000 he grossed annually in the 1940s. His voice on a phonograph record first landed a solo job with CBS. Bill Paley heard the disk, "I Surrender, Dear," from a nearby stateroom aboard ship. He inquired about the name of the vocalist, and then started arrangements to sign him for his network. "I eventually agreed to what seemed the fantastic sum of $1,500 a week, wondering why I

**Church records at Tacoma's St. Patrick Parish have revealed an earlier date: May 3, 1903.*

was doing it," Paley revealed years later.

Bing's nightly 15-minute sustainer first aired on September 2, 1931. Laryngitis and nervousness had delayed the debut a few days, but with the renditions of "Just One More Chance" and "I'm Through with Love" his intimate, intense style caught fire. By November, he had American Cigar as a sponsor.

Earlier, as part of Paul Whiteman's Rhythm Boys, he had performed on that conductor's Old Gold broadcasts in 1929–30, and appeared briefly on screen in *King of Jazz*. As a CBS personality, Bing sang periodically on *California Melodies* while starting his film career at Paramount in 1932. Taking over *Kraft Music Hall* from Whiteman in 1935, he enjoyed a decade as host of this Hollywood-based Thursday night variety show. Only when Kraft and NBC refused to pre-record his program to allow more freedom to enjoy the golf course and his Nevada ranch did he leave that series. Crosby persuaded Philco and ABC to let him make transcriptions so he would not have to be tied down to a weekly schedule. His ABC show is reputedly the first transcribed program fed commercially to a network in prime time, and started an irreversible trend toward ETs. Bing remained with radio throughout the next decade, attracting top-flight guests as he always had. He, in turn, made many guest appearances, including 25 with screen "Road" partner Bob Hope beginning in March 1941. Crosby's last series of light music with a small combo aired five times a week over CBS, and was not unlike his initial 15-minute segments a quarter-century earlier. He received a Peabody Award in 1969.

An Academy Award recipient for *Going My Way*, he starred in dozens of musical films, and a number of dramatic features, and recorded regularly until a week before his death. His Decca version of "White Christmas" remains an all-time best seller. Introduced early in World War II, it brought sentimental thoughts of home to millions of GIs, many of whom also heard "Der Bingle" during his many personal appearances in service camps.

211. CROSBY, Bob (bandleader, singer [signature song: "Summertime"]' b. Aug. 23, 1913, Spokane, WA; d. March 9, 1993, La Jolla, CA). *Camel Caravan* (1939–41); *Three-Ring Time* (1941–42); *Bob Crosby Show* (1943–44, 1946–47, 1949–50); *Club 15* (1947–49).

By 1936 this popular swing-era bandleader-vocalist was heard on many late-night remotes. Significant record sales of his 11-piece Bobcats led to commercial series, including a Camel-sponsored program (with Johnny Mercer) and the first major transcontinental show offered by Mutual from the West Coast, *Three-Ring Time.* In 1944 Bob entered the Marines. Two years later a new group with arranger Jerry Gray doing most of the conducting capitalized on the postwar Dixieland jazz revival and enjoyed air time into the 1950s.

Resembling brother Bing in appearance, mannerisms and voice compounded Bob's sense of frustration, and was the reason he chose to be a bandleader, first and foremost. "They could say Bing was a better singer than I," Bob stated, "but they couldn't say he had a better band. I was going to top him at something." Audiences found the comparison readily at hand; Bob substituted for Bing on his *Kraft Music Hall* during the summer of 1942 and on other occasions. He also filled in for Walter O'Keefe as emcee on *Double or Nothing* in 1951 and with his band backed Jack Benny for a time.

212. CROSS, Milton J. (announcer, commentator [The Voice of the Met] [catchphrase: "Good afternoon, opera lovers from coast to coast."]; b. April 16, 1897, New York, NY; d. Jan. 3, 1975, New York, NY). *A & P Gypsies* (1926–36); *Slumber Hour* (1930–32); Metropolitan Opera broadcasts (1931–73); *General Motors Concert* (1934–37); *Information Please* (1938–40); *Metropolitan Opera Auditions of the Air* (1939–42).

For the purity of diction and the fine quality of his voice, the American Academy of Arts and Letters in 1929 conferred upon Cross the highest honors possible to a radio announcer. His resonance, indeed, almost as much as the words used, created a picture in the listener's mind. Moreover, his voice often brought instant recognition.

Fine music and outstanding artists became associated with this onetime early wireless ballad singer. When broadcasting was in its infancy, Cross went to WJZ Newark in 1922, combining singing with announcing. Especially valued, he was able to bridge mechanical difficulties or non-appearing performers with a song or two.

On NBC staff, later ABC, he had one of the longest tenures of any radio broadcaster. As announcer-commentator, he inaugurated Metropolitan Opera broadcasts in December 1931, and did more than any individual to make the Met a national institution with a listening audience of between 12 and 15 million. Cross was still on the job 43 years later, preparing for the Saturday matinee broadcast when he suffered a fatal heart attack.

213. CRUMIT, Frank (singer, emcee [signature song: "Sweet Lady"]; b. Sept. 26, 1889, Jackson, OH; d. Sept. 7, 1943, New York, NY). *Blackstone Plantation* (1929–34); *Battle of the Sexes* (1938–43); *The Singing Sweethearts* (1943).

For 14 years musical comedy recording stars Crumit and wife Julia Sanderson devoted themselves to radio. Their initial series was the Blackstone cigar show at CBS, followed by a Bond Bread-sponsored show. They were among the first established names to emcee a quiz format. At Frank's death, the duo was appearing on a daily daytime program and a weekly nighttime game.

Crumit studied electrical engineering at the University of Ohio but chose vaudeville as a workplace. He made his radio bow at WJZ in 1925. His stock-in-trade — novelty tunes — was sung in a soft voice accompanied by his ukelele.

214. CUGAT, Xavier (bandleader [King of the Rhumba] [signature song: "My Shawl"]; b. Jan. 1, 1900, Tirona, Spain; d. Oct. 27, 1990, Barcelona, Spain). *Let's Dance* (1934–35); *Camel Caravan* (1941–43).

Born into a family of struggling painters and musicians, he studied the violin in Spain, Germany and America. He became acquainted with Caruso, who engaged him to play his violin between the tenor's concert numbers. Caruso started him drawing, an art that brought him much acclaim as a caricaturist. Then came a job as a cartoonist at the *Los Angeles Times.* But music was his first love, so he gave up art for com-

Milton Cross

posing and leading a small Latin American band. His group plus a handful of dancers demonstrated the tango to audiences at the Cocoanut Grove. As a rhumba band, it moved to New York to open the new Starlight Roof of the Waldorf-Astoria Hotel in 1933, and later broke attendance records during his 13 seasons there. NBC took notice and hired Cugat to appear on a weekly three-hour Saturday night program, *Let's Dance,* which also featured a relatively unknown Benny Goodman and his swing aggregation.

Cugat actually had become one of the first instrumentalists to be heard on radio when he broadcast a recital over WDY at Roselle Park, New Jersey in 1917. But not until 1941 did he rise to the highest big-band ranks. That year ASCAP banned its music from the air after a dispute over fees. Overnight Cugat drew on a pre-existing library of hundreds of non-ASCAP Latin tunes. He was quickly signed to one of the most popular coast-to-coast programs, *Camel Caravan.* It brought him a national following to such a degree that the movies utilized his band and music in a string of first-rate productions, including the Fred Astaire-Rita Hayworth film *You Were Never Lovelier* and Esther Williams extravaganzas *Bathing Beauty* and *Neptune's Daughter.* His band featured such singers as Desi Arnaz, Miguelito Valdes and Lina Romay, and several of his wives, Carmen Castillo, Abbe Lane and Charo.

Cugat once played an eight-week symphonic concert tour of 50 U.S. cities, highlighting his own *Latin Suite* in three movements (Afro-Cuban, bolero and conga) but audiences preferred Cugie on a dance floor. He, too, remarked: "I'd rather play 'Chiquita Banana' and have my swimming pool than play Bach and starve." In 1949 he wrote the autobiographical *Rumba Is My Life,* a gossipy reflection of his showmanship and musical specialties.

215. CULLEN, Bill (host, announcer; b. Feb. 18, 1920, Pittsburgh, PA; d. July 7, 1990, Los Angeles, CA). *Winner Take All* (1946–49); *Walk a Mile* (1953–54); *Roadshow* (1954–55).

Emcee of more game shows than any entertainer in radio and television. By age 60 he looked toward retirement. But as one series would end another idea-proposal-offer inevitably came along to lull him on.

In 1944 he was hired as an announcer by CBS. When the emcee for *Winner Take All* resigned, he was made a temporary host and did so well that he was hired full-time. His off-the-cuff wit established his reputation and led to many programs: *Hit the Jackpot, Give and Take, Arthur Godfrey Show, This Is Nora Drake, Walk a Mile.* Cullen, at first, remained aloof from television because of a decided limp from a childhood bout of polio. But by 1959 his programs, including *The Price Is Right* and *I've Got a Secret,* added up to a total of 25 hours of TV time each week. His activities included a morning wake-up show over WNBC in the mid-50s.

Son of a Pittsburgh Ford dealer, he initially worked without pay at WWSW, a local 250-watt station. An early assignment with producer Walt Framer, circa 1939, focused on man-in-the-street interviews and games. KDKA soon hired him. Aiming for the networks, Cullen was helped by the wartime shortage of young staff announcers. His indispensable talents — an adept sense of format and a keen recall of names and details — made the emcee with big horn-rimmed glasses and elfin grin a sought-after game host and panelist.

216. CURTIN, Joseph (actor; b. July 29, 1910, Cambridge, MA; d. April 5, 1979, Los Angeles, CA). *Second Husband* (1937–46); *Stella Dallas* (1937–38); *Mr. and Mrs. North* (1942–53).

Originator of title-role character Jerry North, a down-to-earth publisher whose hobby was crime, especially murder. The Norths — Pamela and Jerry — were taken from mystery novels by Frances and Richard Lockridge, and as radio sleuths bowed over NBC in 1942. Curtin also carved a solid niche as a daytime serial actor on *Young Widder Brown, Backstage Wife* and other perennials. When soaps neared the end of their run, he joined a family insurance agency in Massachusetts.

A graduate of Yale School of Drama, he played opposite Maude Adams in the early 1930s' *Merchant of Venice* production. A part in *Roses and Drums* in 1934 first placed him at the mike. In person he bore a startling resemblance to Bob Hope.

217. DALEY, Cass (comedienne [catchphrase: "I said it and I'm glad."]; b. July 17, 1915, Philadelphia, PA; d. March 22, 1975, Hollywood, CA). *Maxwell House Coffee Time* (1944–45); *New Fitch Bandwagon* (1945–46); *Cass Daley Show* (1950).

Knockabout comic whose inelegant facial expressions caught the public eye. A club and vaudeville singer, she added raucous sight gags to an act that led centerstage in *The Ziegfeld Follies of 1936* and *Yokel Boy.* No audience could forget her prominent buckteeth and backside. A dozen Paramount Pictures (*Riding High, The Fleet's In*) followed in the 1940s, as did many guest spots on *Kraft Music Hall* and *Bob Burns Show.* An ongoing role as Frank Morgan's niece on *Maxwell House Coffee Time* led to her own series. Its cast included John Brown, Arthur Q. Bryan and Frank Kinsella, who was Daley's husband at the time.

Just as television was taking over living rooms, Daley retired, thus missing out on what might have been a major career in that medium. She re-entered show business in the 1970s to good notices. But before her comeback gained momentum, she died in a freak accident. Alone at her apartment, she fell, hit her head on a table, and imbedded a shard of glass in her neck.

218. DALY, John Charles (newscaster, emcee [catchphrase: "Sign in, please."]; b. Feb. 20, 1914, Jo-

What's My Line? contestant Shirley Morabito with Keenan Wynn, Arlene Francis, Bennett Cerf, John Charles Daly

hannesburg, South Africa; d. Feb. 25, 1991, Chevy Chase, MD). *What's My Line?* (1952–53).

Host of the enduring TV game show with such popularity that it was broadcast over radio at one point in the 1950s — a very unusual step when most series were moving from radio to video. Daly's father was an American-born geologist in South Africa. When he died there, his mother took him to Boston where he completed his education. He became a reporter for NBC, then CBS. After serving as White House correspondent, he traveled the globe for CBS. His statesman-like demeanor on the *Line* panel game led to a vice presidency at ABC in charge of news, special events, public affairs, religious programs and sports. In 1954 Daly received a Peabody Award for Radio-Television News coverage. In the late 1960s he served one year as director of the Voice of America.

219. DALY, William (conductor; b. Sept. 1, 1887, Cincinnati, OH; d. Dec. 4, 1936, New York, NY). *Raleigh Review* (1930); *Voice of Firestone* (1931–36).

Generally unknown by the public at large, Daly enjoyed a close association with George Gershwin. He conducted four of the composer's Broadway productions from 1924 to 1928, apparently orchestrated his concert works, and occasionally performed with him. The Harvard-trained musician once pursued a literary career, but Paderewski advised him to conduct. He directed both popular and classical programs at NBC, including the coveted Firestone series for five years.

Shortly before his death in 1936, New York *Post* critic Aaron Stein wrote of Daly: "He is one of radio's brighter and more versatile musicians, and he brings intelligence and careful attention to all his assignments."

220. DAME, Donald (singer; b. June 1, 1917, Titusville, PA; d. Jan. 21, 1952, Lincoln, NE). *Mu-

sic for an Hour* (1943–44); *American Album of Familiar Music* (1946–49).

A young tenor on the Met roster, he replaced Frank Parker as the star of *American Album*. His pleasing voice with its clear diction was well suited to the traditional love songs and ballads featured on this Sunday night staple. As a teenager, he had approached station WHK Cleveland for a singing job. Later, while attending Western Reserve University on a musical scholarship, he sang on several ongoing programs in that city. He also organized a male chorus for radio concerts. Dame studied in Juilliard's opera school, and soon joined the chorus of NBC's *Salute to Youth* in 1943, and occasionally was a featured soloist. That same year he made both his Town Hall and Met debut.

In the fall of 1951 he joined the Met's *Fledermaus* cast for an extensive tour in the role of Dr. Eisenstein. Ten days before the last performance of the production, the 34-year-old singer, who had long suffered from high blood pressure, was found dead of a heart attack in his hotel room. His last broadcast, with the NBC Symphony as Pedrillo in *The Abduction from the Seraglio,* took place on September 15, 1951.

221. DAMERAL, Myrtle Vail (actress [signature song: "Poor Butterfly"]; b. Jan. 7, 1888, Joliet, IL;

Myrtle Vail Dameral (courtesy of Steve Jelf)

d. Sept. 18, 1978, Kansas City, MO). *The Story of Myrt and Marge* (1931–42, 1946).

Dameral devised her popular serial when vaudeville work declined. The story about the backstage adventures of two sisters attracted CBS in Chicago. She played Myrt, a good-natured woman looking out for younger sister Marge, who was played by her actress-daughter Donna Dameral. The program ran opposite *Amos 'n' Andy* at 7 p.m. until 1937, then moved to daytime.

Donna died after the birth of a third child in 1941. The show continued out the season with Helen Mack as Marge, then signed off. But in 1946 Myrtle revamped it for a syndicated version with a new cast. Its run lasted less than a year.

222. DAMON, Les (actor; b. March 31, 1908, Providence, RI; d. July 20, 1962, Hollywood, CA). *The Adventures of the Thin Man* (1941–44, 1946–47); *The Adventures of Christopher Wells* (1947–48).

Radio's Thin Man — private eye Nick Charles — at its premiere over NBC. A soap opera actor in Chicago in the late '30s, he once ridiculed these daytime cliffhangers which provided his bread and butter. Having spent part of his youth as an Old Vic Theatre player, he felt degraded by work in *Lone Journey* and *Girl Alone,* and so took to drink. Damon was, by his own admission, on his way to becoming a full-fledged bum — until he swallowed some of his youthful ideals and learned respect and pride in his craft.

In New York by 1940 he landed the part of Bill Baker in *Portia Faces Life* and the coveted *Thin Man* lead. U.S. Army duty — with the AFRS in the China-Burma-India war zone — took him away for two years. He returned as the *Thin Man* and picked up the lead in the detective mystery, *The Falcon.* Stage roles for this Brown University and Rhode Island School of Design alumnus included Babyface Martin in *Dead End* and Curley in *Of Mice and Men.* He was an original cast member of the TV serial *As the World Turns.*

223. DAMONE, Vic (singer; b. June 12, 1928, Brooklyn, NY). *Saturday Night Serenade* (1947–49).

Vocally adept romantic baritone. Teenage Damone ushered at the Paramount Theatre when Sinatra and Como were making their first big impact. From observing them, he learned how to put across a ballad and pace a show. At 17 the inexperienced choir singer won on Arthur Godfrey's *Talent Scouts* by singing "Prisoner of Love." That led to a Mercury Record hit, "I Have But One Heart" and CBS's *Saturday Night Serenade.*

As an Army PFC, he sang ballads and spoke recruiting messages for the 1952 summer series *Stars in Khaki 'n' Blue.*

224. DAMROSCH, Walter (conductor, commentator [catchphrase: "Good morning, my dear children."]; b. Jan. 30, 1862, Breslau, Germany; d. Dec. 23, 1950, New York, NY). *Baulkite Hour* (1926–27); *Music Appreciation Hour* (1928–42).

NBC's very first broadcast (November 15, 1926) featured Damrosch and the New York Symphony Orchestra. Earlier that year over WEAF he had conducted his first radio concert — interspersing genial remarks about the music between the numbers. From 1927 to 1931, he directed several series over NBC for RCA and General Electric. Then after 42 years as a full-time conductor, he retired to spread good music by radio. "It is possible for me to make this the most music-loving country in the world," he said as he turned to educate millions — especially young people — in the understanding and appreciation of fine music.

His father, Leopold Damrosch, had come to New York in the 1870s to conduct a German choral society and to popularize the music of his friends, Liszt and Wagner, and to conduct German opera. Young Walter filled his father's place at the Met when he died suddenly in 1885. In 1903 he was appointed conductor of the New York Symphony for which he later established children's concerts.

Dr. Damrosch attained national renown and deepest personal satisfaction in a pioneering series of Friday morning broadcasts over NBC where he served as music counsel. With an estimated audience of five million, many of whom sat before school auditorium loudspeakers, "Papa" Damrosch in a rolling, Teutonic voice explained some passage or refrain from the classical repertoire. The perfect conception of an old-time German professor, Damrosch was tall and stocky with white hair thick about the eyes and bushy brows crowning his sharp, gray-blue eyes. He sounded strong but kind. During the first year of the program NBC decided to make a test of listener reaction, and as a proving ground, network president Merlin H. Aylesworth chose Iowa, because he was born there. The results — 400,000 letters — astounded him.

It was said that American school children knew the voice of Dr. Damrosch better than that of anyone in the United States.

Active into old age, he wrote the opera *The Man Without a Country* in 1937. The Met produced it, casting an unknown soprano named Helen Traubel in a debut role that launched her operatic career. Damrosch Park at Lincoln Center was named in honor of this influential conductor-instructor and other members of his musical family.

225. DARBY, Ken (singer, choral conductor; b. May 13, 1909, Hebron, NE; d. Jan. 24, 1992, Sherman Oaks, CA). *Kraft Music Hall* (1934–35); *Fibber McGee and Molly* (1940–55); *Westinghouse Program* (1943–46).

He led, and arranged for, The King's Men, successors to The Revelers in the top ranks of male quartets from the mid-30s to 1950s. They were tenors Bud Linn and John Dodson, baritone Rad Robinson, and

The King's Men: Bud Linn, Jon Dodson, Rad Robinson, Ken Darby

phony, Robert Weede, Dorothy Sarnoff and Daum. But her Met career lasted only one season.

In the 1920s she pursued musical studies at the Ithaca Conservatory and later after it became part of Ithaca College served as a trustee. Daum retired to Florida in the mid-50s where she managed a hospital gift shop and judged garden club flower shows.

227. DAVIES, Gwen (actress; b. June 19, 1922, New York, NY). *The Adventures of Helen and Mary* (1929–34); *Let's Pretend* (1934–54); *The Class of '41* (1941).

Versatile child actress and occasional singer. As Estelle Levy (until age 19), she played Mary in *The Adventures of Helen and Mary,* the children's program that evolved into Nila Mack's *Let's Pretend* in 1934. Her roles ranged from sprightly elves and fairies to aged ladies and crones. She sang the opening theme song during its long run for Cream of Wheat cereal. Levy had running parts on *Mrs. Wiggs of the Cabbage Patch* and *Hilltop House.* In the opera *Second Hurricane,* written by Aaron Copland in 1937, Orson Welles directed her in the role of Gwen.

Darby, a bass. They began on KFWB Hollywood as staff singers for station manager Jerry King — hence the origin of their name. The foursome were brought to New York by Paul Whiteman for his *Kraft Music Hall* and paid $100 a week each. NBC contributed to their build-up with four spots a week on a sustaining basis.

An on-going attraction on *Fibber McGee and Molly,* they were a summer replacement in 1949. Darby, also a composer, did musical arrangements that included McGee's annual "Night Before Christmas" presentation. From time to time he directed the 60-voice Ken Darby singers and the Westinghouse Chorus. He won three Oscars for scoring of a musical picture (*The King and I, Porgy and Bess, Camelot*) and wrote the Elvis Presley film title song "Love Me Tender."

226. DAUM, Margaret (singer; b. March 25, 1906, Pittsburgh, PA; d. Feb. 23, 1977, Clearwater, FL). *Musical Comedy Revue* (1940); *American Album of Familiar Music* (1943–51).

Soprano soloist on many concert programs conducted by Gus Haenschen who teamed her on duets with tenors Frank Munn and Donald Dame on *American Album.* With Haenschen and baritone Thomas L. Thomas, she commuted for nearly six years in the 1940s from New York to Detroit for the weekly (and costly) All-String Orchestra semi-operatic series sponsored by Stroh Brewery from WJR. Daum competed twice in the *Met Opera Auditions of the Air,* in 1936 and 1939. Her efforts led to a Met debut as Musetta in *La Boheme,* just weeks after she had created the title role in Menotti's *Amelia Goes to the Ball,* first performed in a New York theatre. Its success led to a radio opera by Menotti commissioned by NBC. A satirical farce in English, *The Old Maid and the Thief* aired in 1939 with Alberto Erede and the NBC Sym-

Margaret Daum

She appeared as Little Cosette in Welles's serial *Les Miserables.*

When her brief career as a CBS staff and band vocalist started, Estelle took the name of Gwen and changed Levy to Davies. In the 1950s she continued with cartoon voices ("Casper the Friendly Ghost") and singing commercials ("Sound Off" for Chesterfield). Gwen played the lead in the first original TV musical—DuMont network's "The Boys from Boise."

228. DAVIS, Elmer (newscaster; b. Jan. 13, 1890, Aurora, IN; d. May 18, 1958, Washington, DC). *Elmer Davis and the News* (1939–42, 1945–53).

Within two years of his first broadcast, David had an audience of more than 12 million listeners for his CBS daily five-minute distillation of war news and evening broadcasts. He brought an incisive, analytical mind to the air. He said he never overcame his fright of the microphone, yet the dry, calm voice was seldom ruffled. He had been asked to broadcast the news as a fill-in for H. V. Kaltenborn in the summer of 1939, less than ten days before Germany invaded Poland. The following year he won the first of three Peabody Awards for reporting and interpretation of the news.

Foreign correspondent and editorial writer for the *New York Times* from 1914 to 1924, then a freelance journalist and novelist, Davis quit his $53,000 a year job with CBS to accept the post as director of the Office of War Information. He coordinated all Government news and propaganda and supervised 3,000 employees. President Truman called his work an outstanding contribution to victory. Davis returned to radio with nightly broadcasts for ABC.

As a Rhodes Scholar at Oxford in 1910, he began cultivating an interest in foreign affairs and politics, and spent his summers traveling abroad. Described as a "horse-sense liberal," he came across as a rational, straight-from-the-shoulder speaker especially during times of great calamities and national disasters.

229. DAVIS, Joan (comedienne; b. June 29, 1907, St. Paul, MN; d. May 23, 1961, Palm Springs, CA). *Sealtest Village Store* (1943–45); *Joan Davis Show* (1945–48).

Beginning in 1934 for seven years, Davis played comic supporting roles in films, mostly second features. Then, in 1941 she made an appearance on Rudy Vallee's Sealtest show. Her raucous voice and swooping delivery, marked her as a promising star for a series. When Vallee joined the Coast Guard in 1943, she took over his program. That year she was voted top comedienne in a Scripps-Howard newspaper poll. Davis was also called the world's funniest woman by some aficionados of broad slapstick humor.

In 1945 at CBS she began the *Joan Davis Show* with singer Andy Russell, comic-announcer Harry Von Zell and conductor Paul Weston's orchestra. Davis also made guest appearances with Bob Hope, Dean Martin & Jerry Lewis and Tallulah Bankhead, then moved

Joan Davis

into television. She formed her own production company for her series *I Married Joan.*

A vaudeville performer from six until high school age, she toured as "The Toy Comedienne." Later, in 1931, she teamed up with actor Si Wills, whom she married that year. Before heading for Hollywood, they barnstormed as Wills & Davis, and played the Palace.

230. DAY, Dennis (singer [catchphrase: "Gee, Mr. Benny."]; b. May 21, 1917, Bronx, NY; d. June 22, 1988, Brentwood, CA). *Ray Bloch's Varieties* (1938–39); *Jack Benny Program* (1939–54); *A Day in the Life of Dennis Day* (1946–51).

A sweet Irish tenor and a breathlessly funny comic, Dennis Day spent a quarter century as Jack Benny's adolescent sidekick. A choirboy in The Bronx and later a member of the choir at St. Patrick's Cathedral, Day, whose name originally was Owen Patrick McNulty, entertained family and friends by singing popular songs, playing the accordion and dancing. He graduated from Manhattan College and was headed for Fordham Law School. Meanwhile he got a part-time job at WNYC, the municipal station. It took him to the networks where with Ray Bloch at CBS he earned $21 a show.

When he learned Jack Benny needed a singer to replace Kenny Baker, he sent a recording of his singing to Mary Livingstone, the comedian's wife and a cast member. Day was invited to an audition, where Benny called out, "Oh, Dennis." Day bounded up, saying, "Yes, please." Benny cracked up and announced, "That's it . . . a character who would be deferential and perhaps show up with his mother."

He won a two-week tryout, appearing first on October 8, 1939 to sing "I'm Afraid the Masquerade is Over." It certainly wasn't; he remained until Benny's TV show ended in the mid-60s. His renditions of "Danny Boy," "McNamara's Band" and "Peg o' My Heart" endeared him to listeners who also tuned into his own series in the 1940s. He raised ten children and, in spite of his fame and fortune, his Bel Air home was one of the few in the area without a swimming pool.

231. DAY, Doris (singer [signature song: "Que Sera, Sera"]; b. April 3, 1924, Cincinnati, OH). *Fitch Bandwagon* (1944); *Your Hit Parade* (1947); *Bob Hope Show* (1948–50).

When an auto crash shattered her right leg, she gave up all hope for a dancing career and turned to singing. A local WLW amateur program, *Carlin's Carnival* featured her rendition of "Day After Day" which was heard by bandleader Barney Rapp. He hired her for his new club near Cincinnati at $25 a week. When that folded, 17-year-old Day joined Bob Crosby, then Les Brown. Her mesmerizing vocal on Brown's 1945 waxing of "Sentimental Journey" proved a breakthrough into the star ranks. For 20 years, from 1948 to 1968, the gold-blonde, all-American singer continued to introduce major song hits.

Co-starred with Frank Sinatra on the *Hit Parade*, she teamed up with many baritones for recordings and pictures. Her sense of comedy and timing made her an even bigger box office draw in non-musicals. The book *Doris Day: Her Own Story* revealed her tragic

Doris Day

family life, several bad marriages and financial reversals, well-hidden behind a well-scrubbed, freckled face and sunny, care-free disposition.

232. DEANE, Martha (commentator [The First Lady of Radio]; b. Nov. 21, 1908, Star Lake, NY; d. Dec. 9, 1973, New York, NY). *Martha Deane Show* (1941–73).

In 1941 the role of "Martha Deane," a WOR commentator, became vacant when Bessie Beatty left. (She had replaced the original "Deane," Mary Margaret McBride.) Newspaper editor and foreign correspondent Marian Young moved into the job, and shortly, thereafter left journalism to concentrate on radio. Deane presided before a microphone five mornings a week for 32 years. Some 10,000 guests, many among the most famous people in the world, sat across from her. Listeners seldom knew in advance who the guest would be. Usually it was somebody in the news: a prime minister, a president, an actor, a musician, a poet.

Not unlike a schoolmarm with charm and brains, she was considered the most acute interviewer on radio. With a few pertinent questions she could get her guests talking volubly. Her secret was preparation: "I do my homework. I never have movie stars unless I've seen their movies; actors whose plays I have not seen; authors whose books I have not read. And I don't do froth." Her guests discussed pressing issues in life, politics and culture. And Deane never went out of her way to cater to the supposed "women's angle." In 1942 radio editors of the U.S. and Canada voted her as originator of the "best women's program" and five times Ohio State Institute for Education by Radio cited her as "the best woman commentator."

233. DECAMP, Rosemary (actress; b. Nov. 14, 1910, Prescott, AZ). *Dr. Christian* (1939–53).

Dr. Christian's nurse-secretary, Judy Price, was well cast when DeCamp won the role opposite the kindly and generous physician, played by Jean Hersholt. She reputedly auditioned for three days and outstayed all comers. Earlier, she had flunked her first screen test, which, oddly enough, was for the same Nurse Price in a film based on the series.

Her initial radio job, on *One Man's Family* in 1933, proved brief. She was fired because she could not resist telling the director how to run the program. She joined a touring company, then played on Broadway and at the Pasadena Playhouse. Next came radio (*Easy Aces*) and films (*Cheers for Miss Bishop*). She specialized in mother roles to such diverse screen children as James Cagney, Sabu, Ronald Reagan, Doris Day and Robert Alda. At the mike, she handled character parts on *Columbia Workshop, Gangbusters* and *The Goldbergs*. Her significant television parts were Bill Bendix's wife (*Life of Riley*) and Marlo Thomas's mother (*That Girl*).

Rosemary DeCamp, Jean Hersholt (courtesy of Rosemary De-Camp)

DeCamp majored in drama and psychology at Mills College which also gave her a master's degree.

234. DECORSIA, Ted (actor; b. Sept. 29, 1903, Brooklyn, NY; d. April 11, 1973, Encino, CA). *March of Time* (1937–38); *Joe and Mabel* (1941–42); *Ellery Queen* (1942–44).

Perennial player of villains, thugs, crooks and bad guys. He first made an impression in portrayals of Mussolini on *March of Time*. In the early 1940s DeCorsia was a regular on *Manhattan at Midnight* and *Grand Central Station*. He turned detective for *Ellery Queen*. For *Pursuit* he played Scotland Yard Inspector Peter Black during the 1949–50 season. On television he starred as daredevil sleuth Mike Hammer in *Mickey Spillane Mysteries* and Police Chief Hagedon in *Steve Canyon*.

235. DEKOVEN, Roger (actor; b. Oct. 22, 1907, Chicago, IL; d. Jan. 28, 1988, New York, NY). *Against the Storm* (1939–42); *Stella Dallas* (1943–46).

Beginning in radio in 1935, DeKoven was best known as the outspoken, antiwar Professor Allen on *Against the Storm,* the only daytime serial to win a Peabody Award. It adopted a strong anti-Hitler stand at its inception in 1939 — considered courageous at a time of U.S. neutrality. In December 1941 President Roosevelt had agreed to speak on the program but had to cancel because of the Japanese attack on Pearl Harbor. DeKoven also played in *Gangbusters* and *Brave Tomorrow,* and narrated *Famous Jury Trials*. Beginning

in 1944, he made many appearances on *The Eternal Light*.

A graduate of the University of Chicago and Theatre Guild School, he appeared in such Broadway productions as *Once in a Lifetime, The Lark* and *Funny Girl.* In the early 1950s the tall, dark-haired actor was blacklisted as a Communist sympathizer in the witch-hunting newsletter "Red Channels" after reading a poem at a peace conference. His career halted until he signed a statement denying any communist ties. Television work came later, with *Edge of Night, Ben Casey* and *Ironsides.*

236. DELEATH, Vaughn (singer [The Original Radio Girl]; b. Sept. 26, 1896, Mt. Pulaski, IL; d. May 28, 1943, Buffalo, NY). *Voice of Firestone* (1928–30).

Believed to be the first woman to speak into a microphone (December 1919), she climbed three flights of stairs to a small, stuffy wireless room at the top of the old World Building in New York to talk a bit and sing "Swanee River" *a capella* for an audience of no more than two or three dozen listeners. The engineer that day: Lee De Forest.

Her next foray on the air was at WDY Roselle Park, New Jersey, then at WJZ Newark where she learned the technique of broadcasting. She ventured briefly into directing programs and managing a station (WDT New York), along with announcing.

But as a singer with a warm, throaty voice, she is best remembered from many early programs. Apparently she adopted a crooning technique in order to avoid breaking expensive radio tubes with her unusually high soprano register. Composer of "It's a Lonely Trail," "At Eventide" and many other songs, she ended her broadcast days with a series of programs at WKY Oklahoma City, WICC Bridgeport (CT) and WBEN Buffalo.

237. DELLA CHIESA, Vivian (singer [America's Great Lyric Soprano]; b. Oct. 9, 1915, Chicago, IL). *Contented Hour* (1937); *American Album of Familiar Music* (1940–43); *American Melody Hour* (1941–42).

She first performed over the air at age 19 in Chicago as part of a WBBM "unknown singer" competition. Winning over several thousand aspirants — judges were James Petrillo and John Boles — she made her debut with the Chicago Civic Opera as Mimi in *Boheme* in 1936, and became a regular on *Musical Footnotes, Saturday Night Party* and *Contented Hour.* A quick-study, confident performer, she learned *The Magic Flute* in four days for Alfred Wallenstein's Mozart opera series, a weekly one-hour program over Mutual in 1940. With a repertoire of arias and pop tunes, the high-spirited strawberry-blond soprano attracted the attention of producer Frank Hummert. Signed to his *American Album of Familiar Music,* she was praised and admired for her solos ("Habinera"

Vivian Della Chiesa

from *Carmen*) and duets with Frank Munn ("Our Love"). Guest with Toscanini and the NBC Symphony for Brahms's *Requiem* (January 1943) and on the world premiere of Montemezzi's opera *L'Incantesimo* (October 1943), Della Chiesa was also a frequent singer on Cities Service *Highways in Melody.*

She quit radio on a regular basis to do concerts, and especially to break away from the ongoing cycle of religious and spiritual songs she was required to sing during wartime. "I wanted to reach more people with personal appearances. Ironically, I would have been heard by more people if I had stayed on the air. And, in the long run, probably performed more serious music." In the 1960s she became the singing hostess of *Vivienne,* a five-day-a-week TV talk show out of Cincinnati.

By 1970 Della Chiesa had established herself as a vocal teacher on Long Island. Her philosophy, she states, is to make singing seem "so natural, so spontaneous, so real, that the listener is quite unconscious of the fact that tone production is the result of hard work."

238. DELMAR, Kenny (actor, announcer [catchphrase: "That's a joke, son."]; b. Sept. 5, 1910, Boston, MA; d. July 14, 1984, Stamford, CT). *Mercury Theatre on the Air* (1938); *Cavalcade of America* (1940–41); *Fred Allen Show* (1945–49).

A character in Allen's Alley, Delmar played the blustery Southern Senator Beauregard Claghorn. This bombastic, chauvinistic character, who drank only from Dixie Cups and refused to drive through the Lincoln Tunnel, was mimicked by children and adults alike. He was also Fred Allen's announcer. As a youngster he had toured the country with his mother and aunt's vaudeville act. By the late 1930s, Delmar combined acting with announcing. He portrayed Commissioner Weston on *The Shadow* and played three roles on the classic Orson Welles Halloween eve broadcast "War of the Worlds." He appeared with Henry Morgan in various parts, delivered commercials for *Your Hit Parade,* and emceed *The RCA Victor Show* in the 1945–46 season.

239. DE MARCO SISTERS (Ann, Gene, Gloria, Marie, Arlene) (singers). *Your Hit Parade* (1937); *Fred Allen Show* (1945–49).

Close harmony sister act. Born in Rome, New York between 1925 and 1933, these five daughters of an Italian-born jeweler auditioned for Al Goodman, Fred Allen's conductor, and won a contract for $750 a week in 1945. The sisters, who had a flair for comedy, remained with Allen's show until he left radio four years later.

Originally a trio, the De Marcos came to New York for jobs in 1937, first appearing on the air with Mary Small and Her Juveniles on *Show Boat.* One-night stands paid the rent on a Brooklyn apartment. Eventually they landed guest spots with Kate Smith, Paul Whiteman, Joe Cook, Perry Como, and by the 1950s, Eddie Fisher, plus TV with Ed Sullivan. A major theatre and hotel act, they broke up in 1957 while in Las Vegas. The sisters briefly re-united in 1980 for a New York engagement, but never regained the acclaim that radio had brought the quintet.

240. DEMILLE, Cecil B. (host [catchphrase: "Greetings from Hollywood, ladies and gentlemen."]; b. Aug. 21, 1881, Ashfield, MA; d. Jan. 21, 1959, Hollywood, CA). *Lux Radio Theatre* (1936–45).

An authoritative, ingratiating voice that each Monday evening invited listeners to enjoy an hour of film stars recreating roles in adaptations of memorable motion pictures. A pioneer movie producer-director, DeMille was a showman without equal in Hollywood. Beginning in 1913, the onetime actor produced more than 70 major films, including *The Squaw Man, The Ten Commandments, Cleopatra, Union Pacific* and the Oscar-winning *Greatest Show on Earth.* All were costly — many on an epic scale.

His radio association with Lux Soap commanded a reputed $2,000 a week. But it paid off in sales and ratings. The program had originated in New York for two seasons with stage performers. In 1936 it relocated to the West Coast where movie stars could readily go from sound stage to radio studio. With DeMille as the centerpiece, the series extolled Hollywood.

Censorship over radio, DeMille discovered, was greater than in films. After featuring an unwed mother in *The Old Maid,* DeMille was told by CBS censors he couldn't do it again. By chance, the following week aired *Only Yesterday,* a film plot with a similar situation. DeMille was forced to change the script, confusing many listeners who had seen and remembered the original script.

A member of AFRA, DeMille refused to pay a $1 assessment to that union's political fund. He made a colossal issue of the levy by this performers' group, and carried it to the courts in 1944. He was defeated. As a result, he lost his commanding role as an emcee. He was replaced by another statesman-like voice — that of stage and film director William Keighley's.

241. DENNIS, Clark (singer; b. Dec. 19, 1911, Roscommon, MI). *Breakfast Club* (1936–37); *Fibber McGee and Molly* (1938); *Chesterfield Presents* (1939); *Name The Movie* (1949).

Swing era vocalist with major assignments on various types of programs into the 1950s. "He has one of those voices that runs off the top end of the keyboard," *Variety* wrote in 1939, "and he knows how to sell it." Paul Whiteman featured Dennis with Joan Edwards along with the orchestra's Bouncing Brass, Swinging Strings and Saxophone Socktette on the Chesterfield show. Jane Vance, a former Whiteman vocalist whom Clark married in 1938, had sent the bandleader an unlabeled recording of Clark's radio singing. Whiteman telegraphed an offer. In 1939 he traveled with Whiteman on a 27-week concert tour with many dates on college campuses.

When Whiteman broke up his orchestra, Dennis, a tenor, sang on *The Song of Your Life* with Harry Salter, and on NBC sustainers. He joined the Army in 1943 and returned to radio three years later as a guest for Alec Templeton and Bob Hope. ABC utilized him as host-singer on the musical quiz *Name The Movie.* The show welcomed film stars who phoned VA hospitals and asked convalescing ex-GIs to identify a particular film. Dennis starred in "Brigadoon" on *The Railroad Hour* and in the 1950s was a featured vocalist on *Bob Smith Show* and *Dial Dave Garroway.*

He broke into radio in 1930 in Flint where he attended college. He sang on WJR and KHJ before joining Ben Pollack's orchestra in Chicago in 1935. Appearances on *Climalene Carnival* led to *Fibber McGee* as Perry Como's replacement. He introduced the Tin-Pan-Alley classic "Tenderly" on the Capitol label in 1946.

242. DENNY, George V., Jr. (moderator [catchphrase: "Good evening, neighbors."]; b. Aug. 29, 1899, Washington, NC; d. Nov. 11, 1959, Sherman, CT). *America's Town Meeting of the Air* (1935–52).

At its peak, Denny's *Town Meeting* aired over 170 stations to some ten million listeners. The hour-long spontaneous debate presented two or more speakers

George V. Denny (courtesy of Capital Cities/ABC)

on different sides of a controversial issue. Denny pioneered in audience participation by calling for unscreened questions from the 1,000 or more persons present at Town Hall in New York where most broadcasts originated, beginning in 1935. He got the idea for the no-holds barred series from a narrow-minded neighbor's remark that he never listened to Roosevelt because he disagreed with the President.

The first broadcast, heard on 18 stations of the Blue network, raised the question: "Which Way America? Fascism, Communism, Socialism or Democracy?" Speakers were Lawrence Dennis, A. J. Muste, Norman Thomas and Raymond Morley. The fast-paced program provided a platform to show the debating skills of leaders in many areas, especially politics. Telecasts were added in 1948 and 1952. By then, the proceedings began to lose steam and Denny was forced out in an internal dispute, but the series continued until 1956.

Denny's background included drama instructor, lecture bureau manager and political education league director. In the late '50s he was head of International Seminars, Inc., which planned overseas town meetings in a similar vein.

243. DE ROSE, Peter (pianist, singer; b. March 10, 1900, New York, NY*; d. April 23, 1953, New York, NY). *Sweethearts of the Air* (1923–29).

Teamed with May Singhi Breen, singer and ukelele player in 1923. "Sweethearts of the Air," they were married in 1929 by a retired minister who initially

*Another source gives 1896.

wrote them of his pleasure over hearing May's own arrangement of "The Rosary" as a ukelele and piano duet. He said that he hadn't thought it possible to play a piece of that type on "that little music box." Their harmony vocals proved a staple on radio, and particularly affordable for small regional sponsors along the lines of Father John's Medicine for head and throat colds.

De Rose gained noteworthy acclaim as a composer. His output included "Deep Purple," "Memphis Blues," "Have You Ever Been Lonely" and "Wagon Wheels." His introduction to the business was as a stock clerk for a publishing firm.

244. DESANTIS, Joseph (actor; b. June 15, 1909, New York, NY; d. Aug. 30, 1989, Provo, UT). *This Is Nora Drake* (1947–48); *Dimension X* (1950–51); *X-Minus One* (1955–58).

Cast member of hundreds of programs but few running parts. DeSantis played many dialect parts: a Lithuanian on *Eternal Light*, a French diplomat on *Around the Town*, a Danish writer on *Home Is What You Make It*, a Spaniard on *Your United Nations*. During the 1950s he was featured on the science fiction series, *Dimension X* and its successor *X-Minus One*.

His first professional broadcast was in Italian language radio in 1931, two years after his stage debut at Columbia University. DeSantis' legit theatre credits included *Othello* and *Cyrano de Bergerac*. In 1949 he joined *Photocrime*, an early TV mystery. It led to guest roles on *The Untouchables* and *Bonanza*. DeSantis studied sculpture and exhibited his work in galleries, and taught acting.

245. DESMOND, Johnny (singer; b. Nov. 14, 1920, Detroit, MI; d. Sept. 6, 1985, Los Angeles, CA). *I Sustain the Wings* (1943–45); *Philip Morris Frolics* (1946); *Breakfast Club* (1947–51); *Songs for Sale* (1951–52).

Son of a Detroit grocer, Desmond broke into local radio at eleven (*Uncle Nick's Children's Hour*) and into the band vocalist ranks as a teenager with Bob Crosby's Bob-O-Links and Gene Krupa. When he went into the Army, Desmond wrote Glenn Miller to ask for a chance to audition as a replacement for Tony Martin in the Miller Air Force Band. Known as "The G.I. Sinatra" during his stint with Miller over the Armed Forces Radio Network, he sang popular tunes in French, German and Italian so that the European populace would tune in.

Immediately after the war, he came into his own, working with conductor Jerry Gray and hosting *Teentimers Club*. Nightclubs, recordings, Broadway musicals and TV's *Hit Parade* followed for this smooth-styled, goodlooking baritone who was once tagged by *Time* as "The Creamer" when that magazine was searching for a title to equate with Crosby's "The Groaner" and Sinatra's "The Swooner." He ended his radio days as a frequent guest on *NBC Bandstand* in 1956–57.

246. DEUTSCH, Emery (conductor [signature song: "When a Gypsy Makes His Violin Cry"]; b. Sept. 10, 1904, Budapest, Hungary).

A relatively anonymous musical director for CBS in the 1930s who reputedly arranged for 30 programs a week, such as *Arabesque* and *Let's Pretend*. His native Hungarian background influenced his playing as a violinist, and he spent some time as a member of the A&P Gypsies at NBC. In 1940 he switched to jazz but won no converts. He returned to Gypsy pop music with remotes from such romantic settings as the Rainbow Room. As a composer, he wrote his theme song and collaborated on "Play, Fiddle, Play."

247. DEVOL, Frank (conductor; b. Sept. 20, 1911, Moundsville, WV). *Rudy Vallee Drene Show* (1944–45); *Sealtest Village Store* (1947–48); *Dinah Shore Show* (1953–55).

Musical director-arranger with a flair for comedy. He started playing with bands at 14, following the lead of his father, conductor at the Canton, Ohio, Grand Opera House. A professional musician and teacher after studies at Miami University in Ohio, he joined the staff of WTAM. DeVol was alto sax player-arranger for the orchestras of George Olsen, Horace Heidt and Alvino Rey in the 1930s. As part of Don Lee operations, he presented *Adventures in Rhythm* and *California Melodies*.

Rudy Vallee sought him out as conductor in 1944. That led to several seasons with Jack Carson, Ginny Simms and Dinah Shore. An executive with Columbia Records, he also provided scores for *Pillow Talk*, *Cat Ballou*, *My Three Sons* and other films and TV series. His comic side surfaced with parts on many broadcasts, particularly TV's *I'm Dickens—He's Fenster* and *The Betty White Show*.

248. DICKENSON, Jean (singer [Nightingale of the Airwaves]; b. Dec. 10, 1914, Montreal, Canada). *Hollywood Hotel* (1936); *American Album of Familiar Music* (1937–51).

A coloratura soprano with a clear, bell-like tone that was compared to the voice of Lily Pons who, in the words of Dickenson, "proteged me." Daughter of an American mining engineer, she lived in India and California before studying music in Denver. There, she sang over KDA on *Golden Melodies* and performed Gilda in *Rigoletto* with the San Carlo Opera Company. CBS brought her to *Hollywood Hotel* for vocals with Dick Powell, but it was NBC that launched her as its prima donna on *American Album*.

The slim, dark-haired singer held a prominent niche as a high-note operatic contrast to the mainstream ballads and traditional melodies regularly featured on that long-running Sunday night program.

Jean Dickenson (courtesy of Jean Dickenson)

Marlene Dietrich (courtesy of Capital Cities/ABC)

Although she made concert appearances and sang Philine in a 1940 Met production of *Mignon,* Dickenson never recorded and rarely ventured into the radio guest spotlight. When *American Album* ended in 1951 so did her noteworthy career.

249. DICKSON, Donald (singer; b. Nov. 6, 1910, Clairton, PA; d. Sept. 21, 1972, Brooklyn, NY). *Sealtest Party* (1937); *Chase & Sanborn Hour* (1939–41); *Blue Ribbon Town* (1943–44).

Met Opera baritone who enjoyed brief popularity with mainstream radio audiences. Dickson was featured as Bergen and McCarthy's vocalist, following in the footsteps of Nelson Eddy and John Carter. A Juilliard graduate, he made his Met bow in *Faust* during the 1936–37 season and his Town Hall debut in 1941.

Dickson appeared with symphony orchestras and opera companies and recorded for Victor. He was heard on the only Met broadcast of Walter Damrosch's *The Man Without a Country* in May 1937.

250. DIETRICH, Marlene (actress [signature song: "Falling in Love Again"]; b. Dec. 27, 1901, Berlin, Germany; d. May 6, 1992, Paris, France). *Café Istanbul* (1952–53).

Exotically romantic screen idol. Her seductive portrayals of cabaret entertainers (*Blue Angel, Morocco, A Foreign Affair*) were delicious images of wanton, high-

spirited femme fatales. One of the few Hollywood icons who relished radio work, Dietrich regularly stood beside the microphone of Abbott and Costello, Rudy Vallee, Eddie Cantor, Jimmy Durante, Tommy Dorsey, Bing Crosby and others. Her appearances for War Bond, Red Cross and Armed Services appeals were frequent and genuinely enthusiastic. According to her biographer Charles Higham, she liked the freedom and imagination inherent in radio and looked upon it as a remarkably high-level medium.

In 1952 she undertook a weekly series for ABC from New York. Called *Cafe Istanbul,* it cast her as a beguiling hostess of a club not unlike Rick's in the film *Casablanca.* Espionage and mystery with a song or two by the sultry Dietrich competed bravely — and rather effectively — against entrenched Sunday night TV offerings. Buick Motors provided the sponsorship. In 1953 the program, retitled *Time for Love,* moved to CBS.

251. DINNING SISTERS
　　Lou (b. Sept. 29, 1922, Franklin, KY).
　　Ginger (b. March 29, 1924, Braman, OK).
　　Jean (b. March 29, 1924, Braman, OK).
National Barn Dance (1940–46); *Dinning Sisters-Songs* (1942–43); *Spike Jones Spotlight Revue* (1949–50); *Eddy Arnold Show* (1953).

A close-harmony Chicago-based act under contract to NBC in the early 1940s. This attractive trio briefly had their own 15-minute daily show but gained prime-time exposure chiefly on the *National Barn Dance* before retiring in 1953. They waxed some 80 songs for Capitol and appeared in several films. The trio had teamed up in 1929, a half-dozen years before their professional debut at a Wichita Theatre.

252. DOBKIN, Larry (actor; b. Sept. 16, 1919, New York, NY). *The Adventures of Ellery Queen* (1947–48); *The Saint* (1950–51); *The Adventures of Nero Wolfe* (1950–51); *Gunsmoke* (1952–61).

Mainstay of detective shows. He played Ellery Queen in New York, moving with the series when it went West. Dobkin was Archie on *Nero Wolfe,* Dave on *The Man from Homicide* and Louis and other characters on *The Saint.* For the adult Western called *Gunsmoke,* he played mostly heavies for all of its radio life.

While still in high school, he did his first acting for Ted Cott's WNYC production, "The Ebony Elephant." Pre-war radio jobs over the Yankee Network helped pay expenses at Yale School of Drama. When fellow Air Force man Perry Lafferty started to produce and direct Elaine Carrington's *Playhouse* in 1945, Larry was hired. He frequently picked up roles on *NBC Theatre* ("Portrait of a Lady"), *First Nighter* ("A Dollar a Second") and *Lux Radio Theatre* ("Shane") as well as for *Eternal Light, Escape* and *Romance.*

253. DONALD, Peter (actor, emcee; b. June 6, 1918, Bristol, England; d. April 30, 1979, Fort Lauderdale, FL). *Can You Top This?* (1940–51, 1953–54); *Fred Allen Show* (1944–49); *Talk Your Way Out of It* (1949).

Dialectician and storyteller, he read listener-submitted gags on the concentrated joke session, *Can You Top This?* and competed against a panel of wits and a "laugh meter." Working with Fred Allen, he was Ajax Cassidy, an old character "not long for this world." A straight dramatic actor as well, he appeared on Norman Corwin presentations, *March of Time* and *Manhattan at Midnight.* TV viewers of the 1950s knew him as panelist-emcee of *Masquerade Party.*

His Scottish parents, the vaudeville team of Donald & Carson, took him to Broadway in 1928 for Noel Coward's *Bittersweet.* He also started in radio as a child. He portrayed Tiny Tim in *A Christmas Carol,* and by 13 was an emcee of a commercial program. For a drama called "The Man Who Was Tomorrow," he portrayed the lead at the ages of 18, 21, 25, 35, 55, 60 and 75.

254. DONALDSON, Ted (actor; b. Aug. 20, 1933, New York, NY). *Father Knows Best* (1949–54).

At four he first faced a mike as he sat on the lap of The Singing Lady. When Ted Malone asked his *Between the Bookends* organist Muriel Pollock to bring her son to a special Christmas broadcast in 1938, Ted's career was launched. Between then and age seven, he appeared on *March of Time, Life Can Be Beautiful, Aunt Jenny* and *Our Gal Sunday.* In December 1941 Ted played in a five-episode presentation of *A Christmas Carol* with Edmund Gwenn over Mutual. That year his career went in a new direction when he was

cast as the captivating Harlan, the youngest of the four Clarence Day sons in *Life with Father.* It led to Hollywood and co-starring roles in *Once Upon a Time* and *A Tree Grows in Brooklyn.* He returned to radio as teenage Bud Anderson in the long-running *Father Knows Best.* His own father was singer-composer Will Donaldson.

255. DORSEY, Jimmy (bandleader [signature song: "Contrasts"]; b. Feb. 29, 1904, Shenandoah, PA; d. June 12, 1957, New York, NY). *Kraft Music Hall* (1935–37); *Your Happy Birthday* (1941).

First rank musician-leader in the days of the big bands through the era of progressive jazz. Early lessons on the cornet by his father led to participation in local parades and dances in the coal mining area of eastern Pennsylvania. Jimmy switched to saxophone and clarinet when he and younger brother Tommy became professionals with the Scranton Sirens; their own group, Dorseys' Wild Canaries, became one of the first jazz outfits to broadcast. Jimmy played with Jean Goldkette, Paul Whiteman and Red Nichols. By the early 1930s a top-notch radio and recording musician, Jimmy with Tommy established a full-time orchestra with Bob Crosby on vocals. A headstrong disagreement between the two brothers led to a split in 1935.

Jimmy took the band to Hollywood without Tommy and appeared with Bing Crosby. Tommy on his own soon surpassed his brother in popularity. Then, in early 1941, when ASCAP music was banned from the air, Jimmy's arrangements of non-ASCAP Latin American tunes caught on overnight. For the first time his records ("Green Eyes," "Amapola" and

Tommy & Jimmy Dorsey

"Maria Elena") with vocals by Bob Eberly and Helen O'Connell, outsold Tommy's discs by several million. The following year Jimmy broke the attendance record at the Palladium Ballroom. His moderate tempo and melodious style brought him many guest bookings: *Fitch Bandwagon, 400 Club, Teentimers Club, Saturday Dance Date.* In 1943 the Dorsey feud ended. Jimmy subbed for Tommy from time to time, and together they co-starred in a film bio, *The Fabulous Dorseys.* As the big band era faded they joined forces for a combined co-directed orchestra that flourished from 1953 to late 1956. That November Tommy died; six months later Jimmy was gone. His 1957 recording of "So Rare" was then one of the most popular in the country.

256. DORSEY, Tommy (bandleader [Sentimental Gentleman of Swing] [signature song: "I'm Getting Sentimental Over You"]; b. Nov. 19, 1905, Shenandoah, PA; d. Nov. 26, 1956, Greenwich, CT). *Jack Pearl Program* (1936–37); *Fame and Fortune* (1940–41); *Tommy Dorsey Show* (1942–43); *Music America Loves Best* (1945).

Leader of a jazz-influenced dance aggregation that was second to none as the choice of top radio sponsors. He featured himself as a trombone player. "His forte was the legato approach," wrote John Lissner in *The New York Times* in a posthumous review of his recordings, "and for sheer beauty, purity of tone and complete technical mastery of his instrument, he was unequalled." Dorsey's sentimental swing reigned for over 20 years, beginning with a guest spot on *RCA Magic Key* in November 1935 and continuing to *The NBC Bandstand* in October 1956, just weeks before choking to death in his sleep at age 51.

With older brother Jimmy, he learned to handle a number of instruments from their father, a part-time bandmaster. They joined the Scranton Sirens, playing terrifically together but often fighting like tigers. During 1927–28 the Dorseys worked with Paul Whiteman, and made many superb discs as jazz sidemen. That led to freelance jobs in radio and house bands, orchestra pits, and their own Dorsey Brothers combo. One of their first contracts was with the Boswell Sisters at NBC. On Memorial Day 1935 at the Glen Island Casino, the boys disagreed over the tempo of "I'll Never Say Never Again." When Tommy got up to play his solo, he lit into it fireman-style, playing even twice as fast as usual. Jimmy, holding his saxophone, shook his head from side to side as a signal to slow down. "You can go to hell," quick-tempered Tommy yelled and walked off.

Dorsey formed his own outfit, soon becoming nationally acclaimed. He launched to success a notable group of singers: Edythe Wright, Jo Stafford, Jack Leonard, Connie Haines, Dick Haymes and Frank Sinatra. Beginning in 1938 his musicians made nine appearances on *Fitch Bandwagon,* and were summer replacements for Hope (1940), Skelton (1942) and

Allen (1946). In 1953 the brothers reunited with a combined orchestra, billed as "The Fabulous Dorseys," with radio pickups from the Palladium and Hotel Statler, and on the *All Star Parade of Bands.*

257. DOUGLAS, Paul (announcer, sportscaster; b. Apr. 11, 1907, Philadelphia, PA; d. Sept. 11, 1959, Hollywood, CA). *Fred Waring Program* (1939–42); *Paul Douglas' Sports Column* (1940–41); *Abie's Irish Rose* (1944).

A proficient, likeable sportscaster-announcer, the six-foot, 200-pound Douglas had played professional football briefly with a Philadelphia team. In addition to game coverage, he worked with Jack Benny and Burns and Allen. In 1935 he had a small part as a radio announcer in the Broadway production of *Double Dummy* which lasted less than a month. (By arrangement, his understudy did the part so that he could broadcast Saturday afternoon football games.)

Blunt and outspoken with the voice of a stevedore, he had tried to become a stage actor but didn't make it until he got the lead in the witty, entrancing comedy *Born Yesterday* in 1946. In a masterful portrayal of the heel Harry Brock, he arrived as an actor and received immediate offers from Hollywood. His successes on screen included *A Letter to Three Wives, Executive Suite* and *The Solid Gold Cadillac.* But he turned down the film adaptation of *Born Yesterday,* believing his part had been downplayed in favor of his co-star's (Judy Holliday). Douglas often appeared in radio versions of his screen roles.

258. DOWNEY, Morton (singer [The Irish Thrust] [signature song: "Wabash Moon"]; b. Nov. 14, 1901, Wallingford, CT; d. Oct. 25, 1985, Palm Beach, FL). *Morton Downey Show* (1930–36); *Songs by Morton Downey* (1948–50).

One of America's most popular radio singers, he rose by drive and luck to earn a reputed $250,000 a year at CBS and attract some 10,000 fan letters a week. A natural Irish tenor, he melted the most brittle audiences with a smile in his voice and heartfelt renditions of "Mother" and "moon" ballads. As a youth he sang in amusement parks and at annual gatherings of his Connecticut hometown firemen. Out of high school, Downey left for New York where he performed at clubs, restaurants, theatres and political rallies until Paul Whiteman heard him. Hired for his S.S. *Leviathan* orchestra, he made more than 20 transatlantic crossings and toured as one of the earliest big-band vocalists and received billing with the band — something never before accorded a singer. As bandstand vocalists were still uncommon, Whiteman decreed that Downey be equipped with a silent saxophone before he could sit with his orchestra while waiting to sing. (Whiteman later provided him with a similarly plugged French horn.) Downey left the band to work in a Ziegfeld revue in Palm Beach where he made a lasting impression among the international set.

The affable blue-eyed Downey journeyed to England where he first sang on radio and made some of the earliest of his more than 1,000 recordings. He returned to sing in three early talkies in Hollywood that proved artistically unsuccessful. But it was as a crooner on the air that he achieved his greatest fame. CBS in New York put a wire into the Club Delmonico where he was performing in 1930. He sang four times a week for the network. Perhaps his most notable and lucrative sponsorship was with the Coca-Cola Company, under whose aegis he received $4,500 a week and also a directorship in one of its bottling companies. An astute businessman, he had real estate properties, and ownership in a perfume concern and chemical patent-holding firm. He retired from singing in the mid-50s, after several series on television. He married first wife Barbara Bennett of the theatrical Bennetts in 1929. One of their four sons became talk show maverick and disc jockey Morton Downey, Jr.

A popular raconteur and practical joker, he and Broadway columnist Earl Wilson once ambushed Ted Husing in a broadcasting booth. Waiting until he was well into his scheduled sportscast, they suddenly pounced on him, stripped him to his shorts, and left him stranded at the mike just as a studio audience came by.

259. DOWNS, Bill (newscaster; b. Aug. 14, 1914, Kansas City, MO; d. May 3, 1978, Bethesda, MD).

Recruited from the United Press in London by Edward R. Murrow for radio reporting at CBS. He began on the air in 1942 with an assignment in Moscow. He represented the network at the surrender of Japan in 1945 and at the 1946 atomic bomb tests off Bikini Atoll in the Pacific. In 1950 he received an Overseas Press Club award for coverage of the Berlin blockade and airlift. Later Downs went to Rome for CBS and became a specialist in diplomatic events reporting. In November 1963 he joined ABC, just in time to cover the swearing-in of Lyndon B. Johnson in the wake of the Kennedy assassination in Dallas.

260. DOWNS, Hugh (announcer, emcee; b. Feb. 14, 1921, Akron, OH). *Doctors Today* (1948); *Surprise Symphonette/Serenade* (1948–49); *Dave Garroway Show* (1948–50).

Growing up on a farm near Lima, Ohio, he stuck close to home, listening day after day to the radio set his father had built. "It was pure magic," Downs says, "sitting there in our living room and hearing those voices coming from exotic faraway places like Cincinnati." He won a public-speaking contest scholarship to a local college but quit after a year to help out at home. One day in 1939 he passed the local station, WLOK, walked in to ask for a job, and to his amazement started work at $12.50 a week.

By 1943 Downs had moved on to NBC Chicago, after program directing at WWJ Detroit and serving a hitch in the military. He announced for *The Woman*

in White and *Story for Tonight* in Chicago. It took him years to learn to relax at the mike, he admits. Assignments as a light classical music announcer-narrator helped, as did occasional acting with Dave Garroway.

In 1954 he entered television in New York with the *Home Show*. He achieved fame as Jack Paar's announcer on *Tonight*. He was quizmaster on *Concentration* and co-host on *Today* and *20/20*. His honest and direct approach to a subject attracted large audiences. A serious interest in science led to graduate studies in gerontology and the presidency of the National Space Society. He also taught at Arizona State University.

261. DOYLE, Len (actor; b. Feb. 2, 1893, Toledo, OH*; d. Dec. 6, 1959, Port Jervis, NY). *Mr. District Attorney* (1939–51).

Originator of Harrington, "ace investigator," for *Mr. District Attorney*. According to a 1943 press release, he hung around police stations, "listening to cop talk and watching the lineups" to get into the part. Doyle played the archetypical crime snoop opposite leads Ray Jackson and Jay Jostyn on radio and television for a total of 13 years.

At 17 he made his stage bow in *The Auctioneer* with David Warfield. He attended the American Academy of Dramatic Arts and acted with the Lancaster Stock Company in Pennsylvania before settling on Broadway in a string of plays, including *Three Men on a Horse, Run, Thief, Run* and Saroyan's prize-winning *Time of Your Life*, in which he created the colorful saloon character Kit Carson.

262. DRAGON, Carmen (conductor; b. July 28, 1914, Antioch, CA; d. March 28, 1987, Santa Monica, CA). *The Passing Parade* (1943); *Maxwell House Coffee Time* (1947); *Baby Snooks Show* (1949–51); *Railroad Hour* (1949–54).

A composer-conductor, he mastered the piano, string bass, trumpet, trombone and accordion. A protege of Meredith Willson, he went to Hollywood as an arranger for Judy Garland, Dick Powell, Nelson Eddy and Mary Martin on radio and in films. His patriotic work "I'm an American" became a standard with symphonies and bands. Dragon won an Oscar for scoring (with Morris Stoloff) the 1944 musical *Cover Girl*. His wife Eloise Dragon sang on his Maxwell House series and *Starlight Concert*. Their son Daryl was half of the music team, The Captain and Tennille.

263. DRAGONETTE, Jessica (singer [signature song: "Alice Blue Gown"]; b. Feb. 14, 1904, Calcutta, India; d. March 18, 1980, New York, NY). *Philco Hour Theatre of Memories* (1927–29); *Cities Service Concert* (1930–37); *Palmolive Beauty Box Theatre* (1937); *Saturday Night Serenade* (1941–45).

*Other sources give 1899 and 1902.

The public's devotion to this petite blonde soprano was deeper than to most early broadcasters. Perhaps more ethereal, angelic-sounding than her musical contemporaries, she inspired unusual admiration and loyalty — sort of a spiritual coupling with an airborne disembodied voice. Her worshipful fans sent her handmade quilts, scarves, afghans and dolls, designed personalized lamps, sun dials and bookplates, and named hybrid roses and prized heifers in her honor. This deification from afar actually continued beyond her active days of singing, which ended a decade before the fade out of the type of musical features she helped to introduce and popularize.

Her rise to "Queen of Radio" stemmed from seven years as star of *Cities Service Concert,* a prestigious, hour-long NBC show on which she sang popular songs, arias, folk melodies and sacred selections, backed by a 40-piece orchestra led by Rosario Bourdon. Then, in 1937 came a lucrative and challenging offer to both sing and act in a series of weekly operettas for Palmolive. Squeezed into a half-hour format, the CBS program proved ineffectual and lasted the proverbial 39 weeks. A pioneer at NBC, Jessica also felt kind of an adopted child at the rival network. Not until the 1940s did she connected with another series. *Saturday Night Serenade* brought her back to audiences but her selections were few and generally in the popular mode. By mid-1946 her on-going radio work ended.

Born of Italian-American parents in India, she grew up in Philadelphia where she took vocal lessons. Her Catholic upbringing included attendance at Georgian Court Convent in New Jersey and an intensified curriculum of music studies. That led to New York and the solo part as the off-stage angel in Max Reinhardt's *The Miracle* and a role in the 1926 edition of *Grand Street Follies.* Auditions at WEAF lead to a musical comedy hour, Shakespearean roles and one-act plays, the part of Vivian: the Coca-Cola Girl, and a guest spot on *General Motors Family Party.* Her breakthrough came with an engagement as the soprano star of *Philco Hour Theatre of Memories,* a weekly presentation of well-established operettas. In two and a half years, she sang 75 roles.

Jessica made recordings of her oft-performed songs for Brunswick and Victor, and made lengthy concert tours in 1937–39 during a break from radio. In 1929 she participated in rudimentary RCA telecasts. Her wartime morale-building and bond-selling appearances were recognized by the military branches and Treasury Department. Spain honored her for introducing Spanish music on radio. Pope Pius decorated her for her professional and humanitarian achievements.

Her autobiography, *Faith Is a Song,* is an engaging memoir of broadcasting's earliest decades and her pride of association with them. In her story she took pains never to disclose her age, carefully omitting early dates. But she was 25 in 1929 when she remarked: "I'm young and radio is young. I think radio will advance

Galen Drake (courtesy of ABC Capital Cities/ABC)

just as the movies did. Maybe as it develops, I will develop with it."

264. DRAKE, Galen (commentator; b. July 26, 1907, Kokomo, IN; d. June 30, 1989, Long Beach, CA). *Galen Drake* (1945–57).

Talk show host with a wide following among American housewives. He began on Saturday mornings on ABC in 1945, speaking easily and honestly in a "me-to-you" style. Moving to CBS in 1950, Drake was hyped as the spokesman-guardian of the Housewives Protective League on Monday-to-Friday afternoon airings. He also passed on his homey philosophy and kitchen-table observations locally at WOR. In the late '50s he brought his commentary to ABC-TV with *This is Galen Drake.*

He had begun broadcasting as a teenager and continued as a student while at UCLA. Drake also sang, and briefly conducted the Southern California Symphony before concentrating on talk radio.

265. DUCHIN, Eddy (bandleader [The Ten Magic Fingers of Radio] [signature song: "My Twilight Dream"]; b. April 1, 1909, Cambridge, MA; d. Feb. 9, 1951, New York, NY). *LaSalle Style Show* (1936–37); *Eddy Duchin Orchestra* (1938–39); *Kraft Music Hall* (1946–47).

Sweet music's number-one glamour boy of the 1930s. Duchin began study of piano at age five, played for high school dances in Boston, and organized his own band at a summer camp shortly before entering Massachusetts College of Pharmacy. He planned to become a druggist and join his father's pharmacy. But he auditioned for Leo Reisman and began playing piano with his orchestra just before his senior year. Reisman convinced him his real career lay in music, so he went to New York's Central Park Casino where he remained four years, succeeding Reisman as leader in 1931. Within months he broadcast for CBS at midnight on Sunday and Wednesday and at 5 p.m. on Saturday. Duchin married his first piano "pupil," New York socialite Marjorie Oelrichs, in 1935. She died shortly after the birth of their son (and future bandleader) Peter Duchin in 1937.

Goodlooking and well-mannered, with a unique keyboard style that he described as "breathing with the piano as I would with my voice," he interpreted a song through his "humming." This habit created a curious problem when the band first went on the air in 1932. A strange buzzing sound accompanied the music. The band spent many days trying to find out what caused the annoyance. In the end, the source proved to be Duchin's humming.

He broadcast regularly for such major sponsors as Texaco, American Cigarette and Cigar, and Cadillac Motor Car. His singers, Dorothy Lamour, Patricia Norman, Durelle Alexander, added plenty of sex appeal to the bandstand.

Shortly after the attack on Pearl Harbor, he joined the Navy, spending nearly four years overseas and away from a piano. But he returned to music and radio at the war's end, and gained much of his preeminence. Duchin died of leukemia at 41. Tyrone Power portrayed him in the 1956 film biography *The Eddy Duchin Story* (and prepared for his piano playing by studying with former Duchin pianist Nat Brandwynne who worked out the precise synchronization of Power's hands on a dummy keyboard; the actual sound track was performed by Carmen Cavallero).

266. DUEY, Phil (singer; b. June 22, 1902, Macy, IN; d. April 7, 1982, Chapel Hill, NC). *Lucky Strike Dance Orchestra* (1928–31); *Leo Reisman Orchestra* (1933–37); *Manhattan Merry-Go-Round* (1940–41).

Baritone soloist and member of various small vocal groups. His first radio appearance was in 1926, while singing at the Roosevelt Hotel. He enjoyed a three-year run with Lucky Strike and B. A. Rolfe, and sang often for Atwater Kent and Fred Allen in the early 1930s. Duey was also featured with Leo Reisman for Philip Morris.

A well-educated musician (Indiana University AB '24, AM '38 and Juilliard Graduate School) he aimed for the Met and reached the highly competitive finals of the 1938 *Auditions of the Air.* But pop-ular music seemed his forte, especially on *Manhattan Merry-Go-Round* and its spinoff, *Monday Merry-Go-Round.* He sang in the Happy Wonder Bakers trio and Men About Town quartet, and subbed for Frank Munn on *Waltz Time* in 1941–42.

Duey went to the University of Michigan as a professor of vocal music in 1947. There he directed the Men's Glee Club and prepared many arrangements for the internationally acclaimed 45-voice group.

267. DUFF, Howard (actor; b. Aug. 24, 1913, Bremerton, WA; d. July 8, 1990, Santa Barbara, CA). *Dear John* (1941); *Woman in White* (1946–47); *Adventures of Sam Spade* (1946–51).

At age 18 he was on radio at KOMO Seattle, and with the Seattle Repertory Theatre. By 1940 he moved to network soap operas, and was soon attached to the Armed Forces Radio Service during World War II. After military duty he gained prime-time popularity at the mike, through the role of hard-boiled detective Sam Spade. The show ran until Duff found himself listed in "Red Channels" as a communist sympathizer. He refused to sign a loyalty oath.

His picture parts ranged from character roles to B-picture leads in the late 1940s. His classic *films noir* were *Brute Force* and *The Naked City,* both of which meshed well with his tough guy radio role on the Dashiell Hammett private eye series. His television and movie features were often with his wife from 1951–73, the actress-director Ida Lupino.

268. DUMKE, Ralph (comedian; b. July 25, 1899, South Bend, IN; d. Jan. 4, 1964, Sherman Oaks, CA). *Sisters of the Skillet* (1930–37); *We, the Abbotts* (1941–42); *Studio X* (1941–42); *The Two Minute Man* (1943–44); *Hook 'n' Ladder Follies* (1943–44).

Dumke and partner Ed East were billed as 500 pounds of comedy on the hoof. The hefty duo, best

Ed East, Ralph Dumke

known as Sisters of the Skillet, entertained listeners with chatter and songs, and by kidding household "hinters." Previously in vaudeville as "The Mirth-quakers" for ten years, they improvised their jovial daytime program, first at WGN. Their act was on the opening bill of Radio City Music Hall in December 1932.

The team broke up in 1938, and Ralph went on to a busy schedule at NBC, including emcee of *Funny Money Man, The Two Minute Man* and *Hook 'n' Ladder Follies* (as Cap'n Walt). He appeared in the cast of such 1940s Broadway musicals as *By Jupiter* and *Helen Goes to Troy,* and early TV sitcoms *December Bride* and *My Little Margie.* A frequent guest of Mary Margaret McBride, Indiana-born Dumke once played football for Knute Rockne's team at Notre Dame.

269. DUNNINGER, Joseph (mentalist [Master Mind of Mental Mystery]; b. April 28, 1892, New York, NY; d. March 9, 1975, Cliffside Park, NJ). *Dunninger Show* (1943–44).

Mind-reader, hypnotist and magician. His popularity as a theatre and club attraction carried him to radio where he periodically broadcast chiefly as a curiosity. Suddenly, in the early 1940s, his own show at ABC turned into an overnight sensation. His appeal on a weekly basis, however, proved short-lived, and he only returned as a summer fill-in for *Amos 'n' Andy* in 1945 and 1946.

Dunninger promoted himself as "a mentalist, a demonstrator of telepathic communication." He remained a welcomed guest, continuing into early television which provided the visual mien essential to magicians.

A magic act in vaudeville, he became so widely known that he was invited to the White House to perform for President after President. He often began his performances with random readings from the audience — names, addresses, occupations, birthdays. Dunninger frequently offered $10,000 to any one who could prove he had an accomplice.

270. DUNSTEDTER, Eddie (organist, conductor; b. Aug. 22, 1897, Edwardsville, IL; d. July 30, 1974, Tarzana, CA). *Gold Medal Fast Freight* (1931–33); *It Happened in Hollywood* (1939–40); *The Lineup* (1950–53).

Major CBS West Coast organist-musical director. At its Sunset Blvd. studios, he performed on one of the largest organs in any station, and for such programs as *Pursuit* and *Yours Truly, Johnny Dollar.* In 1930 he had inaugurated the first coast-to-coast hookup from WCCO Minneapolis with General Mills' *Gold Medal Fast Freight.* Dunstedter made numerous record albums of Christmas, religious and popular music. His single of "There's a Gold Mine in the Sky" with Bing Crosby sold several million copies. He composed scores for television shows and films. During World War II he served as an Army Air Corps

colonel in charge of all Corps orchestras on the West Coast.

In the mode of most radio organists, he began as a church musician and movie house accompanist.

271. DURANTE, Jimmy [The Schnozz] [signature song: "Inka Dinka Doo"] [catchphrases: "Goodnight, Mrs. Calabash, wherever you are."; "Everybody's gettin into de act."; "I've got a million of 'em."]; b. Feb. 10, 1893, New York, NY; d. Jan. 29, 1980, Santa Monica, CA). *Jumbo Fire Chief* (1935–36); *Durante-Moore Show* (1943–47); *Jimmy Durante Program* (1947–50).

His song-piano-joke act transferred easily from speakeasy to vaudeville to radio for this brash, loveable comic. Born in the Bowery to Italian immigrant parents, he turned his fractured English with mispronunciations and malapropisms and honky-tonk piano into a winning routine that never failed to charm an audience. He teamed up with singer Eddie Jackson and dancer Lou Clayton in speakeasy days, then soloed on Broadway and in films, proudly recognizing his greatest assets were his huge nose and raspy voice. Durante joined with young Garry Moore at NBC, and the resulting chemistry between the duo pushed the program to high ratings.

In November 1950 he made the first of 11 appearances on *The Big Show* that included a take-off of "Anne of the Thousand Days" with Judy Holliday. A sought-after guest, Durante traded jokes with Vallee, Hope, Cantor and Canova, and appeared on many humanitarian and public service specials. The "Goodnight, Mrs. Calabash, wherever you are" was no secret signoff according to Durante's second wife, Margie Little. "It meant 'all you lonely people out there.'" One of show business's legendary performers, he gained a new generation of fans from television appearances. A stroke in 1972 left him partially paralyzed, ending his "Inka Dinka Doo" singing days.

272. EARL, Craig (quizmaster; b. Sept. 5, 1895, Boston, MA; d. Aug. 1985, Great Barrington, MA). *Professor Quiz* (1937–41, 1946–48).

A magician, he succeeded Jim McWilliams as quizmaster of an early basic guessing game called *Professor Quiz.* Craig's questions were "not too far over the brain-power of average listeners" (*Variety*), some being in the nature of riddles and trick puns. His persistent jollity kept the show in motion, although he sounded to some a trifle anxious to seem all-wise, never to be topped by any of his contestants.

Earl entered radio in the early 1920s to conduct health exercises. They continued until the day he received a letter from an indignant listener who wrote: "How the dickens do you expect me to do setting-up exercises with earphones attached?" A cursory investigation disclosed that there were only a handful of loudspeaker amplifiers in the still-primitive period of broadcasting; awkward headphones were the norm.

273. EAST, Ed (comedian; b. April 4, 1894, Bloomington, IN; d. Jan. 18, 1952, New York, NY). *Sisters of the Skillet* (1930–37); *Name It and It's Yours* (1939–40); *Breakfast in Bedlam* (1939–45); *Ladies Be Seated* (1943–45).

A major vaudeville act with Ralph Dumke led to a WGN microphone. Their *Sisters* daytime show in NBC kidded prevailing programs aimed at houswives. The duo also made guest appearances on *Fleischmann Hour* and *Show Boat*. Once a carnival barker and a pianist with a dance orchestra, jovial, 260-pound Ed broke up with Dumke in 1938, then teamed with wife Polly Smith for *Ed and Polly*. They originated *Ladies Be Seated* at the Blue Network.

A tenacious composer, Ed claimed authorship of about 500 songs, and at one point dashed off ten a week for *Sisters of the Skillet*.

274. EDDY, Nelson (singer; [signature song: "Short'nin' Bread"]; b. June 29, 1901, Providence, RI; d. March 6, 1967, Miami, FL). *Voice of Firestone* (1934–36); *Vick Open House* (1936–37); *Chase & Sanborn Hour* (1937–39).

The Telephone Hour engaged him regularly in the 1940s and '50s, and his 25 appearances brought this series its largest audiences. By then, he was one of the screen's most beloved singers, having co-starred with Jeanette MacDonald in a string of charmingly romantic operettas and musicals at MGM. He sang on President Roosevelt's Inauguration Concert in 1941 and at his Diamond Jubilee Birthday Celebration in 1942, both aired by NBC. His broadcast fee soared to $5,000 by 1944.

The model of a wholesome, all-American type, he combined sturdy masculinity with a deep baritone voice. Self-assured and unpretentious, he figured a natural adjunct to the comedy of Bergen and McCarthy. He maintained guest shots as a serious artist. He also starred on *Kraft Music Hall* summer series 1947–49.

Eddy studied voice to the degree where he learned 32 operatic parts and made a debut as Tonio at the Met in 1924. Concert recitals and radio work supported him in the early days of the Depression. But in 1933 — the year he sang on *Soconyland Sketches*—Hollywood discovered him. Once audiences saw him in *Naughty Marietta,* his reputation as a singing idol was quickly established.

Nelson Eddy, Margaret Speaks

275. EDWARDS, Douglas (newscaster; b. July 14, 1917, Ada, OK; d. Oct. 13, 1990, Sarasota, FL).

At age 15 he was already at a microphone, working as a junior announcer at a makeshift 100-watt station in Troy, Alabama. The transmitter, started by a group of older friends, was over a firehouse and next door to a church where young Edwards was assigned

Douglas Edwards, Ben Lochridge, Richard C. Hottelet

to announce the selections played by the church organist. He attended the University of Alabama, Emory University and the University of Georgia, combining his studies with work at WSB Atlanta and other stations. In the 1930s he joined WXYZ Detroit. In 1942 he commenced a 46-year career with CBS.

The dependable and diligent Edwards was assigned to Edward R. Murrow's London staff near the end of World War II. He covered the 1948 Presidential conventions, and soon was chosen by CBS president Frank Stanton to anchor *Douglas Edwards with the News,* TV's first nightly network news program. Yet he maintained strong ties to radio through frequent in-depth newscasts. His straightforward, highly credible delivery never got too fancy. The news business, he once said, "can be dull, but most times it's interesting."

276. EDWARDS, Joan (singer; b. Feb. 13, 1920, New York, NY; d. Aug. 27, 1981, New York, NY). *Chesterfield Presents* (1938–39); *Girl About Town* (1941); *Your Hit Parade* (1941–47).

Edwards sang the nation's most popular tunes on *Your Hit Parade* longer than other vocalist. And for nearly two years she shared the mike with Frank Sinatra. Born into a family of songwriters and publishers — including her uncle, Gus Edwards — she majored in music at Hunter College and juggled her classes to do piano and vocal interludes at local stations. She sang and directed the orchestra of a network show before joining Paul Whiteman's Chesterfield-sponsored swing aggregation. An accomplished song arranger and composer for nightclubs, Broadway revues and product jingles, the versatile vocalist was a favorite of '40s bobbysoxers. She made guest appearances on a diverse spectrum of programs, ranging from *Ellery Queen* and *The Contented Hour* to *Bill Stern Sports Newsreel* and *Truth or Consequences.* Her three-a-week *Girl About Town* featured accompaniment by duo-pianists Cy Walters and Johnny Garde.

277. EDWARDS, Ralph (host, announcer [catchphrase: "Aren't we devils?"]; b. June 13, 1913, Merino, CO). *Heinz Magazine of the Air* (1936); *Original Amateur Hour* (1936–39); *Truth or Consequences* (1940–54); *This Is Your Life* (1948–50).

An announcer on the West Coast until the mid-1930s, Ralph Edwards hitchhiked to New York determined to break into the big time. Pursuing numerous leads and enduring countless auditions, he picked up jobs at NBC and CBS in 1936. As a voice for hire, Edwards was soon announcing 45 shows a week. They included *Life Can Be Beautiful, Town Hall Tonight, The Children's Hour, The Gospel Singer* and *Major Bowes Original Amateur Hour.* Analyzing the rise of broadcast leaders, he concluded that those performers who had contributed to the development of a unique format or approach were usually among radio's well-heeled royalty.

Ralph Edwards (courtesy of Ralph Edwards Productions)

Edwards came up with the fresh idea of a truth or consequences sessions, based on the old parlor game of forfeits. As an audience-participation show inflicting indignities and pranks on contestants, it got on CBS in March 1940. An overnight success, *Truth or Consequences* carried quiz programs to a new, and madcap, plateau. Assigned offbeat and often humorous tasks, contestants reveled in the challenge, delighting studio observers and most importantly at-home listeners who from the show's vocal cues and sounds issuing from the harried participants used their imagination to embellish the laugh-filled antics. The phenomenally popular series made Ralph Edwards a household name. For his efforts as owner, producer, writer and master of ceremonies, he became radio's youngest entrepreneur. Consequences ranged from the challenge of eating a cream puff in one hand and drinking a glass of milk from the other while singing and skipping rope, to washing an elephant, running a locomotive engine, pushing a walnut by the nose, diapering a young pig, playing a piano upside down, and even increasingly more elaborate challenges. Edwards' morale-building stunts and features during World War II won high praise and awards, as did his postwar fund-raising-for-charity giveaways via riddle-solving contests (Mr. Hush, The Walking Man, Miss Hush, Mr. Heartbeat). Another segment — emotion-filled salutes to a contestant's individual achievements — led to the spinoff of *This Is Your Life,* which like *Truth or Consequences* moved easily into television. Both shows made excellent use of the media's remote pickup abilities.

Edwards remains active in Hollywood where his solid-gold broadcast properties built a lucrative production company. Today his only foray with *Truth or Consequences* comes about each year when he travels

Charles Egelston (courtesy of Photofest)

posite Dennis Day, and Olive of the Sycamore family on *You Can't Take It with You.*

In 1948 she headlined *Rexall Summer Theatre* and appeared on the *New Mel Torme Show.* Her TV credits include *Wagon Train* and *Donna Reed Show.*

280. ELLEN, Minetta (actress; b. Jan. 17, 1875, Cleveland, OH; d. July 2, 1965, Hollywood, CA). *One Man's Family* (1932–55).

For decades she played the understanding and wise mother, Fanny Barbour, on Carlton Morse's *One Man's Family,* the story of an average American family. The half-hour "chapters" began in 1932 at KGO San Francisco. It became the first West Coast serial to have nation-wide sponsorship. The whole cast went to Hollywood in 1937, expecting to make the program into a movie. But the plans fell through, and Minetta and the actors voted to stay in Los Angeles. In 1939 she began to appear on *I Love a Mystery,* another Carlton Morse production.

Ellen never set foot on a stage until after she married and raised a family. Mother parts with University of California Berkeley Players led to radio. The highly esteemed actress retired at age 80 after 23 years as the memorable matriarch.

281. ELLIOT, Win (sportscaster, emcee; b. May 7, 1915, Chelsea, MA). *Fish Pond* (1944); *County Fair* (1946–50); *Quick as a Flash* (1948–51).

A public speaking course in his junior year at the University of Michigan proved to Elliot that he could talk on his feet and be entertaining in the process. He also studied radio writing and announcing, and did some work over WJR before returning to Boston and a job on a small 100-watt hometown station. Work as a staff announcer in Washington, and news editor and

with a road show for a fiesta in Truth or Consequences, New Mexico, a town that changed its name in 1950 to commemorate the tenth anniversary of his well-remembered, zany series.

278. EGELSTON, Charles (actor; b. July 16, 1882, Covington, KY; d. Oct. 31, 1958, New York, NY). *Ma Perkins* (1933–58); *Uncle Ezra* (1939).

Character actor with long-running part as Shuffle Shober on *Ma Perkins.* He also played Pop, the stage doorman, on *Backstage Wife* and Burt on *Portia Faces Life.* Egelston was credited with having been the first person on radio to portray the character of Scrooge in Dickens' *A Christmas Carol.* It was broadcast by WLW in 1929. He spent 20 years on the stage and in silent films before his microphone audition in Cincinnati that year.

279. EILER, Barbara (actress; b. July 27, c1928, Los Angeles, CA). *Masquerade* (1946–47); *Life of Riley* (1946–51); *A Day in the Life of Dennis Day* (1947–51).

Perennial teenage daughter-girlfriend on West Coast comedies. Eiler played Babs Riley, Mildred and Gloria op-

Sportscasters Win Elliot, Jim Kelly

Bob Elliott and Ray Goulding (courtesy of Bob Elliott)

emcee (for an afternoon variety show called *Club 1300*) in Baltimore attracted the attention of the Blue Network.

In New York he took over the quiz *Musical Mysteries* and inaugurated the audience-participation *Fish Pond*. After serving in the Merchant Marines, he connected with *County Fair* at CBS and *Quick as a Flash* at Mutual — both game-filled sessions suited Win's glib and breezy style. His later assignments include *Winner Take All* and *Break the Bank*. He was also announcer for *The Gillette Cavalcade of Sports* for 12 years. His own creation, *Win with a Winner,* fell victim to the NBC ax in the wake of the TV quiz scandal cleanup.

As a radio and TV sports reporter, he covered a myriad of events, particularly hockey and horseracing. For CBS he was heard regularly on sports roundups into the 1980s.

282. ELLIOTT, Bob (comedian; b. March 26, 1923, Boston, MA). *Bob and Ray* (1951–c75); *Monitor* (1955–c60).

During his long heyday with Ray Goulding on radio, they wrote and performed many hours of stellar comedy every week. One of radio's last funny-men duos, they created a collection of memorable airborne characters. Bob was the voice of the bumbling Wally Ballou, recipe-crazed Mary McGoon, dim-witted Harry Backstayge and the fugue-talking McBeebee Twins.

Bob and Ray met while working at WHDH Boston in 1946, and soon discovered they were on the same wavelength for comic effects. Bob, the more introverted and pessimistic of the team, was influenced by radio comedian Raymond Knight and his *KUKU Hour* and *Wheatenaville*. (They later became close friends and Bob married his widow.) Just prior to

World War II, he worked as an usher at Radio City Music Hall and NBC page. His first air assignment was a weekly show at WINS billed as "a page boy's impressions of radio." After military duty in Europe, he met newscaster Gould. The outcome was *Matinee with Bob and Ray*. NBC heard a recording of their guest appearance on WMGM New York and hired them for a daily 15-minute show at 5:45 p.m. Their series brought them the most respected prize in broadcasting, a Peabody Award, in 1951 and again in 1957. Bob and Ray TV appearances continued their mix of nonsense and satire.

"Their jokes, for all their contemporary universality," Kurt Vonnegut, Jr., wrote in 1983, "began as caricatures of radio when it was as densely packed with situation comedies and quiz shows and variety shows and dramas and big time sports events as television is today. Radio was startlingly successful at creating excitement and emotional involvement with sounds alone."

283. ELLIOTT, Larry (announcer; b. Aug. 31, 1905, Washington, DC; d. July 27, 1957, Port Chester, NY). *Texaco Star Theatre* (1938–c41); *American Melody Hour* (1942–c45); *Barry Cameron* (1945).

CBS Washington news reporter and its White House radio announcer in the mid-1930s. He came to New York where he originated the 6:30 a.m. *Rising Sun Show* in 1938. He was an announcer for Fred Allen, Bob Hawk, Alan Young and Andre Kostelanetz. During World War II he became the official Voice of the U.S. Treasury in the sale of war bonds via "*Millions for Defense*" pitches on the *Treasury Hour.*

Irrepressible as his early Washington radio cohort, Arthur Godfrey, Elliott often filled in when Arthur failed to show up on time. On the first such morning Elliott told early risers: "If you're silly enough to get out of a nice warm bed at this ungodly hour, it's your fault. Don't expect me to entertain you. I'm tired, too."

A tenor, Elliott had studied voice for five years in Washington while working as an auto salesman. He sold a car to a radio executive, but overnight the dealership failed and he was out of work. The sympathetic radio man offered him an announcer's job.

284. ELLIS, Herb (actor; b. Jan. 17, 1921, Cleveland, OH). *Dragnet* (1949–52); *The New Adventures of Nero Wolfe* (1950–51); *Tales of the Texas Rangers* (1950–52).

Supporting and character player on many West Coast programs from the late 1930s to 1960s. His longest association, *Dragnet,* encompassed the role of Sgt. Frank Smith and other parts and associate director, as well as the early TV run and feature film. He played Archie on *Nero Wolfe,* and regular parts on the Frank Sinatra dramatic series *Rocky Fortune* and Brian Donlevy thriller *Dangerous Assignment.* He contributed scripts to *Jason and the Golden Fleece* and *Nightbeat.*

Ellis pursued theatre and radio work (WTAM) as a pre-teen in Cleveland. Acting in stock in California a few years later, he joined Jack Lescoulie's *Grouch Club* in San Francisco where he also did AFRS productions with William Conrad. For television he enjoyed running character parts on *Peter Gunn, Dobie Gillis* and *Hennesey.* His motion pictures include *Peter Kelly's Blues* and *Blueprint for Murder.*

285. ELLIS, Robert (actor; b. Aug. 24, 1933, Chicago, IL; d. Nov. 24, 1973, Los Angeles, CA). *Life of Riley* (1949–51); *Aldrich Family* (1952–53).

Best remembered as Henry Aldrich in the 1950s, on radio and television. A child actor since age five, Ellis played in over 50 films, including *April Showers* (juvenile lead) and *Gidget.* He was teenage Junior Riley on *Life of Riley* and Alexander of *Blondie.* On the late '40s annual *Duffy's Tavern* Christmas presentation of "Miracle in Manhattan," he played Jimmy, the crippled lad. For several seasons he was Dexter on TV's *Meet Corliss Archer.* After leaving acting, he became president of Tellet Communication, a firm producing educational films and audiovisuals.

Anne Elstner (courtesy of Steve Jelf)

286. ELMAN, Dave (emcee [The Dean of American Hobbyists]; b. May 6, 1900, Park River, ND; d. Dec. 5, 1967, Clifton, NJ). *Hobby Lobby* (1937–43, 1945–46, 1948–49).

Kindly impresario who introduced a cross-section of the country's vast army of collectors and their diverse hobbies. Nearly 3,000 applications rolled in weekly for the program. A collector himself, he introduced six unusual hobbies per show. Editors voted it outstanding new "idea" show in 1938.

At an early age Elman ran off from his Dakota home to land a job in show business. A hypnotist, he was billed in vaudeville as the "Boy Wonder." He freelanced at small stations and served an apprenticeship in stock and repertory. A sketch for Earl Carroll's *Vanities* gave him a boost, along with work in ad agencies. But not until he sold his *Hobby* idea to radio did he strike gold (with initial sponsor Hudson Motors). The show, which he also wrote, produced and directed, began as a $35 a week sustainer on WOR and led to a $3,500-a-week network feature on CBS. It led to books, newspaper columns, film shorts, vaudeville unit and World's Fair attraction.

287. ELSTNER, Anne (actress; b. Jan. 22, 1899, Lake Charles, LA; d. Jan. 29, 1981, Doylestown, PA). *Hillbilly Heartthrobs* (1933–35); *Stella Dallas* (1937–55).

Actress in the title role of one of the most memorable soap operas of all time, Elstner portrayed the beautiful daughter of an impoverished farmhand who had married above her station in life. During the show's run on NBC, Elstner, who took the part very seriously, is believed to have missed only one week of episodes.

A stage performer, she had re-created a scene from her Broadway play *Sun-Up* on radio, and later joined the cast of *Moonshine and Honeysuckle* in 1930. She periodically played on *Pages of Romance, The Fat Man* and *Great Plays.* In retirement, she operated a New Jersey restaurant where diners were invited to "come and meet Stella Dallas."

288. EMERSON, Joe (singer; b. Aug. 9, 1892, Grand Rapids, MI; d. Sept. 30, 1969, Waynesville, NC). *Hymns of All Churches* (1935–47); *Hymn Time* (1951–54).

Gospel singer with an inspirational weekday morning program. Emerson and an eight-voice choir started as a Mutual sustainer and within a year were bought by General Mills for CBS. His was one of the few daytime light music series with a sponsor. At one point he had both morning and afternoon programs on NBC and ABC, totalling nine 15-minute shows a week. He also appeared on *General Mills Family Party* in 1942.

A baritone, Emerson fell into radio after having lost his real estate holdings in the market crash. He bowed over a Miami station in 1929, then moved to

Chicago. A Navy pilot during World War I, he once taught aviation at MIT. At one point he traveled on a Chautauqua circuit throughout the Midwest.

289. ENNIS, Skinnay (bandleader, singer [signature song: "I've Got a Date with an Angel"]; b. Aug. 13, 1910, Salisbury, NC; d. June 3, 1963, Beverly Hills, CA). *Bob Hope Show* (1938–46); *Abbott and Costello Show* (1946–47).

Ennis became friends with Bob Hope when they appeared together in the 1938 Paramount picture *College Swing.* Hope encouraged him to organize his own orchestra. He had just left the Hal Kemp band where he had been a vocalist in a breathless, throaty, half-whispered fashion that enthralled audiences. When Hope got his own show for Pepsodent, Skinnay's outfit was one of those offered to the producers.

Known as Skinnay since his college days at the University of North Carolina, he suffered good-naturedly under Hope's ribbing about being a thin, asthmatic "dishrag." His band also toured widely, and enjoyed a five-year run at the Statler-Hilton in Los Angeles. In 1963, dining in a restaurant, Ennis choked to death on a piece of roast beef that had lodged in his trachea.

290. ERIC, Elspeth (actress; b. c1906, Chicago, IL). *Betty and Bob* (1939–40); *Crime Doctor* (1942–43); *Road of Life* (1948–49); *Young Dr. Malone* (1952).

Usually cast as the other woman or cantankerous wife in soaps and serials. In the role of Joyce Jordan, the deep-voiced actress, however, played an admirable intern who fought for and won the right to work side by side with men. Eric broke into radio in 1934, six years after graduating from Wellesley College and a stint with the Woodstock Summer Theatre. In 1940–41 she appeared often on *Murder at Midnight, Johnny Presents* and *Grand Central Station.* She also played social reformer Emily Olson in *Central City* and the female lead in *Crime Doctor.* By mid-1950 she could be heard regularly on *The Falcon* mysteries.

While seeking theatre jobs, Elspeth worked as a governess, stenographer, phone operator and model. A breakthrough role on Broadway in *Dead End* in 1935 led to stage assignments in *Margin for Error* and *Snafu.* In the 1960s she turned to scriptwriting for TV soaps (*Another World*), and found it easier to write than act. "The words seem to come effortlessly as though the characters were just talking, and I was putting down what they say. But acting is much more complicated. First, you have to memorize the lines, and then you have to try to convey the sense of character, and adjust to the situation and the other actors."

291. ERICKSON, Louise (actress; b. Feb. 28, 1928, Oakland, CA). *A Date with Judy* (1942–50); *The Great Gildersleeve* (1944–48); *Alan Young Show* (1949).

The adventures of high school teenager Judy Foster and her boyfriends provided Erickson with the defining role of her comparatively short career. To promote the series, she was depicted as being very much like this 1940s radio junior miss. She also made a well-defined impression in the supporting role of Marjorie, Gildersleeve's niece.

Her 14 years in West Coast radio encompassed appearances with Durante and Sinatra, and a short run as Babs on *Life of Riley.* She made her radio bow at age seven in Hollywood as a fairy princess and played in *Dramas of Youth* over Mutual before joining the *Judy* cast in 1942.

292. ETTING, Ruth (singer [signature song: "Shine On, Harvest Moon"]; b. Nov. 23, 1896, David City, NE; d. Sept. 24, 1978, Colorado Springs, CO). *Music That Satisfies* (1932); *Oldsmobile Show* (1934); *Kellogg College Prom* (1935–36).

She helped glamourize the jazz age through appearances as a torch singer in nightclubs, in Ziegfeld shows and on recordings. Her relaxed, easygoing delivery transferred readily to radio where she stressed simple, sentimental songs in the vein of "At Sundown" and "I Cried for You." She first sang on the air in Chicago in 1922 and made frequent guest appearances on KYW, WLS and WQJ and for Chase & Sanborn until CBS and Chesterfield made her one of the stars of its *Music That Satisfies.* In 1930 she was the first guest on Walter Winchell's opening broadcast.

Etting was managed by Martin (Moe the Gimp) Snyder whom she wed in 1922. The stormy marriage ended shortly after her jealous spouse tried to shoot her pianist and arranger Myrl Alderman. She and Alderman were married during Snyder's trial in 1938.

Ruth Etting

When the war forced a cancellation of an 18-month tour of the British Isles, Australia and South Africa in 1939, she retired to a chicken farm in Colorado.

At age 50 in 1947 she attempted a comeback on radio with the help of Rudy Vallee on his new program for Philip Morris. But the outcome was only a weekly 15-minute sustainer with Alderman at WHN New York. Her voice came across as a bit flat and stilted, and appealed mainly to those who remembered her in the 1930s. Etting was rediscovered on a much broader scale when the story of her life was made into a popular MGM film called *Love Me or Leave Me* with Doris Day in 1955. The surprisingly accurate biography created a nostalgic interest in her vintage discs, many of which were commercially reissued.

293. EVANS, Dale (actress, singer [Queen of the Cowgirls]; b. Oct. 31, 1912, Uvalde, TX). *That Girl from Texas* (1940–41); *Chase & Sanborn Hour* (1942–43); *Saturday Night Roundup* (1946–47); *Roy Rogers Show* (1948–55).

A singer on many popular programs before she went into Westerns with future husband Roy Rogers in 1944. At one point she was the featured vocalist for 39 weeks with Bergen and McCarthy, and sang on the shows of Durante and Moore, and Jack Carson. She

Dale Evans

first performed on a local program in Memphis, sponsored by an insurance company where she worked as a stenographer. That led to stints at WHAS Louisville and WFAA Dallas, and a job as vocalist with Anson Weeks' orchestra in Chicago. In 1940 as a CBS staff singer the network picked her as star of *News and Rhythm,* and Fox signed her to a one-year contract. With only two small parts to her credits, she moved to Republic for a varied lineup of pictures: musicals, melodramas, and Westerns.

Her debut role with Rogers was in *The Cowboy and the Senorita,* and dozens more followed. Her favorite film *Don't Fence Me In* had her cast as a newspaper woman. During World War II Evans recorded many overseas broadcasts and entertained at GI camps. Married to Rogers in 1947, she co-starred on his radio and TV shows, and wrote the lyrics to the program's theme "Happy Trails to You." Her other songs ranged from "Will You Marry Me, Mr. Laramie?" (1940) to "The Bible Tells Me So" (1955). The only woman to receive star billing at a Madison Square Garden rodeo, she recorded many Western and religious compositions.

Active in humanitarian and charitable organizations, Evans has received numerous public service and woman-of-the-year awards. She has also written books on personal and family crises. Her first, *Angel Unaware,* stemmed from the death of her two-year-old retarded daughter, Robin.

294. EVANS, Wilbur (singer; b. Aug. 5, 1908, Philadelphia, PA; d. May 31, 1987, Elmer, NJ). *Vick Open House* (1937–38); *Stars from the Blue* (1943–44).

Evans won the first Atwater Kent national singing competition in 1927. The finals were broadcast by Kent, a radio set manufacturer who advanced classical and semi-classical music over the air. Evans' prize included $5,000 and a scholarship to Curtis Institute of Music. As a professional, he concertized across the country and made his operatic debut in *Tristan* with the Philadelphia Orchestra. He signed with CBS for a series of broadcasts with Jeanette MacDonald, soon after three guest appearances on *Show Boat* in 1933.

A six-foot-tall baritone, he starred on Broadway in *Up in Central Park* and *Mexican Hayride,* in which he introduced Cole Porter's "I Love You." He sang in the London production of *South Pacific* opposite Mary Martin, and in many operettas, often with soprano (and second wife) Susanna Foster. He later taught voice in Philadelphia, then worked as an officer in charge of USO shows from 1967 to 1974.

295. EVERETT, Ethel (actress; b. Oct. 13, 1913, New York, NY*; d. April 2, 1973, New York, NY). *Show Boat* (1936–38); *True Story* (1936–39); *Stella Dallas* (1945–46).

Her first radio experience began in 1931 with an NBC sustaining program as the result of an audition

*Another source gives 1909.

and led to 8,000 broadcasts over the next 40 years. Active in college dramatics as Hunter, she first acted professionally in stock. Her numerous credits included *Hilltop House, Believe It or Not, David Harum* and *Kate Smith Show.* Everett was narrator of the 1940 series *By Kathleen Norris.* A decade later she continued as a dramatic actress on TV's *Studio One, Big Story* and *As The World Turns.*

296. FADIMAN, Clifton (emcee; b. May 15, 1904, Brooklyn, NY). *The Book Report* (1931); *Information Please* (1938–48, 1950); *RCA Magic Key* (1938); *Conversation* (1954–57).

Literary critic Fadiman gave a large part of the American public new role models drawn from the country's intelligentsia. As the charmingly pedantic emcee of *Information Please,* he brought to the microphone individuals who were thought unlikely to build a meaningful rapport with most radio listeners. The NBC program's fast-cracking panel of regulars — Franklin P. Adams, John Kieran and Oscar Levant — and its ingratiating host moved briskly along an intellectual race track that few parallel series could tread upon. A 1941 *Current Biography* profile noted Fadiman's "perfect mixture of bright interest and delicate malice that spurs the experts to do their desperate best." He considered himself a purveyor of culture to the masses through a showmanship-like stump-the-pros panel game. At its peak some ten million listeners tuned in.

Educated at Columbia University where he edited an undergrad publication and sold rare books, Fadi-

Clifton Fadiman (courtesy of Broadcast Pioneers Library at University of Maryland)

man taught English, lectured on literary classics and edited books. In 1933 he joined the *New Yorker* as a reviewer, and briefly read his criticisms over the air. Producer Dan Golenpaul thought up *Information Please* in 1938. Fadiman did not see it lasting beyond its first sustaining week. But it quickly developed a cult, gained good press pickup, and became one of the five best programs on the air.

The series enjoyed a decade of wide acclaim, then tried to transfer its allure to TV screens. It proved unsuccessful. Fadiman, however, moved into that medium as a host of a talent show and a quiz panel. He also presided over *Conversation,* a radio series devoted to informal talks on almost everything (except politics) with one or more guests. He was also heard on NBC's *Monitor.* A prolific author and editor into the 1990s, he once said, "I'm a writer and kept working at it."

297. FAIRCHILD, Edward (Cookie) (conductor; b. June 1, 1898, New York, NY; d. Feb. 20, 1975, Los Angeles, CA). *Time to Smile* (1938–44); *Take It or Leave It* (1942–44, 1947–50); *Johnny Presents Ginny Simms* (1942–45); *Eddie Cantor Show* (1946–49).

Perennial, workmanlike musical director for Eddie Cantor. Fairchild appeared on Broadway in George White's *Scandals* and led film studio orchestras for Deanna Durbin. A pianist, he often teamed up with Adam Carroll for twin piano selections.

298. FAITH, Percy (conductor; b. April 7, 1908, Toronto, Canada; d. Feb. 9, 1976, Los Angeles, CA). *Carnation Contented Hour* (1940–47); *Pause That Refreshes on the Air* (1947–51); *Woolworth Hour* (1955–56).

When conductor Josef Pasternack died suddenly, Faith stepped in to direct the *Contented Hour* over NBC. A native of Toronto, he had arranged and conducted some of Canada's most popular music programs during the 1930s. His weekly shows from there (*Music by Faith*) were picked up by Mutual. "Faith," wrote an observer, "can make even 'Dancing in the Dark' sound like a little something by Stravinsky, only more familiar to the masses." His easy listening sounds assured a place on the dial until television pushed aside live music. Faith's full-scale orchestrations were heard on more than 45 albums for Columbia which he joined as musical director in 1950.

299. FARRELL, Eileen (singer [signature song: "Let My Song Fill Your Heart"]; b. Feb. 13, 1920, Willimantic, CT). *Eileen Farrell Sings* (1941); *Songs of the Centuries* (1941); *American Melody Hour* (1943); *Prudential Family Hour* (1943–46).

A CBS staff singer who honed her magnificent operatic voice by performing everything from Gershwin to Gluck in the 1940s. She auditioned for a radio chorus in 1940, but within months emerged as a

Eileen Farrell

Alice Faye

soloist. CBS director of music Davidson Taylor, who gave her this opportunity, remarked that her rendition of a Stephen Foster melody could bring tears to a listener's eyes. A soprano, she made her formal debut impersonating Rosa Ponselle on a *March of Time* broadcast.

In 1947 Farrell turned to the concert hall and opera, making her Met debut in 1960. Her five seasons there embraced such dramatic soprano roles as Leonora in *La Forza del Destino* and the name part in *La Gioconda*. Her performances of Wagner opera were outstanding. Toscanini chose her as a soloist with the NBC Symphony's broadcast of Beethoven's Ninth Symphony. She also sang with the New York Philharmonic under the baton of Leonard Bernstein. Later, she taught voice at Hartford's Hartt School of Music.

300. FAYE, Alice (singer, actress [signature song: "You'll Never Know"]; b. May 5, 1915, New York, NY*). *Phil Harris—Alice Faye Show* (1946–54).

In 1946 with two young daughters to raise and nearly 30 films to her credit, Alice Faye left the movies and settled into a weekly radio series with husband-bandleader Phil Harris. Based on their home life in Hollywood, the program stressed domestic felicity to good advantage and wide acclaim (not withstanding critic John Crosby who severely trashed it as "the crudest and least inhibited comedy show in the first fifteen of the Hooper ratings and my only explanation for its persistently large audience is the fact that

At the start of her career Faye gave 1912 as her year of birth.

it reposes comfortably between Jack Benny and Edgar Bergen").

Faye began her stage career at age 14, chiefly as a dancer in a Chester Hale vaudeville unit. While in the chorus of George White's *Scandals* starring Rudy Vallee, she sang at a backstage party. That led in 1933 to appearances on his *Fleischmann Hour* and in nightclubs. When *Scandals* went into production at Fox in 1934, she was given a role. Before the first week's shooting ended the studio handed her a term contract.

Within short order, the flaxen blonde with the misty, expressive eyes improved consistently in her singing and dancing. She co-starred with Shirley Temple, George Murphy, Tyrone Power, Don Ameche, Betty Grable, John Payne and Carmen Miranda in a dazzling string of well-mounted musicals with scores by Irving Berlin, Harry Warren, Harry Revel and Mack Gordon. Comedian and co-star Jack Oakie introduced her to Phil Harris, and they were married in 1941. She had recently been divorced from singer Tony Martin whom she met when both appeared in *Sing, Baby, Sing* in 1938.

301. FELTON, Verna (actress; b. July 20, 1890, Salinas, CA; d. Dec. 14, 1966, No. Hollywood, CA). *Death Valley Days* (1932–36); *Tommy Riggs and Betty Lou* (1942–43); *Sealtest Village Store* (1942–45); *Judy Canova Show* (1945–53); *Red Skelton Show* (1945–53); *A Day in the Life of Dennis Day* (1950–51).

Motherly character actress who was much in demand as a cast member by West Coast comedians. She played Blossom Blimp with Rudy Vallee, Red Skelton's grandmother, Dennis Day's mom, a member of Gracie Allen's Woman's Uplift Society, Judy Canova's Aunt Agatha, and Don Ameche's mother-in-law. On specials her warm, engaging voice was heard as fairy godmothers and queens. On screen she was heard as the Queen of Hearts in Disney's *Alice in Wonderland.*

For the TV series *December Bride* and *Pete and Gladys,* the cherub-faced stock company-trained Felton gained a reputation as a tireless performer, always game for physical stunts.

302. FENNEMAN, George (announcer; b. Nov. 19, 1919, Peking, China). *You Bet Your Life* (1947– 60); *Dragnet* (1949–56).

Announcer and sidekick for the Groucho Marx-hosted series. Fenneman introduced the contestants, made pitches for the sponsor, and traded quips with Groucho on over 500 shows. TV magazine writer Fredda Balling wrote of their association: "The relationship between George and Groucho is roughly that between wingman and squadron leader. The speed is terrific, so there must be no doubt as to who shall call the next maneuver. George is present to preserve order, to protect the rear . . . and sometimes, unexpectedly, to tow the target."

The suave, handsome Fenneman briefly hosted his own game for ABC-TV, *Anybody Can Play.* His decades of voice-overs, commercials and spokesman roles made him one of broadcasting's longest-working announcers.

303. FENNERLY, Parker (actor [catchphrase: "Howdy, bub."]; b. Oct. 22, 1891, Northeast Harbor, ME; d. Jan. 22, 1988, Peekskill, NY). *The Stebbens Boys* (1931–32); *Snow Village Sketches* (1942–43); *Fred Allen Show* (1945–49).

Known for his portrayal of doleful old Yankee characters, the Maine-born actor is best remembered as Titus Moody, the cryptic New Englander of Allen's Alley. His earlier performances as crusty Down East types were heard on *Ellen Randolph* and *The Stebbens Boys of Bucksport Point.* He also appeared on *Grand Central Station* and *Cavalcade of America,* on Broadway and films, and as the TV spokesman for Pepperidge Farm products. He played the title role in the short-lived *Lawyer Dan Tucker* over CBS in 1947. "I was born old," he said at age 90, "and I played old parts most of my life."

304. FIDLER, Jimmie (commentator [catchphrase: "Good night to you, and you, and I do mean you!"]; b. Aug. 24, 1900, St. Louis, MO; d. Aug. 9, 1988, Los Angeles, CA). *Jimmie Fidler* (1934–40, 1942–50).

Purveyor of Hollywood gossip, he "dished the dirt" in Winchell-like style over some 500 stations each week to 20 million people. His column appeared in 360 newspapers at its peak in 1950. He reputedly recruited a network of studio spies to give him the bits

of gossip that often infuriated members of the Hollywood community. From his broadcasts and columns, he earned more than $250,000 a year. His major sponsors were Tangee lipstick and Arid ("To be sure") deodorant. His gossip-gathering rivals were Winchell, Louella Parsons and Hedda Hopper.

Under the name James Marion, he appeared in a few silent films, then became Sid Grauman's publicity manager. When his own publicity firm folded in the 1929 crash, he turned to writing. It led to his first broadcast, a segment on *Hollywood on the Air* in 1932.

305. FIEDLER, Arthur (conductor; b. Dec. 17, 1894, South Boston, MA; d. July 10, 1979, Brookline, MA). *Robert Merrill with the Boston Pops Orchestra* (1948–49); *Boston Pops* (1951, 1955, 1957).

Venerated, vigorous purveyor of familiar light classical and popular music through Boston Pops concerts for over 50 years. A viola player in the Boston Symphony, Fiedler set up an outdoor concert series in 1929 and was rewarded with the conductorship of the Pops the next year. His performances were periodically broadcast in the 1930s but not until the late '40s did they tie up with radio on a weekly basis. He felt his field of good light music was sadly neglected and was proud to bring it to thousands of Bostonians and millions of listeners.

The U.S. Bicentennial concert of the Pops on July 4, 1976 gathered an estimated 400,000 admirers on Boston's Esplanade. It was believed to be the largest audience for a musical event in U.S. history. The city's most famous and most recognizable resident, he also expanded the fame and scope of the Pops through regular PBS telecasts. "I tried to plan every concert to give variety and to please everybody," he remarked at

Arthur Fiedler

the start of his 50th season in 1979. "I like to play music that I like, and I like a lot of music." RCA often sponsored Fiedler, and in 1955 presented him with a silver baton to commemorate the long association which began in 1935.

306. FIELD, Charles K. (Cheerio) (host; b. Sept. 18, 1873, Montpelier, VT; d. Sept. 1, 1948, Newfane, VT). *Cheerio* (1927–40); *Arco Birthday Party* (1930–32).

Purveyor of uplifting philosophy and verse, particularly for shut-ins and the downcast. Cheerio's early morning broadcasts at the "psychological moment" of each day — 8:30 — carried the support of public-service radio advocates. As editor for the National Health Council, he donated his services to radio, initially as a memorial to his mother; the Child Health Association and NBC provided backing, including musical accompaniment and vocal soloists.

Field's identity was a well-kept secret at the start of his morning messages at KGO San Francisco in 1925. At the suggestion of Herbert Hoover, his Stanford University 1895 classmate (they were in its first graduating class), he took the program to NBC New York as a coast-to-coast feature, giving hope, inspiration and comfort to a wider listenership. The series generated several books by Field: *The Story of Cheerio* and *Cheerio's Book of Days*. He retired in 1940. At the end of World War II he volunteered at an Army rehabilitation hospital near San Francisco. He instructed blind veterans in announcing, producing and writing radio scripts, and assisted in putting on shows in the hospital radio workshop.

At the turn of the century, Field had been a life insurance agent and editor of *Sunset*, a magazine created by the Southern Pacific Co. to promote the attractions and resources of the West. In ill health by 1948, Field hanged himself at his summer place in Vermont — a sad ending for one who had devoted years to brightening up the lives of millions of people.

307. FIELDS, Shep (bandleader [signature song: "Fire Dance"]; b. Sept. 12, 1910, Brooklyn, NY; d. Feb. 23, 1981, Los Angeles, CA). *Rippling Rhythm Revue* (1937–41).

Fields said he got the idea for the Rippling Rhythm introduction in 1936 when he saw and heard his wife blowing on a straw into an ice cream soda. It caused the soda to gurgle musically. The next day at rehearsal, he brought a small goldfish bowl filled with water and two straws. From then on, Fields produced the distinctive sound of a babbling brook before every performance — and the unique musical style changed the course of his activities.

The rippling rhythm, with the reeds, a violin and a sharply muted trumpet playing staccato melody, went out over the air in hundreds of broadcasts. The unusual approach brought him extensive theatre and supper club engagements and the films *Rippling Rhythm*

Shep Fields

and *The Big Broadcast of 1938*. His first commercial program was *Radio Guide's Court of Honor*, and he made several appearances on *RCA Magic Key* to showcase his rickety-tick arrangements and promote his Victor discs. In the 1960s he joined the Hollywood talent agency, Creative Management Associates, as vice president in charge of TV specials.

308. FIO RITO, Ted (bandleader [signature song: "Rio Rita"]; b. Dec. 20, 1900, Newark, NJ; d. July 22, 1971, Scottsdale, AZ). *Presenting Al Jolson* (1932–33); *Hollywood Hotel* (1934–35); *Jack Haley Show* (1937–38).

A pianist, he started out in a movie house, then had an orchestra at 18 in Atlantic City. It evolved into Russo-Fio Rito orchestra until Ted bought out Dan Russo. In 1919 he ventured into a makeshift radio studio for his first broadcast, and operated his own station, WIBO while playing at Edgewater Beach Hotel in Chicago. His roaring '20s compositions — "Toot Toot Tootsie," "Laugh, Clown, Laugh" and "Charley, My Boy" — became popular favorites.

In the 1930s Fio Rito had a knack for discovering talent. They included eyecatching vocalists Betty Grable, June Haver and Lucille Ball, and able pianist David Rose. Thirty years later Las Vegas audiences were still enjoying his sweet music.

309. FISHER, Eddie (singer [signature song: "Any Time"]; b. Aug. 10, 1928, Philadelphia, PA). *Capitol Serenade* (1951); *Stars in Khaki 'n' Blue* (1952); *Eddie Fisher Show* (1953–56).

Network radio's biggest male singer-teen idol of the 1950s. Discovered by Eddie Cantor at Grossinger's in the Catskills during the 1949 Labor Day weekend, Fisher joined his radio show and made a cross-country tour, and within a year disc jockeys proclaimed him "America's Most Promising Male Vocalist." For RCA Victor, Fisher tallied 22 hits in a row in a clear, bold style, a departure from the then-prevailing subdued approach to a crooner's song.

His own series for Coca-Cola in 1953 followed a two-year stint as a GI vocalist with a U.S. Army Band and songs on NBC's *Stars in Khaki 'n' Blue.* By 1955 his *Coke Time* broadcasts were the audio portion of his TV show. His well-publicized marital alliances and breakups soon overshadowed his fine voice — one of the best of the era that preceded the birth of rock and roll.

At 13 Fisher sang on the *Children's Hour,* and as a teenager was on the bandstands of Buddy Morrow and Charlie Ventura.

310. FITZGERALD, Pegeen (host [catchphrase: "We're the Fitz-G's."]; b. 1910, Norcatur, KS; d. Jan. 30, 1989, New York, NY). *The Fitzgeralds* (1945–53).

At-home format pioneer. Longtime talk show co-host, she, with husband Ed Fitzgerald, broadcast mainly on WOR from the couple's Manhattan apartment. Beginning in 1940, they traded commentary on local happenings and events, laced with Gaelic wit and homespun wisdom. Chiefly a morning feature, the program moved onto the ABC network in the mid-40s but never built a big following outside the metropolitan New York area. Their only script was commercials, which they themselves styled and wove in at random.

The Fitzgeralds married in San Francisco in 1930. He was a theatrical press agent and began in 1936 at WOR with *Book Talk, Back Talk and Small Talk* and the all-night *Almanac de Gotham.* Pegeen, an advertising copywriter and department store fashion director, started a WOR show from the 1939 World's Fair. They soon teamed up. Periodically, station executives phased them off the dial but the irremovable duo resurfaced at the insistence of their loyal audience and continued with few breaks until Ed died at 89 in early 1982. Pegeen continued a talk program on WOR — by this point a late evening feature — and later on at WNYC until April 1988, with the long-familiar accompaniment of the purring of a dozen or so household cats.

311. FLIPPEN, Jay C. (emcee, comedian; b. March 6, 1900, Little Rock, AR; d. Feb. 3, 1971, Los Angeles, CA). *Stop Me If You've Heard This One* (1939–40); *Battle of the Sexes* (1943–44).

Versatile broadcaster with a minstrel show-vaudeville background. In 1926 he achieved a measure of acclaim on Broadway in *The Great Temptations* with Jack Benny. Radio work, often at local New York transmitters, proved lucrative in the 1930s. He introduced amateur program contestants, presided as quizmaster, acted as an interlocutor, appeared as a panelist, sang novelty numbers, and pitched in as a sportscaster. In 1931 he participated in the inauguration of "radio talkies," the pioneering sound television experiments in which performers were seen on a primitive TV screen and heard via a radio beam.

After World War II Flippen left New York for Hollywood where he made over 50 films and played in TV's *Ensign O'Toole.* The raspy voice matched the craggy face in roles as ranch foreman, baseball coach and sheriff.

312. FLYNN, Bernardine (actress; b. Jan. 2, 1904, Madison, WI; d. March 10, 1977, Clay City, IL). *Vic and Sade* (1932–44).

As Sade, this Chicago performer launched one of that city's keystone programs. Sponsored by Proctor & Gamble's Crisco, it reached seven million listeners from WMAQ for a dozen years. The show was created and written by Paul Rhymer.

At the University of Wisconsin, Flynn had majored in speech and acted in plays with fellow student Don Ameche. Campus productions brought wide acclaim and led to minor roles in several Broadway plays. She entered radio after winning an audition at NBC on the strength of her French accent. She worked for a time in such soaps as *Public Hero No. 1* and *Right to Happiness,* and on the talk show, *Daytime Newspaper,* with Durward Kirby. In 1950 NBC cast her in the lead of its early TV serial *Hawkins Falls.*

313. FOLEY, Red (singer; [signature song: "Peace in the Valley"]; b. June 17, 1910, Blue Lick, KY; d. Sept. 19, 1968, Fort Wayne, IN). *National Barn Dance* (1941–44); *Grand Ole Opry* (1946–53); *Red Foley Show* (1950–51, 1957–59).

Red Foley (courtesy of Capital Cities/ABC)

Country and western music Hall of Famer. Foley was a major influence during the formative years of contemporary country music. He appeared in the early 1930s on the WLS *Barn Dance* with a group called the Cumberland Ridge Runners. A decade later he was one of its headliners with his guitar and vocals. A baritone, he is believed to have made the first commercial country recordings (1945) in Nashville. At the session, Foley sang "Tennessee Border," "Blues in the Heart" and "Tennessee Saturday Night."

In 1946 he became singing emcee of the *Opry*, replacing Roy Acuff on the network part of the show. He also had his own show, recorded chiefly at the Jewell Theatre in Springfield, Missouri, and his TV series, *Ozark Jubilee*, both in the 1950s. Foley, who had much success on pop and gospel numbers, later returned to Nashville for *Opry* broadcasts and made personal appearance tours.

314. FORD, Edward (Senator) (comedian; b. 1887, Brooklyn, NY; d. Jan. 27, 1970, Greenport, NY). *Can You Top This?* (1940–48, 1950–51, 1953–54).

Permanent member of the panel of joke tellers on *Can You Top This?* Ford apparently created the informal joke sessions with cronies Joe Laurie, Jr. and Harry Hershfield and got them on WOR-Mutual. For years he had entertained at banquets and conventions, and from the vaudeville stage as a monologist. He added the "Senator" prefix to enhance his status as an after-dinner speaker. Listed as a commentator by NBC Artists Service, Ford was famous for his wit, drolleries and pronouncements of plain Yankee common sense, all reinforced with a dour demeanor.

315. FORD, Whitey (comedian [Duke of Paducah] [catchphrase: "I'm going to the wagon, these shoes are killin' me."]; b. May 12, 1901, DeSoto, MO; d. June 20, 1986). *Plantation Party* (1938–43); *Grand Ole Opry* (1943–47).

Emcee and comedian of *Grand Ole Opry* in the 1940s. A banjo player, he toured as Ford & Van and with the Oklahoma Cowboys. Ford first appeared on radio with his own band in 1925 at KTHS Hot Springs. As a single, he became Gene Autry's emcee at WLS and originated Mutual's *Renfro Barn Dance* in 1938. Ford did many local shows over KMOX and WLW, and remained a constant *Opry* visitor until 1959. Locke Stove Co. sponsored his *Duke of Paducah & Opry Gang* series in 1952.

316. FOSDICK, Harry Emerson (preacher; b. May 24, 1878, Buffalo, NY; d. Oct. 5, 1969, Bronxville, NY). *National Vespers* (1927–46).

Pragmatic urban preacher. His theological liberalism on social and economic issues led *The New York Times* in 1969 to describe him as a "pivotal figure in American Protestant history." Founding pastor of New York's Riverside Church in 1927, Dr. Fosdick began

his weekly *National Vespers* that year and widened his audience via NBC in 1930. In addition, he was a frequent speaker on NBC's *National Radio Pulpit.*

A graduate of Union Theological Seminary, he first reached listeners in 1922 while minister at Manhattan's First Presbyterian Church. A traditionist in his sermons and writings—his book *The Meaning of Prayer* became a best-selling classic in its field—he, nonetheless, often expressed disdain for contemporary radio preacher-fundamentalists who bespoke basic intolerance.

317. FOSTER, Cedric (commentator; b. Aug. 31, 1900, Hartford, CT; d. March 12, 1975, Denver, CO). *News & Commentary* (1940–67).

News analyst for Mutual and the Yankee Network. The first daytime news commentator on MBS, he had the same radio time, 1 p.m. Eastern, for some 20 years. Foster was heard on a co-op basis over 300 stations, Monday through Friday, in every state of the Union by 1948.

He started his broadcast career in 1935 as manager of WTHT Hartford, where he had his own nightly commentary on international affairs. Just before World War II, he joined Mutual in Boston. His assignments led to 50 transatlantic crossings and three trips around the world. He was also a correspondent in the Philippines in 1945.

Retiring from Mutual in 1967, he settled in Denver where he continued as a personality on KTLN and KVOD. In 1975 Foster was honored by the Colorado Broadcasters Association for his lifetime of dedication to broadcast news. He had attended Dartmouth Col-

Cedric Foster (courtesy of Broadcast Pioneers Library at University of Maryland)

lege for a year, then traveled around the country. He returned to Connecticut to become a police reporter and financial editor for the *Hartford Times.*

318. FRANCIS, Anne (actress [The Little Queen of Soap Operas]; b. Sept. 16, 1930, Ossining, NY). *When a Girl Marries* (1943–46).

From age five, a model and actress. The honey blond-haired youngster began on *Coast-to-Coast on a Bus, Let's Pretend* and the *Madge Tucker Show,* and advanced to such soaps as *Aunt Jenny* and *When a Girl Marries* (as Kathy). In 1941 Anne had her own TV storytelling show at CBS and a part on Broadway in *Lady in the Dark.* Film roles (*Lydia Bailey, Blackboard Jungle*) and video work (*Versatile Varieties*) led to her first regular TV series, *Honey West;* she played the sexy sleuth. She built a solid reputation as a forthright, honest and unpretentious performer. Her autobiography *Voice from Home,* was published in 1982.

319. FRANCIS, Arlene (emcee, actress; b. Oct. 20, 1910, Boston, MA). *What's My Name?* (1938–43); *Betty and Bob* (1939–42); *Portia Faces Life* (1941–42); *Light of the World* (1942–43); *Blind Date* (1943–46).

Her experience as one of radio's earliest game show emcees provided excellent training for future spontaneous ad-libbing assignments as a talk show moderator, interviewer, hostess and panelist. Co-emcee with Budd Hulick on *What's My Name?* over Mutual, the vivacious and witty Francis handled this audience-participation quiz with smooth professionalism as was further displayed on *Blind Date* in the 1940s.

In the early 1930s she studied for a year at the Theatre Guild Dramatic School, and was allowed by her father, who disapproved of an acting career, to perform on radio. Roles on *March of Time* and *Beatrice Lillie Show* helped persuade him that her talent would take her far in show business. On television she was best known for *What's My Line?* where she appeared as a panelist, beginning in 1950 for a quarter of a century. In 1957 she became moderator of NBC Radio's *Family Living.*

320. FRANKEL, Harry (singer [Singin' Sam]; b. Jan. 27, 1888, Hillsboro, OH; d. June 12, 1948, Richmond, IN).

Forever linked to Barbasol shaving cream and its enduring singing jingle, the deep-voiced Frankel sold tons of this popular men's product through his frequent musical series. A bass, he sang "Bar-ba-sol . . . Bar-ba-sol. No brush, no lather, no rub in, wet your razor, then begin," to the melody of a turn-of-the-century song entitled "Tammy," beginning in 1930 for CBS. At one point he was on both Columbia and NBC for this sponsor.

A minstrel man and vaudeville singer, he was first heard on radio while playing with black-face comic partner Joe Dunlevy in Minneapolis. It was a means of advertising the theatre. The duo used only a ukelele for accompaniment. The station manager, so impressed with their songs and jokes, offered them a contract. They could not accept it because of their agreement with the Keith circuit, but Harry gave it a great deal of thought. In 1929 he alone auditioned at WLW Cincinnati. It started a career that carried his folksy voice from coast to coast and sold everything from lawn mowers to coffee.

In 1936 his wife, vaudeville singer Helene "Smiles" Davis, persuaded him to end his ties with the Barbasol Company because he was losing his identity. He signed with Coca-Cola to promote the new six-bottle carton. His programs of old-time songs were transcribed, enabling him to live in his favorite place, Richmond, Indiana, in a large southern colonial home on 49 acres. Three days out of every two weeks he would go to New York to record the shows. In the 1940s Frankel made a series of 260 transcriptions through his own company for world-wide syndication. For years after his death, local stations continued to contract for segments of this troubadour, "Your old friend Singin' Sam."

321. FRAY, Jacques (pianist, disc jockey [signature song: "Frere Jacques"]; b. Feb. 18, 1903, Paris, France; d. Jan. 20, 1963, New York, NY). *Fray and Braggiotti* (1931–37).

With no formal training in music, this well-to-do banker's son picked up popular tunes by observing and playing with accomplished pianists, including his two-piano partner Mario Braggiotti. They had met in 1927 in a Paris cafe noted for piano entertainment. Together, they introduced much of George Gersh-

Jacques Fray (courtesy of Mario Braggiotti)

win's music to European audiences, and were the first to play both popular and classical music on the same program. Internationally known as "The first team — the last word" from their concerts, recordings and broadcasts.

Network radio embraced their talents for regular series and guest spots. These skillful keyboard giants briefly broke up in the mid-30s when Mario wanted to perform more classical pieces. But they soon reunited until the war took them in different directions. In 1947 Fray began a run of nearly 16 years as a classical disc jockey each afternoon at WQXR New York. At his sudden death in 1963, his ex-partner took his place at the microphone for several seasons.

322. FREBERG, Stan (comedian; b. Aug. 7, 1926, Los Angeles, CA). *That's Rich* (1953–54); *Stan Freberg Show* (1957).

Satirist-comic who is generally acknowledged as the last network radio comedian. Freberg replaced Jack Benny in mid-1957. In spite of rave critical reaction, he failed to pick up a sponsor and was dropped after three months. Wrote critic John Crosby: "Freberg is not only a satirist but a man with a great gift for fantasy, which is sometimes delightful and sometimes gets him into trouble. . . . He is essentially a sound man, and he knows how to call into play the imagination of his listeners."

He first jumped into radio as an early a.m. man-on-the-street interviewer. It was difficult to find people so he became a "one-man mob," supplying voices as needed. By 1947 CBS employed him to produce animal sounds, namely Black Beauty's whinny. He graduated to bird watcher Richard E. Wilt on *That's Rich.* Stan struck paydirt with his parodies on Capitol Recordings of *Dragnet* ("St. George and the Dragonet"), soap operas ("John and Marsha"), DJ payola scandals ("The Old Payola Roll Blues") and Sen. Joe McCarthy ("Point of Order"). Writer of offbeat advertising for such companies as Kaiser Aluminum, Mars Candy and GM, he started his ad firm with the straightforward motto: "Ars Gratia Pecuniae" (Art for Money). His autobiography was called *It Only Hurts When I Laugh.*

323. FREDERICK, Pauline (news analyst; b. Feb. 1908, Gallitzin, PA; d. May 9, 1990, Lake Forest, IL).

In the 1940s and early '50s, she was the only woman network news analyst and diplomatic correspondent in American radio. She considered law as a career before deciding to pursue journalism. Based in Washington as a reporter for *U.S. News and World Report* and the North American Newspaper Alliance, she made her first network broadcast in 1939 and did occasional interviews for NBC.

At all three networks Frederick had her own program, chiefly covering world affairs, the UN and political conventions. Her first overseas broadcast originated in China in 1945. She served as NBC's correspondent at the UN from 1953 to 1974, and received a Peabody Award (1954) and the Paul White Radio-TV News Directors Association Award (1980). "I never believed there was such a thing as 'women's news.'" she said in 1956. "I think news is news; that's all."

324. FREEMAN, Florence (actress; b. July 29, 1911, New York, NY). *Young Widder Brown* (1937–56); *A Woman of America* (1944–46); *Wendy Warren and The News* (1947–58).

Dramatic actress who created the lead Ellen Brown on the durable soap *Young Widder Brown.* She began the role as *Young Widder Jones* on Mutual in 1937; Jones segued into Brown when NBC picked up the series in September 1938. Freeman also played Wendy Warren, a radio news reporter, on a serial that was preceded by five minutes of actual news aired by CBS newsman Douglas Edwards. Her other credits include the title role on *Valiant Lady,* and supporting parts on *Jane Arden, David Harum* and *Abie's Irish Rose.*

After studying for a teaching career at Wells College and Columbia University, Freeman taught English for several years. In 1933 she auditioned and was hired at a small station. A typical broadcast day extended from 9 a.m. to midnight. Her network activities began two years later in New York.

325. FROMAN, Jane (singer [signature song: "With a Song in My Heart"]; b. Nov. 10, 1907, St. Louis, MO; d. April 22, 1980, Columbia, MO). *Florsheim Frolic* (1931–32); *Bromo Seltzer Hour* (1934–35); *Gulf Musical Playhouse* (1939).

Jane Froman

Her near-death experience in a USO plane crash overseas during World War II and her painful recovery and courageous struggle to return to singing largely overshadowed her earlier accomplishments. She started out as a journalism student at the University of Missouri but teachers and choral groups always invited her to sing. After playing the contralto lead in her senior class operetta, the Cincinnati Conservatory of Music awarded her a scholarship to study voice. There she worked for WLW, sponsored by a maker of toasted peanuts, and soon had 22 commercial programs a week at ten dollars a broadcast.

Her one a.m. WLW show was piped into New York where Paul Whiteman heard her. He wired asking if she would meet him in Chicago for an audition. Jane was hardly off the train in Chicago when she fell down a flight of stairs and broke her ankle — just 15 minutes before her appointment with the conductor-showman. But she made her date and sang in spite of the pain shooting through her leg. Jane got through 12 songs before she lost consciousness. To Jane, Whiteman seemed more concerned with getting a doctor than with critiquing her voice. When finally offered a contract she signed for a prime-time build-up.

A popular pre-war radio star, she appeared on *Palmolive Beauty Box Theatre* and *The Pause That Refreshes.* Jane often sang for President Franklin D. Roosevelt; in 1940 he asked her to appear in the first USO show at Ft. Belvoir, Virginia. In 1943 she forfeited nightclub engagements and a Ziegfeld Follies role to answer an overseas call for USO volunteers to entertain troops in Europe. As her Yankee Clipper flight prepared to land in Lisbon, the airplane crashed and exploded in the Tagus River, killing 24 of the 39 persons aboard. A survivor, co-pilot John Burn, swam to Jane's side and held her head above water for 45 minutes until they were rescued. She suffered two broken legs, a broken arm, fractured ribs and other injuries. She subsequently underwent over 25 operations. After years in a wheelchair and on crutches, she eventually walked unaided. But she never let her strong, melodious voice get out of form. Froman returned to Broadway, supper clubs, radio and military base tours. She added television appearances in the early '50s. Her life story became a box office success in 1952. Susan Hayward starred in the film depiction, *With a Song in My Heart,* with Jane dubbing the 26 musical numbers.

Froman was married to radio singer Donald Ross, then in 1948 wed Burn, the pilot who pulled her from the air crash wreckage. After paying medical bills estimated at $500,000 over a period of 15 years, she retired in 1962 and settled in Columbia, Missouri with third husband Rowland Smith, a college friend and journalist.

326. FROST, Alice (actress; b. Aug. 1, 1910, Minneapolis, MN). *Big Sister* (1936–42); *Town Hall Tonight* (1937–40); *Mr. & Mrs. North* (1942–50).

Alice Frost

A mainstay at CBS, she played a variety of roles on the *Columbia Workshop, Mercury Theatre on the Air* and *Suspense.* She entered radio in 1935 after bit parts in five Broadway plays. A master dialectician, Frost portrayed female stooges with Fred Allen, Walter O'Keefe, Ken Murray and Robert Benchley. While starring in *Big Sister,* she met and married its director, Wilson Tuttle. As Pamela North she helped husband Jerry (Joseph Curtin) solve the weekly whodunit on *Mr. & Mrs. North.*

Frost also had recurring roles on *David Harum* and *Lorenzo Jones.* Voted the best dressed woman in radio, she once played the gold-digging Lorelei in a Chautauqua circuit tour of *Gentlemen Prefer Blondes.* She first reached Broadway via the Theatre Guild's *Green Grow the Lilacs* in 1931.

327. FULLER, Barbara (actress; b. July 21, 1921, Nahant, MA). *Madame Courageous* (1938); *Light of the World* (1942–43); *His Honor, the Barber* (1945–46); *One Man's Family* (1945–59).

As a young child, Fuller was always reading — never without a book in her hands. An observant actor-friend, Harvey Hayes of NBC, asked her mother if he could audition her to see if she read well aloud. She did, and joined NBC Chicago in 1932. Her first program, *The Eye of Montezuma* — a daily children's show — featured Joan Blaine and George Gobel. Her second, *Salty Sam,* starred Cliff Soubier, a favorite of youngsters.

By her late teens, Barbara had ingenue leads on *Painted Dreams* and *Stepmother* — her father was played

Barbara Fuller (courtesy of Barbara Fuller)

Jack Fulton (courtesy of Michael S. Fulton)

by Francis X. Bushman, and later by Willard Waterman. In 1942 she moved to New York for *Manhattan at Midnight* and *Armstrong Theatre of Today*. On the West Coast three years later, Fuller assumed the part of Claudia on *One Man's Family*, her longest-running role. Republic Pictures signed her for films while prime time featured her on *Lux Radio Theatre* (opposite Ronald Reagan, Jeff Chandler, Mickey Rooney) and with Abbott and Costello. "I never kept much in the way of scrapbooks," she recalled in 1995, "because I thought radio would go on forever and I had so many credits, they just piled up."

During her career she studied acting with George Shdanoff and Michael Chekhov, and once worked under the direction of Charlie Chaplin in a Los Angeles Circle Theatre production (one of his sons had a supporting role). Since the 1970s Fuller has produced and marketed inspirational radio talks and audio tapes of Dr. William Hornaday, a leading metaphysical teacher.

328. FULTON, Jack (singer; b. June 13, 1903, Philipsburg, PA; d. Oct. 17, 1993, Rancho Bernardo, CA). *Old Gold Hour* (1929–30); *Paul Whiteman's Painters Show* (1931–32); *Poetic Melodies* (1936–38); *Moon River* (1941–42).

Romantic tenor featured by Paul Whiteman from 1926 to 1935. He often harmonized with the orchestra's "sweet trio" in contrast to the jazz-oriented Rhythm Boys, sparked by Bing Crosby. Originally a trombone player-vocalist with George Olsen, Fulton became a bandleader and program host-soloist, chiefly

out of WBBM Chicago. His *Penthouse Serenade* and *Poetic Melodies* showcased his soft-voiced approach to love and sentimental songs. He composed some 120 songs, including the popular "Wanted," "Until" and "My Greatest Mistake." Fulton continued as a staff musician to the mid-50s.

329. FUNT, Allen (host; b. Sept. 16, 1914, Brooklyn, NY). *Candid Microphone* (1947–48, 1950).

Imaginative creator, producer, director and host. His clever hidden mike idea to capture human interest situations became an enthusiastically received series. His recorded interviews and encounters without being recognized proved highly amusing and refreshingly natural. They transferred well to television in the late 1940s as *Candid Camera,* and continued as a practical joke series or segment periodically for many years. TV co-hosts ranged from Garry Moore and Arthur Godfrey to Bess Myerson and Dorothy Collins.

Prior to World War II, Funt, a Cornell graduate, started as a gimmick man who created ideas and stunts for radio shows. He wrote and produced the audience-participation program, *The Funny Money Man,* on which listeners were paid odd amounts for odd objects sent to the show. He also wrote the continuity for one of Eleanor Roosevelt's programs. Service in the U.S. Army ultimately led to his "candid" career. As part of the Signal Corps, he recorded soldiers' voices for back home. Funt discovered that, to avoid mike fright and self-consciousness, concealed equipment produced spontaneous and often hilarious remarks.

In 1946 Mutual hired him to carry out in-the-field experiments with hidden mikes and to record off-the-cuff responses to his badgering. Before his idea of eavesdropping came into full play, that network dropped him. But ABC shaped the format into an half-hour show. Since the 1950s his broadcasts have been used in psychology, sociology and speech courses in many colleges.

330. GALLOP, Frank (announcer; b. June 30, c1910, Boston, MA). *An Evening with Romberg* (1945); *Milton Berle Show* (1947–48); *Monitor* (1955–56).

Foreboding, shuddery voice as announcer, commentator and narrator on soaps, crime thrillers, comedies and concerts. His deep portentous, patrician tone gained the tag as "inventor of instant gooseflesh." Listeners heard Gallop on *Gangbusters, Hilltop House, Stella Dallas* and New York Philharmonic broadcasts. On television with Perry Como, he became the show's "invisible" offscreen announcer-foil. He played a similar meddling voice vis-a-vis Milton Berle on radio.

Gallop started out as a brokerage firm customer's man. He entered radio as the result of a client's complaint over program announcing, circa 1935. Gallop was urged to try for a job at the mike. He won an audition at WEEI Boston but kept his daytime stock trading work. Ten months later he moved on to CBS New York. Because of his princely intonation he was often mistaken for an Englishman.

331. GAMBARELLI, Maria (ballerina [Gamby]; b. 1900, La Spezia, Italy; d. Feb. 4, 1990, Huntington, NY). *Roxy's Gang* (1922–28); *Dance with Gamby* (1930).

Samuel (Roxy) Rothafel's premiere danseuse at New York's Capitol Theatre in shows that accompanied silent films and in broadcasts with his Gang. Roxy promoted his screen-stage presentations by a backstage WEAF hookup featuring his regular performers. Maria felt radio offered no room for a dancer. She sat in an obscure corner of the broadcast room, enjoying all the other artists. "Suddenly, like a bolt from the blue, I heard Roxy say one evening: 'Well, there's little Gamby; come here, Gamby.' I turned from pink to red when I realized I was discovered sitting on the sidelines. Although I can't remember what I did that first broadcast, the fans seemed to like it, and from that time on I broadcast regularly, singing Italian songs and reciting little poems."

In a light soprano voice, she often sang with Roxy baritone Douglas Stanbury. When Roxy opened his Roxy Theatre in 1927, she continued with the Gang for another year. In 1930 Gamby gave over-the-air dance lessons — an eight-week course at WJZ. But as a dancer on stage, she made her greatest impression. As a child, she had received ballet training as a member of the Metropolitan Opera dance ensemble. She was determined to return as its prima ballerina — and did in 1939 for two seasons. Gamby also directed pre-

Maria Gambarelli

cision dance groups, choreographed for ballet companies, and performed in films. Putting aside her dancing shoes in the 1940s, she acted on television and in summer stock.

332. GAMBLING, John B. (host [signature song: "Pack Up Your Troubles in Your Old Kit Bag"]; b. April 9, 1897, Norwich, England; d. Nov. 21, 1974, Palm Beach, FL). *Your Personal Program* (1936–37); *John B. Gambling Club* (1952).

Scion of three generations of broadcasters. The Gambling name is closely identified with talk radio, particularly in metropolitan New York. In 1925, John B., a wireless operator-radio technician, stepped in as an impromptu host for absent physical culturist Bernarr Macfadden on WOR's morning exercise class. His articulate British voice caused a flurry of calls from listeners who wanted to know his name. Management signed him for wake-up news, weather reports, music intros and general chatter along with calisthenics.

A regional program, it was called *The Musical Clock,* prior to becoming *Rambling with Gambling* in 1948, and remained the early bird slot of Gambling for over three decades. He celebrated his 30th anni-

Food commentator Alfred W. McCann, Jr., John B. Gambling

versary in 1955 with a record-breaking party at Madison Square Garden. Some 27,000 fans turned out to honor him. One of his few network series, *Your Personal Program,* was sponsored by Beneficial Management at NBC.

Gambling's son, John A. (b. 1930) inherited the morning spot in 1959 and made it the highest rated a.m. program in the country. Grandson John R. (b. 1950) came to WOR as a staff announcer in 1978 and soon filled the shoes of his father and in the 1990s his twin sons, teenagers Andrew John and Bradley John (b. 1980) were already warming up in the wings.

John B. Gambling went to sea with the Royal Navy in World War I, and later served as the wireless chief on British and American passenger ships. When his American-born wife insisted he work on land, he found a job in broadcasting. In 1951 he described the most embarrassing incident that ever happened on his show. One morning a Western Union boy walked into the WOR studio with a telegram. Gambling said to him, "Sonny, wouldn't you like to say something to the radio audience?" He faced the mike and yelled: "Aw get up, you lazy bums!"

333. GARBER, Jan (bandleader [The Idol of the Air Waves] [signature song: "My Dear"]; b. Nov. 5, 1897, Norristown, PA; d. Oct. 5, 1977, Shreveport, LA). *Jan Garber Supper Club* (1934–35).

Chiefly a "sweet style" outfit heard on many remotes, Garber's dance orchestra enjoyed a short stint with Burns and Allen (1938), but had few other commercial series. He remained an "idol" for late-night fans who picked up his broadcasts from ballrooms and dance halls around the country. A violinist, he briefly played with the Philadelphia Orchestra and served as

a band director for the armed forces during World War I. He formed the "semi-hot" Garber-Davis Orchestra in the early 1920s.

334. GARDE, Betty (actress; b. Sept. 19, 1905, Philadelphia, PA; d. Dec. 25, 1989, Sherman Oaks, CA). *Mrs. Wiggs of the Cabbage Patch* (1936–38); *Lorenzo Jones* (1937–40); *Quaker Party with Tommy Riggs* (1939–40); *Aldrich Family* (1946–47).

Usually cast as a mother, an aunt or a middle-aged friend of the family, the tall and lively Garde was ideally cast in the role of the rough and ready Aunt Eller in the original Broadway production of *Oklahoma.* Radio serials had given a solid foundation, particularly from portrayals of Mrs. Wiggs and Lorenzo Jones's wife Belle. She often performed on Orson Welles specials and with comedians Henry Morgan and Eddie Cantor. Hers was the voice of the Jergens commercial on the Walter Winchell program. She both starred in and directed the soap *My Son and I* in 1939–40. Her later acting credits included *The Big Story, Theatre Guild on the Air* and *Cavalcade of America.*

When Betty was new to radio, she had not had a chance to learn the director's signals. On a CBS program, he gave her the sign from the booth to stretch, but she thought he was telling her she was too close to the microphone and backed up. As the signal continued so did Garde. Finally the director came out of the booth with a hastily printed sign, and lay flat on his back and held it under her chin telling her to stretch for *time* and come back to the mike.

335. GARDINER, Don (newscaster; b. Jan. 10, 1916; d. March 27, 1977, Quoque, NY). *Monday Morning Headlines* (1944–58).

His Sunday evening news program ran on ABC from the war years to the close of the Eisenhower era. His sponsors for the weekly 15-minute staple included Air Wick, Old Gold and Mutual of Omaha. Gardiner also was announcer on *Gangbusters, When a Girl Marries* and *Counterspy.*

He started as a page with NBC. Before joining the Blue Network in New York in 1943, he was an announcer with WAIR Winston-Salem and WRC Washington. He covered special events, such as the inauguration of President Franklin D. Roosevelt in 1941.

336. GARDNER, Ed (comedian; b. June 29, 1901, Astoria, NY; d. Aug. 17, 1963, Los Angeles, CA). *Duffy's Tavern* (1941–51).

The world never heard Duffy but they relished the pure New Yorkese of Archie the manager of the Third Avenue saloon ("where the elite meet to eat"). The program began with Gardner answering the phone and playing it straight as the colorful barkeep who dispensed a mix of practical wisdom and zany advice to a host of regulars — Clancy the Cop, Finnigan and Eddie the Waiter — and a guest star.

The New York-born actor created the picturesque character in the late 1930s but found no one to play him. While demonstrating the voice he wanted, Gardner noticed the guys in the control room having hysterics. The role became his, and he built a whole show around the bartender. An immediate success, it attracted seven million listeners, became a movie and turned up in a TV version.

Gardner started out as a salesman of pianos and miniature golf courses, then switched to show business in 1929 after marrying Shirley Booth (she created the part of Miss Duffy). He directed WPA shows and worked for an ad agency. His first radio venture, *This Is New York,* at CBS never found a sponsor. But its focus on city people from cabbies to celebrities inspired Gardner's Archie.

In the late '50s brief taped segments of *Duffy's Tavern* ran on NBC's *Monitor.* He later worked as a producer-director in the TV department of J. Walter Thompson.

337. GARGAN, William (actor; b. July 17, 1905, Brooklyn, NY; d. Feb. 16, 1979, San Diego, CA). *I Deal in Crime* (1945–47); *Martin Kane, Private Eye* (1949–50).

A leading sleuth on radio (*Barrie Craig, Murder Will Out*) and in television's first popular detective series (*Martin Kane, Private Eye*). The latter also played on Mutual in 1949. Gargan actually worked as an investigator for a credit agency before landing his first acting role at 20. The part in *Aloma of the South Seas* on Broadway led to other stage roles in *Chicago* and *Animal Kingdom* and screen work in *They Knew What They Wanted* and *A Close Call for Ellery Queen.* Gargan's face became familiar to audiences as he portrayed a range of characters from policemen to a U.S. President.

His career ended in 1960 when he was stricken with cancer of the larynx. Losing his voice box, he mastered the technique of esophageal speech. The once-heavy smoker became a spokesman for the American Cancer Society, demonstrating the ability to overcome his handicap. Returning to California from a fundraising tour for the group, he died on a flight from New York.

338. GARLAND, Judy (singer, actress [signature song: "Over the Rainbow"]; b. June 10, 1922, Grand Rapids, MI; d. June 22, 1969, London, England). *Jack Oakie's College* (1937); *Good News of 1938* (1937–38); *Bob Hope Show* (1939–40).

MGM turned young Judy into a workhorse, casting her in 12 musicals in less than five years during her teens. After signing her studio contract in 1935, she made a guest appearance on *Shell Chateau,* hosted by Wallace Beery on October 26. For her broadcast debut, she sang "Broadway Rhythm," a song from a current MGM musical. Her rigorous picture schedule left little time for a weekly radio series in the mode of Bing Crosby's *Kraft Music Hall.* The studio, however, did showcase her remarkable talent on its star-filled program *Good News,* beginning in November 1938. In early 1939 — the year she mesmerized audiences as Dorothy in *The Wizard of Oz* — 16-year-old Judy sang on Bob Hope's show. That fall she joined his cast, performing a veritable Hit Parade of song.

Over a 20-year period she made nearly 200 radio appearances, often on *Lux Radio Theatre, Command*

Radio columnist Harriet Van Horne, William Gargan (courtesy of Capital Cities/ABC)

Judy Garland

Performance and Bing Crosby's shows. At the mike she eagerly promoted her films and recordings, and during World War II saluted the Armed Forces and sold bonds. After 1952 when exhaustion and nervous collapse frequently interrupted her career, radio played a secondary part in Garland's star-crossed, self-destructive life. The first Judy Garland TV special aired on *Ford Star Jubilee* in 1955, but on that medium, too, her appearances were sporadic.

339. GARROWAY, Dave (emcee, announcer [catchphrase: "Peace"]; b. July 13, 1913, Schenectady, NY; d. July 21, 1982, Swarthmore, PA). *World's Great Novels* (1946–47); *Dave Garroway Show* (1947–51); *Reserved for Garroway* (1949–50); *Dial Dave Garroway* (1950–53).

Whimsical, genial host-raconteur. Beginning in 1937 as a page boy for NBC and a special events announcer at KDKA, he broke into Chicago radio as announcer and sports reporter, specializing in horse racing and golf tournaments (often assisting Bill Stern). In 1940 he was the Voice of Westinghouse for *Musical Americana.*

A Navy man during the war, he broadcast five nights a week in Honolulu. There, he began to develop his low-key personal style and offbeat commentary. His career took off in 1947 when he hosted a nighttime popular music show, augmented by a daytime series. The latter was picked up by Armour & Co. as a major feature for which Garroway traveled to reach a variety of subjects.

By the late '40s his *Garroway at Large* made him an early TV favorite. He inaugurated NBC's *Today*

show in 1952. Radio, however, remained on his agenda with *Sunday with Garroway* and *Monitor* segments. He once jumbled prefixes in the introduction of a ballet sequence: "And now we present Maria Firechief in 'The Tailbird Suite.'"

340. GERSHWIN, George (pianist, composer; b. Sept. 26, 1898, Brooklyn, NY; d. July 11, 1937, Los Angeles, CA). *Music by Gershwin* (1934).

Prolific composer and frequent guest artist. He made many appearances on variety shows, beginning with the *Eveready Hour* in the mid-1920s. Roxy, Rudy Vallee and Paul Whiteman vied for his keyboard talent. General Motors aired several concert programs of his own works with Gershwin as soloist. In 1934 he launched a musical series interwoven with backstage anecdotes and informal remarks, and unceremonious interviews with other composers. His sponsor, the chewing gum laxative called Feen-A-Mint, broadcast the 15-minute program Monday and Friday over WJZ. After a summer break, during which George and his brother Ira concentrated on writing *Porgy and Bess,* the series resumed at CBS as a half-hour Sunday segment. Louis Katzman conducted an orchestra that included such high-caliber players as Tommy and Jimmy Dorsey.

At the time, Gershwin spoke of radio's influence on the tastes of the average listener. "Before the microphone carried the masters to rub elbows with the jazz singers, many people attended the opera or allowed themselves to be lured to a concert because it was the thing to do or the place to be. But the democracy of the radio waves has raised the people to a level where the tastes are more cosmopolitan as well as more discriminating."

George Gershwin with young fan Doris Hewes (courtesy of Doris Hewes)

An important influence in musical comedy and the concert hall, he wrote "Rhapsody in Blue" in 1924 for Whiteman's "Experiment in Modern Music" at Aeolian Hall. After the opening (and short run) of *Porgy and Bess,* the Gershwins settled in Hollywood to work on film scores. While in the early stages of *Goldwyn Follies,* George at age 38 died following the removal of a fulminating brain tumor.

341. GERSON, Betty Lou (actress; b. April 20, 1914, Chattanooga, TN). *First Nighter* (1935–36); *Grand Hotel* (1937–40); *Story of Mary Marlin* (1938–41).

Heroine of numerous radio plays. Chicago-based in the 1930s, she appeared regularly on *First Nighter* and *Grand Hotel.* Her daytime roles included Constance on *Arnold Grimm's Daughter,* Helen on *Road of Life* and Laura for *Ma Perkins,* as well as the lead on *Mary Marlin.* Gerson performed on *Knickerbocker Playhouse, Cavalcade of America* and *The Railroad Hour* into the mid-50s. She studied at the Goodman Theatre School in Chicago where she auditioned for NBC in 1934. "It was a new medium then," the onetime soap queen of Chicago remarked in 1991. "I didn't get to do much theatre because I was so successful in radio. It's a dreadful thing, though — success where you can't do anything else."

For Disney she created the booming voice of the mean but ridiculous Cruella for *101 Dalmatians.* Gerson married Chicago radio producer-director Joseph Ainley in the mid-1930s, and ex-actor and artists directory publisher Lew Lauria in 1966.

342. GIBBONS, Floyd (commentator; b. July 16, 1887, Washington, DC; d. Sept. 24, 1939, Saylorsburg, PA). *Headline Hunter* (1929–30); *World Adventures* (1930–31); *Nash Program* (1936–37).

Gibbons' staccato, machine-gun discharge of words attracted listeners. His rapid fire record was 217 words a minute. A war correspondent and roving reporter, Gibbons delivered exciting, breathtaking news commentary that sometimes embraced unverified material. Part of the colorful "front page" school of journalism, this "headline hunter" elaborated on his eyewitness accounts. They included high seas disasters, such as the German torpedo attack and sinking of a British liner.

His fame rested in part on his appearance. He habitually wore a patch over his left eye, apparently lost from trying to observe a German machine gun too closely during the historic battle at Belleau Wood in World War I. Broadcasts of current events and true-life "thrillers" brought notoriety. He died in 1939, just as war broke out again in Europe.

343. GIBBS, Georgia (singer [Her Nibs] [signature song: "Kiss of Fire"]; b. Aug. 17, 1920, Worchester, MA). *Your Hit Parade* (1937–38); *Melody Puzzles* (1938); *Camel Caravan* (1942–43); *Philco Hall of Fame* (1945).

Up-beat, dynamic interpreter of both ballads and rock. As Fredda Gibson, she had steady jobs with bands, 13- and 26-week runs on musical games and revues, and a stint with the *Hit Parade.* Typed as that fast-singing Lucky Strike girl, she remodeled herself into a lusty, slower-paced stylist under a new name, Georgia Gibbs. In 1941, after recording with Artie Shaw, he called her "the greatest singer of American songs."

In 1945 she joined Jimmy Durante. Periodic guest visits on Crosby and Hope shows continued until television and nightclub engagements took her into the early rock 'n' roll era.

344. GILMAN, Page (actor; b. April 18, 1918, San Francisco, CA). *Penrod and Sam* (1931); *One Man's Family* (1932–59).

Jack Barbour of *One Man's Family,* beginning as a young teenager in 1932 in San Francisco. He played this key role for 27 years with only a break for wartime service in the Army. Carlton Morse also cast him in recurrent roles for *I Love a Mystery.* Gilman began on radio as a juvenile under the name Billy Page in 1927 and appeared on the NBC West Coast's *Memory Lane* and *Ship of Joy* during high school and college (Stanford, UCLA). He also played Penrod on *Penrod and Sam.*

For each broadcast of *One Man's Family,* there originally were at least two rehearsals. "Later on we had just one rehearsal," Gilman points out, "and at the very end of the program's run, we often started recordings without any rehearsal at all. We had to record ten shows in two days."

On his return from military duty, he worked as a

Page Gilman (courtesy of Page Gilman)

linotype operator and later as a national ad manager for a daily newspaper. It overlapped his radio career for 13 years.

345. GILMORE, Art (announcer; b. March 18, 1912, Tacoma, WA). *Dr. Christian* (1937–54); *Meet Me at Parky's* (1946–47); *Amos 'n' Andy* (1947–48).

West Coast announcer, beginning in 1934 as a singer, reader of poetry and reporter of Hollywood news in Tacoma. Later that year he went back to college (Washington State) where he worked as an announcer on the state-owned, on-campus KWSC. In 1935 Gilmore joined KOL Seattle. "We just had to do the best we could and often it was right," he says. "I do think that 'live' radio put you on a little edge and as a consequence many people probably did better because of that." KFWB hired Art as staff announcer but he soon went to KNX where he was chosen to announce *Dr. Christian.* He was closely associated with the Saturday series, *Stars Over Hollywood.* For *Red Ryder,* he both announced and whistled its theme song.

In 1941 he became a free-lancer; it allowed him to seek acting work on *Lux Radio Theatre* and *Pacific Story.* For television Gilmore narrated the police drama *Highway Patrol,* and announced *Climax,* and the shows of Red Skelton, George Gobel and Fred Astaire. For *Dragnet* he played LA Police Captain Didion.

Gilmore's credits include narration for thousands of motion picture trailers and hundreds of documentaries, travelogues and children's albums. After service in the U.S. Navy, he taught returning GIs radio announcing at USC and co-authored the text, *Television and Radio Announcing.* Gilmore was founding president of Pacific Pioneer Broadcasters, and president of AFTRA, and its Los Angeles branch.

346. GLUSKIN, Ludwig (conductor [signature song: "On the Air"]; b. Dec. 16, 1898, New York, NY; d. Oct. 13, 1989, Palm Springs, CA). *Hollywood Showcase* (1937–38); *Amos 'n' Andy* (1945–47); *Adventures of Sam Spade* (1949–50).

After a time as a drummer with Paul Whiteman in the 1920s, he settled in France where he led The Playboys. This jazz band made hundreds of recordings in Berlin and Paris where he also performed on Radio-Paris in 1928. He returned to New York and was hired by CBS in 1934. Named director of music two years later, he conducted the music for Orson Welles' "War of the Worlds" broadcast. From 1948 to 1958 he served as music director for CBS-TV.

347. GOBEL, George (comedian, singer [Lonesome George]; b. May 20, 1920, Chicago, IL; d. Feb. 24, 1991, Encino, CA). *National Barn Dance* (1931–35); *Tom Mix* (1935).

Little Georgie Gobel went on radio at age eleven, singing and playing guitar on the WLS *Barn Dance* in Chicago. There, he sang in a church choir and played juvenile roles in *Tom Mix.* During World War II he entertained his Army buddies with songs and bits of comedy. Audiences opted for his humor over his music. Television proved his best medium when he was given his own comedy show in 1954. It won instant praise and for Gobel an Emmy for Outstanding New Personality. Later he was a regular on *Hollywood Squares.*

348. GODFREY, Arthur (emcee, disc jockey [The Old Redhead] [signature song: "Seems Like Old Times"]; b. Aug. 31, 1903, New York, NY; d. March 16, 1983, New York, NY). *Professor Quiz* (1937–38); *Arthur Godfrey Time* (1945–72); *Arthur Godfrey's Talent Scouts* (1946–58).

Master of the ad lib and commercial banter. A legendary communicator, Godfrey built a morning audience of 40 million people and more than 80 sponsors (Chesterfield Cigarettes, Lipton Tea) by his peak in the early 1950s. His revolutionary style — folksy, candid and irreverent — placed him as the biggest performing asset of CBS for whom he contributed some $27 million a year. It netted him $1 million annually by 1950 from a lineup of daytime and evening variety shows totalling nearly nine hours a week. One of the best-loved men in America, the onetime cook, radio operator and cemetery lot salesman became a powerful superstar whose clout and ego eventually alienated many within the broadcast industry.

In 1929 Godfrey drifted into radio while a Coast Guard enlistee who liked to sing and plunk a banjo. His companions urged him to perform in an amateur show at WFBR Baltimore. The station brought the freckle-faced redhead back for a sponsored series as

Art Gilmore (courtesy of Art Gilmore)

Arthur Godfrey

the Warbling Banjoist. His casual, raspy speaking voice outshone his low-key and limited-range vocalizing. In 1930 he was hired as an announcer. Assigned to a station break for *The National Farm and Home Hour,* one day he blurted the words "National Harm and Foam Hour." Not long after, he was injured in an auto accident and hospitalized for a broken hip and pelvis. For months he listened to the radio; it occurred to him that broadcasts were aimed at mass audiences and too little to individual listeners. Thereafter, on most programs, he conversed with people in a homespun, joking and sometimes shocking way. His kidding remarks on the content of radio advertisements took the stuffiness out of commercials.

From Baltimore "Red" Godfrey went to Washington and NBC. His personal remarks and tardiness in 1934 got him fired, but CBS's WJSV took him on. A local wake-up disc jockey, he worked the daily 2½ hour *Sun Dial.* Walter Winchell boosted his broadcasts to the degree that WOR added him to its New York lineup with a 15-minute spot. The show flopped. He had better luck as an announcer for *Professor Quiz.* In 1941 he finally broke into the CBS New York schedule as an early morning feature, while still beaming his well-established WTOP broadcasts to Washington listeners. He captured nationwide attention in 1945, when he was chosen to give the commentary on the funeral procession for President Franklin D. Roosevelt.

CBS placed *Arthur Godfrey Time* on the network in 1945. His popular *Talent Scouts* discovered such new performers as Vic Damone, Steve Lawrence, Pat Boone, Van Cliburn and the McGuire Sisters (Elvis flunked his audition). His other discoveries included

"The Little Godfreys:" Marion Marlowe, Carmel Quinn, Jeanette Davis, The Mariners and Julius LaRosa, whom he fired in a celebrated on the air incident for that singer's lack of humility.

In the 1950s Godfrey remained in the top ten in TV ratings in spite of debilitating bouts with cancer and hip operations, widely publicized and foolhardy incidents as an airplane pilot, and temperamental run-ins with CBS boss William Paley. (The net once admitted it had a vice president in charge of Arthur Godfrey.) But in 1958 he ended his simulcasts and went with an hour every morning on radio and a half hour on television. A year later he dropped the latter but kept his radio show until 1972.

He also ventured into films (*The Glass Bottom Boat*), played on Broadway (*Three To Make Ready*), recorded popular songs ("Too Fat Polka"), promoted aviation (with the rank of colonel, USAF Reserve), and spoke out on environmental issues (Nixon-appointed member of Citizens' Advisory Committee on Environmental Quality). Godfrey was once described by *Time* magazine as "the greatest salesman who ever stood before a microphone." Fred Allen aptly called him "the man with the barefoot voice."

349. GOFF, Norris (actor; b. May 30, 1906, Cove, AR; d. June 7, 1978, Palm Desert, CA). *Lum and Abner* (1931–54).

The bumbling shopkeeper, Abner, of the Jot 'Em Down Store, on the long-running comedy *Lum and Abner.* An Arkansas wholesale grocer's son, he and Chester Lauck as Lum created the easy-going cracker barrel humor from their own days as youths together in rural Mena, Arkansas. Their characters came about one evening when asked to take part in an amateur talent program over station KTHS Hot Springs in April 1931. The two friends decided to imitate a couple of aged farmers at the last minute; they went on the air without script or rehearsal — and ad libbed what turned out to be the hit of the evening. They became a weekly feature on the station. A network audition soon followed and a series of Lum and Abner sketches went on the Blue network from the Midwest. An enormous success, the duo settled in Hollywood in 1937, where they also appeared in seven movies.

Goff subscribed to many rural Arkansas papers to keep in touch with his roots and to develop routines, many of which were worked up by him and Lauck around their kitchen tables. Goff also played such country characters as Mousey Grey, Ulysses S. Quincy and Squire Skimp. Several TV projects were proposed when the show left the air, but none made it past the pilot stage.

350. GOODMAN, Al (orchestra leader; b. Aug. 5, 1890, Nikopol, Russia; d. Jan. 10, 1972, New York, NY). *Lucky Strike Dance Orchestra* (1933); *Gulf Headliners* (1933–34); *Your Hit Parade* (1935–38); *Palmolive Beauty Box Theatre* (1935–37); *Show Boat* (1936–

37); *Fred Allen Show* (1940–49); *Prudential Family Hour* (1941–49); *Al Goodman's Musical Album* (1951–53).

One of the hardest-working, most versatile conductors in radio. His father, a cantor, brought five-year-old Al and other family members from Russia to Baltimore where Al studied at the Peabody Conservatory. A piano player and song plugger, he was asked by a young lyric writer, Earl Carroll, to collaborate on a show called *So Long Letty* that proved a hit in 1916. During rehearsals Goodman demanded that the pit leader put more spirit into the work. The annoyed conductor taunted him to come down and see if he could do better. Goodman did, and that started him on a new career. After a performance in Los Angeles, Al Jolson offered him a contract to conduct *Sinbad*. He soon developed into a music "doctor," handling rehearsals and conducting opening nights of many revues and musicals — as many as ten shows during the 1930–31 season.

His first radio program was the *Chrysler Hour* with Ziegfeld and Jack Pearl in 1931. His music backed George M. Cohan and Irwin Cobb. He inaugurated *Your Hit Parade* in 1935. Goodman made numerous records for RCA Victor, once asserting that if a tune became a hit, it was on the strength of its melody, not the orchestration.

351. GOODMAN, Benny (bandleader [King of Swing] [signature song: "Let's Dance"]; b. May 30, 1909, Chicago, IL; d. June 13, 1986, New York, NY). *Let's Dance* (1934–35); *Eddie Dowling's Elgin Revue* (1936); *Camel Caravan* (1936–39); *The Victor Borge Show* (1946–47).

Radio fans chiefly discovered Goodman and his new kind of jazz. Called swing, it gained the tall, commanding clarinetist the cognomen, King of Swing. His band rolled out a definite contagious beat that first caught on from appearances on NBC's *Let's Dance,* a three-hour Saturday night session from New York with Benny's tempo, and for contrast, Xavier Cugat's rhumba beat and Murray Kellner's fox trot mode. West Coast listeners especially tuned in for the fast-paced, post-midnight "repeat." They were very familiar with his spirited music when on tour in August 1935 at the Palomar Ballroom in Los Angeles

Al Goodman

he dug into his favorite Fletcher Henderson swing arrangements at the end of a lackluster junket that had stressed sweet dance tunes. The Ballroom crowd responded to the change of pace with a tremendous roar and surged around the bandstand. Stunned by the

Benny Goodman

cheers and acclaim, Goodman admitted later that the roar "was one of the sweetest sounds I ever heard in my life."

California disc jockeys also propelled the band into prominence. The first celebrity DJ, Al Jarvis, had been plugging the Goodman band records in Los Angeles, and when the musicians reached the Palomar, the audience knew and was anxious to hear his choice hot numbers and his lively, jubilant way of playing his clarinet.

Goodman had been a bandstand professional since 1924, joining up with teenage jazz musicians in Chicago. He signed with Ben Pollack's band; Glenn Miller and Jack Teagarden were members. In 1929 he started to freelance on radio and records. But not until five years later did he organize his own band, in which every man would be a top-flight soloist. But bookings at Billy Rose's Music Hall and the Roosevelt Grill offered little chance for his new upbeat arrangements of "King Porter Stomp" and "Stompin' at the Savoy"—until the breakthrough in Los Angeles. That led to an extended stay in Chicago where he was first billed as a "swing" band and plugged into a radio series for Elgin Watch.

The band rode on the crest of the big-band wave, and moved into the forefront of commercial programs. Goodman soon hired brilliant black musicians like Teddy Wilson and Lionel Hampton to play alongside Harry James and Gene Krupa in previously segregated hotel ballrooms and radio studios. Goodman waxed some 2,000 recordings, many with his small combos, and played his clarinet with symphonies and swing quartets. His life was filmed as *The Benny Goodman Story* in the 1950s, with Steve Allen in the title role. His music stopped many shows. The Carnegie Hall concert of January 16, 1938 with the extraordinary "Sing, Sing, Sing" made history and marked the beginning of formalized jazz concerts.

352. GOODWIN, Bill (announcer, actor; b. July 20, 1910, San Francisco, CA; d. May 9, 1958, Palm Springs, CA). *Burns and Allen* (1934–39); *Bob Hope Show* (1939–41, 1952–58); *Bill Goodwin Show* (1947, 1957).

An appealing, well-modulated spokesman on commercials and popular all-round announcer who often participated in situation plots with many comedians. He enjoyed a long association with Burns and Allen on radio and TV, first in New York at CBS. He joined Bob Hope in a similar capacity in his second season for Pepsodent and later in the 1950s. The personable Goodwin worked with Bergen and McCarthy, Paul Whiteman, Eddie Cantor and Dinah Shore, taking part in many gags. He briefly starred in his own series.

School theatricals led to jack-of-all-trade jobs at a station in Sacramento. He joined the Don Lee Network and moved to one of its stations in Hollywood. At age 25 Goodwin was in charge of production. CBS brought him to New York in 1934. He had occasional leads in dramatic programs (*Atlantic Spotlight, Skippy Hollywood Theatre*) and performed in motion pictures (*Spellbound, The Jolson Story*).

353. GORDON, Bert (comedian [catchphrase: "How doo you DO!"]; b. April 8, 1900, New York, NY; d. Nov. 30, 1974, Duarte, CA). *Time to Smile* (1935–46); Eddie Cantor Show (1946–49).

A vaudeville trouper and George White's *Scandals* (1921) comic, he created the zany character called "The Mad Russian." For nearly 15 years the wide-eyed eccentric entertained audiences as Eddie Cantor's stooge. His popularity took him to such special hookups as "Salute to President Roosevelt" on FDR's 60th birthday and "Let's Talk Turkey to Japan" for the Sixth War Loan Drive. By 1951 he had settled in *Duffy's Tavern* as the character Yasha.

354. GORDON, Dorothy (moderator; b. April 4, 1889, Odessa, Russia; d. May 11, 1970, New York, NY); *Dorothy Gordon's Youth Forum* (1943–70).

An authority on folk songs for children as well as a singer, Gordon made her first radio appearance on WEAF on April 4, 1924. Her musical features were regularly heard on WJZ. While in London she prepared programs for children on the BBC, beginning in 1929. Having grown up in Europe where her father was an American lawyer associated with the diplomatic service, she learned songs in seven languages and from 14 different countries in their original tongue.

She returned to America in 1931 and became director of music programs for *American School of the Air*. She persuaded Sir James Barrie to allow a broadcast of *Peter Pan* for the first time, won permission from A. A. Milne to sing *Winnie the Pooh* songs and obtained approval from Rudyard Kipling to air his *Just So Stories*. She also produced *Yesterday's Children* and *Children's Corner*.

In 1943 she organized youth forums in lecture halls. Many were broadcast over WMCA. Asked to join the staff of *The New York Times* and to moderate its forums, Gordon began a weekly series when the *Times* bought station WQXR. Difficult questions and current topics were discussed by students selected from New York area schools and colleges. "To keep things going in the discussion, so there are no lulls, is something like being the conductor of an orchestra," she said. Gordon helped to establish similar youth forums in other cities. She presided over two generations of panelists before the program ended in 1970 at NBC. Gordon and her Forum received the coveted George Foster Peabody Award in 1951, 1963 and 1966.

355. GORDON, Gale (actor; b. Feb. 2, 1906, New York, NY; d. June 30, 1995, Escondido, CA). *Irene Rich Dramas* (1938–42); *Fibber McGee and Molly* (1941–42, 1945–56); *The Fabulous Dr. Tweedy* (1946–47); *Burns and Allen* (1947–49); *Phil Harris-*

Alice Faye Show (1947–50); *Judy Canova Show* (1948–51); *My Favorite Husband* (1948–51).

A career as a humorous character and foil was evenly balanced between radio and television roles. His mother, Gloria Gordon, blazed a "regular" trail with Benny and on *My Friend Irma* (Mrs. O'Reilly). Her son took on parts as officious lawyers, stiff bankers and big-shot businessmen, playing against the likes of Dennis Day and Judy Canova — although he once played the title role in *Flash Gordon*. As Mayor La Trivia in Fibber McGee's town, he created one of radio comedy's best-remembered supporting characters — a part he played for 15 seasons with only a break for war service as a Coast Guard seaman. In the last decade of net prime time, he appeared as Mr. Merriweather on *Halls of Ivy,* Mr. Scott for Phil Harris and Alice Faye, Bill Cole on *Mr. & Mrs. Blandings,* and Judge Grundle on *Penny Singleton Show.*

Lucille Ball wanted the glowering facade of her radio foil in the part of Fred Mertz on *I Love Lucy,* but Gordon opted for the school principal Osgood Conklin on *Our Miss Brooks.* He later joined *The Lucy Show* and its successors as Mr. Mooney. In between, he replaced Joe Kearns as Mr. Wilson on *Dennis the Menace.*

Educated in England and on Long Island, he landed a part on Broadway at 17 in *The Dancers* starring Richard Bennett. He worked in stock companies and films before beating out a dozen Hollywood actors to become Mary Pickford's romantic lead in her first radio show in the mid-1930s. "I was paid $100 a week, a fantastic salary in those days," Gordon notes. His wife Virginia Curley appeared with him on *Death Valley Days.*

356. GORDON, Richard (actor; b. Oct. 25, 1882, Bridgeport, CT; d. Dec. 1967, New York, NY). *Adventures of Sherlock Holmes* (1930–36); *Valiant Lady* (1938–39); *Knickerbocker Playhouse* (1942).

Radio's first Sherlock Holmes. His nearly six years in the role of the master detective made the character so real that he removed his telephone listing because his listeners called him for his opinion on murder cases. In 1932 he won the coveted American Bosch Radio Star Popularity Poll in the category of dramatic actor. (Other winners that year were Morton Downey, Jessica Dragonette, Rudy Vallee, Ed Wynn, Rubinoff and

John S. Young.) Gordon was a featured player on *Big Sister, Our Gal Sunday, Hilltop House, Aunt Jenny's Real Life Stories* and many historical dramas.

He started out as a newspaper reporter and cartoonist, then briefly studied at Yale Art School. His first professional work was on Broadway in *Her Lord and Master* in 1902. Gordon spent 15 years in stock, at one time with his own company in Ottawa. Some 50 productions later, he entered radio.

357. GOSDEN, Freeman F. (comedian [signature song: "The Perfect Song"]; b. May 5, 1899, Richmond, VA; d. Dec. 10, 1982, Los Angeles, CA). *Sam 'n' Henry* (1926–28); *Amos 'n' Andy* (1928–60).

The Southern-raised, stage-struck Gosden played the role of Amos Jones, a hardworking, churchgoing Negro who believed in the basic goodness of others. First broadcast by NBC in August 1929, *Amos 'n' Andy* with Charles Correll as Andy centered around the co-proprietors of the Fresh-Air Taxi Company in Harlem, which took its name from its single asset, a broken down cab with no windshield. Gosden also played the role of the conniving George "Kingfish" Stevens and Lightnin', a shuffling character with a high-pitched drawl.

The team had been amusing friends in Chicago with improvised dialogue set in the Southern Negro dialect that Gosden had been mimicking since his youth. They first appeared on radio as a singing act, but borrowed the black characterizations for *Sam 'n' Henry* in 1926. After moving to WMAQ in 1928,

Richard Gordon

they reached a wider audience, soon becoming a national addiction. Stores, restaurants, bars and theatres virtually stopped activity at 7 p.m. each night and turned on the radio to keep their customers happy.

Gosden and Correll missed only one show during its long run. Even when Gosden was in the hospital in February 1947 for a kidney operation, he was heard by special pickup from his hospital bed.

The TV version without its originators enjoyed a brief success in the early 1950s. However, it was forced off the air by the NAACP which felt it was a gross libel on the Negro and an insult to the race. Earlier, Gosden and Correll had sold their popular program and all legal rights to CBS for $2.5 million. Periodic attempts to revive or re-syndicate the classic serial or its key characters have been blocked by the network which believes any Amos 'n' Andy projects could only bring a lot of negative press in the black community.

358. GOTHARD, David (actor; b. Jan. 14, 1911, Beardstown, IL; d. Aug. 2, 1977). *Romance of Helen Trent* (1936–37, 1944–60); *Woman in White* (1938–39); *The O'Neills* (1939–43).

Helen Trent's ever-faithful suitor, Gil Whitney, for 17 years. One of radio's last daytime actors, Gothard endured the daily soap saga of romance with the seemingly sophisticated but vacillating Helen, forever age 35. Some four million listeners tuned in over the 200-station hookup. Gothard also played in *The Right to Happiness* and *The Adventures of the Thin Man,* both opposite Claudia Morgan.

Following high school in Los Angeles, Gothard appeared with community theatre groups. Interested in radio, he hitchhiked to Chicago where he got his first job, as announcer, in 1932.

359. GOULD, Morton (conductor, composer; b. Dec. 10, 1913, Richmond Hill, NY; d. Feb. 21, 1996, Orlando, FL). *Music for Today* (1934–42); *Original Amateur Hour* (1941); *Cresta Blanca Carnival* (1942–44).

This versatile man of music studied at New York Institute of Musical Art (now Juilliard) before taking his piano skills to vaudeville, movie houses and radio. He often performed as a piano team with Bert Shefter while on staff at Radio City Music Hall and NBC. In 1936 he was hired to conduct and arrange a series of orchestral programs for Mutual. They brought him national prominence. His Cresta Blanca show, for which he created the famous C-R-E-S-T-A jingle, featured outstanding popular and concert artists.

Guild composed his first piece at age six, and went on to create symphonic works, movie and Broadway scores, and ballet music, and conduct on some LP 100 albums. From 1986 to 1994 he served as President of American Society of Composers, Authors & Publishers (ASCAP), the oldest performing rights organization in the world.

Morton Gould

360. GOULD, Sandra (actress; b. c1920, Brooklyn, NY). *Duffy's Tavern* (1944–47); *A Date With Judy* (1945–49); *The Sad Sack* (1946); *Life of Riley* (1947–48).

Comedienne-supporting player, chiefly remembered as the Brooklyn accented Miss Duffy of *Duffy's Tavern* in the mid-40s. She also played Mitzi, Judy's chum on *A Date with Judy* and Minerva, Babs' friend on *Life of Riley.* Gould worked with Dennis Day and Bob Hope, and on *Women of Courage* and *My True Story.*

A student at the American Academy of Dramatic Arts, she bowed on Broadway at age 11 and by 16 had worked in a dozen productions. For television she created Gladys Kravitz, the neighbor on *Bewitched,* and was seen on the *Joan Davis Show* and *Our Miss Brooks.* In 1960 Gould wrote *Always Say Maybe,* a humorous "modern girls' guide to almost everything — but mostly men."

361. GOULDING, Ray (comedian; b. March 20, 1922, Lowell, MA; d. March 24, 1990, Manhasset, NY). *Bob and Ray* (1951–c75); *Monitor* (1956–c60).

Half of the networks' last great comedy team, Goulding and partner Bob Elliott evolved at station WHDH Boston in the late 1940s. Ray was a newscaster; Bob, a disk jockey. They started bantering from time to time. Nobody told them to stop, so they just kept on. It led to *Matinee with Bob and Ray.* Building a legion of fans in New England, the duo moved to the NBC network in New York. Their improbable yet recognizable characters — Wally Ballou, Mary McGoon, Mary Backstayge — and their satirical, low-keyed routines—on giveaways, home dismantling kits—bolstered radio in the wake of TV comedy.

Although they made video appearances, it was in radio that they said they felt most comfortable and considered it their real home. A specialty of the team was the interview of an expert in an unlikely field of endeavor (Ray) by an often perplexed radio reporter (Bob). "We really appreciated each other, as opposed to some comedy teams," Elliott said in 1990. "We had no rivalry, just great mutual respect. We always got along well." They were given a Peabody Award as the foremost satirists in radio in 1951, and again for radio entertainment in 1957.

Goulding began as an announcer in 1939 when he finished high school. Before U.S. Army service, he worked at WEEI Boston.

362. GRAHAM, Billy (preacher; b. Nov. 7, 1918, Charlotte, NC). *Hour of Decision* (1950–).

Evangelistic crusader and gospel preacher whose Sunday afternoon broadcasts brought him a wide following and a statesman-like pre-eminence. Over 150 ABC-linked stations carried his *Hour of Decision* sermons. His program later went into syndication, augmenting its broad reach and becoming the second rated religious program, surpassed only by *The Lutheran Hour*.

Graham was ordained as a Southern Baptist minister in 1939, and was drawn to tabernacle preaching that led to his "Crusades for Christ" throughout the United States and overseas. Beginning in 1951 he was periodically on television.

Billy Graham (courtesy of Capital Cities/ABC)

363. GRAHAM, Ross (singer; b. Aug. 8, 1905, Benton, AR; d. Jan. 5, 1986, Fort Worth, TX). *Cities Service Concert* (1935–44); *Show Boat* (1936).

Bass-baritone who won state and regional finals of the 1930 Atwater Kent competition in San Francisco. Two years later, while singing at a banquet in the resort-spa of Hot Springs, Ross was discovered by a vacationing Roxy. Hearing Ross sing "Old Man River," Roxy took him aside and promised a place on the opening night bill of the Radio City Music Hall. Graham soon left for the choice assignment in New York and remained a featured attraction in its stage presentations.

In 1935 Graham joined the *Cities Service Concert.* He appeared on the *Met Opera Auditions of the Air* in 1936 and 1937, and sang with the NBC Symphony and on the *Prudential Family Hour.* His deep voice was also heard on the salient Barbasol shaving cream commercial over Mutual. He retired from professional singing in 1947 and moved to Texas for a job with an electric service company.

Graham had sung as an amateur over KTHS Hot Springs where he was employed at a bank and with a utility company. The son of an evangelistic singer, the tall, blond-haired performer grew up on an Arkansas farm, and always recalled the day, when riding a large disc harrow behind four mules, he was thrown and the harrow passed completely over him. He escaped with only a few tears in his clothing.

364. GRANIK, Theodore (moderator; b. 1906, Brooklyn, NY; d. Sept. 21, 1970, New York, NY). *American Forum of the Air* (1937–c56).

A successful lawyer and counselor, Granik had a life-long fascination with radio. While at CCNY he took a job as secretary to Lee Adam Gimbel, vice president of Gimbel Brothers. The store had set up its own small station, WGBS, and Ted was spending more of his time at the studio than at his desk. He wrote scripts, reported prize fights and filled in as a performer (often reading from the Bible). He started *Law for the Layman.* When the station was sold in 1928, he continued it on WOR. The discussions on law led to an unrehearsed, non-scripted debate on a controversial topic, a practice all but unknown at the time. The program received wide publicity, and WOR approved Granik's idea to start a radio forum to debate issues.

Throughout the 1930s, the series flourished but paid no salary to its originator. Not until June 1939 did it become sponsored over Mutual. The Forum achieved semiofficial status in that it was the only program which was reprinted word for word in the *Congressional Record.* It received a Peabody Award in 1940. Ten years later the Forum moved to NBC where under the sponsorship of American Trucking Association it became a simulcast. Granik's *Youth Wants to Know* and *All America Wants to Know* were Forum offshoots. At the time of his death, Granik owned WGSP-TV Washington, and was planning to go back on the air with the kind of program that made him the "champion of plain talk."

365. GRAUER, Ben (announcer, emcee; b. June 2, 1908, Staten Island, NY; d. May 31, 1977, New York, NY). *Walter Winchell* (1933–39); *Pot o' Gold* (1939–41); *NBC Symphony* (1942–54); *Information Please* (1943–46); *Chesterfield Supper Club* (1947–48); *Boston Symphony* (1949–51, 1954–57).

NBC staff announcer who by 1941 had handled 70 commercial programs since joining the network eleven years earlier. He became as much an aural identification mark for NBC as the roar of Leo the Lion for MGM.

A child actor on the stage and in films, he graduated from City College of New York. Erudite, ebullient and energetic, Grauer quickly advanced from routine chores as station breaks and time checks to challenging assignments, including coverage of the maiden flight of the dirigible *Akron,* horse racing from Aquaduct, the first UN Conference from San Francisco and New Year's Eve celebration in crowded Times Square. Ben called himself "a utility man"—a special events reporter for any and all situations. His enthusiastic approach and unpretentious delivery and good humor placed him in the forefront of broadcasters, in both radio and television (and there at its startup with the opening of the 1939 NY World's Fair). His voice was called "the most authoritative in the world" by the National Academy of Vocal Arts and won him the H. F. Davis Award in 1944 as the best NBC announcer.

His love of music helped to secure him the prized job as announcer-narrator for Toscanini's NBC concerts. "He was unquestionably the one genius with whom I worked," Ben said. Even the able Grauer made a mistake or two. Signing off for Walter Winchell, he said: "This is Ben Grauer squeaking." And a minute before the Eddy Duchin orchestra went on the air one night, he stepped up to the mike for the usual voice balance test. Using his most austere WJZ voice, he proclaimed sonorously, "This is W. J. Zilch, Hoboken." At that moment, the mike went "live." "W. J. Zilch" bounced off eardrums all over the eastern seaboard.

Grauer retired from Radio City in 1974 but remained active for the Voice of America, commercials and occasional TV assignments.

366. GRAY, Glen (bandleader [signature song: "Smoke Rings"]; b. June 7, 1903, Metamora, IL; d. Aug. 23, 1963, Plymouth, MA). *Camel Caravan* (1934–36).

His danceable, riff-styled Casa Loma Orchestra had unusual flair. Its off-beat rhythm, particularly on "Casa Loma Stomp," defined the emerging swing period of the big bands. Gray's suave, polished treatment on popular ballads — often sung by Kenny Sargent — were broadcast highlights. In 1940 Gray appeared on United Drug Company's *Parade of Stars,* a program transcribed over NBC; he played often on *Fitch Bandwagon.* Known on almost every college campus, the group broke up in 1950. The band had been established as a cooperative — the first such venture in the business with its musicians sharing in the profits.

An acknowledged early jazz musician, Gray played several reed instruments with the Orange Blossoms, a jazz unit of the Jean Goldkette organization.

367. GRAY, Jerry (bandleader; b. July 3, 1915, Boston, MA; d. Aug. 10, 1976, Dallas, TX). *I Sustain the Wings* (1945); *Philip Morris Frolics* (1946); *Club 15* (1951–52).

Big band composer-arranger as well as conductor. Hired by Glenn Miller in 1939, he contributed "String of Pearls" and "Pennsylvania 6-5000" at the height of Miller's popularity. An Army Air Force lieutenant, he was assigned to Miller's wartime AAF band heard on many broadcasts and recordings. When Miller's plane disappeared en route to France, Gray took over as leader with drummer Ray McKinley.

By 1946 Gray had formed his own band for radio, chiefly for Philip Morris. He also conducted for Marine Corps broadcasts and Bob Crosby's *Club 15.* With the major revival of Glenn Miller music in the early 1950s, Gray scored the film bio *Glenn Miller Story* and stressed his mentor's indelible arrangements on discs and tours.

He started as a violinist at seven, and was concertmaster and soloist with the Boston Junior Symphony Orchestra. In 1936 Gray joined Artie Shaw's string section. As chief arranger he created Shaw's breakthrough theme "Begin the Beguine."

Ben Grauer

368. GREEN, John (Johnny) (conductor, composer [signature song: "Body and Soul"]; b. Oct. 10, 1908, New York, NY; d. May 15, 1989, Beverly Hills, CA). *In the Modern Manner* (1934); *Jack Benny Program* (1935–36); *Packard Hour* (1936–37); *Johnny Presents* (1938–40); *The Man Called X* (1946).

As an up-and-coming bandleader he entered radio in 1933. His first network program, *In the Modern Manner,* had Green announcing, explaining the music, and conducting. This CBS feature won a *Radio Stars* magazine award. With Green at the piano, his band enjoyed a season with Jack Benny and with Fred Astaire. He helped to inaugurate the NBC Melrose studios in Hollywood in 1935 (the network had been broadcasting from what many have described as a "shack" on the RKO lot). As the star of three Philip Morris programs, he conducted three nights a week for 104 weeks on three separate networks in 1938–39. The series aired the radio premiere of *The Wizard of Oz.*

By the early 1940s Green was on the music staff of CBS where in 1942 his Fantasy for Piano and Orchestra, "Music for Elizabeth," was given its world premiere by the CBS Symphony with Vera Brodzky as soloist and Green on the podium.

Composer of the all-time classic "Body and Soul," he headed the MGM music department for L. B. Mayer and won four Academy Awards for his film scores, including an Oscar for *An American in Paris*. His first hit song, "Coquette," was written (with Carmen Lombardo) while he was studying economics at Harvard in the late 1920s. He was pulled between Wall Street and Tin Pan Alley, but shortly after the stock market crash he joined Paramount's Astoria studios on Long island as a composer-conductor. An admirer of Paul Whiteman — who commissioned his "Night Club Suite" for a Carnegie Hall concert — Green enjoyed a similarly long and multifaceted career, including conductor of the Los Angeles Philharmonic for more than 20 seasons at the Hollywood Bowl.

369. GREENWOOD, Charlotte (comedienne; b. June 25, 1893, Philadelphia, PA; d. Jan. 18, 1978, Beverly Hills, CA). *Life with Charlotte* (1944). *Charlotte Greenwood Show* (1944).

Greenwood's high kicks and gangly mannerisms made her a delightful addition to over 30 films and a dozen musical revues. Her Letty character in a series of stage comedies (*So Long Letty*) established her as a major star. Although she pleased many loyal fans over radio, she never caught on with younger listeners as did Joan Davis.

With three pictures in release including *The Gang's All Here,* Pepsodent signed her as Bob Hope's summer replacement in 1944. A variety show set against the background of a boarding house, *Life with Charlotte* cast her with Arthur Q. Bryan and Shirley Mitchell and Matty Malneck's orchestra. The same year she played in a comedy drama as a cub reporter on a small

Virginia Gregg (courtesy of Steve Jelf)

town newspaper. It ran briefly on ABC. Greenwood made her final bow as Aunt Eller in the movie version of *Oklahoma* in 1955. Oscar Hammerstein had written the part for her but she was unable to appear in the groundbreaking Broadway musical a dozen years earlier.

370. GREGG, Virginia (actress; b. March 6, 1916, Harrisburg, IL; d. Sept. 15, 1986, Encino, CA). *Rudy Vallee Drene Show* (1945–46); *Richard Diamond, Private Detective* (1949–52); *One Man's Family* (1952–54).

Greatly admired supporting player on many radio theatre presentations, notably *Screen Directors' Playhouse, Anacin Hollywood Star Theatre* and *Escape.* Her ongoing roles included Helen Asher on *Richard Diamond,* Betty Barbour on *One Man's Family,* Miss Wong on *Have Gun, Will Travel* and Betty on *Yours Truly, Johnny Dollar.*

Gregg started out as a bass viola player in the Pasadena Symphony. With five other young women she formed the Singing Strings for CBS and Mutual. Her acting career encompassed television (*Dragnet*) and films (*Body and Soul*). Gregg's 45 pictures include the chilling off-screen voice of the mummified mother in three *Psycho* movies. As a pastime during World War II she learned to send and receive Morse Code.

371. GREY, Nan (actress; b. July 25, 1918, Houston, TX; d. July 25, 1993, San Diego, CA). *Those We Love* (1938–44).

Leading lady on screen and radio. With John

Wayne and Deanna Durbin in late 1930s films, she
played the female lead, Kathy Marshall, in *Those We
Love,* a soap opera aired from Hollywood for seven
years. Her co-stars were Donald Woods and Richard
Cromwell. She married singer Frankie Laine in 1950
and retired. She later invented a cosmetic mirror for
near-sighted women.

372. GRIFFIN, Robert E. (actor; b. July 31,
1903, Hutchinson, KA; d. c1960). *Story of Mary
Marlin* (1935–45); *Tale of Today* (1935–39); *Dr. Paul*
(1951–53).

Griffin sang his way through two years at the University of Kansas, taught voice and bowed as a radio
vocalist in 1923. But it was as an actor that he made
his mark. His longest and best role, U.S. Senator Joe
Marlin and husband of Mary Marlin, began locally at
WMAQ Chicago in October 1934 and quickly moved
to network. He enjoyed solid runs in *Road of Life* and
Grand Hotel, and once had a poetry-reading program.
Griffin married serial actress Margaret Fuller (*Ma Perkins, Guiding Light*).

A stage hand at the Pasadena Playhouse, he had secured an important part in the Mission Play at San
Gabriel. It led to *This One Man* with Paul Muni in
New York in 1931. At KNX Griffin both sang and
acted. In studios he preferred to use a rack for his
script because he believed he could give a more relaxed
performance if his hands were free.

373. GRIMES, Jack (actor; b. April 1, 1926,
New York, NY). *Let's Pretend* (1937–54); *The Adventures of Superman* (1938–40); *Second Husband* (1938–
46); *Lorenzo Jones* (1939–41).

Specialist in feisty child parts that often had a comic
twist. Grimes worked on as many as 40 shows a week,
including repeats from the West Coast, and reputedly
played close to half of the male child roles in New
York radio, circa 1940. From his extensive radio jobs,
at age 14 or 15 he supported seven family members.
He enjoyed long runs on *Let's Pretend* (his favorite role
was the lead in "Jack and the Beanstalk") and *Second
Husband* (which starred Helen Menken with whom
he had appeared in the mid-30s play *The Old Maid).*

Grimes' first appearance on radio was an interview
on child actors in 1934. He was both the original
Jimmy Olsen (*Superman*) and Archie Andrews (1943
at Mutual). Along with parts in a half-dozen Broadway plays and films, he had assignments on over 220
TV programs. He stopped counting his radio credits
after 12,000 shows. A graduate of the Professional
Children's School, he found time to complete four
years at Columbia University.

374. GROFE, Ferde (conductor, composer [sig-
nature song: "On the Trail"]; b. March 27, 1892, New
York, NY; d. April 3, 1972, Santa Monica, CA). *Florsheim Frolic* (1931–32); *Lucky Strike Dance Orchestra*
(1932–33); *Saturday Night Party* (1936–37).

Grofe spent the years 1919–31 as pianist and
arranger and "symphonic jazz" composer for Paul
Whiteman. He helped develop an American school of
contemporary music, and created such enduring compositions as "Grand Canyon Suite" and "Mississippi
Suite." He orchestrated Gershwin's "Rhapsody in
Blue" for its premiere performance.

After working in the shadow of Whiteman, he left
to perform on his own. "All I ever wanted to be was a
bandmaster," he once remarked. Grofe conducted on
many radio series in the 1930s, while continuing to
compose orchestral pieces and arrange versions of tunes
brought to him by other composers. "On the Trail,"
the most famous part of "Grand Canyon Suite," provided the theme for Philip Morris tobacco programs
and commercials.

From a show business background, Grofe played
as a violinist with the Los Angeles Symphony for ten
years while working at a pit piano in silent movie
houses and cabarets. He teamed up with Whiteman
shortly before his orchestra went East and achieved its
trailblazing success in popular music.

375. GUEST, Edgar A. (commentator [The Poet
of the People]; b. Aug. 20, 1881, Birmingham, England; d. Aug. 5, 1959, Detroit, MI). *Musical Memories* (1932–35); *Welcome Valley* (1935–37); *It Can Be
Done* (1937–39).

Writer-broadcaster of inspirational verse. At his
peak he was syndicated in 300 newspapers and aired
coast to coast by NBC and Household Finance Corporation. A newsman who started as an office boy
posting baseball scores at Detroit's *Free Press* in 1895,
Guest turned out at least one poem a day for his
"Breakfast Table Chat" column. His best-remembered
lines "It takes a heap o' livin' in a house t'make it
home" became a title for his first commercially published book; it subsequently ran through more than
30 editions.

Guest first recited poetry on broadcasts of the Detroit Symphony in 1930–31. His Depression-era fan
mail to NBC grew to tremendous proportions. Most
of the letters were from persons who wanted nothing,
save to tell him how much his words cheered and
helped them.

376. HAENSCHEN, Gustave (conductor; b.
Nov. 3, 1889, St. Louis, MO; d. March 27, 1980,
Stamford, CT). *Palmolive Hour* (1927–31); *Chase &
Sanborn Choral Orchestra* (1929–30); *American Al-
bum of Familiar Music* (1931–51); *Show Boat*
(1934–37); *Saturday Night Serenade* (1936–48).

A song he composed as an undergraduate at
Washington University — "Underneath the Japanese
Moon" — became the foundation on which he built a
long and very productive career as a musical director
for recordings and radio. The tune formed the basis
for a number in the 1914 edition of the *Ziegfeld Follies,*
and opened many show business doors. A director of

popular releases for Brunswick Records throughout the 1920s, Haenschen employed many young performers for jazz numbers and mainstream ballads, and brought them to radio when that label began to promote its releases over the air via *Brunswick Hour of Music.* He also was responsible for the arranging and conducting of discs made by established star Al Jolson.

Haenschen presented sponsored features on WJZ before the networks came into place and achieved national prominence by 1929 with *Palmolive Hour* and Brunswick co-artists: Frank Munn, Virginia Rea and Elizabeth Lennox. These singers remained on the shows he planned and conducted into the 1940s, most notably the Frank and Anne Hummert production *American Album of Familiar Music.* In 1930 he became vice president-musical director of World Broadcasting Company which turned out thousands of recordings from the classical, operatic and light classical repertoires to form basic music libraries for hundreds of small stations.

An unusual affiliation occurred in 1940 when Detroit's WJR and Stroh Beer signed him to air a program by a 35-piece string ensemble whose members were from the Detroit Symphony. The expensive single-station series entailed a weekly "flying allotment" to and from New York for Haenschen and the two imported singers, Thomas L. Thomas and Margaret Daum. Moreover, the Stroh brothers insisted on original arrangements of light concert music and theatre audiences for both the dress rehearsal and broadcast.

During his 30 years on radio, the constantly busy and invariably cheerful businessman-artist conducted for sponsors Coca-Cola, Standard Brands, Pet Milk, Sterling Drug and General Foods, and for performers Lanny Ross, Jessica Dragonette, Vic Damone, Kitty Carlisle, Vivian Della Chiesa, Lucy Monroe, Felix Knight and Vivienne Segal. "If I have a formula for success in radio," he asserted in 1946, "it is to be satisfied with nothing less than musical perfection, which also means musical beauty." He concluded: "Do not cheat the composer and the hearers by an extravagant performance. Do the job simply, but remember that simplicity can have as many facets as there are selections in a musical catalogue."

377. HAINES, Larry (actor; b. Aug. 3, 1917, Mt. Vernon, NY). *Joyce Jordan, M.D.* (1945–46); *Big Town* (1948–51); *Easy Money* (1954–55).

Quirky and quaint characterizations highlighted his broadcast credits: Charlie the Crooner on *The Falcon,* Mozart on *Big Town,* Lefty on *Rosemary.* Often cast as a villain or the villain's victim, Haines balanced a lineup of soap operas (*David Harum, Pepper Young's Family*) and crime dramas (*Mr. District Attorney, Counterspy*). In 1951 he played the narrator—the boatswain "Boats"—on *Now, Hear This.* In 1953 he starred as Mike Hammer, private eye, on *That Hammer Guy.* In 1950 he joined the first daytime TV series, *The First Hundred Years,* then moved into the

Larry Haines (courtesy of Larry Haines)

part of Stu Bergman on *Search for Tomorrow,* winning two Emmys during his 35 years as this character. Haines also worked the last soap opera of radio, *The Second Mrs. Burton,* which CBS dropped in November 1960 along with five other serials.

Haines studied at the Westchester branch of City College of New York where he was offered a dramatic scholarship. But he decided to try his luck in show business right away. He started working at WWRL New York, from 10 a.m. to past midnight seven days a week. "I auditioned for everything—and if you asked me for the number of shows I eventually did, I'd have to say something like 15,000. I love radio because it allows the audience to paint its own sets."

On Broadway Haines contributed Tony-nominated performances in *Promises, Promises* and *Generation,* and played in the comedy hit *A Thousand Clowns.* When audio drama was revived by Himan Brown in the 1970s for the *CBS Radio Mystery Theatre,* he was among the old-timers recruited for the full-hour presentations.

378. HALEY, Jack (comedian [signature song: "Button Up Your Overcoat"]; b. Aug. 10, 1899, Boston, MA; d. June 6, 1979, Los Angeles, CA). *Log Cabin* (1937–38); *The Wonder Show* (1938–39); *Sealtest Village Store* (1943–47).

A breezy, light comic with inexhaustible good spirits. His Broadway and film appearances were entertaining and tuneful yet forgettable — until he played a strange, lovable character called the Tin Woodsman in the all-time screen classic *The Wizard of Oz* with

Judy Garland and fellow comedians Ray Bolger and Bert Lahr. The delightful musical fantasy brought renewed popularity. His radio guest spots multiplied, and in 1943 he replaced Rudy Vallee on the Sealtest show, which co-starred Joan Davis. He appeared with Fred Allen shortly before retiring in the early 1950s.

Once a song plugger, Haley turned to musical comedy routines in vaudeville with Charlie Crofts and Benny Rubin. His earliest Broadway success was in *Follow Through* in 1929, also his film debut a year later.

379. HALL, Robert (actor, host; b. c1925, Rochester, NY; d. Sept. 25, 1967, New Rochelle, NY). *The Green Hornet* (1944–47); *Music 'til Dawn* (1953–67).

One of several actors who played Britt Reed, *The Green Hornet.* An announcer for WXYZ Detroit where the show originated, he had also worked at stations in Rochester, Syracuse and Warren, Ohio.

At CBS he inaugurated the disc-spinning *Music 'til Dawn* in a relaxed, low-key manner. It won a Peabody Award in 1965 and was sponsored by American Airlines. A graduate of The Eastman School of Music and an accomplished singer, Hall performed with light opera, civic music and church groups.

380. HALL, Wendell (singer [The Red-Headed Music Maker] [signature song: "It Ain't Gonna Rain No More"]; b. Aug. 3, 1896, St. George, KS; d. April 4, 1969, Mobile, AL). *Eveready Hour* (1924–25); *Red-Headed Music Maker* (1933–36); *Gillette Community Sing* (1936–37).

Ukulele-playing vocalist, he popularized that

Wendell Hall

stringed instrument among flappers and sheiks in the 1920s. He started his career as a singing xylophonist in vaudeville in 1917 but found a brighter future with a uke and a song. In 1921 he bowed over KYW Chicago and by 1924 had migrated to WEAF. There, on the *Eveready Hour* on June 24, 1924, he became the first to marry in a ceremony broadcast over radio; he had courted his wife over the air. An early crooner, the tall and lanky Hall wrote his theme song, and became a mainstay on *Majestic Theatre of the Air* and *Sign of the Shell.*

381. HALOP, Florence (actress; b. Jan. 23, 1923, Jamaica Estates, NY; d. July 15, 1986, Los Angeles, CA). *Duffy's Tavern* (1943–44, 1947–49); *Jimmy Durante Show* (1948–50).

Child performer at age five on Milton Cross's *Coast-to-Coast on a Bus,* where often joined by brother Billy Halop (and future Dead End Kid). In 1943 she took over the role of the Brooklynese-speaking Miss Duffy on *Duffy's Tavern.* For Durante she played sultry-voiced Hotbreath Houlihan and had supporting roles with Jack Paar on his 1947 summer show. In 1951 Halop made seven appearances in crime cases on *The Falcon.* She worked with Orson Welles, Agnes Moorehead and Ed Begley. "I watched, I listened and I did. That is how I learned to act."

In 1952 she switched to television and the role of the mother on *Meet Millie.* Other notable continuing parts were the outspoken Mrs. Hufnagel on *St. Elsewhere* and the raspy-voiced bailiff on *Night Court.*

382. HAMILTON, Gene (announcer; b. Feb. 22, 1910, Toledo, OH). *General Motors Concert* (1935–37); *Voice of Firestone* (1938–42); *Chamber Music Society of Lower Basin Street* (1940–42, 1950); *What's the Score?* (1952); *Dr. Norman Vincent Peale* (1955).

This NBC announcer-commentator-emcee started with the network at WTAM Cleveland in 1929 after a brief run as a singer and guitarist in vaudeville and radio at WAIU Columbus. Gene handled Tom Waring's program and Cleveland Orchestra broadcasts, then in 1931 moved to Chicago's Merchandise Mart for NBC assignments on *First Nighter, Clare, Lu and Em, Lum and Abner* and Whiteman band remotes from the Edgewater Beach Hotel. The next stop, Radio City, in 1934 led to *Music Appreciation Hour* and *General Motors Concert* ("Safe Driving" segments). Meanwhile, he continued his singing, winning an audition as a basso in the Fred Waring Glee Club but soon dropped the idea of juggling two careers. Of announcing in those days, he has said: "It was a very funny profession. It attracted a strange group of men. Nobody in the beginning set out to become an announcer; one just drifted into it accidentally. There were no experts."

His deep stentorian voice seemed ideally suited for serious music programs, and by 1939 he had replaced

Gene Hamilton (courtesy of Gene Hamilton)

ning over his allotted program time, the comedian had been warned by the network time and again not to let it happen. Gene, instructed to sound the NBC chimes precisely at 9:30, broke in with the prescribed station break. Cantor's staff went ballistic. One aide called Gene a S.O.B. Hearing those words, he landed a punch, causing a fistfight on the studio stage. Cantor's sponsor wanted Hamilton fired immediately, but NBC vice president John Royal admitted he'd do the same if anyone called him a S.O.B. Gene kept his job.

Under an AFTRA accord, Gene and a number of other broadcasters were guaranteed lifetime employment at NBC. In exchange, the network gained the right to pre-record and broadcast station identification at will. Gene retired in 1975 after a monumental 46 years with NBC.

Howard Claney (in Europe to study painting) on Firestone and for NBC Symphony broadcasts. He developed a knack of how to pronounce foreign words for these assignments and for Philadelphia and Boston Symphony programs. It was often a challenge. "If, for example, you were presenting a Hungarian composer, some hunky in the orchestra invariably would tell you their idea of how a name should be pronounced. You could go along with him or go by the rule book. Listeners, too, loved to detect what they considered a slip of the tongue."

Hamilton also introduced and narrated *Concert Time* (ABC Symphony), *Promenade Concerts* and *NBC String Symphonette*. He reached out to pop music fans as Dr. Gino, the satirical, verbose commentator on Dixieland, jazz and blues, and interviewer of long-haired musicians, on *Chamber Music Society of Lower Basin Street*. For the Blue Network, just prior to Army service, he was assistant production manager.

During a broadcast in Studio 8H, he once cut off Eddie Cantor in the middle of a joke. Notorious for run-

383. HANNON, Bob (singer; b. Feb. 9, 1912, Chicago, IL; d. Feb. 16, 1993, New York, NY). *Frank Fay Show* (1941–42); *American Melody Hour* (1943–48); *Manhattan Merry-Go-Round* (1943–49); *Waltz Time* (1945–48).

A tall, engaging baritone with a clear tone and fine diction, he attracted the attention of producer Frank Hummert who featured him on shows throughout the 1940s. Born Lacy R. Bohannon, he also sang under the name Barry Roberts on *Manhattan Merry-Go-Round*.

A choir singer in Kansas City, he quit school at 15 to plug songs locally in theatres and over WDAF with the Nighthawks, then tried vaudeville. In the big-

Evelyn MacGregor, Bob Hannon

band era, he vocalized with Harry Sosnick, Henry Busse, Wayne King and Buddy Rogers, and emceed at Chicago's Chez Paree where he broadcast over Mutual. He was leading his own orchestra in 1939 when Paul Whiteman insisted he join his aggregation. That led directly to contracts with NBC and CBS on sustaining and commercial programs, including tenor Frank Munn's *Waltz Time.*

In the early 1940s Hannon performed as singing host for Roxy Theatre stage revues for a record-breaking 62 weeks. He later formed a harmony act with Jimmy Ryan, recorded many children's records and commercial jingles, and managed and performed with USO units overseas.

384. HANSHAW, Annette (singer; b. Oct. 18, 1910, New York, NY; d. March 13, 1985, New York, NY). *Show Boat* (1932–37).

Heard singing at a party in 1928 by Pathe Records executive Waldemar Rose (whom she married several years later), Hanshaw signed a recording contract. Her many jazz discs under her own name and pseudonyms Dot Dare, Gay Ellis and Patsy Young carried her into radio. She initially sang on broadcasts in Clearwater, Florida, then in 1930 was invited to appear on the Cliquot Club Eskimo program. As part of *Show Boat* she rendered blues numbers to contrast with Lanny Ross's love ballads. At 26 she retired, citing extreme stage fright before a microphone. Her last program, *Camel Caravan,* aired in 1937.

385. HARE, Ernie (singer [signature song: "How do you do everybody, how do you do?"]; b. March 15, 1883, Norfolk, VA; d. March 9, 1939, Jamaica, NY).

He and Billy Jones formed the radio harmony team, The Happiness Boys, in the early 1920s. They made over 2,000 broadcasts on which they sang an estimated 10,000 songs. Their first, on October 18, 1921, was at newly opened WJZ Newark. When WEAF opened in Manhattan, they began a five-year stint sponsored by the Happiness Candy Stores, and were said to be the first radio entertainers to be sponsored commercially.

The two met in 1920 at the Brunswick phonograph studios when the manager asked Ernie if he would make a record with Jones, another Brunswick artist. They waxed numerous discs during their 18-year partnership. It included broadcasts as the Interwoven Pair ("I'm heel'; I'm toe"), the Tasty Breaders and the Gillette Gentlemen.

There were a number of odd similarities between Hare and Jones. Both had sung in church choirs. Both were born on March 15, and the maiden name of both their mothers was Roberts. Both were 5 feet 6½ inches tall, wore size 7½ shoe and size 16½ collar. For a long time both weighed 175 pounds. Hare's last broadcast was for the Sachs Furniture Company over WMCA New York on January 29, 1939.

386. HARRICE, Cy (announcer; b. March 1, 1915, Chicago, IL). *RCA Victor Show* (1945–46); *The Big Story* (1947–55); *Cavalcade of America* (1950–53).

Deep-voiced commercial announcer and product spokesman. From 1946 to 1970 he delivered Pall Mall

Annette Hanshaw

Cy Harrice (courtesy of Cy Harrice)

cigarette advertisements for radio and television, speaking the indelible tag line "and, they are mild!" Many of these tobacco commercials were delivered in tandem with announcer Ernest Chappell. Harrice also had longtime contracts with Du Pont, GM and Proctor & Gamble, and announced Walter Winchell, *Grand Central Station, Quick as a Flash* and *The Thin Man.*

While a student at Northwestern in 1936, he free-lanced nights and weekends as WLS, becoming one of the first to handle fizzing Alka Seltzer tablet commercials for Miles Laboratories, who sponsored *National Barn Dance* and *Uncle Ezra.* On staff, he became a copywriter, newsman and programmer. From 1942 to 1945 he was a lead news broadcaster at WGN. He left to freelance in New York. After a lean three months, he suddenly began assignments on many top shows. His own production, *What's the Good Word,* aired as 30-second spots, circa 1960.

At short notice, Harrice once stepped in to star opposite Ginger Rogers in "700 Boiled Shirts," a presentation on *Cavalcade of America.* "Acting wasn't my bent," he emphasized. "My specialty was selling over the air."

387. HARRIS, Arlene (comedienne; b. July 7, 1898, Toronto, Canada; d. June 12, 1976, Woodland Hills, CA). *Al Pearce and His Gang* (1935–c45); *Baby Snooks* (1949–51).

Known as "the human chatterbox" on the Al Pearce shows. A monologist and impersonator, she toured in vaudeville as Arlene Francis in the 1920s, before retiring to recover from injuries in an auto accident. When the Depression hit her household, she decided to re-capitalize on her talent. Her first radio appearance was in 1933 at KFWB Hollywood. Pearce heard her "bright and diverting" monologues and signed her. Harris later played Mummy Higgins on *Baby Snooks.* Her initial stage appearance was in *The Girl from Vagabondia* in Toronto in 1916.

388. HARRIS, Phil (bandleader, singer [signature song: "Rose Room"] [catchphrase: "Hiya, Jackson."]; b. June 24, 1904, Linton, IN; d. Aug. 11, 1995, Rancho Mirage, Ca). *Let's Listen to Harris* (1933–34); *Jack Benny Program* (1936–51); *Phil Harris-Alice Faye Show* (1946–54).

Musical staple and individual comic foil with Jack Benny. Harris emerged as a drummer-bandleader in Los Angeles in the early 1930s, becoming a popular attraction in Hollywood, particularly at the Cocoanut Grove. Chosen for Benny's show in 1936, he quickly built up box-office appeal through radio.

Married to actress Alice Faye in 1941, Harris passed up band tours to concentrate on the mike. The couple soon had their own show on Sunday nights. After a tepid beginning, this domestic comedy improved as the scripts got better. A key performer was the sardonic character Frankie Remley, portrayed by

Elliot Lewis, who played off against the blustery and brash Phil.

Harris was a frequent guest on *Fitch Bandwagon* from 1939 to 1946, and replaced Kay Kyser on *Kollege of Musical Knowledge* for summer runs in 1944 and 1945. As a musician, he performed best in a half-talking manner on such novelty numbers as "That's What I Like About the South," "Goofus" and "The Thing."

389. HART, Kitty Carlisle (singer; b. Sept. 3, 1914, New Orleans, LA). *Song Shop* (1937–38).

Musical comedy star, Kitty Carlisle made radio guest appearances with Ed Wynn and Rudy Vallee. During its Broadway run she and William Gaxton reprieved a segment of the operetta *White Horse Inn* on an October 1936 broadcast of *RCA Magic Key.* The young soprano was already well known from her film work opposite Bing Crosby, Allan Jones and the Marx Brothers. A series for Coca-Cola, *The Song Shop,* placed her at a CBS mike with Frank Crumit and Gus Haenschen's orchestra.

In the early TV era her weekly turns as a panelist (*To Tell the Truth*) developed into a major career. Still later, with an interest in women's affairs, Carlisle serves as special consultant to Governor Nelson Rockefeller. In 1976 Governor Hugh Carey appointed her chairman of the New York State Council on the Arts, and in that post she has devoted most of her time and energy to public service.

Her earliest stage credits include the title role in an abridged version of *Rio Rita* at the Capitol Theatre between picture shows. She and her husband, playwright Moss Hart, once portrayed "Mr. & Mrs. Hush" on a celebrity-guessing contest benefiting the American Heart Association on *Truth or Consequences* in October 1948.

390. HARVEY, Paul (commentator [catchphrase: "Stand by . . . for news!"]; b. Sept. 4, 1918, Tulsa, OK). *Paul Harvey News* (1951–).

From twice daily, 15-minute Chicago-area news commentaries in the 1940s, Harvey branched out to become the voice of middle America via the ABC network. He built an audience of over ten million listeners on a chain of some 1,000 stations, beginning in 1951 for sponsor Dixie Cup. Called a "maverick conservative," he delivered a provocative and entertaining tabloid newspaper of the air in a style of homespun eloquence.

Except for a stint of Army service in 1943–44, Harvey has been connected to broadcasting since he was 14 and a gofer at KVOO Tulsa. A champion orator in high school, he was allowed to fill in at the mike for announcements and news. He was promoted to KVOO staff announcer while studying at the University of Tulsa. From there, he held jobs as manager, newscaster and special events director at stations in Abilene, Oklahoma City and St. Louis. From 1941 to

Paul Harvey (courtesy of ABC Capital Cities/ABC)

1943 he worked as program director at WKZO Kalamazoo. His Chicago broadcasts began at WENR and topped the local ratings. Harvey's agenda later added television, a newspaper column, books, and lectures, but radio remained the keystone of his long career.

391. HASKELL, Jack (singer; b. c1920). *Dave Garroway Show* (1947–51); *Music from the Heart of America* (1948–49); *NBC Bandstand* (1957).

Vocalist closely linked with Dave Garroway and other Chicago programs of the 1940s. While at Northwestern as a music major, he did *Fitch Bandwagon* commercials and vocal numbers over WBBM and WGN. Naval flight instructor duty followed until 1946. Vocals with Les Brown led to numerous NBC Chicago series as a baritone soloist: *Bits of Hits, Design for Listening, Pastels in Rhythm,* and his own summer series in 1950 and 1951. Haskell joined Garroway in 1947 and followed him to New York for TV's *Garroway at Large* and *Today.* Apart from recordings and summer stock, his Broadway exposure came as the Secret Service man in love with the President's daughter in Irvin Berlin's 1962 musical *Mr. President.*

392. HASTINGS, Bob (actor; b. April 18, 1925, Brooklyn, NY). *The Sea Hound* (1942–44); *Adventures of Archie Andrews* (1946–56); *Eternal Light* (1955–57).

Juvenile singer-actor on many children's shows. A Let's Pretender, he also periodically appeared on *The Lady Next Door, Our Barn* and *Coast-to-Coast on a Bus*

at NBC, and made a half-dozen appearances on *National Barn Dance* in 1939–40. Hasting's chief role, the comic book teenager. Archie Andrews, ran for ten years. After U.S. Army World War II service he graduated to adult characters on *Nora Drake* and *Search for Tomorrow.* His various *Aldrich Family* assignments included Bob McCall and George Bigelow.

By the late 1950s he was on daytime TV's *Kitty Foyle* and primetime's *Phil Silvers Show*— and then on to *McHale's Navy* and *All in the Family* (as Kelsey). His younger brother Don Hastings originated the Video Ranger on *Captain Video* in 1949.

393. HATCH, Wilbur (conductor; b. May 24, 1902, Moken, IL; d. Dec. 22, 1969, Studio City, CA). *Calling All Cars* (1935–40); *Gateway to Hollywood* (1939); *Screen Guild Theatre* (1942–50).

Director of music at KNX and CBS, beginning in 1930. Hatch composed background music for thrillers, Westerns and heavy dramas. He created the special mood music for the suspenseful *Whistler* in the 1940s. He conducted for the network's comedies, *Sweeney and March* and *Our Miss Brooks,* and later on TV's *I Love Lucy.*

Hatch first appeared as a pianist in 1922 at KYW Chicago and began a commercial series in 1927.

394. HATFIELD, Lansing (singer; b. c1910, Franklin, VA; d. Aug. 22, 1954, Asheville, NC).

Bass-baritone winner of the 1941 *Met Opera Auditions of the Air.* He made his Met debut that December in the role of Monterone in *Rigoletto* but had more exposure in Broadway musicals including *Show Boat, Rio Rita* and *Sadie Thompson.* His radio appearances, on *Fireside Recitals, Chase & Sanborn Hour* and *Telephone Hour,* spanned the years 1937 to 1942. In World War II he made USO tours of Army camps and the Southwest Pacific.

A soloist with New York Symphony and Philadelphia Orchestra, he also appeared with light opera groups. Hatfield studied at Lenoir-Rhyne College and Peabody Conservatory of Music in Baltimore where in the mid-1930s he was a church soloist. In the early 1950s he worked for radio stations in Asheville, North Carolina.

395. HAUSNER, Jerry (actor; b. May 20, 1909, Cleveland, OH; d. April 1, 1993). *Lum and Abner* (1934); *Fleischmann Hour* (1936); *Silver Theatre* (1937–41); *Capt Flagg & Sgt. Quirt* (1941–42).

Character actor specializing in juvenile and light comedy parts. Regularly cast as a baby ("Butch Minds the Baby," *Screen Directors' Playhouse*), a little brother (of *Baby Snooks*) or a dwarf ("Snow White," *Railroad Hour*), Hausner also played reporters, circus barkers and bums. "I became well known as a guy who sounded as if he just walked in off the street," he said in 1986. "I realized that was a salable commodity—

that there were very few actors who could sound like non-actors."

During World War II he produced the AFRS *Yank Swing Session* and *Personal Album*. The Hollywood-based performer worked with Burns and Allen, Jack Benny, Bob Hope, Alan Young, Ronald Colman and Howard Duff well into the 1950s. Once a stock and vaudeville actor, Hausner first went on the air at WJAY Cleveland. His network break came with *Lum and Abner.*

396. HAVRILLA, Alois (announcer; b. June 7, 1891, Pressov, Hungary; d. Dec. 7, 1952, Engle-wood, NJ). *Campbell Soup Orchestra* (1930–32); *Jack Benny Program* (1933–34); *Colgate House Party* (1934–35).

Havrilla came to the United States as a young boy. He spoke no English. But by 1930 he was a leading announcer and commentator, who in 1935 won the American Academy of Arts & Letters gold medal for diction. Growing up in Bridgeport, Connecticut, he was discovered to have a fine alto voice, with a range of three octaves. He sang in a church choir while learning English from his music teacher. In 1923 he appeared as soloist with Percy Grainger at Carnegie Hall where he met Graham McNamee and Elliot Shaw who suggested he pursue a job opening at WJZ.

Havrilla, however, continued his music studies at NYU, then taught — but only for eight weeks. Radio again beckoned and in 1924 he joined WEAF's staff. Assignments with the Atwater Kent concerts, Jack Benny, *Eveready Hour* condensed opera presentations and other important shows followed. Havrilla also narrated movie travelogues and shorts. In 1946 he began an association with WPAT and WNJR Newark.

Alois Havrilla

397. HAWK, Bob (quizmaster; b. Dec. 15, 1907, Creston, IA; d. July 4, 1989, Laguna Hills, CA). *Name Three* (1939–40); *Take It or Leave It* (1940–41); *Thanks to the Yanks* (1942–45); *The Bob Hawk Show* (1946–53).

First emcee of the eventful $64 Question double-or-nothing quiz. At its start, *Variety* described it as "good-natured and semi-simpleminded" and noted Hawk's fresh manner and weakness for puns. But it all seemed right for radio in 1940, and right with Ever-sharp Pen, its sponsor whose net sales soared from $2 million to $30 million from radio advertising in less than a half-dozen years.

Hawk was working on *Name Three* over Mutual when chosen over several hundred prospective em-cees. He apparently suggested the seven step-ups in money from $1 to $64, and thought up the idea of placing the questions in categories (although the format's creator was actually Peter Cranford, a clinical psychologist in Georgia). Within a year the game was so popular it packed studios and auditoriums to capacity. When Hawk's initial agreement came up for renegotiation, he opted for a much bigger paycheck. Meanwhile he sold himself to another sponsor, quitting his already established, top-drawer contest for an untested format elsewhere.

His *How 'm I Doin'?* floundered, but six months later his *Thanks to the Yanks* proved a well-timed and lively game that handed out bundles of Camel Cigarette cartons to servicemen. That series segued into the postwar *Bob Hawk Show,* a diverting potpourri of questions and gags.

The radio bug bit Hawks in 1926. On Chicago stations he was an announcer, poetry reader and disc jockey. The next step, emcee, led to *Fun Quiz* and *Foolish Questions.*

398. HAY, Bill (announcer [catchphrase: "Heah they ah."]; b. 1887, Dumfries, Scotland; d. Oct. 12, 1978, Santa Monica, CA). *Amos 'n' Andy* (1928–42).

As station manager of WGN, Hay met Amos and Andy (then known as Sam and Henry) and announced their first program. In 1928 he moved with the duo to WMAQ and continued as an integral part of their broadcasts into the 1940s.

Hay was sales manager and treasurer of a piano company in Hastings, Nebraska, when KFKX came into being in 1922. The company gave the station a piano and Hay went along announcing, arranging programs, singing and directing.

Scottish-born Hay came to America in 1909, studied the violin, took vocal lessons, and sang in churches before radio. His brogue-style station breaks readily identified the Hastings transmitter among early listeners.

399. HAY, George D. (host [The Solemn Old Judge]; b. Nov. 9, 1895, Attica, IN; d. May 9, 1968,

Virginia Beach, VA). *WSM Barn Dance* (1925–27); *Grand Ole Opry* (1927–51).

Originator, director and emcee of the *Opry,* the foremost network program of American country music. To many citizens of Nashville, it seemed just another hillbilly program in 1925, but it soon became a wide-ranging platform for outstanding native talent, and made the city the capital of country and western music and tourist mecca for its sounds and culture.

Hay started as a reporter for the Memphis *Commercial Appeal,* and was named radio editor and program director-announcer for its station WMC in 1923. The following year, he joined WLS Chicago as announcer and helped begin the *National Barn Dance.* In 1925 he was guest announcer at the opening of WSM Nashville. They offered him a job, and six weeks later on November 28, 1925, he inaugurated the *Opry* forerunner, *WSM Barn Dance,* with an old-time fiddler, Jimmy Thompson.

The homespun Saturday night hoedown was soon heard over much of the country, breaking down urban barriers against earthy country and folk music, and bringing it into the mainstream of America. Hay hired the first and only Black to be a regular on the *Opry,* harmonica player DeFord Bailey, who along with banjoist Uncle Dave Macon, was the most popular performer in the early 1930s. During Hay's 26 years with WSM, he served as publicity director, Artists Service manager and audience relations director.

400. HAYES, Helen (actress; b. Oct. 10, 1900, Washington, DC; d. March 17, 1993, Nyack, NY). *The New Penny* (1935–36); *Bambi* (1936–37); *Helen Hayes Theatre* (1940–42); *This Is Helen Hayes* (1945); *Textron Theatre* (1945–46); *Electric Theatre* (1948–49); *Weekday* (1956).

Called "The First Lady of the American Theatre," this dedicated actress won both great acclaim and many awards from her roles, ranging from Victoria Regina and Cleopatra to Madelon Claudet and Mrs. McThing. The ladylike Hayes often recreated her brilliant portrayals over the air, beginning on *Collier's Hour* in 1930. Her own series broadcast dramatizations of popular contemporary stories. "She produces it instinctively and with personal delight," said an observer. She also supervised the *Helen Hayes Theatre* including casting. Radio serials intrigued her as well, and she performed on several in the mid-30s.

Her generosity was equally legendary. At the microphone she spoke in behalf of numerous causes: child health, Red Cross nurse recruitment, Girl Scout activities, war bond sales, Salvation Army. In 1947 she was heard as a presenter on the first annual Antoinette Perry Awards — and won that night the best actress Tony for her performance in *Happy Birthday.* A 1950s transcribed series told dramatic stories of unusual human-interest appeal. As late as 1963, Hayes headed a radio repertoire company called *The G.E. Theatre* for FM station syndication.

Dick Haymes

401. HAYMES, Dick (singer [signature song: "The More I See You"]; b. Sept. 13, 1918, Buenos Aires, Argentina; d. March 28, 1980, Las Vegas, NV). *Tommy Dorsey Show* (1942–43); *Here's to Romance* (1943–44); *Dick Haymes Show* (1944–48); *Carnation Contented Hour* (1950).

Light, high baritone with a sensuous quality, gaining national attention as a 1940s crooner. Trained by his mother, a vocal coach, he followed Sinatra as a vocalist with Harry James, then replaced him again in the Tommy Dorsey band. On his own in 1943, he signed for a show with Ray Bloch's orchestra, and a year later as emcee-singer with Gordon Jenkins. Haymes was well represented on recordings and motion pictures. His Decca discs and Fox films rivaled Sinatra's. He once subbed for Andy Russell on four *Hit Parade* airings in 1947.

Haymes and his younger brother, the singer-DJ Bob Haymes (a.k.a. Bob Stanton), grew up in London and Paris before settling in America. As a teenager, he secured his first vocal job with Johnny Johnson's band. An engagement at New York's La Martinique nightclub quickly led to stardom — and seven marriages (number four was Rita Hayworth), tax problems, alimony claims and an unsuccessful Federal attempt to deport him as an alien who had claimed draft exemption in World War II. He ended his radio career as a "Mr. Music" guest on *NBC Bandstand* in 1956–57.

402. HAYTON, Lennie (conductor [signature song: "Times Square Scuttle"]; b. Feb. 13, 1908, New York, NY; d. April 24, 1971, Palm Springs, CA). *Old Gold Hour* (1929–30); *Ipana Troubadors* (1933–34); *Your Hit Parade* (1935); *Show of the Week* (1940).

Topline orchestra leader-pianist. His smooth and lilting piano work with Cass Hagan attracted Paul Whiteman. In 1928 he joined his orchestra, and soon became one of the chief arrangers and broadcast conductors. He formed his own outfit to appear on a series with Whiteman alumnus Bing Crosby who also made him musical supervisor on the Crosby-Marion Davies film *Going Hollywood.* By 1937 his 16-piece orchestra was noted for imaginative arrangements, especially on the programs of Fred Allen, Ed Wynn, Fred Astaire and Ruth Etting. In April 1935 he inaugurated Lucky Strike's *Hit Parade.*

In 1940 Hayton left radio to become a musical director at MGM. During his 13 years on the lot, he arranged and conducted for *The Barkleys of Broadway, The Pirate, The Harvey Girls* and *On the Town,* for which he won an Oscar for scoring (and again for *Hello, Dolly*). He met singer Lena Horne at Metro. They were married in 1947, and he became her arranger-accompanist on records and tours.

403. HAYWARD, Thomas (singer; b. Dec. 1, 1918, Kansas City, MO, d. Feb. 1, 1995, Las Vegas, NV). *Serenade to America* (1945–47); *The Name Speaks* (1946).

Lyric tenor with 334 performances of 32 parts with the Met Opera — an association lasting from 1945 to 1957 and stemming from emergence as co-winner (with Robert Merrill) on the *Auditions of the Air.* He bowed as Tybalt in *Romeo et Juliet,* following a season with the New York City Opera. Hayward had more than 400 concert performances with major symphony orchestras along with solo assignments with the NBC Concert, Cities Service and Bell Telephone orchestras. In 1944 NBC first featured him on *Encores.* He soon became a regular on *Serenade to America.*

Born Thomas Tibbett, he took his stepfather's surname. After high school he worked as an office boy at General Electric. Two GE executives urged him to pursue a singing career and arranged an audition with NBC Chicago. Unsuccessful there as well as in New York, he tried a third time and did achieve radio bookings and an opera contract. Upon his retirement in 1964, Hayward joined the music faculty at Southern Methodist University and remained as professor of voice and opera for 30 years.

404. HEALY, Tim (commentator; b. 1891, Sydney, Australia; d. Oct. 12, 1947, Ft. Worth, TX). *Ivory Stamp Club* (1934–36); *Calling All Stamp Collectors* (1938–41); *Captain Tim Healy Spy Stories* (1943–44).

Founder of a radio stamp club in the 1920s, this world traveler and war hero told stamp stories as well as spy yarns chiefly on the Blue Network. This Uncle Don of the postage-stamp set broadcast in the early evening hours several times a week. Once asked how a mere postage stamp could generate as many as 50,000 fan letters a week, the former Australian Army captain replied: "Where in fiction can you find anything like the bloody battles, exotic foreign lands and heroes of every time and place that are recorded for eternity on postage stamps?"

At one time he presided over four shows simultaneously in New York. They included a stint as morning news commentator. For his *Stories Behind the Stamps* at Mutual in 1938, Henry Morgan did his Kellogg commercials. The adventurous Captain Tim wrote his autobiography, *More Lives Than One,* shortly before he ended his broadcast career in 1945. His son Tim, Jr. a priest, became president of Georgetown University and The New York Public Library.

405. HEARN, Sam (actor; b. March 5, 1900, New York, NY; d. Oct. 27, 1964, Universal City, CA). *Jack Benny Program* (1934–38); *Show Boat* (1936); *A Day in the Life of Dennis Day* (1950–51).

Specialist in comic parts in Broadway musicals and radio. He created Sam Schlepperman on Jack Benny's show, after introducing the character in a Friars Club revue. Schlepperman later made the rounds as guest of Fibber McGee, Tommy Riggs and Rudy Vallee, and segued into Mr. Jacoby for Dennis Day.

406. HEATHERTON, Ray (singer, host; b. June 1, 1909, Jersey City, NJ). *Old Gold Hour* (1929); *Castles of Romance* (1934–36); *Musical Cruise with Spearmint Crew* (1934–35).

Youthful tenor-band vocalist whose ease at a mike led to host assignments for luncheon- and breakfast-time programs. As a teenager he was soloist with Fa-

Sam Hearn (courtesy of Broadcast Pioneers Library at University of Maryland)

ther Finn's Paulist Choristers. One evening while listening to Paul Whiteman's orchestra in a nightclub, Heatherton looked over his shoulder and saw the bandleader right behind his chair. Whiteman had heard about his singing, and insisted he do a number with the band. Ray did, and a week later was singing on Whiteman's Old Gold show. Not long after, Ray complained about guitarist Eddie Lang's jazz chords as accompaniment. Paul wasn't pleased, so he sent Ray back to Long Island, without a job.

Following a lean period centerstage, Ray at 22 obtained an audition at NBC through the efforts of James Melton. The network signed him for light musical series, chiefly as vocalist with the Ipana Troubadors and Eddy Duchin. Heatherton was featured in the Rodgers & Hart show *Babes in Arms* and in 1940 led an orchestra at the Rainbow Room (his return engagement was 36 years later).

After serving in the Marines, he returned to New York radio (and added TV) as *The Merry Mailman* and hosted *Luncheon at Sardi's*. By the 1960s he was a Long Island bank publicist with a local hour-long feature called *Breakfast Show*. Heatherton's daughter Joey became a singer-actress; his son Dick, a disc jockey.

407. HEATTER, Gabriel (news commentator [catchphrase: "Ah — there's good news tonight!"]; b. c1890, New York, NY; d. March 30, 1972, Miami, FL). *News and Comment* (1935–51); *We, the People* (1937–41).

His optimistic, reassuring voice aired world, national and local news through the Depression to the Cold War. Unfailingly upbeat with a depth of feeling for every subject, he personified the energetic newscaster. One year the Women's National Committee in Radio chose him as one of the two outstanding reporters, citing his colorful presentation, his high standard of English and his excellent diction. His home was wired for the latest radio and news bulletins so that he could be on top of news stories. He usually broadcast from his apartment.

The high point of his early radio years occurred when, for MBS in 1936, he covered the trial of Bruno Hauptmann, kidnapper of the Lindbergh baby. He unexpectedly set a record for ad libbing. When Hauptmann's execution was delayed for nearly an hour, Heatter had to keep talking. His performance caused such comment that sponsors lined up for his services.

He had worked for the *Herald* and Hearst papers in New York and as Paris representative for the Foreign Language Publishers Association. In 1932 he wrote for *The Nation*. WMCA owner Donald Flamm gave him air time for a speech and was so impressed that he signed him on as a commentator. Six months later, Heatter joined WOR, earning $150 for two broadcasts a week. Known for his keen predictions of major international events, he also interviewed guests from various walks of life on *We, the People*. Heatter

moved to Miami in 1951 and conducted a daily radio news segment and TV program until the mid-60s.

408. HEFLIN, Van (actor; b. Dec. 13, 1910, Walters, OK; d. July 23, 1971, Hollywood, CA). *Mrs. Wiggs of the Cabbage Patch* (1936–38); *The Man I Married* (1939–40).

While a young actor in New York, Heflin became immersed in radio drama, especially soap opera. Playing Bob on *Betty and Bob,* Fred on *Central City,* and Sammy on *The Goldbergs,* he matured as a performer and demonstrated genuine talent as a lead and supporting character. The role as the reporter opposite Katharine Hepburn in *Philadelphia Story,* a hit on Broadway, changed the direction of his career toward Hollywood. He won an Academy Award in 1942 for *Johnny Eager* and accolades as a homesteader in *Shane* a decade later.

Heflin played detective Philip Marlowe in a 1947 summer series. The Oklahoma native starred in "Arrowsmith," a presentation of *NBC University Theatre,* as Pat in "State Fair" on *The Theatre Guild on the Air,* and as Jim Fallon in "The Big Trees" for *Lux Radio Theatre.* He also appeared in works of Arthur Miller and Rod Serling.

409. HEIDT, Horace (bandleader [signature song: "I'll Have You in My Dreams"]; b. May 21, 1901, Alameda, CA; d. Dec. 1, 1986, Los Angeles, CA). *Horace Heidt Brigadiers* (1935–38); *Pot o' Gold* (1939–41); *Treasure Chest* (1940–44); *Original Youth Opportunity Program* (1947–53).

Middle-of-the-road music, augmented by a troupe of very talented performers who were featured acts,

Horace Heidt

placed Heidt and his Musical Knights in the league with Waring's Pennsylvanians. He also devised one of the first radio shows to conduct ad-lib interviews with an audience. Called *Answers By the Dancers,* it got started in the mid-30s by accident when a WGN microphone from the bandstand at the Drake Hotel in Chicago fell to the dance floor. Heidt jumped down, grabbed the mike and began chatting with bystanders. He soon originated other interview programs while bringing to the forefront such entertainers as Al Hirt, Art Carney, Gordon MacRae, Frankie Carle, Larry Cotton and the King Sisters.

His most popular show was *Pot o' Gold,* a breakthrough series on which for the first time money was given away by a telephone call. Listeners' hopes for a $1,000 windfall led to high ratings throughout the country. Not since the early days of *Amos 'n' Andy* had there been such a runaway success. The spinning of a giant numbered wheel, keyed to individual phone directories, page and listing line, selected the number that Heidt called each Tuesday evening from NBC. The scheme gave rise to many similar radio games. Characterized by the FCC as an illegal lottery, the government attempted to crack down on the increasingly controversial proceedings. Lawsuits by would-be winners plagued Lewis-Howe, its sponsor, and the giveaway ended after a sensational two-year run.

Heidt wound down his broadcast activities with a talent scout program that went on the road in search of newcomers. An athlete-musician, he had begun his own career by playing in dance clubs in the 1920s, after a serious back injury in a football game at the University of California at Berkeley ended his sports feats.

410. HEMINGHAUS, Paula (singer; b. Dec. 31, 1897, Columbus, OH). *Philco Hour* (1927–29); *American Album of Familiar Music* (1937–50); *National Radio Pulpit* (1943–50); *Highlights of the Bible* (1945–49).

Steadfast member of many program choruses, a key ingredient in musical presentations. She is representative of those musicians who made a business out of singing as a chorister on a round of daytime and evening shows — *Cities Service Concerts, Music Appreciation Hour, Saturday Night Serenade, Telephone Hour, Voice of Firestone.* Heminghaus, a contralto, emerged from the choral ranks from time to time, as a soloist on *Met Auditions of the Air* in 1936 and in a double quartet performing Brahms "Liebeslieder" with Toscanini and the NBC Symphony in 1939, 1942 and 1948.

She received her musical education at the University of Toledo of which her father was president. She began at WEAF at 195 Broadway in 1926 with a contract for three performances a week in grand and light opera and oratorio. She first appeared on the *NBC Grand Opera* series conducted by Cesare Sodero and on the earliest Radio City studio broadcasts directed by Frank Black. Heminghaus spent many seasons as a member of the Radio Choristers on *National Radio Pulpit.* At the beginning of television she sang in NBC's production of *The Mikado*—and lost some ten pounds from the extreme heat emanating from banks of studio lights. For a special broadcast of the *Davey Tree Hour* in 1931, pioneer aviator Clarence Chamberlain flew the cast to Ohio in a small plane from an airstrip that later became Newark Airport.

411. HENDERSON, Skitch (conductor [signature song: "Anita"]; b. Jan. 27, 1918, Birmingham, England*). *Dial Dave Garroway* (1952); *Best of All* (1954–55); *NBC Bandstand* (1957–59); *It's Network Time* (1959).

A rehearsal pianist at MGM and standby pianist at NBC Hollywood in 1938, he first was featured on 1940 sustainers *Spotlight on Youth* and *Hollywood Tomorrow.* Following flight duty with the U.S. Army Air Force Training Command, he formed an orchestra and joined Bing Crosby on his unprecedented prime-time transcribed series at ABC. He also conducted on *Light Up Time* for Frank Sinatra; in 1950 he had his own disk-jockey raconteur show at WNBC from 6 to 8 each morning, with an additional hour at noon.

Skitch became an engaging personality beyond his music making, exchanging pleasantries and chatting with guests. By 1954 he was co-emcee on *The Bob Smith Show.* For two years he led the NBC Band of Stars on *The NBC Bandstand,* the net's last major popular music series.

The English-born, U.S.-raised Lyle C. Henderson once saluted the three-note chimes of NBC with his own composition on the network signal. TV musical director for Steve Allen and Johnny Carson, Skitch in 1983 founded the NY Pops Orchestra and regularly conducted its 70 musicians at Carnegie Hall.

412. HENRY, Bill (commentator; b. Aug. 21, 1890, San Francisco, CA; d. April 24, 1970, Northridge, CA).

All-round broadcaster-reporter with an unpretentious, low-key style. When his paper, *Los Angeles Times,* established a radio station in 1922, he began doing programs. He helped cover the 1936 Olympics in Berlin for CBS, the R.A.F. in France at the start of World War II for CBS, and the 1956 national political conventions for NBC. He often broadcast, filed stories and recorded shows on the same day. In 1947 he was president of the Radio Correspondents Association in Washington where he was chief CBS correspondent. His broadcasts won him a Headliners Award in 1948.

Henry had covered Occidental College sports for the *Los Angeles Times* and joined its staff after graduation in 1914. In 1939 he began writing his column "By the Way," a popular feature. It also became a 15-minute CBS Pacific Coast series. At the time of his

*Other sources give Halstad, MN.

death, he was to be honored with the Medal of Freedom, the highest award a U.S. President can bestow on a civilian.

413. HERLIHY, Ed (announcer, host; b. Aug. 14, 1909, Dorchester, MA). *Your Radio Reporter* (1943–45); *Army Hour* (1944–45); *Kraft Music Hall* (1946–47); *Honeymoon in New York* (1947–49); *The Big Show* (1950–52); *Weekend* (1953–55).

A studio workhorse with the versatility to handle a broad spectrum of general utility chores at the NBC microphone, day and night. A heavy-set man with a large friendly face, he exuded good humor and jollity, be it around tart Tallulah Bankhead (who called him "Herliheee-hi-ho") or a raft of eager-to-perform youngsters.

Joining NBC staff in 1935, he sold some 1,000 products over the years, but he chiefly was associated with Kraft foods as its spokesman for 42 years. "You need a good voice, of course," Ed pointed out in 1952, "but the announcer's personality is more important. The next step is experience." His training began while at Boston College, playing bad guys on local shows. Then he worked at WLOE Boston at $10 a week. He found a radio job in Worchester before chief NBC announcer Pat Kelly hired him.

Each Sunday morning for some 15 years, he presided over the cast of the Horn & Hardart *Children's Hour,* aired locally from WNBC and for a decade on its New York TV station. Herlihy was also the voice of Universal newsreels for some 25 years. He returned to acting in the 1970s in summer stock, road companies and movies. The latter included the *Police*

Academy series. His brother Walter Herlihy was a radio and TV announcer at ABC.

414. HERRMANN, Bernard (conductor-composer; b. June 29, 1911, New York, NY; d. Dec. 24, 1975, Los Angeles, CA). *Columbia Workshop* (1936–40); *Mercury Theatre on the Air/Campbell Playhouse* (1938–40).

Chief symphonic conductor at CBS from 1934 to the early 1950s. He wrote, arranged and conducted scores for more than 1,200 programs, including *Invitation to Music* (featuring Eileen Farrell), *American School of the Air* and *Exploring Music.* Herrmann helped convince Paley that it was important for Columbia to expand its staff orchestra for broader musical purposes. Persuading him to program new music and obscure old music that the public might not otherwise hear, he aired Copland, Hindemith, Ives and Milhaud.

In an association with Orson Welles, he wrote the music for the "War of the Worlds" broadcast of the Mercury Players and went West with him to do the score for *Citizen Kane,* the first of 61 film scores (including his Oscar-winning *All That Money Can Buy* and Hitchcock's *Psycho* and *The Man Who Knew Too Much*).

Herrmann studied composition at NYU with WOR conductor Philip James. He founded and led the New York Chamber Orchestra in 1931–32. As an assistant to Johnny Green, he conducted studio musicians on popular and light classical music programs before directing the CBS Symphony for nearly 20 years.

Ed Herlihy

415. HERSHFIELD, Harry (comedian; b. Oct. 13, 1885, Cedar Rapids, IA; d. Dec. 15, 1974, New York, NY). *Stop Me If You've Heard This One* (1939–40); *Can You Top This?* (1940–51, 1953–54).

Raconteur and humorist, he began as a newspaper artist and cartoonist in Chicago. He also wrote a weekly humor column, and the book *Laugh Louder, Live Longer.* His quick wit and droll stories led to participation on *Stop Me If You've Heard This One,* then as a panelist on *Can You Top This?* Listeners sent in jokes, which were read on the air. Hershfield and fellow resident joke-swappers, Senator Ed Ford and Joe Laurie, Jr., would in turn tell anecdotes in the same general category to top the listener's joke. The audience reaction was measured on a "laughmeter"—merely a volume-gauging device linked to a special microphone.

His popularity at this comic game show and his famous Pinkus stories made him a sought-after toastmaster and after-dinner speaker at hundreds of gatherings. He contributed his time and money to many charities, including the McCosker-Hershfield Cardiac Home, which he and Alfred J. McCosker, chairman of Mutual Broadcasting, founded in 1946 for needy adults suffering from heart disease.

416. HERSHOLT, Jean (actor; b. July 12, 1886, Copenhagen, Denmark; d. June 2, 1956, Hollywood CA). *Dr. Christian* (1937–53).

His philanthropic and civic activities, including president of the Motion Picture Relief Fund and Academy of Motion Picture Arts & Sciences, led to the establishment of the prestigious Jean Hersholt Humanitarian Award at the annual Oscar ceremony. Hersholt's long and consistently successful career began in his native Denmark where he played in the first picture made there (1906). By 1914 he was in Hollywood under contract to Thomas Ince. He made an impression in *Greed, Grand Hotel* and *The Country Doctor,* the story of the physician who delivered the Dionne quintuplets. That role led to radio and his portrayal over CBS of *Dr. Christian,* a homey drama of a small-town general practitioner. Other M.D. parts included Dr. Hans on a *Fleischmann Hour* in 1937.

417. HICKS, George F. (announcer; b. Aug. 26, 1905, Tacoma, WA; d. March 17, 1965, Jackson Heights, NY). *Death Valley Days* (1932–41); *Seth Parker* (1938–39).

First string announcer at NBC New York. He started in 1928 at WRC Washington, and moved to WEAF the following year. He handled many prize fights and special events (political conventions, trans-Atlantic flights, eclipses), along with the shows of Jack Benny and Larry Clinton.

In 1942 he switched to the Blue Network as its London office chief. He covered the Normandy invasion from the signal bridge of a warship, utilizing a film recording machine for the first time in a war zone. For his dramatic on-the-spot remarks he won a National Headliners Club award. He also conducted a series in which seamen of all Allied countries told stories of the horrors of war on the high seas. To prepare for it Hicks spent four weeks on a convoy vessel. A commercial spokesman, he was employed for ten years on the *United States Steel Hour* TV show, touring mills to do individualized commercials.

Hicks attended several colleges in the state of Washington but finished up at George Washington University as preparation for a career in the consular service. While studying he wrote to Washington stations for an announcing job. He was unsuccessful until he answered an ad by WRC. Two hundred applied; he won the audition.

418. HIGBY, Mary Jane (actress; b. May 29, 1909, St. Louis, MO; d. Feb. 1, 1986, New York, NY). *When a Girl Marries* (1938–56); *Nora Drake* (1958–59).

For 18 years she played the lead, Joan Davis, on the popular soap opera *When a Girl Marries.* She landed the role at CBS for $105 per week, the union minimum. Appearing on many soaps, including *David Harum, Thanks for Tomorrow* and *Helen Trent,* she worked on these daytime cliffhangers until they faded from radio.

Higby at age ten or so appeared in a few silent films; her father was a director. In 1932 the director of a Los Angeles dramatic show called in urgent need of replacement for an ill leading lady. Higby took over 28 minutes later. She hit the mark on *Shell Chateau, Hollywood Hotel* and *Lux Radio Theatre.* In 1937 she switched coasts, moving into such dramatic shows as *Nick Carter, Grand Central Station* and *Five Star Matinee.*

In her amusing, episodic memoir *Tune in Tomorrow,* published in 1968, she wrote of life in and around the studios. The relationship between actors and their various employers, she noted was simple and direct. "No middlemen intervened. We simply got in touch with the directors by phone or in person. Most actors made routine calls to the advertising agencies and networks every few weeks."

Married to actor Guy Sorel, she returned to the

Mary Jane Higby

screen in 1970 in a highly praised portrayal of a 66-year-old widow who proved especially difficult to kill in the cult film, *Honeymoon Killers.*

419. HILDEGARDE (singer, pianist [The Incomparable Hildegarde] [signature song: "Darling, Je Vous Aime Beaucoup"]; b. Feb. 2, 1906, Adell, WI). *Beat The Band* (1943–44); *Raleigh Room* (1944–46); *The Hildegarde Program* (1946–47).

Called by Walter Winchell, "the girl who sings the way Garbo looks," Hildegarde Loretta Sell started as a pianist for a silent movie theatre, then joined a vaudeville act known as Jerry and her Baby Grands. Following several lean years as an accompanist, song plugger, and sustaining radio singer, she sailed to London with a four weeks' contract in the ultrasmart Cafe de Paris and stayed three years. In England and France she was soon hailed as one of the greatest new entertainers in show business — the darling of British society and European royalty.

On her return to New York in 1936 she appeared on Rudy Vallee's program and *RCA Magic Key.* NBC gave her a build-up through guest appearances on *Show Boat* and *Your Hit Parade,* and her own program on Saturday night. Her interpretation and diction, her charm and versatility, registered well with audiences. Known as The Incomparable Hildegarde, she wore

Hildegarde

long white gloves for piano solos — a trademark that fell into her act years before when during a fast-paced finale she didn't have time to take them off. She emceed the top rated musical quiz *Beat the Band* and hosted the variety series, *Raleigh Room,* favorite shows of GIs who doted on her hauntingly expressive renditions of "All the Things You Are" and "I'll Be Seeing You." A very popular guest, she shared a mike with Crosby, Cantor, Bergen & McCarthy, Kay Kyser, Fred Allen and Henry Morgan.

Musical since the time she hummed an opera at 18 months, she grew up in Milwaukee and studied at Marquette University. A press agent once referred to her as "The Dear That Made Milwaukee Famous," while others have called her "The Milwaukee Chantootsey."

420. HILL, Edwin C. (news commentator; b. April 23, 1884, Aurora, IN; d. Feb. 12, 1957, St. Petersburg, FL). *The Human Side of the News* (1932–45, 1949–52); *Real Silk Program* (1936–37); *Your News Parade* (1937–38).

One of New York's best reporters, with a flair for human interest. He made his debut in 1931 and continued broadcasting until the summer of 1956 when he was a vacation replacement for Winchell at Mutual. His voice, described as deep, rich and sonorous, won a large following. Hill's recordings of old-fashioned Christmas and Thanksgiving stories were aired annually.

A top writer for the New York *Sun,* he left in 1923 to become a director of Fox newsreels and scenario editor for Fox Films but returned to journalism in 1927. As a reporter, he interviewed about 1,000 noteworthy men and women and covered major news stories, including political campaigns, shootings, executions and trials.

In 1951 he broadcast weekly for NBC, and simultaneously had five programs a week over ABC.

421. HILLPOT, Billy (singer; b. July 31, 1904, Red Bank, NJ; d. Feb. 25, 1985, New York, NY). *The Smith Brothers: Trade and Mark* (1926–34); *Camel Pleasure Hour* (1930).

Hillpot started his singing career with fellow Rutgers graduate, Scrappy Lambert. In the mid-1920s orchestra leader Ben Bernie signed the duo as a special attraction. They became widely popular as radio's Trade and Mark. This series cast them to represent the two founders of the sponsor's cough drop company, the Smith Brothers who were long identified from their product container likenesses. Hillpot often accompanied himself on guitar for solos and made many records. He later joined Lord and Thomas as head of programming, then went to NBC in a similar position. In that capacity he brought to the air *Information Please.*

422. HIMBER, Richard (bandleader [signature song: "It Isn't Fair"]; b. Feb. 20, 1906, Newark, NJ;

d. Dec. 11, 1966, New York, NY). *Studebaker Champions* (1934–37); *Your Hit Parade* (1937).

Manager and booking agent-sideman for Rudy Vallee and Russ Colombo, Himber formed his own band in 1932 and lined up work at New York's Essex House. A violinist, he provided sweet, swing-flavored music with vocals by Joey Nash. In 1938 radio columnists voted his the top band in the field. But he seemed happier as a magician, prankster and bon vivant. Nonetheless, the prestidigitatorial maestro was frequently able to obtain corporate sponsorship for his musical endeavors into the 1950s. They included open-air concerts by a 25-man orchestra in Rockefeller Center.

423. HITZ, Elsie (actress; b. July 21, 1902, Cleveland, OH). *Dangerous Paradise* (1933–36); *An Evening in Paris* (1934); *Ellen Randolph* (1939–40); *Stella Dallas* (1944–45, 1947–c49).

Heroine in daytime serials. Her portrayal of Ellen Randolph led *Variety* to comment: "Miss Hitz occasionally suggests Katharine Hepburn's elfin moments." She played Anne Howe in an adaptation of the comic strip Joe Palooka and Gail Brewster in *Dangerous Paradise,* one of her longest-running roles. Other assignments included the mystery thriller *Follow the Moon* with Richard Gordon and *True Story Hour with Mary and Bob* at CBS.

Elsie Hitz (courtesy of Broadcast Pioneers Library at University of Maryland)

Hitz started in stock in Cleveland while still in high school, and in the 1920s enjoyed parts on Broadway in *Reckless Woman* and *The Butter and Egg Man.* A singer on occasion, Hitz bowed in radio when an agency cast her with Lionel Atwill in a condensation of "Show Boat" on the *Eveready Hour.*

424. HODIAK, John (actor; b. April 16, 1914, Pittsburgh, PA; d. Oct. 19, 1955, Tarzana, CA). *Li'l Abner* (1939–40); *Wings of Destiny* (1940–42).

Growing up in Detroit, he played roles in Ukranian folk plays at a local church. English was a second language in his household, so John, even after winning a college scholarship in dramatics, had to forgo the award because of poor diction. While working as a budget manager at an auto assembly plant, he doggedly studied English. His efforts paid off with part-time jobs at WXYZ (*Green Hornet*). Leaving Detroit for Chicago radio in 1935, he won roles on *Mary Marlin, Bachelor's Children* and other serials. But by mid-1939 he faced a lack of parts and was ready to quit broadcasting and go back home. "As my last stab, I went to the auditions that had been going on spasmodically for over a year, to cast a cartoon character — and so help me, they picked me as Li'l Abner."

In 1942 Hodiak signed a contract with MGM. He contributed strong, well-praised characterizations to *Lifeboat* (his debut), *Command Decision* and *Battleground.* His wife Anne Baxter co-starred in *Sunday Dinner for a Soldier.* He was hailed for his 1954 Broadway performance in *The Caine Mutiny Court Martial.* His career was cut short by a fatal heart attack at age 40.

425. HOFF, Carl (bandleader; b. Sept. 25, 1905, Oxnard, CA; d. Oct. 15, 1965, Ventura, CA). *Your Hit Parade* (1935–38); *Al Pearce and His Gang* (1937–40).

One of a half-dozen conductors of *Your Hit Parade* orchestra in the 1930s. He led a peppy, fast-tempo outfit that by the 1940s reflected his skill as an arranger, developed through association with Paul Whiteman, Vincent Lopez and Paul Ash. It was the insistence of Ash, for whom he played saxophone, that brought about Hoff's own band in 1934 in Chicago. A mainstay of Al Pearce's show, Hoff was a guest on *Fitch Bandwagon* and spotlighted young vocalist Bob Haymes.

426. HOFFA, Portland (comedienne; [catchphrase: "Mr. A-a-allen!"] b. Jan. 25, 1910, Portland, OR; d. Dec. 25, 1990, Los Angeles, CA). *Town Hall Tonight* (1934–40); *Texaco Star Theatre* (1940–45); *Fred Allen Show* (1945–49).

A chorus dancer in Broadway revues, she met her radio partner-husband Fred Allen in 1922 when they both appeared in *The Passing Show.* Portland assisted him in his juggling act in vaudeville. On his programs she often accompanied Allen as they strolled down Allen's Alley, talking in a high-pitched voice to the resident characters. She also shared the microphone with him on the all-star *Big Show* in the early 1950s. After Allen's death in 1956 she married Joe Rines, a bandleader.

427. HOLTZ, Lou (comedian; b. April 11, 1893, San Francisco, CA; d. Sept. 22, 1980, Century City, CA). *Fleischmann Hour* (1934, 1939).

Storyteller-dialectician. Closely associated with Rudy Vallee's *Fleischmann Hour,* beginning in the early 1930s. He started out as a singer in vaudeville with Elsie Janis. That led to comedy in several editions of the *Scandals* from 1919 to 1921 and the revue *You Said It.* Between theatre and night club engagements, he appeared on *Kraft Music Hall.* In the 1950s he was rediscovered by Jack Paar who brought him on his late-night television show 18 times.

428. HOPE, Bob (comedian [signature song: "Thanks for the Memory"]; b. May 29, 1903, Eltham, England). *Atlantic Family* (1935–36); *Rippling Rhythm Revue* (1937); *Bob Hope Show* (1938–55).

"There was nothing like radio," Hope replied to a question at a Museum of Broadcasting seminar in 1986 on his many years in radio and television. "One of the greatest things in radio was that you could create your sense of things. With Amos and Andy: you could see the Fresh-Air Taxi Company." In a profession noted for change and desuetude, he stayed on top, surrounded by loyal and talented associates — especially writers who fed him timely, and often spicy, lines and sketches. Hope's typical season consisted of

39 programs with 40 hours of preparation for each, and about 115 gags per show.

Beginning with a guest shot for Rudy Vallee in June 1933, Hope chalked up over 1,200 broadcasts, chiefly at NBC for Pepsodent toothpaste. Before the launch of this tremendously popular program by adman Albert Lasker of Lord & Thomas in 1938, he was a "13-week kid." He would last about that long on a show and that was it. "My radio show for Bromo Seltzer was so bad that the sponsor wound up taking the product," Hope once quipped.

His arduous apprenticeship in vaudeville, followed by solid musical comedy roles on Broadway in *Roberta* and *Ziegfeld Follies of 1936,* put him in good stance for the microphone. His fresh and spirited wartime broadcasts deified the indefatigable trouper. As early as May 1941, his Tuesday night shows from training camps and bases — later from far-flung GI outposts — were eagerly anticipated by the troops and at-home listeners.

Surrounded by the fine musicianship of Skinnay Ennis and Les Brown, and vocalists Judy Garland, Marilyn Maxwell and Frances Langford, Hope packed more fast-paced, uplifting entertainment into a half hour than most comedian-emcees in the 1940s. His regularly scheduled radio program — it included several seasons on daytime — continued 17 years, and outlasted all the comedy variety shows except Bergen and McCarthy. In 1956 he continued to broadcast tapes of former programs, and in 1957, they were integrated into the Friday segment of *Monitor,* and later into NBC's *Nightline.*

Hope's family had settled in Cleveland when the British-born youngster was four. By 16 he was into amateur prizefighting and dance instructing. Then came a job in touring musicals and chorus work on Broadway, and finally leading roles. His feature debut in Hollywood, *The Big Broadcast of 1938,* went so well he stayed. With Bing Crosby, he was cast in their first team comedy, *The Road to Singapore,* in 1940. He made the first of eight guest appearances on Bing's *Kraft Music Hall* in July 1938.

Hope made an easy transition into television; early on, Paramount had a station on the lot, and he went before the TV cameras to inaugurate the new medium for local viewers.

Hope has performed at

Bob Hope

countless charitable and public service events. Early in his career, many were broadcast. He has received more honors and accolades than any other entertainer of the 20th century. He has penned more than a dozen books, usually co-written with his highly skilled writers. But like his stand-up routines, his biographies are self-deprecating and glib, yet not very revealing of the man who became a show business, living legend and a contemporary American patriot.

429. HOPPER, Hedda (actress, columnist; b. June 2, 1890, Hollidaysburg, PA; d. Feb. 1, 1966, Hollywood, CA). *Brent House* (1939); *Hedda Hopper Show* (1939–42, 1944–46, 1950–51).

Hollywood actress-gossip writer. Her daily column endeared her to some 30 million readers in scores of papers. A film colony personality, she reigned as co-queen (with Louella Parsons) of Hollywood chatter.

She began as a chorus singer and stage actress, then in 1915 appeared in Louis B. Mayer's first production, *Virtuous Wives*. She made more than 100 films and built up numerous contacts in all phases of the movie business. Hedda, who had been married to the renowned actor De Wolf Hopper, started writing when, in her 40s, she realized stardom was out of reach. Within a half-dozen years, she scored a coup by winning contracts with the Chicago Tribune-Daily News Syndicate. Hedda began her own gossip series in 1939—a three-a-week airing of off-the-set tattle—and appeared as celebrity guest on such audience-participation shows as *Double or Nothing, People Are Funny* and *Welcome, Travelers*. Her outlandish, conversation-piece hats often inspired scripts for the programs of Bob Hope, Rudy Vallee and Dinah Shore. She called her autobiography *From Under My Hat.*

430. HORLICK, Harry (conductor [signature song: "Two Guitars"]; b. July 20, 1896, Tiflis, Russia; d. July 1970, Cedarhurst, NY). *A&P Gypsies* (1924–36).

Leader of early radio's finest salon orchestra. He escaped from Bolshevik Russia to Turkey in the early 1920s, and as a violinist earned enough to pay his passage to America. Engagements with the City Symphony and a Russian club in New York attracted the attention of WEAF. His gypsy melodies and Hungarian folk tunes were distinctly different from anything that had been heard in mainstream musical circles.

The Great Atlantic & Pacific Company signed Horlick and five of his compatriots to an attention-getting and appealing series. As its popularity grew so did its personnel, expanding to 26 players and a varied repertoire of dance and novelty numbers and symphonic-like selections. His Gypsy tenors included Oliver Smith and Frank Parker. Announcer Milton Cross once introduced the aggregation as the "A & G Pipsies." When A & P withdrew sponsorship, Horlick's radio work became sparse. He conducted spo-

Harry Horlick

radically into the 1950s, being represented on the MGM label with a LP disc of Strauss waltzes.

431. HOTTELET, Richard C. (news correspondent; b. Sept. 22, 1917, New York, NY).

CBS correspondent in Europe and New York for more than 30 years. While a graduate student in Berlin in 1938, he joined the Berlin bureau of United Press to report on Hitler's war-making efforts. He was arrested in 1941 for alleged espionage by the Nazis, and after being placed in solitary confinement was exchanged for a German newsman-prisoner. Following assignments with OWI in London, Hottelet joined CBS News there in 1944. For the next dozen years he reported from London, Moscow, Berlin and Bonn. He flew missions with the Ninth Air Force, including a D-Day flight over Normandy that produced an eye-witness account of the seaborne invasion.

His New York assignments, beginning in 1956, encompassed coverage of the UN for CBS. He capped his many years reporting on international affairs as moderator of NPR's *America and the World*.

432. HOWARD, Bob (pianist-singer [Jive Bomber]; b. June 20, 1897, W. Newton, MA; d. Dec. 4, 1986, Bronx, NY). *Gliding Swing* (1938–39); *Calsodent Presents Bob Howard* (1939–40); *Sing It Again* (1948–51).

Described as a comic-on-the-keys. Howard was one of the first and very few black performers to have a sponsored radio series. It aired for Williams shaving cream and Muriel cigars over NBC on Thursday nights in the late 1930s. He became a regular on WHN's daily *Gloom Dodgers* with Don Bestor and Morey Am-

Bob Howard

434. HOWARD, Joe E. (singer, composer; b. Feb. 12, 1867, New York, NY*; d. May 19, 1961, Chicago, IL). *Gay Nineties Revue* (1940–44).

His 1906 standard "I Wonder Who's Kissing Her Now," sung in every barroom in America, periodically brought Howard to the forefront of show business, well into old age. His other songs numbered over 500, for such musicals as *Brown of Harvard* and *The Time, the Place and the Girl,* in which he had a leading role. Once a very rich man, he was left broke by a half-dozen marriages and the Wall Street crash.

From 1930 to 1938 he toured on the fringes of vaudeville. But he never stopped rehearsing his old songs ("Goodbye, My Lady Love," "What's the Use of Dreaming"). Then in late 1938, the tall, still-youthful-acting Howard landed an engagement at Billy Rose's Diamond Horseshoe, singing turn-of-the-century ballads and dancing the cakewalk. This comeback led CBS to sign the veteran star for its *Gay Nineties Revue,* a nostalgic songfest down memory lane that proved very popular among war-weary listeners. It was one of the very few shows with a costumed cast. In 1947 George Jessel produced his movie bio *I Wonder Who's Kissing Her Now.* The well-received musical film and TV appearances kept Howard and his vintage songs in the limelight for another dozen years. The venerable song and dance man died on stage of the Chicago Civic Opera House while singing at a benefit advertised as "A Great Old Vaudeville Night."

sterdam. In 1948 Ray Bloch asked him to join a new musical quiz called *Sing It Again.* It became a CBS simulcast, bringing the 320-lb. jazz musician much popularity among early viewers. His solos led to his own CBS-TV show — 15 minutes in the early evening, six days a week, and running for seven years.

Howard started in vaudeville in 1923 after studies at the New England Conservatory of Music. He worked with Jimmie Lunceford, Bunny Berigan and Fats Waller (whom he resembled in style and appearance). He appeared in clubs (Copacabana), on discs (Decca) and on Broadway (*Early to Bed*).

433. HOWARD, Eddy (bandleader, singer [signature song: "Careless"]; b. Sept. 12, 1914, Woodland, CA; d. May 23, 1963, Palm Springs, CA). *Carton of Cheer* (1944–45); *The Gay Mrs. Featherstone* (1945); *Sheaffer Parade* (1947–48).

A vocalist-guitarist with Dick Jurgens from 1934 to 1940. An impressive and attractive singer, Howard began doing solo spots, then formed his own band in 1941. Backed by his sweet-sounding musicians, he appeared on several Brown & Williamson Tobacco shows during the war years. He wrote his theme, and in 1946 became the band of the year with his outstanding recording of "To Each His Own." Howard often broadcast from Chicago, and was emcee, vocalist and conductor of *Just for You* in 1954.

435. HOWARD, Tom (comedian; b. June 16, 1885, County Tyrone, Ireland; d. Feb. 27, 1955, Long Branch, NJ). *Fleischmann Hour* (1931–35); *Sunday Night Party* (1936–37); *Model Minstrels* (1939); *It Pays to Be Ignorant* (1942–51).

Ringmaster and guiding spirit of the madcap and mock quiz panel, *It Pays to Be Ignorant.* The thin, irascible comic with the dry, high-pitched voice presided over three other old vaudeville troupers, including his foil and longtime partner George Shelton. The duo had made many appearances with Rudy Vallee from 1933 to 1938.

In 1943 he described his initial step into radio. "I just went up to the studio one morning, read over some gags that were typewritten on a sheet of paper a couple of times, went out, had some lunch, then came back and read the jokes over a microphone, which took at the most six or seven minutes, then went home after being told I didn't have to come back till the following week. Well, this was something!" And it paid several thousand a week.

On Broadway in the 1920s he had appeared as a star or featured player with Marilyn Miller, Fred and Adele Astaire, Joe Cook and Ted Healy. He was a Philadelphia grocery store clerk when he got his first job in vaudeville in 1905.

*Other dates range from 1865 to 1878.

His daughter Ruth Howard wrote much of the *Ignorant* script and gags. The program idea stemmed from her husband Bob Howell, commercial manager at WELI New Haven, where she was working. Originally called *Crazy IQs,* it rescued Tom's slumping radio career.

436. HOWE, Quincy (newscaster; b. Aug. 17, 1900, Boston, MA; d. Feb. 19, 1977, New York, NY). *Quincy Howe: Comment* (1943–46).

An author and book editor up until World War II, he said, "For me, life began in 1939, at the age of 39, when I began broadcasting news and commentary on radio." This experience at WQXR New York, led to his joining CBS in 1942. Howe helped to make analysis an accepted part of news reporting, previously delivered as much as possible without comment. His services were in constant demand for documentaries, educational features and panel discussions. He was dropped in 1947 from the CBS evening news spot, however, at the request of a sponsor—an action that brought criticism of the network and probably led to more independence for the news division. He left CBS in 1949 to teach journalism, but returned to the microphone at ABC, from 1954 to 1968.

437. HOWELL, Wayne (announcer, disc jockey; b. 1921; d. July 8, 1993, Pompano Beach, FL). *Wayne Howell Show* (1950–51); *Pickens Party* (1951); *Chamber Music Society of Lower Basin Street* (1952).

NBC New York announcer, beginning in the mid-1940s for 39 years. Howell also spun records, handled guest interviews and occasionally subbed for Clem McCarthy, Bill Stern and Bert Parks on their sports and music features. He also announced TV programs, including *Broadway Open House* and *Concentration* in the 1950s, and the annual Miss America Pageant from 1966 to 1985.

438. HUGHES, Arthur (actor; b. June 24, 1893, Bloomington, IL; d. Dec. 28, 1982, New York, NY). *Just Plain Bill* (1932–55); *Stella Dallas* (1939–40).

Lead on *Just Plain Bill* for 23 years. As Bill Davidson, a small town barber he was the serial's beloved character, part-philosopher, part-good samaritan, on nearly 6,000 broadcasts. A graduate of the Academy of Dramatic Arts, he appeared on Broadway in the cast of *Mourning Becomes Electra, Golden Boy* and *Idiot's Delight,* and other outstanding dramas over a period of 40 years. On *Collier's Hour,* an early radio potpourri, he played both the host-editor and lead character, Fu Manchu.

439. HULICK, Wilbur Budd (comedian; b. Nov. 14, 1905, Asbury Park, NJ). *Stoopnagle and Budd* (1931–37); *Show of the Week* (1939–40); *What's My Name?* (1939–40, 1943); *Studio X* (1941–42).

Slim, easygoing Hulick teamed up with corpulent, cavorting F. Chase Taylor as the satirical comedy headliners, Stoopnagle and Budd. The partners met at WMAK Buffalo where Budd was an announcer and disc jockey. They liked to clown around. When a regularly scheduled network feature met with a line breakdown, they rushed into a studio and successfully ad libbed a fill-in broadcast. Taylor was the better humorist while Budd proved a better performer.

As the *Gloom Chasers,* the duo had a long series of radio ups and downs. There were periods when their wit came over intact and other times when their talents were soft-pedaled beyond recognition. Stoop and Budd broke up in the late '30s. Hulick then rode the early wave of game shows as emcee of *What's My Name?* and *Quizzer Baseball.* He played Mortimer Meek on *Meet Mr. Meek* and Thimbledrip on Goodyear's *Hook 'n' Ladder Follies.* Reviewing *Boredom By Budd* in 1938, a critic noted his "knack of dry humorizing and ability to go along with absurdliness."

440. HULL, Warren (host, announcer; b. Jan. 17, 1903, Gasport, NY; d. Sept. 14, 1974, Waterbury, CT). *Good News of 1939/1940* (1938–40); *Vox Pop* (1942–48); *Strike It Rich* (1948–55).

A popular figure from the mid-1930s to 1950s, first as announcer (*Your Hit Parade, Good News*) and lastly as quizmaster (*Strike It Rich, Mother Knows Best*). His earliest work in radio included singing, pro-

Warren Hull (courtesy of Charles Rhodes)

ducing, writing and the proverbial sweeping the studio floor. He later appeared with Bea Lillie and Jack Haley, and on *Show Boat.*

Hull broke into the emcee ranks with audience-participation *Vox Pop* and its coast-to-coast hookup of 117 stations. It broadcast interviews from headline locations — remotes that co-host Hull handled well during the war years. His best-known series was *Strike It Rich,* a "helping hand" quiz that tended to exploit people in dire straits. This "misery" show featured a "heart line" through which pitying listeners could help with offers of cash, goods and jobs. Hull's genuinely sympathetic approach to the worries and woes of contestants counterbalanced some of the public attack on the commercialization of the plight of despondent people.

Hull studied voice at the Eastman School of Music near his upstate New York home. His first stage appearances were in operettas and musical comedies. He achieved leads in dozens of second features, including the *Green Hornet* and *Spider* serials.

441. HURT, Marlin (actor; b. May 27, 1904, Du Quoin, IL; d. March 21, 1946, Hollywood, CA). *Home Town Unincorporated* (1939–40); *Fibber McGee and Molly* (1944–45); *Beulah* (1945–46).

His soprano-voiced portrayal of a Negro maid was bizarre casting — and as a leading role short-lived. *Beulah* stemmed from a character on *Show Boat* and *Fibber McGee and Molly,* then became a CBS summer comedy series and was retained that fall.

In the 1930s Hurt had performed as Dick in the trio Tom, Dick and Harry (with Bud and Gordon Vandover), on Chicago radio, and on *College Humor* and *That's Life* as Fred Brady's girl. Out of his dialect and cross-over parts was born the amusing and loveable Beulah. This character received much mail from black listeners, even a serious proposal of marriage! At his death, the starring role went to the Negro actress, Hattie McDaniel, in a groundbreaking assignment for a member of her race.

442. HUSING, Ted (announcer; b. Nov. 17, 1901, Bronx, NY; d. Aug. 10, 1962, Pasadena, CA). *Sportslants* (1928); *The March of Time* (1931).

One of the best sports announcers on radio. Husing's control and accuracy made his dramatic, resonant voice sought-after by stations for 30 years. In preparing to cover football games he would sometimes spend most of the preceding week with one of the teams, observing their practice and studying their plays. In 1931, however, he was barred from Harvard stadium because he happened to describe the performance of its football captain as "putrid." He also broadcast political conventions and Olympic games, and interviewed U.S. presidents and foreign dignitaries.

His early endeavors read like a Walter Mitty script: airline aviator, pro football player, policeman, Wall Street runner, Florida real estate salesman. In

Ted Husing

1924 on his way to New York from Miami, he read a help wanted ad for an announcer at WJZ, and got the job. In 1925 he broadcast the first football game (University of Pennsylvania vs. Cornell). After a brief spell as an executive with WHN he joined CBS in 1927, advancing to the highest paid sportscaster in radio. He quit sports to become a disk jockey in 1946 at WHN. His shows aired 3 hours a day for 11 sponsors. A brain tumor knocked him off the dial six years later. A comeback at CBS in 1957 led to local appearances for KFI on the Pacific Coast. But he lost his $150 a week job in less than six months.

Husing's last years were spent writing his autobiography, *My Eyes Are in My Heart,* a sequel to his earlier reminiscences, *Ten Years Before the Mike.*

443. IDELSON, Billy (actor; b. Aug. 21, 1920, Forest Park, IL). *Vic and Sade* (1932–42); *One Man's Family* (1951–59).

Young actor best remembered as Rush, son of the quirky Vic and Sade. At age 22 he left the series for wartime duty in the U.S. Navy. In 1951 he began a long run as Hank Murray, one of Hazel Barbour's twin sons on *One Man's Family.* He also played Hugo on *The Truitts,* Emil on *Those Websters* and Clay on Carlton Morse's *Woman in My House.*

In 1931 Idelson had started out as Skeezix in a version of the comic strip *Gasoline Alley.* A graduate of Northwestern, he capped his career as a TV writer-producer (*Bob Newhart Show*).

seven musicals and was the uncredited, off-screen pianist who played the music of Chopin in *A Song to Remember.*

He began playing the piano at age three, studied in Barcelona and Paris before taking over as head of the Geneva Conservatory. He began concertizing and at his peak played an average of 183 concerts a year. A number of his performances combined conducting and playing. ("The result . . . does not need the apology of being a visual tour de force," noted *The New York Times.*) He regularly appeared with his sister, Amparo Iturbi, in duo-piano recitals, and recorded many best-selling singles, capped by a million copies of Chopin's Polonaise in 1945 for RCA-Victor. One of his last associations was as conductor-musical director of the Greater Bridgeport (CT) Symphony from 1967 to 1972.

445. IVES, Burl (singer [signature song: "Blue Tail Fly"]; b. June 14, 1909, Hunt Township, IL; d. April 14, 1995, Anacortes, WA). *Columbia County Journal* (1944); *Radio Reader's Digest* (1945).

Program innovator CBS gave Ives his own folk song and ballad series *The Wayfarin' Stranger* in 1940 when other booking agents viewed him as just another hillbilly act. He had learned many of his folk songs from his grandmother, who had mastered hundreds of American ballads of Scottish, English and Irish origin. A cross-country hitchhiker, young Ives supported himself by singing and playing the guitar and banjo, and doing odd jobs. Along the way he added cowboy and lumberjack songs.

Jose Iturbi

444. ITURBI, Jose (pianist-conductor; b. Nov. 28, 1895, Valencia, Spain; d. June 28, 1980, Hollywood, CA). Rochester Philharmonic Orchestra (1935–37, 1939–42).

Concert hall performer with a flair for screen acting. Pianist Iturbi made his U.S. debut in 1929 with the Philadelphia Orchestra, playing Beethoven's G Major Concerto, then in 1933 in Mexico City bowed as a conductor. He led many of the world's foremost orchestras, but is closely identified with the Rochester Philharmonic and its weekly Thursday evening broadcasts over NBC Blue. In 1942 he made the first of 21 guest appearances at the keyboard over a 15-year period on *The Telephone Hour.* His music — embracing boogie woogie as well as the classics — and scripted repartee popped up on the comedy-variety shows of Vallee, Crosby, Bergen & McCarthy, and Amos 'n' Andy.

Described as a "restless musician" — he once took boxing lessons and became a licensed pilot — Iturbi broke into the movies in 1943 at MGM with *As Thousands Cheer* and *Two Girls and A Sailor.* He went on to make

Burl Ives

Stage appearances and club dates led to the microphone. But he was soon drafted. He was assigned to *This Is the Army* on Broadway, and for a time had a program, *G.I. Jive,* broadcast to overseas military outposts.

Ives rejoined CBS, making network appearances on *Chesterfield Supper Club, National Barn Dance, Johnny Presents.* In 1946 he introduced a series of recorded song shows over Mutual. By then, he had settled in Hollywood for film work which culminated in an Oscar in 1959 for a supporting role in *The Big Country.*

446. JAMES, Harry (bandleader [signature song: "Ciribiribin"]; b. March 15, 1916, Albany, GA; d. July 5, 1983, Las Vegas, NV). *Spotlight Bands* (1943–44); *Everything for the Boys* (1944); *Call for Music* (1948).

One of the biggest names of the swing era. In the early 1940s he made at least three broadcasts a week, frequently on the *Fitch Bandwagon.* A virtuoso on the trumpet, he was admired for his ability to play lead horn and take all the hot choruses, as well as conduct his highly successful 18-piece band.

James started out in his father's circus band, then at age 12 led a similar group for the Christy Brothers Circus. In 1935 he was hired by Ben Pollack, and two years later, joined the brass section of Benny Goodman's band where he became widely known as a jazz soloist. In 1939, with Goodman's encouragement and financial help, James organized his own Music Makers.

A rough-and-ready swing band, it soon turned to a sweeter, smoother style, featuring its singing discov-

Harry James

eries, Frank Sinatra and Dick Haymes. James mixed hot numbers ("Two O'Clock Jump") with light fare ("I Had the Craziest Dream"). "I've Heard That Song Before" became Columbia Records first million seller. His assignment to the CBS series vacated by Glenn Miller when he received an Army captaincy skyrocked James to the top ranks.

One of the few bandleaders to make more than token appearances in movies, James played supporting roles, usually with his musicians, in a dozen major films. He gained vast publicity due to his marriage to cinema star and pinup queen Betty Grable in 1943. Not long before his death, he headlined the touring musical *The Big Broadcast of 1944,* with Dennis Day, Hildegarde, Don Wilson and the Ink Spots.

447. JAMES, Hugh (announcer; b. Oct. 13, 1915, Bronx, NY). *Voice of Firestone* (1939–54); *Three Star Final* (1944–49); *Big Town* (1948–49).

His strong, baritone voice proved highly marketable. For 15 years he did four daily network shows, including the intro to Lowell Thomas's NBC newscast. While still in high school, James set out to make radio his career. He started as a page, then advanced to tourist guide, at NBC. In 1933 he conducted the first group of sightseers through the network's new studios in Radio City. Pat Kelly, supervisor of announcers, overheard him and thought his voice had possibilities. Soon he was doing station breaks.

In 1935 NBC placed him as staff announcer at WFIL Philadelphia, and less than a year later at WORC Washington. There, he broadcast the second term inauguration of President Roosevelt from a post in the Capitol dome, standing in a frigid wind for hours, and consequently catching pneumonia. In August 1937 James came back to New York for Lowell Thomas's broadcasts.

Called the master of the "mellow sell," he believed "sincerity is the most important quality an announcer can possess." His was the only speaking voice on Firestone in a two-fold capacity as host and announcer. On that prestigious concert series, he once introduced baritone Igor Gorin as "Igor Baritone." After the show Gorin returned the compliment by addressing him as "Hugh Announcer."

448. JAMES, Philip (conductor, composer; b. May 17, 1890, Jersey City, NJ; d. Nov. 1, 1975, Southampton, NY). *Bamberger Little Symphony* (1929–36).

James considered radio work the finest school, technically, for the embryonic American conductor and orchestral musician. "We must look to our radio stations, unorganized and inconsistent as they are in many cases, for an American school of conductors," he said in 1936. The one-time Army band master and musical director for Victor Herbert put this theory to the test, becoming conductor of WOR's Bamberger Little Symphony Orchestra in 1929 — the first chamber ensemble to broadcast weekly. He made it a point to present one American composer each week. He himself was one of five American composers to share $10,000 in a NBC symphonic composition contest in 1932. James's winning work was an impression of a day in a radio studio and called "Station WGZBX." The piece was first performed by the NBC Symphony Orchestra under the direction of Eugene Goossens.

In 1933 James, an academically trained organist, assumed the chairmanship of the music department of New York University. By the early 1940s he was an occasional guest conductor of WOR's Sinfonietta and Symphonic Strings, and commentator on *Wellsprings of Music* at CBS.

449. JAMESON, House (actor; b. Dec. 17, 1902, Austin, TX; d. April 23, 1971, Danbury, CT). *Renfrew of the Mounted* (1936–40); *Young Widder Brown* (1938–42); *The Aldrich Family* (1939–53); *Marriage for Two* (1949–50).

Father Sam Aldrich in *The Aldrich Family,* he created one of radio's most memorable parental roles. The series stemmed from a Broadway play, and lasted a dozen years, into early television. Before joining this domestic comedy, Jameson had the lead as Renfrew, his first major radio assignment. The Texas-born actor had begun on Broadway as a spear carrier in the Theatre Guild's *St. Joan.*

During World War II he was called upon to give special savings bond appeals and patriotic readings on *Cities Service Concert,* and to star in dramatizations on *Worlds at War* and *Lands of the Free.* For Du Pont's *Cavalcade of America,* the statesmen-like actor played Jefferson Davis, James Madison and Thomas Jefferson.

450. JANNEY, Leon (actor; b. April 1, 1917, Ogden, UT; d. Oct. 28, 1980, Guadalajara, Mexico). *The Parker Family* (1939–42); *Right to Happiness* (1947–48); *Ethel Merman Show* (1949).

Child actor in films, he faced unemployment at age 15 because he had outgrown kid roles. Vaudeville, where he had made his debut at two in hometown Ogden, offered few prospects by the mid-1930s. Radio proved his best bet, especially when he became Richard Parker, the all-American lad of *The Parker Family.* Janney performed on as many as 63 different shows, including *The Shadow, Charlie Chan, Quick as a Flash* and *Mr. District Attorney,* and frequently using one of 20 different accents or dialects, ranging from a fresh-voiced youngster to a whinning old man.

Between 1947 and 1956 he made more than 40 appearances on *The Eternal Light,* a series of Biblical, historical and modern-day dramas presented by the Jewish Theological Seminary. He moved into early television dramas and soap operas. Janney was a member of the national board of AFTRA for 30 years.

451. JENKINS, Gordon (conductor, composer [signature song: "You Have Taken My Heart"];

Gordon Jenkins

b. May 10, 1910, Webster Groves, MO; d. May 1, 1984, Malibu, CA). *Hall of Fun* (1938–39); *Everything for the Boys* (1944–45); *Bob Burns Show* (1944–46).

A relief organist for his father in a Chicago movie theatre at age 10, he dropped out of school to play the piano in a St. Louis speakeasy, and later found work at KMOX in 1927. He opened the St. Louis station at 9 a.m. by singing and playing organ, piano and accordion until the regular staff arrived. "By 10 o'clock, if no one else had shown up yet, I would take it from the top and do the whole thing over again." It was his first steady musical job and gave him, if nothing else, "a sense of my own worth — that I was somebody who could do something."

Jenkins turned to arranging for bandleaders Isham Jones, Benny Goodman, Paul Whiteman and Vincent Lopez, conducting for Beatrice Lillie's musical *The Show Is On,* and scoring films. His first major hit, "You Have Taken My Heart," was introduced by soprano Jessica Dragonette on a 1934 *Cities Service Concert.* He was named West Coast musical director for NBC, offering *Rhythm and Romance* and *Time and Tempo* to fill the sustaining schedule. He left to conduct a 31-piece orchestra on the *Dick Haymes Show* where he also collaborated on "capsule operettas," an eagerly anticipated feature. His "Manhattan Tower," a four-selection tribute to New York, became his best known semi-serious work. As a Decca conductor and musical director in the 1940s, he showcased Louis Armstrong, Peggy Lee and The Weavers. He also wrote a cluster of Top 10 tunes, including "My Foolish Heart," "P.S., I Love You" and "San Fernando Valley."

Helen Jepson

452. JEPSON, Helen (singer; b. Nov. 28, 1906, Titusville, PA). *Kraft Music Hall* (1934–35); *Show Boat* (1936).

Both Rudy Vallee and Paul Whiteman claimed her as their discovery in the 1930s. But conductor Philip James first featured this lyric soprano with his Bamberger Little Symphony Orchestra on June 24, 1933 at WOR — months before she attracted the interest of those two impresarios. Her broadcast debut came even earlier, as a pupil at Curtis Institute in 1929. Nonetheless, Vallee called himself "her Columbus" since she made her coast-to-coast debut on his *Fleischmann Hour* on Columbus Day 1933. She sang the "Jewel Song" from *Faust*.

The tall, blonde Jepson had appeared with the Philadelphia Grand Opera before its financial collapse. Settling in Manhattan with her husband, flutist George Possell, she struggled for vocal engagements while continuing voice lessons. Her weekly appearances with Whiteman changed her luck and attracted the interest of the Met where she bowed in 1935 in the premiere of the one-act American opera *In the Pasha's Garden* with Lawrence Tibbett. She brought beauty, voice and charm to such roles as Violetta, Nedda, Louise and Desdemona. Her popularity among radio listeners led to the frequent bookings on *The Telephone Hour*, *RCA Magic Key*, *Echoes of New York* and *Your Hit Parade*.

Divorced and remarried in the early 1940s and plagued by a throat ailment, Jepson retired by the end of that decade. She taught singing — Edie Adams was a student — and lectured on operatic subjects. She also returned to college in New Jersey to train as a speech therapist for handicapped children.

453. JESSEL, George (comedian, emcee [Toastmaster General of the U.S.A.] [signature song: "My Mother's Eyes"]; b. April 3, 1898, New York, NY; d. May 23, 1981, Los Angeles, CA). *For Men Only* (1939–40); *Here's Looking at New York* (1941–42); *Hollywood Calling* (1949–50).

Jessel bounced from one corner of show business to another during a life in the limelight that began at age 10. He teamed up with other adolescent hopefuls to play vaudeville as part of Gus Edwards' kid revue. Eddie Cantor was on the same bill. In 1915 he played in London for eight weeks, but not until the lead in *The Jazz Singer* came his way did Broadway seem hospitable. Nonetheless, he lost out to Jolson in the film version. His early talkies were undistinguished.

Radio filled in the gaps between personal appearances and his most successful period as a motion picture producer at 20th Century–Fox in the 1940s. Yet he was never really comfortable on radio or television. On the air he always had an impulse to ad lib, and the rigid schedules in broadcasting chafed. The loquacious Jessel was a radio guest for Ruby Vallee in 1934, Hildegarde in 1944 and Bob Hope in 1954, among many others. He often opened and closed his appearances with his familiar telephone routine with his mama.

His popularity as a speaker at banquets and celebrations kept him busy to the point where it blossomed into a fulfilling vocation. His mix of comedy, eloquence and sentimentality as a toastmaster never went out of favor, and in *Variety*'s summation, "He was a showman to the end."

454. JOHNSON, Parks (emcee, interviewer; b. May 22, 1891, Sheffield, AL; d. Oct. 4, 1970, Wimberley, TX). *Vox Pop* (1935–48).

Acknowledged originator of the forerunner of all the quiz and game shows. He started his Voice of the People remotes as a local show in Houston in 1932. An advertising and newspaper man, he had joined KTRH a few years earlier and decided on man-on-the-street interviews with questions and prizes to participants.

With Jerry Belcher, station engineer who helped carry it out, Johnson and *Vox Pop* came to New York as a 1935 summer fill-in for Joe Penner's hour over NBC. "We were just a couple of country boys," Parks once said, "and we were scared of what some of these smart New Yorkers might say to us. So we broadcast the first time from Columbus Circle, keeping the site of the show a strict secret in advance." The enlightening and amusing series moved with the times — and at the rate of about 1,000 miles a week — turning up at odd but important and widely separated points.

As early as July 1940 Johnson embarked on subjects and locales related to the war effort, reporting

Parks Johnson, Guy Lombardo, Howard Barlow, Wally Butterworth, Graham McNamee, Lowell Thomas (courtesy of Bill Johnson)

from training bases, military hospitals and defense plants. His broadcasts particularly focused on the achievements of service men and women and factory workers. "The Show That Travels America" went to Detroit Tank Arsenal, Quantico Marine Base, Walter Reed Hospital and Houston Shipbuilding Corporation, and many other war-related locations. Although his broadcasts were not done from scripts, Johnson gave careful preparation for each interview from information collected from advance men who selected the most engaging prospects. Above all, he wanted the program to help Americans understand their fellow Americans a little better. And sometimes these Americans were household names: Jack Dempsey, Rita Hayworth, Duke Ellington, Jimmy Doolittle, Gypsy Rose Lee.

In May 1939 at the New York World's Fair, *Vox Pop* conducted its interviews as part of the first lineup of telecasts comprising sponsored network programs. Hundreds of Fair visitors viewed the show over a battery of TV sets in the RCA exhibit. On camera, Parks loaded and smoked a pipe with the sponsor's Kentucky Club Pipe Tobacco. The program became a regularly scheduled TV feature at NBC studios that year.

By 1948 Johnson was tired of New York, and the hassle with networks, agencies and sponsors. He retired to a ranch in Wimberley, Texas, where in the true Vox Pop mode, he became involved in just about everything to make this community a better place to live.

455. JOHNSON, Raymond Edward (actor [catchphrase: "Good e-e-evening, and how are you this evening?"]; b. July 24, 1911, Kenosha, WI). *Today's Children* (1936–38); *Girl Alone* (1936–39); *Inner Sanctum Mystery* (1941–45); *Young Widder Brown* (1942–44, 1947); *The Crime Club* (1946–47).

As Raymond the host of *Inner Sanctum,* he guided his listeners through the dark and winding caverns of mayhem and mystery. A squeaking door signaled the beginning of each hair-raising show, followed by Raymond's soft and eerie welcome and sinister laugh. His weekly intro inscribed his name and voice into the annals of radio lore.

Johnson performed on many soaps and in *Mr. District Attorney, The Aldrich Family,* and *Arch Oboler's Plays,* but it was the mystery program that placed him in the mind of his audience. And also saddled him with a sinister image he could not shake. "My whole career changed," he said years later "Up to this time I was the leading man, the boy friend. But even unknown to me, I became the scarey guy, the bogey man." He left the show to serve in the Army, and on his return began doing *Joyce Jordan, M.D.* But stricken with multiple sclerosis in his 40s, he was forced to limit his work and finally retire. In later years he performed at radio conventions where he recreated his old macabre tales and recited dramatic monologues.

456. JOHNSTON, Johnny (singer; b. Dec. 1, 1914, St. Louis, MO; d. Jan. 6, 1996, Cape Coral, Fl.). *Club Matinee* (1937); *The Breakfast Club* (1937–38); *Chesterfield Time* (1944–45); *Rhapsody in Rhythm* (1947).

Capable pop star, he had his own prime-time CBS program *Rhapsody in Rhythm* with Peggy Lee and The Pied Pipers. His vocal numbers first came over the air from Chicago, chiefly with *The Breakfast Club.* For the summer of 1945 he took over for Perry Como on *Chesterfield Supper Club.*

Johnston introduced the enduring classic "That Old Black Magic" in Paramount's wartime *Star Spangled Rhythm* and also recorded "Laura," a hit that sold a million copies. He was one of the first artists that Capitol Records signed in 1942.

457. JOHNSTONE, William (actor; b. Feb. 7, 1908, Paisley, Scotland). *There Was a Woman* (1938); *The Shadow* (1938–43); *Today's Children* (1946–48); *Bob Hope Show* (1953–54).

Supporting character on numerous series, from *Six-Gun Justice* and *The Fabulous Dr. Tweedy* to *Valiant Lady* and *The Silent Men,* and an occasional lead, notably as *The Shadow,* replacing Orson Welles in that coveted role.

Johnstone made various appearances on *March of Time, Johnny Presents* (28 roles from September 1940 to April 1942) and *Cavalcade of America* (as Jean Laffite and Zachary Taylor). For daytime television, he played Judge Lowell on *As The World Turns* from 1957 to the late '70s.

458. JOLSON, Al (singer [The Jazz Singer] [signature song: "Swanee"] [catchphrase: "Folks, you ain't heard nothin' yet!"]; b. May 26, 1886, St. Petersburg, Russia; d. Oct. 23, 1950, San Francisco, CA). *Al Jolson Show* (1932–33, 1936–39, 1942–43); *Shell Chateau* (1935–36); *Kraft Music Hall* (1933–34, 1947–49).

One of the great entertainers of all time, Jolson worked in minstrel shows, vaudeville, Broadway musicals, recording studios and movies. By 1928 radio was the natural next step. Over the air his exuberant singing and frentic repartee registered well, particularly on *Shell Chateau* and *Kraft Music Hall.* His radio work continued into the early 1940s. A pause during World War II gave him an opportunity to travel close to the front lines as an entertainer — a commitment he continued when the Korean conflict broke out.

In the wake of the 1946 autobiographical film *The Jolson Story,* he made a monumental comeback. Being a radio guest star became a very lucrative assignment; he received $10,000 per spot, the highest pay of any entertainer at that time. Jolson soon settled for two seasons — and $7,500 a week — on the *Kraft Music Hall* (which he had helped inaugurate back in 1933). He re-popularized many of his earlier hits:

Al Jolson (courtesy of Steve Jelf)

"April Showers," "California, Here I Come," "Avalon," "Sonny Boy."

Jolson had made his network bow singing Irving Berlin's "What Does It Matter?" on a NBC program to aid Mississippi Valley flood victims in April 1927. That year he had taken a chance with the untried medium of talking pictures. His *Jazz Singer* is considered a milestone in the motion picture arts, and Jolson is credited with introducing the "talkies." In 1950 not long after the release of the eagerly awaited sequel, *Jolson Sings Again,* and following an exhausting trip to entertain troops in Korea, Al stopped in San Francisco to be guest on Bing Crosby's show. The pre-recorded session was set for October 24, 1950. Jolson died of a heart attack on the eve of the taping.

459. JONES, Billy (singer; b. March 15, 1887, New York, NY; d. Nov. 23, 1940, New York, NY).

Comic-patter and musical entertainer of radio's early decade with partner Ernie Hare. The "Happiness Boys" began in a recording studio and hit its stride at a radio microphone. Beginning in August 1923 at WEAF, they are considered to be the first comedy show. The duo were especially adept with catchy opening and closing tunes, and with satire of the early wireless.

Hare died in 1939; his 16-year-old daughter Marilyn replaced him. When she left for Hollywood, Jim Brennan joined Jones on the *Billy Jones Review* each Sunday afternoon over WMCA. A radio script for the November 24, 1940 program was found in Jones's pocket when he collapsed and died while walking along Broadway.

460. JONES, Spike (bandleader [signature song: "Hotcha Cornia (Black Eyes)"]; [catchphrase: "Thank you, music lovers"]; b. Dec. 14, 1911, Long Beach, CA; d. May 1, 1965, Bel Air, CA). *Bob Burns, The Arkansas Traveler* (1943–44); *Spike Jones Show* (1947–49).

Spike Jones's musical mayhem carried on by his check-suited City Slickers made millions laugh, especially during a time of war-weariness. He broadcast his first show in 1941 using washboards, cow bells, small cannons and bird whistles to make wacky music. He had played drums for what he called "soup music" with the likes of John Scott Trotter on the *Kraft Music Hall,* and it bored him. Soon after organizing his own merrymen, this musical Robin Hood stole from the rich repertoire of classics and mainstream standards, and began to spread his satirical spoofs by West Coast radio appearances.

Their biggest break came with the waxing of an anti-Hitler burlesque called "Der Fuehrer's Face" for Victor. The polka-flavored song injected a rubber "razzer" emitting a spirited Bronx cheer whenever the word "Heil" was sung. Victor had little confidence in the nutty tune, so it pressed only 500 discs. Jones took one to Martin Block at Station WNEW who in-

Spike Jones

Jim & Marian Jordan

troduced it on his *Make Believe Ballroom.* Block created a stampede when he offered a free record to anyone who brought a $50 war bond. The New York disc jockey gave away 289 records the first day and sold more than $60,000 worth of bonds in two weeks. The novelty number reportedly sold more than 1.5 million copies, and gained a measure of immortality when a similarly titled Disney cartoon featured the patriotic novelty.

After the war Jones toured with his Musical Depreciation Revue, featuring comedian Doodles Weaver and singer (and Jones's wife) Helen Grayco. The show's finale "Cocktails for Two" with an entire chorus of hiccups was one of his greatest put-ons. Jukeboxes spun this City Slickers disc to such a degree that Victor made 150,000 pressings with it on both sides. As soon as one side wore out, the other could be played to death. And few listeners ever forgot his rendition of "You Always Hurt The One You Love," in which the "beloved" is shot, stabbed and poisoned, or his schmalzy "Blue Danube" with four strategically placed belches.

461. JORDAN, Jim (comedian [catchphrase: "Dad-rat the dad ratted. . . ."]; b. Nov. 16, 1896, Peoria, IL; d. April 1, 1988, Los Angeles, CA). *Smackouts* (1931–35); *Mr. Twister* (1933); *Fibber McGee and Molly* (1935–57); *Kaltenmeyer's Kindergarten* (1936–37).

Jordan and wife Marian began appearing on radio in 1925 while trodding the boards in vaudeville. During ten years of skits, they gradually developed the Fib-

ber McGee and Molly characters. Chicago radio featured them often as a comedy team on *Breakfast Club* and *National Barn Dance.* In 1935 NBC picked up the duo who quickly became a classic American couple. Residing at radio's 79 Wistful Vita, they opened their door to a lineup of memorable "visitors:" the Old-Timer, Wallace Wimple, Mayor La Trivia and Throckmorton P. Gildersleeve. McGee's overstuffed closet, which frequently unloaded on Jordan's character, was a sound effects man's challenging moment of glory.

Their familiar, well-accepted routines readily translated into a series of movies (*Heavenly Days, Here We Go Again*) but a 1959–60 TV version without the Jordans didn't measure up. In the late 1950s they appeared each weekend on NBC's *Monitor* as part of the "Stardust Edition" concept of scheduling top-flight talent in five-minute segments scattered throughout the program.

462. JORDAN, Marian (comedienne [catchphrase: "'Tain't funny, McGee."]; b. April 16, 1898, Peoria, IL; d. April 7, 1961, Encino, CA). *Smackouts* (1931–35); *Fibber McGee and Molly* (1935–37, 1939–57); *Kaltenmeyer's Kindergarten* (1936–37).

Warm-hearted, perceptive Molly on the long popular program of small-town life with the raffish, boastful Fibber, played by husband Jim Jordan. The closely knit couple met when they sang in a church choir while still in their teens, and married in 1918, just before Jim went off to war. Singing at community socials led to vaudeville, although Marian periodically stayed home to raise their two children (and did so again from November 1937 to April 1939).

They first stood at a microphone as the singing "O'Henry Twins" on a Chicago station in 1926. The Jordans returned, doing musical programs and children's shows, until starting *Smackouts,* about a small-town grocer. Four years later, in 1935, with the help of writer Don Quinn, the McGees burst forth over NBC Chicago. The series was a backdrop for many memorable characters at 79 Vistful Vista. They included the little girl next door, Teeny, whose whispery voice was Marian and who forever asked "Whatcha doin', mister, whatcha doin', huh?"

The McGees figured prominently on many NBC specials: 15th and 25th anniversary shows, *Parade of Stars,* "All Star March of Dimes," *Radio City Previews,* and "Hollywood Salutes FDR." On a CBS *Suspense* episode in 1949,they played straight mystery roles — a rare opportunity for serious drama.

463. JOSLYN, Allyn (actor; b. July 21, 1901, Milford, PA; d. Jan. 22, 1981, Woodland Hills, CA). *Island Boat Club* (1932); *Pages of Romance* (1932–33).

Between 1928 and 1937 he appeared in more than 3,500 radio shows, according to an account filed by the AP at his death. They included leading roles in *Royal Canadian Mounted Police Stories* and *The Court of Human Relations.* For the first two years of *Show Boat,* he was Lanny Ross's speaking voice and handled similar assignments for other singers. His radio work lessened when he scored a success on Broadway in *Boy Meets Girl* (1935) and made his movie debut as a cold-blooded newspaperman in *They Won't Forget* two years later. He went on to establish himself as one of Hollywood's most versatile character actors.

464. JOSTYN, Jay (actor; b. Dec. 13, 1905, Milwaukee, WI; d. July 24, 1977). *Mrs. Wiggs of the Cabbage Patch* (1936–38); *Mr. District Attorney* (1939–51); *The Mystery Man* (1941–42).

NBC's anti-crime program, *Mr. District Attorney,* became so real to millions of listeners that the actor Jay Jostyn in the title role regularly received letters asking for legal advice and help on such problems as boundary disputes and marital impasses. Some listeners even thought Jostyn was crimebuster Thomas E. Dewey off duty. "When the Republicans had their convention in 1940 I had letters from several voters telling me they had instructed their delegates to vote for Dewey because he put on such a swell radio show." In fact, the racket-busting work of Dewey inspired series producer Ed Byron.

Jostyn assumed the D.A. role on October 1, 1939 with the episode "The Accident Racket." Besides his weekly prosecuting triumphs, he appeared as the father on *The Parker Family,* and on *Second Husband* and *Our Gal Sunday.* Occasionally he played a defense lawyer on *Famous Jury Trials.* But its sponsor specified that in this role he must never lose a case.

A graduate of Wisconsin Conservatory of Music, he broke into show business as a Hollywood stock actor and started on New York radio in 1936.

465. JOY, Dick (announcer; b. Dec. 28, 1915, Putnam, CT; d. Oct. 31, 1991, Medford, OR). *My Secret Ambition* (1937–38); *Vox Pop* (1939–43, 1945–46); *The Saint* (1945); *Danny Kaye Show* (1945–46).

West Coast regular who started as a member of the original CBS-KNX staff for local news and special events in 1937. By 1940 he was announcer for all West Coast originations of the traveling interview show, *Vox Pop,* becoming the personal choice of the show's creator Parks Johnson. During the 1945–46 season Joy handled its broadcasts from the East Coast where Pabst Beer had hired him for the Danny Kaye program. When the *Telephone Hour* aired from Hollywood, he announced this prestigious great artist series. In 1946 he became co-owner of KCMJ, Palm Springs' first station, and commuted for two years for freelance work on *Sam Spade* and Spike Jones. Selling his transmitter in 1951, Joy moved into television at KTTV. For 17 years at KFAC he held the job of news director and principal newscaster.

On a New Year's Eve 1945 broadcast for *Vox Pop* Dick came down with a severe sore throat — every announcer's nightmare. *Vox Pop*'s director Fran Harris, taking a look at the wobegone Joy, ordered him to go to a nearby bar for a cherry cordial to "warm him up." Back in the studio, with one minute to airtime, his stomach and the cordial came into conflict. The result: hiccups. Harris viewed the situation with a grain of salt. "My God — New Year's Eve, coast-to-coast, Bromo-Seltzer the sponsor, and your mother in LA doesn't know you drink! What a headline!" Each time Joy read the commercials he was so nervous the hiccups stopped — but in-between, and afterwards, they came back. "I don't think Parks Johnson ever knew about it," he remembered years later, "and neither did my mother."

As an undergrad at USC, he covered radio for the student paper, and decided on broadcasting instead of journalism. His earliest work was at KEHE and KHJ.

466. JULIAN, Joseph (actor; b. c1911, St. Marys, PA; d. March 11, 1982, New York, NY). *Lorenzo Jones* (1944–49); *Call the Police* (1947); *Hearthstone of the Death Squad* (1948–53).

Frequent narrator-actor in Norman Corwin dramas and war documentaries for CBS. During World War II he journeyed to England to appear on the series "An American in Great Britain," heard both there and in the United States. In 1945 from Japan he taped human-interest interviews with GIs for a Red Cross-sponsored series. Julian's credits, circa 1940, read like a weekly program log: *Young Doctor Malone, Front Page Farrell, The Goldbergs, Nero Wolfe, Inner Sanctum, Superman, The Greatest Story Ever Told.* One of

Joseph Julian (courtesy of Steve Jelf)

467. KABIBBLE, Ish (comedian; b. Jan. 19, 1908, Erie, PA; d. June 4, 1994, Palm Springs, CA). *Kollege of Musical Knowledge* (1938–48).

Nonsensical comic and cornet player. His real name was Merwyn Bogue but he took a stage name from the lyrics of one of the goofy songs in his act. Ish joined Kay Kyser's band in 1931, doing everything short of the laundry. As the troupe's comedian he combed his hair straight down toward his eyebrows and was always introduced as "the guy with the low-cut bangs and the high-kicking cornet." Although he played occasional jazz solos, he is remembered as a silly character who sang such songs as "Three Little Fishes." Ish stayed with the Kollege into its television runs in 1949 and 1951, then went into the real estate business.

468. KADELL, Carlton (announcer; b. Aug. 21, 1906, Danville, IL; d. March 14, 1975, Chicago, IL). *Kitty Keane* (1939–41); *Amos 'n' Andy* (1945–47); *Masquerade* (1946–47).

Chicago and Hollywood announcer-actor for more than 40 years. His choice assignment was *Amos 'n' Andy;* other major shows were *Mayor of the Town* and *Big Town.* KaDell announced for Dorothy Lamour, Jack Carson and Edgar Bergen. He also played title roles in *Tarzan, Red Ryder* and *Right to Happiness.* In the 1950s KaDell returned to Chicago where he had started out doing time signals at WJJD in 1931. He appeared there in the mystery-detective program *A Life in Your Hands.* His *Classical Kaleidoscope,* over KEFM, built a loyal audience and aired until the very day of death in 1975.

KaDell's father had operated a chain of movie theatres, and Carlton turned down several screen contracts over the years. Before radio, he enrolled in a speech enhancement school, then acted with a Chautauqua company. He reached Broadway in *Ladies of the Jury.*

469. KAHN, Joseph (pianist; b. June 7, 1903, New York, NY). *Voice of Firestone* (1928–29); *NBC Symphony* (1938–41, 1954); *Information Please* (1938–46); *Cameos of Music* (1947–50).

NBC staff musician, beginning in 1928. Already there were three pianists on staff at the new network but all were concert-level performers. A jazz player was needed. Kahn did an "on the air" audition and was hired. A quick study, he had gained invaluable experience by playing with his violinist-father for silent movie pictures. He soon accompanied both pop and concert and opera singers, and worked on some 30 programs per week. That included "stand-by" duty in a small studio (2B) in case a performer failed to show up or technical problems knocked a program off the line.

During his 26 years at NBC Kahn also directed serious music and rhythm groups, including Joe Kahn and His Kilocycle Kids for Lee Sullivan's *Vest Pocket Varieties.* He also played under Toscanini in the NBC Symphony and post-Toscanini Symphony of the Air.

his talents was playing music by squeezing his palms together. He once performed this feat on the *Fred Allen Show,* giving rise to the comedian's question, "What kind of music are you going to palm off on us tonight? Handel?"

In the 1940s he wrote articles published in *Variety* and *The New York Times* that claimed most actors on radio were conscious of "lack of inner satisfaction after doing a radio job" and "didn't take themselves seriously as artists." His views outraged many in the business. Julian promoted the idea of memorizing a radio role, and gave several performances without a script in hand — and in the process scared the hell out of other cast members.

In his personal memoir *This Was Radio* (1975), he recalled the time on *Radio Reader's Digest* when to simulate an operating room they held a stethoscope to an actor's heart and the other end to the mike. After the program, the telephone rang. "Twenty-two doctors warned us to get that man to a hospital. They all detected a malfunction of the heart. It probably saved that actor's life."

Blacklisted in "Red Channels," a handbook used by the networks for screening out controversial artists, he found few jobs open. He sued the publishers. After a four-year struggle he was exonerated and resumed his once-flourishing career.

His pre-network assignments included skits and disc intros at WNYC and sound effects and acting at WLW.

In the 1950s on a U.S. State Department-arranged Symphony of the Air tour of the Far East, Kahn performed "Rhapsody in Blue" 17 times. He provided music for *The Story of Mary Marlin* at both CBS and NBC for ten airings a week. During the run of *Information Please* he played musical questions at a piano to stump such panel guests as Artur Rubinstein and Leonard Bernstein.

While on the *Atwater Kent Hour* in 1930, he met and married that year's Atwater Kent national contest winner, soprano Carol Deis of Dayton, Ohio. She received first prize by singing the "Bell Song" from *Lakme* and in 1931 signed contracts with NBC and the Philadelphia Opera Company. Her radio credits included *Your Hit Parade* and *Met Auditions of the Air.*

470. KALTENBORN, Hans (H.V.) (commentator; b. July 9, 1878, Milwaukee, WI; d. June 14, 1965, New York, NY). *Current Events* (1927–36); *Editing The News* (1930–55).

His reporting and commentary on the Munich crisis in the fall of 1938 stands as his most notable achievement. With Europe on the edge of war, he made 102 broadcasts ranging from two minutes to two hours over a period of 18 days. He scarcely left the CBS studios in New York, sleeping on a cot and subsisting on sandwiches and coffee. Kaltenborn was able to translate German, French and Italian as it was heard on the short wave, and thus gave listeners an instant summary of the talks of world leaders.

A journalist on the staff of the *Brooklyn Eagle,* Hans Von Kaltenborn came to a microphone in April 1922

H. V. Kaltenborn

when he broadcast a news roundup for WYCB. Two years later he became a weekly commentator for WEAF. The well-traveled, Harvard-educated correspondent refused to use notes or prepared material. "I would say whatever came into my head," he explained, "however, I had my head trained so that I didn't get into too much trouble."

By 1930 he had joined CBS as news editor and covered political campaigns and national elections. He handled like assignments for NBC through 1956. He also interviewed many heads of state. Kaltenborn helped to organize the Association of Radio News Analysts as well as the Radio Pioneers. His books included the autobiographical *Fifty Fabulous Years.*

He insisted on speaking his mind despite the occasional shudders in executive offices. His listeners either forgave or ignored his mistakes. Harry S. Truman, for one, never forgot Kaltenborn's broadcast of 1948 Election Night returns and his declaration that Truman had been defeated by an overwhelming vote — when, in fact, the President had scored a celebrated victory.

471. KATIMS, Milton (violist, conductor; b. June 24, 1909, Brooklyn, NY). *NBC Symphony* (1943–54); *Serenade to America* (1944–46); *Eternal Light* (1946–48, 1952–54).

Cited as one of the most eminent American artists in the music of the viola. Toscanini invited him to join the NBC Symphony in 1943 after nearly eight years as a soloist and conductor at Mutual. Beginning in 1947 for seven years, this trusted associate periodically led the NBC orchestra for a total of 52 broadcasts. Katims' staff assignments ranged from the war-related (*We Came This Way*) to audience participation (*Honeymoon in New York*) to comedy (Henry Morgan, Jack Pearl). From 1940 to 1954 he also played with the Budapest String Quartet. He ended his yeoman service at Radio City in 1954 when he became conductor of the Seattle Symphony.

A Columbia University graduate, Katims taught at The Juilliard School, founded the Chamber Music Society and served as artistic director, School of Music, University of Houston.

472. KAUFMAN, Irving (singer; b. Feb. 8, 1890, Syracuse, NY; d. Jan. 3, 1976, Indio, CA). *Champion Sparkers* (1928–30); *Lazy Dan* (1933–36); *Broadway Vanities* (1934–35).

Best known as an old-time minstrel man with a "familiar style of easy jollity." He started as a vocalist with Gus Haenschen's orchestra on WJZ in 1922. He had his own programs as Lazy Dan, Johnny Prentiss, Happy Jim Parsons and Salty Sam — often using many different accents. He appeared on commercials, most notably as the crazy Frenchman singing about Chateau Martin Wine.

Kaufman started as a boy soprano in vaudeville and with a circus. Work as a New York song plugger led to an audition and contract with the Edison Company in 1911. Under different names, he waxed a grand total of some 6,000 songs. In 1913 he joined the Avon Comedy Four, a top vaudeville act that included the team of Smith and Dale. Five years later Irving, with brother Jack, formed the Kaufman Brothers, singing on many records. Kaufman retired in 1949, after appearing in the Broadway musical version of *Street Scene.*

473. KAY, Beatrice (singer; b. April 21, 1907, Bronx, NY; d. Nov. 8, 1986, No. Hollywood, CA). *Gay Nineties Revue* (1940–44); *Gaslight Gayeties* (1944–45); *The Beatrice Kay Show* (1946).

Through her radio, club and recording work, the diminutive, husky-voiced singer became a living symbol of the Gay '90s in the 1940s. Her admirers persisted on adding 30 or 40 years to her age, pegging her a survivor of the Diamond Jim Brady era; others accused her of fraud when she insisted that she was really a much younger woman. And when she left a broadcast people confused her mother with herself— and often asked Mama for her autograph. It all stemmed from an engagement doing turn-of-the-century songs at Billy Rose's Diamond Horseshoe in the late 1930s. Night after night, the 32-year-old soubrette performed a steam-heated "Ta-Ra-Ra-Boom-De-Aay" or a wistful "Bird in a Gilded Cage," drawing a future out of yesterday.

Bill Paley caught her act and was struck with Kay's unusual talents. He proposed a Gay '90s show at CBS. She and her husband Sylvan Green, a pianist-arranger,

Beatrice Kay, Joe E. Howard

researched the old songs by digging up and listening to hundreds of old Edison cylinder recordings and by tracking down old-time singers and composers. They included Joe E. Howard who co-starred with Kay on the Monday program, sponsored by Model Pipe tobacco.

Kay started with a stock company as a youngster, played in small time vaudeville, doubled for little Madge Evans in silent pictures, and sang a bit in speakeasys. Radio made her into the "voice with the built-in bustle" and led to 12 record albums and the million-plus seller "Mention my Name in Sheboygan," and a lead in the Betty Grable musical *Billy Rose's Diamond Horseshoe.* She was one of the first headliners to play Las Vegas. One time, after her rendition of "I Don't Care," a gallery heckler yelled, "Hey Beatrice, what keeps those shoulder straps up?" She shot back, "Just your age!"

474. KAYE, Danny (comedian [signature song: "Dinah"]; b. Jan. 18, 1913, Brooklyn, NY; d. March 3, 1987, Los Angeles, CA). *Danny Kaye Show* (1945–46).

Films and television were his forte but he made a detour into radio in 1945 with his own CBS variety show. As a disembodied voice, noted *Time* magazine, "he proved he could be funny in the dark." A few years earlier he had climbed from obscurity to stardom via the Broadway musical comedy *Let's Face It* and the beguiling *Lady in the Dark.* A succession of motion pictures — beginning with *Up in Arms* and *Wonder Man* — captured the antics of this limber-faced, nimbled-footed entertainer and his rapid-fire patter.

Never one to turn down a humanitarian or patriotic request for his talents, he appeared on many special broadcasts for overseas servicemen, community chest drives, USO appeals and UN emergency funds. Kaye also raised more than $6 million for symphony musicians' pension funds by performing at benefit concerts, with epic zaniness and show-stopping vitality.

475. KAYE, Sammy (bandleader [Swing and Sway with Sammy Kaye]; [signature song: "Kaye's Melody"]; b. March 13, 1910, Lakewood, OH; d. June 2, 1987, Ridgewood, NJ). *Sensations and Swing* (1940); *Sunday Serenade* (1941–54); *So You Want to Lead a Band* (1946–48).

Kaye's dance band first got attention on broadcasts from Cleveland in the mid-1930s. His was a sweet-sounding, rhythmically appealing outfit that was remarkably similar to the approach to a song by Kay Kyser who was broadcasting out of Chicago. A clarinetist-alto sax player, he started on the band circuit at Ohio State University where he organized a group to play college dances. But after three years of one-night stands and little money, he was ready to turn to civil engineering, his undergraduate major.

A booking at Bill Green's Casino, just outside of Pittsburgh, turned the tide. Green and Kaye became golfing buddies at a nearby course, and Green got the Mutual network to air Sammy's music direct from the

Sammy Kaye

dance floor. From there, the band headed East to the Sunnybrook Ballroom in Pottstown, then to New York's Hotel Commodore in 1938. It hit upon the distinctive use of spoken intros of vocalists (Tommy Ryan, Don Cornell, Tony Alamo) at the end of the first chorus. And if a tune couldn't be danced to, Kay would not play it.

His most famous gimmick, "So You Want to Lead a Band," let members of the studio audience conduct the band. Chosen at random, they competed against each other for prizes. The audience chose the winner through their applause. In 1953 Kaye estimated that this game had given away more than 200,000 batons to contestants.

Kaye moved into TV with his musical game but continued to broadcast over all four radio networks in the early 1950s: six times a week with Mutual and CBS from the Astor Roof, Monday to Friday at 8:15 p.m. at ABC, and Sundays over NBC. The latter series successfully mixed poetry reading with Kaye's scene-setting music.

While broadcasting his *Sunday Serenade* show from New York on December 7, 1941, the band was interrupted with the news of the sneak attack on Pearl Harbor. Sammy was so touched by the surprise bombing of U.S. Forces that he went home and wrote the song "Remember Pearl Harbor." The tune was introduced eight days later and is considered the first American war song of World War II.

476. KEANE, Teri (actress; b. Oct. 24, 1925, New York, NY). *Life Can Be Beautiful* (1946–53); *The Second Mrs. Burton* (1952–60)

Leads as Chichi on the classic soap *Life Can Be Beautiful,* as Terry Burton on the very last soap on the air, *The Second Mrs. Burton,* and as Jocelyn Brent in the medical world saga, *Road of Life.* Prime time offered appearances in *Cavalcade of America, Inner Sanctum* and *Gangbusters.* She bowed on *Show Boat,* and 40 years later was still at a mike, with *CBS Mystery Theatre.* Her Broadway credits include *What a Life* and *The Vagabond King.* Keane easily moved into television, with running parts in *As the World Turns* and *Edge of Night.* She was married to actor John Larkin, who played *Perry Mason* in the 1950s.

477. KEARNS, Joseph (actor; b. Feb. 12, 1904, Salt Lake City, UT; d. Feb. 17, 1962, Los Angeles, CA). *Judy Canova Show* (1945–53); *Jack Benny Program* (1945–c53); *The Great Gildersleeve* (1949–51); *Honest Harold* (1950–51).

Character parts on golden-age comedies include the keeper of Jack Benny's underground vault; Lukey, a boy friend of Judy Canova; Mr. Thompson, Gildersleeve's friend; Mel Blanc's girlfriend's father, and Melvin Foster on *A Date with Judy.* Kearns periodically surfaced on the shows of *Blondie,* Burns and Allen, Phil Harris-Alice Faye, and Bob Hope. He also played on *Me and Janie,* a 1949 summer replacement for Alan Young; supporting roles on *Railroad Hour* presentations, and was heard as the signature voice on *Suspense.* His serious roles were often in crime-mystery productions *Pursuit* and *Let George Do It.*

Kearns acquired a visual presence as next-door neighbor Mr. Wilson on television's popular *Dennis the Menace,* a role he played for three seasons. He began on radio at KSL in 1932.

478. KEATING, Larry (actor, emcee; b. April 13, 1899, St. Paul, MN; d. Aug. 26, 1963, Hollywood, CA). *Scramby Amby* (1943–45); *Murder Will Out* (1945); *New Fitch Bandwagon* (1945–46); *This Is Your FBI* (1948–53).

Announcer-emcee-actor who later gained wide recognition from films and television. At KPO San Francisco he hosted *American Treasure Chest,* a "hobby lobby" storytelling session that delved into the history of family heirlooms. During World War II he appeared in scores of military base broadcasts with Bob Hope. *This Is Your FBI* provided his best and longest-running radio credit. On TV he played neighbor Harry Morton on *Burns and Allen,* and in the early '60s, neighbor Roger Addison on Alan Young's *Mister Ed.* He often was cast as a businessman, lawyer or doctor.

479. KEECH, Kelvin (announcer; b. June 28, 1895, Hawaii; d. May 1977, Jackson Heights, NY). *Twenty Thousand Years in Sing Sing* (1933–c36); *Popeye the Sailor* (1935–36).

At his retirement from ABC in 1962, Keech remarked, "I'm only five foot six, but my radio listeners always pictured me as a tall, thin fashion-plate and that exercise of their imagination was beneficial to us mortals." He spent 33 years helping listeners conjure up images, beginning at NBC in 1929 (after "mike fright" ruined an early audition). Helped by the network's Peter DeRose and May Singhi Breen, he landed assignments on *Eveready Hour, Popeye the Sailor* and various dance band series, and worked with Irene Rich and Joan Davis. Briefly, he was a freelancer and producer.

From his Hawaiian upbringing, he learned the ukulele, and after graduating as an engineer from Franklin and Marshall College in 1914, and serving as a radio operator in the US Signal Corps, he turned to music. Keech organized a jazz band in Europe, and at one point, while with the BBC, taught the Prince of Wales to play the ukulele. He later sang the theme and strummed the instrument for *Terry and the Pirates.*

480. KELK, Jackie (actor; b. Aug. 6, 1922, Brooklyn, NY). *Hello, Peggy* (1935–38); *The Gumps* (1936–37); *Terry and the Pirates* (1937–39); *Aldrich Family* (1940–51).

High-pitched, quavering-voiced Homer, the 16-year-old buddy of Henry on *The Aldrich Family.* Until age 28 he played the teenager on radio without a break, including two seasons on television. His first show, *Chase & Sanborn Hour,* cast him as a bratty kid stooge opposite Eddie Cantor in 1933. Kelk similarly plagued Bert Lahr, Burns and Allen and Jack Benny in prime time while doing serials during the day. On *The Gumps,* he played Chester; Agnes Moorehead was Min, his mom. He never forgot the day his voice suddenly changed during a broadcast. "I went out of the studio and cried. It was kind of pathetic."

He played the lead in *Terry and the Pirates.* Bud

Jackie Kelk (courtesy of Jackie Kelt)

Collyer, who was Pat, also worked with Kelk (as Jimmy Olsen) on *Superman* for seven years. In the mid-40s he was a frequent guest on *Chesterfield Supper Club* and appeared on the *Theatre Guild on the Air* presentation of "Ah, Wilderness" with Walter Huston and Richard Widmark.

A Professional Children's School graduate, Kelk bowed on Broadway at nine in *Bridal Wise* with Madge Kennedy. His other stage credits include *Goodbye Again, Jubilee* and *Me and Juliet.* At age 12 he appeared on screen as Loretta Young's son in *Born To Be Bad,* and later followed up with adult parts in *Somebody Up There Likes Me* and *Pajama Game. Aldrich Family* sponsor and writers in 1951 mounted *Young Mr. Bobbin* on TV for Kelk, but the situation comedy lasted only one season.

481. KELLY, Joe (quizmaster; b. May 31, 1901, Crawfordsville, IN; d. May 26, 1959, Chicago, IL). *National Barn Dance* (1934–46); *Quiz Kids* (1940–51).

His cheerful disposition and down-to-childhood point of view gained Joe Kelly, the post of chief quizzer on the juvenile counterpart of *Information Please.* News commentators and college professors were looked over as possible emcees by creator Lou Cowan but Kelly put the Quiz Kids at ease better than anyone auditioned. An unlikely choice, considering his formal educational qualifications were practically nil. He quit school at age nine to sing as "The Irish Nightingale" in a touring company. The jovial Kelly was never very far from show business, even after he promised his wife he would stick to 9-to-5 jobs.

His radio career had a small beginning when he teamed up in a comedy singing act, "The Two Lunatics of the Air," broadcasting six shows a week from Battle Creek, Michigan. Four years later, he left to join the announcing staff of WLS, from which he was subsequently chosen as emcee for *National Barn Dance.* His success with this Saturday night country music staple put him in the running for other Chicago-based shows.

Quiz Kids went on as an NBC Blue summer fill-in. Its knowledge-spouting youngsters drew a large, and often incredulous, audience. But for Kelly the opening broadcasts did not auger well. He seemed incapable of dealing with the strain of monitoring the often esoteric and intricate responses from his ultra-bright charges. But sets of cards prepared in advance with all possible answers at his fingertips revitalized the effervescent, easygoing personality of Kelly. His motto during his long tenure was "Treat children as equals, don't talk down to them, and you'll create a healthy 'pal' relationship."

482. KELTON, Pert (actress; b. Oct. 14, 1907, Great Falls, MT; d. Oct. 30, 1968, Ridgewood, NJ). *Dough-Re-Mi* (1942); *Milton Berle Show* (1947–49); *The Magnificent Montague* (1950–51).

The child of a vaudeville couple, Pert went into

the family act — singing, acting, tap dancing, and playing the trombone. Successful on Broadway in *Sunny* with Marilyn Miller and in a handful of film musicals, she went into radio in the late '30s. "It took me three years to get started. It was a new medium and it had to be learned."

Milton Berle gave her a chance to play Tallulah Feeney and four other women, just before he broke into television. She had various comedy roles on *Kraft Music Hall* and briefly with Ethel Merman. Kelton hated to see the decline of radio, but switched to TV, where she created the part of the original Alice Kramden with Jackie Gleason on "The Honeymooners," and was featured with Phil Silvers and Danny Thomas.

Pert and actor-husband Ralph Bell (*Valiant Lady, Backstage Wife*) were mentioned in "Red Channels," a publication purporting to tell of communist influence in the media. It injured both professionally in the early 1950s. She bounced back with *The Music Man* and remained a sought-after performer for another decade.

483. KENNEDY, John B. (commentator; b. Jan. 16, 1894, Wales, Great Britain; d. July 22, 1961, Toronto, Canada). *Collier's Hour* (1927–32); *RCA Magic Key* (1935–39)

For *Collier's* Magazine, Kennedy, a writer, set a record for the number of interview features and short stories published. When the magazine inaugurated a general variety program, he was emcee. He later broadcast backstage commentary and interviews, particularly at the opera. In 1934 Kennedy began announcer assignments, news commentary and political analysis for NBC. He appeared on the first RCA TV transmission in Camden, New Jersey in 1936. His manner of speech was described as "direct, sincere and convincing." He moved to CBS, then to WNEW and WOR. At his retirement in 1950, Kennedy was broadcasting from an ABC mike.

A newspaperman in St. Louis, Chicago and New York, he worked with Herbert Hoover in postwar European relief.

484. KENNEDY, John Milton (announcer; b. June 23, 1912, Farrell, PA). *Lux Radio Theatre* (1942–52).

Los Angeles announcer, beginning at KEFJ in 1933 with a salary of $25 for a seven-day week. Work at KFAC and KHJ, and at a Mexican station, led to staff at The Blue Network from 1942 to 1947 and the coveted weekly spot for *Lux*. Within a few seasons he was making $200 a broadcast. For early television he appeared on *Armchair Detective, Life with Luigi* and *You Asked for It*. In the 1960s he joined Southern California Edison as a commercial announcer. He traveled as its spokesman for some 20 years; one year he delivered a record 199 talks throughout the state.

Kennedy studied to be an actor on a Pasadena Community Playhouse scholarship. In 1932 he toured in plays throughout California. His earliest radio job, with Los Angeles high school friends, came about on *Tidbit Revue* at KEFJ.

485. KENTON, Stan (bandleader [signature song: "Artistry in Rhythm"]; b. Feb. 12, 1912, Wichita, KS; d. Aug. 25, 1979, Hollywood, CA). *Bob Hope Show* (1943–44); *Stan Kenton Concerts* (1952–53).

Early proponent of progressive jazz during the last decade of the big bands. Kenton formed a band in 1941, an instant success on the West Coast. At its first New York appearance at Roseland, dancers complained that it was too loud and its tempos were not danceable. But recordings for the newly formed Capitol label built an ardent legion of fans. Guest conductor for Bob Hope in June 1943, Kenton signed on as permanent leader on the Pepsodent series.

As solo pianist Kenton appeared on *Teentimers Club* and *King Cole Trio Time* in the mid-40s. His broadcast concerts of experimental and usually controversial works stressed a symphonic jazz style. Mainstream swinging vocals by Anita O'Day, June Christy and Chris Connor counterbalanced his heavy avant-garde thrust as did imaginative arrangements by Peter Rugolo. The tenacious Kenton continued on the road long past the demise of all but a handful of vintage big bands. He established his own record company to promote and distribute his innovative and often complex music. In the process he regularly visited disc jockeys and talk show hosts.

486. KIERAN, John (panelist; b. Aug. 2, 1892, Bronx, NY; d. Dec. 10, 1980, Rockport, MA). *Information Please* (1938–48, 1950).

A leading New York sports writer with a serious bent toward ornithology and literary classics, among many subjects, he established national fame from participation as a regular panelist on *Information Please*. Kieran had a predilection for collecting knowledge and was considered a walking encyclopedia. Affable and genuinely modest, he joined the program panel weeks after its start. People were convinced that he knew the answer to every question under the sun. They often telephoned him at his *New York Times* office. The day after each *Information Please* show, as many as 200 calls would come in.

Kieran was surrounded by books as a child. His father was president of Hunter College and his mother, a school teacher. John briefly taught in a rural school before joining the sports department of the *Times* in 1915. In 1947 he became editor of an offshoot of the radio series, the *Information Please Almanac*.

Typically he turned to Latin to explain himself: "Homo sum, humani nil a me alienum puto (I am a man, and nothing pertaining to humanity is alien to me)."

487. KIERNAN, Walter (commentator, emcee; b. Jan. 24, 1902, New Haven, CT; d. Jan. 8, 1978, Daytona Beach, FL). *Sparring Partners* (1952–53); *Weekend* (1953–55).

Walter Kiernan, NBC vice president John Royal

talk show. The voices of the young couple over the air seemed to radiate cheeriness despite the fact its co-hosts were well-known first-nighters and night owls. Although few listeners knew it, the daily breakfast show, during much of its run, was actually recorded the previous afternoon, replete with simulated clinking coffee cups.

One summer while still in college, Kilgallen became a New York cub reporter. She never returned to school for the 1931–32 semester. Instead, she aggressively covered trials, politics and police beats, and at one point made an ingenious, fast-paced round the world trip that would have drawn even the envy of the adventurous Nelly Bly.

When TV's *What's My Line?* began in 1950, she became a regular panelist. Participating in 789 programs over the next 17 years, the highly competitive Dorothy guessed more occupations of contestants and identified more celebrity guests than the *Line*'s two permanent co-panelists Arlene Frances and Bennett Cerf. On radio she had made guest appearances on game shows *Uncle Jim's Question Bee* and *Battle of the Sexes*.

Famous for his ability to spin out the news with an easygoing style, and often with a humorous twist. He broadcast on early-morning programs at ABC. "At that hour of the day, if you can let a fellow to listen to you without wanting to cut his your throat, you've done a public service," he observed in 1950. His newspaper column "One Man's Opinion" was circulated by International News Service and led to broadcasts using the same title. His best-remembered show, *Kiernan's Korner,* had only limited network play.

He broke into reporting in New Haven, his hometown. Assignments with AP led to Hartford as INS bureau chief in 1935. He ended his radio career in the 1950s at NBC as a commentator and special events man for *Weekday, Weekend* and *Monitor*.

488. KILGALLEN, Dorothy (commentator; b. July 3, 1913, Chicago, IL; d. Nov. 8, 1965, New York, NY). *Voice of Broadway* (1941); *Breakfast with Dorothy and Dick* (1945–63).

Her widely syndicated "Voice of Broadway" column and CBS series attracted New York's WOR, and together with her actor-producer husband Richard Kollmar, the station broadcast their early morning at-home

489. KING, John Reed (emcee, announcer; b. Oct. 25, 1914, Atlantic City, NJ; d. July 8, 1979, Woodstown, NJ). *What's My Name?* (1941); *Torme Time* (1947); *Go for the House* (1948)

King ran game shows in wholesale lots in the 1940s, chiefly as daytime audience-participation sessions for housewives. His *Missus Goes A-Shopping* aired as a local CBS novelty, transcribed at neighborhood grocery stores in various communities in metropolitan New York. King made it a lively human-interest feature for Pepsi-Cola, and mentioned numerous household products on this 15-minute program.

King's announcing chores include the mauve decade-costumed *Gay Nineties Revue*. In 1945 he sparkplugged Mutual's *Break the Bank* and briefly was the voice of *Sky King*, "America's favorite flying cowboy." At CBS King worked with Edward R. Murrow and Robert Trout, and delivered a weekly wartime news report in French which was beamed into occupied France.

King began with big band remotes from Atlantic City and subsequently read news items for CBS while still a student at Princeton. In the early 1930s he served as the voice of Paramount newsreels.

490. KING, Pee Wee (singer, accordionist; b. Feb. 18, 1914, Abrams, WI). *Grand Ole Opry* (1945–47); *Pee Wee King Show* (1952–55).

Country music entertainer-composer. With his own musicians, Golden West Cowboys, he was often on *Grand Ole Opry,* beginning as guest in 1937 and by the mid-40s, as a regular. His act featured Eddy Arnold and Ernest Tubb at various times, and is believed to be the first to use an electric guitar and drums on the *Opry.* King played on *National Barn Dance* in the early 1930s and joined Gene Autry's show in Chicago. The band followed him to the West Coast for a series of cowboy films. In the 1950s King was emcee, guitarist and orchestra leader of his own program, and was active in television from Louisville and Cleveland.

Born Frank King, he performed over Wisconsin stations as a young teenager. He worked with the Log Cabin Boys on Louisville radio. His compositions began to receive national play with "Tennessee Waltz," written with Redd Stewart. The future Country Music Hall of Famer followed up with more big hits: "Slow Poke" and "You Belong to Me."

491. KING, Wayne (bandleader [The Waltz King]; [signature song: "The Waltz You Saved for Me"]; b. Feb. 18, 1901, Savannah, IL; d. July 16, 1985, Paradise Valley, AZ). *Lady Esther Serenade* (1931–38).

Wayne King

His greatest fame came from a weekly waltz-flavored Chicago show sponsored by Lady Esther Cosmetics. The series mixed dreamy music with sentimental poetry recited by announcer Franklyn Mac-Cormack. King's band initially received $500 a week but that amount grew to $15,000 a week, proof of the broadcasts' broad popularity.

A clarinetist, he first led his own aggregation at Chicago's Aragon Ballroom in 1927. Radio series soon followed for Pure Oil, Sanatron Tube and Armour Ham. He was awarded *Radio Guide's* trophy as radio's most popular dance orchestra for seven consecutive years (1934–40). King made many transcriptions for Ziv at the NBC Chicago studios beginning in the mid-1940s and featuring vocalists Nancy Evans and Larry Douglas.

492. KING SISTERS (Alyce, b. Aug. 14, 1914; Donna, b. Sept. 3, 1918; Louise, b. Dec. 21, 1913; Marilyn, b. May 11, 1930; Yvonne, b. Jan. 15, 1920) (singers). *Horace Heidt and His Brigadiers* (1936–38); *Al Pearce and His Gang* (1939).

Captivating vocal group featured with bands and variety show series. Their father, William King Driggs, a college voice teacher in Salt Lake City, gave them their early training. Just out of high school, they joined Heidt's troupe, and appeared with Al Pearce, Phil Harris and Meredith Willson. A major attraction with the band of guitarist Alvino Rey (Louise's husband) in the early 1940s, the sisters also made many Bluebird discs. Yvonne married Rey's pianist Buddy Cole.

On television in the mid-60s, the Kings had expanded into a large, visually attractive musical family in the mode of Lawrence Welk.

493. KINGSTON, Lenore (actress; b. Oct. 4, 1916, Los Angeles, CA; d. May 5, 1993, Van Nuys, CA). *Dan Harding's Wife* (1937–38); *Ma Perkins* (1937–47); *Fibber McGee and Molly* (1938); *The Affairs of Anthony* (1938–40).

Dramatic actress on numerous Proctor & Gamble daytime offerings. One of her longer-running roles was Jane Daly on *The Affairs of Anthony.* She played Mercedes on *Don Winslow of the Navy* and Ebba on *Against the Storm.* Kingston first appeared on radio in Hollywood in 1930 as a substitute for a friend on vacation. She attended LA City College, then worked in films at Universal for a year. Her TV credits included *Hazel* and *General Hospital.*

A ham operator, Kingston was the subject of *This is Your Life* for her work as a radio link between overseas servicemen and their state-side families.

494. KINSELLA, Walter (actor; b. Aug. 16, 1900, New York, NY; d. May 11, 1975, Englewood, NJ). *Dick Tracy* (1938–39); *Joe and Mabel* (1941–42); *Abe's Irish Rose* (1942–43); *Mr. & Mrs. North* (1942–46). One-time Arrow Shirt model and amateur track star, he moved into acting in 1924 with the hit play *What Price Glory?* He played the part of Pat Patton on *Dick Tracy* at NBC and worked as a regular on *Abie's Irish Rose* and *Stella Dallas*. Early television's *Martin Kane, Private Eye* utilized Kinsella as announcer for commercials and actor in the role of a retired police lieutenant, Happy McMahon, who operated a tobacco shop. The sponsor was U.S. Tobacco Company which first had brought the detective series to radio in 1949.

495. KIRBERY, Ralph (singer [The Dream Singer]; [signature song: "Day Dreams"]; b. Aug. 24, 1900, Patterson, NJ). *Mohawk Treasure Chest* (1934).

Introduced as a late-night singer of romantic songs. His lilting "dream" ballads won over listeners, first on a sustaining basis at NBC with five-minute interludes at midnight in 1931. He picked up sponsors — Enna Jettick Shoes, Mohawk Carpets, Piso Syrup — for various light music series. Kirbery was also a guest on the pioneering transcription series *Musical Moments Revue*. Chevrolet presented these pre-recorded programs at different times over 400 U.S. stations in 1937.

Before signing with NBC, baritone Kirbery worked as an auto salesman and flour broker. An expert pilot, he entered the Army Air Corps at the beginning of the war and remained a military officer.

496. KIRBY, Durward (announcer, emcee; b. Aug. 24, 1912, Covington, KY). *Club Matinee* (1939–43); *Meet Your Navy* (1943–44); *Honeymoon in New York* (1945–47).

High-spirited, versatile broadcaster-sidekick. Best remembered as Garry Moore's pal on *Club Matinee* and on his CBS-TV variety shows of the 1950s, Kirby delivered commercials, interviewed guests and traded punchlines with warmth and ease. Early in his career, in 1941, he won the coveted H.P. Davis Announcer Award. His voice was heard on *Quiz Kids, Hilltop House, Fred Waring Show* and *Break the Bank*. For WHN he hosted a unique daily program called *Wings Over New York,* consisting of interviews of arrivals at LaGuardia Airport in 1947–48.

Kirby joined the campus radio station while at Purdue and singing with its glee club. He started out at WBAA in West Lafayette, Indiana in 1931, then spent several years as a morning DJ at WFBM Indianapolis. His salary was $25 a week. "The Depression had just ended for me. Man-o-man, I was walking on the gold-paved streets of heaven," he wrote in his memoir *My Life . . . Those Wonderful Years.* He switched to WLW as staff announcer in 1935. Chicago's *Club Matinee* brought him to network audiences. He served in the Navy, for which he emceed *Meet Your Navy* over ABC Chicago. *Honeymoon in New York* opened a door for his success as a performer-host. A daily a.m. audience participation show, it bowed on December 31, 1945. Kirby never forgot the program's first week. "Nobody in his right mind, in-

cluding tourists, would be caught at a radio show at 9 a.m. on New Year's Day. There were about 25 people in the theatre and I seem to recall we spent the whole time glaring at each other."

497. KIRSTEN, Dorothy (singer; b. July 6, 1910, Montclair, NJ; d. Nov. 18, 1992, Los Angeles, CA). *Keepsakes* (1943–44); *Kraft Music Hall* (1948–49); *Light Up Time* (1949–50).

Gifted and glamorous lyric soprano, she paid for her vocal lessons and Juilliard studies by appearing in choral groups backing Kate Smith and singing with dance orchestras. Met star Grace Moore heard her in 1938. As her mentor, she sent Dorothy to study in Rome. When the war forced her to return, she made her New York debut with the San Carlo Opera Company as Mimi in *La Boheme* in 1942. She bowed at the Met in the same role in 1945. The radiant, charming singer enjoyed an unprecedented 30-year Met run, biding farewell in the role of Floria Tosca "with the vocal control and dramatic acuity of a prima donna in mid-career," (wrote *New York Times* critic Allen Hughes). She always considered herself a singing actress rather than an opera singer. Her radio co-stars included pop singers Frank Sinatra, Nelson Eddy and Gordon MacRae. Kirsten frequently sang on *Highways in Melody* and the *Railroad Hour.* She was also seen in films with Bing Crosby (*Mr. Music*) and Mario Lanza (*The Great Caruso*).

498. KITCHELL, Alma (singer, commentator; b. June 29, 1893, Superior, WI). *Melody Hour* (1936–37); *Brief Case/Streamline Journal* (1938–42); *Pin Money Party* (1940–41).

Contralto capable of performing opera, oratorio, light melodies and sacred songs. In 1930 she joined NBC after well-received recitals in New York, and studies at the Cincinnati Conservatory and with vocal teacher and future husband George Kitchell. Her ease as a public speaker and ability as a spokesperson for a product led to informal talk shows on "subjects dear to a woman's heart" on *Woman's Exchange* and *Streamline Journal.* Kitchell also became assistant director of women's programs at NBC and later a commentator at ABC in the 1940s. Her commercial television series, *In the Kelvinator Kitchen,* in 1947 attracted early viewers.

She once sang from an airplane flying over New York with an accompaniment by a studio orchestra below at Radio City. In 1996 she celebrated her 103rd birthday still delivering straight talk and clear-cut opinions and achieving a record of longevity that no other radio pioneer had surpassed.

499. KNIGHT, Felix (singer; b. Nov. 1, 1908, Macon, GA). *Schaefer Revue* (1938); *American Album of Familiar Music* (1949–50).

Versatile lyric tenor who sang light classics, pop ballads and grand opera. His career began in California at a small CBS station in Santa Barbara where he

Felix Knight

was a music student. He made his network bow with Raymond Paige on *Shell Mountain House* in Los Angeles. NBC brought him to New York in early 1938 for *RCA Magic Key, Music Appreciation Hour* and *Schaefer Revue.* His NBC Artists build-up included *Metropolitan Opera Auditions of the Air.* He reached the finals with Leonard Warren, John Carter and Phil Duey. Losing by a single vote of the judges (one of whom, Earle Lewis, had a personal contract with contender Carter and apparently swung the decision to him over Knight).

His singing activities broadened after Special Services tours in World War II. He made his debut at the Met in *The Barber of Seville,* recorded operettas and show tunes, sang with Toscanini, and gained choice radio assignments. Knight also appeared with major U.S. symphonies. In the late 1940s he moved into supper clubs and summer stock and returned to television where he had sung on the first opera on NBC television (*Carmen*). Among his seven films of the 1930s, *Babes in Toyland* with Laurel and Hardy remains an audience favorite. In retirement he spent many years teaching voice in New York. His wife, actress Ethel Blume, appeared on *The Adventures of Helen and Mary* and *The Aldrich Family.*

500. KNIGHT, Frank (announcer, actor; b. May 10, 1894, St. John's, Newfoundland, Canada; d. Oct. 18, 1973, New York, NY). *Literary Digest* (1930–31); *Arabesque* (1937–40).

Knight came to radio from the legitimate stage

and was heard on dramatic programs *The First National Hour, Collier's Radio Review* and *Arabesque* (in the leading role of Dr. Billbert). He found his voice more in demand as an announcer; it bordered on the pompous with an almost cathedral formality, which was *de rigeur* in early radio. A slip of the tongue by Knight once brought forth this weather report: "Tomorrow rowdy, followed by clain."

The British-accented Knight had joined WABC in 1928 just before Columbia purchased the station as its flagship. His first big remote assignment was the arrival of the dirigible *Graf Zeppelin.* Stationed atop a hangar at Lakehurst, New Jersey, he gave a description of the big airship's completion of a transatlantic trip from Germany.

A principal "voice of Columbia," he maintained an appearance of elegance, wearing, as did most staff announcers, a dinner jacket after six p.m. In 1936 he began a long association with the Longines Watch Company's *Symphonette* and *Choraliers.* He also announced the first CBS Sunday broadcast of the New York Philharmonic in 1930. That year he remarked, "I shall remain with radio just as long as it will have me." He outlasted all his early CBS colleagues.

501. KNIGHT, Ray (comedian; b. Feb. 12, 1899, Salem, MA; d. Feb. 12, 1953, New York, NY). *Ingram Shavers* (1930–31); *Cuckoo (KUKU) Hour* (1932); *Wheatenaville Sketches* (1932–35).

Writer-actor-director with versatile productions ranging from comedy sketches (Hour of Detachment with the Kiddies) to dramatic shows (Billy Batchelor series). After practicing law in Boston, Knight had studied playwriting at Yale. In 1927 he won the Drama League's prize for the best one-act play of the year. Titled "Strings," it was broadcast by NBC. His first radio appearance, "Embarrassing Moments in History," brought his offbeat comedy to the air. Knight soon created and portrayed Ambrose J. Weems, manager of station KUKU, and major domo of the *Cuckoo Hour,* sponsored by Blue Moon Cheese. He and his associates, writer Ward Byron and conductor Robert Armbruster, helped set the stage for his caricatures. This comic thrust was successfully pursued by Jack Benny and Fred Allen with the interplay of such characters as Rochester and Mrs. Nussbaum. His other shows were *Good Morning, It's Knight, Raising Junior, The Joke's on You* and *House in the Country.* One of his mythical sponsors was Little Gem Mouth Stretcher Company, makers of mouth-stretchers for people who put their foot in their mouth every time they open it.

In the 1940s Knight played supporting roles in serials. For Young & Rubicam he directed the Ed Wynn and Allan Young shows at NBC. His satirical wit as a writer contributed to the network success of *Bob and Ray.* An unique figure in early radio, this clever jack-of-all-trades combined creative talent and endless energy to turn out a succession of original offerings.

502. KOLAR, Victor (conductor; b. Feb. 12, 1888, Budapest, Hungary; d. Jan. 16, 1957). *Ford Sunday Evening Hour* (1938–39).

In 1934 he was engaged to direct the Detroit Symphony at Ford Gardens, Century of Progress Exposition, Chicago. During this engagement the European-trained violinist conducted a record 162 two-hour concerts — including 48 national broadcasts — over a period of 86 days. More than 800 different compositions were performed.

Kolar came to the United States in 1904, was a violinist and assistant conductor with the Pittsburgh Symphony. Walter Damrosch brought him to New York in the same dual capacity for his Symphony. By 1920 he had established himself as associate conductor in Detroit. In 1936 he became principal conductor and remained an inextricable part of that city's musical life. Ford Motor sponsored a number of his programs over CBS.

503. KOLLMAR, Richard (actor, host; b. Dec. 31, 1910, Ridgewood, NJ; d. Jan. 7, 1971, New York, NY). *John's Other Wife* (1937–38); *Claudia and David* (1941); *Boston Blackie* (1945); *Breakfast with Dorothy and Dick* (1945–63).

Kollmar studied drama at Yale, and made his radio debut in 1935 as emcee for a fashion show. Heard on many programs, including *Gangbusters, The March of Time* and *Grand Central Station,* he was best known for his portrayal of private detective Boston Blackie on a syndicated Mutual series. On Broadway Kollmar had a measure of stardom in *Too Many Girls.* During the run of this George Abbott musical in 1940, he married Dorothy Kilgallen, a reporter and "Voice of Broadway" columnist for *The New York Journal-American.*

They began a morning talk show on WOR that invariably started with the exchange of salutations: "Good morning, darling — good morning, sweetie." The couple chatted about parties, family incidents and plays (Kollmar produced a few — *By Jupiter, Are You with It?, Plain and Fancy*). Apart from the mike their lives took distinctly separate and less domestic directions. One of the reasons apparently was because Kilgallen became the better known and more visible through her weekly participation as a TV panelist on the top-rated game *What's My Line?*

Kollmar appeared on Ray Knight's *Cuckoo Hour,* and handled dialect parts for Fred Allan and Ben Bernie. He often dubbed the dialogue for baritones Charles Kullman, Conrad Thibault and Robert Weede on *Palmolive Beauty Box Theatre.* He got to sing for a Sunday morning program of Southern mountain songs called *Dreams of Long Ago.* Its script writer Ethel Park Richardson found him an agent who took him to audition for composer Kurt Weill and director Joshua Logan. They cast him in *Knickerbocker Holiday* as the youthful Dutch hero who defies Peter Stuyvesant. While studying the script his mother reminded Kollmar that his great-great-grandfather was buried right next to the colorful 17th-century Dutch governor at St. Mark's-in-the Bouwerie. This ancestor, Daniel D. Tompkins, was Vice President under James Monroe and four times Governor of New York.

504. KOSTELANETZ, Andre (conductor; b. Dec. 22, 1901, St. Petersburg, Russia; d. Jan. 13, 1980, Port-au-Prince, Haiti). *Chesterfield Hour* (1934–38); *Tune-Up Time* (1939–40); *The Pause That Refreshes* (1940–43).

Hired by CBS to conduct its symphony orchestra in 1930, he shaped it into a popular, commercially-sponsored aggregation. His arrangements of light music sung by major operatic artists gave rise to the well-known "Kostelanetz sound." He developed microphone techniques that were adopted by other radio orchestras, which also copied his choice of instrumentation. He used numerous and varied instruments in all notes of any harmony. Similarly, his name and sound met success in the recording studio. He sold 52 million records, a figure believed surpassed only by that of the Boston Pops Orchestra.

"The microphone is an extraordinary medium," he said in an interview in 1976. "It's like a second orchestra. The colors that you can obtain by the use of microphones are just extraordinary. I could not play it in a concert; it would mean nothing. But through the medium of the microphone, and by keeping in close contact with the orchestrator, we can get new sounds."

He married Met coloratura soprano Lily Pons in

Andre Kostelanetz

1938. They formed one of the most brilliant musical teams on radio and in the concert world, and toured extensively for the USO through the Middle and Far East in 1944–45.

Kostelanetz studied piano as a child and at 20 became assistant conductor of the Imperial Grand Opera in St. Petersburg. When he arrived in the United States in 1922, he worked as an accompanist and repertoire coach to several stars of the Met and Chicago opera houses. He made his radio bow in early 1928 at the Atlantic Broadcasting Company in Steinway Hall (This small chain joined Columbia later that year). His broadcasts brought renown and led to conducting orchestras around the world. A highly efficient leader, he knew how to generate good performances with a minimum of rehearsals — a skill that made him well liked by cost-conscious networks and sponsors.

With the end of live radio concerts, he conceived and conducted the Lincoln Center "Promenades" of the New York Philharmonic. These presentations mixed symphonic music with dance, narration, mime and folk singing, and proved a sellout for 15 seasons, beginning in 1963. His memoirs, entitled *Echoes,* were published posthumously in 1981.

505. KRUGER, Alma (actress; b. Sept. 13, 1871, Pittsburgh, PA; d. April 5, 1960, Seattle, WA). *Pages of Romance* (1932–33); *Show Boat* (1937); *Those We Love* (1938–45).

Solid acting experience in Shakespearean plays and as part of The Theatre Guild and Eva Le Gallienne's Civic Repertory Company brought her to radio at age 60. She played in *The Goldbergs* and as Captain Henry's wife on *Show Boat.* Her longest-running part was Emily Mayfield on *Those We Love.* On screen at MGM Kruger portrayed head nurse Mollie Byrd in the Dr. Kildare series. She retired in 1947 and died 13 years later at age 88.

506. KUPPERMAN, Joel (panelist; b. May 18, 1936, Chicago, IL). *Quiz Kids* (1942–52).

Quintessential Quiz Kid who personified brilliance, precocity, and even eggheadedness for 1940s audiences. A supercharged mathematical wunderkind, he was at six the youngest participant. His I.Q. was above 200, and according to Kids' historian Ruth Duskin Feldman, his mental development was the highest that ever had been tested in the 25 years of child study by the Chicago public schools. Before he was ten, he had a vocabulary at least ten percent greater than the average adult's. By 1946 the gangling and bespectacled Kupperman appeared almost weekly, becoming perhaps the best known of the dozens of youngsters who fielded questions from emcee Joe Kelly.

Kupperman's inquisitiveness and wit brought guest spots with Fred Allen, Bill Stern and Ralph Edwards, and a part in the Donald O'Connor film, *Chip Off the Old Block.* At 16 he graduated from *Quiz Kids* and two years later picked up an A.B. degree from the Univer-

sity of Chicago. He remained in academe, receiving S.B., A.M. and Ph.D. degrees by 1963. He became a professor of philosophy at the University of Connecticut where alumni once voted him an award for excellence in teaching. At age 45 he looked back with a clear lack of enthusiasm. "Being a bright child among your peers was not the very best way to grow up in America."

507. KYSER, Kay (bandleader, emcee [The Old Perfessor] [signature song: "Thinking of You"] [catchphrase: "Evenin' folks, how y'all?"; "That's right — you're wrong."]; b. June 18, 1906, Rocky Mt., NC; d. July 23, 1985, Chapel Hill, NC). *Elgin Football Revue* (1935–36); *Kollege of Musical Knowledge* (1938–48).

Kyser led a band like a college cheerleader at a football game, and his exuberance and good humor went over in spades. His musical group was formed while he was a student at the University of North Carolina. He developed a local following before touring the country and hitting on the idea of singing song titles as an intro to a number. In 1934 the band broke attendance records at the Blackhawk in Chicago. There, Lew Wasserman of MCA asked Kay to do a Professor Quiz-type program with popular music questions and fans as "students."

Kyser's *Musical Klass* had trial runs over WGN before being sold to American Tobacco and airing over Mutual in 1938. *Variety* called the novelty "an intelligent example of combining a stunt idea with a standard entertainment item." It quickly occupied a mid-

Kay Kyser

week niche on NBC, providing brisk melodies with vocals by Harry Babbitt, Ginny Simms, Sully Mason and Georgia Carroll (Kay's wife). Kay's bubbly way of handling contestants and his method of practically giving answers to slow quizees endeared him to all. His more than 700 camp shows and hospital visits at home and overseas brought cheer to millions of Americans. He made numerous appearances on *Fitch Band-wagon* from 1940–44, and played at the opening of the Stage Door Canteen in Hollywood.

Kysers's recordings — ranging from the nonsensical "Three Little Fishes" to the inspirational "Praise the Lord and Pass the Ammunition" — and films — including the all-star *As Thousands Cheer* and the tuneful *Carolina Blues* — augmented his well-earned fame. His *Kollege* on television, however, did not catch on. Not long after, Kay was ready to retire as the old Perfessor and settle in his college town, Chapel Hill. He became an accredited Christian Science practitioner and teacher, and in the 1970s that church's head of film and broadcasting.

508. LA CENTRA, Peg (singer, actress; b. 1913, Boston, MA). *Court of Human Relations* (1934–39); *For Men Only* (1938–39); *Gulden Melodeers* (1938–40).

Song stylist with acting assignments. With Benny Goodman and Artie Shaw in the late 1930s, she also appeared as musical guest for Fleischmann, Palmolive and Wrigley, and as dramatic player for Campbell Soup, Pepsodent and Time-Life. One of her last roles was on a 1951 episode of *Counterspy*. She married actor Paul Stewart in 1939.

La Centra attended Katharine Gibbs School. Before finishing her studies there and at New England Conservatory of Music, she auditioned at WNAC Boston. A job as announcer resulted. She subsequently did roles on various local stations before going to New York. In 1935 she made tabloid headlines. In an improvised radio studio at an Asbury Park, New Jersey hotel, she and boxer Max Baer were slightly injured by gunpowder when a sound effects man accidentally fired a blank cartridge from a pistol during a dramatic show.

509. LAKE, Arthur (actor; b. April 17, 1905, Corbin, KY; d. Jan. 10, 1987, Indian Wells, CA). *Blondie* (1939–50).

In 1939, a year after Columbia Pictures produced the first of 28 Blondie films, CBS aired the series with Lake in the role he created on screen. As Dagwood Bumstead, he was perfectly cast to portray the bumbling husband of Blondie, played by Penny Singleton.

At age five Lake had joined his parents' vaudeville act and toured the South until settling in Hollywood in 1917. In the 1920s he played in two reelers, Westerns and college musicals but by 1937 his roles had become smaller and smaller. When he landed the part of Dagwood, from the popular comic strip, his luck

turned. The first Blondie film grossed $9 million, and a string of low-budgeted, high-profit sequels followed. The radio version caught on and continued for eleven seasons. It first bowed as a skit on Bob Hope's Pepsodent Show in December 1938. Lake recreated the character with the high pitched "Blonnndie" call for help on television but it lasted only a year. His wife, Patricia Van Cleve, played Blondie on the series' final radio season.

510. LAMBERT, Harold "Scrappy" (singer; b. May 12, 1901, New Brunswick, NY; d. Nov. 30, 1987, Palm Springs, CA). *Smith Brothers: Trade and Mark* (1926–35); *Manhattan Merry-Go-Round* (1932–33, 1938–39); *Town Hall Tonight* (1934–38); *Your Hit Parade* (1936–37).

When music filled nearly two-thirds of all air time, Lambert sang on at least one show each night. He joined the trios and quartets added to the cast of most musical variety and comedy programs. He sang with the Songsmiths for Ed Wynn, The Men About Town for *Manhattan Merry-Go-Round,* the Show Boat Four for the Maxwell House *Show Boat,* the Town Hall Quartet for Fred Allen, and Hit Paraders for Lucky Strike. "Many nights, I ran from one Radio City studio to another to shows that were back to back," he related in 1979. "And repeat broadcasts for the West Coast added a full late-night schedule."

His radio work had begun with fellow Rutgers University pal Billy Hillpot for the Smith Brothers coughdrop makers. This song-and-patter act expanded to a full-scale musical show with a large orchestra conducted by Nat Shilkret and a young Met Opera contralto named Rose Bampton.

From 1926 — beginning with Ben Bernie's band — to 1933, Lambert recorded an estimated 2,500 songs on dozens of labels, using a half-dozen pseudonyms as male vocalist for Red Nichols, Joe Venuti, Ben Pollack, Abe Lyman and others. In 1943 he became agent in MCA's radio department in Beverly Hills, and later worked in real estate and oil leasing.

His clown-like grin and hijinks were legendary along radio row. One time, he and quartet baritone Len Stokes brought gales of laughter to a *Show Boat* audience by greeting each other by shaking hands through the legs of conductor Gus Haenschen as he stood high above them on a podium. When on the air Fred Allen reputedly shunted him to the sidelines for fear he'd break up by merely looking in his direction.

511. LAMOUR, Dorothy (singer, actress [signature song: "The Moon of Manakoora"] b. Dec. 10, 1914, New Orleans, LA; d. Sept. 22, 1996, North Hollywood, CA). *Chase & Sanborn Hour* (1937–39); *Front and Center* (1947); *Sealtest Variety Show* (1948–49).

Vocalist with Herbie Kay (her first husband), she left for New York and a radio build-up as *The Dreamer of Songs* over NBC-Blue in 1935. When the show relocated to Hollywood, a screen test followed at Paramount and the lead in the first of her sarong-costumed films, *The Jungle Princess.* She worked well as a dramatic actress on screen with Jon Hall, Ray Milland and Henry Fonda. She co-starred with Crosby and Hope in six *Road* pictures . . . and made eight guest appearances on Bing's *Kraft Music Hall* in 1940 alone. A regular with Bergen and McCarthy, she sang one or two songs each week and appeared in skits. Paramount's *The Big Broadcast of 1938* included this bona-fide radio discovery. Every radio comedian vied for this vivacious pin-up girl at his mike — Abbott and Costello, Ed Gardner, Jack Benny, Eddie Cantor.

An enduring favorite of GIs, Lamour had her own postwar program under the auspices of US Army Recruiting Service. It led to a variety show as emcee-singer for Sealtest in 1948. She retired in 1952 but resumed her career a decade later with occasional film and TV work. Her autobiography, *My Side of the Road,* provided a self-portrait of a performer of extraordinary versatility.

512. LANDT, Daniel (singer; b. Oct. 25, 1901, Scranton, PA; d. Feb. 24, 1961, Mount Kisco, NY). *Doc Pearson's Drug Store* (1936); *Bob Hawk Show* (1948).

Member of the Landt Trio, song-and-patter act, with brothers Karl and Jack. The group played vaudeville circuits, including the Palace, and performed at WEAF in the late 1920s. A solid string of NBC sustaining and commercial programs kept the trio on the airwaves year after year. Pianist Howard White backed them for these light music segments. They originated *Sing Along* at CBS, and did early television and children's records before retiring in 1953. Dan became a Westchester real estate broker and town assessor.

513. LANGFORD, Frances (singer [signature song: "I'm in the Mood for Love"]; b. April 4, 1914, Lakeland, FL). *The Spartan Hour* (1933–34); *Hollywood Hotel* (1935–40); *Bob Hope Show* (1941–46); *The Drene Show* (1946–47).

Her singing over a Tampa station while in college was heard by the vacationing Rudy Vallee who brought her to his variety hour in 1931. At 17 she had her own series over WOR. By 1934 and under the management of NBC Artists Service, she began putting songs across on prime-time programs. Her low, melodious contralto voice and dream-girl looks attracted movie scouts. Together with screen work, she broadcast regularly on *Hollywood Hotel* and *Texaco Star Theatre.* Bob Hope added her to his troupe, and when war came she remained a stellar part with her sentimental ballads. Entertaining from the front lines in numerous faraway places and on the homefront for war loan drives, she won a special place in the hearts of GIs. Langford and Don Ameche made a popular duo as "The Bickersons" in the post-war years; the domestic sketches revealed her ability as a comedienne.

Frances Langford

Langford was married to film actor Jon Hall from 1938 to 1955. Her career took second place when she wed outboard motor manufacturer Ralph Evinrude and returned to Florida and ownership of a coastal resort-restaurant.

514. LANIN, Howard (conductor; b. July 15, 1897, Philadelphia, PA; d. April 26, 1991, Philadelphia, PA). *Atwater Kent Hour* (1929–30); *Campbell Soup Show* (1931–32).

Called King of Society Dance Music and one of six Lanin brothers who were ballroom and resort bandleaders for most of the 20th century. He joined the Philadelphia musician's union in 1913 and played his last gala 73 years later in 1986. With Sam Lanin he opened Roseland in Philadelphia (1918) and in New York (1919). His orchestra grew to some 40 musicians for private parties of the Great Gatsby era.

In 1922 at WDAR (later WFIL) he claimed to have broadcast the first "live" music in Philadelphia. It aired nightly from Arcadia Cafe. After playing at the National Sales Meeting of the Atwater Kent Radio Company, Lanin took over that manufacturer's key radio series. Soup tycoon John T. Dorrance similarly engaged him as leader of the Campbell Soup orchestra

Howard Lanin (courtesy of Howard Lanin Productions, Inc.)

Snooky Lanson

for five nights weekly over NBC. From 1934 to 1945 he played for President Franklin D. Roosevelt's Birthday Ball, an annual benefit for the March of Dimes at the Waldorf Astoria Hotel (which he had helped open in 1931). A stage show-type booking by General Motors in 1940 led to a production company to service business clients, chiefly for banquets and conventions.

515. LANIN, Sam (bandleader [signature song: "Smiles"]; b. Sept. 4, 1891, Philadelphia, PA; d. May 5, 1977, Hollywood, FL). *Ipana Troubadors* (1925–31); *Benrus Ticksters* (1930–31).

One of seven brothers who were professional musicians, notably conductors-bookers Howard and Lester Lanin. The first Lanin orchestra in America was formed by their father Benjamin Lanin in 1892 in Philadelphia. Sam concentrated on radio with three programs a week by 1929. His melodic Ipana series helped popularize the medium. (Frank Black, then Lennie Hayton, took over this aggregation for radio in 1933.) Lanin also led the Gillette Blades between frequent recordings sessions. He used a half-dozen aliases for his discs of sweet and semi-jazzy tunes.

Shortly after World War I, he was hired to lead a band at the Roseland Ballroom in New York. He opened that dance hall, and stayed for over a dozen years. In the late '30s he moved to Florida.

516. LANSON, Snooky (singer; b. March 27, 1914, Memphis, TN; d. July 2, 1990, Nashville, TN). *Snooky Lanson Show* (1946–50); *Your Hit Parade* (1950–57).

Vocal star in the last decade of *Hit Parade* broadcasts. Lanson often sang the No. 1 tune of the week. He replaced Frank Sinatra in 1950. When the series added television, it became the most popular simulcast of its time.

A singing emcee at WSM, where he also worked with Beasley Smith's orchestra, he was little known until he landed the *Hit Parade* spot. His hit record "The Old Master Painter" showcased his singing ease. Lanson returned to Nashville in the 1960s, did nightclub singing, hosted a syndicated DJ show, and sold Ford automobiles.

517. LANZA, Mario (singer; b. Jan. 31, 1921, So. Philadelphia, PA; d. Oct. 7, 1959, Rome, Italy). *Mario Lanza Show* (1951–52).

This tenor's brief radio series for Coca-Cola at NBC showcased his unusual vocal prowess. Guest appearances on *Great Moments in Music* with Jean Tennyson had first brought him to the air in 1945. Critics, however, were divided on his voice. Some called it great and full of power; others claimed it lacked musical taste and discipline.

Lanza had been discovered by conductor Serge Koussevitzky who arranged a scholarship at the 1942 Tanglewood Music Festival. He began a national tour but was drafted into the Army. His professional activities languished at war's end. Not until solo appearances at Grant Park in Chicago and the Hollywood Bowl drew record crowds did studio doors open. Lanza was regarded by many as the greatest tenor since Caruso. A radio appearance on "Two Hours of

Mario Lanza

Stars," a special 1948 Thanksgiving Day program from Elgin Watch Company gave him an opportunity to sing opera arias, popular tunes and sacred music on a single broadcast. His RCA Victor recordings of "Be My Love" and "Loveliest Night of the Year" and his MGM films, led by the high-grossing *The Great Caruso,* proved to be his lasting legacy.

The handsome Lanza photographed well but his weight — at times more than 250 pounds — led to arguments with producers. He was compelled to go on rigid diets to lose as much as 60 pounds in order to appear before the movie cameras. In 1957 he shed some 75 pounds and embarked on a new career in Europe, combining films with concert tours. He died there from a heart ailment at age 38.

518. LA PRADE, Ernest (conductor; b. Dec. 20, 1889, Memphis, TN; d. April 20, 1969, Sherman, CT). *Collier's Hour* (1927–32).

Violinist in Walter Damrosch's New York Symphony Orchestra, he helped that conductor's *Music Appreciation Hour* as assistant and editor of instruction books for classroom teachers. At NBC he served as music director for *Collier's Hour,* an early variety show. For his supervision of *Orchestras of the Nation,* he received a 1947 Peabody Award. La Prade was NBC Director of Musical Research from the early 1940s to retirement in 1954. His brother, Malcolm La Prade, conducted radio travelogues as *The Man from Cook's* at WEAF-NBC from 1925 to 1939.

La Prade was a strong proponent of audience participation. He encouraged amateur musicians to play along at home in a synchronized performance of a Brahms or Mozart symphony. He was the author of the children's book *Alice in Orchestralia* and the comic opera *Xantha.*

519. LASSIE (actor; b. June 4,1940, North Hollywood, CA; d. 1958). *The Lassie Show* (1947–50).

The world's best-known and most-beloved canine. Pal, the first of a long line of male dogs who played the heroic Lassie, was an eight-month-old collie placed in the hands of Hollywood dog trainer Rudd Weatherwax for obedience sessions. He failed to break the animal's habit of chasing motorcycles. Pal's owner gave him to Rudd in lieu of paying for the job. But with no movie work for the highly intelligent dog, Rudd turned him over to a friend.

Then, in the early 1940s, Eric Knight's best-seller, *Lassie Come Home,* was picked up by MGM for the movies. Rudd quickly reclaimed Pal and won him the lead as Lassie. MGM filmed four more audience-pleasing Lassie sequels, making this easy-to-direct performer a canine star on stage and radio as well as the screen, and beginning in 1954 on television. Age 14, Pal (Lassie I) retired that year after completing the pilot of the video series.

On his radio adventure series, sponsored by Red Heart Dog Food, Lassie barked, whined, growled and cried. Announcer-narrator Charles Lyon kept the listener informed of what the spunky dog was doing. Other cast members — Marvin Miller, Betty Arnold — filled in with dialogue. ABC first presented these dog dramas as a 15-minute Sunday afternoon show; NBC moved it to Saturday mornings in its second season. Lassie's feats amazed audiences and co-workers. But when network and film directors asked Lassie to do the impossible, Rudd would explain, "she's only human, you know."

520. LAUCK, Chester A. (actor; b. Feb. 9, 1902, Alleene, AK; d. Feb. 22, 1980, Hot Springs, AK). *Lum and Abner* (1931–54).

As Lum he enjoyed a 24-year run with Ozark partner Abner (Norris Goff). Both were from Mena, in western Arkansas, and utilized country village life to create the series' focal point, Jot 'em Down Store, in Pine Ridge, Arkansas.

The two men had been entertaining each other and their friends with imitations and impersonations for years before their radio debut. Their first broadcast, a Mena amateur talent show, aired over KTHS Hot Springs in April 1931. Quaker Oats soon signed the duo as a NBC series. Their Lum and Abner characterizations remained high in ratings into the 1950s and spun off a handful of feature films. After their retirement, Lauck became public relations director for Conoco Oil in Houston.

521. LAURIE, Joe, Jr. (comedian; b. 1892, New York, NY; d. April 29, 1954, New York, NY). *Can You Top This?* (1940–51).

Joe Laurie, Jr., Paula Stone, Jimmy Walker, Fred Stone

Thomas, Earl Wrightson, Vivian Della Chiesa, Dorothy Kirsten and Robert Merrill. This series for Cities Service segued into Lavalle's *Band of America,* also sponsored by that oil company. Television appearances and tours for the 48-member outfit (one for each State) led to a seven-year contract to direct the Radio City Music Hall orchestra.

The Juilliard-trained musician composed a number of band marches, gaining him the tag, "America's Second Sousa." Lavalle frequently worked with young people through his All-American High School Band and received many honors for activities related to youth and music.

Comedy-act vaudevillian who filled in time between shows by writing skits for others, a column for *Variety* and eventually a 572-page history of show business, *From Vaude to Video,* with co-author Abel Green. He was playing in *The Gingham Girl* in Chicago in the early 1920s when he got into radio as emcee of a show put on over KYW by members of the cast. He insisted on an audience and convinced the station to admit spectators. In 1937 Rudy Vallee brought him to the *Fleischmann Hour* for eight consecutive appearances.

His inexhaustible supply of jokes made him a natural participant on *Can You Top This?* He relished the challenge of talking on any subject. As such, he provided entertainment both over the air, and at benefits and special shows.

522. LAVALLE, Paul (conductor; b. Sept. 6, 1908, Beacon, NY). *Chamber Music Society of Lower Basin Street* (1940–43); *Silhouettes in Music* (1941); *Stradivari Orchestra* (1943–45); *Highways in Melody* (1944–48); *Band of America* (1948–56).

Hired in the 1930s by NBC as a staff clarinetist, under his real name Joseph Usifer, he played in numerous aggregations, including the NBC Symphony under Toscanini and Stokowski. He urged the network to let him organize and lead ensembles. Many conducting assignments were on short-lived sustainers, including those of his wife Muriel Angelus and Ted Steele. But a jazz outfit for which he also arranged, broke new ground on *Chamber Music Society of Lower Basin Street.* Next came his all-string orchestra (with rare instruments) to promote Stradivari Perfume, and a concert group to play light classical music on *Highways in Melody* with soloists Thomas L.

523. LAWES, Lewis E. (commentator; b. Sept. 13, 1883, Elmira, NY; d. April 23, 1947, Garrison, NY). *Twenty Thousand Years in Sing Sing* (1933–39).

Crime prevention in the 1930s led to a broad interest in penal life and prisoner rehabilitation. Warden Lewis Lawes wrote several books from an insider's viewpoint, including the best-selling *20,000 Years in*

Paul Lavalle

Sing Sing. He had become warden of the 2,000 or more prisoners in that stronghold in 1920. His well-received accounts — stressing inmate rehabilitation — provided grist for films and broadcasts. Sloan Lina-ment sponsored the common-sense penologist as storyteller on a weekly dramatized series. He wanted to teach the public that prisoners were neither heroes nor lunatics nor "poor sick boys" and to show how easy it was for normal men and women to "go wrong."

By sheer merit, Lawes had risen from prison guard to the post of warden of one of America's most chal-lenging penal environments. An early career achieve-ment involved the building of a reformatory with-out walls for youthful inmates. It was said that he stretched humanitarianism to the limits of the law, with a stiff punch always in reserve.

524. LEAF, Ann (organist; b. June 28, 1906, Omaha, NE; d. April 3, 1995). *Ann Leaf at the Or-gan* (1929–32).

Columbia's premier organist in the 1930s with her nightly *Nocturne* series coast-to-coast from the Para-mount organ studios. "She makes the organ sing like a mighty orchestra or whisper like water rippling in moonlight," exclaimed *Radio Guide.* She also ap-peared with Fred Allen and Tony Wons. As the num-ber of soaps grew, she began to supply background music for a daily handful, such as *Women of Courage, Lorenzo Jones, Doc Barclay's Daughters, Ellen Randolph.* She started in radio in 1929 after extensive motion pic-ture theatre experience. Less than five feet in height, Leaf was dubbed "Little Organ Annie" and "The Mighty Mite of the Organ."

Ann Leaf

She displayed an aptitude for the organ at a young age and was soloist with the Omaha Symphony at eleven. The Juilliard-trained Leaf once played a duet in perfect synchrony with another organist at a distant station. Neither could hear the other. On the *Carna-tion Contented Hour,* Leaf premiered her composition, the samba "Rio Coco."

525. LEE, Peggy (singer; b. May 26, 1920, Jamestown, ND). *Summer Electric Hour* (1947); *Jimmy Durante Show* (1947–48); *Chesterfield Supper Club* (1948–49).

Big band experience with Will Osborne and Benny Goodman provided the foundation that took this de-liberate, studied song stylist to the top ranks of re-cording and club artists. At one point she seemed pegged as a radio standby for Jo Stafford or Perry Como. Then, in 1946 Durante added her as his fea-tured vocalist, and that brought her solo status on the *Supper Club.* With first husband Dave Barbour, Peggy Lee sang/hosted *King Cole Trio Time.* In *Pete Kelly's Blues,* she proved herself a fine actress in the role as the sultry speakeasy entertainer. Her songwriting collabo-rations with Barbour and others resulted in the oft-re-quested "Manana," "It's a Great Day" and "Golden Earrings."

526. LEEDS, Peter (actor; b. c1920, Bayonne, NJ). *Rogue's Galley* (1945–47); *Alan Young Show* (1946–47); *Bob Hope Show* (1953–55); *Stan Freberg Show* (1957).

Regular cast member for Bob Hope radio, TV and USO shows, beginning in the early 1950s. A performer skilled in many voices and dialects, he played Eugor, the conscience of Detective Rogue, and Joe, "the yes man," of Alan Young, and many supporting characters on *The Railroad Hour* and *Nightbeat.* He estimated that his radio appearances to-talled 3,000 and his TV expo-sure reached 600 programs, including *The Untouchables.*

Leeds studied at the Neighborhood Playhouse af-ter one year on a basketball scholarship to John Marshall Law School. An Air Corps veteran, he served as presi-dent of the Los Angeles Lo-cal of AFTRA.

527. LEIBERT, Rich-ard (organist; b. April 29, 1903, Bethlehem, PA; d. Oct. 22, 1976, Fort Myers, FL). *Organ Rhapsody* (1933–36);

Dick Leibert's Musical Revue (1934–35); *Music by Leibert* (1943–51); *Still of the Night* (1952–53).

Chief organist at Radio City Music Hall from its opening in 1932 into the 1970s. He made organ music from its magnificent consoles as a featured part of the stage presentation. In that role it was a short hop to NBC studios and dozens of jobs over the air. He provided solo interludes and background music. In addition, he recorded more than 200 transcriptions for NBC Thesaurus.

Leibert studied at the Peabody Conservatory and worked for Loew's at the opening of new "atmospheric" movie theatres in various parts of the country. He briefly conducted a band of college youths on barnstorming tours, but returned to the console. That led to organs at the Brooklyn Paramount and Radio City.

528. LENNOX, Elizabeth (singer; b. March 16, 1894, Ionia, MI; d. May 3,1992, Southport, CT). *Palmolive Hour* (1928–31); *Lucky Strike Dance Orchestra* (1928–31); *American Album of Familiar Music* (1933, 1938–40); *Broadway Varieties* (1934–37).

Her splendid contralto voice of great range and flexible tone attracted the attention of pioneer radio stations as well as early phonograph makers. An artist with Brunswick Records, she began broadcasting for them in the mid-1920s. Also a church soloist and concert hall recitalist, she joined William Paley's newly formed Columbia chain as a staff vocalist in 1927. A year later conductor Gustave Haenschen brought her to the *Palmolive Hour*, a program built around the talents of his Brunswick singers. At NBC Lennox performed on one of the first major short-wave programs to Europe, a Christmastime 1929 presentation that included her Lucky Strike Dance Orchestra co-vocalist Gladys Rice.

Her remarkable enunciation was ideally matched with the clear diction of tenor Frank Munn with whom she sang weekly duets on *American Album.* She also co-starred with Everett Marshall and Oscar Shaw on *Broadway Varieties* (aka *Vanities*) at CBS. When her singing career ended in 1941 Lennox retired to Connecticut, devoting herself to the recently established Fairfield County (later Greater Bridgeport) Symphony as president and program chairman, and to presenting young professional artists in concert. A graduate of the Cosmopolitan School of Music in Chicago, she made her recital debut there in 1916 and waxed her first discs for the Edison Company three years later.

529. LEONARD, Sheldon (actor; b. Feb. 22, 1907, New York, NY). *A Day in the Life of Dennis Day* (1948–51); *Martin and Lewis Show* (1949–50); *Judy Canova Show* (1949–53).

His Runyonesque comic flair, honed in such Broadway hits as *Three Men on a Horse, Having Wonderful Time* and *Kiss the Boys Goodbye,* carried him to

Elizabeth Lennox

an equally solid niche in films and radio. He had first turned to the theatre as head of the dramatic society while on an athletic scholarship to Syracuse University. Leonard was in much demand by comedy show writers for supporting roles that he played to good advantage with the likes of Hope, Burns and Allen, Phil Harris and Alan Young. He also appeared on the daytime lineup: *Aunt Jenny, Big Sister* and *David Harum,* and as downright heavies on *The Shadow* and *The Saint.* His 140 films included *Lucky Jordan, Tortilla Flat* and *Guys and Dolls.* Leonard began writing scripts for *Suspense*—a step that led to directing, then producing TV shows for Danny Thomas, Andy Griffin and Dick Van Dyke.

It was Leonard in the part of a holdup man who

stuck a gun in front of Jack Benny and spoke the classic line: "Your money or your life!" And waited in silence until Benny replied, "I'm thinking."

He summed up his career in the book *And The Show Goes On.* "Radio was nice easy work," he wrote in 1995, "no lines to memorize, no early makeup calls, no distant locations. In fact, it was too easy. Most of my work was done on two or, at most, three days in the week."

530. LESCOULIE, Jack (announcer, emcee; b. Nov. 17, 1911, Sacramento, CA; d. July 22, 1987, Memphis, TN). *Grouch Club* (1938–40); *Meet the Champions* (1956–57).

Good-humored announcer and interviewer. After attending Los Angeles City College and studying at the Pasadena Playhouse, he auditioned with a band for jobs at KGFJ Los Angeles in 1932. Instead, he ended up an announcer and all-night DJ at one dollar a broadcast. During a career with many ups and downs, Jack did pre-broadcast warm-ups and commercials. He originated the *Grouch Club,* a comedy series he hosted on CBS and NBC. It made fun of commonly unpleasant things and of early morning "happiness shows."

During World War II he was a combat reporter with the Air Force. Afterwards, he teamed up with Gene Rayburn for *The Jack & Gene Show,* an early morning program on WOR. But he is chiefly remembered as a co-host of television's *Today* from its beginning in 1952 with Dave Garroway and later with Hugh Downs from 1962 to 1966.

531. LEVANT, Oscar (panelist, pianist; b. Dec. 27, 1906, Pittsburgh, PA; d. Aug. 14, 1972, Beverly Hills, CA). *Information Please* (1938–44); *Kraft Music Hall* (1947–49).

Clownish wit with a genius-level brilliance, Levant brought an in-depth knowledge of the entertainment field to *Information Please.* A musician-composer, he had little formal education but picked up a lot of information and facts from talking with people, especially celebrities. He also remembered just about everything he read, particularly from the sports pages. The panel's "bad boy," the bombastic, skeptical Levant gave the program its "difficult moments." Emcee Clifton Fadiman once observed: "You never could tell what would come out of his mouth, largely because his conscious mind and subconscious were on the same level. He was unpredictable in his answers."

Questions of music popped up on nearly every broadcast with panelist Levant in residence; often they required the services of NBC staff pianist Joseph Kahn. Levant would be slouched in his chair, sometimes with his head down on the table in front of him. But he'd look up suddenly and raise his hand to identify a secondary theme from a seldom-played symphony.

Levant's initial break came when he was called in

Oscar Levant

as a last-minute substitute for a recording of "Rhapsody in Blue." His friendship with its composer George Gershwin proved a turning point, and he built a concert hall career on the Gershwin repertoire that carried over into radio (*Telephone Hour*) and films (*The Barkleys of Broadway*). His autobiographical book *The Memoirs of an Amnesiac* included an account of his experiences as *Information Please's* "l'enfant terrible." An objective and entertaining look at his musical virtuosity and caustic wit was called *A Talent for Genius,* published two decades after his death.

532. LEVIN, Sylvan (conductor; b. May 2, 1903, Baltimore, MD; d. Aug. 10, 1996). *Sinfonietta* (1944–45); *Brownstone Theatre* (1945); *Let's Go to the Opera* (1946).

Musical director of Mutual, via WOR, in the 1940s. He followed Alfred Wallenstein in that post. Levin made his musical reputation by starting and conducting the Philadelphia Opera in the 1930s. During his watch, the company presented a number of operas in English translations and several productions of new works by Deems Taylor, Menotti and other American composers. From 1929 to 1932 he served as associate conductor of the Philadelphia Orchestra under Stokowski, leaving to organize and lead the York (PA) Symphony. In 1944 he rejoined Stokowski, then with the New York City Symphony.

At MBS he broadcast *Sinfonietta* as well as popular music features and dramas. He also conducted

Great Moments in Music at CBS. "There is a huge audience to whom good music is still foreign," he observed in an interview in 1946, "and who have therefore the advantage of not being 'ossified' in their taste. They must be attracted to good music by way of the familiar and popular."

Levin studied piano at both Peabody Conservatory and Curtis Institute of Music. He joined the Curtis faculty as a vocal coach and opera instructor while still a graduate student in 1928.

533. LEVINE, Henry ("Hot Lips") (trumpeter, conductor; b. Nov. 26, 1907, London, England; d. May 6, 1989, Las Vegas, NV). *Chamber Music Society of Lower Basin Street* (1940–42, 1950, 1952); *Strictly from Dixie* (1941–42); *Solitaire Time* (1946–50).

NBC house musician who rose from the ranks to lead Dixieland groups. Beginning in 1934, trumpeter Levine played on scores of programs under Damrosch, Black and Toscanini. In the early 1940s he helped to create two popular music series, utilizing his early experience as a member of the rejuvenated Original Dixieland Jazz Band. The Basin Street series, appropriately aired on the Blue network, showcased newcomers Dinah Shore and Lena Horne, and tantalized listeners with hip and slightly sardonic intros to a session of barrelhouse, boogie woogie and the blues. RCA recorded several albums using Levine and the cast before military service interrupted his career for four years.

Levine grew up in Brooklyn where he blew his horn in boys' high school bands and by 17 was a professional. Engagements with George Olsen and Vincent Lopez, and the English orchestra of Ambrose (for the opening of London's Mayfair Hotel in 1927) led to pit jobs for Broadway musicals and to staff at Radio City.

Following the war, he worked as musical director for NBC in Cleveland, then held similar posts for a number of resort hotels in Miami and Las Vegas. Before retiring in 1982, Levine returned to Dixieland and jazz as both an instrumentalist-leader and instructor.

534. LEWIS, Cathy (actress; b. 1918, Spokane, WA; d. Nov. 20, 1968, Hollywood, CA). *The Drene Show* (1944–45); *The Great Gildersleeve* (1949–54); *My Friend Irma* (1947–54); *On Stage* (1953–54).

At one point in the mid-1940s Lewis was juggling five radio shows a day in Hollywood where she had started in films at age 19. Best known as Jane Stacy, the dependable roommate and confidante of hairbrained Irma, played by Marie Wilson, she also did the TV version. A teenage singer with the bands of Herbie Kay, Ted Weems, and Glen Gray, she appeared as leading lady in *Suspense* and *Whispering Streets*. She played Gildersleeve's girl friend, Nurse Kathy Milford, for five seasons.

Her stage credits included *Winterset, Bitter Sweet,* *Stage Door* and *The Man Whom Came to Dinner* (on tour with Alexander Woollcott). In *Hazel* on television, she played the sister of Hazel's boss. From 1943 to 1958 Lewis was married to actor-producer Elliott Lewis. Together, they produced and co-starred on the CBS anthology *On Stage.*

535. LEWIS, Elliott (actor; b. Nov. 28, 1917, New York, NY; d. May 20, 1990, Gleneden Beach, OR). *Midstream* (1939–40); *Meet Me at Parky's* (1946–47); *Phil Harris—Alice Faye Show* (1946–54).

High-rated programs, from comedy to suspense, filled Lewis' acting days. His best featured role, the guitar-playing Frankie Remley, was with Phil Harris and Alice Faye. He also co-starred and produced with one-time wife, Cathy Lewis, Columbia's *On Stage.* Writing, producing and teaching augmented his performing credits on *Arch Oboler's Plays* and *Capt. Flagg and Sgt. Quirt.*

Elliott studied dramatics and music at Los Angeles City College. He made his debut in 1936 over KHJ in "The Life of Simon Bolivar." The fee was five dollars. Devoted to radio, he worked in Chicago on *Knickerbocker Playhouse* and in New York with *Big Town.* During World War II he served in the Army with the Armed Forces Radio Service. For TV he co-produced *Climax,* and later wrote mystery novels.

Said Lewis in 1978 of his favorite medium: "Radio gives out a series of impulses in the form of a story that allows or insists that its audience create a picture in their mind of what the people in the story and events look like. Listeners have to create their own geography, even the wardrobe."

Elliott Lewis (courtesy of Steve Jelf)

536. LEWIS, Fulton, Jr. (commentator [catch-phrase: "That's the top of the news as it looks from here."]; b. April 30, 1903, Washington, DC; d. Aug. 21, 1966, Washington, DC). *News and Comment* (1938–66).

A politically conservative news commentator who targeted many New Deal programs and liberals for criticism. Often referred to as "the voice with a snarl," he attracted listeners with an almost religious zeal for his opinions.

In 1937 he had resigned from the Hearst organization to become a $25-a-week replacement with Mutual's Washington affiliate, WOL. Two months later, his broadcasts were a network fixture. A leading Washington correspondent and columnist from 1924 to 1937, Lewis was carried by 460 stations on his Mutual hookup. He founded the Radio Correspondents' Association, the official accrediting agency for admission to the correspondents galleries of Congress.

In 1950 he attacked almost nightly the re-election of Sen. Millard Tydings of Maryland. When the Senator was defeated, he blamed Lewis for unfair commentary.

537. LEWIS, Jerry (comedian; b. March 16, 1926, Newark, NJ). *Martin and Lewis Show* (1949–53).

Chaplinesque clown who first achieved success as the partner of singer Dean Martin. A club comedian, he teamed up with Dean at Atlantic City in 1946 in an improvised session of songs and slapstick. Major night club bookings, TV spots and motion pictures followed. Bob Hope signed the duo as his guests in 1948–49. For *The Big Show* they joined with Hope in a take-off of *The Women* called "The Fellers," and appeared on Elgin Watch's "Two Hours of Stars" 1948 Thanksgiving program (Jerry cavorted with Vera Vague and Don Ameche; Dean sang "Rambling Rose"). Their own show followed in the spring of 1949 with Dean as emcee. After a string of phenomenally popular films, the partnership broke up in 1956 when each was anxious to try a career on his own.

Lewis proved a viable solo performer on screen in *The Sad Sack, Ladies Man* and *The Bellboy,* especially building a loyal following in Europe for his unsubtle brand of contorted pantomime and idiocy. He personally spearheaded the annual telethon to raise funds for the Muscular Dystrophy Associations of America.

Jerry first sang at age five at a hotel in the borscht circuit. His father was the show's emcee-singer. His mother, Mona Lewis, played the piano at WOR. Jerry began as a "record" act, mouthing the lyrics of songs played on a phonograph off stage. His own singing voice later sold over 1,000,000 copies of his Decca release of the old Jolson standard, "Rock-a-Bye Your Baby."

538. LILLIE, Beatrice (comedienne; b. May 29, 1894, Toronto, Canada; d. Jan. 20, 1989, Henley-on-Thames, England). *Bea Lillie Show* (1934–37).

Often called one of the world's funniest women, Lillie performed best when her physical gestures, especially her facial comments, registered with an audience. Nonetheless, her barbed riposters and witty songs became the solid foundation for a comedy-variety series, initially sponsored by Borden Milk. During that mid-1930s period she combined broadcasts with stage runs in *At Home Abroad* and *The Show Is On.* She regularly moved back and forth between London and New York, after first bringing British humor to America in *Charlot's Revue of 1924.* Dressed as Britannia, Queen of the Waves, she sang a song called "March with Me," a rowdy satire on Britain's sacred symbol of naval strength, and garnered rave reviews as the show's lead.

Lillie began singing in local Toronto soirees, then studied music in England where in 1914 Andre Charlot hired her for his revues. Her Broadway hits included *Inside USA* and *High Spirits;* her famous songs, "Mad Dogs and Englishmen" and "There are Fairies in the Bottom of My Garden." Married to Sir Robert Peel, she never took her official title, Lady Peel, seriously and called her autobiography *Every Other Inch a Lady.*

539. LINDLAHR, Victor (commentator; b. Feb. 14, 1897; d. Jan. 26, 1969, Miami Beach, FL). *Talks on Diet* (1936–53).

Food and nutrition commentator. His talks on diet began at Mutual with a Monday noontime series and soon grew to five times a week. Serutan sponsored him in the mid-40s. His best-known book was *You Are What You Eat,* published in 1941.

Lindlahr graduated from Chicago College of Osteopathy in 1918. His early broadcasts gained listenership from the introduction of his 600-calorie, seven-day reducing diet.

540. LINKLETTER, Art (emcee; b. July 17, 1912, Moose Jaw, Saskatchewan, Canada). *People Are Funny* (1942–60); *House Party* (1945–63).

Host of two of radio's longest-running, best-loved audience-participation shows. Both stemmed from a partnership with John Guedel and stressed situation gags. The series contained the nucleus of a dozen or more game show formats, including *To Tell the Truth, Password* and *The Price Is Right.* Linkletter's ability to talk extemporaneously at length in any situation with people of all ages and backgrounds kept the programs fresh and spontaneous.

His rise to radio stardom followed a classic route: 1933, KGB announcer while at nearby San Diego State; 1936, radio director, Texas Centennial Exposition; 1937, radio director, San Francisco World's Fair; 1939, freelance announcer and emcee; 1942, co-host, NBC network. Linkletter announced almost every known type of sports, and broadcast from planes, battleships and submarines. His ad-lib training was honed

Art Linkletter (courtesy of Steve Jelf)

on *Who's Dancing Tonight?* aired by KSFO from the ballroom of San Francisco's St. Francis Hotel.

House Party continued the good-spirited thrust of *People* on a Monday-through-Friday afternoon basis, and added homespun humor. His off-the-cuff interviews with groups of young schoolchildren delighted listeners and inspired books on "kids say the darnest things." Linkletter also wrote *People Are Funny*, a backstage view of his work, and appeared in a movie based on his popular show. Television successfully embraced both of his blockbuster programs. But by 1970 they were off the air, and Art was content to give his time to lecturing and writing, and to extensive business interests and investments.

541. LISS, Ronald (actor; b. 1931, New York, NY; d. c1970). *Peables Takes Charge* (1938–39); *Portia Faces Life* (1941–42).

Child actor-singer, beginning at age four on Madge Tucker's variety show *Coast-to-Coast on a Bus.* He later appeared on *Let's Pretend,* and as Ned on *Peables Takes Charge* and Crutch on *Bess Johnson,* both at NBC. Liss often played a Buddy, Bobby or Scotty on such soaps and serials of the 1940s as *Buck Rogers* and *Mark Trail.* As a teenager, he added roles on *Eternal Light, Studio One,* and *Living.*

542. LITTLE, Little Jack (singer [Cheerful Little Earful] [signature song: "Little by Little"]; b. May 28, 1902, London, England; d. April 9, 1956, Hollywood, FL). *Little Jack Little Show* (1930–35).

His "intimate personality" technique worked well in his role as singer-pianist. Known as a mike-hugging

artist, he had a low, husky voice. One observer wrote: "He tips the mike to his lips and sways with it in a manner that is almost amorous." Born John Leonard, he worked for publishing houses, playing songs over radio. In the 1930s, he had 15-minute broadcasts many times a week, often from WLW. A composer, Little contributed "A Shanty in Old Shanty Town" and "Jealous" to the charts. In the late '40s his knowledge of music proved valuable as a disc jockey in Washington.

At the University of Iowa, he had organized a campus orchestra and took it to New York. He returned to a podium from time to time, and once toured with Paul Small as Little and Small.

543. LIVINGSTONE, Mary (comedienne; b. Nov. 27, 1908, Seattle, WA; d. June 30, 1983, Holmby Hills, CA). *Jack Benny Program* (1934–55).

A fixture of husband Jack Benny's show for 21 years. She played his wisecracking cohort, first in vaudeville and then on radio at NBC. Initially reluctant to be part of Benny's act, she agreed to join him when no other partner measured up. During their heyday, they were among radio's reigning families, which also included their good friends George Burns and Gracie Allen. She made few appearances when the Benny troupe moved into television, and retired in the 1960s.

Married to Benny in 1927, Sadye Marks (her real name) had first met the comedian at age 12 when he called on her oldest sister. A half-dozen years later, they met again at the May Company store in Los Angeles, where she sold women's hosiery, and began dating.

544. LLOYD, Rita (actress; b. Jan. 16, 1930, Brooklyn, NY). *Let's Pretend* (1948–54).

Television had already started to take off by the time Lloyd passed the CBS and *Let's Pretend* auditions. She had in the words of Pretender historian Arthur Anderson, "a mature voice, good speech, and the ability to play emotional parts." After being in the American Theatre Wing's training program, she landed parts on *Portia Faces Life, Suspense, Eternal Light* and *Backstage Wife.* Television soon beckoned with soap roles on *Guiding Light* and *Edge of Night* (as the wicked spy Jessica Webster), as did work as a stage performer and TV series narrator.

Teenage Rita first appeared on mike in a high school show at NBC and participated in an all-city radio workshop at WNYC. She studied drama at City College, then decided to become a professional. In the 1970s she helped to create Command Performance, a company designed to show out-of-towners aspects of life in New York and introduce them to their favorite soap stars.

545. LOMAX, Stan (sportscaster; b. May 20, 1899, Pittsburgh, PA; d. June 26, 1987, Ossining, NY).

Mutual network's first and best-known early sports broadcaster. He started his 15-minute sports results programs in 1932 on WOR and left the station 45 years later in 1977. The show aimed at providing thorough coverage, giving ample time to college and sometimes high school scores, at a time when other shows concentrated primarily on professional sports. He chiefly reported on football, baseball and basketball.

After studying at Cornell and Hobart, he became a sports writer and later covered Brooklyn Dodgers baseball and college football. Lomax began his radio career by filling in for Ford Frick on *Evening Journal Sports.*

546. LOMBARDO, Guy (bandleader [The Sweetest Music This Side of Heaven] [signature song: "Auld Lang Syne"]; b. June 19, 1902, London, Ontario, Canada; d. Nov. 5, 1977, Houston, TX). *Burns and Allen* (1932–34); *Roosevelt Grill Orchestra Program* (1946–50); *Lombardoland USA* (1949–57).

A dominating influence among dance bands, the Lombardo style focused on a direct singable interpretation of easily comprehended melodies. A distinctively mellow sound, the music of Guy's Royal Canadians never fell out of favor in the hard-driving swing era or beyond into the age of rock. "We lose 'em in the teens often times," he said, "but we catch 'em again later on." He never lost a large radio following during his four decades on the bandstand.

Guy's group started with his brothers Carmen (on sax and vocals) and Lebert (on trumpet) and two friends in Ontario. An audition across the border brought them an engagement in Cleveland where Guy

Guy Lombardo

persuaded a station to let him broadcast without pay. This spread his fame and led to more bookings, including the Granada Cafe in Chicago. There, for CBS he made his first network broadcast in 1927 — the start of a long relationship with that chain and many consumer product advertisers.

He arrived in New York in October 1929 for an engagement at the Hotel Roosevelt Grill (he stayed for 33 seasons) and a program sponsored by Robert Burns Panatella cigars. William Paley asked him to close the year, playing from 11:30 to 12:00. "And NBC asked us to *open* the New Year," Guy recalled. "It was flattering — the two biggest networks wanting us on each side of midnight." For the next 48 New Year's Eves listeners eagerly tuned in the Royal Canadians and "Auld Lang Syne," perhaps to be reassured that the old year had, indeed, ended and a new one had begun.

His danceable records ("Coquette," "Boo Hoo," "Easter Parade"), often with smooth vocals by Kenny Gardner and Rosemarie Lombardo, numbered in the thousands and remained popular with disc jockeys decades after their first release. A showman and entrepreneur, Lombardo produced many summer extravaganzas at the Jones Beach Marine Theatre, a short distance from his Long Island waterfront home, restaurant, and racing circuit speedboats. He was an honor guest on *This Is Your Life* in 1949. His autobiography, *Auld Acquaintance,* was published in 1975.

547. LOPEZ, Vincent (bandleader [signature song: "Nola"] [catchphrase: "Hello everybody — Lopez speaking."]; b. Dec. 30, 1894, Brooklyn, NY; d. Sept. 20, 1975, North Miami, FL). *Luncheon with Lopez* (1947–48).

A headliner at the Pennsylvania Hotel Grill, beginning in 1921, the year he first played on radio from a makeshift studio of WJZ Newark. He suffered from mike fright, and all he could manage in that initial broadcast were four words of greeting that became his official sign-on for the next 50 or so years. His smooth dance rhythms went over the air as the first remote pickup, if not in the country, at least in New York. His earliest sponsor was Gimbel Brothers department store. The genial pianist-conductor was often heard from the Astor Grill, St. Regis Roof and his own Club Lopez. In November 1926 NBC featured his orchestra on its inaugural program.

Lopez began as a pianist in a Brooklyn saloon; at 22 he led a five-piece orchestra at a Chinese restaurant on Broadway, then moved his outfit into vaudeville with dancer Pat Rooney. Over the years his sidemen included Xavier Cugat, Glenn Miller and Artie Shaw; his most successful discovery was singer Betty Hutton. After seven years of cross-country engagements, he parlayed a three-month booking at the Hotel Taft Grill into a 25-year run.

His tentative plans for a symphonic jazz concert was the catalysis for rival Paul Whiteman's Aeolian Hall concert in 1924. Lopez presented his own large-scale program with 40 musicians at the Metropolitan Opera House later that year. It only brought him a mountain of debts and shortlived recognition as a promoter of America's new musical forms. Lopez put many of his recollections into the autobiographical *Lopez Speaking: My Life and How I Changed It.*

548. LORD, Phillips H. (actor; b. July 13, 1902, Hartford, CT; d. Oct. 19, 1975, Ellsworth, ME). *Sunday Evening at Seth Parker's* (1929–33, 1935–36, 1938–39); *Cruise of the Seth Parker* (1933–34); *G-Men* (1935–36); *We, the People* (1936–39).

Son of a Connecticut Congregational minister and educated at solidly established New England institutions, Lord combined writing and producing with acting. He originated and played Seth Parker in 1929 and became the evangelistic Down East character. Prayers and hymns were part of the folksy, old-fashioned *Sunday Evening at Seth Parker's*— homespun "keeping faith" type of plots for Depression-logged listeners.

His typewriter churned out scripts for similar heartwarming and colloquial characters in the early 1930s: *Uncle Abe and David, The Stebbins Boys* and *Country Doctor* (with Lord as the MD). Then, with Chevrolet as sponsor, he turned to stories of crime-busting with *G-Men*. That quickly evolved into *Gangbusters,* based on files of the FBI. Next came *Mr. District Attorney* in 1939 and *Counterspy* during World War II. Lord constantly pursued true stories. He brought many people and their real-life experiences to *We, the People.*

In 1934 the flamboyant Lord set out to sail around the world in his four-masted schooner, *Seth Parker.* Cables and shortwave pickups kept him in the script each week. The highly publicized voyage made headlines when the vessel floundered in a storm off Tahiti and Lord was rescued by H.M.S. *Australia.* Unfailingly entrepreneurial, this shrewd Yankee made a fortune with his radio properties and spin-offs by age 40.

549. LOVEJOY, Frank (actor; b. March 28, 1912, Bronx, NY; d. Oct. 2, 1962, New York, NY). *Mr. District Attorney* (1939–40); *We Love and Learn* (1942–44); *Mr. & Mrs. North* (1943–45); *Murder and Mr. Malone* (1947–48); *Nightbeat* (1950–52).

Crime fighting-law enforcement series and daytime soaps formed the bulk of his 4,000 or more network appearances. Roles, too, on *Arch Oboler's Plays* and *Manhattan at Midnight* displayed his tough, cynical demeanor. Lovejoy tried Broadway in 1934 but did not make an impression. The film *Home of the Brave* 15 years later opened jobs beyond radio. He often acted with his wife, Joan Banks. They were appearing in a New Jersey production of *The Best Man*— his most famous stage role — when he died at age 50.

Often the first choice of radio casting directors, he stepped into broadcasting by happenstance. In 1934 Lovejoy became stranded in Cincinnati for a fortnight

Frank Lovejoy (courtesy of Capital Cities/ABC)

while waiting for other members of a stock company to assemble. To pay his expenses, he applied for work at WLW — and stayed a year.

550. LUDDEN, Allen (host; b. Oct. 5, 1918, Mineral Point, WI; d. June 9, 1981, Los Angeles, CA). *Mind Your Manners* (1947–48); *College Bowl* (1953–58).

Described by a critic as "the happy highbrow," the ingratiating Ludden brought a gentle professorial demeanor to game shows. A glib, effortless talker, the erudite emcee generated high ratings for the spirited, fast-paced undergraduate question-and-answer context, *College Bowl.* Its popularity as a Sunday afternoon sporting event was so well established by the mid-50s that General Electric took it to television.

Shortly after receiving bachelor's and master's degrees in English from the University of Texas, and performing and teaching a bit, Ludden entered the military. He assisted actor Maurice Evans who was a major in the Pacific directing troop entertainment. After the war, Evans made him his personal manager. Part of the job was to build up interest in his production of *Hamlet* by talking at clubs, luncheons and in high school auditoriums.

He joined WTIC Hartford in 1947, and because of his experience with teenage groups, became moderator of *Mind Your Manners,* a Saturday talk show picked up by NBC. Ludden served in administrative posts with CBS before achieving much acclaim as host of TV's *Password,* starting in the 1960s. The Emmy-

Allen Ludden

Frank Luther

winning game was on weekday afternoons as well as in prime time once a week. After the death of his first wife in 1961, he married actress Betty White.

551. LUDDY, Barbara (actress; b. May 25, 1907, Helena, MT; d. April 1, 1979, Los Angeles, CA). *First Nighter* (1936–1949, 1952–53).

Leading lady of half-hour plays on *First Nighter*. Her regular co-stars were Les Tremayne and Olan Soule. The scripts were particularly good and often had amusing twists; the action moved at a fast pace, backed by the music of a large orchestra (Caesar Petrillo was often on the podium). Whenever there were tall actors in the cast, the petite Luddy had to be provided with a box to reach the mike.

Luddy started out as a child singer in vaudeville and movie extra in Hollywood. She toured with a stock company production, *Lombardy Ltd*, in Australia while still a teenager. With radio Chicago became her homebase.

552. LUTHER, Frank (singer; b. Aug. 4, 1905, Lakin, Kansas; d. Nov. 16, 1980, New York, NY). *Happy Wonder Bakers Trio* (1928–31); *Manhattan Merry-Go-Round* (1932–33); *Luther-Layman Singers* (1939–41); *Frank Luther Show* (1947–48).

Called the "Bing Crosby of the sandpile set" for bringing more stories in song to children than anyone else on radio and records. To young listeners he was familiar as the voice of nursery rhymes and "Mother Goose" tales, and of lessons in song about health, diet, arithmetic and manners.

He studied piano and singing at Kansas State Normal College, spent three years as an evangelist, and appeared as a tenor in touring choral groups. He was top tenor for one season with The Revelers with whom he made his first radio appearance. A prolific composer of children's songs, including the enduring "Barnacle Bill the Sailor," he got his first inkling of power over youngsters' minds in the 1930s when he used the phrase "friendly darkness" in a song. Child psychiatrists who were treating children for fear of darkness wrote him to keep up the good work.

He often teamed up on radio with his wife Zora

Layman on folk songs and old ballads. Luther wrote the book *Americans and Their Songs* and lectured on American music.

553. LYMAN, Abe (bandleader [signature song: "California, Here I Come"]; b. Aug. 4, 1897, Chicago, IL; d. Oct. 23, 1957, Los Angeles, CA). *Waltz Time* (1933–48); *Melodiana* (1936–37); *Your Hit Parade* (1937).

A flashy drummer determined to organize and lead a band, Lyman after several false starts succeeded with his Californians, a 20-piece orchestra. It moved into the Cocoanut Grove in 1921 and remained there with renewed engagements for a record five-year period. During this time Brunswick Records musical director Gus Haenschen added the group to the company's popular music lineup. They were known for their snappy dance rhythms.

The ebullient leader did not sign for an ongoing network series until he left the West Coast for New York in the early 1930s. There, thrice-weekly CBS broadcasts segued into *Waltz Time,* a Friday night mainstay produced by Frank Hummert who kept a proprietary grip on its musical contents. Lyman conducted this perennial for some half-dozen years. Although the billing remained "Abe Lyman's orchestra," for the rest of its run, Victor Arden actually led a studio-recruited group that included oft-featured accordionist Charles Magnante. Lyman, it seems, preferred playing in night clubs and on the road, as well as overseeing the operation of family restaurants in California.

554. LYNCH, Christopher (singer; b. c1920, County Limerick, Ireland; d. April 15, 1994, Worcestershire, England). *Voice of Firestone* (1946–50).

Irish tenor chosen by Harvey Firestone to succeed Richard Crooks as ongoing lead on *Voice of Firestone.* This sponsor booked Carnegie Hall on September 30, 1946 to introduce its new singer. It was also Lynch's American debut. He had been named by John McCormack as his vocal "successor," after Lynch had studied with the peerless Irish tenor in Ireland. That season the 26-year-old Firestone tenor often alternated with soprano Eleanor Steber, although there were many shared programs.

In a 1947 review of *The Voice of Firestone,* John Crosby spoke of Lynch "who sings 'Beautiful Isle of Somewhere' so you can smell the shamrocks in it . . . he has a lovely full tenor, which is enough to be thankful for in this era of thin barytones."

By 1949 his Firestone appearances became less frequent. That year he went on a two-month concert tour to the Western states, and he customarily spent the summer in Ireland. More and more the program featured guest artists — photogenic singers seemed in favor as the *Voice* added television to become a simulcast. Lynch also recorded for RCA and Columbia but never achieved the star status of his mentor McCormack or predecessor Crooks in the United States.

Peg Lynch, Alan Bunce (courtesy of Peg Lynch)

555. LYNCH, Peg (actress; b. Nov. 25, 1916, Lincoln, NE). *Ethel and Albert* (1944–50); *The Couple Next Door* (1957–59).

Her classic domestic human comedy had its roots early in her broadcast career. She amused herself with an imaginary couple in a three-minute sketch, when, shortly after college graduation, she was employed on KATE in Albert Lea, Minnesota. Lynch wrote 250 spot commercials and four regular shows a week, and did some acting. The series which she called *Ethel and Albert,* was expanded to five minutes when she moved to WCHV Charlottesville, Virginia, to do a women's variety program. It soon became a daily feature, then in 1944 moved to the Blue Network in New York.

Richard Widmark was the first Albert for eight months, but Alan Bunce was the second and last. In 1950 the duo moved on to television with a segment on Kate Smith's program. In 1952 *Ethel and Albert* became a half-hour show for Sunbeam. Five years later they were back on radio at CBS. By 1953 Lynch had written and acted in more than 3,000 of her droll and usually plotless scripts. "I'm opposed to plot because things don't happen that way to me," she once explained. "I never like to have Ethel and Albert do anything we wouldn't do at home."

556. LYTELL, Bert (actor; b. Feb. 24, 1885, New York, NY; d. Sept. 28, 1954, New York, NY). *Bert Lytell's Adventures* (1938–39); *Stage Door Canteen* (1942–45).

Debonair stage and film star who emceed the wartime morale-boosting variety show, *Stage Door Can-*

Bert Lytell

teen, a radio version of the actual GI center near Times Square. As executive vice president of USO Camp Shows, he arranged entertainment for servicemen at posts stateside and overseas, as well as for listeners over the CBS series. While playing on Broadway in *Margin for Error* and *Lady in the Dark* in the years 1939–41, he worked in radio appearances. Lytell's films included the lead in *Alias Jimmy Valentine* which spun off a radio series. Active in television, he played Father Barbour in *One Man's Family* and emceed *Philco Television Playhouse.*

Both parents were actors. At age three Bert had a walk-on part, and his first regular role in stock in Newark at 17.

557. McBRIDE, Mary Margaret (commentator; b. Nov. 16, 1899, Paris, MO; d. April 7, 1976, West Shokun, NY). *Mary Margaret McBride* (1934–54).

First-rate newspaper and magazine writer, Mary Margaret came on the air as "Martha Deane" with a chatty women's program at WOR Mutual in 1934. The station soon decided that she did not have a good radio personality — she spoke in a high-pitched rural twang, stumbled over words, often giggled. But a complimentary write-up in the *Daily News* gave it pause for a trial period. Sponsors adored Mary Margaret, and that spoke the loudest. She became the female Arthur Godfrey — a super saleswoman and pioneer in daytime talk shows. Her daily 45-minute sessions of revealing interviews and homespun advice proved outstandingly popular.

In 1940 she moved to CBS with a 15-minute format, then switched to a longer, better-suited time frame at NBC. In retirement she eased into regional radio, broadcasting thrice weekly on WGHO Kingston, NY from her Catskill Mountain home.

558. McCAFFREY, John K. M. (newscaster, moderator; b. Nov. 30, 1913, Moscow, ID; d. Oct. 3, 1983, Torrington, CT). *The Author Meets the Critics* (1947, 1949–51).

Newsman with assignments as emcee, host and quizmaster. He took over the lively literary series that placed an author at a table of book critics for an exchange of opinions and criticism. Teacher and editor as well as journalist, McCaffrey worked as an early TV newscaster for NBC with *11th Hour News.* A graduate of the University of Wisconsin and Columbia, he figured prominently in New York's publishing world.

559. McCAMBRIDGE, Mercedes (actress; b. March 17, 1918, Joliet, IL). *Girl Alone* (1937–39); *Big Sister* (1944–46); *I Love a Mystery* (1949–52); *Defense Attorney* (1952); *Family Skelton* (1953–54).

Performer active in the three busiest radio broadcast centers of the country at their productive peaks. While at Mundelein College and a member of its speaking choir, McCambridge signed an NBC contract in Chicago in 1936 to do soaps and serials. Four years later, in Los Angeles, she appeared with Rudy Vallee and Ben Alexander. In 1942 the future Oscar winner settled in New York and parts in *The Thin Man, Dick Tracy, Inner Sanctum* and *Carrington Playhouse* — and the title role in *Big Sister* at CBS. She also played Rosemary in *Abe's Irish Rose.* The focal point of many melodramatic scripts, she was described as "a sort of latter day Pearl White of the air lanes."

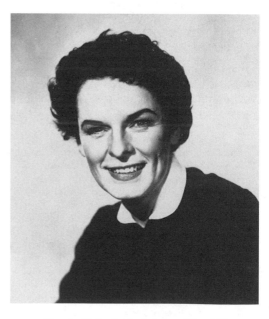

Mercedes McCambridge (courtesy of Steve Jelf)

Determined to try Broadway, McCambridge worked into her schedule a string of plays, virtually all of which closed within days of their openings. She had better luck with her movie debut, *All The King's Men;* it brought her a best supporting-actress award. Radio remained an important part of her activities, with television, into the 1950s.

560. McCARTHY, Clem (sportscaster [catch-phrase: "R-r-r-racing fans, this is Clem McCarthy."]; b. Sept. 9, 1882, East Bloomfield, NY; d. June 4, 1962, New York, NY).

Gravel-voiced, rapid-fire reporter of horse races. His speedy description (224 words a minute) began with the 1928 Kentucky Derby, aired by KYW Chicago. He proceeded to cover the next 22 annual runs of the Churchill Downs classic, chiefly for NBC. McCarthy also handled blow-by-blow accounts of prizefights.

The son of a horse dealer, he aspired to be a jockey but grew too big. He turned to track reporting. When Arlington Park, Chicago, installed an up-to-date PA system in 1927, he tried announcing. Clem was soon a familiar sight with binoculars in one hand and mike in the other.

561. McCONNELL, Ed (singer, host; b. Jan. 12, 1892, Atlanta, GA; d. July 24, 1954, Newport Beach, CA). *Smilin' Ed McConnell* (1936–44); *Buster Brown Gang* (1944–53).

Children's show host with make believe characters: Tige the dog, Froggy the gremlin, Squeekie the mouse, Midnight the cat, Grandie the piano. His well-dramatized stories of adventure, interlaced with songs, drew a large kiddie following, especially when Buster Brown Shoes came on as sponsor for a Saturday morning session and offered free comic books and such premiums as orange, green and brown neckerchiefs. Casual and heavy set Smilin' Ed later took his unpretentious program to NBC-TV with animated visual representations of his Gang.

A onetime song leader for evangelists, he was drawn to vaudeville. In 1922 he entertained with a banjo over WSB Atlanta. He soon went to Orlando after signing a contract with a phonograph company. It specified that he go on the air in Florida at least once a week. To do so, he leased an unused transmitter from Rollins College and built his own station. The husky-voiced, down-to-earth McConnell appeared on WSM, WWJ, WLW before connecting with NBC in 1932. On his early song sessions he was billed as "The Singing Philosopher."

562. McCONNELL, Lulu (comedienne [catch-phrase: "Hey, honey are you married?"]; b. April 8, 1882, Kansas City, MO; d. Oct. 9, 1962, Los Angeles, CA). *It Pays to Be Ignorant* (1942–49, 1951).

The brunt of numerous scripted insults by other panelists on *It Pays to Be Ignorant,* a travesty on quiz shows. Her gravel-voiced retorts unfailingly generated waves of laughter. She had bowed on Broadway in *Poor Little Rich Girl* in 1920 and played a lady buffoon in vaudeville. Radio came along and provided parts in 1933 with Isham Jones and Gertrude Niesen. Once tested for Marie Dressler film roles, Lulu opted for broadcast characters.

563. MacCORMACK, Franklyn (announcer; b. March 8, 1908, Waterloo, IA; d. June 12, 1971, Chicago, IL). *Myrt and Marge* (1932); *Easy Aces* (1935); *Poetic Melodies* (1936–38).

Narrator-commentator-announcer, he was well known as a reader of poetry to music accompaniment. Wayne King's orchestra often provided the melodic backing. A recording of his recitation of "Why Do I Love You?" with King's "Melody of Love" reputedly sold four million copies.

Starting out as an actor, MacCormack had turned to broadcasting in 1930 when stage roles became sparse. St. Louis radio gave him a

Ed McConnell

foothold; Chicago's WBBM offered the foundation of a career as announcer and producer. In 1937 he welcomed listeners to *Jack Armstrong*. His *Poetic Melodies* with singer Jack Fulton attracted Wrigley Company as sponsor.

In 1959 at WGN he inaugurated *All Night Showcase* which he aired until the day he died a dozen years later.

564. McCRARY, Jinx Falkenburg (hostess; b. Jan. 21, 1919, Barcelona, Spain). *Hi! Jinx* (1946–49); *Tex & Jinx* (1949–56); *Weekend* (1953–55).

A model and film actress prior to her marriage to Air Force Colonel Tex McCrary in June 1945, Jinx retired as a young bride to suburban Long Island. But that fall an NBC executive asked if they would be a New York area husband-and-wife talk show team. Tex, a newspaper and magazine editor, thought it sounded like fun. For the next dozen years, they broadcast five or six mornings a week from their home. When the show went on the network as a summer replacement for *Duffy's Tavern*, Tex and Jinx became coast-to-coast household names through their scintillating conversation and headline guests. Her earliest radio appearance had been guest shots with Eddie Cantor, Bob Hope, Bing Crosby and Bill Stern, with whom she covered the 1942 National Singles & Doubles Tennis matches from Forest Hills. A serious case of hepatitis ended Jinx's broadcasts in 1958; Tex did the show alone for two more years.

Born to American parents living overseas, Jinx had grown up in South America and California, becoming a well-tanned tennis champion. While playing in Los Angeles, photographer Paul Hesse shot the tall, raven-haired athlete for a *Saturday Evening Post* magazine cover. Chosen the first Miss Rheingold for a 1940 beer ad campaign, she took a part in Al Jolson's Broadway show *Hold on to Your Hats*. She could neither sing nor dance, and had had no acting training, but Columbia Pictures signed the Latin-looking starlet for *Two Latins from Manhattan*. Ten more low-budget pictures and one major musical (*Cover Girl*) made her a favorite GI pinup girl and popular USO trouper. Jinx met Tex in 1941 when he called for a backstage interview and wrote a story, "The Girl of Two Americas."

565. McCRARY, Tex (interviewer; b. Oct. 13, 1910, Calvert, TX). *Hi, Jinx* (1946–49); *Tex & Jinx* (1949–58).

Outstanding interviewer-multimedia pro who nurtured the radio-TV talk show into a viable mainstream feature. With his wife, the former actress Jinx Falkenburg, they had a daily NBC ad-lib breakfast show. "We'd chat about current news and ourselves, and interview guest stars," McCrary explained in a 1993 profile. "We didn't sidestep controversial issues. My newspaper experience had convinced me that the radio executives were all wrong when they said that

people, particularly women, didn't want weighty stuff in the morning; I believe that minds were fresh and particularly open to the consideration of serious subjects in the morning."

Tex went from Yale '32 to a job as copy boy and cub reporter on *The New York World-Telegram*, then to the editorship of the *Literary Digest*. In 1936 he went to work at the *Daily Mirror*, a major Hearst paper. He met Jinx for a feature in that tabloid in 1941, and four years later they wed between his Air Force assignments and her movie and USO commitments. Their bright, fast-moving programs lasted for a dozen years until Jinx's ill health broke up the highly appealing duo.

566. McDANIEL, Hattie (actress; b. June 10, 1895, Wichita, KS; d. Oct. 26, 1952, Woodland Hills, CA). *Beulah* (1947–51).

McDaniel stepped into the Beulah role to become the first Negro actress to star on a prime-time network show. Actor Marlin Hurt had first created the maid as a character on Fibber McGee during World War II. A singer with George Morrison's orchestra and on the Pantages and Orpheum circuits, she first worked on radio at KNX in 1931. The show, sponsored by Optimistic Donuts, was announced by Tom Breneman. Hattie would get so enthusiastic singing that she'd start to dance, and move away from the microphone. Breneman would have to lead her back to the mike. "On our first show he gave me a nickname. . . . I thought the cast would wear formal dress so I was in evening gown. But everyone else wore street clothes,

Hattie McDaniel (courtesy of Steve Jelf)

and when I arrived Tom said: 'Well, look at our High Hat Hattie.'"

In 1940 she was the first Black to receive an Oscar from her role of Scarlett O'Hara's mammy in *Gone with the Wind*. McDaniel, who appeared in nearly 300 films usually as a cook or maid, shared the air with *Amos 'n' Andy*, Eddie Cantor and the Black Gospel music choir on *Wings Over Jordan*. Of radio she observed: "Radio is not physically harder work than other entertainment media, but it is more exacting."

567. McGRATH, Paul (actor; b. April 11, 1904, Chicago, IL; d. April 13, 1978, London, England). *Crime Doctor* (1944–50); *Big Sister* (1944–54); *Inner Sanctum Mysteries* (1945–52).

The host of the mystery series *Inner Sanctum*. His grim-voiced introductory set the scene for some of the most spine-tingling tales ever broadcast. His soap opera assignments were many: *David Harum, Lora Lawton, Stella Dallas, Young Widder Brown*. Apart from the microphone, he appeared with the foremost ladies of the stage: Ruth Gordon, Ina Claire, Helen Hayes, Ilka Chase, Shirley Booth.

McGrath was one of the very first radio performers to appear on television. He made his debut in 1938 when he was playing on Broadway opposite Gertrude Lawrence in *Susan and God*. NBC presented this telecast, the first of a Broadway play. He returned to video in the live drama showcases of the 1950s and on CBS soap operas.

568. MacGREGOR, Evelyn (singer; b. Nov. 2, 1899, Pittsfield, MA; d. July 1967, Sun City, CA). *Waltz Time* (1942–48); *American Melody Hour* (1942–48); *American Album of Familiar Music* (1943–50).

Her straightforward interpretations of both established and new songs on three Hummert-produced musical shows were greatly admired in the 1940s. MacGregor's career had progressed from church singing and vaudeville stints to serious recitals and *The Metropolitan Opera Auditions of the Air* in 1937. She joined Frank Munn on *Waltz Time* in 1942, then became its co-star with Bob Hannon. She subbed for Vivian Della Chiesa on *American Album* in 1943 and was soon added to the permanent cast. Her sonorous and velvety-smooth voice proved an asset to *American Melody Hour*.

569. MacHUGH, Edward (singer; b. May 26, 1893, Dundee, Scotland; d. Feb. 3, 1957, Fort Lauderdale, FL). *The Gospel Singer* (1933–43).

A five-day-a-week hymn singer at NBC. His widowed mother had brought him and six other young children from Scotland to Canada. MacHugh worked as a railroad car cleaner and sang in his spare time. While a ticket-taker at a Royal Hunt Club reception in Montreal, he was asked to sing "God Save the King." His rendition won the attention of the Governor General, who encouraged his pursuit of singing. After voice training in London, he came to the United States in 1921 with an acting troupe presenting Robert Burns' *Cotter's Saturday Night*. He began singing over Boston's WEEI and WBZ, first with a department store choral group, then as a soloist. Each program featured a hymn or two with organ accompaniment. A flood of requests for more sacred songs convinced him that an all-hymn program would fill an important void in radio. His series went coast-to-coast over NBC, first from Boston, then from WJZ. His most requested hymn among the 3,000 that he had sung by the mid-1930s was "The Old Rugged Cross."

At one point he was ordered by the Immigration Department to return to Canada when it was discovered that he had never taken out U.S. citizenship papers. NBC broadcast MacHugh's program from Canada until he successfully re-entered the country.

Because some NBC stations were unable to carry his show in the morning, discs of his program were cut each day and sent to transmitters as far off as Hawaii for broadcast in various time frames. By 1940, his voice was one of the most-recorded in the world.

570. McINTIRE, John (actor; b. June 27, 1907, Spokane, WA; d. Jan. 30, 1991, Pasadena, CA). *Cavalcade of America* (1940–41); *This Is My Best* (1944–45); *One Man's Family* (1946–47).

Part of the lively coterie of acting pros who dominated New York radio, circa 1940. They included his wife and frequent co-performer Jeanette Nolan whom

John McIntire (courtesy of Capital Cities/ABC)

he married in 1935. For DuPont's *Cavalacade of America* he portrayed such historical figures as Lincoln, John Adams and Andrew Jackson. He emceed *The Hour of Charm* and *Wings Over America,* and in 1941 became the Industrial News Editor on *News of the Week in Industry,* sponsored by GE.

For the dramatic series *This Is My Best,* he was host-announcer. A character actor often handling movie parts as a law officer or politician, McIntire made an impression in *Winchester 73, The Far Country, Psycho* and scores of other films. On television, he replaced Ward Bond as the wagonmaster on *Wagon Train* and helped make *Naked City* a much-praised police drama.

McIntire grew up in Montana where he was a bronco riding champ. As a USC student he gave dramatic readings at a Los Angeles station. Following a two-year hitch as a seaman on a cargo ship, he went back to the mike as an actor-announcer.

571. MACK, Ted (emcee; b. Feb. 12, 1904, Greeley, CO; d. July 12, 1976, North Tarrytown, NY). *Original Amateur Hour* (1948–52).

Major domo of amateur performers, taking that post after Major Bowes died. Mack joined the program as its talent scout in 1935, soon after its debut on NBC. Under his aegis the series gave an airing to such young hopefuls as Pat Boone, Ann Margaret and Jerry Vale. The *Hour* transferred well onto the TV screen in 1948, and was that medium's oldest entertainment program when it went off in 1970.

The amiable emcee dispensed with Bowes' trademark: the clanging of the show's gong. "Too cruel," he explained. Mack played the clarinet and saxophone in his youth and was associated with Red Nichols, Ben Pollack, Benny Goodman and Glenn Miller. At

Ted Mack

one time he led his own outfit: Edward Maguiness and His Band. Lack of space on the marquee caused a name change to Ted Mack.

572. McLAUGHLIN, Don (actor; b. Nov. 24, 1906, Webster, IA; d. May 28, 1986, Goshen, CT). *Story of Mary Marlin* (1941–42); *Counterspy* (1942–57); *Young Widder Brown* (1946).

Dramatic lead as chief agent David Harding of *Counterspy.* A regular on soap operas *Helen Trent, Lora Lawton* and *Mary Marlin,* he was cast in a handful of wartime khaki and camp serials: *You're in the Army Now, Buck Private and His Girl* and *Chaplain Jim* (described in the script as "kindly, rugged, with a sense of humor"). McLaughlin played roles on Broadway in *Fifth Column* and *South Pacific.* But as Chris Hughes on *As the World Turns* for 30 years, he established a visual presence matched by few daily soap characters. The series was the first half-hour daytime TV drama, beginning in 1956.

An English and speech major at the University of Iowa, he taught and coached but left the schoolhouse in 1933 for a New York career in acting. After his network audition McLaughlin was chosen to play a Confederate cavalryman, but just before air time the role was cut, and he ended up helping the sound man imitate the whinny of a horse.

573. McNAMEE, Graham (announcer [catchphrase: "Goodnight all and goodbye."]; b. July 10, 1889, Washington, DC; d. May 9, 1942, New York, NY). *Fleischmann Hour* (1929–c1935); *The Fire Chief* (1932–35); *Treasury Hour* (1941–42).

Like many early announcers, he entered radio as a singer, and soon moved into non-musical assignments. In 1923 he had entered the WEAF studio out of curiosity one lunch hour, auditioned and was hired to both sing and announce. He turned to sports broadcasting that year, covering a prizefight and the World Series. By his own account, the most exciting moment in his career was the famous "long" count for the second Dempsey-Tunney fight in Chicago in September 1927. His descriptions of Rose Bowl and similar football contests helped sell many early radio receivers. His longest and most exhausting assignment was the 1924 Democratic National Convention in Madison Square Garden. He handled the microphone from a booth with an assist from Phillips Carlin for 15 hours a day for 15 days.

Sports fans, however, were often critical of his coverage; he tended to embellish play-by-play description for dramatic effect, and added fanciful sidelights when the contest proved dull. He later modified his breathless enthusiasm and curbed his capricious comments to conform to more objective reporting.

McNamee had made his recital bow as a baritone in Aeolian Hall, New York in 1920, and for three years sang on tour and in many large churches. But few mainstream bookings came along. His first radio

Graham McNamee

Sidney Ellstrom, Don McNeill, Fran Allison

job as a singer was viewed as a stop-gap between concert seasons. His interaction with comedian Ed Wynn (Texaco's *Fire Chief*) helped to establish the announcer as an integral personality on a program. His book, *You're On the Air,* published in 1928, was one of the first on broadcasting. He began a new series at the Blue Network, *Party Line* with Elsa Maxwell, shortly before his death at age 52.

574. McNAUGHTON, Harry (comedian [catchphrase: "I have a poem, Mr. Howard."]; b. April 29, 1896, Surbiton, England; d. Feb. 26, 1967, Amityville, NY). *Phil Baker Show* (1933–39); *It Pays to Be Ignorant* (1942–49, 1951).

From a British show business family, he opened in the classic play *The Better 'Ole* in New York in 1919, and stayed to appear in Shubert revues, Cohan plays and *Ziegfeld Follies.* McNaughton specialized in giving audiences a true picture of an Englishman and not a caricature. In the 1930s he was "Bottle," the blundering British butler of Phil Baker. In 1951 he played the lead, again as an English butler, in *It's Higgins, Sir.* But as a nitwitted panelist on *It Pays to Be Ignorant,* emceed by Tom Howard, he reached his greatest popularity.

575. McNEILL, Don (host; b. Dec. 23, 1907, Galena, IL; d. May 7, 1996, Evanston, IL). *Breakfast Club* (1933–68).

Host of one of network radio's durable and established institutions, *The Breakfast Club* ... by 1950, ABC's most valuable commercial daytime property. His reputation with listeners, the love and respect for him, gave such sponsors as Swift and Philco an impact they could not get elsewhere. McNeill offered generous helpings of music ("hymn time"), sentiment ("memory time"), fun ("march time") and prayer ("silent prayer"—"each in his own words, each in his own way, for a world united in peace").

It all began in 1932 when Don auditioned for a nondescript Chicago network show, *Pepper Pot.* He got the emcee job and changed the program's name to *Breakfast Club.* His unscripted remarks and good-natured humor made it a success. Audiences were added in 1937, making it a coveted place to gather for a morning variety show, highlighted by audience participation and name guests.

McNeill, a journalism school graduate, accepted a job doing a radio column in the *Milwaukee Journal* in 1929. To augment his salary, he doubled as an announcer and emcee. A year or so later, he moved to the *Louisville Times,* then returned to radio with a comedy act on the West Coast. His on-the-road *Breakfast Club* appearances drew thousands of fans throughout the Midwest until his retirement after nearly 7,500 broadcasts.

576. McNELLIS, Maggi (hostess, panelist; b. c1916, Chicago, IL; d. May 24, 1989, New York, NY). *Maggi's Private Wire* (1944–47); *Leave It to the Girls* (1945–49).

Society's craze for debutantes as supper club singers launched her career in Chicago, then New York. She switched to radio with a WINS gossip and interview program in 1943. Her first network show, *Maggi's Private Wire,* stressed the chatter of society and the celebrity world. Billed as NBC's Gal About Town, she was a top fashion commentator and on her own made the list of best-dressed women in the country. She co-hosted the noonday audience-participation program, *Luncheon at the Latin Quarter* with Herb Shelton over ABC. Participation in *Leave It to the Girls,* which offered women advice on romance and marriage, introduced her to a wide audience. She was the moderator of the TV version in the late 1940s and co-author of the home-entertainment guidebook *Party Games.*

577. MACON, "Uncle Dave" (banjo player [Dixie Dew Drop]; b. Oct. 7, 1870, Smart Station, TN; d. March 22, 1952, Readyville, TN). *Grand Ole Opry* (1926–44).

Early and enduringly popular entertainer on *Opry.* Macon strummed a banjo and sang, usually wearing a plug hat and kicking time with one foot at the base of the stand-up mike. A regular cast member for several decades, jovial "Uncle Dave" built up a large national following through his country-style banjo wizardry. He made his last *Opry* appearance on March 1, 1952, just weeks before his death at age 81.

In his younger days he operated a mule and wagon transport company. He was discovered by a talent scout at a farmer's party and offered a theatre engagement. Macon and fiddler Sid Harkreader cut their first discs for Vocalion in 1924.

578. MacRAE, Gordon (singer; b. March 12, 1921, East Orange, NJ; d. Jan. 24, 1986, Lincoln, NE). *Teentimer's Club* (1946–47); *Texaco Star Theatre* (1947–48); *The Railroad Hour* (1949–54).

His boy-next-door personality coupled with a rousing baritone voice brought stardom in every medium. From a musical family in Syracuse, New York, he studied piano and clarinet but passed up a college

Gordon MacRae

degree to go to New York to pursue an interest in acting. He got no farther ahead than a page at NBC. Elsewhere, at the 1939–40 World's Fair, he entered an amateur singing contest and won a two-week stint at the fair with the Harry James band. A scout for Horace Heidt heard him vocalize, not on a bandstand, but in a Radio City men's room. MacRae sang with Heidt for two years. In early 1943 at CBS he picked up a quarter-hour nightly for ballads and romantic songs.

After military service he returned to the microphone and small roles on Broadway. When Warner Bros. handed the tall, good-looking singer-actor a seven-year contract in 1948, radio gave him a big buildup. It led to *The Railroad Hour* where he starred in well-crafted condensed versions of well-known operettas and popular musical shows with singers Lucille Norman, Dorothy Kirsten, Dorothy Warenskjold and Annamary Dickey. In his films he often teamed up with Doris Day, and in nightclubs and television with his wife Sheila MacRae. As Curly, the cowhand, in the screen version of *Oklahoma!* he co-starred with Shirley Jones in her film debut.

579. MacVANE, John (newscaster; b. April 29, 1912, Portland, ME; d. Jan. 28, 1984, Brunswick, ME). *United or Not* (1950–52).

UN correspondent for 32 years, first for NBC and later ABC (until 1977). A reporter for *The Brooklyn Eagle, The New York Sun* and *The London Daily Express* in the 1930s, this Williams College-Oxford-educated writer also served on the Paris desk of International News Service. He was hired by NBC to cover the war in Europe, initially reporting "live" from London rooftops during the Blitz.

The authoritative, deep-voiced MacVane went to North Africa in 1942 with U.S. troops, and was the first radio newsman ashore on D-Day and the first American correspondent to enter Paris with the Allied liberating forces in August 1944. He was among the first four journalists to move into Berlin while the city was still in flames in 1945. A year earlier, when ground forces assaulted the beaches of Normandy, he spent five days with them. But due to a lack of short-wave equipment, his D-Day broadcasts reached only the BBC and the U.S. Signal Corps, and they refused to transmit them on to New York for American audiences. His days overseas were recalled in his 1979 book *On the Air in World War II.*

580. McVEY, Tyler (actor; b. Feb. 14, 1912, Bay City, MI). *Glamour Manor* (1944–46), *Today's Children* (1947–50).

Oft-featured Los Angeles actor. His 1,000 broadcasts with Jack Benny, *Dr. Christian, One Man's Family, Fibber McGee and Molly,* Gene Autry, Red Skelton, *The Great Gildersleeve* and *Burns and Allen* began in 1937. "'Live' radio was the greatest way in the world to make a living," he remarked in 1994. "There were probably 150 of us in Hollywood that worked quite steadily on the many shows that emanated from there — some more successful than others."

McVey began in hometown amateur theatricals, then at 21 joined a company that staged shows throughout upper New York State and New England. He produced, directed and performed in a show called *The Trial of the Century, or Who is Nellie Bly.* He lost his shirt in the venture but two years later moved on to Los Angeles. His first job was a recorded series, *Jerry of the Circus.* In 1939 he made the first of many *Lux Radio Theatre* appearances; it was a presentation of "Stage Door" with Ginger Rogers. McVey worked in over 300 TV films (*Bonanza, Lassie*) and live TV

Tyler McVey (courtesy of Tyler McVey)

(*My Friend Irma, Climax*) and feature films (*Patton, Hello, Dolly*).

581. McWILLIAMS, Edward "Jim" (quizmaster; b. c1886, Cleveland, OH; d. Oct. 14, 1955, Virginia Beach, VA). *Professor Quiz* (1936); *Uncle Jim's Question Bee* (1936–39); *Ask-It-Basket* (1938–39).

Combining inquiring mike and spelling bee techniques, *Professor Quiz* was a pioneering game show, said to be the first as a network quiz-program series. It aired locally in Washington in 1934 before switching to the CBS net. Ex-vaudeville monologist, McWilliams had a kindly way and steered clear of tripping up contestants. He was once described as a Will Rogers sort of man in appearance and philosophy.

When *Professor Quiz* moved to NBC, McWilliams was dropped. His question-and-answer sessions continued elsewhere on his academia-style *Uncle Jim's Question Bee.* His last I.Q. testing series, *Correction, Please,* stressed word definitions and war personalities. In 1948 he retired to a farm in Virginia.

582. MADISON, Guy (actor; b. Jan. 19, 1922, Pumpkin Center, CA; d. Feb. 6, 1996, Palm Springs, CA). *The Adventures of Wild Bill Hickok* (1951–56).

Western hero of film, radio and television in the 1950s. He played the part of U.S. Marshall Hickok for home audiences. The series revitalized a languishing movie career for this boyishly handsome yet blandly mannered actor. The Kellogg-sponsored daytime thriller aired three afternoons a week over Mutual for most of its five-year run, while syndicated TV episodes totalling 113 lasted another two years into 1958. The character of Wild Bill meshed well with Guy's stiff, tight-lipped acting style. His clownish sidekick, Jingles, was played by Andy Devine.

Madison, who changed his name from Bob Moseley when he was discovered by a talent scout in 1944, bowed on screen in David O. Selznick's wartime drama *Since You Went Away.* He played a lonely sailor, reflecting his then-existing military stint as a member of the Coast Guard. His popularity as Hickok led to leads in many Westerns in Hollywood and Europe, including the starring role in the early 3-D opus *The Charge at Feather River.*

583. MAIER, Rev. Walter A. (preacher; b. Oct. 4, 1893, Boston, MA; d. Jan. 11, 1950, St. Louis, MO). *Lutheran Hour* (1930–49).

Old-time evangelist on the most-listened-to weekly religious series. His low-key nondenominational approach to a sermon built an enormous following that generated some 15,000 letters a week, most of them containing cash contributions to finance his broadcasts.

Maier was an executive secretary of the young people's auxiliary of the Missouri Synod of the Lutheran Church when he first stepped up to a microphone to address its 1922 convention. The favorable response led to the establishment of a station at St. Louis's Concordia Seminary. From KFUO he sought to extend the range of his sermons. In 1930 CBS agreed to schedule his program as a paid religious show via WHK Cleveland. The Depression cut short the necessary outlay of $200,000 at the end of that first year.

In 1935 Maier inaugurated a two-station hookup in Detroit and Cincinnati with the underwriting of a benefactor. In five years it grew to a 200-station enterprise attracting Mutual which took over the ready-made network. Maier also began to syndicate his program and to beam it over shortwave as the International Lutheran Hour. Soon it was heard over 1,200 stations throughout the world. Transcriptions offered Dr. Maier's sermons in 36 languages by 1950. Maier's voice was one of the few broadcast engineers did not try to modulate at the mike; listeners were attuned to its old-fashioned acoustical delivery. It was his weekly impassioned sermons that inspired Billy Graham to pursue a career as a preacher.

584. MAITLAND, Arthur (actor; b. 1874; d. May 23, 1959, New York, NY). *David Harum* (1937–50); *Adventures of Archie Andrews* (1945–47, 1951–52); *Marriage for Two* (1949–50).

Veteran character actor. He portrayed Zeke, an old rascal and skinflint on *David Harum,* and Mr. Weatherby on *Archie Andrews.* His other ongoing roles were Mr. Lewis on *Just Plain Bill,* Mr. Crane on *Stella Dallas* and the minister on *Marriage for Two.*

A stage performer for David Belasco, he also directed Little Theatre movements in New Orleans, Atlanta and Chattanooga. He ran his own playhouse in San Francisco before World War I.

585. MALBIN, Elaine (singer; b. May 24, 1932, New York, NY). *Serenade to America* (1946–47); *Saturday Matinee with Elaine Malbin* (1947); *Music for Today* (1947–48); *Al Goodman's Musical Album* (1951–52).

Precocious lyric soprano who at age 14 became a featured singer at NBC. An innate musicality shone brightly in classical arias for *The RCA Show* as early as December 1945. A year later her unusual vocal ability was a highlight of *Music for Tomorrow* and *Music As You Like It.* The Brooklyn teenager sang on over 125 broadcasts of *Serenade to America,* and on WNBC's inaugural "Hail & Farewell" and the 20th anniversary salute to the net's affiliates in 1947. Recognized as a dependable singer and able actress, she co-starred on *The Railroad Hour*'s "Smiles," "Sweethearts" and "Rosalinda."

Malbin also played leads in operettas and with the NY City Opera Company. In 1952 she had the title role in the Broadway musical *My Darlin' Aida,* loosely based on the Verdi opera. She was an acknowledged pioneer on presentations of opera on television decades before regular Met telecasts. A career land-mark was the world-premiere performance as Joan of Arc in *The Trial at Rouen* by Norman Dello Joio on NBC-TV in 1956.

586. MALNECK, Matty (bandleader; b. Dec. 9, 1903, Newark, NJ; d. Feb. 25, 1981, Los Angeles, CA). *Campana Serenade* (1942–43); *Duffy's Tavern* (1944–49).

Violinst and composer who directed music for *Duffy's Tavern,* and the programs of Charlotte Greenwood and Bob Crosby. Beginning in 1926 Malneck spent ten years as jazz violinist and arranger for Paul Whiteman. He provided music for many TV shows and films. His hit tunes included "Goody-Goody" and "Stairway to the Stars." The Denver-raised musician organized his own swing band in 1939.

587. MALONE, Pick (comedian; b. June 23, 1895, nr. Dallas, TX; d. Jan. 22, 1962, New York, NY). *Friendship Village* (1932); *Show Boat* (1932–37); *Chesterfield Supper Club* (1945).

Teamed with Pat Padgett for blackface routine as Molasses 'n' January. They had joined up in New York in 1926 for vaudeville bookings. On *Show Boat* they found their biggest audience. As Pick and Pat, they played hayseeds on *National Barn Dance.*

Speaking with a slow Southern drawl, Andrew Pickens Maloney exemplified the old-time minstrel comedian that radio often showcased.

588. MALONE, Ted (commentator; b. May 18, 1908, Colorado Springs, CO; d. Oct. 20, 1989, Stratford, CT). *Between the Bookends* (1935–43, 1945–58); *Pilgrimage of Poetry* (1939–40); *American Pilgrimage* (1940–41); *Yankee Doodle Quiz* (1943–44).

In 1929 he was called on to fill a vacant 15 min-

Ted Malone (courtesy of Capital Cities/ABC)

utes of air time at KMBC Kansas City with poetry. He was working there as an announcer, utility man, writer and singer under his real name, Alden Russell. He agreed, but, embarrassed by the task, insisted on another name. At the end of the broadcast, announcer Hugh Studebaker called him Ted Malone, and it stuck, especially as fan mail arrived.

The daily series continued as *Between the Book-ends,* and was piped West to regional CBS outlets. But it was another local program, an historical series built around an imaginary time machine and called *Phenomenon,* that first took Malone to New York in 1935. It had an utilities association standing by as a sponsor but President Roosevelt criticized light and power companies that week and the project fell apart. However, the poetry readings did attract a sponsor. Hinds Cream picked it up at CBS five times each week at 12:15 p.m. When the midday broadcasts moved to NBC-Blue three years later, an organ for background music became an integral part. In due course, Malone's sincere and friendly voice and Rosa Rio's mood-setting music were so well meshed that many listeners assumed they had to be a married couple.

Malone read poems of famous writers and those of listeners. His feeling for people and keen story sense made him a natural raconteur, and he varied his formula with philosophy, humor and tall tales. He also edited poetry anthologies and served as poetry editor for *Good Housekeeping.* He extended his airborne literary thrust with *Pilgrimage of Poetry* and *American Pilgrimage,* on which he visited the homes of best-known American writers.

During World War II a determined Malone persuaded the very reluctant ABC to send a "poetry reader" to Europe as a roving correspondent, specializing in interviews with GIs. For the cost-conscious network to agree, he had to provide some of his own money — in this case, a book advance from a publisher interested in his war experiences. He continued for a time as an overseas reporter for ABC at the end of the war. Westinghouse had signed on as his chief sponsor, bringing Ted the most money he'd ever received from broadcasting.

Malone had began making use of his voice in his high school days in Independence, Missouri. Thoroughly enamored with radio, he got a job at KMBC doing a 5 a.m. farm program while a student at nearby William Jewell College. He was still talking over regional stations some 50 years later.

589. MANNERS, Lucille (singer; b. May 21, 1912, Newark, NJ). *Cities Service Concert* (1937–44).

A stenographer in Newark, New Jersey, she gained a foothold in music by using her lunch hour to sing at WOR. Evenings were spent with a small semi-professional opera company. The ambitious Manners took music lessons three or four times a week for eight years. Her voice teacher wangled an audition at NBC. Accepted by the network, she began on morning sus-tainers and appeared occasionally as a guest on *Voice of Firestone* and *Palmolive Beauty Box Theatre.*

Described as a girlish soprano with a sympathetic feeling for music, she attracted the attention of Cities Service. This sponsor, seeking a vacation substitute for Jessica Dragonette, heard Manners sing "One Night of Love" and picked her as a fill-in. When Dragonette sought a different musical format and left the Friday night program in 1937, the blonde, blue-eyed Manners became the oil company's new concert star under the aegis of conductor Frank Black. This association lasted until the mid-40s. She later appeared with the New York City Opera in productions of *Boheme* and *Faust.*

590. MANNING, Knox (announcer; b. Jan. 17, 1904, Worcester, MA; d. Aug. 26, 1980, Woodland Hills, CA). *Headlines on Parade* (1937–39); *Melody and Madness* (1939); *Adventures of Sherlock Holmes* (1939–43).

Originally hired as a radio actor in Boston in 1930, he added announcing, then commentary and narration. Knox worked on many programs over the Yankee and Don Lee networks. He settled on the West Coast where he was a screen narrator and bit player. At one point KNX featured him on two daily broadcasts.

During World War II he served as a commander with the 12th Combat Camera Unit in North Africa and Italy. In 1952 Manning became the first president of the American Federation of Radio Artists when it added television performers to its ranks.

591. MARAIS, Josef (singer; b. Nov. 17, 1905, Sir Lowry's Pass, South Africa; d. April 26, 1978, Los Angeles, CA). *African Trek/Sundown on the Veld* (1939–41); *Meredith Willson Show* (1949).

Marais and his wife and partner Miranda, born Rosa Baruch de la Pardo (1912–1986), were a distinctive duo specializing in folk music. They met at the Office of War Information in New York where he had developed a reputation as a singer of songs from the South African veld. American listeners were soon fascinated by the treasure trove of multi-cultural folk songs and folk lore from a series of novel programs at NBC that included his violin or guitar accompaniment, and a South African Bushveld band.

Josef came to the United States in 1939 after studying music in Prague and London. Earlier, for several years he had given a series of musical programs over the BBC.

As a team Marais and Miranda appeared with Meredith Willson, but gained their greatest following in concert halls. Josef recorded and wrote music for stage productions and symphonies, and with Miranda wrote plays with music.

592. MARSH, Audrey (singer; b. March 18, 1911, New York, NY). *Schaefer Revue* (1938); *Johnny Presents* (1940–42).

Singing ingenue with acting roles. Stage work, including the part of Rosemary in *Abie's Irish Rose,* led to radio in the early 1930s. Called the "female Rudy Vallee," she handled solos and leads in such shows as *Jeddo Highlanders, Nat and Bridget* (for Natural Bridge Shoes), *Fox Fur Trappers, Harv and Ester* (for Harvester Cigars) and *Boy and Girl Next Door.* For *Show Boat* she played Mary Lou. A soprano, Marsh sang on *Hits and Misses, Schaefer Revue* with Felix Knight, and *Johnny Presents,* backed by Ray Bloch and joined by sister Beverly Marsh. She was closely identified with the 1939 song "We've Come a Long Way Together."

Marsh wanted to be an actress but Frank Marvin, head of the radio department at DeSylva, Brown & Henderson, sent her to CBS for a singing audition. "Through no desire on my part, I was suddenly a contracted singer at CBS." Radio became her forte — "my performing life, and oh, how enjoyable it was. I loved every minute of it. There has never been a medium that gave so much satisfaction to both performers and audience. Radio jiggled your imagination — you had to use your brain and listen."

A featured and ensemble singer, she performed on *Chorus of Stars, Prudential Family Hour, Kate Smith Show* and *The Big Show,* as well as on record albums. In the 1940s Marsh added singing commercials and voice-overs and dialect parts to her repertoire.

593. MARSHALL, Everett (singer; b. Dec. 30, 1900, Lawrence, MA; d. April 1965). *Broadway Vanities/Varieties* (1934–35).

Opera and musical comedy baritone who briefly headlined several radio series and sang for Atwater Kent, Vallee and Whiteman. Marshall started his career in European opera houses and made his American debut at the Met in *Lohengrin* in 1927. After four years there, he widened his fame through the *George White Scandals of 1932* and *Ziegfeld Follies of 1934,* and an early movie musical, *Dixiana.*

For *Vanities* at CBS he made curtain speeches and took speaking roles in scenes from musical shows, both of which distracted from his better-handled singing assignments. In 1936 and 1937 he starred in the Casa Manana Revue at Ft. Worth's Centennial fairgrounds and introduced the enduring melody "The Night is Young and You're So Beautiful."

594. MARSHALL, Herbert (actor; b. May 23, 1890, London, England; d. Jan. 22, 1966, Beverly Hills, CA). *The New Old Gold Show* (1941–42); *The Man Called X* (1945–48, 1950–52).

Many-sided trouper in every media, particularly films for 39 years. Sophisticated and gentlemanly, he played with and against the most glamorous female stars of stage and screen, among them Garbo, Dietrich, Hepburn and Crawford. Marshall was very effective on radio, where his velvety voice and precise British diction came over the air often in juxtaposition to bombastic comedians. Dramatic presentations of "Goodbye, Mr. Chips" and "Stairway to Heaven" properly utilized this worldly-wise actor. In a radio tribute to the King and Queen of England during

Everett Marshall

Herbert Marshall (courtesy of Capital Cities/ABC)

their 1939 U.S. visit, he did the farewell scene from *Romeo and Juliet* with Judith Anderson.

In his own series he was cast as the adventurous Ken Thurston in *The Man Called X.* It first aired as a summer replacement for Bob Hope.

595. MARTIN, Dean (singer; b. June 17, 1917, Steubenville, OH; d. Dec. 25, 1995, Beverly Hills, CA). *Martin and Lewis Show* (1949–53).

On the same Atlantic City bill with zany comic Jerry Lewis in 1946, he started horsing around in Jerry's act, doing anything that came to mind, and Jerry did likewise. They proved such a draw that they were signed as a team, and were paid $5,000 a week at New York's Copacabana. While performing on the West Coast, the duo was signed by producer Hal Wallis and made 16 movies that were major box office successes, starting with *My Friend Irma* in 1948.

On radio Bob Hope welcomed them as his guests on four shows in the 1948–49 season. It led to their own series at NBC with Martin as emcee, vocalist and straight man. Dissension between the two grew. Lewis was eager to prove his worth on his own. Martin felt shunted into the background as a singer. One of show business's greatest partnerships broke up in 1956.

Dean, well established as a pleasurable pop singer with such hits as "That's Amore" and "Three Coins in the Fountain" surprised audiences — and himself — with highly praised acting performances on screen. Beginning with *The Young Lions* opposite Marlon Brando and Montgomery Cliff, the newly discovered dramatic side of Martin took him to major roles in *Some Came Running, Rio Bravo,* and important films of the 1960s. His casual ease as singer and host remained in view on his television variety programs.

596. MARTIN, Freddy (bandleader [signature song: "Tonight We Love"]; b. Dec. 9, 1906, Cleveland, OH; d. Sept. 30, 1983, Newport Beach, CA). *Penthouse Serenade* (1936–37); *Fitch Bandwagon* (1943); *Jack Carson Show* (1943–46); *NBC Bandstand* (1956–57).

Martin started playing a dance version of the classical Tchaikovsky "Piano Concerto in B Flat" in 1941. Introduced at the Cocoanut Grove, his arrangement startled the audience. But it soon realized the piece had a dance-floor beat. He called the piece "Tonight We Love." His inspiration, so he claimed, had been a performance of the concerto by Toscanini and the NBC Symphony. His new theme put his 18-piece, highly melodic aggregation on the map and produced one of the record hits of the 1940s. Other conductors jumped on the bandwagon, extracting themes from Debussy, Ravel, Greig and Rachmaninoff (areas that Whiteman and a few others had successfully tapped 20 years earlier).

Freddy grew up in an orphanage and joined its school band as a drummer. He picked up the C-melody saxophone as a teenager, then formed a dance

Freddy Martin

band. After jobs with Jack Albin and Arnold Johnson, he led a group at the Bossert Roof in Brooklyn from 1931 to 1934. It attracted the interest of CBS, MCA and hotels on the West Coast. His recordings of "Intermezzo" and "The Hut Sut Song" sold in the hundreds of thousands; in 1947 his disc and transcription royalties brought in nearly $200,000, placing him among the five best-selling Victor artists (outdistancing Perry Como and Vaughn Monroe).

Martin enjoyed much radio exposure, beginning with *Lady Esther Serenade.* He considered the Cocoanut Grove his homebase, playing there between an annual tour into the 1960s.

597. MARTIN, Ian (actor; b. April 29, 1912, Glasgow, Scotland; d. July 25, 1981, New York, NY). *Against the Storm* (1942); *Adventures of Archie Andrews* (1946–47); *RCA Victor Show* (1946–47); *True Confessions* (1957).

Character roles requiring dialects and portrayals of older persons kept him on a different daytime show every day of the week in the 1940s. His parts ranged from Nathan on *Against the Storm* and Arnold on *Right to Happiness* to Archie Andrews' father and Johnny Victor, RCA's *Man About Music*. Martin studied at Harvard before going to Broadway (*Victoria Regina*) and radio (*Great Plays*). He spent three years in the U.S. Army, assigned to Special Services as emcee for numerous broadcasts and Bond drives. While appearing regularly on *Ford Theatre* and *Radio City Playhouse,* he originated the role of Finian in *Finian's Rainbow* on Broadway.

Turning to television, he was a member of the original cast of *Edge of Night*. Martin was seen on many video soaps, including *The Nurses* for which he was chief script writer. A child actor in Glasgow, he came to America in 1929 and two years later started as actor-announcer at WTAM Cleveland.

598. MARTIN, Mary (singer; b. Dec. 1, 1913, Weatherford, TX; d. Nov. 4, 1990, Rancho Mirage, CA). *Lifebuoy Health Soap Program* (1939); *Good News of 1940* (1940); *Kraft Music Hall* (1942).

Radiant first lady of musical comedy with legendary performances in *South Pacific, The Sound of Music, Peter Pan,* and her initial success — singing "My Heart Belongs to Daddy" — in Cole Porter's *Leave It to Me* in 1938. She began as a dancer and started her own dancing school in Texas where she also sang on radio. Her straightforward, self-confident delivery of a song's lyrics won club and stage auditions and led to guest spots on General Foods' *Good News of 1938;* by 1940 she was a *Good News* regular while making pictures at Paramount (*The Great Victor Herbert, Love Thy Neighbor*). Studio star Bing Crosby added her to *Kraft Music Hall*. But in 1943 she returned to the stage in *One Touch of Venus,* and radio chiefly became an occasional vehicle for songs (*Stage Door Canteen*) and interviews (*Monitor*).

Tony Martin

599. MARTIN, Tony (singer; b. Dec. 25, 1912, Oakland, CA). *Burns and Allen* (1936–39); *Tune-Up Time* (1939–40); *Tony Martin from Hollywood* (1941); *Carnation Contented Hour* (1951); *Tony Martin Show* (1953).

Stalwart baritone and proficient actor. With his pre-Hollywood name, Al Norris, he played tenor sax and sang in Tom Gerun's band, chiefly in Chicago. In the mid-30s Hollywood began to capitalize on his good looks and vocal ease. He entered radio, too, beginning with Burns and Allen. Martin did guest shots on *Good News of 1938,* and for Bob Hope, Kay Kyser and Eddie Cantor. On the set of *Sing, Baby, Sing,* he met and courted its star Alice Faye. As soon as filming was completed, they eloped. Martin's nightclub singing tours kept them apart most of the time, and they were divorced in 1940. He married dancer Cyd Charisse in 1948.

During AAF service, Tony sang on weekly coast-to-coast recruitment broadcasts with Glenn Miller and his GI aggregation. On post-war radio, he was an emcee-singer, and a favorite recording artist ("I Get Ideas," "There's No Tomorrow") of disc jockeys. His films include *Ziegfeld Girl, Casbah* and *Hit the Deck*.

600. MARTINI, Nino (singer; b. Aug. 8, 1905, Verona, Italy; d. Dec. 9, 1976, Verona, Italy). *Seven Star Revue* (1933–34).

In 1933 he was the first radio-honed artist to step from a microphone to centerstage of the Met, where he made his debut in December in *Rigoletto*. That year CBS honored him with the Columbia Medal for

Mary Martin

distinguished contribution to radio. He had become well known for his bi-weekly radio recitals, and his broadcast repertory included 15 operas in French or Italian. A lyric tenor, he stayed at the Met for 13 seasons. His radio work never again reached the frequency of his pre-Met days.

The handsome, photogenic Martini had come to the United States in 1929 to sing in Hollywood-produced Italian movie shorts. He starred in several American feature films, notably *The Gay Desperado*.

601. MARX, Groucho (comedian [catchphrase: "Hooray for Captain Spaulding"]; b. Oct. 2, 1890, New York, NY; d. Aug. 19, 1977, Los Angeles, CA). *Flywheel, Shyster and Flywheel* (1932–33); *Blue Ribbon Town* (1943–44); *You Bet Your Life* (1947–60).

One of radio's unsolved puzzles was the full utilization of the talents of Groucho. After years of hit-and-miss exposure, chiefly through guest-shot routines, he got his break as a comic quizmaster of *You Bet Your Life*. At its premiere, *Variety* gave it mild praise. However, it noted that "he has the happy faculty to extract laughter, not at the expense of the contestants, but from an off-guard zanyism that has a quality of freshness about it." Year after year, people listened to, and beginning in 1950 viewed, the basic, low-stakes question-and-answer format laced with Groucho's uniquely snappy and impertinent banter. The imaginative selection of contestants — team members generally had opposite tastes or vocations — and the inclusion of "the secret word" as a special $100 reward contributed to its ongoing success. Apart from

Bing Crosby's program, it was among the very first transcribed/taped network prime-time features.

Groucho had faced a radio mike in the early 1930s with Chico in the zany Flywheel series on *Five Star Theatre*. But the show about a malpractice lawyer and his bungling assistant seemed ahead of its time as a "sound-only" comedy for the outrageous behavior of the wacky Marx Brothers. With Chico, he tried again for six months with *The Circle* in 1939.

Born in a New York tenement, Groucho and his brothers were pushed into show business by their mother. At ten he was a singer with the Gus Edwards vaudeville troupe. The boys teamed up for an act that led to Broadway and films (the earliest were their stage hits *The Cocoanuts* and *Animal Crackers*). By the early '40s their movies had lost much of their original zing, and Groucho turned to radio as a single. He made frequent guest spots with Rudy Vallee and Dinah Shore, and starred on a shortlived series for Pabst Beer. The closest to a game show was an appearance on the panel of *Information Please* in 1941.

You Bet Your Life brought Marx's insult humor and eccentric antics to a new generation who could tune him in on both and TV during the 1950s (and decades later from syndication). He won an Emmy as the most outstanding TV personality in 1950, and wrote his autobiographical *The Secret Word is GROUCHO* in 1976.

602. MASSEY, Curt (singer; b. May 3, 1910, Midland, TX; d. Oct. 21, 1991, Rancho Mirage, CA). *Show Boat* (1935–36); *Curt Massey Show* (1939–56).

Groucho Marx

Curt Massey (courtesy of Capital Cities/ABC)

Easy-voiced, ingratiating baritone. In 1930 he joined the musical staff of KMBC Kansas City, supplying daily presentations of country songs. But as a violin-playing member of his sister Louise Massey's Westerners, he came to New York for *Show Boat.* In 1939, again a vocalist, he replaced Red Foley on *Avalon Time.* That year he began his own program of light songs over NBC and CBS. At one point he worked 19 shows a week from Chicago. Curt also co-starred on a daytime series with Martha Tilton, and in 1956 settled into a long run on television. He composed the theme song for the TV comedy *Petticoat Junction,* created by KMBC coworker Paul Henning.

603. MASSEY, Raymond (actor, host; b. Aug. 30, 1896, Toronto, Canada; d. July 29, 1983, Los Angeles, CA). *The Doctor Fights* (1944); *Harvest of Stars* (1945–46).

Imposing and impressive actor whose portrayals of Abraham Lincoln defined that President for the ages. He first played the 16th President in the Pulitzer Prize–winning play *Abe Lincoln in Illinois* in 1938 and recreated the tall and somber figure on screen a year later. On radio Massey's vibrant voice captured the essence of Lincoln on over 20 broadcasts. They began as scenes from his stage success, then expanded to encompass recitations of Lincoln's Gettysburg Address, and Civil War stories centered around the White House. He once played Lincoln in a wartime script, "The People vs. Adolph Hitler," aired on *The Day of Reckoning. Cavalcade of America* presented the Canadian-born war veteran in a half-dozen dramatizations of Lincoln's life. His other radio roles included Mark Twain and Walt Whitman. For a 1952 summer run of *Eternal Light* entitled "Words We Live By," he read a Psalm each week. For the first generation of TV viewers, Massey was better known as Dr. Gillespie on the *Dr. Kildare* series of the 1960s.

604. MATTHEWS, Grace (actress; b. Sept. 3, 1910, Toronto, Canada; d. May 15, 1995, Mount Kisco, NY). *Just Plain Bill* (1946–47); *The Shadow* (1946–49); *Big Sister* (1946–51).

Beginning in 1939, she spent six years on CBC daytime and evening programs. She played the lead on the wartime *Soldier's Wife* and *The Story of Dr. Susan,* a series whose announcer was actor Court Benson. They were married in Toronto in 1940. Following World War II they began active careers at the microphone in New York. Grace's credits include the lead in *Big Sister* and the part of Liz Dennis on *Brighter Day* (also on the CBS-TV version, using similar daily scripts).

For three years in the 1940s, she played the lovely Margo Lane opposite *The Shadow,* Brett Morrison. There were few New York-based dramatic shows of the period that did not cast Matthews. She re-located to London in 1959 for some three years, doing theatre, and BBC and ITV programs. Her U.S. televi-

Grace Matthews (courtesy of Michael Stevenson)

sion credits included *Road of Life* and *As The World Turns.*

Having studied at the Royal Academy of Dramatic Arts, she worked in stock in Manitoba and Ontario for two years and at Hart House Theatre, Toronto, for one season. When World War II broke out in September 1939, she was doing summer stock in Saratoga, New York and quickly returned to Canada to aid the war effort.

605. MAXWELL, Marilyn (singer, actress; b. Aug. 3, 1920, Clarinda, IA; d. March 20, 1972, Beverly Hills, CA). *Beat the Band* (1940–41); *Kraft Music Hall* (1944); *Abbott and Costello Show* (1946–47); *Bob Hope Show* (1950–53).

Maxwell advanced from capable band singer to accomplished actress. Her breezy, sensuous manner captivated audiences, as did her attention-getting blonde looks on screen. In demand for comic repartee and musical numbers with Crosby and Cantor, she was most often paired with Hope on his Chesterfield show. They also co-starred in films (*The Lemon Drop Kid, Off Limits*) and entertained troops in Korea. Her radio drama credits include leads in *Double Indemnity* and *Champion.*

As early as 1927 under the name Marvel Maxwell, she appeared on WOWO Fort Wayne. An Indianapolis bandleader signed her as featured vocalist

Marilyn Maxwell

when she was 16. A year later she joined Buddy Rogers' orchestra, and in 1938 Ted Weems' band and its musical quiz *Beat the Band*.

606. MEAKIN, Jack (conductor; b. Sept. 28, 1906, Salt Lake City, UT; d. Dec. 30, 1982, Rancho Mirage, CA). *The Great Gildersleeve* (1945–52); *You Bet Your Life* (1952–61).

Musical director-composer with a hand in producing *Hour of Charm, Your Hit Parade* and *Kollege of Musical Knowledge*. This Stanford graduate started as a pianist at NBC San Francisco in 1929 and rose to music chief by 1938. After a stint at WOV and NBC New York as producer-director he moved to Hollywood in 1944 for Foote, Cone & Belding agency assignments with Hedda Hopper and Hoagy Carmichael, and Lever Bros., Campbell Soup and Armour.

Meakin composed and conducted the music for *Great Gildersleeve* and for Groucho Marx's *You Bet Your Life*. He also created the catchy theme for *Thanks to the Yanks* with Bob Hawk. In the 1960s he ran his own company to produce commercials, musical scores and sound effects for radio, TV and films.

607. MEIGHAN, James (actor; b. Aug. 22, 1906, New York, NY; d. June 20, 1970, Huntington, NY). *Lora Lawton* (1943–45); *The Falcon* (1945–47); *Backstage Wife* (1945–51).

Perennial daytime lead, notably as matinee idol Larry Noble in *Backstage Wife*. Nephew of silent film star Thomas Meighan, he honed his craft with the Yonkers Stock Co. and in eight O'Neill plays, includ-

ing *Desire Under the Elms*. Prior to radio he appeared on Broadway in *My Maryland* and *Hamlet in Modern Dress* in the 1920s. Meighan played opposite Helen Hayes in her 1936 radio series and took over from Bert Lytell the lead in *Alias Jimmy Valentine* at WJZ. In the mid-40s he played *The Falcon*, a private detective. His cast assignments ranged from *Death Valley Days* to *Mohawk Treasure Chest*. During World War II he portrayed General Eisenhower on a broadcast of *These Are Our Men*.

608. MELTON, James (singer; b. Jan. 2, 1904, Moultrie, GA; d. April 21, 1961, New York, NY). *Palmolive Hour* (1927–31); *House of Wrigley* (1927–29); *Telephone Hour* (1940–42); *Texaco Star Theatre* (1943–46); *Harvest of Stars* (1946–50).

Melton first sang over WSM Nashville for $25 from sponsor Ideal Laundry. His desire was to become a serious singer but he performed light music to earn a living. In 1927 he secured an engagement on stage at the Roxy Theatre and work at the microphone with *Roxy's Gang*. At age 23 he became first tenor with the already famous quartet, The Revelers. They sang for Palmolive, Wrigley and Raleigh.

These broadcasts led the tall, darkly handsome Melton to solo recordings for Columbia, concert tours with George Gershwin, and movies at Warner Bros. A highly driven, keenly competitive singer, he ingratiated himself into the radio hierarchy of producers and sponsors, who presented him on a string of coveted shows. He was Jack Benny's vocalist in 1933–34. As star of the *Palmolive Beauty Star Theatre*,

James Melton

he performed some 55 operettas. For *The Telephone Hour,* he sang programs of light and serious selections for 104 consecutive weeks, and from 1942 to 1946 appeared regularly as its guest soloist.

In 1936 he decided to sing in opera, applying himself with the study of roles and stage techniques. Two years later he made his debut in Cincinnati as Pinkerton in *Madama Butterfly,* followed by engagements with the Chicago Opera. His radio sponsor Texaco — which also presented the Saturday matinee broadcasts from the stage of the Met — apparently influenced the management in the signing of Melton to its roster in 1942. His style and delivery, at least in the early stages of his career, were modeled after John McCormack. His voice was light, flexible and well produced but often lacked variety, range of color and refinement. In the early 1950s when his television show failed to gain an audience, he turned to road tours and pop concerts. Melton collected vintage automobiles that for a time were housed in a museum near his Connecticut home.

609. MENKEN, Helen (actress; b. Dec. 12, 1902, New York, NY; d. March 27, 1966, New York, NY). *Second Husband* (1937–44).

Acclaimed Broadway star who embarked on a radio career in the 1930s. She created the role of Brenda Cummings, portraying the problems of a woman with two children who ventured into a second marriage. *Second Husband* was initially broadcast serially Tuesday nights by CBS. By 1943 it had switched to a morning time, five days a week. "The series was a de luxe example of the radio soap opera," *The New York Times* noted at her death. "Yet Miss Menken brought to the role the same kind of dignity, emotional fire and dash that she was to employ in the legitimate theatre."

Growing up in Manhattan, she went on the stage at the age of five in *A Midsummer Night's Dream,* then played in *Ben Hur* at the Hippodrome and on Broadway in *The Red Mill.* Menken won praise from leads in *The Old Maid* and *Mary of Scotland* before turning to radio. Outspoken and hot tempered, she once told other actors in a broadcast studio exactly what she thought of radio scripts and scriptwriters. One of them whispered that the mike was turned on and that everyone was listening to every word she said. "I'm glad of it," she exclaimed. "I want them to hear what I'm saying. I wouldn't say anything behind anyone's back that I wouldn't say to his face."

During World War II she helped organize the Stage Door Canteen for GIs in New York and its morale-lifting, all-star program for CBS. Menken served as head of the American Theatre Wing and expanded its annual Tony awards and community service programs.

610. MERCER, Johnny (singer, composer; b. Nov. 18, 1909, Savannah, GA; d. June 25, 1976,

Johnny Mercer

Bel Air, CA). *Camel Caravan* (1939–40); *Johnny Mercer's Music Shop* (1943); *Chesterfield Music Shop/Supper Club* (1944, 1949); *Your Hit Parade* (1946); *Call for Music* (1948).

Oscar-winning tunesmith and laid-back vocalist. His first big hit, "Lazybones," was written with Hoagy Carmichael who helped secure him a vocal audition for Paul Whiteman. Accepted as part of Whiteman's large aggregation, he sang in a high-pitched, rhythmic style with a strong and sensitive Southern country lilt. Mercer wrote material for Whiteman's *Kraft Music Hall,* particularly numbers for the orchestra's singers and jazz instrumentalists. He soon became established in Hollywood as a prolific songwriter, contributing solid, catchy tunes ("I'm an Old Cowhand") for Bing Crosby and ("Cowboy from Brooklyn") for Dick Powell. After working with Benny Goodman in *Hollywood Hotel,* he joined his *Camel Caravan* as a vocalist. By 1943 he had his own show, a summer fill-in for Bob Hope. He co-starred with Dinah Shore on his 1948 series.

He co-founded Capitol Records at a time of wartime scarcities for the industry yet quickly built the company into a leading label for artists. His lyrics to the memorable song "Moon River" from the picture *Breakfast at Tiffany's* won an Academy Award in 1961.

611. MEREDITH, Burgess (actor; b. Nov. 16, 1909, Cleveland, OH). *Red Davis* (1933–35); *The Pursuit of Happiness* (1939–40); *We, the People* (1941–42).

An apprenticeship in Eva Le Gallienne's Civic Repertory Company led to summer stock and Broad-

Burgess Meredith, Betty Field (courtesy of The Museum of Modern Art/Film Stills Archive)

A commission in the U.S. Army led to pickup assignments as an *Army Hour* announcer and field reporter. Captain Meredith returned to lighter fare as guest of Cantor and Hildegarde. In the early 1950s he led the cast of versions of the plays, *Hobson's Choice* and *Biography.*

612. MERMAN, Ethel (singer; b. Jan. 16, 1909, Astoria, NY; d. Feb. 15, 1984, New York, NY). *Rhythm at Eight* (1935); *Ethel Merman Show* (1949).

Singing star of Broadway's greatest musicals, from 1930 to the 1960s. Merman was a distinctive stage personality with a powerful voice, bringing life to such shows as *Anything Goes, Panama Hattie, Annie Get Your Gun* and *Gypsy.* Her overnight success came with George and Ira Gershwin's *Girl Crazy* and the show-stopping song "I Got Rhythm." During its 1930–31 run she appeared at WEAF on the *Bond Program* and *RKO Hour.* Guest spots followed with Vallee. She sang "The Animal in Me" in Paramount's all-star *Big Broadcast of 1936.* Its premiere was broadcast on *Your Hit Parade* with Merman at the mike.

way in the early 1930s. Many productions flopped but the ambitious and persistent Meredith usually received good notices, especially for *Little Ol' Boy* and *She Loves Me Not.* It brought him the part of Red Davis, a typical American boy in a program sponsored by Beech-Nut chewing gum and a series that evolved into *Pepper Young's Family.* The show paid a Depression-defying $350 for three broadcasts a week plus 11 p.m. repeats. One night he completely missed the second airing. The director had to step in and try to imitate him on the spot. The sponsor was furious and fired him.

His breakthrough soon came as Mio in the Maxwell Anderson award-winning play *Winterset.* It led to films (*Of Mice and Men* with Betty Field). Vallee aired Burgess and co-star Margo in a scene from *Winterset* and followed up in 1937 with excerpts from his next Broadway success *High Tor.* On April 11, 1937 he appeared with Orson Welles in Archibald MacLeish's classic story "The Fall of the City" on *Columbia Workshop.* That year he performed on Columbia's *Shakespeare Festival,* aired in direct opposition to NBC's John Barrymore and *Streamlined Shakespeare.* By 1941 he was combining movies and the stage with acting and emceeing on *Cavalcade of America, Spirit of '41, Lincoln Highway* and *Inner Sanctum Mysteries.*

For Norman Corwin's *Pursuit of Happiness*—a CBS program of fine drama, music and poetry—he faced a studio-auditorium audience of some 400 people as well as millions of listeners with at most two days of rehearsal. "And the audience listened carefully in those pristine days," Burgess recalls in his book *So Far, So Good.* "Radio is an old story now, but when it first arrived it was exciting to hear words and music come out of the air. It was the edge of the miraculous."

Ethel Merman

This one-time cabaret and vaudeville performer had a NBC situation comedy in 1949. But it short-changed listeners who expected more songs from Ethel, plot or no plot. Her brassiness and bravado played well opposite emcee Tallulah Bankhead on frequent *Big Show* guest appearances in the early 1950s. Her clarion-call delivery of Irving Berlin's "I Like Ike" in *Call Me Madam*—a musical bankrolled largely by NBC—helped draw attention to the 1952 Eisenhower presidential bid. She reprieved the tune at the 1956 Republican National Convention, broadcast from the Cow Palace, San Francisco. Merman's best and most magical media moment came in a lengthy duet with Mary Martin on the 1953 Ford 50th anniversary show on CBS-TV.

613. MERRILL, Robert (singer; b. June 4, 1919, Brooklyn, NY). *Serenade to America* (1943–46); *An Evening with Romberg* (1945); *Robert Merrill Show* (1945–46); *RCA Victor Show* (1946–49).

His rendition of the Figaro aria from *The Barber of Seville* won a place on Major Bowes' *Original Amateur Hour.* Solo appearances with the NBC Concert Orchestra followed, plus first place in *The Metropolitan Opera Auditions of the Air.* In 1945 he bowed at the Met as the elder Germont in *La Traviata.*

Toscanini chose the "borscht" circuit-trained baritone for an NBC Symphony two-part broadcast of *Traviata* in December 1946. NBC featured his vigorous and versatile voice on *Music for a Summer Evening* and *Music for Tonight,* and in the early 1950s as

singing host of *Encore.* He appeared in Toscanini's final opera performance and recording as Renato in *Un Ballo in Maschera.* The first American singer to give 500 performances at the Met, Merrill was the official singer of the National Anthem for the New York Yankees baseball team.

614. MERRIMAN, Nan (singer; b. April 28, 1920, Pittsburgh, PA). *Serenade to America* (1943–46).

A soloist with Toscanini and the NBC Symphony in the 1940s and early '50s. This mezzo-soprano performed in motion picture choruses while a student in Los Angeles. In 1942 she won a Cincinnati Opera contest, made her debut in *La Gioconda,* and gained the backing of a group of music patrons who paid for a year of work at the Cincinnati College of Music. Upon the completion of her studies, she emerged as the winner of a Federation of Music Clubs competition.

With her success came a NBC contract, and periodic solos on *Music of the New World.* Toscanini engaged her for an all-Verdi program on July 25, 1943 (during the broadcast, there came the news of the fall of Mussolini), and more appearances followed with the NBC Concert Orchestra, as did recordings for Victor and engagements by Rodzinski and Bernstein.

"Radio is about the best vocal mirror we have," Merriman said in a 1945 *Etude* article. "If people listen to you at all, they listen to you intently. They have nothing else to do, and there is nothing to distract them. For that reason, anything you do, whether good or bad, seems intensified."

Robert Merrill

Nan Merriman

615. METZ, Stuart (announcer; b. March 20, 1908, Buffalo, NY). *Pepper Young's Family* (1937–40); *Mr. Keen, Tracer of Lost Persons* (1939); *Waltz Time* (1939–c42).

NBC staff announcer. With a background as a ham radio operator from his home in Williamsville, New York, he joined Buffalo Broadcasting Corporation in 1929 as an engineer. It led to announcing and programming assignments. An audition record for Pat Kelly at NBC New York resulted in a job there, beginning with *Betty Moore Triangle Club* in 1937. He later announced *Road of Life, Light of the World,* and narrated *Grand Central Station.*

616. MICHAUX, Elder Solomon Lightfoot (preacher [signature song: "Happy Am I"]; b. Nov. 7, 1883, Newport News, VA; d. Oct. 20, 1968, Washington, DC). *Elder Michaux Happiness Church Service* (1948–53).

His message of earthly contentment and heavenly optimism sparked his frequent broadcasts, drawing audiences of white as well as Black adherents. A theme of cheerfulness despite the Depression uplifted many. A backer of President Franklin D. Roosevelt, Michaux was credited with prompting large numbers of Negro voters to support him in elections. His Good Neighbor League in Washington fed, housed and clothed countless people, and his seven churches stressed good works.

Elder Michaux's Radio Church of God went on Mutual in the 1940s after years of local airings. It featured much joyful music and handclapping. Michaux continued to broadcast "The Happy Am I Preacher and His Famous Choir" from Washington until 1968.

617. MILLER, Glenn (bandleader [signature song: "Moonlight Serenade"]; b. March 1, 1904, Clarinda, IA; d. Dec. 15, 1944, on a military flight from England to France). *Moonlight Serenade* (1939–42); *USO Matinee* (1942).

Miller last led his legendary band on a BBC broadcast three days before leaving on a military plane that was lost without a trace during World War II. An Army major assigned to direct the American Band of the Allied Supreme Command, he was keeping a promise to GIs to broadcast from Paris on Christmas Day. Both as a commissioned officer and as a civilian, the trombonist-bandleader broadcast almost on a daily basis—from studios, hotels, dance halls, military bases. Chiefly through radio his was a rags-to-riches rise.

Spring bookings at Frank Dailey's Meadowbrook and Glen Island Casino in 1939 enthralled the ears of the late-night listeners and first gained Miller a nationwide reputation. Broadcasts from the Cafe Rouge of the Pennsylvania Hotel were soon augmented by a CBS series for Chesterfield cigarettes, paying him $5,000 for three 15-minute shows a week. He introduced from five to seven new songs every week, and by year-end one of every three recordings in juke boxes sported a Glenn Miller label. And just about everywhere the band appeared, it broke attendance records. At the 1939 State Fair in Syracuse, the biggest dance crowd in the history of central New York turned out to see him.

A musical perfectionist, he studied phrasing, interpretation and tonal color in order to develop an unusual yet popular swing style and harmonic structure. "Swing, as such, will never die," he predicted in 1941, "though of course its name may be changed."

Ben Pollack signed Glenn to his first big-band contract. By the mid-30s he was arranging for Ray Noble, Benny Goodman and Red Nichols, and building the basis for his own outfit with its distinctive singing reed effect. Long after Miller's death, his orchestra continued to have a wide and loyal following. His methodical orderliness and unique creativity, in the words of music critic John S. Wilson, "have given Mr. Miller a longevity of appeal that is without precedent in popular music."

618. MILLER, Jack (conductor; b. Sept. 4, 1895, Dorchester, MA; d. March 18, 1985, Los Angeles, CA). *Kate Smith and Her Swanee Music/New Star Revue/Coffee Time/A&P Bandwagon* (1931–38); *Aldrich Family* (1939–40, 1943–44, 1946–51).

Musical director for Kate Smith from her start in radio in 1930 and on her Columbia recordings, and later TV. Her sponsor, General Foods, also signed him for its long-popular *Aldrich Family* series. Miller conducted an orchestra on *Molle Mystery Theatre* from 1943–46 and *Confidentially Yours, Jack Lait* in 1950.

619. MILLER, Marvin (actor, announcer; b. July 18, 1913, St. Louis, MO; d. Feb. 8, 1985, Santa Monica, CA). *Romance of Helen Trent* (1939–42); *The Whistler* (1942–45); *Duffy's Tavern* (1945–46, 1948–49); *Smilin' Ed McConnell and His Buster Brown Gang* (1948–51).

By 1940 Miller, a freelance announcer, tallied some 40 radio shows a week in Chicago (*First Nighter, Chicago Theatre of the Air, Helen Trent*'s love interest Gil Whitney). He relocated to Los Angeles where he added acting assignments. For *Coronet Storyteller* he worked as narrator and played many parts. He announced *The Whistler,* and when the lead actor, Bill Forman, went into the Army, Miller became *The Whistler.* He served as announcer, and periodic cast member, for Red Skelton, Billie Burke, Lassie, *The Crisco Kid* and *Railroad Hour.*

Beginning in 1955 he starred as the personal secretary who delivered a million dollars to some lucky person each week on TV's dramatic series *The Millionaire.* He portrayed many Oriental characters on television and in films. They included his first feature, *Blood on the Sun.* Miller's voice was heard on *The F.B.I.* and Mr. Magoo cartoons.

While a student at Washington University, he did

radio at KWK and WIL. His professional credits began at KMOX. In the mid-1980s he regularly recorded a five-minute syndicated show called "Almanac," used as a lead-in to weather reports.

620. MILLS, Billy (conductor; b. Sept. 6, 1894, Flint, MI; d. Oct. 21, 1971, Glendale, CA). *Myrt and Marge* (1934–36); *Fibber McGee and Molly* (1938–52); *The Great Gildersleeve* (1941–43); *Amos 'n' Andy* (1944–45).

Arranger, staff conductor and general music supervisor at CBS Chicago from 1932 to 1937. Hired by Johnston's Wax as music director for Fibber McGee, Mills moved to NBC. "His is a good, workmanly pit job," *Variety* noted. He also conducted for Alex Templeton, Victor Borge, and *The Great Gildersleeve*.

A theatre pianist, church soloist and military bandleader, Mills made orchestrations for Isham Jones in the 1920s before forming his own orchestra. He broadcast from Chicago's Marigold Gardens, a famed dance pavilion of that period. He attended the University of Michigan and Syracuse where he composed student operettas.

621. MILLS BROTHERS (singers [signature song: "Goodbye Blues"]).

JOHN C. (b. Oct. 19,1910, Piqua, OH; d. Jan. 24, 1936, Bellefontaine, OH).

HERBERT B. (b. April 12, 1912, Piqua, OH; d. April 12, 1989, Las Vegas, NV).

HARRY F. (b. Aug. 19,1913, Piqua, OH; d. June 28, 1982, Los Angeles, CA).

DONALD F. (b. April 29, 1915, Piqua, OH).

JOHN H. (b. Feb. 11, 1882, Bellefonte, PA; d. Dec. 8, 1967, Bellefontaine, OH). *Mills Brothers Quartette* (1931–33).

The Mills Brothers (Herbert, tenor; Donald, second tenor; Harry, baritone; John C., bass) formed a quartet in Ohio in the mid-1920s. Emphasizing barbershop harmonies, they were billed as Four Boys and a Guitar. At the time the brothers ranged in age from 11 to 15. They began broadcasting in 1928 at WLW where, unable to get a sponsor, management nonetheless, kept them on the air for ten months. Duke Ellington and Seger Ellis heard their carefully measured three- and four-part modulated harmonies and facilitated their initial success in New York in 1929–30. In 1932 they had the first commercially sponsored (Proctor & Gamble) network show (CBS) for black artists. The quartet often appeared on Bing Crosby's programs, and sang on AFRS's *Mail Call* and *G.I. Jive* and USAF's *Manhattan Melodies*.

The brothers had great success on recordings, beginning with "Tiger Rag" and "Sweet Sue" for Brunswick and continuing with "Paper Doll" and "Glow Worm" for Decca. When oldest brother John Mills died in 1936, their father John H. took over as bass. They appeared in the first of the "Big Broadcast" films in 1932; nearly 50 years later they were doing personal appearances and television commercials, still using their original arrangements.

622. MINER, Jan (actress, b. Oct. 15, 1917, Boston, MA). *Lora Lawton* (1945–49); *Hilltop House* (1948–57).

Voted favorite dramatic actress of radio throughout the 1950s. She played the lead in *Lora Lawton* and Girl Friday roles on *Boston Blackie, Perry Mason* and *Casey, Crime Photographer*. She frequently appeared on *Radio City Playhouse* and *My Secret Story*. Her first major role, *Linda Dale*, came in the early 1940s.

"When we saw television coming along, we all went to acting class to work physically," Miner recalled in Ted Sennett's *The Old Time Radio Book* (1976). "When you stand in front of a microphone, you do it vocally, and you do it with your imagination. But you don't do it physically. So we went to class to move our bodies."

At 16 she had started acting at Boston's Copley Theatre, playing maternal parts and continuing in that vein on Broadway (*Watch on the Rhine*) and films (*Lenny*). She portrayed Gertrude Stein on stage and film in a critically acclaimed performance. Viewers in many countries know her as Madge the Manicurist in the long-running commercials for Palmolive liquid detergent.

Mills Brothers: Herbert, John C., Donald, and Harry (courtesy of Daniel R. Clemson)

Mischa Mischakoff

The personable, authoritative-sounding Mitchell had left the Army as soldier and entertainer in 1919, and joined Paul Whiteman, doing orchestrations and directing a Whiteman band unit for seven years. He then settled in New Haven where he conducted and managed stage shows in picture houses. Just prior to his break in radio, he was manager of a Major Bowes touring unit. When *The Answer Man* ended, he joined the European offices of the Marshall Plan. His daughter Dolly Mitchell was a blues singer with Whiteman in the 1940s.

623. MISCHAKOFF, Mischa (violinist; b. 1895, Proskourov, Russia; d. Feb. 1, 1981, Petoskey, MI). *NBC Symphony* (1937–51); *NBC String Trio* (1943–46).

Concertmaster of the NBC Symphony. He held similar posts with the New York Symphony (1924–27), Philadelphia Orchestra (1927–29) and Detroit Symphony (1951–58). For a dozen years, beginning in 1940, he taught at Juilliard. He often appeared a soloist for Toscanini and played in the NBC String Trio and Quartette. During this period he could be heard on *Serenade to America* and *Shostakovich Chamber Music Festival.*

Mischakoff studied at the St. Petersburg Conservatory, and in 1917 became concertmaster of the Moscow Grand Opera. He emigrated to America in 1922, changing his name from Fishberg because of the many string players with that surname.

624. MITCHELL, Albert (host; b. May 31, 1893, Elsberry, MO; d. Oct. 4, 1954, Paris, France). *The Answer Man* (1937–50).

Mitchell, orchestra leader in vaudeville and songwriter, originated *The Answer Man* at WICC Bridgeport, Connecticut in 1936. He had applied for a weekly unsponsored program, answering any questions which might be sent to him. About four weeks after his start, he was signed by WOR and sponsor Provident Loan Society for three broadcasts a week. During most of its run on Mutual, Bruce "Ben" Chapman asked the 40 or so questions on each show; the answers were researched by a large, diligent staff who often called upon experts in every imaginable field. Mitchell was not the first or only Answer Man. As early as 1931 WJZ and *The Gruen Watch Answer Man* (Earl Gilbert) and regional clones appeared periodically.

625. MITCHELL, Shirley (actress; b. c1920, Toledo, OH). *The Great Gildersleeve* (1941–58); *Fibber McGee and Molly* (1943–46); *Young Love* (1949–50).

Audibly etched in radio annals as the widow Leila Ransome, the good-natured, vivacious girl friend of Gildersleeve. Mitchell enjoyed other running parts as lovable albeit ditsey characters in the lives of Rudy Vallee (as Shirley Whirley), Fibber McGee (Alice Dar-

Shirley Mitchell (courtesy of Shirley Mitchell)

ling), Red Skelton (Mrs. Willy Lump Lump) and Jack Benny (Mabel, the telephone operator). She played Joan Davis' rival Shirley Anne, and the mouse (Kitty Archer) of *McGarry and His Mouse* as well as featured roles for Bing Crosby, Jack Carson, Phil Silvers and Amos 'n' Andy.

Starting out on WSPD's *Children's Hour,* Shirley later went on to study at the Universities of Toledo and Michigan. She appeared at the Cleveland Playhouse but switched to Chicago radio in 1942. *First Nighter* was her first network show. After stints on *Mary Marlin, Road of Life* and *Ramson Sherman Show,* she relocated to Los Angeles, and by the 1950s recreated many of her radio roles on TV and added new ones for *Bachelor Father, I Love Lucy* and *Pete and Gladys.* Her films included *Desk Set* and *Cross Current.*

626. MOHR, Gerald (actor; b. June 11, 1914, New York, NY; d. Nov. 10, 1968, Stockholm, Sweden). *The Lone Wolfe* (1948); *Adventures of Philip Marlowe* (1948–50).

Hailed as a young Bogart, Mohr moved into detective roles in films and radio as the Lone Wolfe, then at the mike as Philip Marlowe. Charming yet sinister characterizations carried him into TV's *Foreign Intrigue* and similar offerings on European video.

While at Columbia University, he had been hospitalized. In a room next to Mohr's, announcer Andre Baruch overheard him talking and decided to persuade him to audition for radio. CBS hired Mohr as an announcer, and at age 20 he covered the Morro Castle ship disaster off the New Jersey coast. Work with Orson Welles' Mercury Theatre led to Hollywood and to appearances on *Lux Radio Theatre, Suspense, Rogue's Gallery* and *The Whistler,* and movie parts in *Lady of Burlesque, Gilda* and *Detective Story.*

Of radio Mohr observed: "The supreme test is when the theatre snob is cut down to his voice and shorn of gallery gestures and has nothing but a microphone to rely on. How good is he? This is when the cords in the neck of the ham begin to show. No actor worthy of the name is lessened by his medium, whether it be radio, pictures, stage or television."

627. MONROE, Lucy (singer; [The Star-Spangled Soprano]; b. Oct. 23, 1906, New York, NY; d. Oct. 13, 1987, New York, NY). *Hammerstein's Music Hall* (1935); *Lavender and Old Lace* (1935); *American Album of Familiar Music* (1935–37); *Manhattan Merry-Go-Round* (1941–42).

Beginning in 1938, for the next 30 years, she spent much of her time singing "The Star-Spangled Banner"—often on broadcasts for National Defense Day, the President's Birthday Ball, Armistice Day, Army Day, War Bond Drives and USO benefits. She estimated that she had sung the National Anthem more than 5,000 times. They included every New York Yankees opening day and World Series between 1945 and 1960.

Daughter of actress Anna Laughlin, the original Broadway star of *The Wizard of Oz,* Lucy headed for a theatrical career upon graduating from high school. Musical comedy parts came along in the mid-1920s, in Ziegfeld's *Louis the Fourteenth* and the *First Little Show.* Around 1930 she got a sustaining spot over NBC, but operatic roles became her major interest. She made her debut as Marguerite in *Faust* at the Hippodrome in New York in 1932 and appeared with the St. Louis Opera in *Boheme,* giving rise to the consensus that she was the best-looking girl in American opera. Monroe's soprano voice—full, somewhat limpid in tone—and unusually clear articulation attracted radio producers Anne and Frank Hummert who teamed her with the equally intelligible tenor, Frank Munn. Popular prima donna of *Lavender and Old Lace* and other Hummert shows, she was abruptly dropped by them when her widowed mother left a suicide note blaming Lucy for outright neglect and misbehavior. At the time the 30-year-old singer was seemingly having an affair with a man whom her mother had hoped to wed. Without a radio series, Monroe freelanced as guest soloist with the Philadelphia Orchestra on the *American Banker's Hour,* did operettas at the Jones Beach outdoor theatre, and appeared as Jenny Lind in *American Jubilee* at the New York World's Fair. Her patriotic penance convinced the Hummerts to rehire her in 1941 for their Sunday tune-filled *Manhattan Merry-Go-Round.*

628. MONROE, Vaughn (singer, bandleader [signature song: "Racing with the Moon"]; b. Oct. 1,

Vaughn Monroe

1911, Akron, OH; d. May 21, 1973, Stuart, FL). *Penthouse Party* (1941); *Vaughn Monroe Show* (1946–54).

A serious-minded musician, he started out as a trumpet player in the 1930s but ended up combining that job with vocalizing and bandleading. He worked his way through Carnegie Tech by means of professional engagements with dance bands but gave up all idea of being an engineer soon after joining Larry Funk. He reluctantly substituted as conductor for Boston society leader Jack Marshard. The experience led to his own outfit, designed both to please conservative dancers and rhythm-bent younger fans.

Radio pickups gained him wide recognition, especially among college students. His deep-voiced renditions of "Riders in the Sky" and "Ballerina" won the tall, goodlooking crooner matinee-idol status. By 1946 he had his own program for Camels, first as a summer replacement for Abbott and Costello. The exposure took him into the movies and television. In 1956–57 *The NBC Bandstand* featured him often as their "Mr. Music" guest, and RCA utilized him as its commercial spokesman.

629. MOORE, Garry (host, comedian; b. Jan. 31, 1915, Baltimore, MD; d. Nov. 28, 1993, Hilton Head Island, SC). *Club Matinee* (1939–42); *Beat the Band* (1940–41); *Everything Goes* (1942–43); *Camel Caravan* (1943–47); *Take It or Leave It* (1947–49); *Garry Moore Show* (1949–51).

A reluctant radio comedian, he planned on being a continuity writer, but was astonished to find people laughing at his jokes. His first job at WBAL Baltimore in the mid-30s led to St. Louis as a news announcer and sports commentator for KWK. Using his real name Thomas Garrison Morfit, he went on a network in 1939 as a comedian and writer on *Club Matinee*, a daily afternoon variety show at NBC Chicago. That year he hosted *Fitch Summer Bandwagon*. A contest for a new name won a Pittsburgh woman $50 and Garry a stage name. Emcee of *Beat the Band*, a musical game show, followed, as did *Service with a Smile* from Army camps.

In 1943 the crew-cut, bow-tied Moore co-starred with Jimmy Durante as a replacement for Abbott and Costello. The show built up an estimated four million listeners a week and ran until 1947 when Moore struck out on his own as emcee of *Take It or Leave It.* When Tom Breneman died suddenly in 1948 Moore stepped in on *Breakfast in Hollywood* for 15 weeks. *Variety* noted his "infectious and ingratiating quality . . . that must inevitably invite a healthy femme response." This role encouraged him to go back to daytime radio with his own variety show with an accent on music and comedy. In 1950 CBS worked out a similar series for its TV network. That breezy low-keyed presentation led to additional contracts as game show moderator.

The likable, unassuming Moore had a reputation for being unfailingly considerate and understanding.

Because of his alertness and innate good taste, he always knew what to say in every situation, and whenever necessary, gently got a contestant, panelist or performer off the hook.

630. MOORE, Grace (singer [signature song: "One Night of Love"]; b. Dec. 5, 1901, Jellico, TN; d. Jan. 26, 1947, Copenhagen, Denmark). *Vick Open House* (1935–36).

With an abundance of vitality and ambition, this indomitable diva epitomized the tag line, "star of stage, screen and radio." From Broadway musical (*Music Box Revue*) to the Met (*Boheme*) to Hollywood film (*New Moon*), the exuberant and attractive soprano added broadcasting in the 1930s, commanding a large fee from Vick Chemical for a weekly series. A decade later she was still captivating listeners from appearances on *The Telephone Hour*. Above all, Moore knocked the high hat off grand opera by her melodic joie de vivre in the trailblazing and broadly appealing operatic movie *One Night of Love* (1934). She told her success story of a small-town girl who made good in *You're Only Human Once,* published in 1944, just three years before her death in a plane crash.

631. MOOREHEAD, Agnes (actress; b. Dec. 6, 1906, Clinton, MA; d. April 30, 1974, Rochester, MN). *Charis Players* (1930–31); *The Shadow* (1937–40); *Bess Johnson* (1941); *Mayor of the Town* (1942–49).

Established and versatile star in every medium, Moorehead originated the suspenseful role of the bedridden woman about to be murdered in the radio classic, "Sorry, Wrong Number." The monologue was first aired on *Suspense* on September 15, 1945. With Orson Welles she was a founder of the Mercury The-

Agnes Moorehead (courtesy of Steve Jelf)

atre, and appeared on its CBS broadcasts. She also played his girlfriend in *The Shadow*. Her film debut was in Welles's *Citizen Kane*.

A strong and authoritative individual, she earned a doctorate in literature, taught high school, and studied at the American Academy of Dramatic Arts before winning parts in Broadway plays. Moorehead could perform the gamut from comedy to tragedy, and from young heroines to old witches. She portrayed Eleanor Roosevelt on *The March of Time*, and played opposite radio comedians, among them Hope and Benny. In the 1940s she became a regular on *Cavalcade of America* and *Mayor of the Town* (as Lionel Barrymore's housekeeper).

632. MORGAN, Claudia (actress; b. Nov. 12, 1911, Brooklyn, NY; d. Sept. 17, 1974, New York, NY). *Against the Storm* (1937–42); *Adventures of the Thin Man* (1941–50); *Right to Happiness* (1942–60); *Adventures of the Abbotts* (1954 -55).

Workaday, workanight actress in New York, often appearing in two regular radio series while simultaneously acting in one or two Broadway plays. She was actually dismissed from *Ten Little Indians* after a spell because her Nora Charles role in the *Thin Man* held up the curtain every Friday night. The popular detective program was her best-known radio part — the wry and wisecracking wife of Nick Charles. On Broadway at age 16, Morgan spent her daytime hours in soaps. She played Nicole Scott and Christy Allen in *Against the Storm*, Nita Bennett in *Lone Journey* and Carolyn Cramer on *The Right to Happiness*. Periodic roles in *The Falcon* and *Radio City Playhouse* augmented her schedule.

From a theatrical family, she was the daughter of actor Ralph Morgan and niece of Frank Morgan. One of her best and most frequently performed roles was Maggie Cutler in *The Man Who Came to Dinner*, opposite Monty Woolley, first on Broadway, then on the road.

633. MORGAN, Edward P. (newscaster; b. June 23, 1910, Walla Walla, WA; d. Jan. 27, 1993, McLean, VA). *News and Commentary* (1954–67).

Reporter, anchor and commentator. A World War II and foreign correspondent, Morgan joined CBS in 1951, and soon became director of news for radio and TV. His broadcasts switched to ABC Washington in 1955, and continued into the 1970s. His reports and commentary were sponsored by the AFL-CIO and had a liberal view point. He also broadcast as a correspondent for public radio. Morgan won many honors for coverage of such events as the assassination of President Kennedy and the sinking of the passenger ship *Andrea Doria*. Morgan received a Peabody Award for radio news in 1956, the Sidney Hillman Foundation Award for radio news analysis in 1959, and Alfred I. du Pont Award for best broadcast commentary in 1960.

After studies at Whitman College and the University of Washington, he was a reporter in Seattle, correspondent for UPI and associate editor of *Collier's*.

634. MORGAN, Frank (actor; b. June 1, 1890, New York, NY; d. Sept. 18, 1949, Beverly Hills, CA). *Good News of 1938/1939* (1937–39); *Maxwell House Coffee Time* (1941–45); *The Fabulous Dr. Tweedy* (1946–47).

A contract in 1937 at MGM, where he would play *The Wizard of Oz* and 67 other roles, extended to the studio's *Good News* program. Morgan appeared regularly, and co-starred on its successor for Maxwell House with Fanny Brice. He subbed for Bing Crosby on *Kraft Music Hall* for four months during the 1945–46 season.

Beginning as a Broadway juvenile in 1914, Morgan had leads in *The Firebrand, Topaze* and *The Band Wagon*. On radio he specialized in blustery, easily confused nabobs, such as Dean Tweedy of Pots College. His last broadcast was on the quiz show *Hollywood Calling* in July 1949. His brother Ralph Morgan, an actor, first induced him to discard life on a cattle ranch to try his luck on stage.

635. MORGAN, Henry (comedian; b. March 31, 1915, New York, NY; d. May 19, 1994, New York, NY). *Here's Morgan* (1941–43); *Henry Morgan Show* (1946–47, 1949–50).

Radio's sharp-tongued "bad boy" of the 1940s. Satirist, raconteur and writer, Morgan reflected the acerbic, unpredictable personas of Arthur Godfrey and Oscar Levant. On his own comic platform, more

Henry Morgan (courtesy of Capital Cities/ABC)

in the mode of Fred Allen, he built a reputation for insubordination, especially to sponsors and broadcast executives. He always bit the hand that fed him, and as a result often lost prime-time advertisers initially willing to take a chance on the offbeat ad libs and monologues. His wry ways won over most listeners and critics yet his course on the airwaves proved bumpy and erratic.

At the age of 17 Morgan started out as a page at WMCA. a year later he secured an announcer's job at WCAU Philadelphia where in a script for a broadcast about missing persons he included the names of station personnel. It ended his work in that city. Following jobs in Boston and Duluth, he joined the announcers staff at WOR. He pestered its management for a show of his own, and in 1940 he had a weekly quarter-hour called *Meet Mr. Morgan*. He built up a solid cult of listeners—a dedicated following that convinced Mutual to launch his *Here's Morgan*. Morganphiles remembered their idol's weather reports: "High winds . . . followed by high skirts . . . followed by men." The broadcast on which he auctioned off the entire Mutual network, with the announcers sold in pairs "so they won't get lonely"—all for $83, including good will—is a radio legend.

Morgan's best period came after his return from a two-year stint in the Army. ABC gave him a half-hour on Sunday evenings. Schick Injector Razor sponsored his iconoclastic sketches but took offense at his zestful jabs at its product ("It's got an automatic blade changer so simple a child can change it. But what child shaves?") Bristol-Myers launched his 1949 variety show, seemingly better equipped to handle his "kidding the sponsor" segment. His sidekick, Gerard, was playing by Arnold Stang.

"His mordant humor did not sit well with certain people, and some of them concluded that he must be either a Communist or friendly to Communists," Richard Severo wrote in his *New York Times* obituary. Morgan was named in the career-destroying book "Red Channels" as seemingly unsuitable for the media. Yet he found work in the 1950s and '60s as a regular panelist on the TV game shows *I've Got a Secret* and *What's My Line?*

636. MORGAN, Russ (bandleader [Music in the Morgan Manner] [signature song: "Does Your Heart Beat for Me?"]; b. April 29, 1904, Scranton, PA; d. Aug. 8, 1969, Las Vegas, NV). *Russ Morgan Orchestra* (1937–39).

Sweet-jazz style trombonist and leader. A Pennsylvania coal miner, Morgan formed his first band, the Scranton Sirens, with Tommy and Jimmy Dorsey. He toured Europe with Paul Specht and played in the Goldkette band in Detroit where he broadcast at WXYZ. A pianist and composer-arranger, he organized a hotel orchestra in 1936 at the insistence of Rudy Vallee who gave it airplay on his program and lined up a booking at New York's Biltmore that

lengthened into two years. Philip Morris presented him on Tuesday over NBC and Saturday from CBS for several seasons.

Noted for his waah-waah mute on the trombone, the tall, broad-shouldered musician was featured on *Fitch Bandwagon* and *NBC Bandstand* In the 1960s Morgan led his orchestra at the Dunes Hotel on the Vegas Strip. His compositions "Somebody Else is Taking My Place" and "You're Nobody Till Somebody Loves You" became pop standards.

637. MORRISON, Brett (actor; b. May 5, 1912, Chicago, IL; d. Sept. 25, 1978, Hollywood, CA). *First Nighter* (1937–41); *Arnold Grimm's Daughter* (1938–42); *Road to Danger* (1942–44); *The Shadow* (1945–54).

He portrayed *The Shadow* (Lamont Cranston), a wealthy man who played at the job of detective. Cranston solved crimes that the police could not, and in the process often protected the innocent. Morrison was particularly noted for his horrific laugh that would open each broadcast. Morrison essayed his role with aplomb and forcefulness; his predecessors included Frank Readick, Orson Welles and Bill Johnstone.

Brett entered radio fulltime in Chicago in 1937 as Mr. First Nighter, and worked on *Best Sellers, Listening Post, Stella Dallas, Mary Marlin* and other serials. In the 1940s he was narrator for Bible dramatizations on *Light of the World* and of word-color backgrounds for the salutes to American cities and industries on *Carnation Contented Hour*. At his death from a heart attack on Hollywood's Vine Street, Morrison had just finished an episode for the resuscitated radio drama, *Heartbeat Theatre*.

638. MOSS, Arnold (actor; b. Jan. 28, 1909, Brooklyn, NY; d. Dec. 15, 1989, New York, NY). *Jane Arden* (1938–39); *Against the Storm* (1939–40); *Story of Mary Marlin* (1942–43); *Light of the World* (1947); *Cafe Istanbul* (1952–53).

Multifaceted artist, best know for interpretations of Shakespearean roles. After obtaining a Ph.D. in theatre, he served a two-year apprenticeship at the Civic Repertory Theatre. He taught speech and drama at Brooklyn College in the 1930s, and had parts on Broadway. That led to a performance as Prospero in *The Tempest* in 1945.

Producers brought him to radio soaps (*Stella Dallas*) and dramatic shows (*The March of Time*). His voice often narrated anthologies and commemorative and anniversary events. For *Molle Mystery Theatre*, he wrote and starred in "To the End of the World," and appeared as villainous characters. Moss broadcast as spokesman for the New York Philharmonic Orchestra and was a staff announcer for CBS.

As head of his own repertory company, the Shakespeare Festival Players, he toured some 50 U.S. colleges in 1959.

639. MOYLAN, Marianne (singer; b. Aug. 16, 1932, Southampton, NY; d. July 25, 1990, Southampton, NY).

MOYLAN, Peggy Joan (singer [Angels of the Airwaves] [signature song: "Sittin' on a Log Pettin' My Dog"]; b. Oct. 2, 1934, Sag Harbor, NY). *The Moylan Sisters* (1939–44).

Radio's youngest harmony duo. Their natural ability was first noticed when the sisters, sitting on their living room floor, suddenly joined a quartet singing over the radio and harmonized in near perfection. Five-year-old Marianne had said to three-year-old Peggy Joan, "You sing the downstairs notes and I'll sing the upstairs ones." Their parents soon obtained an audition at NBC.

They began on the Horn & Hardart *Children's Hour* at WEAF and in 1939 signed for their own series (sponsored for several seasons by Thrivo dog food with the intro: "Children and dogs. Symbols of affection. They both bring happiness to the home"). Their captivating personalities and amazing vocal clarity and flexibility brightened many Sunday afternoons. They always included a hymn, such as "The Rosary" or "I Need Thee, Heart of Jesus."

Their unique vocal career ended as suddenly as it had begun. The Moylans faced their teen years, weary of long commutes from eastern Long Island to Radio City and anxious to leave show business and go off to school. Marianne became a lab technician; Peggy Joan, a medical secretary. Both married and between them raised five sons and three daughters.

640. MUNN, Frank (singer [The Golden Voice of Radio]; b. Feb. 27, 1894, Bronx, NY; d. Oct. 1, 1953, Queens Village, NY). *Palmolive Hour* (1927–31); *American Album of Familiar Music* (1931–45);

Waltz Time (1933–45); *Lavender and Old Lace* (1934–37).

One of the most perfect voices for early radio and recording microphones. A tenor with crystal-clear enunciation and highly expressive phrasing, Munn never lacked a commercial sponsor once he became a professional in the mid-1920s. His mentor, conductor Gus Haenschen, featured his vocals on Brunswick discs and that phonograph company's pre-network broadcasts. They consistently worked together on a half-dozen well-received musical programs, most notably the long-running *American Album* at NBC. At one point, Munn sang on three weekly prime-time series, building a repertoire of frequently requested ballads, especially "When Irish Eyes Are Smiling," "Sylvia," "Forgotten," "Something to Remember You By" and "Trees." His duets as Palmolive's Paul Oliver with soprano Virginia Rea as Olive Palmer were highlights of early coast-to-coast radio.

A major attraction for Hummert-produced, over-the-counter drug-sponsored vehicles, he, unlike most singers, made very few guest appearances across the dial. A soloist or band vocalist on more than 350 recordings, Munn continually turned down offers to perform on stage, in nightclubs and concert halls, and on screen. Self-conscious of his unromantic roly-poly shape, the short and stocky singer preferred to appeal only to the ear.

His vocal dexterity came naturally and was extended by mimicking the artistry of John McCormack from recordings. A World War I factory worker, he suffered an on-the-job injury to his hand, necessitating a long recuperation that led to singing jobs to pay his rent. An untypical star, he shunned publicity, guarded his privacy, and saved his large earnings. At 51, and at the peak of his popularity, he quit show business and never sang again in a retirement as complete as Garbo's.

641. MURPHY, George (actor, emcee; b. July 4, 1902, New Haven, CT; d. May 3, 1992, Palm Beach, FL). *Let's Talk Hollywood* (1948); *Hollywood Calling* (1949).

The first professional actor elected to the U.S. Senate (1964). His speaking ability, and fund-raising and public relations skills placed him in the role of a politician as well as an entertainment industry spokesman. A vaudeville and Broadway song-and-dance man, Murphy did mostly guest spots on such shows as *Kraft*

Frank Munn

Music Hall and *Cavalcade of America*. He skillfully handled pleas to buy war bonds, save waste paper, and give blood. In 1948 he filled in as summer replacement for Jack Benny on *Let's Talk Hollywood*. Active in the Republican Party, he began to appear at conventions in 1952. He also served as president of the Motion Picture Industry Council.

At the height of the give-away craze, Murphy signed for a movie quiz, called *Hollywood Calling*. After several weeks he realized the answers to jackpot questions were being "planted" in newspapers. He wanted out, and was released only when he told NBC that he would disclose the deliberate practice of press leaks.

While in the Senate, he had throat surgery that left him only with the capability to speak in a whisper. After his defeat in 1970, he wrote his autobiography, *Say, Didn't You Used to Be George Murphy?*

Murphy & Lodge

642. MURRAY, Jan (comedian, emcee; b. Oct. 4, 1917, Bronx, NY). *Songs for Sale* (1950–51); *Meet Your Match* (1952–53).

Standup comic in theatres and nightclubs, he then sought a major radio or TV series. It turned out to be *Songs for Sale* for which he introduced five or six amateur song writers in a competition for the best tune on each broadcast. Murray thought the producers would quickly run out of would-be tunesmiths, but the CBS show became a runaway hit, and attracted musical contestants from all walks of life.

A popular simulcast, it featured two young vocalists, Rosemary Clooney and Johnny Desmond. Jan never lacked for TV game shows in the 1950s. He handled *Dollar a Second* and *Treasure Hunt* with commendable ease, proving he knew his way around audience-participation proceedings.

Earlier, Murray made a half-dozen guest appearances on the *Penguin Room with Hildegarde* in 1946 and did solo comedy spots on *Hollywood Open House* and *Chesterfield Supper Club*.

643. MURRAY, Ken (comedian; b. July 14, 1903, Nyack, NY; d. Oct. 12, 1988, Burbank, CA). *New Royal Vagabond* (1933); *Hollywood Hotel* (1937–38); *Texaco Star Theatre* (1939–40); *Which Is Which?* (1944–45).

A second-generation vaudevillian who during a long career returned to his early show business roots, on stage and television, and with homemade films. His most successful presentation, *Ken Murray's Blackouts,* a revolving format revue, ran for 3,844 performances at Hollywood's El Capitan Theatre in the 1940s. After a brief engagement in Las Vegas, he brought the variety show to CBS-TV as *The Ken Murray Show,* a top ten-rated program from 1950–52.

Murray required a visual presence to showcase his talents—and his proverbial unlighted cigar—to best advantage; his radio series never made it into the big leagues with Cantor, Benny or Allen. Ken's sidekick Tony "Oswald" Labriola once targeted the problem when he cracked his favorite motor car was "Ken Murray's radio script car, because it had had the same lines for ten years." Briefly a quiz show emcee, he fared better as a guest of Rudy Vallee and Bob Hope.

An amateur movie enthusiast, he made a name for himself as a Hollywood historian. He captured the town's vintage days in candid homemade scenes of movie colony celebrities, then edited the footage, added commentary, and presented these anthology pictures in theatres and on TV. Film work also brought him an Academy Award in 1947 as a producer of an unusual feature with trained birds as the leading characters (*Bill and Coo*). His book, *The Golden Days of San Simeon,* became a perennial best-seller at the Hearst Castle.

644. MURRAY, Lyn (conductor, b. Dec. 6, 1909, London, England; d. May 20, 1989, Los Angeles, CA). *Bill and Ginger* (1932–36); *Chesterfield Presents* (1936–37); *Your Hit Parade* (1939–47); *Ford Theatre* (1947–48).

His choral group, the Lyn Murray Singers, was highly praised for its contribution to *Voice of Firestone, Your Hit Parade, 99 Men and a Girl* and *Moods for Moderns*. As a conductor-composer, he provided background music for *Radio Reader's Digest, Columbia Workshop* and *Ellery Queen*. On staff at CBS, he led its symphony, dance bands and string ensembles, and backed singers Eileen Farrell and Frank Sinatra. He began as a choral coach at $100 a week in 1934; by 1943 his CBS commercial shows paid him more than $1,000.

Murray left New York in the late 1940s for Hollywood where he prepared music for the *Hallmark Playhouse* (hosted by novelist James Hilton) and for feature films and television series. "In radio they spent a great deal of money on music," he remarked in 1975, "but in television, it's the bottom of the totem pole."

Murray toiled as a sailor and newspaperman before radio staff jobs came along in 1928 at WGH Newport News and WCAU Philadelphia. He teamed up for comedy and songs on *Bill and Ginger* (Virginia Baker) which was picked up by the networks and took him to New York.

645. MURROW, Edward R. (newscaster [catchphrase:"Good night, and good luck."]; b. April 25, 1908, Pole Cat Creek, NC; d. April 27, 1965, Pawling, NY). *Edward R. Murrow with the News* (1946–59).

Journalistic giant and broadcast catalyst. His calm, terse voice, tinged with an echo of doom, delivered world news at pivotal moments in America's history, especially during the battles and bombings of World War II.

An independent, incisive reporter, Murrow became a commanding figure in his field and the top broadcaster at CBS. At the start of the European war he gathered together a talented group of correspondents — Sevareid, Collingwood, Hottelet — to cover global events. Based in London as CBS news chief, he vividly described the frequent air raids and incendiary fires in that city and reported firsthand air missions over enemy targets. Murrow received the first prize for best radio foreign news reporting by the Overseas Press Club in 1946.

Returning to the United States that year, he became vice president of CBS in news operations. But he soon asked to return as a reporter with an evening news broadcast. On this report Murrow did not allow his sponsor to break into the news with a middle commercial. Only a closing message would be read by the Campbell Soup commercial announcer. To hold the audience, he would then come back with a short "Word for Today" item.

An outstanding graduate of Washington State College, he became assistant director of The Institute of International Education in 1932. Three years later Murrow joined CBS as director of talk and education. In 1937 while attending a meeting of the National Education Association, he received a call from New York asking if he would go to Europe. He later called the move as taking a front row seat for some of the greatest news events of history. When the Germans invaded Austria, he was allowed to broadcast the swift collapse of that country for ten consecutive days to listeners at home.

In the post-war period, Murrow, the highest paid newscaster, earned $112,000 a year. It jumped to nearly $250,000 when he became the only major radio news figure to make a fully successful move to television. His series, *See It Now,* ranked as the best documentary on TV, and his *Person to Person* at-home celebrity interviews attracted large audiences. He left a strong stamp on both media that was duly recognized with the Peabody Award for excellence in 1943, 1949, 1951 and 1954. His 25-year association with CBS ended in 1961 when President John F. Kennedy chose him as director of the U.S. Information Agency. Among his duties was the supervision of Voice of America whose broadcasts he made more plain speaking and straightforward, encompassing both the bad as well as the good.

646. NAGEL, Conrad (actor, emcee; b. March 16, 1897, Keokuk, IA; d. Feb. 24, 1970, New York, NY). *Silver Theatre* (1937–42, 1945–46); *The Passing Parade* (1938); *Radio Reader's Digest* (1942–45).

Conrad Nagel

200 films, beginning with the silent version of *Little Women* in 1919. His Broadway career extended from *Forever After* in 1918 to *The Skin of Our Teeth, State of the Union* and *Goodbye, My Fancy* in the 1940s. His commanding voice introduced broadcast adaptations of plays and short stories on the popular *Silver Theatre* and *Radio Reader's Digest.* He was cmcee for pianist Alec Templeton's 1939 summer series. For a 1949 presentation on *Cavalcade of America,* he portrayed Dr. Oliver Wendell Holmes. In 1949 Nagel became host of *Celebrity Time,* an early ABC-TV game-variety show, and of *Silver Theatre* for the 1949–50 season at CBS-TV.

Nagel served on the national and local board of AFTRA and on the committee that originated the Oscar awards. He made his professional debut playing juvenile leads with the Princess Stock Company in 1914, the year he left Highland Park College.

647. NAISH, J. Carroll (actor; b. Jan. 21, 1900, New York, NY; d. Jan. 24, 1973, La Jolla, CA). *Life with Luigi* (1948–53).

A familiar face in films, speaking various dialects in numerous supporting roles, Naish never became a household name until 1948. CBS cast the dark-haired, swarthy actor as Luigi, an Italian immigrant living in Chicago and looking at his new homeland with wonder and confusion. The comedy-drama brought fame to this native New Yorker of Irish extraction, who on screen had played a sea-raiding pirate, Chinese businessman and French legionnaire, among some 250 parts.

During World War I he enlisted in the Navy and was sent to Europe. He deserted to join a buddy in

J. Carroll Naish (courtesy of Steve Jelf)

the Army, flew missions with the Aviation Section, and finally wound up with a discharge in France. He roamed about the Continent, picking up jobs and a command of eight languages. This al fresco dialectician ended up in Hollywood where he put his years abroad to good use in early talkies.

648. NASH, Clarence (actor; b. Dec. 7, 1904, Watonga, OK; d. Feb. 20, 1985, Burbank, CA). *Mickey Mouse Theatre of the Air* (1938); *Burns and Allen* (1942–43); *Bob Burns Show* (1947).

The Voice of Donald Duck for 50 years. In more than 150 cartoons and several full-length features, beginning in 1933, Nash spoke Donald's lines and those of his nephews, Huey, Dewey and Looey. He carried the role to radio on Walt Disney programs. For Burns and Allen, he played Gracie's pet duck; a pet frog for Bob Burns, and the Rinso White bobwhite on *Amos 'n' Andy.*

Following high school Nash did animal imitations at fairs and on the Chautauqua circuit. While working for Adohr Farms dairy products, he drove a pony and cart for special promotions, performing bird and animal imitations at Los Angeles schools. One day he stopped by the Disney Studio, and tried out his baby-goat voice for "Mary Had a Little Lamb." "Stop!" cried Disney. "That's our talking duck." Six months later Donald Duck made his debut in "The Wise Little Hen." In 1984 "Ducky" Nash celebrated Donald's 50th birthday with a visit to The White House where President Reagan presented him with a plaque commemorating his unique place in family entertainment.

649. NEELY, Henry (emcee [The Old Stager]; b. Nov. 5, 1878, Philadelphia, PA; d. May 1, 1963, Elmhurst, NY). *Philco Theatre of Memories* (1927–30); *Two Seats in the Balcony* (1932–35); *Fitch Bandwagon* (1937–40).

Writer, director, producer and actor as well as emcee. His first network connection was in 1927 with Philco programs. Known as The Old Stager, he presented *Garden of Tomorrow, Home on the Range* and *Eversharp Penman* in the 1930s. He wrote for *Show Boat,* spoke during intermissions of *General Motors Concert,* and acted on *Hilltop House, This Life Is Mine* and *Just Plain Bill.* He travelled the country to emcee big band features on *Fitch Bandwagon.* Neely ended his broadcast activities in 1946. He then became a writer-lecturer on astronomy, chiefly at the Hayden Planetarium with as many as 12 lectures a week. Known as "the dean of New York's star gazers," Neely wrote a number of easily understood books on astronomy.

A newspaperman and author of novels and short stories, he published and edited one of radio's pioneer fan magazines, *Radio in the Home.* In 1921 he was director of WIP Philadelphia, and became the first to syndicate a daily radio column while with the *Public Ledger.*

650. NELSON, Frank (actor; b. May 6, 1911; d. Sept. 12, 1986, Hollywood, CA). *Flywheel, Shyster & Flywheel* (1932–33); *Blondie* (c1945–49); *Life of Riley* (1946); *A Day in the Life of Dennis Day* (1949–51).

Freelance actor on numerous golden-age comedy shows. His best-remembered association, *Jack Benny Program,* began in 1946. He usually made his entrance in a squeal that came out "yeeeeeess?" He was also at the mike with Eddie Cantor, Fanny Brice, Bob Hope, Jimmy Durante, Burns and Allen and other headliners. He played Chester Riley's "conscience" on Bill Bendix's *Life of Riley.* His wife, actress Veola Vonn, often appeared in the same cast. In the 1950s Nelson served as local and national president of AFTRA. During his term he established a pension and welfare fund for fellow performers.

Nelson started out at KOA Denver in 1926; three years later he reached Hollywood where local station dramatic performances led to the networks.

651. NELSON, John (emcee; b. 1915; d. Nov. 3, 1976, Palm Springs, CA). *Bride and Groom* (1945–50); *Know Your NBC's* (1953–54).

Host of Hollywood-based *Bride and Groom.* It generally featured a couple celebrating their golden wedding anniversary, a newly married couple on their honeymoon, and a couple who married on the show in a ceremony performed at the invitation of the sponsor. Nelson delighted participants with a truckload of send-off presents. He held the reins as quizmaster of *Know Your NBC's* and announcer of *Live Like a Millionaire,* which transferred to TV screens with John as emcee.

He attended Gonzaga University. After three years in the Navy, he produced radio and TV shows for the Air Force. A program executive at NBC, Nelson later managed KPLM Palm Springs.

652. NELSON, Ozzie (bandleader, actor [signature song: "Loyal Sons of Rutgers"]; b. March 20, 1907, Jersey City, NJ; d. June 3, 1975, San Fernando Valley, CA). *Bakers Broadcast* (1933–38); *Red Skelton Show* (1941–44); *The Adventures of Ozzie and Harriet* (1944–52).

Leader of an early 1930s orchestra on a circuit of hotel ballrooms, dance halls and school proms. It made extra money to supplement his earnings as a recent Rutgers law school graduate. A capable singer, Nelson caught on with his Rudy Vallee-like approach to a song. He gained popularity when he hired an Iowa beauty queen and vaudeville performer named Harriet Hilliard (1909–94) as his vocalist. Comedian Joe Penner added the band to his show in 1933; two years later Nelson and Hilliard were married.

The Nelsons were worked into skits on the Red Skelton program in the early 1940s, proving to be identifiable comic personalities on their own. These segments led to the creation of their own family *Ad-*

Ozzie & Harriet Nelson

ventures on CBS Sunday evenings. Incidents in the Nelson household, which included young sons David (b. 1936) and Ricky (1940–85), were incorporated in the scripts. "We stay within what I call 'farce believ-ability,'" explained Ozzie in 1947. That year the Intercouncil Committee on Christian Family Life selected the program as one of the ten radio shows best liked by church people for depiction of family life. During the show's first four years the Nelson boys were played by child actors (Tommy Bernard and Henry Blair) but David and Ricky successfully took over the roles themselves. The high-rated series transferred well to television in 1952 where it was produced and directed by Ozzie, and launched the wise-cracking Ricky's rock-and-roll singing career.

653. NESBITT, John (commentator; b. Aug. 23, 1900, Victoria, British Columbia, Canada; d. Aug. 10, 1960, Carmel, CA). *The Passing Parade* (1937–40, 1942–46).

Dramatic storyteller of startling yarns. He took lengthy tales and told them with split-second exactness. His fans and his friends provided him with material for his *Passing Parade.* From 1943–46 it was part of John Charles Thomas's Westinghouse program.

A newspaper reporter and stock actor, Nesbitt started on the air in 1930, and joined NBC in San Francisco in 1933 with his special series. It went on the Red Network in 1937 and was a summer fill-in for *Fibber McGee and Molly* in 1942 and 1943. His *Passing Parade* film shorts for Metro won three Academy Awards.

654. NIESEN, Claire (actress; b. 1920, Phoenix, AZ; d. Oct. 4, 1963, Encino, CA). *The O'Neills* (1939–41); *Backstage Wife* (1945–59); *The Second Mrs. Burton* (1946–c50).

At 16 Niesen had a running part as Peggy in *The O'Neills.* She originated the well-crafted title role of *The Second Mrs. Burton* and played in *Light of the World, Life Can Be Beautiful* and *The Right to Happiness.* But it was as Iowa girl Mary Noble (*Backstage Wife*) that she fought for 14 years to keep her matinee-idol husband's love amid the distractions of Broadway.

655. NIESEN, Gertrude (singer [signature song: "I Wanna Get Married"]; b. July 3, 1914, mid-Atlantic Ocean; d. March 27, 1975, Los Angeles, CA). *Songs by Gertrude Niesen* (1932–33); *Good News of 1939* (1939).

Torch singer, once described as having a lush, cello-like voice "with the rhythm of the surf pounding a cliff." (Niesen said tennis and swimming were her favorite sports because they were rhythmic.) Imitations of Lyda Roberti's "Sweet and Hot," Polish accent and all, at parties, led to four-a-day stints in New Jersey, then better billings in New York theatres and nightclubs.

In 1932 CBS hired her to sing on a sustaining program. That year Rudy Vallee's *Fleischmann Hour* began to feature Niesen, who also appeared in *The Ziegfeld Follies of 1936* with Bob Hope and Fanny Brice. Following several dismal films, she ventured to Paris and London for club and stage bookings. In 1939 she re-entered radio with *Good News* and guest spots for Alec Templeton, Colonel Stoopnagle and Curt Massey. Her Broadway role as a burlesque queen in the musical comedy *Follow the Girls* ran for more than 800 performances in the mid-40s.

Niesen was born prematurely aboard ship in 1914. Her parents were on a belated honeymoon trip to Europe. When talk of war spread across the Continent, they started to hurry home to Brooklyn, believing their baby was still two months off.

656. NILES, Ken (announcer; b. Dec. 9, 1906, Livingston, MT; d. Oct. 31, 1988, Santa Monica, CA). *Hollywood Hotel* (1934–38); *Rudy Vallee Show* (1946–47); *Take It or Leave It* (1947–48); *A Date with Judy* (1947–49).

An early announcer and producer for the Don Lee network, he began broadcasting in the late 1920s at KJR Seattle. His 1928 show, *Theatre of the Mind,* was one of the first to present original dramas on the West Coast. For CBS he was host and producer, with Louella Parsons, of *Hollywood Hotel.* Based in the film capital, he introduced the radio shows of many stars: Bing Crosby, Danny Kaye, Edward G. Robinson, William Bendix, Hattie McDaniel, Abbott and Costello. His brother, Wendell Niles, was also a leading announcer.

Wendell Niles (courtesy of Steve Jelf)

657. NILES, Wendell (announcer; b. Dec. 29, 1904, Twin Valley, MN; d. March 28, 1994, Toluca Lake, CA). *Bob Hope Show* (1943–48); *The Man Called X* (1946–48); *Hollywood Star Playhouse* (1952–53).

West Coast free-lance announcer. Starting in 1935 he joined Burns and Allen. Assignments followed with Bergen and McCarthy, Tommy Dorsey, Al Pearce and Bob Hope. He was heard on many Hollywood TV shows. As a character actor, he appeared in more than 30 films, including *Knute Rockne, All American* in 1940. His younger brother was announcer Ken Niles.

A lightweight boxing champion of Montana and aeronautics school instructor, he first appeared on the air as an orchestra leader in Seattle in 1923.

658. NILSSON, Norma Jean (actress; b. Jan. 1, 1938, Hollywood, CA). *Blondie* (1947–48); *Father Knows Best* (1949–52).

Child actress beginning at age five with Arch Oboler. She played Cookie on *Blondie* and appeared with Jack Carson for several seasons. Her role as pre-teen Kathy Anderson was pivotal on many episodes of *Father Knows Best.* In the 1950s Nilsson worked on some 300 shows of the TV version of *Our Miss Brooks.* She made her film debut in the 1945 MGM musical *Anchors Aweigh.*

659. NOBLE, Ray (bandleader, composer [signature song: "The Very Thought of You"]; b. Dec. 19, 1907, Brighton, England; d. April 3, 1978, Lon-

Ray Noble

don, England). *The Coty Program* (1935); *Burns and Allen* (1937–40); *Chase & Sanborn Hour* (1941–48).

British-born Noble had built up such a following in the United States through his Victor recordings that he and vocalist Al Bowlly came to New York in early 1935. With the help of Glenn Miller, he put together an all-star unit that opened in the Rainbow Room. Edgar Bergen was part of the show. Noble later conducted the orchestra for Bergen's program throughout the 1940s, and served as a foil for Charlie McCarthy and Mortimer Snerd. He also played for the Alec Templeton and Burns and Allen shows, and gained a measure of approval as a comedian. His first American broadcasts were sponsored by Coty Perfumes on Wednesdays, and NBC aired his sparkling and well-textured dance music four other nights as a remote from the Rainbow Room atop the RCA building.

At 19 Noble won an arrangers competition sponsored by the English music publication *The Melody Maker.* At 21 he was a staff arranger for the British Broadcasting Corporation. In 1929 he became musical advisor for His Master's Voice records, and in that capacity conducted its house band, billed as the Mayfair Orchestra. Among his most successful compositions is the enduring "Goodnight Sweetheart."

660. NOLAN, Jeanette (actress; b. Dec. 30, 1911, Los Angeles, CA). *Young Dr. Malone* (1939–40); *Cavalcade of America* (1940–41); *One Man's Family* (1947–50); *The Great Gildersleeve* (1949–52).

One of the most successful supporting cast members on radio, she was frequently heard on *Manhattan*

at Midnight, Big Sister, The Railroad Hour,* and *Lux Radio Theatre.* Her role as Nicolette Moore, a governess at Jack Barbour's house, on *One Man's Family* ran for several seasons. On *Cavalcade of America,* she once played Ann Rutledge to husband John McIntire's Abe Lincoln. Together the McIntires played on *Crime Doctor, Tarzan, Frontier Gentleman* and *This Is My Best.* They worked on the TV western, *The Virginian,* in the 1960s.

On *March of Time* Nolan portrayed Eleanor Roosevelt, Queen Marie of Roumania and the Duchess of Windsor. She appeared in Orson Welles' film version of *Macbeth.*

The McIntires frequently retreated for months each year to a log cabin on their 640-acre ranch in the Yaak Valley of Montana.

661. NORMAN, Lucille (singer; b. June 15, 1929, Lincoln, NE). *Names of Tomorrow* (1946–47); *The Time, the Place and the Tune* (1947); *Railroad Hour* (1950–54); *Al Goodman's Musical Album* (1952–53).

Co-star with Gordon MacRae on *Railroad Hour* musical presentations. Initially a guest in the role of Julie for "Showboat" in October 1949, she soon appeared weekly throughout much of 1950 in such familiar offerings as "The Red Mill," "The Pink Lady" and "H.M.S. Pinafore." MacRae hoped to sing on screen with the photogenic soprano but her few movie parts were with others and generally undistinguished.

In early 1945 Norman sang on a weekly regional show over KNX and for Al Goodman at NBC, as well as in concert halls doing light opera. As a young woman she studied at the Cincinnati Conservatory of Music and won a talent contest on a local program. Shortly after a performance at age 14 with the Columbus Symphony, she was selected for *The Met Opera Auditions of the Air.* The Sunday afternoon broadcast for her coast-to-coast debut encountered unexpected and earthshaking interruptions. The date was December 7, 1941 — and the Japanese had just attacked Pearl Harbor.

662. NOVIS, Donald (singer; b. March 3, 1906, Hastings, England; d. July 23, 1966, Norwalk, CA). *Colgate House Party* (1934); *Fibber McGee and Molly* (1938–39).

A lyric tenor, Novis won the Atwater Kent national radio auditions in 1928 and was designated "America's most promising youthful vocalist." But the coveted prize failed to open doors to the musical stage or broadcast studios. During the next two years the one-time professional boxer sang only three concerts, did occasional local programs near his Pasadena home, and received five dollars a week as church soloist.

In 1930 the tenor got a break: a tryout at the Cocoanut Grove in Los Angeles that led to an 18-month engagement. A turning point, it led to an NBC contract for three or four concert broadcasts a week

Freddy Martin, Donald Novis

in New York where in 1932 he also sang "Trees" for a segment in the first of the "Big Broadcast" films. Novis appeared in Billy Rose's *Jumbo* at New York's Hippodrome and on the 1935 radio series spinoff. He retired in 1963 after 11,000 appearances at Disneyland's Golden Horseshoe, then served as recreation director in Newport Beach.

663. OAKIE, Jack (actor, comedian; b. Nov. 12, 1903, Sedalia, MO; d. Jan. 23, 1978, Northridge, CA). *Jack Oakie's College* (1936–38).

Screen favorite with leads in mid-30s campus musical comedies (*College Humor, College Rhythm*). He

Walter O'Keefe

proved an ideal host for a variety show built around a collegiate theme. Sponsored by Camel Cigarettes, his Hollywood-based series added George Stoll's orchestra and Benny Goodman's swing band, at that point the most popular new dance sensation among undergraduates. Comedians and singers from nearby movie studios — including 13-year-old Judy Garland and humorist Robert Benchley — made guest appearances as did special college-recruited talent.

Oakie had left a job as a Wall Street clerk to join a Broadway chorus, then vaudeville. With the advent of "talkies," his facility with comic dialogue and song lyrics made him one of the busiest stars on sound stages. (He averaged five pictures a year from 1929 to 1937). Because he was making movies all day, *Oakie College* rehearsed as well as aired at night. After two seasons as host of the weekly one-hour broadcast, the versatile performer limited his radio work to guest appearances. He was part of Paramount's *Big Broadcast of 1936*.

664. O'BRIEN, Edmond (actor; b. Sept. 10, 1915, Brooklyn, NY; d. May 9, 1985, Inglewood, CA). *Mrs. Wiggs of the Cabbage Patch* (1936–38); *Betty and Bob* (1939–40); *Yours Truly, Johnny Dollar* (1950–52).

Leading man in many film-noir productions of the 1940s. O'Brien impressed movie audiences with roles in *The Killers, D.O.A.* and *White Heat*. As the Hollywood press agent in *Barefoot Contessa,* he won the 1955 best supporting-actor Oscar and a nomination for his portrayal of an aging, alcoholic senator in *Seven Days in May.*

A student at Fordham and the Neighborhood Playhouse, he picked up the recurrent role of Gregory on *Mrs. Wiggs* at NBC. O'Brien joined Orson Welles' Mercury Players in 1937 for its modern-dress stage version of *Julius Caesar*. In the 1950s he starred as Johnny Dollar and in dramas aired by *Screen Directors' Playhouse, Hollywood Star Theatre* and *Lux Radio Theatre*. In 1939 he had entered films at Fox, playing the poet Gringoire in *The Hunchback of Notre Dame.* O'Brien joined the Army Air Force and appeared in its 1943 Broadway show *Winged Victory* and the screen version.

665. O'KEEFE, Walter (comedian, emcee; b. Aug. 18, 1900, Hartford, CT; d. June 26, 1983, Torrance, CA). *Camel Caravan* (1934–36); *Town Hall*

Tonight (1937); *Battle of the Sexes* (1942–43); *Double or Nothing* (1947–53); *Monitor* (1957–59).

Gifted comedian, quizmaster, commentator, emcee, columnist, songwriter and singer. For nearly 70 years O'Keefe commanded the spotlight, with radio a major arena. Guest shots began in the mid-1920s, but he did not land a regular series until he replaced an ill Walter Winchell on *The Magic Carpet*. Next, he starred for Nestle with Don Bestor's orchestra, then on *Camel Caravan* with Glen Gray and the Casa Loma Orchestra. After filling in for Fred Allen and replacing Fred Astaire, he had a show with Mary Martin in 1939. Playing against the first coast-to-coast telephone giveaway, *Pot 'o Gold,* it never found an audience.

After a stint on *Battle of the Sexes* and wartime camp tours, Walter took over the *Breakfast Club* in Chicago for vacationing Don McNeill. Here he found his natural metier. His agent lined up a quiz show, *Double or Nothing,* a high-rated daytime contest that provided a six-year run.

After prep school in England, Walter enrolled at Notre Dame, where he boarded with football coach Knute Rockne. O'Keefe traveled with Rockne on lecture dates to provide comedy relief, but his undergrad days were soon interrupted by service in the Marines.

A monologuist, he performed in vaudeville, speakeasies and revues, and often featured his hit song "I Wanna Dance Wit' Da Guy What Brung Me" and his widely imitated version of "The Man on the Flying Trapeze." In 1937 his humor column ran in daily newspaper syndication. In 1940 he headed up the radio, stage and screen division of Wendell Wilkie's presidential campaign.

His greatest achievement, he admitted in 1982, was overcoming alcoholism. "When I began drinking in the morning, I realized something was drastically wrong. Then, I went to see the movie *The Lost Weekend,* and immediately saw myself. It was the beginning of my long recovery."

666. OLSEN, George (bandleader [signature song: "Beyond the Blue Horizon"]; b. March 18, 1893, Portland, OR; d. March 18, 1971, Paramus, NJ). *Lucky Strike Orchestra* (1932–33); *Jack Benny Program* (1932); *Royal Gelatine Revue* (1933); *Royal Crown Revue* (1938).

His band reflected the spirit of popular music in the 1920s and early '30s. It featured a soft, close harmony

trio and novelty effects — overall, a balanced and inviting musical aggregation. Its Victor discs included the top sellers "Who," "Varsity Drag" and "Beyond the Blue Horizon" (with train whistle and chugging sounds).

Olsen conducted several numbers on the 1926 Inaugural of NBC, and when B. A. Rolfe left the Lucky Strike dance series, he took over part of the programs. Olsen appeared in a string of musicals (*Kid Boots, Good News*) and in hotel ballrooms (Edgewater Beach, Claridge). He conducted for Jack Benny for a season.

A drummer, Olsen stayed in the business for 30 years, then entered the restaurant field in 1951. His first wife was Ethel Shutta, a popular singer.

667. OLSEN, Johnny (emcee, announcer; b. c1910, Windom, MN; d. Oct. 12, 1985, Santa Monica, CA). *Ladies Be Seated* (1944–49); *Get Rich Quick* (1948); *Whiz Quiz* (1948).

In 1944 Olsen came to New York as a staff announcer at ABC, and added duties as host of audience-participation shows. Emcee of *Ladies Be Seated,* he charmed grandmothers, mothers and assorted children while putting them through their paces.

He started as the Buttermilk Kid on radio in Madison, Wisconsin, then went to KGDA Mitchell, South Dakota, home of the Corn Palace, to manage, sell, announce and sing — and preach a morning religious service. His next move — to WTMJ Milwaukee as chief announcer — led to Hollywood for a year. Back in Milwaukee, he aired his *Rumpus Room.* At ABC Olsen warmed up and announced *Swingshift Frolics, On Stage Everybody* and *True or False.* In dealing with contestants on radio and television for over 40 years, he broke a rib, an arm and an ankle (the last injury placed him in a wheelchair from where he emceed).

Johnny Olsen, Janice Gilbert, Bert Parks (courtesy of Temple University Libraries Photojournalism Collection)

Olsen's *Ladies Be Seated* was one of the first game shows in television, broadcasting weekly from WRGB Schenectady in 1945 when that city encompassed some 300 sets. By 1950 his weekly schedule read, as follows: *Ladies Be Seated, Get Together* and *What's My Name,* ABC; *Prince Charming,* Mutual; *Fun for the Money,* ABC-TV; *Rumpus Room,* WABD-TV; *Luncheon Club,* WMGM. His wife Penny Olsen appeared on a number of these programs. Olsen (a.k.a. Olson) ended his long career as the buoyant "Come on down" TV announcer on *The Price Is Right.*

668. ORMANDY, Eugene (conductor; b. Nov. 18, 1899, Budapest, Hungary; d. March 12, 1985, Philadelphia, PA). *Roxy's Gang* (1922–27); *Philadelphia Orchestra* (1937–38).

Ormandy came to the United States in 1921 for a concert tour that did not materialize. The almost penniless musician took his first American job as violinist in the orchestra of the Capitol Theatre, New York's leading motion picture house. He was quickly made concertmaster, then principal conductor. As Jeno Blau his real name he acquired a measure of fame as a member of Roxy's Gang, playing readily recognized melodies on his violin. (In later years as musical director of the prestigious Philadelphia Orchestra, he did not wish to be reminded of his fledgling days as an off-the-cuff backstage broadcaster.) He acquired an extensive repertoire at the Capitol where concert manager Arthur Judson heard him and took the fast-study maestro under his wing. Engagements with the New York Philharmonic and Philadelphia Orchestra followed as did concerts over CBS.

From 1931 to 1935 he led the Minneapolis Symphony which he transformed into an ensemble commanding wide respect. From there he went to Philadelphia as co-conductor with soon-to-retire Leopold Stokowski. In 1938 he assumed the post of music director. He maintained "the Philadelphia sound" lush, sonorous, homogeneous — during a 44-year stewardship that took his orchestra on many U.S. and international tours and into millions of homes via radio and recordings.

669. ORTEGA, Santos (actor; b. 1906, New York, NY; d. April 10, 1976, Fort Lauderdale, FL). *Myrt and Marge* (1939–42); *The Man I Married* (1939–42); *Light of the World* (1941–42); *Mr. & Mrs. North* (1942–43); *Ellery Queen* (1942–44).

Skilled in handling a great variety of accents, he never lacked roles in dramatic serials and thrillers. In his first series *Blackstone Plantation,* he played a part calling for a Spanish accent. He was much in demand for detective roles. He was the original Inspector Queen in *Ellery Queen,* and the first Perry Mason and the first Nero Wolfe. Ortega also portrayed Charlie Chan and Bulldog Drummond, and acted in *Boston Blackie.* He got his show business start at 17 singing at New York's Hippodrome Theatre. When television brought soaps to daytime viewers, he created the character Grandpa Hughes in *As the World Turns* in 1956.

Ortega compared the two mediums from the standpoint of the range and number of roles. He popped up on *Myrt and Marge,* for example, in various dialect parts which disguised his normal voice. "When I portrayed Jack Arnold on that show," he explained, "I was shot in the back and killed. Later on at the trial, it was quite simple for me to play the role of the stage doorman who witnessed the murder. It would, of course, be impossible on TV for me to give testimony on my own slaying."

670. OSBORNE, Will (bandleader, singer [signature song: "The Gentleman Awaits"]; b. Nov. 25, 1905, Toronto, Canada; d. Oct. 22, 1981, Santa Monica, CA). *Abbott and Costello Show* (1945).

Crooner-bandleader contemporary of Vallee, Osborne enjoyed frequent radio exposure yet never attained the idolized status of his fierce musical rival. A drummer, he set out by foot and thumb for Broadway from Canada, and by 1924 had organized his own four-piece unit, first broadcasting over WMCA the following year. By 1930 CBS scheduled seven programs a week from the Park Central Hotel; locally, several were sponsored by Herbert's Blue-White Diamonds, an early Vallee backer. He maintained his swing-oriented band into the 1940s and appeared with Abbott and Costello.

Composer of "Beside an Open Fireplace" and "Pompton Turnpike," he later became a house bandleader in Las Vegas and Lake Tahoe, and a talent agent.

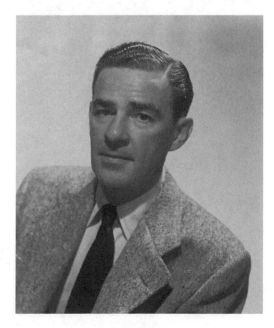

Will Osborne

671. OWEN, Ethel (actress; b. March 30, 1892; d. Dec. 28, 1990). *Valiant Lady* (1939–40); *The Man I Married* (1940–41); *Helpmate* (1941–44).

Owen claimed 13 different radio voices — for women of all ages and in every station of life. "I have a mental picture of every character. I know in my mind just how she looks, feels and acts," she said in 1942. "The voice just comes naturally." Her voices ranged from Mrs. Stanton Grey on *Houseboat Hannah* and Aunt Matt of *The Man I Married* to Carrie, the Emersons' maid on *Helpmate,* and Beverly Boulevard of the *Jackie Gleason-Les Tremayne Show.*

A native of Racine and a student at Northwestern from 1911–12, she started out at WTMJ Milwaukee in dramatic shows, plus *Morning Melodies* with singer-actor Dennis Morgan. In Chicago she joined *First Nighter* and *Fibber McGee and Molly.* On her first network soap, *Helen Trent,* Owen rehearsed with the cast, thinking it was a run-through of the whole show. It actually was that day's broadcast — a fact she only discovered at the sign-off. In the 1940s she combined radio with Broadway — with stage roles in *Three's a Family* and the 1946 revival of *Show Boat* (as Parthy Ann).

672. OWENS, Harry (bandleader [signature song: "Sweet Leilani"]; b. April 18, 1902, O'Neill,

Harry Owens

NE; d. Dec. 12, 1986, Eugene, OR). *Hawaii Calls* (1935–41, 1945–49).

Owens and his Royal Hawaiians fashioned a setting of hula skirts and trade winds by tropical island music from Waikiki Beach's famous Royal Hawaiian Hotel. A Midwesterner, he had played trumpet in Los Angeles bands before starting his own in the mid-1920s. In 1933 Owens was asked to organize a hotel orchestra at the Royal Hawaiian, combining island sounds with mainland fox trots. So successful was he that his four-month contract was continued on for seven years. Beginning in 1935 he appeared on a short-wave transmission of *Hawaii Calls* for the West Coast.

Owens toured the states on a yearly basis. In late 1941, as he prepared to return to Honolulu, Pearl Harbor was bombed, ending his association with the Royal Hawaiian for the duration. He returned in 1945, and began a coast-to-coast version of his pre-war series. He brought his entertainers to television on the West Coast in 1949. Later he operated a tour agency and music publishing firm. He wrote "Sweet Leilani" for his daughter the day she was born in 1934. Some 20 million recordings of the song, including the very popular Bing Crosby version, have been sold.

673. PAAR, Jack (comedian; b. May 1, 1918, Canton, OH). *The Jack Paar Show* (1947); *Take It or Leave It* (1950–52).

Paar's frequent and general undistinguished forays into radio were readily forgotten in the wake of his remarkable acclaim as host of TV's *Tonight* show. A hardworking announcer at a half-dozen Midwest stations in the late 1930s, he served as a noncombatant soldier, entertaining troops in the South Pacific for two years. His verbal improvisation got him many auditions and in 1947, the coveted spot as summer replacement for Jack Benny. But it only led to a 13-week stint at ABC that fall. He built an uncertain reputation as temporary fill-in for Benny, Don McNeill and Arthur Godfrey. He fared better as quizmaster with the long-established $64 Question, lasting beyond the summer into several half seasons.

Early television provided many opportunities, from morning to prime time. But Paar failed to find an audience until 1957 and *Tonight.* His unpredictability, whimsical humor, and knack for choosing guests defined late-night TV viewing for the country.

674. PADGETT, Pat (comedian; b. Dec. 29, 1898, Atlanta, GA; d. Feb. 6, 1990, Fort Myers, FL). *Friendship Village* (1932); *Show Boat* (1932–37); *Chesterfield Supper Club* (1945).

Padgett ran away from Georgia Military School to join a minstrel troupe. He entered many amateur nights before jobs in vaudeville provided a living. In 1926 he met up with Pick Malone to become half of Pick and Pat. They also worked as Molasses 'n' January, a blackface act. *Show Boat* featured their comedy on many broadcast "voyages" in the '30s.

675. PAGE, Gale (actress; b. July 23, 1910, Spokane, WA; d. Jan. 8, 1983). *Climalene Carnival* (1934–36); *Hollywood Playhouse* (1939–40); *Today's Children* (1946–47).

Film actress-singer, Page was regularly featured on *Hollywood Playhouse* when her screen career flourished at Warner Bros. For that series she worked in such recreations of "Lost Horizon" and "The Man from Yesterday." She broke into radio via a breakfast show in Spokane. In 1933 she joined KYW Chicago and soon moved to NBC and broadcasts with Fibber McGee and Don McNeill. In the late '40s she played the lead in *Story of Holly Sloan,* a serial about a young radio singer. It provided Page an opportunity to display her solid vocal talent. As a Warner contractee she portrayed the wife of Knute Rockne in his film bio, with Pat O'Brien and Ronald Reagan.

676. PAIGE, Raymond (conductor; b. May 18, 1900, Wausau, WI; d. Aug. 7, 1965, Larchmont, NY). *Hollywood Hotel* (1934–38); *Musical Americana* (1940–41); *Stage Door Canteen* (1942–45); *Salute to Youth* (1943–44).

Leader of large, versatile radio orchestras, including the 99-man aggregation for *99 Men and a Girl* (Hildegarde) and the 100-piece symphony for *Musical Americana.* Both encompassed some 24 violin players. He presented many works of American composers, and often introduced tunes from Disney films.

His first outstanding program was *California Melodies* which spotlighted Bing Crosby and the Boswell Sisters. Next came *Hollywood Hotel,* an all-star variety show from the film capital. Settling in New York, he contributed to a string of wartime morale boosters: *Salute to Youth, Star-Spangled Vaudeville* and *Stage Door Canteen.* He led the *Kraft Music Hall* orchestra during the summer of 1945. Following a series for RCA Victor, he became music director of Radio City Music Hall and its 60-man symphony in 1950, and continued until his death 15 years later.

Reared in Los Angeles, he studied the violin and played in local theatre pits for silent pictures. He took over as conductor at the Paramount Theatre but lost the job when talkies came along. Paramount studios hired him as a violinist. One day in 1930 a fellow violinist asked him to substitute on a broadcast at KHJ. When Don Lee, owner of a 13-station chain, heard that the ex-conductor was in the studio, he offered Paige a job as head of the network's music department. During his 45-year career, he led the Los Angeles Philharmonic, Pittsburgh Symphony, Hollywood Bowl Orchestra and NBC Symphony.

677. PALMER, Effie (actress; b. June 20, c1890, nr. Albany, NY; d. Aug. 19, 1942, New York, NY). *The Road of Life* (1937–38); *Orphans of Divorce* (1939–42); *This Small Town* (1940–41).

Frank Parker

Her radio work took root from an appearance at New York's Wanamaker store station in 1922. Twenty years later, at the time of her death, this broadcast veteran was still at the mike, specializing in mother roles in soaps. She played the feminine title role on *Mother and Dad,* Ma Parker on *Seth Parker* and Mother Nora on *Orphans of Divorce.* Palmer, described as an Albany "farm girl," attended the School of English Speech and Expression in Boston and worked in stock. Her broadcasts numbered over 1,000 on the likes of *Just Plain Bill, March of Time, Soconyland Sketches* and *The O'Neills.*

678. PARKER, Frank (singer; b. April 29, 1906, New York, NY*). *A & P Gypsies* (1927–35); *Jack Benny Program* (1934–35); *Frank Parker Show* (1936, 1947); *Paul Whiteman's Musical Varieties* (1936–37); *American Album of Familiar Music* (1945–46); *Arthur Godfrey Time* (1950–56).

A conservatory-trained voice, he spotted the tremendous future of radio and edged off the musical comedy stage. In 1926 Parker eagerly filled in for a tenor with Hope Hampton on an Eveready program. That break led to a quartet — and taking incidental solos — with the A & P Gypsies. He augmented his schedule by joining the Revelers quartet on Jessica Dragonette's *Cities Service Concert.* In 1934 he moved to featured billing on *Gulf Headliners* and *Jack Benny Program.* When Benny and his troupe headed for Hol-

Another source gives 1903.

lywood, the photogenic Parker picked up a few movie roles, then returned East for a year's run with Paul Whiteman.

In 1936 he also had his own NBC series with Red Nichols and a young Bob Hope who made an impression as comic relief. Next came a run as vocalist for *Burns and Allen,* and in 1941, top billing on *Golden Treasury of Song* at CBS. The cheerful tenor made numerous guest appearances, then at age 39 joined the Merchant Marines. But within a year he was subbing for Thomas L. Thomas on *Manhattan-Merry-Go-Round.* He next replaced Frank Munn on *American Album,* and moved on to his own transcribed series with Paul Baron's orchestra.

When the trend turned to radio baritones, the brush off was compounded by a costly divorce, a disastrous business venture and a failed club act. Desperate to work, he asked Arthur Godfrey for a behind-the-scenes job. But Godfrey put him on stage — an appearance that began a six-year run on Arthur's various CBS radio and TV shows. A dozen years before, Godfrey, then on a local Washington outlet, boosted Parker's appearance as Alfredo in the Chicago Opera production of *La Traviata.* And when Arthur came to New York in 1940 to break into a network lineup, Parker introduced him to the right people. He never forgot the favor. Parker's re-discovery — especially underscored by his frequent duets with Marion Marlowe — added another decade to his career.

679. PARKS, Bert (emcee, announcer; b. Dec. 30, 1914, Atlanta, GA; d. Feb. 2, 1992, La Jolla, CA). *Camel Caravan* (1938–42); *Break the Bank* (1945–50); *Stop the Music!* (1948–52); *Double or Nothing* (1953).

Full of pep and bounce, Parks rode the crest of the postwar quiz wave. He had served a long apprenticeship as announcer, chiefly at CBS in the 1930s. Back from Army service, he landed the job of host on a new series called *Break the Bank.* A supercharged emcee with a winning smile, he had a great interest in people — at least on stage — and in liking to entertain them and in making them like him. When he was chosen to emcee another giveaway, *Stop The Music!* he became the leading audience-participation showman on radio. Both made a happy transition to television, widening his fame as an entertainer-quizmaster. He once boasted, "I created a whole era. I started the pattern . . . everything was the MC. When you did a quiz, there was no support. Just you and those questions."

When a contestant hesitated with an answer, Bert acted concerned, even sad. His gyrations, noted *The New York Times,* were terpsichorean. "He rolls his eyes, his feet stamp rhythmically, he anxiously eyes the clock, gently whispers: 'Think hard.'"

His career began at age 16 when he picked up a job as singer on Atlanta's WGST. He also was staff announcer, and two years later went to CBS at $50 a week. Young Parks was hired by Eddie Cantor as an-

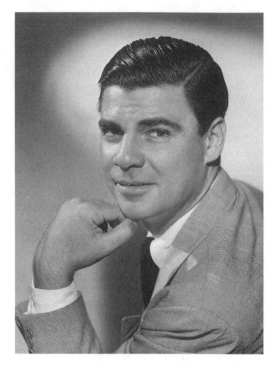

Bert Parks

nouncer and vocalist. He also appeared as emcee with Benny Goodman and Xavier Cugat, and for *Camel Caravan.*

A free-lance performer, Parks appeared on every network and New York flagship station and beyond to Newark's WAAT where he started *Second Honeymoon* in 1947. His frenetically folksy manner carried many weak game formats to good ratings. By the 1950s he was on 12 shows a week in radio and television. His broadcasts included *Bert Parks Bandstand,* a daily radio show. He became familiar to millions as the perennial emcee of the Miss America Beauty Pageant and serenader of the annual winner with his musical trademark, "There She Is."

680. PARKYAKARKUS, (Harry Einstein) (comedian; b. May 6, 1908, Boston, MA; d. Nov. 24, 1958, Beverly Hills, CA). *Eddie Cantor Show* (1935–37); *Al Jolson Show* (1937–38); *Meet Me at Parky's* (1945–47).

His Greek-inspired Parkyakarkus on the *Eddie Cantor Show* was one of the more entertaining dialect comedians of the 1930s. A character of twisted verbiage and low-drawer humor, he was also heard with Jimmy Durante and Al Jolson. His popularity led to stardom on his own series. But it never took him into television along with his contemporaries. He died of a heart attack after finishing a humorous monologue at a Friars Club banquet attended by 1,200 show business figures.

Louella Parsons, Dick Powell, Frances Langford, Raymond Paige

681. PARSONS, Louella (commentator; b. Aug. 6, 1881, Freeport, IL*; d. Dec. 9, 1972, Santa Monica, CA). *Hollywood Hotel* (1934–38); *Louella Parsons* (1945–51).

Pioneer movie gossip columnist who broadcast the news of Hollywood at the peak of its studio-dominated era. As a Hearst syndicated writer with much feared power and a commanding position, she came to radio as the centerpiece of *Hollywood Hotel.* The CBS variety program — one of the first from the West Coast — attracted the reigning stars who found a top-rated platform to perform a brief sketch and talk about their latest picture. They received no fees for their work. By 1938 its wide popularity spun off a movie extravaganza with the hit tune "Hurray for Hollywood."

The shrewd, matronly chronicler enthralled readers and listeners. Her folksy 15-minute Sunday night broadcast at ABC reported "exclusives" from the glamorous make-believe land of the silver screen. Parsons gathered items from her active participation in parties and premieres, and from the help of five staff associates and countless press agents.

682. PASTERNACK, Josef (conductor; b. July 1, 1881, Czenstachowa, Poland; d. April 29, 1940, Chicago, IL). *Atwater Kent Concert* (1930–31); *Carnation Contented Hour* (1937–40).

Conservatory-trained conductor-viola player. Pasternack directed the Metropolitan Opera Orchestra, Boston Symphony and Philadelphia Orchestra while concentrating on radio in the 1930s. An early series, the *Hoffman Program,* featured Nelson Eddy and the

*Some sources give 1890 and 1893.

Philadelphia Grand Opera Company.

At age ten, he began music studies in Warsaw and learned to play every orchestral instrument except the harp. Toscanini urged him to become a conductor. He began at the Bremen Opera. Later he conducted the Boston Pops, and was chief musical director of Victor Records. He died while rehearsing for the *Contented Hour* at NBC Chicago studios in 1940.

683. PAUL, Les (guitarist; b. June 9, 1915, Waukesha, WI). *Fred Waring Show* (1936–41); *Drene Show* (1944–45).

Instrumental combo leader and guitar-playing partner of singer-guitarist Mary Ford. Les, an electronics whiz, built special guitars and recording equipment that enhanced multitrack vocals and echo chamber effects. With Ford to whom he was married from 1949 to 1964, he sold millions of Capitol discs of their unique renditions of "Vaya Con Dios," "How High the Moon" and "The World is Waiting for the Sunrise." The influential duo performed on mid-50s radio with Dave Garroway and Bob and Ray, and on a five-minute MBS program 12 times weekly.

In his teens Paul had had a show as "Rhubarb Red" over WHAD Milwaukee. He played guitar and harmonica at WRJN Racine, KMOX St. Louis and WIND Chicago. He appeared on NBC's *National Barn Dance* and with Ben Bernie over CBS. In 1936 his combo — rhythm guitar, electronic guitar, bass fiddle, piano — caught the ear of Fred Waring. As featured Pennsylvanians for five years, they learned precision timing and showmanship, Waring-style.

During the last years of World War II, Les served in the Army, chiefly waxing ETs for overseas, then backed Bing Crosby on radio and recordings and enjoyed a run on Rudy Vallee's show. Les set up a studio workshop in his garage. His recording method breakthroughs were interrupted in 1948 by serious injuries from an auto accident. His return to the microphone signaled the beginning of major musical accomplishments and international acclaim.

684. PAYNE, Virginia (actress; b. June 19, 1910, Cincinnati, OH; d. Feb. 10, 1977, Cincinnati, OH). *Ma Perkins* (1933–60); *First Nighter* (1936–38); *The Carters of Elm Street* (1939–40); *Brighter Day* (1952).

By dispensing sage and optimistic advice as "Oxydol's own Ma Perkins" for 27 years, Payne built a loyal audience of 18 million at the soap opera's peak. For many years the true identity of Ma Perkins remained an industry secret. In response to her fans' demands, CBS reluctantly put the young blond actress in a gray wig, steel-rimmed glasses, low-heeled Oxfords and dowdy dresses, and sent her out to make public appearances. At the beginning of the series at WLW in 1933, she successfully had changed the timbre of her voice to that of a mature and cheerful woman. And apparently she never missed a performance of the Proctor and Gamble program—one of radio's longest-running serials.

Apart from the microphone, Payne became interested in a plan for organizing radio performers, and joined with 15 others in the founding of a union that became known as the American Federation of Radio Artists. She became a member of the AFRA national board in 1940, and also took part in negotiating contracts with the networks to encompass television performers as well as radio artists. For the last 16 years of her life she performed in the legitimate theatre, including a Broadway musical debut in 1964 in *Fade Out-Fade In* with Carol Burnett.

685. PEABODY, Eddie (banjoist [The Banjo King]; b. Feb. 19, 1902, Reading, MA; d. Nov. 7, 1970, Covington, KY). *National Barn Dance* (1940–46).

Best known and most acclaimed banjoist of his time. An energetic showman, he helped to popularize playing the banjo with the use of a soft plectrum, rather than the fingers. Throughout the 1930s, he was a frequent soloist on *Fleischmann Hour* and *Show Boat,* and for a time NBC featured him as a late-night interlude, and with Richard Himber's Orchestra. He soon became a regular on *National Barn Dance.*

Stationed at the Great Lakes Training Center during World War II, Lt. Cmdr. Peabody managed to return to the program a dozen times while in uniform and between a tour to entertain troops in the Pacific.

A talented musician, he had performed in vaudeville on violin and guitar but the banjo drew the most audience response. An announcer in a slip of the tongue once introduced his act: "And now ladies and gentlemen, Eddie Playbody will pee for you!"

686. PEALE, Norman Vincent (preacher; b. May 31, 1898, Bowersville, OH; d. Dec. 24, 1993, Pawling, NY). *The Art of Living* (1931–60).

Influential religious leader and popular preacher-writer. Not long after he became pastor of Marble Collegiate Church in New York, he began appearing weekly on *The Art of Living,* sponsored by the National Council of Churches (and briefly in 1935 by Doeskin Products) and heard by an estimated five million people on the NBC network. His messages stressed applied Christianity to help one tap reservoirs of power within themselves and how religion could combat problems. He also answered questions sent in by listeners.

His best-seller, *The Power of Positive Thinking,* published in 1952, placed him in the forefront of American clergymen and predated the late 20th-century flood of self-help books and movements.

His many inspirational books and *Guideposts* spiritual magazine led to appearances as guest expert on family problems on *For Better Living* in the 1950s. He and his wife also appeared on the weekly TV program *What's Your Trouble?* from 1952 to 1968.

A graduate of Ohio Wesleyan and Boston University School of Theology, he had spent a year as a newspaper reporter to earn money. Peale served parishes in Rhode Island and Brooklyn and from 1927 to 1932, the University Church in Syracuse, where he became one of the first clergymen in the country to preach on his own radio program.

687. PEARCE, Al (comedian [catchphrase: "I hope, I hope, I hope. . . ."]; b. July 25, 1900, San Francisco, CA; d. June 2, 1961, Newport Beach, CA). *Al Pearce and His Gang* (1932–42).

Jovial, boyish Pearce and his brother Cal and soon-to-expand Happy-Go-Lucky Hour gang were first heard in San Francisco in 1929. The NBC Pacific network featured his troupe but not until 1935 did it go coast to coast from New York as a daily sustainer. Pearce introduced Morey Amsterdam, Bill (Tizzy Lish) Comstock, and Mel Blanc, and gave Amos 'n' Andy a boost when they surrendered the Sam and Henry characters.

On his variety show, Pearce enacted Elmer Blurt, a "low-pressure" door-to-door salesman who hoped and hoped nobody would answer the door. The close knit "all for one, one for all" troupe enjoyed a long run for top sponsors (Ford, General Foods, R. J. Reynolds) but lost its appeal in the early war years. A decade later Al tried television with morning and afternoon exposure at CBS. But by then his extensive real estate investments took priority.

Al's bow at the mike is the earliest of any performer. He claimed to have participated as a youngster in an experimental broadcast at San Jose in 1912.

688. PEARL, Jack (comedian [catchphrase: "Vas you dere, Sharlie?"]; b. Oct. 29, 1894, New York, NY; d. Dec. 25, 1982, New York, NY). *Jack Pearl—Baron Munchausen* (1932–34); *Jack Pearl Program* (1936–37, 1948); *Cresta Blanca Carnival* (1941–42); *The Baron and The Bee* (1953–54).

When Lucky Strike was looking for something different to sponsor, Pearl's gag writer submitted the Baron Munchausen character, the biggest liar in the world. In 1932 the comedian had a weekly spot to tell the Baron's tall tales and exploits. They were always greeted with skepticism by the straight man, Cliff Hall. Then Pearl would pause and utter the catchy phrase, "Vas you dere, Sharlie?"

Before radio, the comedian was in 19 Broadway shows, including *A Night in Paris* and *Ziegfeld Follies.*

Jack Pearl (courtesy of Steve Jelf)

His first stage appearance, in Gus Edwards' *School Days,* led to his adopted German dialect when the show's lead, a German comic became ill and Pearl got his part.

His irascible Munchausen was periodically reprieved for short seasonal runs and nostalgic guest spots, particularly on *The Big Show.* But television passed him by, and the Baron sustained a premature retirement.

689. PEARL, Minnie (comedienne [Queen of Country Comedy] [catchphrase: "Howdeeee. I'm just so proud to be here."]; b. Oct. 25, 1912, Centerville, TN; d. March 4, 1996, Nashville, TN). *Grand Ole Opry* (1939–1990).

The first comedienne hired for the *Opry.* Well bred and educated, Sarah Ophelia Colley accepted an invitation to audition on the celebrated Nashville program. The producers agreed to allow her a one-shot opportunity because they had doubts whether she would be perceived as a putdown of country people. Although scheduled late in the program, long after the NBC segment was over, she achieved immediate

success, and a contract to perform regularly. Minnie became a familiar character in folk humor through radio, road shows (with Roy Acuff and Pee Wee King) and stage appearances.

Her down-home broadly humorous storytelling was based on an old woman from the remote mountains of Alabama with whom she once stayed. Minnie Pearl began as a one-woman feature at women's clubs, community gatherings and conventions. She gradually eased into new material, changing with the social climate of the time to be a bit more raucous and somewhat risque. Over the years of extensive touring, she always returned to the *Opry* broadcast on Saturday night, wearing the familiar dime-store hat with the dangling $1.98 price tag. A favorite for decades, she was inducted into the Country Music Hall of Fame in 1975 as "exemplifying the endearing values of pure country comedy."

690. PEARY, Harold (actor [catchphrase: "You're a hard man, McGee."]; b. July 25, 1905, San Leandro, CA; d. March 30, 1985, Torrance, CA). *Adventures of Tom Mix* (1937–38); *Fibber McGee and Molly* (1937–41); *The Great Gildersleeve* (1941–50); *Harold Peary Show* (1950–51).

Star of one of the first spinoffs created from another radio series. His Throckmorton P. Gildersleeve, the next-door neighbor of Fibber McGee, came on that show in 1937. The character was a blundering baritone whose heart of gold usually was well concealed. It was such a hit that Peary became the centerpiece of a new series which proved to be one of the last great comedies of radio. Peary ranked as one of the most welcomed visitors to the shows of fellow comedians.

Peary left the role in 1950, and was replaced by Willard Waterman, an actor who sounded so much like the original Gildersleeve that their voices were nearly indistinguishable. Peary made several movies based on the character and played other roles in many TV series.

His radio bow occurred in January 1923 as a boy soprano on an Oakland, California station. In 1929 in San Francisco he sang as NBC's Spanish Serenader. His NBC Pacific credits ranged from *Little Orphan Annie* and *Wheatenaville* to *Spotlight Revue* and *Roads to Romance.*

691. PEERCE, Jan (singer [signature song: "The Bluebird of Happiness"]; b. June 3, 1904, New York, NY; d. Dec. 15, 1984, New York, NY). *Music Hall of the Air* (1934–41); *A & P Gypsies* (1935); *Golden Treasury of Song* (1940–41).

An experienced lyric tenor a half-dozen years before his Met debut as Alfredo in *La Traviata* in November 1941, Peerce under various names had never been vary far from a microphone since the beginning of broadcasting. His earliest exposure to music was as a youngster in a lower East Side synagogue. Violin

Jan Peerce

lessons followed, and 15-year-old Pinky Perelmuth joined the musicians union to play jobs in a Catskill Mountains camp. He settled down to be a singing fiddle player and occasional jazz band leader. Shortly before Radio City Music Hall opened in late 1932, Samuel L. (Roxy) Rothafel heard him sing at a banquet for Weber and Fields. Soon he performed on several of Roxy's informal programs as John Pierce. Then as Jan Peerce, he almost sang at the opening of the vast new showplace but at the last minute Roxy cut his solo because the program ran well beyond midnight. Engaged as a vocal soloist for four stage shows a day seven days a week, he was also picked by musical director Erno Rapee to sing on his Sunday afternoon *Music Hall of the Air.* He often sang on Consolidated Edison's *Echos of New York, Palmolive Beauty Box Theatre, Great Moments in Music* and *Harvest of Stars.*

On a broadcast shortly before his 1941 Met bow, a *Variety* critic tuned in and wrote: "Jan Peerce almost blew the radio apart with a tremendous rendition of 'Rachel Quand Du Seigneur' from 'Juive,' in which his golden tones rang the bell time and time again with top 'A's and 'B' flats. The 'La Donna e mobile' from 'Rigoletto' was equally good, and Peerce concluded his program with 'El relato de Rafael' from 'La Dolorosa,' with a seat-lifting top 'C'."

In 1938 Toscanini summoned him to sing for a broadcast of the Beethoven Ninth Symphony. It was the first of 13 performances with the NBC Symphony. Peerce was hailed as a bona fide American tenor at his concert debut at Town Hall in 1939, and began recitals from coast to coast as well as leading roles in Verdi and Puccini operas at the Met. His last

performance with the company was at a New York parks concert in 1968 in *Faust.* Not long after, he had his Broadway debut as Tevye in *Fiddler on the Roof*— and sang as technically secure and musically convincing as he had since his earliest performances as young Jascha Pearl with Jewish songs beamed to WEVD listeners.

692. PELLETIER, Vincent (announcer; b. March 21, 1908, Minneapolis, MN; d. Feb. 25, 1994). *Contented Hour* (1935–45); *Hymns of All Churches* (1938–46); *Dr. Paul* (1951–53).

Announcer, narrator and emcee, beginning in 1927 after a stint in vaudeville. Inspired by his mother, concert singer Mabel Pelletier, he first worked on the air as an amateur singer in 1923. As staff announcer at NBC Chicago, Pelletier enjoyed long associations with Carnation Milk and General Mills. In the early 1950s, he announced *First Nighter,* hosted *Hollywood Searchlight,* and narrated *Hollywood Bowl Concerts.* He even filled in as an actor on *Father Knows Best* and *Railroad Hour.*

693. PELLETIER, Wilfred (conductor; b. June 30, 1896, Montreal, Canada; d. April 9, 1982, New York, NY). *Roses and Drums* (1934–36); *Metropolitan Opera Auditions of the Air* (1935–42); *Vacation Serenade* (1943–44).

Conductor and coach for numerous established operatic stars and promising young artists. As maestro of an annual series that brought singers with hopes of a Met contract to audition over the air, he was paterfamilias to such new performers as Richard Tucker, Leonard Warren and Rise Stevens.

Wilfred Pelletier

The series featured many performers from NBC musical shows, a number of whom placed high in the annual contest and thus advanced their career, if not in opera, usually in radio and recital halls.

In 1917 Pelletier had joined the Met as an assistant conductor and coach for the likes of Caruso and Martinelli, often toured with the company and conducted its spring season. For four years he composed the music used as background for *Roses and Drums,* a light drama aired Sunday afternoons at CBS, and was well known for his work on the Packard and Firestone programs. He often led the NBC Symphony as guest conductor. French-Canadian, he maintained close ties as director of symphony orchestras, festivals and conservatories in Montreal and Quebec, as well as with the NY Philharmonic young people's concerts.

From 1925 to 1936 Pelletier was married to soprano Queena Mario of the Met who sang on its first network broadcast, a performance of *Hansel and Gretel,* on Christmas Day 1931. In 1937 he wed soprano Rose Bampton, for whom he conducted often at the Met, in concert and on radio.

694. PENNER, Joe (comedian [catchphrase: "Wanna Buy a Duck?"]; b. Nov. 11, 1904, Nagybecskereck, Hungary; d. Jan. 10, 1941, Philadelphia, PA). *Joe Penner Program* (1933–38); *Penners of Park Avenue* (1939–40).

Secondary bookings in carnivals, burlesque, vaudeville and nightclubs happily led to radio where Penner came to national prominence. In 1933 Rudy Vallee brought him to a microphone, and later that year, Vallee's agency starred the comic in his own show for Fleischmann Yeast. Subsequent programs for the products Cocomalt and Tip-Top Bread brought him a box office value that netted him more than $13,000 a week for personal appearances.

A hard worker and constant worrier, he was so agitated about scripts and general composition of his shows that at the conclusion of a program he sometimes would have to repair to a hospital for a stay of several days. At age 36 Penner died suddenly of a heart attack while in his musical roadshow, *Yokel Boy.* His catch phrase and pet duck "Goo-Goo" helped propel him to overnight stardom but his career went down hill when his series turned to situation comedy.

695. PERKINS, Ray (emcee, singer; b. Aug. 23, 1896, Boston, MA; d. Jan. 31, 1969, Bradenton, FL). *Crush Dry Cronies & Old Topper* (1930); *National Amateur Night* (1934–36); *Show of the Week* (1938–40); *The Nickel Man* (1941).

Pianist-singer-comedian, Perkins had been a songwriter until switching to the microphone in the mid-1920s. He was featured on many short-lived series, and in 1932 sang as "The Barbasolist" for Barbasol Co. and subbed as emcee for Rudy Vallee. The amateur hour craze led him to host a Major Bowes-like open house. By 1939 Perkins was a sustaining per-

former at NBC, but then had a five-month run for Pepsi Cola as *The Nickel Man* in 1941.

Perkins' first appearance was in the role of Judge Jr. for a *Judge* magazine series over WJZ in 1925. From 1946 to 1959 he was a disc jockey at KFEL Denver and columnist on records for the *Denver Post.*

696. PERRIN, Vic (actor; b. April 26, 1915, Menomonee Falls, WI; d. July 4, 1989, Los Angeles, CA). *Story of Holly Sloan* (1947–48); *Peter Kelly's Blues* (1951); *CBS Radio Workshop* (1956).

Frequent performer on westerns and detective stories. He became a regular on *Dragnet, Fort Laramie, Gunsmoke, One Man's Family* (as Ross Farnsworth) and *Yours Truly, Johnny Dollar.* He was a staff junior announcer for NBC Hollywood in the early 1940s, then chief announcer at The Blue Network (*Coronet Story Teller*). Perrin joined Charles Laughton's repertory group and worked on *CBS Radio Workshop,* a critically praised experimental series considered one of the most ingenious shows ever on the air. Drama and classics were broadcast, namely Huxley's "*Brave New World,*" Ray Bradbury's science fiction, an interview with Shakespeare. In the 1960s Perrin was known to TV viewers as the other worldly voice that introduced each episode of *The Outer Limits,* a science fiction series.

A graduate of the University of Wisconsin, he was a sought-after voice—but never seen—on many TV commercials. "If they see me," he explained, "they can't believe me as an actor."

697. PETRIE, George O. (actor; b. Nov. 16, 1912, New Haven, CT). *Philo Vance* (1948–49); *Amazing Mr. Malone* (1949–50); *The Falcon* (1953–54).

From 1945 to 1955, lead in a half-dozen mystery adventures. Chiefly detective and private investigator series, they included *Call the Police, Charlie Wild, Private Eye* and *The Falcon.* As the fifth and last Falcon (Mike Waring) he slugged it out with villains "with wisecracks as well as with his ready fist." Creators of the daytime soaps *Joyce Jordan, M.D., Backstage Wife* and *Romance of Helen Trent* utilized his talents as did directors of dramas for *Theatre Guild on the Air, The Big Story* and *Silver Theatre.* For Petrie, working at a mike was a breeze. "I never trained for it; I just did it." He described the work as an interlude, albeit an extremely important one. His activities were preceded, accompanied and followed by work on Broadway, in summer stock and with the Federal Theatre. Then came television (*The Honeymooners, Dallas*) and films (*At Sword's Point, Gypsy*).

Petrie's first radio experience was with the Guy Holland Players at WTIC Hartford in 1937. The $5 pay for 15-minute dramas augmented the $15 a week from the Federal Theatre. From 1940 until he was drafted into the Army in 1942, he was part of a stock company at WMCA doing a series called *Five Star Fi-*

George Petrie (courtesy of George O. Petrie)

nal which dramatized news events six days a week with an expanded version on Sundays. During this period he sporadically found parts on the networks' *We, The People* and *Lincoln Highway*.

698. PETRIE, Howard (announcer; b. Nov. 22, 1907, Beverly, MA; d. March 24, 1968, Keene, NH). *The Show Without a Name* (1942–43); *Jimmy Durante Show* (1947–50); *Judy Canova Show* (1947–51).

Personality announcer in the 1940s. Petrie joined NBC in 1930, after working at WBZ for a year. Earlier, he had been a security salesman who happened to visit that station in Boston. Petrie traded jokes with Garry Moore on a string of shows including the *Durante-Moore Show*. He occasionally sang on the air with comic quartets with names "From Hunger" and "Gwine to Heaven on a Mule."

Petrie won the H. P. Davis Announcer Award in 1942. Six feet four inches tall and 240 pounds, he drifted into films when a producer in search of a tall man for a character part spotted him on a radio stage. He appeared in some 20 pictures.

699. PEYTON, Patrick (preacher [The Rosary Priest]; b. c1909, Carracastle, County Mayo, Ireland; d. June 3, 1992, Los Angeles, CA). *Family Theatre* (1947–63).

Father Peyton coined the saying, "The family that prays together stays together." This message permeated his radio addresses, which began in 1945 over Mutual. He encouraged Catholics to pray at home

daily and recite the rosary, and urged followers of other religions to join in praying according to their beliefs. His broadcasts included religious dramas or stories illustrating group prayer or family values. Hollywood stars — Bing Crosby, Loretta Young, Rosalind Russell, Gregory Peck, Frank Sinatra and others — donated their talents.

Peyton had left his native Ireland as a teenager. He worked as a coal miner and church sexton before studying for the priesthood at Holy Cross Seminary and Notre Dame. Ordained in 1941, he traveled from parish to parish in upstate New York until he convinced MBS to let him present his message of the value of family prayer. His anthologies also ran on television, and were recorded for audio and video cassettes.

700. PICKENS, Jane (singer [signature song: "Alone Since We've Parted"]; b. Aug. 10, 1908, Macon, GA; d. Feb. 21, 1992, Newport, RI). *Gulf Headliners* (1934); *Evening in Paris* (1935–36); *Sealtest Party* (1936–37); *Jane Pickens Show* (1948–49, 1954–57); *Pickens Party* (1951–54).

Jane and her comfortably Atlanta-raised sisters Patti and Helen harmonized as children with their father, a cotton broker, at the piano. Jane studied at Curtis Institute and won scholarships at Juilliard. The family moved to Manhattan in 1932, and the sisters made a test recording for Victor that created such an

Jane Pickens

impression with NBC executives that they hired the trio unseen — for competition to the Boswell Sisters at CBS. Jane arranged their songs and accompaniments, and together they produced a very pleasing blend of high and low registers. Their fame was sudden and solid on radio and recordings. And on Broadway they helped to introduce "Autumn in New York" in the revue *Thumbs Up.*

The sisters broke up in 1937 when Patti eloped with tenor Robert Simmons of the Revelers quartet. Jane continued as a solo performer. Indeed, she had never allowed her serious music ambitions to lie dormant during her days with lighter fare. She soon appeared both with the New York Philharmonic and Philadelphia Opera Company, and played the lead in *Regina,* Marc Blitzstein's musical version of *The Little Foxes.* Radio, too, gave opportunities to sing both light and serious compositions. Her own show continued on NBC until the late 1950s.

701. PICKFORD, Mary (actress; b. April 9, 1893, Toronto, Canada; d. May 30, 1979, Santa Monica, CA). *Mary Pickford Dramas* (1934–35); *Parties at Pickfair* (1935).

Screen star Mary Pickford, "America's Sweetheart," reigned over Hollywood from a fabled estate that symbolized the opulence and allure of the movie capital. In the 1930s with her picture career over, the dedicated, hardworking actress turned to radio as hostess of a full-hour dramatic series. That led to *Parties at Pickfair,* a program that originated from her home and played up her role as a partygiver. She later co-starred with husband Buddy Rogers on a variety series, and was regularly sought out for special broadcasts to make appeals for the Red Cross, U.S. Savings Bonds and March of Dimes.

On her earliest broadcasts, she suffered mike fright. To alleviate some of her nervousness, the microphone was camouflaged to look like a floor lamp. It gave rise to the so-called Mary Pickford mike.

Pickford started in one-reel films in New York in 1909 at $5 a day. Her box office appeal grew tremendously over a 194-picture, Oscar-winning career.

702. PIOUS, Minerva (actress; b. March 5, 1903, Odessa, Russia; d. March 16, 1979, New York, NY). *Fred Allen Show* (1933–49); *Snow Village* (1943); *Henry Morgan Show* (1950).

As Mrs. Nussbaum, a Bronx housewife with a heavy Russian accent, Pious was a regular on Allen's Alley where she merrily mangled the English language to the delight of listeners and told absurd stories about her husband Pierre. While working in journalism in New York, she had helped a friend with a comedy script and played a role on its airing at WRNY. Fred Allen heard her and offered her a part on his show. While with Allen, she created dozens of characters, assuming the guise of French, German, Italian, English and other nationalities. Pious also appeared in

an array of totally different parts with Tommy Riggs, Sammy Kaye, Bob Hope and Jack Benny, and in 1936 replaced Fanny Brice on Broadway in *The Ziegfeld Follies.*

Pious explained her entry into the theatre. "I sort of edged into show business, by way of radio. I suppose my father thought it was more refined because people didn't see your face or your figure — only your voice. In a way it wasn't like show business at all."

703. POLESIE, Herb (panelist; b. July 3, 1899; d. June 8, 1979, Marina Del Rey, CA). *Twenty Questions* (1946–54).

Polesie began as an announcer in Pittsburgh in 1924. He also directed Bing Crosby, Al Jolson, Jimmy Durante, Frank Sinatra and Fanny Brice, and produced a number of their shows. He created and directed *It Pays to Be Ignorant.* In 1946 Polesie, a quick man with a spontaneous joke, joined the panel of *Twenty Questions.* Its creator Fred Van Deventer picked him because he sounded like panelist Oscar Levant of *Information Please,* a prototype for the series.

704. PONS, Lily (singer; b. April 12, 1904, Draguignan, France; d. Feb. 13, 1976, Dallas, TX).

Pons compared her voice to a flute. "It has projection," she said at the close of her career in 1972. "No matter how loud the conductor, I never force my voice." It was as Lucia with pristine flute-like range

Lily Pons

that she made her Met debut and her first American recordings, both in 1931. The challenging high-note coloratura passages proved to be her forte, and the diminutive French singer with a dazzling smile went on to a solid repertory of bel canto roles and to adoring acclaim as a prima donna in opera houses and concert halls. An idolized figure in music, she once sang to more than 300,000 Chicagoans in a Grant Part concert in the summer of 1939.

Her phenomenal voice, enchanting personality and keen showmanship took her to films and radio. She first sang at WEAF on Easter Sunday 1931 with the Victor Orchestra, then dashed to the Met to perform the mad scene from *Lucia* at a Sunday night concert with Gigli and Swarthout. She starred in three pictures in Hollywood and sang regularly with the orchestra of Andre Kostelanetz whom she wed in 1938 after a cross-country courtship. Her guest appearances on *The Telephone Hour* from 1942 to 1957 totaled 50 — more than any other artist. And her work on *Voice of Firestone* in the 1940s drew large audiences. On a special Liberation of Paris broadcast in 1944, she sang "La Marseillaise."

Lily's early musical studies on the piano won her a prize at the Paris Conservatoire. During World War I she entertained wounded veterans by singing and was told she had an extraordinary voice. After three years of hard work, she made her debut in Alsace and performed intermittently in the French provinces. Still unknown and inexperienced, she was persuaded to audition for the Met along with a dozen other nervous aspirants. Her effortless singing of the Bell Song from *Lakme,* the Mad Scene from *Lucia* and a Rigoletto aria — all challenging physical feats that she repeated for the quickly summoned Met president Otto Kahn — led to manager Gatti-Casazza's remarks: "The perfect voice. She is for the Met."

705. POST, Emily (commentator; b. Oct. 3, 1873, Baltimore, MD; d. Sept. 25, 1960, New York, NY). *Emily Post* (1930–33, 1937–38); *The Right Thing to Do* (1938–39).

Arbitress of etiquette and good manners. The basic premise of Emily Post was that "no one should do anything that can either annoy or offend the sensibilities of others." Her name became synonymous with correct deportment. Through her widely known book *Etiquette,* published in 1922, daily column, and radio program, she reached untold numbers of people with firm but gentle common-sense advice.

Beginning in 1930, Mrs. Post aired a series of do's and don'ts commentary sponsored by Proctor & Gamble, General Electric and DuPont over CBS and NBC. Her pet dislikes, listeners learned, were pretentious people, dirty silver and hostesses who served themselves first.

706. POWELL, Dick (singer, actor; b. Nov. 14, 1904, Mt. View, AR; d. Jan. 2, 1963, Hollywood, CA). *Old Gold Program* (1934); *Hollywood Hotel* (1934–37); *Campana Serenade* (1943–44); *Fitch Bandwagon* (1944–45); *Rogue's Gallery* (1945–46); *Richard Diamond, Private Detective* (1949–52).

When Powell asked his studio, Warner Bros., for straight parts in dramatic pictures, they said they could not build him into a serious actor so long as he was crooning on the radio. So he quit his starring role on the top-rated *Hollywood Hotel* in 1937. Warners still didn't give him what he wanted. "To them, I was a silly squawking actor," he said in a 1945 interview. "But I knew there were cycles in pictures. I was on a dying vine — they would have let me die on that vine." He finally purchased the remainder of his contract and briefly freelanced, but all the good scripts went to the regular stars, not singers. By 1938 Powell was back on radio as an emcee — and still pushing for a heavy part. Then came *Murder, My Sweet* at RKO, a successful breakthrough in which he played a tough private eye named Philip Marlowe. That broke the cherub-looking crooner mold. From then on he had a better choice of dramatic roles in films (*Cornered*) and radio (Detective Richard Rogue).

Powell had organized his own band in high school and sang in a church choir before traveling as vocalist with an orchestra. He continued to study voice with a view to opera. He spent three years as an emcee and singer in a Pittsburgh theatre. A Warner scout signed him in 1932. A string of outstanding musicals, most often with Ruby Keeler and a bland script, included *42nd Street* and *Footlight Parade.* Before his surprising change-over, the singer introduced such Al Dubin-Harry Warren hits as "Honeymoon Hotel," "I Only Have Eyes for You" and "Lullaby of Broadway." Years later his Four Star Productions brought many detective and western anthologies to television, with Powell as host and frequent lead.

707. POWELL, Jane (singer; b. April 1, 1929, Portland, OR; *Chase & Sanborn Hour* (1943–44).

Perennial teenage soprano who looked like the girl next door in some 20 films. Born Suzanne Burce, she started out on a children's program at age seven and was said to have a voice rated at the two-and-a-half-octave range. An audition at KOIN Portland, arranged by her vocal teacher, landed her a program. She became one of the city's most tuned-in local performers. During a visit to Los Angeles, she and her parents got on *Hollywood Showcase,* a series for new talent. The following week, among six finalists, she won top honors, and as an encore, thrilled the audience with an aria from *Carmen.* Talent scouts pursued her for the networks and movies. She signed as Charlie McCarthy's girl friend at NBC and for a studio build-up at MGM.

The gifted 15-year-old star-to-be was farmed out for *Song of the Open Road* with W. C. Fields. The girl she played was called Jane Powell, and to her surprise that became her professional name. MGM made it clear that full time movie-making ruled out a weekly radio show. There would be guest shots on *Carnation Contented Hour* and *Harvest of Stars,* and starring roles on *The Railroad Hour* ("Student Prince," "Little Nellie Kelly," "Brigadoon"). And she once subbed as Judy for Louise Erickson on *A Date with Judy,* the title of her 1948 film in which she introduced "It's a Most Unusual Day." Her string of charming musicals ended on a high note with *Seven Brides for Seven Brothers.* Concert dates, night club engagements, TV shows and a Broadway revival fueled a mature and ongoing singing career. In 1988 she found time to pen the autobiographical *The Girl Next Door . . . and How She Grew.*

708. PRENTISS, Ed (actor; b. Sept. 9, 1909, Chicago, IL; d. March 18, 1992). *The Guiding Light* (1937–46); *Captain Midnight* (1938–49); *General Mills Hour* (1944–46).

Exploits of daring pilot Captain Midnight enthralled young listeners in the time between homework and supper five days a week. Chicago-trained actor Ed Prentiss originated the lead role and played the stalwart air hero for most of its ten-year Mutual run. The serial particularly stirred youthful imaginations with breathtaking wartime adventures of brave, noble and heroic protagonists.

A daytime mainstay, Prentiss played the orphaned Ned Holden on *The Guiding Light* and Alice's husband in *Painted Dreams.* As host for General Mills he

introduced and tied together their three daily back-to-back soaps: *Guiding Light, Today's Children* and *Woman in White.* He later served as announcer and fill-in emcee for Dave Garroway. On television he regularly appeared as the banker on *Bonanza.*

709. PRESCOTT, Allen (host [catchphrase: "Hello, girls."]; b. Jan. 21, 1904, St. Louis, MO; d. Jan. 27, 1978, New York, NY). *The Wife Saver* (1932–42); *Yours Sincerely* (1941–42); *Prescott Presents* (1941–42).

Light-hearted purveyor of household hints. Several mornings a week he delivered flip, breezy suggestions on how to clean kitchen utensils, slice vegetables and hang pictures, in contrast to the heavy-handed commentary of some of his distaff colleagues. His frank admission that he knew nothing about homemaking endeared him to an audience that wrote him several hundred letters a week. His popularity led to reference books on candy recipes and home-making tips. His *Wife Saver* broadcasts were interrupted for two years' service in the Navy. On his return his program moved from the Blue Network to WNEW.

Working as a New York *Mirror* reporter in 1929, he appeared on a WMCA news program with Walter Winchell. By 1931 Prescott broadcast as a WINS newsman, and covered such special events as aerial maneuvers over Manhattan and polo matches from Governors Island.

Ed Prentiss

Allen Prescott (courtesy of Steve Jelf)

710. PRESTON, Walter (singer; b. Feb. 9, 1901, Quincy, IL; d. Aug. 7, 1982, Greenport, NY). *Philco Hour* (1927–29).

Preston made his first radio appearance in August 1925 at WEAF when he was told it might lead to concert hall bookings. What resulted was a long association with NBC, then in the early stages of organization. A baritone, he sang as a soloist on the *Philco Hour* with Jessica Dragonette and in many quartets (New Yorkers, American, Armchair) and larger groups (Modern Choir, Sixteen Singers) on *Show Boat* and *Saturday Night Serenade*. In later years he researched, wrote, produced and hosted a revue of Broadway show music on WOR called *The Show Shop*. In November 1948 he directed a chorus of 17 voices on an NBC Symphony broadcast.

He received his musical education at Juilliard, and won the gold medal of the New York Music Week Association competition at Carnegie Hall. The prize included a one-hour recital program on radio. He wrote the lyrics for "Slumber On," the theme for the landmark late-night *Slumber Hour*.

711. PRICE, Vincent (actor; b. May 27, 1911, St. Louis, MO; d. Oct. 25, 1993, Los Angeles, CA). *Valiant Lady* (1939); *Helpmate* (1942–43); *The Saint* (1947, 1949–51).

Macabre villain and flamboyant archfiend in many films. His pre-ghoulish acting successes were often as historical figures—Sir Walter Raleigh, King Charles II, Richelieu and Prince Albert. The latter role won

Vincent Price

praise in London and New York, and brought Price to the prestigious *RCA Magic Key* where he recreated with Helen Hayes and George Macready the proposal scene from *Victoria Regina* in June 1937. (It was repeated in 1939 on the *Chase & Sanborn Hour* with Hayes and Don Ameche.) That fall he returned for a scene from *The Lady Has a Heart* with Elissa Landi.

While cultured, Yale-educated Price prepared for his screen bow, he briefly played Paul Morrison on *Valiant Lady*. In demand for adaptations from the Hollywood screen, he was frequently heard on *Johnny Presents* in 1942 and *Sealtest Village Store* in 1947. His well-mannered lead as debonair sleuth Simon Templar (*The Saint*) enhanced the dial for several years. During the 1955–56 season he substituted as host in the absence of Herbert Marshall on *Your Radio Theatre* and also acted in its dramas.

712. PRUD'HOMME, Cameron (actor; b. Dec. 16, 1892, Auburn, CA; d. Nov. 27, 1967, Pompton Plains, NJ). *Stella Dallas* (1943–46); *David Harum* (1944–47, 1950–51); *A Woman of America* (1944–45); *Backstage Wife* (1945–46).

Cast in many of the major soaps, including the title role of *David Harum,* a small-town banker who acted as a fatherly adviser to his neighbors. Such roles were his forte. They ranged from Father McCary on *Life Can Be Beautiful* to Asa Walker on *Young Widder Brown.* His dramatic parts—as fathers and doctors—continued on *Cavalcade of America* and *Theatre Guild on the Air* into the 1950s. On stage and in films the rugged middle-aged actor was father to Katharine Hepburn, Tammy Grimes, Shirley Booth and Geraldine Page.

He broke into radio in San Francisco in 1931, and played on *Winning the West* for the NBC Pacific network.

713. PRYOR, Roger (actor; b. Aug. 27, 1901, New York, NY; d. Jan. 31, 1974, Puerta Valarta, Mexico). *Screen Guild Theatre* (1939–42); *Theatre Guild on the Air* (1949–51); *NBC Summer Symphony* (1949–51).

Dependable, businesslike performer-emcee. Pryor played on Broadway (*The Royal Family*), in films (*Belle of the Nineties*) and on bandstands (trombonist-leader). Radio work assumed an important part of his latter career, chiefly as producer, host and narrator. In 1947 he joined the ad firm Foote, Cone and Belding as vice president in charge of broadcasting and retired 15 years later. During his Hollywood years, he was wed to actress Ann Sothern. His father was Arthur Pryor, early 20th-century bandmaster in the mode of John Philip Sousa.

714. QUINN, Bill (actor; b. May 6, 1912, New York, NY; d. April 29, 1994). *Just Plain Bill* (1936); *When a Girl Marries* (1939–41); *Home of the Brave* (1941–43).

Juvenile-character actor with numerous appearances on serials and dramas. They ranged from *Against the Storm* to *The Man Behind the Gun.* Educated at Professional Children's School, he bowed on Broadway at age six in David Belasco's *Daddies,* and went on to appear in *The Bluebird, Gentlemen of the Press* and *Winterset.* By 1937 he was a regular on *Renfrew of the Mounties* at CBS and a frequent cast member on the programs of Irene Rich and Kate Smith. In 1945 he played the lead in *Front Page Farrell.* Beginning in the mid-40s Quinn made many appearances on *Molle Mystery Theatre* and *The Big Story.*

His TV work included Sweeney, the bartender on *The Rifleman* and Mr. Van Rensselaer on *All in the Family.*

715. RAFFETTO, Michael (actor; b. Dec. 30, 1899, Placerville, CA; d. May 31, 1990, Berkeley, CA). *One Man's Family* (1932–51, 1954–56); *I Love a Mystery* (1939–43).

Originator of the role of Paul Barbour, the eldest son of *One Man's Family.* The series was started in San Francisco and carried by NBC's West Coast net for its first year. In 1951 because of illness, his character was written out of the script. Raffetto, however, assisted program creator Carlton E. Morse with writing and directing the show. He returned to his speaking role on a regular basis in 1954. He also portrayed the globe-trotting hero Jack Packard on *I Love a Mystery,* a series for which he contributed scripts. Its sequel, *I Love Adventure,* aired in 1948.

Raffetto appeared in University of California theatricals, and his interest in acting continued after he had taken up the practice of law. He tried to carve out a place in silent films, but without success. He made out better as a diction teacher. Impressed with his voice as well as a script he had written in 1930 called *Arm of the Law,* NBC engaged him as an actor in this serial about a picturesque old lawyer.

716. RAHT, Katherine (actress; b. May 8, 1901, Chattanooga, TN; d. Dec. 2, 1983, Chattanooga, TN). *Aldrich Family* (1939–51); *Snow Village* (1943).

Her stentorian voice opened *The Aldrich Family* with the motherly call: "Henry-y-y! Henry Aldrich!" Her longest-running role, Alice Aldrich, started out in a 1939 summer series. Between mothering one of America's most famous adolescents, Raht turned up on *Crime Doctor, Counterspy* and *Aunt Jenny's True-Life Stories.* During World War II she was a senior hostess at the Stage Door Canteen two nights a week. GIs were amused when she told them she had three sons in service — all named Henry. They were the three actors (Ezra Stone, Norman Toker, Dickie Jones) who had played the role of Henry Aldrich before going into uniform.

After graduation from Bryn Mawr College, Raht taught history and French at the University of Chattanooga and Foxcroft School. Drawn to acting, she pursued jobs in summer stock, then took a year off in New York to job-hunt and take voice training. After two plays that opened and closed almost simultaneously, she had a long run on Broadway in *Our Town* as the lady in the box and as understudy — and eventual replacement — for Evelyn Varden (Mrs. Gibbs). The role led to a radio audition. Typecast as a dowager, she also appeared on stage in *The Heiress, Sabrina Fair* and *The Happiest Millionaire.*

717. RAMONA (singer, pianist; b. March 11, 1909, Lockland, OH; d. Dec. 14, 1972, Sacramento, CA). *Kraft Music Hall* (1933–35); *Paul Whiteman's Musical Varieties* (1936).

Ramona and Her Grand Piano brought dazzling keyboard rhythm and mesmerizing vocal intonation, not to mention a glamorous stage presence, to the famous bandstand of Paul Whiteman. She caught his ear while singing over WLW in 1932. She replaced Mildred Bailey as the distaff star of his large aggregation. When Whiteman returned to the victor label and inaugurated the *Kraft Music Hall,* Ramona enjoyed her greatest success. The dark-eyed performer with her dark hair parted in the middle gave a mysterious Latin look that projected well in night clubs and concert halls.

Released from a paltry $125-a-week contract with Whiteman, who also managed all her performances, she failed to maintain a fast-track momentum. In 1938 she formed an all-male band at WOR; in 1941 she and her Tune Twisters broadcast six unsponsored 15-minute shows a week from Mutual. Later, from Cincinnati's WLW the sophisticated singer-pianist broadcast a chatty musical program *Rendezvous with Ramona,* and with her husband, announcer-sportscaster Al Helfer, aired a local morning show.

She had entered radio on the *Nighthawk Frolic* at WDAF Kansas City in 1926 while still in high school. Don Bestor first engaged her as a pianist.

718. RANDALL, Tony (actor; b. Feb. 26, 1920, Tulsa, OK). *Light of the World* (1948); *I Love a Mystery* (1949–51).

Two decades before the role of fastidious Felix in TV's *The Odd Couple,* Randall portrayed pedantic Reggie in the radio revival of *I Love a Mystery.* In the early 1940s he carved out a livelihood from announcing and from acting in soap operas *Portia Faces Life* and *When a Girl Marries.* Following service as a lieutenant in the Signal Corps, he returned to perform on Henry Morgan's program and on Broadway with Katharine Cornell in *Antony and Cleopatra* (as Scarus). At NBC he played Jarrod in a 13-week dramatization of "Samson and Delilah" on *Light of the World.*

His stage and film work displayed an exceptional versatility: serious drama in *Inherit the Wind,* deft comedy in *Will Success Spoil Rock Hunter?,* debonair

Tony Randall (courtesy of Steve Jelf)

song and dance in *Oh Captain!* For early TV he appeared as the swaggering sidekick of Mr. Peepers (Wally Cox).

719. RANDOLPH, Isabel (actress; b. Dec. 4, 1889; d. Jan. 11, 1973, Burbank, CA). *Dan Harding's Wife* (1936–38); *Story of Mary Marlin* (1936–39); *Fibber McGee and Molly* (1936–43); *A Day in the Life of Dennis Day* (1947–48).

Soap opera-comedy show character. Her first radio work began in 1932 following an audition at NBC Chicago. The lead in *Dan Harding's Wife* led to concurrent parts on *A Tale of Today* (Harriet Brooke) and *Mary Marlin* (Margaret Adams). Randolph added comedy as Mrs. Uppington with the McGees and Agatha Frost with Judy Canova. The very names of her characters — Mrs. Beachwater, Mrs. Piddleton — signified the arrival of authoritative, imperious matrons.

Based in Hollywood after 1939, the onetime Broadway cast member of *The Noose* and *Bird of Paradise* appeared in several Gene Autry and Roy Rogers Westerns. For television she worked on *I Love Lucy* and *Robert Cummings Show,* and played Dick Van Dyke's mother in his first comedy series.

720. RANDOLPH, Lillian (actress; b. Dec. 14, 1898; d. Sept. 12, 1980, Los Angeles, CA). *The Great Gildersleeve* (1941–58); *Billie Burke Show* (1944–46).

As Birdie, the jocular cook and housekeeper for the Gildersleeve household, Randolph enjoyed her best

and longest radio role. In the 1950s she briefly essayed the lead in *Beulah.* Busy in films (*At the Circus, It's a Wonderful Life*), she moved into early television as Madame Queen on *Amos 'n' Andy* and as Birdie for a season. Decades later, this Black Film Hall of Fame honoree was still on camera with *The Jeffersons* and *Roots.*

She was the sister of stage and radio actress Amanda Randolph, who also played in TV's *Amos 'n' Andy.*

721. RAPEE, Erno (conductor; b. June 4, 1891, Budapest, Hungary; d. June 26, 1945, New York, NY). *Roxy's Gang* (c1922–25); *Music Hall on the Air* (1933–44); *General Motors Concert* (1935–37).

Each Sunday afternoon he conducted the Radio City Music Hall Symphony orchestra in programs that widened most listeners' musical sphere. Rapee owed his career as house conductor to stage production manager S. L. (Roxy) Rothafel who in 1918 offered him a post at the Rivoli. Wherever Roxy went, the one-time European piano prodigy followed — to the Capitol, to the Roxy, and finally to the Music Hall where he stayed until his death. In the process Rapee developed an orchestra that was at home in Wagner or the jazz of the day. One of the first to synchronize scores for motion pictures, he contributed music to 750 full-length films and some 1,000 newsreels over a ten-year period. In 1931, after working in Hollywood in the actual production of sound pictures, he became music director for NBC where he conducted the prestigious General Motors concerts.

Rapee had arrived in New York from Budapest in 1912 and gotten a job as pianist in the orchestra of the Monopol Restaurant, and filled his spare time as an assisting artist with chamber music ensembles and conductor of Hungarian operas.

722. RATHBONE, Basil (actor; b. June 13, 1892, Johannesburg, South Africa; d. July 21, 1967, New York, NY). *Sherlock Holmes* (1939–46); *Tales of Fatima* (1949).

Incarnation of the imaginary detective Sherlock Holmes on radio and screen for a generation or more of mystery fans. He regretted the association with the Baker Street character. "Nobody thought I could do anything else," he said. "When I would come onto a set or into a radio studio, it was never 'Hello, Rathbone'. It was always 'Hello, Holmes.'"

The classically educated Shakespearean performer came to the United States in 1912, and became a dashing figure on Broadway (*Romeo and Juliet*) and a frequently villainous character on screen (*If I Were King*). The Holmes series began in 1939 with *The Hound of the Baskervilles,* and he made 15 more sequels. Dr. Watson was played by Nigel Bruce on both the film and air versions.

The first radio episode, "The Case of the Sussex Vampire," was described by *Variety* as "superior whodunit stuff." The popular role brought Rathbone a

Virginia Rea

considerable income. He gave up the series for a short-lived detective program called *Scotland Yard,* followed by murder mystery series entitled *Tales of Fatima.*

723. REA, Virginia (singer; b. March 28, 1896, Louisville, KY; d. 1941). *Palmolive Hour* (1927–31); *American Album of Familiar Music* (1933–35); *Rubinoff and His Orchestra* (1935–37).

A coloratura soprano, she achieved her greatest acclaim as Olive Palmer of the *Palmolive Hour* with tenor Frank Munn (a.k.a. Paul Oliver). Their duets of romantic ballads made these well-established Brunswick recording artists radio stars of the first magnitude. Rea promoted her releases via Brunswick's musical programs and by concert tours. She sang everything from lieder and operatic arias to art songs and popular tunes. Her solos on *Eveready Hour,* an early variety series, generated much fan mail. By 1929 she reputedly was the highest paid singer on any concert series, receiving more for one song than any other radio performer. Her weekly salary was said to be $1,500.

When Palmolive reclaimed the Olive Palmer moniker in December 1931, she had to return to her own name. But without the magic of the old pseudonym, she seemed to have lost much of her following. Rea re-teamed with Munn for a short run with Paul Whiteman's orchestra, then joined Munn for 16 months in the mid-30s on *American Album.* Her last commercial series with Jan Peerce and Rubinoff's orchestra for Chevrolet displayed a pleasing, albeit light, voice best in the middle register. Although she

returned to the recital hall in 1937 and received favorable reviews, her earlier triumphs were not repeated and her radio engagements—*RCA Magic Key,* NBC Concert Orchestra series—were few and far between. Emotionally hurt and financially crushed from a failed marriage—her third—she apparently took her own life in mid-1941.

724. READICK, Frank (actor; b. Nov. 6, 1896, Seattle, WA; d. c1965). *The Shadow* (1930–35); *Les Misérables* (1937).

Narrator of the pre-Lamont Cranston *Shadow,* among many key roles in the 1930s and '40s. They included Knobby on *Joe Palooka, Eustace Meek* and *Smilin' Jack.* Mutual once broadcast the latter from his apartment because he had the flu. The blood and thunder story drew the police when a neighbor of Readick called over gunshots fired by a sound effects man.

A regular on *March of Time,* Readick met co-actor Orson Welles on that series. In 1938 Welles made him a charter member of *The Mercury Theatre on the Air.* For "War of the Worlds," he played the newsman Carl Phillips who describes with great emotion the horrors of the Martian invasion.

His son, Bob Readick (1924–85), became a busy radio actor in the 1940s with frequent appearances on *Let's Pretend* and *Rosemary.*

725. REED, Alan (a.k.a. Teddy Bergman) (actor; b. Aug. 20, 1907, New York, NY; d. June 14, 1977, Los Angeles, CA). *Abie's Irish Rose* (1942–44); *Life with Luigi* (1948–53).

Straight man-character actor on many comedy shows headlined by Durante, Cantor and Hope. He was the original Daddy to Fanny Brice on *Baby Snooks,* Clancy on *Duffy's Tavern,* Pasquale on *Life with Luigi* and Joe on *Joe Palooka.* For Fred Allen, Reed portrayed Falstaff Openshaw. After moving to Los Angeles in 1943, he appeared in more than 50 films.

Born Teddy Bergman, he changed his professional name to break the trap of his Jewish identity, which he later said limited his early roles to parts in which he mimicked ethnic accents. He was also active on Broadway with Alfred Lunt and Lynn Fontanne, and as the voice of Fred Flintstone on the television series *The Flintstones.*

726. REGAN, Phil (singer [The Singing Cop]; b. May 28, 1906, Brooklyn, NY; d. Feb. 11, 1996, Santa Barbara, CA). *Burns and Allen* (1932–33).

In 1931 columnist Nick Kenny heard Regan, a New York City policeman, sing one night at a party. Kenny advised him to try radio. Guy Lombardo added this Irish tenor to the Burns and Allen program. When the show moved to Hollywood, he was screen-tested and cast in the first of some two dozen films, mostly second-feature quickies (*Laughing Irish Eyes, She Married a Cop*). Regan fully expected to por-

Phil Regan

tray Irish composer Chauncy Olcott in *My Wild Irish Rose* but lost out to Dennis Morgan.

Phil joined Ken Murray on radio in 1936 and had his share of guest spots with Ed Wynn, George Jessel and Paul Whiteman. Then, in 1942, he landed his own daily series. Pepsi-Cola later featured him as singer-emcee in 1951, perhaps as a counter-attraction to Coca-Cola's Irish tenor Morton Downey. In 1940, 1944 and 1948, he sang "The Star-Spangled Banner" at sessions of the Democratic Party National Convention and at the Inauguration of Harry S. Truman, a close friend.

Young Phil never had a singing lesson, but was one of the Paulist Choir Boys and did a brief turn with a Gus Edwards unit. At 13 he went to work as an office boy in an oil refinery, corking sample bottles of oil. One day a bottle broke, and glass went into his hand, cutting all the tendons. He received $2,500 in compensation — a hefty enough sum in 1923 with which to start married life (at age 17) and raise a family (four children). After working as a chauffeur, Regan took a Civil Service exam and became a policeman.

727. REID, Elliott (actor; b. Jan. 16, 1920, New York, NY). *Roses and Drums* (1936); *Grand Central Station* (1938–39); *Theatre Guild on the Air* (1951–52).

In the mid-1930s, he secured parts as a juvenile and character actor in mainstream dramas, including *March of Time, Suspense* and *Cavalcade of America.* His stage bow was in the Mercury Theatre modern

dress version of *Julius Caesar* in 1937. Just before Navy duty, he appeared on screen in DeMille's *Story of Dr. Wassell* and MGM's *Young Idea.* Reid joined the Theatre Guild's radio series as narrator and actor in 1951, the year he played on Broadway in *Two on the Aisle.* On TV he worked with Henry Morgan, Lucille Ball and Dinah Shore. His mimicking of John F. Kennedy opened up a mini-career in clubs in the early 1960s.

His first paying job was on *American School of the Air;* earlier stints on *The Children's Hour* were for free.

728. RESER, Harry (bandleader [signature song: "The Cliquot March"]; b. Jan. 12, 1896, Piqua, OH; d. Sept. 27, 1965, New York, NY). *Cliquot Club Eskimos* (1925–33).

Together with the A & P Gypsies and Ipana Troubadors, the Cliquot Club Eskimos provided early network dialers with peppy melodies on a regular basis. Led by the Big Chief Eskimo Reser, this aggregation featured his virtuoso banjo solos. His self-composed signature with its jingle of sleigh bells and barking huskies to carry out the Arctic motif was a distinctive opener to his NBC program. When audiences were added to the proceedings — by 1931 it aired from the old New Amsterdam Roof studio — Reser's musicians dressed in heavily furred Eskimo outfits. For the first six years, he also produced the show. The series sold carloads of the sponsor's sparkling club soda and ginger ale, although the beverages were only available in the Northeast.

Reser first learned to play the violin and piano, then the banjo when he discovered it was the rage in New York cafes. In the 1920s he made hundreds of up-tempo dance band discs. But by 1940 he had faded from the podium into the pit. One evening while tuning up his guitar in the orchestra pit in preparation for a performance of *Fiddler on the Roof,* he collapsed and died.

729. REVELL, Nellie (commentator; b. March 13, 1873, Springfield, IL; d. Aug. 12, 1958, New York, NY). *Neighbor Nell* (1935–39); *Meet the Artist* (1939–43).

Newspaper reporter, publicist and radio personality. Revell joined NBC in the early 1930s and interviewed notable figures in show business, sports and politics. Her features were 15-minute sustainers on the Blue Network. In 1939 with three interview programs on the air, including *Meet the Song Writer,* she was a guest on *Hobby Lobby* as "a collector of people."

Revell started her career on her father's newspaper in Springfield, Illinois, and left for a string of writing jobs in Chicago, Denver, San Francisco, and lastly New York and *The World.* Demanding equal status with men in reporting, she often quit a post when a paper put her news stories or columns on the woman's page. As a press agent she handled a circus, the Keith-Orpheum picture circuit and Al Jolson.

Harry Reser, John S. Young, top center (courtesy of KDKA Radio)

730. REY, Alvino (bandleader [signature song: "Blue Rain"/"Nighty Night"]; b. July 1, 1911, Oakland, CA). *Horace Heidt and His Brigadiers* (1935–38).

Electric guitarist who built a large band around the innovative and melodic solo sound of this instrument. His four years with Horace Heidt — and his aggregation's frequent broadcasts — led to Rey's own outfit featuring the singing King Sisters (he married Louise King). It played as a studio band at KHJ and recorded many transcribed shows. On the road Rey enjoyed remotes from New York's Biltmore and New Jersey's Rustic Cabin, where one snowy night when the engineer and the announcer could not reach the club, Rey with his electronic know-how set up the broadcast equipment and put the show on the air.

Earlier, at age 20, Rey worked with Phil Spitalny and at NBC San Francisco. World War II broke up his band. A new aggregation of the late '40s failed commercially. A studio musician, he returned centerstage in a very rewarding reprise of the King Family TV series of the 1960s.

Gladys Rice

731. RICE, Gladys (singer; b. Nov. 27, 1890, Philadelphia, PA; d. Sept. 7, 1983, New York, NY). *Roxy's Gang* (1922–27); *Lucky Strike Dance Orchestra* (1928–33); *Voice of Firestone* (1931–32); *Horse and Buggy Days* (1939–40).

Original Roxy cast member. A soprano, she sang all types of music, with emphasis on English and French ballads. Beginning in light operettas, Rice made her first records for Edison just before her start in radio. She followed Roxy from the Capitol to his own theatre. He once remarked to her: "Gladys, you sing 'Ave Maria' like a love song." Her sponsors were among the best-known advertisers: RCA Victor, General Motors, General Electric, Mobil Oil. Such was her following that one fan wrote her in the early 1930s saying, "If you are on for Mobil Oil, we'll buy Mobil Oil, and if you are on for sawdust, we'd buy sawdust."

Rice adored shopping and clothes, and usually was formally dressed when she broadcast. She sang on series with James Melton, Lewis James, Frank Munn and Douglas Stanbury. A Roxy Gang baritone, Stanbury devoted his retirement years to her well-being; neither one ever married. From a theatrical family, she was the daughter of actor John Rice who achieved a bit of movie immortality by becoming the first to kiss his leading lady (May Irwin) on screen.

732. RICE, Grantland (sportscaster; b. Nov. 1, 1880, Murfreesboro, TN; d. July 13, 1954, New York, NY). *Sports Stories* (1943–44).

Renowned sports writer-editor with a celebrated column, The Sportlight. He branched out into one-reel sports films and network sports segments. In the 1930s Rice provided a capsule of seasonal football scores during *Cities Service Concert.* NBC soon gave him a weekly half-hour for sports stories.

His earliest newspaper work began in Nashville and Atlanta. In 1911 he went to New York where he soon joined the *Tribune.* Rice selected all-American football teams and promoted golf, his favorite activity. He referred to Notre Dame's legendary backfield of the 1920s as "the four horsemen," a tagline that caught on.

733. RICH, Freddie (bandleader; b. Jan. 3, 1898, Warsaw, Poland; d. Sept. 8, 1956, Beverly Hills, CA). *Penthouse Party* (1936); *Your Hit Parade* (1936); *Camel Caravan* (1943).

One of the most rhythmic dance aggregations in the 1930s. Rich formed his band after a half-dozen years accompanying Sophie Tucker, Eva Tanguay and Gus Edwards. In 1922 he landed the coveted job as maestro at the Astor Hotel where he stayed seven years and broadcast frequently via WJZ. Sparkling piano arrangements were a feature along with Rich's own novelty "I'm Just Wild About Animal Crackers." In 1928 he joined CBS as a principal conductor, directing as many as 16 programs a week for over a decade.

He seldom used a baton but led with his fingers and marked time with his foot so emphatically that engineers had to cover the conductor's stand with felt to prevent the microphone from picking up the toe-tapping sound.

734. RICH, Irene (actress; b. Oct. 13, 1891, Buffalo, NY; d. April 22, 1988, Hope Ranch, CA). *Irene Rich/Dear John* (1933–42).

A paragon of good manners and charm, Rich winningly convened a sense of warmth and confidence in her long-running dramatic radio series. She had turned to radio near the end of an active film career that had begun as an extra in silent pictures in 1918. Her seven comedies with Will Rogers established her as a role model for the ideal wife. Her network sponsor was Welch's grape juice, and her svelte image became indelibly linked with the product, which she touted as the key to being slender. Welch's said she had increased sales by over 600 percent, and frankly admitted she had saved the company from collapse in the Depression.

735. RIGGS, Glenn (announcer; b. July 24, 1907, East McKeesport, PA; d. Sept. 12, 1975, Malaga, Spain). *Musical Varieties* (1939–40); *Hop Harrigan* (1942–48).

Top NBC-ABC announcer. He began on KDKA as chief announcer and host of *The Musical Clock,* one of the first recorded breakfast programs. He left in 1938 for NBC. When the Red and Blue networks split, he joined the latter, and by 1946 had many free-lance assignments as well, among them *Hop Harrigan, Boston Blackie* and *The Thin Man.* Riggs was a mainstay of *My True Story* and *Philco Hall of Fame.* On February 9, 1942 he rushed to an East River pier to broadcast an on-the-spot description of the burning of the passenger ship *Normandie.* Riggs spent 29 years at ABC radio and television, retiring in 1972.

Growing up in Pittsburgh, he appeared in numerous high school and college plays and glee club concerts. Professional acting jobs dwindled by 1929, so he applied for factory work at Westinghouse. The personnel manager suggested he do something at its station KDKA. At the end of the interview, an office boy ran in excitedly and said, "The announcer hasn't shown up." Riggs was hustled off to a studio, handed the latest stock quotations and told "Read."

736. RIGGS, Tommy (comedian; b. Oct. 21, 1908, Pittsburgh, PA; d. May 21, 1967, Pittsburgh, PA). *Fleischmann Hour* (1937–38); *Quaker Party with Tommy Riggs* (1938–40); *Tommy Riggs and Betty Lou* (1941–43).

A radio ventriloquist without a dummy, Riggs created the voice of a capricious little girl called Betty Lou. The dual-character act originated in 1929 at a rehearsal at WCAE Pittsburgh. While playing the piano, he broke into Betty Lou's authentically placed voice, a diversion he had only engaged in at college parties. The studio manager liked the moppet's expressions so much that he insisted it become part of his act.

Tommy Riggs and Betty Lou became local favorites. "I went on the air at 11 o'clock one night," he recalled, "and a Labor Department representative called on me and demanded I send Betty Lou to bed where she belonged at that hour." Riggs moved to a Cleveland station, then to WLW Cincinnati. He arrived at the time of the 1937 Ohio River floods. On the air all night and the next morning, Betty Lou appealed for aid for flood victims. He went to NBC when Rudy Vallee invited him to appear for Standard Brands, and he stayed 47 weeks. His own show for Quaker Oats followed.

Military service aboard a Navy minesweeper in the Pacific interrupted his series. CBS brought him back but the dual-voice performer never regained his earlier popularity. He had radio and TV shows in Alabama before returning to WCAE as a disk jockey and music director in 1955.

737. RIO, Rosa (organist; b. c1910, New Orleans, LA). *My True Story* (1942–58); *Deadline Drama* (1944); *Between the Bookends* (c1946–56).

A theatre organist supplying music for silent films, she thought her career was over when "talkies" came to the screen. But she was hired to stay on for almost three years, filling in when the sound track broke down. Rosa came to New York in the 1930s and got a job accompanying the students of voice teacher Estelle Liebling. To make ends meet she played an accordion at parties. It all led to an audition at NBC where she endured a very demanding test by network conductor Leopold Spitalny on both a traditional pipe organ and a new electric organ. Because the network had never hired a woman as organist, she was only brought in as a substitute. Rosa told Spitalny: "If I last two weeks, I'll probably be around until I'm 85." Although the 100 or so men on staff had their own dressing quarters, she said to her boss that any old ladies room would do just fine for her.

Rosa remained at NBC and ABC for a total of 22 years, doing five to seven shows a day into the late 1950s and for television's *Brighter Day.* She provided improvised musical background for many soap operas and dramatic programs. At Mutual she freelanced the "eerie," "tense" and "storm-filled" moods of *The Shadow,* played by Orson Welles and Brett Morrison. She accompanied *The Gospel Singer* and *The Mystery Chef,* as well as Myrt and Marge and Bob and Ray. *My True Story* gave her the opportunity to do more interpretative music than any other series. For *Rosa Rio Rhythms,* she simultaneously played the Hammond organ with her left hand and a piano with her right. Aired twice a day with songs of home, it was a favorite of wartime GIs. She worked well translating into musical terms the poetry readings of Ted Malone on the daily and unrehearsed *Between the Bookends.*

Rosa studied at Oberlin Conservatory and Eastman School of Music. In the 1960s she turned to teaching and concertizing. She brought her keyboard wizardry to vintage theatre organ consoles throughout the country. With the advent of video tape, she composed and recorded musical accompaniment for over 400 silent films for Video Yesteryear.

738. RIPLEY, Robert L. (emcee; b. Dec. 25, 1893, Santa Rosa, CA; d. May 27, 1949, New York, NY). *Colonial Beacon Light* (1930–31); *Esso Program* (1931–32); *Bakers Broadcast* (1935–37); *Believe It or Not* (1939–40, 1944, 1947–48).

A sports cartoonist for newspapers in 1918, one day he faced a deadline and had no idea for a subject. He quickly gathered together a few athletic oddities and captioned the drawing, "Believe It or Not." Favorable reaction led to a weekly feature, including oddities of all kinds, then a best-selling book and a syndicated column in 300 publications.

In 1930 he began to make motion pictures and appear on radio. His program was said to be the first sponsored series to use remote pickups consistently. He broadcast from an underwater garden, a snake pit, the rapids of a river, and other out-of-the-way locales. In 1940 his NBC program was described as "the most interesting and thrilling" on the air. It readily transferred to early television. Ironically, the subject of his last program was the story behind the writing of "Taps," the bugle call for the dead. The show closed with "Taps" played by a bugler silhouetted against a background of drifting clouds. Three days later, Ripley died while having a check-up in a New York hospital.

Radio sponsors for his incredulity included Esso, Hudson Motor Car, Standard Brands and General Foods. In 1948 he made an extended expedition to the Orient. Listeners heard him by short wave or transcription every four or five days

Rosa Rio (courtesy of Capital Cities/ABC)

on his afternoon run of *Believe It or Not.* He once aired a special series on venereal disease, discussing little-known facts on the oft-avoided subject, for *The Silent Enemy.*

739. ROBERTS, Ken (announcer, emcee; b. Feb. 12, 1910, Bronx, NY). *Easy Aces* (1937–41); *Quick as a Flash* (1945–47).

As emcee of *Quick as a Flash,* Roberts achieved his long-set goal of having a show of his own. This exceptionally appealing game dramatized moments in history of which contestants guessed the event; songs played by Ray Bloch's orchestra provided clues. Roberts also set the scene for a short whodunit enacted by various dramatic show cast members. He had excellent schooling for the task. He had served as Phil Baker's announcer on *Take It or Leave It.*

Roberts went into radio in 1928, making the rounds at small New York stations. He landed a job at WPCH, then moved to WMCA as an announcer. Following work in summer stock, he was on the air at a Brooklyn station four days a week for six months. His next stop, CBS, placed him in the upper echelon of announcers. He chalked up solid credits on *Crime Doctor, The Shadow, It Pays to Be Ignorant* and *Blind Date.* As an actor, he played next-door neighbor Cokey on *Easy Aces.* Roberts was long regarded as a bounce announcer — someone who put an upbeat lilt and laugh in commercials, to the satisfaction of the sponsor.

740. ROBINSON, Edward G. (actor; b. Dec. 12, 1893, Bucharest, Romania; d. Jan. 26, 1973, Hollywood, CA). *Big Town* (1937–42).

An actor of boundless energy and dynamic toughness who delivered two-fisted type portrayals on screen. He brought his commanding, well-trained voice to radio as crusading newsman Steve Wilson of *Big Town,* his only series. The zealously written CBS program often gave European-born Robinson a soap box to promote the American way while exposing civic scandals, corruption and crime.

He entered dramatic school in New York at 19 and broke into the legitimate theatre in 1915. The Theatre Guild noticed his good reviews and cast him in *The Adding Machine* and a variety of productions. Talking pictures proved worthy of his locutionary talent. *Little Caesar* and *Five Star Final* made him a star, and carried him to choice roles as tough, sinister and cynical characters. He made numerous special appearances on radio for many civic and patriotic causes. On a single day he contributed $100,000 to the USO as "a small down payment on the privilege of being an American."

In his autobiography, Robinson wrote that had television not come along, "radio might have become one of the fine arts. Except for phonograph records, nobody before had ever been asked to listen and not see."

741. ROCKWELL, George L. (Doc) (comedian; b. March 19, 1889, Providence, RI; d. March 3, 1978, Brunswick, ME). *Camel Pleasure Hour* (1930).

Monologuist-writer, often on humorous and philosophical subjects. He performed and collaborated with Fred Allen and appeared with Kate Smith and Rudy Vallee as a guest. Rockwell produced sustaining shows for CBS and NBC in the 1930s. A booking agent and magician, he performed in vaudeville, *George White's Scandals, Greenwich Village Follies* and *Ziegfeld Follies* before retiring in the early 1940s.

The peppery raconteur made his first radio appearance at KDKA when it was barely out of its experimental stage. Later, in 1932, he shared the bill that opened Radio City Music Hall.

742. ROGERS, Charles (Buddy) (bandleader, actor [America's Boyfriend] [signature song: "My Buddy"/"Twelfth Street Rag"]; b. Aug. 13, 1904, Olathe, KS). *Twin Stars* (1936–37); *Pick-A-Date* (1949–50).

Boyish collegiate type with a jazz band in the 1920s. Rogers, who mastered a half-dozen instruments, moved back and forth from conducting to acting with ease. A stage and nightclub musical attraction, the bright-eyed and handsome Buddy co-starred in the classic silent film *Wings.* The 1927 picture *My Best Girl* introduced him to Mary Pickford, at the time the biggest star in Hollywood. They were married in 1937.

Buddy's band aired over remotes and guested on *Fitch Bandwagon* into the 1940s, but never commanded a major sponsor. He emceed an early musical contest from Hollywood called *Scripteasers* and returned in a similar capacity with ABC's *Pick-A-Date.* Television held little appeal after a run as emcee of *Cavalcade of Bands.* By 1955 he devoted much of his time to overseeing the large Pickford-Rogers business holdings and entertaining at their legendary Beverly Hills estate, Pickfair.

743. ROGERS, Roy (actor, singer [King of the Cowboys] [signature song: "Happy Trails to You"]; b. Nov. 5, 1912, Cincinnati, OH). *Roy Rogers Show* (1944–46, 1948–55); *Saturday Nite Round-Up* (1946–48).

While doing odd jobs as a cowhand and a house painter, Rogers formed several country music duos and bands. The first of these was organized for a radio station amateur contest in Los Angeles. He did not win, but someone who tuned in suggested that he join an established singing group. His first professional broadcast was as a member of the *Uncle Tom Murray's Hollywood Hillbillies* in 1931. Roy later organized the O-Bar-O Cowboys with Bob Nolan and Tim Spencer, a vocal trio that performed regularly in Roswell, New Mexico. During a break in the music Rogers revealed his craving for a piece of lemon pie "just like Mom bakes back home." A listener called and said she would deliver the pie if he would sing "The Swiss Yodel." Roy did, and Arlene Wilkins arrived with two lemon pies and an invitation to a chicken dinner. Roy and Arlene were wed in 1936. (She suffered a fatal embolism after childbirth in 1946.)

Roy, Nolan and Spencer revamped their group into the Sons of the Pioneers, and soon achieved prominence over the air, on recordings and in films. Their disc "The Last Roundup" contributed greatly to their initial break. When Republic Pictures sought a new Western personality in 1937, Rogers raced to the studio, was given a test, and won the lead in *Under Western Skies.* He appeared in many singing Westerns with his horse Trigger, and after 1944 with leading lady Dale Evans, whom he married in 1947.

Roy's straight shooting naturalism in singing and acting projected well over radio. Described as the "world's top boots and saddle star" in the 1940s, he won the first position as Western cowboy at the movie box office year after year. With the arrival of television, he went into filming more than 100 half hour episodes for a regular series, and for several seasons had both NBC-TV and radio programs every week.

Roy yodelled and called square dances at a very young age in rural Ohio. He hitchhiked to California in 1930. After he lost a trucking job, he lived in a Depression-era migratory camp and picked peaches. He found out years later that John Steinbeck actually wrote *The Grapes of Wrath* in the same place. Born Leonard Slye, Roy took the name Rogers when Republic came up with a surname reflecting the enormous popularity of the late Will Rogers. He and Dale Evans wrote a joint autobiography *Happy Trails* in 1979. His various business enterprises include a Western museum and fast-food restaurants.

744. ROGERS, Will (humorist [America's Greatest Humorist]; b. Nov. 4, 1879, Oolagah, OK (Indian Territory); d. Aug. 15, 1935, Point Barrow, AK). *Gulf Headliners* (1933–34).

Cowboy philosopher-entertainer. A wealthy rancher's son, Rogers joined a Wild West show in 1903 and soon took his rope tricks into vaudeville. He added homespun commentary on the events of the day, and rose to top-billed star of the Ziegfeld Follies and a sought-after dinner speaker and silent film actor. This shrewd and savvy observer of early 20th-century life and times brought his richly humorous wisdom to nationally syndicated columns and to coast-to-coast broadcasts.

In the 1920s Rogers filled requests by stations to stand at a mike and pass along his down-to-earth views in his own inimitable style. His first broadcast was with a group of Follies girls at KDKA in 1922. On Election Night 1924 he added quips to the coverage of returns by WEAF and Graham MacNamee. It was the first regional network broadcast of national elections.

Will Rogers

Rogers was never entirely at ease behind a mike, especially in a studio, where no audience was present. Used to laughter and applause, he worked best with a sounding board in the manner of Cantor and Wynn. NBC featured his monologue "Fifteen Minutes with a Diplomat" on its Inaugural program in November 1926. On an early large-scale hookup over NBC, the Dodge Brothers *Victory Hour* special, Will mimicked Calvin Coolidge. Speaking from his home in Beverly Hills, Rogers gave the impression that the U.S. President was his houseguest and had agreed to say a few words on the state of the union. A surprising number of people actually believed that Coolidge was part of the remote pickup.

In 1930 Rogers first appeared on a regular series, a 13-week CBS program for Squibb Pharmaceuticals. With few pockets of the country without access to radio, Rogers more and more stood as a VIP guest — for station dedications, NRA galas, Red Cross fundraisers, political conventions and shortwave tributes. In 1933 his own Sunday evening series for Gulf inevitably attracted large audiences. A 15-minute monologue, not unlike his Follies routine, brightened up the lives of countless Depression-dazed Americans.

"The hardest thing over this radio," he observed after forgetting that radio demanded split-second timing, "is to get me stopped. So tonight I got me a clock here. When that alarm goes off, I am going to stop, that is all there is to it."

The man who said he never met a man he didn't like worked on the air well into 1935 and at a period when production of his films demanded much of his time and energy. Nevertheless, he broke away in August 1935 to accompany aviator Wiley Post on a trip to study the feasibility of an air route between Alaska and Russia. Leaving Fairbanks for Barrow where adverse weather conditions prevailed, Post's plane crashed in the bleak Arctic wasteland, ending the remarkable life of one of the country's most original and respected citizens.

745. ROLFE, Benjamin Albert (B.A.) (conductor [signature song: "Happy Days Are Here Again"]; b. Oct. 24, 1879, Brasher Falls, NY; d. April 23, 1956, Walpole, MA). *Lucky Strike Dance Orchestra* (1928–32); *Believe It or Not* (1934–c40).

Exponent of fervent, fast-tempo dance rhythms in early network days. A vaudeville cornetist, film producer and promoter-manager, he led an orchestra at the Palais d'Or restaurant on Broadway where he aired a noonday program. He joined NBC for twice weekly broadcasts hyping American Tobacco's leading brand. His 55-piece orchestra with such master musicians as Ross Gorman, Frank Banta, Milton Rettenberg, Andy Sannella, Phil Napoleon — was the largest dance band in radio — and some say the loudest. A prolific group on the Edison label, Rolfe's aggregation appeared on the NBC Inaugural broadcast in November 1926. Two years later his Lucky Strike series became the first to be broadcast to the West Coast.

The rotund conductor believed dance music should "throb and laugh with happiness." In 1931 with the Depression tempering this overly joyful thrust, and 468 broadcasts under his baton, Rolfe resigned and traveled overseas. In 1932 he participated in one of the first broadcasts from Hawaii to the mainland. He remained active in radio until the early 1940s, then settled in Long Beach, California, as its municipal bandmaster. He returned to the air at WNAC Boston, chiefly as a raconteur.

746. ROOSEVELT, Eleanor (commentator; b. Oct. 11, 1884, New York, NY; d. Nov. 7, 1962, New York, NY). *Eleanor Roosevelt Chats/It's a Woman's World/Talks by Eleanor Roosevelt* (1932–42, 1947–51).

Her "special quality" of saying meaningful things simply and concisely won a large daytime following for this forthright First Lady. She was praised for her mastery of delivery and timing as for her constant awareness of her unseen audience. Sponsors signed her for 15-minute talks while her husband, Franklin D. Roosevelt, was Governor of New York. Although her fees from Simmons Mattress and others were given to charity, she periodically faced criticism for commercial broadcasts. After FDR took office as President, she briefly retired, but by mid-1934 was again broadcasting. In 1935 Selby Shoes offered $72,000 for 16 talks, permitting her to direct all monies to a favorite cause, American Friends Service Committee. Her soft, well-pitched voice heard on topics of interest to women sold tons of Pond's Cream and Sweetheart Soap. The Pan American Coffee Bureau spon-

Eleanor Roosevelt (courtesy of Capital Cities/ABC)

sored her series of talks on current events on the eve of World War II.

After the death of FDR, Eleanor's daughter Anna joined her for an ABC morning series over 200 stations. For the first time, she failed to attract a sponsor. In 1950 NBC placed her at a WNBC mike with son Elliott Roosevelt for a daily 45-minute program, and that network also featured her on a Sunday TV discussion show. Eleanor Roosevelt made frequent radio talks and guest appearances on current issues programs, among them *America's Town Meeting of the Air, University of Chicago Round Table, Meet the Press* and *The UN is My Beat.* She often visited the *Mary Margaret McBride Program* to discuss human rights in her role as U.S. Representative on the Social, Humanitarian and Cultural Committee of the United Nations.

747. ROSE, David (conductor; b. June 15, 1910, London, England; d. Aug. 23, 1990, Burbank, CA). *California Melodies* (1940–41); *Red Skelton Show* (1947–53); *David Rose Show* (1950); *Bold Venture* (1950–51).

Orchestra leader-composer with many credits for TV background music and film scores. In one week he wrote eight tunes for broadcast, including the hit "Holiday for Strings." Rose joined Red Skelton for a radio-TV collaboration that lasted for some 25 years. Earlier, he had been with NBC's staff orchestra in Chicago for eight years, four of them as arranger. Mutual hired him as musical director in 1938. During military service, he composed music for *Winged Victory,* an AAF benefit show brought to Broadway and to the movie screen. A performance of his work "Waukegan Concert," inspired by the comic violin playing of Jack Benny, was performed by an orchestra conducted by Leopold Stokowski at the Hollywood Bowl.

Rose described his musical style as "in-between," neither jazz nor classical. He studied at the Chicago College of Music and played piano with Ted Fio Rito. His music for Danny Kaye's 1945 film *Wonder Man* was nominated for an Oscar.

748. ROSS, David (announcer; b. 1891, New York, NY; d. Nov. 12, 1975, New York, NY). *The Shadow* (1931–32); *Fred Waring Show* (1934–39).

A book and play reviewer in 1926, he happened to be visiting the old WABC studios in New York one day when there was a point on the day's schedule for which nothing had been planned. Ross volunteered to do a short dramatic reading. The result was an offer to join the station as a staff announcer. He soon became part of CBS with recitations as a poet-announcer. He also did commercials and made recordings of poetry. Notwithstanding the classic fluff—a recommendation for a new "mouse wash"—Ross received the American Academy of Arts and Letters diction award in 1932.

His well-modulated voice and fervent phrases on *Words in the Night* and *A Rendezvous with David Ross*

attracted a large following who stayed with him as he moved to other networks. Ross retired as a freelance announcer at age 81, but continued to write verse for literary periodicals and books until his death three years later.

749. ROSS, Lanny (singer [signature song: "Moonlight and Roses"]; b. Jan. 19, 1906, Seattle, WA; d. April 25, 1988, New York, NY). *Troubadour of the Moon* (1930–31); *Maxwell House Show Boat* (1931–37); *Hollywood Mardi Gras* (1937–38); *Your Hit Parade* (1938–39); *Lanny Ross Program* (1948–52).

All-American scholar-athlete-musician at Yale, he held the national 300-yard track championship, led the glee club and belonged to the Whiffenpoofs. He gave up a chance for the 1928 Olympic team to make an undergraduate concert tour. Between track training and classes, Lanny commuted to New York once each week to sing on the air with the Jeddo Highlanders, an octet from Yale. While at Columbia Law School, he made his expenses by appearances at NBC. In 1931 he put aside his LL.B. and began as tenor soloist at a salary five times greater than that offered by a law firm. His *Show Boat* series quickly achieved the second highest Hooper rating for any program.

Ross had hopes of becoming a classical singer like his idol John McCormack but the tall lyric tenor won acclaim for his mainstream American love songs. Nonetheless, he studied at Juilliard for his Town Hall recital. He also turned to acting in films (*Melody in Spring, College Rhythm*) and on Broadway (*Petticoat*

Lanny Ross

Fever). Yet by 1940 he was busier than ever on radio, singing on ten CBS programs a week for Franco-American Spaghetti (with separate East and West Coast broadcasts Monday through Friday night). Lanny Ross moved into early television after World War II military service. He married his manager Olive White in 1935.

750. ROTHAFEL, Samuel "Roxy" (emcee; [catchphrases: "Hello, everybody. This is Roxy speaking."; "Goodnight . . . pleasant dreams . . . God bless you."]; b. July 9, 1881, Stillwater, MN; d. Jan. 13, 1936, New York, NY). *Roxy's Gang* (1922–32); *Roxy Revue* (1934–35).

A radio editor described Roxy as "sedately humorous, gently witty" as he presided before the microphone with his gang of entertainers. The first host of an ongoing variety series, he summoned his troupe to broadcast over WEAF between shows at the Capitol Theatre in New York. Like a proud parent, this stage manager-impresario informally introduced them, described their costumes, and chatted about their musical selections and accomplishments. "My gang," he called them, and the name stuck to soprano Gladys Rice, baritone Douglas Stanbury, ballerina Maria Gambarelli, cellist Yascha Bunchuck, tenor Wee Willie Robyn, basso Jim Coombs, concertmaster Eugene Ormandy and a score of others.

The whole business of broadcasting from the Capitol evolved from experiments by Bell Telephone engineers on a public address system for that large movie house. To save his voice at a rehearsal, ex-marine Rothafel gave up shouting through a mega-

S. L. Rothafel

phone and used a microphone and amplifier. He was so pleased that he gave the company permission to use an offstage dressing room as a permanent place to house their equipment. The sound engineers soon installed microphones around the proscenium to pick up the music of the orchestra, and relay it to the laboratory downtown. This led to WEAF programs direct from the theatre, beginning on November 19, 1922. The Sunday evening broadcasts increased the number of ticket buyers at the box office — to the surprise of Roxy's boss Edward "Major" Bowes — and generated bushels of letters from listeners near and far. Roxy especially utilized radio to bring cheer to invalids, particularly to veterans in military hospitals for whom he also raised funds for individual bedside radio sets.

By the time NBC came into place with flagship station WEAF, *Roxy's Gang* was heard in over half the United States, and Rothafel himself was an outstanding personality of the airwaves. His fame led in 1927 to a colossal new movie palace called The Roxy — a 6,214-seat, cathedral-like theatre with a large radio studio for the 110-piece Roxy Symphony, the Roxy Chorus and assorted solo performers. But the earlier close-knit feeling of a family gathering was lost in such a grandiose setting. The creative imagination of this master showman took him one block east to manage the world's biggest showplace, Radio City Music Hall, in 1932. But its opening with costly and overextended all-stage entertainment failed to draw sufficient audiences at the depth of the Depression.

Roxy's disagreement over vaudeville acts versus motion picture presentations with Rockefeller Center, Inc., led to a promptly insisted upon semi-retirement. Plagued by illness, he never managed another New York theatre. In 1934 a less ebullient Roxy returned to radio with *The Roxy Revue* and a new gang of young entertainers. Castoria sponsored the CBS show, which never captured public fancy as his early hookups had.

The precision-dancing Music Hall Rockettes — an offshoot of his earlier Roxyettes — remain his only visible legacy and a perennial New York attraction.

751. ROVENTINI, Johnny (commercial announcer; b. Aug. 15, 1910, Brooklyn, NY). *Ferde Grofe Show* (1933); *Johnny Presents* (1939–47).

His "Call for Phil-lip Mor-ress" is one of the well-entranched commercial intros of radio. Philip Morris Tobacco first signed Johnny, a pint-sized bellboy, to pipe his shrill call over the air in 1933. Her perfect B-flat call had an unforgettable ring. Johnny, a 43 inch tall midget, wore a martial-styled bellhop's uniform in his many appearances at trade shows, conventions and festivals as well as broadcasts.

He had started work as a bellhop at the Hotel Manger in New York and later became a page boy at the Hotel New Yorker where he was discovered by the cigarette manufacturer's vice president for sales, Alfred E. Lyon, and ad agency president Milton Biow. Philip

Morris had already adopted the bellboy trademark for window posters and counter signs advertising its cigarette. Now they wanted a living trademark to represent the company and increase product recognition. An actual life-size trademark proved to a clever sales move, and for Johnny, a lifetime of "stepping out of store windows everywhere."

752. ROWE, Genevieve (singer; b. Aug. 28, 1908, Fremont, OH; d. Feb. 26, 1995, New York, NY). *Johnny Presents* (1935–39); *Gay Nineties Revue* (1939–42); *Songs America Loves* (1940); *An Evening with Romberg* (1946).

Rowe won the 1929 Atwater Kent singing contest while a student of piano and voice at The College of Wooster in Ohio where her father served as professor of Music and her mother taught music theory. The $6,000 prize allowed her to study in New York. Rowe made a Town Hall debut in 1934 and soon won a fellowship at the Juilliard School of Opera, and the role as Queen of the Night in its production of *The Magic Flute*. She auditioned regularly for radio, ultimately gaining chorus jobs.

As part of Ray Bloch's Swing Fourteen ensemble, she appeared on *Johnny Presents*. When one of the featured singers became ill, Rowe filled in. It led to solos and her own CBS series. That took her to Alfred Wallenstein's Bach Cantata and Mozart opera programs at

Mutual and the vocal role as Jenny Lind on *Gay Nineties Revue*. A coloratura soprano described as "light, flexible, true and very pleasant," she toured widely for Columbia Concerts. Her husband, Robert P. Hill, was her accompanist. Upon retirement, Rowe became a secondary school music teacher in Westfield, New Jersey and a voice coach.

753. ROWELL, Glenn (singer, comedian [signature song: "Hello, Hello, Hello"]; b. Nov. 2, 1899, Pontiac, MI; d. Oct. 9, 1965). *Quaker Early Birds* (1930–32); *Gene and Glenn* (1933–41).

Member of Ford and Glenn, a close harmony duo on Columbia records and Chicago radio from 1925 to 1930. They added Gene Carroll, and when Ford Rush left to lead an orchestra, the act became Gene and Glenn for an early morning song and humor program and an occasional evening series spot (*National Barn Dance*). Their Jake and Lena situation comedy characters proved popular. They began at WTAM Cleveland and ended the act at WTIC Hartford in the early 1940s.

Rowell studied piano at a St. Louis conservatory. A song plugger and music publisher's rep, he became an organist-pianist in Chicago theatres, and in 1924 on radio. His many compositions included religious songs ("Read Your Bible Every Day," "Next Door to Jesus").

754. ROY, Cecil (actress [The Girl of a Thousand Voices]; b. 1900, St. Paul, MN; d. Jan. 26, 1995, Englewood, NJ).

Known for the ability to play anybody or anything in the space of a single program. She once created 17 voices and a dog for WOR's *Daily Dilemma* in 1946, and claimed a knack to impersonate anyone she ever heard talk. Directors called Roy the "cradle to the grave lady" because of a versatility to portray a crying baby or an old crone. Her credits included *Amanda of Honeymoon Hill*, *Kaltenmyers Kindergarten* and *The Goldbergs*.

After graduating from college, she taught school, then traveled as a book publishers representative. Turning to acting with a stock company, Roy entered Chicago radio with *Clara, Lu and Em* in 1934. Later, she was the cartoon voice of Little Lulu and Caspar the Friendly Ghost. Her recordings for children included a dramatization of Winnie the Pooh.

755. RUBIN, Benny (comedian; b. Feb. 2, 1899, Boston, MA; d. July 15, 1986, Los Angeles, CA).

Dialect comic on Jack Benny's programs. A vaudeville headliner, he began an act in small-time revues and burlesque, then teamed up with Jack Haley in the 1920s. He played the Palace and made numerous two-reel "talkies." Rubin usually played genial ethnic characters in support of other comics. At the height of the amateur hour craze, he hosted the Feenamint *National Amateur Hour* with musical director Arnold Johnson.

Genevieve Rowe (courtesy of Genevieve Rowe)

Rubinoff

756. RUBINOFF, David (violinist, conductor; b. Sept. 3, 1897, Grodno, Russia; d. Oct. 6, 1986, Columbus, OH). *Chase & Sanborn Hour* (1931–35); *Rubinoff and His Violin* (1935–37).

Part of Eddie Cantor's troupe in the early 1930s, Rubinoff was first brought to radio by Rudy Vallee who heard him at New York's Paramount. He also had speaking parts over the air, and was widely impersonated but his Russian accent was far less pronounced in ordinary conversation. His own program, for Chevrolet, started in 1935. It grew into one of the first major transcribed series, heard on hundreds of stations linked together by its auto sponsor. He played himself in the 1935 film *Thanks a Million* with Fred Allen and Dick Powell.

Rubinoff started lessons on the violin at age five and studied at the Royal Conservatory of Warsaw. In 1911 Victor Herbert was so impressed he brought the entire Rubinoff family to America. This teenage protege soon conducted local theatre orchestras and various bands in Pittsburgh and Minneapolis. He left for New York in 1926.

757. RUFFNER, Edmund (Tiny) (announcer; b. Nov. 8, 1899, Crawfordsville, IN; d. Feb. 23, 1983, Mt. Clemens, MI). *Show Boat* (1932–c36); *Captain Diamond's Adventures* (1932–34).

Singer-announcer-director. Ruffner left the stage after several roles in Shubert productions (*Princess Flavia*) to join WEAF in 1927. Also, as assistant to the chief of Judson Radio Bureau, he developed and placed some 20 programs on the air in 1929–30. He became director for Benton & Bowles radio department, with Fred Allen and *Show Boat* under his wing as writer-producer. He was heard on *Palmolive Beauty Box Theatre* and *The Better Half.* Known professionally as Tiny Ruffner, he towered over his confreres at six foot six.

Coming out of the Army in 1918, he had gone to work for Standard Oil of California as a salesman. In 1924 the company aired a show on KFL Los Angeles. Tiny was chosen as leading man, singing Gilbert and Sullivan and Victor Herbert operettas. That led to a brief concert career before he successfully auditioned as announcer for NBC.

758. RUSSELL, Andy (singer; b. Sept. 16, 1919, Los Angeles, CA; d. April 16, 1992, Phoenix, AZ). *Your Hit Parade* (1946–47).

Bilingual singer who popularized Spanish-flavored songs of the 1940s. His romantic renditions of "Besame Mucho," "Amor" and "I Can't Begin to Tell You" placed him among the decade's leading crooners. Born Andres Rabago, he had played drums and sang with Gus Arnheim and Alvino Rey. His best-selling Capitol Records led to contracts for Joan Davis' show and his own program. In 1946 he replaced Tibbett as *Hit Parade* star.

Although his screen appearances were forgettable, he gained a measure of success on television with his singer-wife Della Russell. He enjoyed widespread acclaim with shows, films and recordings in Mexico and Argentina. He also worked on commercials for Spanish-language radio in the United States.

Andy Russell

759. RYAN, Irene Noblette (comedienne, actress; b. Oct. 17, 1903, El Paso, TX; d. April 26, 1973, Santa Monica, CA). *Tim & Irene Sky Road Show* (1934–35); *Royal Crown Revue* (1938).

Vaudeville and tab show veteran with husband Tim Ryan, a singer-comedian. Soon after playing the Palace, the duo moved into radio in 1932 with *Carefree Carnival.* They enjoyed several seasons on the dial, including a summer show for Jell-O in 1936.

The five-feet-tall Irene played old and odd characters in films and made her Broadway bow in *Pippin* in 1972. It won the 69-year-old performer a Tony nomination. Irene achieved her greatest popularity as the irascible Granny on TV's *Beverly Hillbillies.*

As Irene Noblette, she began in amateur nights in San Francisco at age eleven. In the 1940s she was part of Bob Hope's Victory Caravan and overseas trips to Berlin. With her earnings she established the million-dollar Irene Ryan Foundation to provide countrywide scholarships to worthy theatre arts students.

760. RYAN, Patricia (actress; b. Feb. 25, 1921, London, England; d. Feb. 15, 1949, New York, NY). *Let's Pretend* (1934–49); *Claudia and David* (1941–42).

Child performer who began in 1929 in the role of Helen in *The Adventures of Helen and Mary,* a tale of romance and adventure. A forerunner of *Let's Pretend,* it segued into a juvenile repertory company at CBS with Pat playing many leading roles for 15 years. Although she never had any professional training, she matured as an actress into grownup parts on *Joyce Jordan, The Parker Family* and *Girl Alone.* She extended her dramatic range as the child bride in *Claudia and David* opposite Richard Kollmar. Ryan also played Geraldine on *The Aldrich Family* and tried script writing. Her original story called "The Silver Knight" aired on *Let's Pretend.*

On a Valentine's Day 1949 broadcast of "Valentine for Sophia" on *Cavalcade of America,* she played opposite Glenn Ford in the role of a girl who was afflicted with severe headaches. Ironically, she complained of a similar condition just prior to airtime. For the broadcast Pat struggled through her biggest scene before staggering from the mike. Several actresses assumed her part but near the end of the drama she was able to step in and say her last lines. The 27-year-old Ryan returned home and died that night of a cerebral hemorrhage.

761. SALTER, Harry (conductor; b. Sept. 14, 1898, Bucharest, Roumania; d. March 5, 1984, Mamaroneck, NY). *Your Hit Parade* (1935–37); *Hobby Lobby* (1937–43); *Stop The Music!* (1948–52).

Musical director and one of the originators of *Stop The Music!* Salter selected the mystery tunes. "None of us expected the immediate overwhelming response the program got," he wrote in 1950, "and in the beginning I chose the mystery melody by simply rifling

Harry Salter

through my files. It wasn't long before I had to hire three musicologists to assist me." The show created more national excitement than any other post-war game or contest.

Salter and conductor Mark Warnow put together the nucleus of the giveaway, bringing in aspects of *Pot o' Gold, Hit Parade* and *Manhattan Merry-Go-Round.* Producers Lou Cowan and Mark Goodson brought it to life at ABC to run against NBC comedy shows and CBS dramatic offerings. Salter garnered high grades for the all-important musical segments that featured vocalists Kay Armen and Dick Brown.

A violinist, he had played with B. A. Rolfe and led the six-piece Rose Room orchestra over WEAF every evening. For Atlantic Broadcasting Company, he conducted the Atlantic Ensemble for Steinway Hall. His first major network show *Log Cabin* had him back Lanny Ross. While conducting *Hobby Lobby,* he met his wife Roberta Semple who appeared to talk about her hobby of Biblical perfumes. He was also the original producer and conductor for the long-running *Name That Tune* on television.

762. SANDERS, Joe (bandleader [The Ole Left Hander] [signature song: "I Found a Rose in the Snow"]; b. Oct. 15, 1896, Thayer, KS; d. May 14, 1965, Kansas City, KS).

From nighttime broadcasts in 1922 at the Muehlebach Hotel over 500-watt WDAF Kansas City, his Coon-Sanders Band became widely known. Its program, *The Nighthawks Frolic,* issued membership cards to "nighthawks." They eventually totaled 37,000 in every state, Canada and Mexico. Organized in 1919 with Carleton Coon, it was the first dance outfit to play on a regularly scheduled program. Sanders conducted, played the piano, sang, and wrote songs. By the late '20s, the band settled in Chicago, homebase as it toured the country for one-night stands.

Coon died in 1932. Sanders retired but returned to the bandstand two years later. In 1939 his musicians broadcast from an airplane 5,000 feet above San Francisco.

In his youth Sanders, a lefty, pitched for the KC Athletic Club; he once was responsible for a perfect baseball game of 27 consecutive strikeouts.

763. SANDERSON, Julia (singer, emcee [signature song: "Sweet Lady"]; b. Aug. 22, 1887, Springfield, MA; d. Jan. 27, 1975, Springfield, MA). *Blackstone Plantation* (1929–34); *Battle of the Sexes* (1938–40); *Let's Be Charming* (1943–44).

Her cheery rapport and vocal harmony with husband-singer Frank Crumit made them an ideal radio couple with billing as The Singing Sweethearts. They also co-emceed an early audience-participation contest that featured their singing. In 1914 as a musical comedy star of *The Girl from Utah,* Sanderson, a soprano, introduced Jerome Kern's enduring ballad "They Didn't Believe Me." She briefly continued alone on the air after Crumit's death in 1943.

764. SANFORD, Harold (conductor; b. 1879, Florence, MA; d. Jan. 19, 1945, Springfield, MA). *Philco Hour* (1927–30); *Dutch Master Minstrels* (1929–30); *Exploring America with Carveth Wells* (1931–33).

NBC staff conductor from 1927 to 1940. Best known for directing the orchestra and singers for Philco's operetta series and Gilbert and Sullivan works, he composed incidental music for *Great Highways* and theme songs ("Mem'ries," "The Cavalcade March"). Sanford was a close friend of Victor Herbert, for whom he made many orchestrations, conducted and played violin.

765. SANNELLA, Andy (bandleader; b. March 11, 1900, Brooklyn, NY; d. 1961). *Campbell Soup Orchestra* (1931); *Manhattan Merry-Go-Round* (1934–37); *Gillette Community Sing* (1936–37).

Conductor and frequent soloist while a staff musician. He was proficient on saxophone, clarinet and violin. At NBC he inaugurated a series of saxophone recitals and was its first Hawaiian steel guitar soloist. Sannella was featured on the *Lucky Strike Dance Orchestra, Palmolive Hour* and *Armstrong Quakers.* His best stint as conductor came on *Manhattan Merry-Go-Round* as it spotlighted famous acts of the theatre with original headliners Blanche Ring, Fritzi Scheff, Donald Brian and Louise Groody. He settled in Hollywood as a sideman by the late '30s.

At 17 Sannella joined the submarine division of the Navy, and after his discharge at Panama City, obtained a job as a violinist at a local hotel. Back in Brooklyn in the 1920s, he played in the bands of Mike Markel and Ray Miller. He recorded extensively on a dozen labels.

766. SCHNABEL, Stefan (actor; b. Feb. 2, 1912, Berlin, Germany). *Grand Central Station* (1937–38); *The Shadow* (1937–39); *Valiant Lady* (1941–42); *Studio One* (1947–48).

Actor — straight, heavy or character — in over 5,000 shows. A performer in Germany and at London's Old Vic, he landed in New York in 1937 and immediately picked up a part in *Columbia Workshop*'s presentation of "R.U.R." Assignments quickly followed in *We, the People, Johnny Presents, March of Time* and other series. In 1944 he played opposite Gertrude Lawrence in a *Revlon Theatre* version of "Avalanche" over the Blue Network; in 1951 he portrayed Kurtz in *The Theatre Guild on the Air*'s "The Third Man." Schnabel often played Nazi roles and "bleeding victims" on *This Is Our Enemy,* and during World War II broadcast propaganda messages to his native Germany.

While with *The Shadow,* he met Orson Welles who invited him to perform in his Federal Theatre productions. In the Mercury Theatre's "War of the Worlds," Schnabel played a Pennsylvania Dutch farmer who dies at the hands of the Martians. In 1983 he recalled the turmoil at CBS during that 1938 Halloween Eve broadcast. After he had finished his part, he sat in an anteroom at the studio. "A few policemen trickled in,

Stefan Schnabel (courtesy of Stefan Schnabel)

then a few more. Soon the room was full of police, and a massive struggle was going on between the police, page boys and CBS executives, who were trying to prevent the cops from busting in and stopping the show. It was quite a show to witness."

His film bow was in Welles' *Journey into Fear* in 1941. On Broadway he appeared with Welles in the Cole Porter musical *Around the World in 80 Days,* and in *Plain and Fancy* and *The Cherry Orchard.* He enjoyed a long run as Dr. Steve Jackson on TV's *Guiding Light.* His father was concert pianist Artur Schnabel.

767. SCHUMANN-HEINK, Ernestine (singer; b. June 15, 1861, Prague, Czechoslovakia; d. Nov. 17, 1936, Hollywood, CA). *Enna Jettick Melodies* (1930); *Hoover Sentinels Serenade* (1934–35).

International concert and operatic contralto. Her warm motherly cheerfulness endeared her to a wide public. Admired as much for her generosity and spirit as for her artistry, she enraptured audiences with familiar Brahms songs and her annual Christmas Eve rendition of "Silent Night" in her native German. One of the most celebrated heroines of Wagnerian opera at the turn of the century, she ventured into radio when very few great singers approached the unfamiliar and somewhat intimidating microphone.

As early as 1921 while on a West Coast concert tour, Schumann-Heink took time to venture to the new radio station of the Stockton *Record.* Manager of KWG had asked her to stop by and sing a song or two. She agreed, and climbed two steep flights of stairs to

Ernestine Schumann-Heink

the radiophone mike for a mini-program of two well-known selections: "At Parting" and "The Rosary." "I love radio, even without the audience," she said a dozen years and a hundred or more broadcasts later. "In my spirit I see them all, all their faces, and I am inspired."

Not long after NBC was formed, the network added her to its advisory staff as operatic counsel. She continued her vocal career well into her 70s and was still a fine singer, although her range had been compressed to little more than half of its former scope. Whenever she could be induced to sing or to speak, either in person or on the air, she remained a drawing card. Madame Heink sang on many special broadcasts for the American Legion (although her sons fought on both sides in World War I, her loyalty to her adopted country never wavered). At the time of her death, she was beginning a film career in Hollywood.

768. SCHWARZKOPF, H. Norman (narrator; b. Aug. 28, 1895, Newark, NJ; d. Nov. 25, 1958, West Orange, NJ). *Gangbusters* (1938–40).

Investigator-state police officer. As Superintendent of the New Jersey force, he became involved in the Lindbergh kidnapping and trial of Bruno Richard Hauptmann, who was executed in 1936 for the crime. His role in the case brought international prominence and an association with *Gangbusters.* He interviewed a law enforcement officer who figured in the crime re-enacted each week on that series. The program was done in cooperation with police and federal law enforcement departments throughout the country. The lead-in was a simulated prison break with wailing sirens and piercing whistles.

A West Point graduate, Colonel Schwarzkopf served the State Police from 1921 until 1936 when Governor Harold Hoffman replaced him with a political ally. Following work in the life insurance business, he entered the National Guard and was assigned by the Army to Iran to reorganize its police and training program. In the 1950s he served the NJ Department of Law & Public Safety, and as a major general led the 78th Division of the Army Reserve Corps. His son, Norman, Jr., served as commander in chief, U.S. Forces, Operation Desert Shield and Desert Storm, in 1990–91.

769. SCOTT, Raymond (conductor, composer [signature song: "Toy Trumpet"]; b. Sept. 10, 1909, Brooklyn, NY; d. Feb. 8, 1994, North Hills, CA). *Your Hit Parade* (1949–57).

Time magazine once called Scott's jazz style so sophisticated that it seemed almost a caricature of jazz. His quintet concentrated on music specifically written by him for the microphone. His screwball titles — "Dinner Music for a Pack of Hungry Cannibals," "Huckleberry Duck," "Bumpy Weather over Newark" — gained him the reputation of an eccentric wag. In 1938 with CBS recording equipment, engineers and arrangers at his disposal, he created a jazz laboratory to create his uncommon music. A year later he organized a full-size swing-oriented band while a staff conductor at CBS.

Born Harry Warnow, he started as a pianist in his brother Mark Warnow's CBS orchestra. In 1936 he changed his name to Scott. Fifteen years later, when Mark died, Raymond picked up his baton for *Your Hit Parade.* His singing discovery and '50s *Hit Parade* vocalist Dorothy Collins was his second wife. He invented several electronic and keyboard instruments, and contributed background music to cartoons and other films.

770. SCOURBY, Alexander (actor, host; b. Nov. 13, 1913, Brooklyn, NY; d. Feb. 23, 1985, Boston, MA). *Right to Happiness* (1944–46); *The Eternal Light* (1944–57); *Your United Nations* (1946–47).

Famous for his rich bass voice as an actor-narrator and host. He started on the New York stage as a Shakespearean actor in 1936, and soon began working widely in radio using the name Alexander Scott. At one point, he played running roles in five different soap operas, including *Against the Storm.* He also portrayed Superman's father Jor-el. Scourby was regularly heard on *The Eternal Light* for nearly 14 years. During World War II he did broadcasts in Greek for the Office of War Information.

For 40 years he recorded many works for the blind, including all 66 books of the King James version of the Bible; it took four years and on its release in 1966 became a best seller. Active in films and television, he was a host of a National Public Radio *Live from the Met* production, taping in Boston when he died.

771. SEVAREID, Eric (correspondent; b. Nov. 26, 1912, Velva, ND; d. July 9, 1992, Washington, DC).

Recruited as a CBS news reporter by Edward R. Murrow at the outbreak of war in Europe in 1939. He delivered authoritative commentaries spoken in serious tones with an underlining caustic wit. "His writing ability and experience, combined with an ability to project a sense of fairness and sound judgment, brought him the respect of his peers and audiences," wrote Herbert Mitgang of *The New York Times* at his death. Sevareid was the last American to broadcast from Paris when the Nazis invaded in 1940. He reported the Battle of Britain bombing raids in London, and in 1943 headed for the China-Burma-India theatre where he survived the crash of a crippled airplane in a Burmese jungle.

Back in Europe in 1944 he covered the campaign in Italy, landed with the first wave of Americans in southern France and accompanied them across the Rhine into Germany. His rugged good looks and scholarly mien carried him into television, and participation in CBS newscasts. His autobiography *Not So*

Wild a Dream (1946) went through eleven printings and became a reference book for historians and students of the Depression and war years.

772. SEYMOUR, Anne (actress; b. Sept. 11, 1909, New York, NY; d. Dec. 11, 1988, Los Angeles, CA). *Grand Hotel* (1933–37); *The Story of Mary Marlin* (1936–43); *A Woman of America* (1943–45); *My Secret Story* (1951–54).

The seventh generation of her family to be on the stage, she decided to look into radio at WLW in 1932. She played in more than 300 programs within a strenuous three months' period — everything from fashion commentary to mystery thrillers. Moving to Chicago, the summer stock-trained actress co-starred with Don Ameche in *Grand Hotel.* That led to a contract as *Mary Marlin,* one of the most popular soap opera characters of the day. Four years later she went to Broadway where she had acted prior to radio, but soon rejoined the serial when it moved to New York. In the 1940s she periodically filled the lead in *Portia Faces Life,* replacing Lucille Wall and Alice Frost.

Among other assignments was the part of a Japanese woman in the famous John Hersey *Hiroshima* broadcast. Seymour herself voluntarily left what she called "the luxurious rut of obscurity" of daytime drama in 1946, and freelanced and wrote and sold radio scripts. In 1950 she returned full time to the air with the situation comedy *The Magnificent Montague,* opposite Monty Woolley. A character actress in films, she made her debut as Lucy Stark in *All the King's Men* in 1949.

773. SEYMOUR, Dan (announcer, host; b. Feb. 22, 1915, New York, NY; d. July 27, 1982, New York, NY). *Young Man with a Band* (1939–40); *We, the People* (1943–51); *Molle Mystery Theatre* (1945–48); *The Aldrich Family* (1948–50).

After graduation from Amherst College in 1935, he entered radio as an announcer at WNAC Boston of the Yankee Network, and a year later joined CBS as staff announcer. The dulcet-toned Seymour impressed his superiors. He could wax lyrical on a Spry commercial on *Aunt Jenny,* handle popular music jargon as emcee on *Camel Caravan,* and preside over the human interest script of *We, the People.* He was the announcer on Orson Welles's memorable broadcast of "War of the Worlds." It was generally known that he was making better than $100,000 a year before he was 30.

But he was far from satisfied. So as a business executive he moved into production as the supervisor of the wartime series *Now It Can Be Told* and in 1950 *We, the People.* He then switched to Young & Rubicam advertising agency to handle television programming. In 1955 he joined J. Walter Thompson as director of its Radio-TV Department; by 1964 he was chairman of the Executive Committee and president. "I never really enjoyed being a performer," he once

Dan Seymour

told a reporter. "The process of simply reading lines became a bore. I became fascinated with the whole business of mass communication and mass persuasion." And in the process made his firm an influential leader in the development of both programming and advertising for television.

774. SHARBUTT, Del (announcer; b. Feb. 16, 1910, Ft. Worth, TX). *Lavender and Old Lace* (1934–36); *Hobby Lobby* (1937–38); *Your Hit Parade* (1947); *Jack Benny Program* (1947–48).

His career began at WBAP in his native Ft. Worth in 1928. He came to the CBS announcing staff in New York in 1934 at age 24, and did remotes, then shows with Bob Hope and W. C. Fields. A weakness for serious drinking—sometimes between the three-hour frame of the East Coast broadcast and the repeat for the West—eventually brought about a confrontation with his doctor who helped him break the habit.

In a 1978 interview with his son Jay Sharbutt of the AP, he noted that drinking was prevalent around radio studios and sometimes caused mayhem on a repeat. Del recalled an amusing on the air incident that stemmed from the tippling of a musician. "Kostelanetz was conducting a program for Chesterfield when suddenly the baton flew out of his hand, right into the bell of Jack Jenney's trombone. Jack was about half loaded on brandy at the time and whispered under his breath, 'Well, if that ain't throwing a cue, I'll kiss _____.' You didn't hear the remark on the air. All you heard was the band falling apart, first the brass section, then the reeds. The band just disintegrated."

775. SHAW, Artie (bandleader [signature song: "Nightmare"]; b. May 26, 1910, New York, NY). *Melody and Madness* (1938–39); *Burns and Allen* (1940–41).

Music business intellectual who organized a series of unusually creative swing aggregations. His bands filled the spectrum from conventional dance combos to strikingly incongruous strings-added groups. A superb clarinetist, Shaw began as a saxophonist in Irving Aaronson's orchestra, then concentrated on free-lancing with Freddie Rich, Howard Barlow and Kostelanetz for broadcasts, earning as much as $500 weekly in the early 1930s. His first band failed to reach a supportive audience; a revamped group with vocalist Billie Holliday and arranger Jerry Gray in 1938—particularly through radio in Boston—brought solid success, and one of the best-selling records of the decade, "Begin the Beguine." Broadcasts, hotel bookings and motion pictures placed Shaw on the swing era map. There were guest spots for his 23-man orchestra on *Fitch Bandwagon,* an old Gold series, and a contract at NBC with *Burns and Allen.* He discovered the tune "Frenesi," making it an instant hit and establishing his arrangement as an all-time big-band classic. Within the band, Shaw's Gramercy Five revealed his outstanding instrumental flexibility.

Shaw entered the Navy in 1942 and led a service band overseas. From the Naval Air Base at Pearl Har-

Artie Shaw

bor, he helped salute President Roosevelt's birthday on a four-network hookup in 1943. The oft-married, sometimes controversial musician frequently took time off to loaf and relax, and to write. The autobiographical *The Trouble with Cinderella* (1952) was his best-received book.

776. SHAW, Hollace (singer; b. July 24, 1913, Fresno, CA; d. March 2, 1976, Los Angeles, CA). *Hour of Charm* (1940–44); *Saturday Night Serenade* (1945–47); *Pet Milk Show* (1948).

Coloratura soprano, once known as "Vivian" in Phil Spitalny's all-girl orchestra on GE's *Hour of Charm.* A native of California, she attended Pomona College and began her career in 1936 after placing first in a musical competition on *The California Hour,* an amateur program on the West Coast. Shaw was featured on CBS sustainers with Mark Warnow and Howard Barlow, and was a frequent guest of Lyn Murray on *To Your Health.* In 1943, fan magazine *Tune In* captioned her photo with the words "knocks 'em dead with voice and looks."

In 1939 she introduced the song "All the Things You Are" in Jerome Kern's Broadway musical *Very Warm for May,* and also sang in *Higher and Higher* with Jack Haley. She appeared regularly at Radio City Music Hall and with symphony orchestras. Her brother founded and directed the Robert Shaw Chorale which often performed with the NBC Symphony from 1948 to 1954.

777. SHEEN, Bishop Fulton J. (preacher; b. May 8, 1895, El Paso, IL; d. Dec. 10, 1979, New York, NY). *Catholic Hour* (1930–52).

Charismatic, widely listened-to religious speaker. His *Catholic Hour* addresses on "One Lord, One World," "The Seventh Word to the Cross," "You" and other topics attracted an audience representing many denominations. Professor of Philosophy at Catholic University of America, Sheen recognized the vast influence of a radio pulpit early in his priesthood. He first came to the microphone at WLWL New York in 1928 and participated in the Interfaith Dedication of Radio City studios in 1933. As auxiliary Bishop of New York he continued his talks, which were designed to help people cope with life, over NBC into the 1950s.

As early as 1940 he had appeared in an Easter service on television. On that medium, beginning in 1952, Bishop Sheen quickly developed into a forceful

George Shelton & cast

influence through his weekly *Life Is Worth Living.* Sponsored by Philco, the DuMont network series ran remarkably strong against tough competition, namely, NBC's Milton Berle. It earned him an Emmy as Most Outstanding Personality of 1952. In the late 1960s he served as Bishop of Rochester, a post he was reputedly "exiled" to when he incurred the anger of Francis Cardinal Spellman over his anti-Vietnam war stance.

778. SHELTON, George (comedian; b. March 4, 1896, New York, NY*; d. Feb. 12, 1971, New York, NY). *Sunday Night Party* (1936–37); *Model Minstrels* (1939–40); *It Pays to Be Ignorant* (1942–49, 1951).

Expert nitwit on the zany *Ignorant* quiz. He started out as a dramatic actor in a Midwest tent show, then enlisted in the Army which sent him overseas for eight major campaigns and a stint with a troop entertainment unit. Shelton teamed up as straightman for comic Tom Howard in vaudeville, movie shorts and radio. *Variety* called their comedy "a low I.Q. ton of bricks."

His first series, *Music That Satisfies,* for Chesterfield, ran in 1933. During the 1935–36 season he made weekly appearances on Vallee's program.

779. SHELTON, Herb (announcer, host; b. 1913, Brooklyn, NY; d. July 21, 1964, Manhasset, NY). *Maggi's Private Wire* (1944–47); *Honeymoon in New York* (1945–47); *Luncheon at the Latin Quarter* (1947–49).

"A warm mike personality," Shelton broke into the network ranks in 1944 after several years as an announcer, program director and DJ at WINS. His audition at NBC consisted of reading news from a prepared script. He stumbled through it, and Pat Kelly, chief of announcers, came out of the control booth with a "well-kid-I'm-sorry" look in his eyes.

"All the 'o's' are missing from this script," Shelton protested.

*Another source gives 1883.

"Ben Grauer read that cold last night," Kelly replied.

But a week later Herb was hired as staff announcer anyway. Six months later he asked Kelly about the notorious script. "I was only kidding," he laughed. "Nobody could have read that thing."

Shelton proved his worth by winning the H. P. Davis award for best announcer on the NBC network. A year earlier, in July 1945, he had rushed to the scene of the crash of a bomber into the upper floors of the Empire State Building, and interviewed witnesses to the disaster.

Shelton joined Maggi McNellis on two talk shows of the 1940s while announcing for *The Fred Waring Show* and *Teentimers Show*. By 1949 at WJZ he had his own show and in the 1950s added a disc jockey-styled children's program called *Egbert and Ummly*. Next, Herb hosted a TV kiddie show along with a Sunday a.m. DJ feature, totaling 12 hours a week. In 1961 he expanded to 18 hours a week with small talk, traffic, weather and recordings for WFYI, key station of the Herald Tribune Radio Network.

780. SHERMAN, Ransom (actor, host; b. Oct. 15, 1898, Appleton, WI; d. Nov. 26, 1985, Henderson, NV). *Club Matinee* (1937–41); *Sunbrite Smile Parade* (1938–39); *Ransom Sherman Presents* (1938–39); *Fibber McGee and Molly* (1941–44).

Actor, host and writer, Sherman was a mainstay of Chicago radio, chiefly at NBC. For *Fibber* he shared the character of Uncle Dennis with Bill Thompson, and was on the show's 1941 summer replacement, *Hap Hazard*. For Tums he emceed the game show *Quicksilver* in 1939–40.

He started as a member of the Three Doctors comedy team of early radio. His programs were a grab bag of nonsense and non sequitars, best expressed as *Mirth and Madness*. On *Club Matinee* he introduced a young Baltimore broadcaster named Garrison Morfit and had listeners help pick his stage name, Garry Moore. Sherman's deadpan expression was a frequent visage on early television from Chicago.

781. SHIELD, Roy (conductor; b. Oct. 2, 1893, Waseca, MN; d. Jan. 9, 1962, Fort Lauderdale, FL). *This Amazing America* (1940); *Design for Listening* (1943–45); *RCA Victor Show* (1946–47); *Top Secret* (1950); *Eternal Light* (1955–56).

Director of music for the central division of NBC Chicago from 1931 to 1945. A pianist and composer, he contributed to numerous series and specials. When *RCA Magic Key* and *Voice of Firestone* picked up segments from Chicago, Shield led a local orchestra. He was sponsored by Armour and Greyhound on his own shows. At the death of Josef Pasternack in 1940, he stepped in within hours to direct the *Contented Hour* and returned for five succeeding broadcasts. Beginning in December 1945 for some 15 years, he became

musicians contractor for the NBC eastern division in New York where he often contributed background music and led NBC orchestras and subbed on *The Band of America*.

Shield studied organ and piano in Chicago and became a pianist in vaudeville and conductor-arranger for Victor Records in Hollywood in the 1920s. He also composed and scored incidental music for Hal Roach comedies. His 1944 composition "Your America" was introduced on a Union Pacific Railroad program in observance of the 10th anniversary of the country's first streamlined train.

782. SHILKRET, Nat (conductor [signature song: "Dusky Stevedore"]; b. Dec. 25, 1889, Queens, NY; d. Feb. 18, 1982, Franklin Square, NY). *Eveready Hour* (1923–30); *Music That Satisfies* (1931–32); *Smith Brothers: Trade and Mark* (1934–35); *Palmolive Beauty Box Theatre* (1934–35); *Relaxation Time* (1938–39).

Versatile, hardworking conductor-orchestrator who combined recording duties with radio features. At 23 he was musical director of Victor, then manager of the foreign department responsible for directing the music for 35 countries. An instrumentalist with the bands of Sousa, Goldman and Pryor, he also played with the NY Philharmonic and Met Opera Orchestra.

Contralto Elizabeth Lennox, who appeared with Shilkret on a GE series, called him the least temperamental of all the conductors with whom she had worked. "With singers, he is most indulgent and cooperative," she noted in the 1930s.

On radio his music ranged from jazz and operettas to sacred masses and concertos. In 1935 he relocated to Hollywood where he led film studio orchestras and conducted for *Camel Caravan*. By 1939 he was back in New York directing the Victor Concert Orchestra on the *RCA Magic Key*. At one point he had three brothers in his orchestra, including Jack Shilkret, a pianist-bandleader.

783. SHIRER, William L. (news analyst; b. Feb. 23, 1904, Chicago, IL; d. Dec. 28, 1993, Boston, MA). *CBS European News* (1937–45); *W. L. Shirer: News and Comment* (1945–49).

European correspondent for U.S. newspapers and news services in the 1930s, Shirer joined CBS in 1937 to report on political affairs from Vienna. His London-based boss, Edward R. Murrow, initially hired him to arrange for broadcasts and to use independent newspaper correspondents on them. But CBS soon switched to Shirer and Murrow at the mike. Until 1941 and the German occupation of much of the Continent, Shirer roamed from one city to another, chiefly reporting on Hitler and the Axis maneuvers. His book on that period, *Berlin Diary*, became a best seller. His overseas broadcasts brought the holocaust and war closer to Americans. Shirer's postwar programs, however, dropped in the ratings, and his liberal views displeased CBS sponsors. Mutual picked up his news and commentary in 1947.

Leaving radio in 1949, he turned full-time to writing. His popular 1960 history, *The Rise and Fall of the Third Reich,* vividly recorded the evils of Nazi Germany.

784. SHORE, Dinah (singer; b. March 1, 1917, Winchester, TN; d. Feb. 24, 1994, Beverly Hills, CA). *Chamber Music Society of Lower Basin Street* (1940); *Eddie Cantor Show* (1940–43, 1948–49); *Dinah Shore Show* (1941–46, 1953).

One of the ten most admired women in the world, Dinah Shore epitomized the fairy tale-like rise of a small town girl to nationwide prominence. Her talent for singing heartfelt torch songs and blues was the basis of a long and fulfilling career in the entertainment business. She studied voice as a teenager in Tennessee and was invited to perform over WSM Nashville, a job she continued while attending Vanderbilt University. With an eye on New York, she prepared for a radio audition. Her first tryout flopped when she lost her voice. The second a year later, in 1938 led to openings at WNEW and NBC.

Ben Bernie put her on his payroll and Eddie Cantor introduced her as his new discovery. She also had a 15-minute program over the Blue Network and a Victor contract. The renowned *Chamber Music Society of Lower Basin Street* and its music of the three Bs — Barrelhouse, Boogie Woogie and the Blues — featured her. In 1940 the unpretentious, homey Dinah won the Scripps-Howard newspaper poll as the outstanding new radio star. A velvet-voiced mood singer she soon ranked as a favorite of GIs for whom she often sang "I'll Walk Alone" and "I'll Be Seeing You."

By 1944 after co-hosting a summer program with Paul Whiteman, she began her own prime-time series. Her shows transferred successfully to early television, although she always had felt that she had "bombed" visually as a movie star in her seven films. Her singing engagements continued into the 1980s but the direction of her career led to a daily talk show; her leisure-time interests led to golf and cooking. These activities resulted in the sponsorship of a professional golf tournament bearing her name and the publication of a best-selling cookbook *Someone's in the Kitchen with Dinah.*

785. SHRINER, Herb (comedian; b. May 29, 1918, Toledo, OH; d. April 24, 1970, Delray Beach, FL). *This Is the Show* (1940–41); *Camel Comedy Caravan* (1942–43); *Herb Shriner Time* (1948–49); *Two for the Money* (1952–56).

Shriner first made an impression as the Harmonica Humorist on *Camel Caravan* in 1942. He was already an established vaudeville and nightclub performer, and had been heard as a teenager in a harmonica group of *Hoosier Hop,* an Indiana-based show

on the CBS network. For Camel cigarettes he toured Army camps as emcee of an entertainment unit. It was a build-up to his series with that sponsor and Jack Carson, Connie Haines, Ken Niles and Freddie Rich's orchestra.

Herb wrote much of his own material, drawing upon personal observations and a vivid imagination. He spoke with an Indiana drawl, specializing in topical jesting. Arthur Godfrey chose him as summer replacement for *Talent Scouts* in 1951. His casual delivery and superb sense of timing in the manner of Will Rogers led to his own show, then to the simulcast quiz *Two for the Money.*

786. SIMMS, Ginny (singer; b. May 25, 1916, San Antonio, TX; d. April 4, 1994, Palm Springs, CA). *Kollege of Musical Knowledge* (1938–41); *Ginny Simms Show* (1942–47); *Your Hit Parade* (1947); *The Pause That Refreshes* (1947–48).

Romantically imbued vocalist. Especially popular among GIs during World War II, Simms prepared for a solo career at Kay Kyser's *Kollege.* Singing on the Fresno state campus, she joined up with Kyser's unit in 1935 and rose to the highest rank of big-band song stylists before striking out on her own in the early 1940s. Feature movie roles followed in support of Abbott and Costello and George Murphy.

Her CBS solo series with Percy Faith's orchestra provided a freer, and in her eyes, a more effective, platform for her singing. A metronome-like band beat, she pointed out, had placed definite restrictions on her delivery. She also felt studio applause was a discordant element in programs attempting to create a mood, and was gratified by the rule of no spectators applying to her own programs.

787. SINATRA, Frank (singer [The Voice] [signature song: "Put Your Dreams Away"]; b. Dec. 12, 1915, Hoboken, NJ). *Fame and Fortune* (1940–41); *Songs by Sinatra* (1942–43); *Your Hit Parade* (1943–44, 1947–49); *Frank Sinatra Show* (1944–47, 1954–55); *Light Up Time* (1949–50); *Rocky Fortune* (1953–54).

In 1935 he auditioned for Major Bowes' *Original Amateur Hour,* singing Cole Porter's "Night and Day" as part of an aspiring vocal group called the Hoboken Four. It emerged a winner, taking Sinatra on the road with one of the Major's units. He soon pursued solo work and sang on 18 sustaining programs in Jersey City, Newark and New York (namely, WNEW's *Dance Parade*). He then took the job as singing emcee and headwaiter at the Rustic Cabin roadhouse. Harry James caught his act and signed him as his vocalist at $75 a week. When James ran into booking trouble, he tore up Sinatra's contract to let him join Tommy Dorsey where he came into extraordinary prominence, first with the Pied Pipers and then as a soloist.

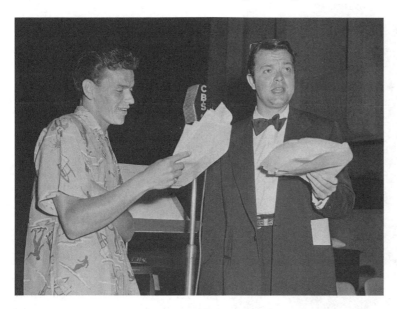

Frank Sinatra, Orson Welles

"Last Night When We Were Young," and "It Never Entered My Mind." And he became in a sense the surrogate for many a tongue-tied male.

A high-living swinger, megabucks businessman and many-sided superstar, Sinatra cast aside retirement several times to bring his electrifying and peerless voice to huge and loyal audiences. To many, he is the legendary Mr. Show Business, the greatest entertainer of their lifetime.

By the time he went on his own in October 1942, Sinatra had caught the attention of the younger set, known as bobby soxers. His first appearance at the New York Paramount Theatre was a sensational success. Teenagers sighed, swooned and yelled, and virtually stampeded to gain admittance to the hottest act in show business. The lean, frail-looking, blue-eyed baritone signed with CBS for his own shows, *Reflections* and *Songs by Sinatra.* In February 1943 he became the main attraction on *Your Hit Parade.* Oddly enough his weekly program, *Broadway Bandbox,* lacked a sponsor that fall. Writer Robert Bagar described Sinatra the singer: "He can croon or he can sing out. He is, specifically, an interpreter who gives you the essence of a song, its meaning and music in a gracious manner. He is always aware of what the orchestra is doing in back of him, in which respect he might be classified as a considerable musician. He does not go in for exaggeration. He phrases as beautifully and as shrewdly as a thoroughgoing instrumentalist."

Bing Crosby, he admits, was his inspiration to become a singer. After seeing that crooner in the movies, Sinatra gave up his job as a sports reporter, and started his own vocal quartet for parties and dances. His recordings — beginning with 84 discs with Dorsey's orchestra in 1940–42 — were phenomenal hits. In 1965, with his record sales in the tens of millions, it was calculated that they would tower in one stack 35½ miles high. His discs have filled countless hours of broadcast time on hundreds of stations, often providing marathon sessions of songs by Sinatra. Three generations have made love to such mellow tunes as "Try a Little Tenderness," "Come Rain or Come Shine," "From Here to Eternity" (the theme from the film that won him an Oscar in a dramatic role in 1953),

788. SINGISER, Frank (newscaster; b. July 16, 1908, Montevideo, MN; d. May 28, 1982, Sudbury, VT). *Mutual News* (1943–46).

After graduating from Brown University, he began as an announcer at WGY Schenectady in the late 1920s. He soon joined NBC as one of the youngest announcers on staff. His friendly, well-modulated voice was heard on the General Electric and General Motors programs and A&P broadcasts. The network promoted him among potential sponsors as a keen salesman who "understands his listeners, never irritates nor over-sells, and can be depended upon to arouse listeners' reaction whether the product is lingerie or motor cars."

After some ten years with NBC in New York, he moved to MBS. There, his evening newscasts were first aired three times a week for Sinclair Oil. Singiser was acknowledged as one of WOR's lead newsmen. He retired in 1971.

789. SINGLETON, Penny (actress; b. Sept. 15, 1908, Philadelphia, PA). *Blondie* (1939–46, 1948–49); *Penny Singleton Story/Show* (1950).

The well-cast movie and radio role of comic-pages' *Blondie,* wife of Dagwood Bumstead, provided a long and successful run for Singleton. There were 28 Columbia features and eleven seasons on the air for the well-loved Chic Young characters. Anxious to try other parts, she left after seven years in the mid-40s but returned to *Blondie* for the 1948–49 season. In 1950 she moved on to play a widowed mother on her own show. Although *Blondie* transferred easily onto TV, she didn't make the move to the video Shadylane Avenue.

Known as Dorothy McNulty when a singer on Broadway and in minor film roles, she changed her professional name about the time *Blondie* came along. Penny capped her career as executive president of the American Guild of Variety Artists.

Sciences named Skelton the best comedian of the year in 1952. By then he was convulsing audiences on both media.

791. SLATER, Bill (emcee, sportscaster; b. Dec. 3, 1902, Parkersburg, WV; d. Jan. 25, 1965, New Rochelle, NY). *Uncle Jim's Question Bee* (1939–41); *Right Down Your Alley* (1946); *Twenty Questions* (1946–54); *True or False* (1948).

His exceptional career ranged from that of a schoolteacher to a sports announcer. He got into radio in the early 1930s by covering a local football contest at the Blake School, Minneapolis. His first network exposure—an Army-Navy football game over CBS—came about while headmaster at Brooklyn's Adelphi Academy. He covered the 1936 Olympics in Berlin and was broadcasting the Dodger-Giant game on December 7, 1941 when it was interrupted by news of the Japanese attack on Pearl Harbor.

As quizmaster of the stimulating *Twenty Questions,* the tall West Point graduate and political science scholar brought many years of classroom experience to a job that demanded scrupulously accurate answers to the panel's queries. Earlier he was the third Uncle Jim on *Question Bee* and emcee of *The Dunninger Show,* a mid-40's summer replacement for *Amos 'n' Andy.* He moved into early television with baseball pickups and to the movie screen as the voice of Paramount newsreels. His brother was announcer-producer Tom Slater.

792. SLOANE, Everett (actor; b. Oct. 1, 1909, New York, NY; d. Aug. 6, 1965, Brentwood, CA). *Inner Sanctum Mysteries* (1941); *Crime Doctor* (1943–47); *Molle Mystery Theatre* (1946–48); *Twenty-First Precinct* (1953–56).

Perspicacious, highly versatile performer. Sloane became firmly established and well regarded in every area of acting. Radio provided many opportunities for supporting and leading roles for a quarter century, from a *Pretty Kitty Kelly* soap character and *March of Time* luminary to *The Goldbergs'* son Sammy and the *Crime Doctor,* Dr. Benjamin Ordway. When a particular part called for it, his belligerent manner and vitriolic voice never failed to capture an audience.

Stage-struck from age seven, he made his professional bow in a Greenwich Village production. He left the theatre for Wall Street but when the Crash brought a 50 percent salary cut in his brokerage job, he turned to radio to augment his income. Richard Mack, a scriptwriter for WOR's *Impossible Detective Mysteries,* engaged him as a supporting character at $20 a show. He was also hired for *40 Fathom Trawler.* For eight years he played a leading role on *The Shadow.* He was heard regularly on *Buck Rogers.*

Sloane made his Broadway debut in *Boy Meets Girl* in 1935 and scored his greatest stage success in *A Bell for Adano* in 1944. Between these two hits, he joined Orson Welles' *Mercury Theatre on the Air* and ap-

Red Skelton

790. SKELTON, Red (comedian [catchphrase: "I dood it!"]; b. July 18, 1913, Vincennes, IN). *Avalon Time* (1939–40); *Red Skelton Show* (1941–53).

Mississippi showboat minstrel and circus clown, teenage Skelton moved into vaudeville where he struggled for jobs. While playing in Montreal, he and his wife and partner at the time, Edna Stilwell, worked up an act involving a doughnut dunker. It proved so hilarious that their short booking turned into a seven-week stay and led to New York's Paramount Theatre.

In 1937 radio (and Rudy Vallee) brought Red to coast-to-coast audiences. The unpredictable antics of various characters—the Mean Widdle Kid, Cauliflower McPugg, Willie Lump Lump and Clem Kadiddlehopper—became eagerly awaited bits. His own series aired from Hollywood where he entered films in 1938. His MGM screen test has become a comedy classic of its type. Red's only break from a string of box-office winners (*Whistling in the Dark, I Dood It*) was an enlistment in the Army in 1944–45.

The Academy of Radio and Television Arts and

peared in many broadcasts, including "War of the Worlds." As a member of the Mercury Players he made his film bow in *Citizen Kane* as the business manager of Kane's publishing interests. He gave other memorable performances in Welles' *Journey into Fear* and *The Lady from Shanghai.* For television he created the part of the dynamic slave-driving businessman in Rod Serling's highly acclaimed *Patterns* in 1955 and repeated his outstanding performance in the movie version. That year Sloane continued on radio as Captain Frank Kennedy on *Twenty-First Precinct.*

In the pre-TV year 1944 he tersely spoke of the three major media. "As a business proposition radio is sound and occasionally satisfying. The theatre is ego-satisfying but otherwise unreliable; the movies are a lump of money." Sloane estimated that he appeared in an average of 20 programs a week, playing approximately 15,000 assorted roles in the years 1930 to 1945. They included Adolf Hitler about 100 times on the air.

793. SMALL, Mary (singer; b. May 10, 1922, Baltimore, MD) *Little Miss Bab-O's Surprise Party* (1934–35); *George Jessel's Jamboree* (1939); *Your Happy Birthday* (1940–41).

Highly engaging child vocalist with her own well-produced "Little Miss Bab-O" show. At six, in Baltimore, she had stood at a studio mike to sing for *Uncle Eddie's Kiddie Hour,* billed as "the miniature Kate Smith." As a network star, she brightened *Show Boat, Saturday Vaudeville* and *Your Hit Parade,* and the programs of Rudy Vallee and Fred Allen. Theatre roles, club dates and voice teaching occupied the grown-up Small.

794. SMART, J. Scott (actor; b. Nov. 27, 1902, Philadelphia, PA; d. Jan. 15, 1960, Springfield, IL). *Town Hall Tonight* (1934–36); *Snow Village* (1943); *The Fat Man* (1946–51).

Best known as *The Fat Man.* This corpulent, clever sleuth had been conceived by author Dashiell Hammett for his novel *The Maltese Falcon.* When auditions for the role were held, Smart was chosen because, as an ABC executive explained, "It takes a fat man to sound like a fat man. His voice is very deep and resonant, quite sinister at times."

Smart got underway at

WPDQ Buffalo. Specializing in dialect parts, he played Senator Bloat on Fred Allen's show, Uncle Walt on *Gasoline Alley* and various names in the news on *March of Time.* In 1936 he left New York for the movies. Success proved elusive so he returned in the early 1940s for roles with *Inner Sanctum Mysteries* and *Grand Central Station.* After starring in the radio-inspired film, *The Fat Man* in 1951, Smart gave up his career as a performer to become a painter. In the 1950s he also operated a summer theatre at Oqunquit, Maine.

795. SMITH, Jack (singer; b. Nov. 16, 1914, Seattle, WA). *Breezing Along* (1939–40); *Prudential Family Hour* (1943–45); *Jack Smith Show* (1946–51); *Jack Smith-Dinah Shore Show* (1952).

Years of ensemble work trained "Smiling Jack" Smith well for solos with Al Goodman on the *Prudential Family Hour.* Soon he was on his own and featured regularly on *Gaslight Gaieties, Glamour Manor* and several transcription series. A part of his popularity stemmed from his flair for singing South American and Afro-Cuban melodies.

An affable tenor, with "a smile in his voice," he sang in a group called the Three Ambassadors with Gus Arnheim at the Cocoanut Grove while still going to Hollywood High School. They teamed up with Anson Weeks and Phil Harris for band tours. In New York they gave broadcasting a try, with Kate Smith, Eddie Cantor, and Ray Bloch's orchestra.

Jack Smith

Kate Smith

796. SMITH, Kate (singer, emcee [Songbird of the South] [signature song: "When the Moon Comes Over the Mountain"] [catchphrases: "Hello Everybody!"; "Thanks for listenin'"]; b. May 1, 1907, Greenville, VA; d. June 17, 1986, Raleigh, NC). *Kate Smith and her Swanee Music* (1931–34); *Kate Smith Revue* (1934–47, 1951–52); *Kate Smith Speaks* (1938–51).

When phonograph company executive Ted Collins heard buxom, broad-shouldered Kate Smith in the 1930 Broadway musical "Flying High," he changed the direction of her career. He led her into radio. No longer would she be the on-stage knockabout comic relief and the target of dumb fat girl jokes (The New York *World* critic wrote that she "weighs as much as four chorus girls") but a wholesome singing mistress of ceremonies. Kate's debut on her own prime-time series occurred in April 1931 on a 15-minute CBS sustainer broadcast several times a week. She had just concluded a month-long sustaining program at NBC, aired Thursdays from 11:30 to 11:45 p.m. She had a sponsor, La Palina Cigars, within two months and on the premiere introduced the song — "When the Moon Comes Over the Mountain" — that became her vocal trademark.

Kate and Ted Collins formed a successful corporation to bring to the air a full hour of variety that at one point required orchestra leader Jack Miller and 27 musicians, Ted Straeter's chorus of a dozen, and five composers and arrangers. Among those who first got their start on her CBS nighttime program were Abbott and Costello, *The Aldrich Family* with Ezra Stone, Henny Youngman and Bea Wain. Smith tallied

more than 10,000 hours of radio broadcasting. Much of this total stemmed from a 15-minute noontime feature as a friendly commentator who chatted with homespun philosophy on current topics. Later she integrated her own music into the program from selections drawn from her many recordings.

Considered the First Lady of Radio and one of the outstanding women in the country, Smith made enormous contributions as War Bond saleswoman, selling more than $600,000,000 in bonds. On a single, 17-hour marathon, she solicited $39,000,000 from listeners. Earlier, during World War I, she performed as a child for troops in the Washington area. In 1938 Irving Berlin granted her exclusive rights to sing "God Bless America" on the air, which she did year after year. Her stirring performances made this patriotic hymn a second national anthem.

Considered a national institution, Smith entered television in 1950 with a daytime program, and later appeared regularly as a guest on Ed Sullivan's variety shows. By age 70 in ill health and thin and almost a recluse, she had lost her great voice. She spent the rest of her years in physical therapy as a result of a diabetic coma, emerging only to appear at the 1982 Emmy Awards ceremony and to receive the Medal of Freedom from President Ronald Reagan (her co-star in the film *This is the Army*). Her pink granite mausoleum at Lake Placid bears the inscription of the words of Franklin D. Roosevelt, "This is Kate Smith. This is America."

797. SMITH, Whispering Jack (singer; b. May 30, 1896, Bronx, NY; d. May 13, 1950, New York, NY). *Whispering Jack Smith* (1932–35).

Soft-voiced crooner with a whispering style. It was WMCA that launched his solo career. His partner failed to appear. The engineer grabbed Smith. "When I tried to sing, the cords in my throat tightened up and I could only whisper," he recalled. The mail brought favorable comments which defined his style permanently.

Smith started professionally in 1915 as part of a quartet in a Bronx theatre. After World War I service, he joined Irving Berlin's publishing house and appeared in the London revue, *Blue Skies*. His disc of "Cecilia" sold several hundred thousand pressings, an unusual feat in that decade.

798. SMYTHE, J. Anthony (actor; b. Dec. 18, 1885, San Francisco, CA; d. March 20, 1966, Los Angeles, CA). *Carefree Carnival* (1930–32); *One Man's Family* (1932–59).

Paterfamilias of *One Man's Family* for a record 27 years, beginning at KGO in March 1932. He played Henry Barbour, a plain and somewhat old-fashioned figure who spoke for a cross-section of American fathers, often in homilies and homespun sermons. For Smythe, the role practically provided a life-time job and comfortable security. In real life he remained a bachelor. Beginning in 1930 in *Split Second Tales* at NBC, Smythe also wrote, directed and played in sketches on *Carefree Carnival,* sponsored by Crazy Water Crystals.

While pursuing law studies at the University of San Francisco, he had performed in campus shows, then managed to get bit parts in regional theatre. Pre-radio, he played leading roles for 20 years, principally in stock with Florence Reed and Holbrook Blinn.

799. SOCKMAN, Ralph W. (preacher; b. Oct. 1, 1889, Mount Vernon, OH; d. Aug. 29, 1970, New York, NY). *National Radio Pulpit* (1928–62).

Methodist pastor who preached Sunday mornings from New York. His programs started in 1928 over NBC and continued for 34 years. He once remarked that his radio "pastorate" began about the same time as *Amos 'n' Andy*—yet his sermons survived the two comedians. RCA's David Sarnoff referred to him as "Broadcasting's most durable character." From 1932 to 1936 he also spoke on a summer series called *The Sunday Forum,* and in 44 years of preaching never missed a sermon because of illness.

His sermon, delivered in a highly personal way, brought in an average of 30,000 letters a year. Dr. Sockman held degrees from Ohio Wesleyan and Columbia, and served as president of the Carnegie Foundation's Church Peace Union and director of the Hall of Fame of Great Americans at New York University.

800. SODERO, Cesare (conductor; b. Aug. 2, 1886, Naples, Italy; d. Dec. 16, 1947, New York, NY).

Ann Sothern

One of the first conductors of opera broadcasts. His series of condensed grand operas ran on WEAF in the 1920s. He also conducted excerpts from *Pinafore* on the NBC Inaugural in 1926. A hardworking perfectionist with absolute pitch, Sodero joined the Met in the 1940s to direct the Italian repertoire, and as such was heard on many Saturday broadcasts. Italian-born, he had left Europe in 1906 to conduct at the Hammerstein Opera Company. As musical director at Edison Records, he waxed over 1,000 discs.

Contralto Elizabeth Lennox sang on his NBC grand opera programs for three years. She recalled that he took infinite pains with individual singers who, if necessary, had to repeat the same passage innumerable times to get it just right. "With his Italian temperament, his explosions were something to be feared. When aroused, he broke batons between his fingers, and once tried to tear a complete opera score in two."

801. SOSNICK, Harry (conductor [signature song: "Lazy Rhapsody"]; b. July 13, 1906, Chicago, IL; d. March 22, 1996, Bronx, NY). *Pennzoil Parade* (1932–33); *Your Hit Parade* (1936); *Beat the Band* (1943–44); *Treasury of Stars* (1954–55).

Orchestra leader-arranger who began in radio as an accompanist and on hotel band remotes in Chicago. In the early 1930s he formed his own outfit for key engagements at Edgewater Beach Hotel and Chicago World's Fair. Sosnick conducted for headliners Olsen & Johnson, Al Pearce and Joe E. Brown, before joining Hildegarde on high-rated quiz and variety shows. He served as musical director for Decca Records and backed many singers from 1937 to 1943.

Following a stint as music chief at Ted Bates ad agency, he joined ABC as vice president for music in the late 1960s.

802. SOTHERN, Ann (actress; b. Jan. 22, 1909, Valley City, ND). *Maisie* (1945–47, 1949–52).

Star of the *Maisie* series on screen and radio. As the amusingly scatter-brained heroine, she captivated the public in ten pictures and on 78 broadcasts. For MGM she first appeared as Maisie in 1939, having been in musical comedy on Broadway (*America's Sweetheart*) and in films (*Kid Millions*). Although Sothern had done guest appearances with Vallee, Cantor and Crosby, *Maisie* at CBS was her first and only radio series; it was a syndicated program of MGM Radio when it returned to the air in 1949 after a 2½-year hiatus. During that break she made *Letter to Three Wives,* an award-winning film. In 1953 she came to television in the role of *Private Secretary,* a popular sitcom, and followed with the *Ann Sothern Show* into the 1960s.

In high school she won prizes for musical composition and upon graduation studied music at the University of Washington. As Harriet Lake, she began in Hollywood's Christie Comedies and first sang in the chorus of Ziegfeld's *Smiles.* Sothern was married to actor-bandleader Roger Pryor from 1936–42. She met second husband, actor Robert Sterling, in 1941 when he had a part in *Ringside Maisie.*

803. SOULE, Olan (actor; b. Dec. 28, 1909, La Harpe, IL; d. Feb. 1, 1994, Corona, CA). *Bachelor's Children* (1935–46); *First Nighter* (1943–49, 1952–53); *Grand Marquee* (1949–47).

Leading roles on the drama series *First Nighter* placed him in the forefront of actors in Chicago radio. Not infrequently his shows were back-to-back yet separated by a mile between the studios of CBS in the Wrigley Building and NBC in the Merchandise Mart. His first break was as Daddy Warbucks' Chinese cook Aha in *Little Orphan Annie.* The slight, bespectacled Soule went on to Coach Hardy in *Jack Armstrong* and performed on the soap *Bachelor's Children* for eleven years. In 1947 he moved with *First Nighter* to Hollywood where he added films and TV parts. In the police drama *Dragnet,* Soule played the lab technician, and continued in that role on television.

Broad acting experience with a touring stock company in the 1920s — he also drove its truck and erected tents — provided a basis for portrayals as a heavy as well as a milquetoast. In 1933 he began appearing at WGN with a five-dollar job here and a ten-dollar job there. Overall, he amassed credits in 7,000 radio shows and commercials.

804. SPAETH, Sigmund (commentator; b. April 10, 1885, Philadelphia, PA; d. Nov. 11, 1965, New

Olan Soule (courtesy of Steve Jelf)

York, NY). *The Tune Detective* (1931–c40); *Fun in Print* (1940).

Musically trained on the piano and violin and as a vocal performer. He taught music and English and coached football before turning to writing books. They included anthologies of old popular songs, biographies, histories and musical guides. His ability to trace popular melodies back to their origination point in classical and folk music became a fascinating radio series. He was a widely used expert witness in plagiarism suits involving hit songs — most pointedly in determining the roots of "Yes, We Have No Bananas" in Handel's "Messiah," several Wagner operas and old ballads.

In 1948 during a TV version of his *Tune Detective* Spaeth, perhaps to bring attention to his new series, revealed the current jackpot mystery tune on *Stop The Music!* It was identified the following night by a New York listener to the giant telephone giveaway.

Spaeth attempted a literary quiz called *Fun in Print* with guest experts. But unlike *Information Please,* it never got off the ground. He once gave a series of piano lessons broadcast to listeners who followed them on their piano using sets of instruction sheets. Spaeth founded the New York Chapter of the Society for the Preservation and Encouragement of Barbershop Quartet Singing in 1945, and contributed arrangements to the organization.

805. SPALDING, Albert (violinist; b. Aug. 15, 1888, Chicago, IL; d. May 26, 1952, New York, NY). *The Pause that Refreshes on the Air* (1940–44).

Internationally acclaimed violinist who in 1939 made his 200th Atlantic crossing for concerts overseas. With the outbreak of war in Europe curtailing these tours, this American virtuoso turned to radio as both instrumentalist and emcee. The program was an unexpected success, and pleased its sponsor Coca-Cola and CBS. Radio was not new to Spalding. He had appeared on the prestigious Atwater Kent concerts a decade earlier and played on *Kraft Music Hall* for Bing Crosby.

As a youngster he spent winter months in Italy where his mother maintained a music salon in Florence. It was there that he began his lessons on a half-sized violin at age seven. A graduate of the Bologna Conservatory at age 14, he made his debut in Paris at 16. His American bow was at Carnegie Hall three years later, in 1908, as a soloist with the New York Symphony under Walter Damrosch. The bilingual Spalding served in Italy as an Army Aviation Corps officer in World War I and in the psychological warfare branch there in the last days of World War II.

During a 45-year career he was much admired for his straightforward, refreshingly unmannered playing.

806. SPEAKS, Margaret (singer; b. Oct. 23, 1904, Columbus, OH; d. July 16, 1977, Blue Hill, ME). *Voice of Firestone* (1935–43).

Paul Specht

sored by Columbia Phonograph, and was a training ground for many who would become important musicians. As a band booker, Specht is believed to have arranged the first broadcast of cornetist Bix Beiderbecke, over WHN. Before World War I Specht and his Society Serenaders featured "classical jazz," starting out in Indiana; by 1925 his pioneer work over the air was done, although he continued to broadcast as often as four times weekly over WJZ.

808. SPITALNY, Phil (conductor [signature song: "Isle of Golden Dreams"]; b. Nov. 7, 1890, Odessa, Russia; d. Oct. 11, 1970, Miami, FL). *Nestles Chocolateers* (1932–33); *Blue Coal Revue* (1933); *Hour of Charm* (1935–48).

Organizer and leader of the best-known all-girl orchestra. A clarinetist, Spitalny played with local bands in Cleveland in the early 1900s and later directed a 50-piece symphony in a Boston movie house. He led his own orchestra into the Depression days but enjoyed only moderate success. Next he formed an all-girl aggregation, first thought a mere novelty but proved itself to be a durable and solidly musical group. It made its debut at the Capitol Theatre in 1934 and radio followed. Sponsored by GE as the *Hour of Charm,* the program won many awards, including the Women's National Exposition of Arts and Industries Achievement Award in 1937.

Composer of "Save the Last Dance for Me" and "It's You, No One But You," Spitalny married his solo violinist Evelyn Kaye Klein, billed as Evelyn and her Magic Violin. His brothers were Leopold, NBC conductor and musicians contractor, and Maurice, musical director at KDKA Pittsburgh.

809. SPIVAK, Lawrence (moderator, panelist; b. June 11, 1900, Brooklyn, NY; d. March 9, 1994, Washington, DC). *Meet the Press* (1945–75).

Originator of *Meet the Press,* a broadcast forum for journalists to question people in the news. The widely imitated program enlarged radio and TV's role in current events. Spivak's "terrier-like tenacity" and objectivity stood in contrast to interviewers who sometimes expressed their own opinions. The discussion series started on MBS with Spivak as producer and panel member; Martha Rountree, the first moderator, helped develop the format and bring many of the world's leaders to its microphone.

A magazine business manager and publisher, Spivak added video to *Meet the Press* in 1948. He lived to see his program become the longest-running program in television history.

810. STABILE, Dick (bandleader [signature song: "Blue Nocturne"] b. May 29, 1909, Newark, NJ; d. Sept. 25, 1980, New Orleans, La). *Martin and Lewis Show* (1949–53).

During a long West Coast engagement at Ciro's nightclub, Stabile met Dean Martin and Jerry Lewis,

Soprano soloist on Firestone's Monday concert series. From a musical family, she was a niece of composer Oley Speaks ("Sylvia," "On the Road to Mandalay"). Her voice was well suited to the microphone and was heard in concert halls until the early 1950s. For the first five seasons on *Firestone,* she alternated broadcasts with Nelson Eddy, Lawrence Tibbett and Richard Crooks, then carried the series.

As an undergraduate at Ohio State, Speaks gained her first experience, singing Sunday night concerts on a program originating at a local hotel and broadcast over a small station. She auditioned for WOR in 1927 and made her first appearance there. Speaks sang briefly in a trio, the Humming Birds, with Whispering Jack Smith on his Absorbine, Jr., program over WJZ.

807. SPECHT, Paul (bandleader [signature song: "Evening Star"]; b. c1895; d. April 11, 1954, New York, NY).

It was said Specht made the very first broadcast of dance music, on September 20, 1920, at WWJ Detroit. He was quick to recognize the value of radio in advertising a name and moved on to play from WJZ Newark and the Waldorf-Astoria. WJZ experimented with Specht's "band within a band"—The Georgians—in early remote broadcasts from the Alamac Hotel, New York. The station also beamed his music across the Atlantic to Europe in 1924.

This six-piece combo had its own program, spon-

whose partnership was moving into high gear. A saxophonist with his own band since 1936, Stabile began conducting and arranging for the duo on radio and television, and in films for nine years. He was often the foil for their comic routines.

As a teenager he played with George Olsen and in 1929 joined Ben Bernie for a six-year run. His danceable, good-sounding ensemble enjoyed extended bookings in hotels (Biltmore, Lincoln) and nightclubs (Copacabana, Cocoanut Grove). When he joined the U.S. Coast Guard, he turned over the band to his talented wife, vocalist Gracie Barrie. Chief Petty Officer Stabile conducted several *Million Dollar Band* shows and war bond specials before revamping his musicians into a solidly attractive and commercial unit for the postwar era.

For the last ten years of his life, he was the bandleader at the Fairmont Hotel in New Orleans.

811. STAFFORD, Hanley (actor; b. Sept. 22, 1900, Hanley, Staffordshire, England; d. Sept. 9, 1968, Hollywood, CA). *Thatcher Colt* (1936–37); *Big Town* (1937–40); *Baby Snooks* (1939–51); *Blondie* (1939–50).

Actor selected to play the harassed Daddy to the impossible Baby Snooks (Fanny Brice). The memorable duo first came into their own on *Good News of 1938.* Stafford also assumed the role of Mr. Dithers, Dagwood's bad-tempered boss on *Blondie* a year later.

Born Alfred John Austin, he took his stage name in honor of his birthplace. He spent his teenage years in Canada and came to radio at KFI in 1930. Stafford was married to Viola Vonn, a radio actress.

For a *Screen Guild Players* program in 1948, he told the story of "Pinocchio" while Brice injected the usual disruptive Baby Snooks asides.

812. STAFFORD, Jo (singer; b. Nov. 12, 1918, Coalinga, CA). *Tommy Dorsey Show* (1940–43); *Chesterfield Music Shop* (1944); *The Ford Show* (1945); *Chesterfield Supper Club* (1945–49).

Singing with the Pied Pipers, a superbly featured vocal quartet with Tommy Dorsey, led to duets with the band's crooner Frank Sinatra. Their well-blended stylish numbers brought her solo status. In 1944 Jo signed for the Johnny Mercer show and began recording for his new company, Capitol. Nightclub work followed. After a dozen guest spots on *Chesterfield Supper Club* in 1945, that year she came on as singing emcee for the 15-minute Tuesday and Thursday broadcasts, alternating with Perry Como. Columbia Records added her to its roster in 1951 and she quickly brought them one of her biggest sellers, "Shrimp Boats." Jo married arranger-conductor Paul Weston, and they often performed together. Their off-key cocktail lounge act, first done for laughs at private parties, proved a particular favorite of audiences.

She and her sisters, Pauline and Christine, started singing together in 1935, and won an amateur con-

Jo Stafford

test and a contract to sing over a local California station. A spot on the Crockett Family program gave them a chance to sing country music. In 1937 Jo teamed up with a male octet. When it reorganized into the Pied Pipers, the comparatively unknown songstress took a big step toward becoming one of the foremost pop artists of her time.

813. STANG, Arnold (actor; b. Sept. 28, 1923, Chelsea, MA). *Eileen Barton Show* (1945–46); *Adventures of Archie Andrews* (1946–47, 1952–53); *Milton Berle Show* (1947–49); *Henry Morgan Show* (1949–50).

A child actor on *Let's Pretend* and *Children's Hour* who continued on to supporting roles in every medium. His high-pitched, nasal comic voice popped up on the programs of Dinah Shore, Kay Kyser, Abbott and Costello and Eddie Cantor. There were also periodic serious portrayals interspersed with weekly episodes of Archie Andrews.

Stang preferred New York radio where he became a regular with Milton Berle. His role as NBC stage hand on Berle's top-rated television show familiarized audiences with his face and characteristic horn-rimmed glasses and bow tie. His voice continued as a key ingredient of many commercials. On screen, he is best remembered as the woeful junkie on *The Man with the Golden Arm.*

Arnold Stang (courtesy of Arnold Stang)

Ted Steele

814. STEBER, Eleanor (singer; b. July 17, 1914, Wheeling, WV; d. Oct. 3, 1990, Langhorne, PA). *Voice of Firestone* (1944–54).

Winner of the 1940 Met Opera Auditions of the Air. This all-American soprano made her debut as Sophia in *Der Rosenkavalier* that year and sang 33 roles — notably Mozart heroines — until her last appearance there in 1966. She had her own radio show, *I. J. Fox Trappers,* in Boston when a scholarship student at the New England Conservatory. Her radio work in New York began with *Home Front Reporter.* For Toscanini she sang on the 1944 NBC broadcasts of *Fidelio,* and gained acclaim in oratorio and lieder recitals in U.S. concert halls and European music festivals. She appeared on about 15 broadcasts a year for Firestone, making the program's theme, "If I Could Tell You," part of her own repertoire. Her later years were devoted to teaching voice and establishing the Eleanor Steber Music Foundation to aid young singers.

815. STEELE, Ted (bandleader, host [signature song: "Love Passed Me By"]; b. July 9, 1917, Hartford, CT; d. Oct. 15, 1985). *Gliding Swing* (1940); *Boy Meets Band* (1941); *Ted Steele's Studio Club* (1942); *Chesterfield Supper Club* (1944–45).

An ability to play the newly developed Novachord — a small piano that creates tones by electrical impulses and amplification — turned this NBC page into a $1,000-a-week performer in 1939. The conservatory-trained Steele provided mood music for daytime serials, starred on swing sessions, wrote and produced middle-of-the-road music features, made Thesaurus recordings, and led a dance band — all before age 23.

As a teenager he played high school and college proms and directed a band on a Cunard liner. His earliest radio jobs took him to Birmingham, Alabama, then to Los Angeles as an assistant program director. NBC wired him to come East — but at Radio City he donned the uniform of a $15-a-week page. When a network sponsor insisted on a Novachord, its manufacturer recommended Steele. In the 1950s he became a popular disc jockey on New York's WMCA, then general manager at WINS.

816. STEHLI, Edgar (actor; b. July 12, 1884, Lyons, France; d. July 16, 1973, Upper Monclair, NJ). *Arthur Hopkins Presents* (1944); *Backstage Wife* (1945–46); *David Harum* (1946–47).

Stehli's stage and radio activities brought him in contact with the best offerings of both. On Broadway he played in John Barrymore's production of *Hamlet* and in the long-running comedy *Arsenic and Old Lace.* At the microphone he portrayed the master scientist, Dr. Huer, in *Buck Rogers* and District Attorney Miller in *Crime Doctor.* The European-born, American-educated actor was often called on for dialect parts, particularly French and German. Stehli found that any similarity between stage and radio work ended when an actor reported for rehearsal. In the theatre he told an interviewer in 1941, an actor has three or four weeks to develop a characterization, while in radio is fortunate to get an hour or so to run through the lines. "You have only your voice to work with — no make-up, costumes or lighting effects. Another handicap — and a tremendous one — is the loss of an audience, a visible, live audience. The response an audience may give the actor can make all the difference in the world in the way he plays a part."

Stehli periodically played on *Life Can Be Beautiful, Stella Dallas, The Aldrich Family* and *Eternal Light,* and historical figures Ben Franklin and Charles Dickens.

817. STEINKE, William (host; b. 1885, Slatinton, PA; d. Jan. 29, 1958, Saco, ME). *Jolly Bill and Jane* (1927–c35); *No School Today* (1939).

Host of an early children's show, *Jolly Bill and Jane,* at NBC New York. "Jane" was Muriel Harbater, age ten in 1930. Steinke took all incidental parts on the show. A newspaper cartoonist, he liked to entertain youngsters in his spare time. Radio offered a broad-reaching opportunity. He began on WOR Newark in 1924, and became the station's first Santa Claus — by temperament and size, it seems. He also started sports programs. In 1929 he moved on to NBC. He also appeared as a cartoonist on WNBC-TV.

In the mid-1930s Steinke and his daughter Bettina, an artist, created colorful Pied-Piper murals for NBC's special children's studio, 9-A, at Radio City.

818. STERN, Bill (sportscaster; b. July 1, 1907, Rochester, NY; d. Nov. 19, 1971, Rye, NY). *Carnival of Champions* (1937); *Colgate Sports Newsreel* (1939–51).

Colorful sportscaster with an endless string of flamboyantly told (and sometimes undocumented) stories and anecdotes about sports and historical figures. His clipped, nasal and pompous style gave authority to the coverage of games and proved popular to fans of his loquacious play-by-play accounts and his dramatic *Sports Newsreel* commentaries. Stern had had ambitions of becoming a movie actor, but had to settle for an usher's job. Radio piqued his interest, and

Bill Stern (courtesy of Steve Jelf)

in 1925 he did his first broadcast for WHAM Rochester, although he had been hired to sweep the floors. Years later, as a sideline, Stern lined up some football announcing on a trial basis for NBC. But he was fired because he had asked friends to write in to NBC saying what a wonderful job he was doing. Unfortunately, they wrote before the broadcasts took place. In 1935 Stern headed South to Shreveport, Louisiana to cover the football games of nearby Centenary College.

Following a contest with the University of Texas at Austin, he was involved in an auto crash that would cost him a leg. He later called this his "big break" because NBC's John Royal relented and rehired him, and before long he was placed in complete charge of all NBC sports broadcasts. Stern remained at that network for 17 years, then moved to ABC, and in the 1960s to Mutual. He broadcast the first television sporting event — a baseball game between Princeton and Columbia in 1939. Of his highly imaginative and occasionally controversial sports talks, he once said: "It isn't a sports show, it's entertainment for the same kind of people who listen to Jack Benny."

819. STEVENS, Julie (actress; b. c1917, St. Louis, MO; d. Aug. 26, 1984, Wellfleet, MA). *Abie's*

Irish Rose (1943–44); *The Romance of Helen Trent* (1944–60); *Stella Dallas* (1945–47).

The third and last actress to portray the long-suffering, middle-aged Helen Trent in its 27-year run. Stevens came to the role after the serial moved from Chicago to New York where she was already a veteran with leads in *Light of the World* and *Kitty Foyle*. At the height of the program's popularity, more than 1,000 letters a week were written, not to Stevens, but to Helen Trent herself. Most either offered or sought advice.

She appeared in the early prime-time television program *Big Town*. In retirement Stevens was a co-host with Ted Bell on the "Ted and Julie" show on WVLC Orleans, Massachusetts and performed in community theatres on Cape Cod.

820. STEVENS, Leith (conductor; b. Sept. 13, 1909, Mount Moriah, MO; d. July 23, 1970, Los Angeles, CA). *Death Valley Days* (1933–35); *Molle Merry Minstrels* (1934–35); *Saturday Night Swing Club* (1936–39).

Conductor-choral director, initially with CBS as an arranger in 1930. He also composed special scores used on *Columbia Workshop*. By 1934 he was staff conductor. His programs included *Magazine of the Air, Big Town* and *Ford Summer Evening Hour*. He started the freewheeling *Saturday Night Swing Club* which brought outstanding swing and jazz performers to the air coast to coast for the first time. Following wartime supervisor of overseas radio for the Southwestern Pacific area, he turned to composing motion picture scores, among them *The Wild One* with Marlon Brando, and directing music for television shows, including *Burns and Allen*.

Stevens started out as a piano accompanist for vocalists in Kansas City, then toured the country in that capacity with Schumann-Heink and Lambert Murphy. In 1927 he won a Juilliard fellowship. His first wife was lyric soprano Mary McCoy.

821. STEVENS, Rise (singer; b. June 11, 1913, New York, NY). *Rise Stevens Show* (1945).

A New Yorker, Stevens witnessed the early growth of broadcasting in that city; as a gifted and ambitious singer, she performed on children's programs and in radio choruses. During the 1935–36 season of the *Met Opera Auditions of the Air,* Stevens reached the semi-finals. She had already sung on a half-dozen operettas of *Palmolive Beauty Box Theatre*. Extensive vocal studies, both at Juilliard and with private teachers in Manhattan and abroad, brought invitations to sing opera in Prague, Vienna and Buenos Aires. An outstanding mezzo-soprano, she signed a Met contract in 1938, bowing in *Mignon* and receiving praise for her unusual range and dramatic presence. In one of her best roles, *Carmen,* she was heard on eleven Met broadcasts.

Stevens remained a frequent guest soloist on *Pru-*

Rise Stevens

dential Family Hour and *Voice of Firestone* well into the 1950s. Through films opposite Nelson Eddy and Bing Crosby, she extended her popularity.

822. STEWART, Paul (actor; b. March 13, 1908, New York, NY; d. Feb. 17, 1986, Los Angeles, CA). *House of Glass* (1935); *David Harum* (1936–38); *The Shadow* (1937–38); *Mr. District Attorney* (1939–40); *Light of the World* (1942).

People knew his face but not his name or voice, Stewart once remarked. His movie roles as villains and heavies overshadowed his earlier work over the air. Part of the Mercury Theatre group, he appeared in its stage and radio productions, including "War of the Worlds" broadcast in 1938. He made his screen debut in Orson Welles' *Citizen Kane*. Serials and soaps were a mainstay as well as various assignments on *March of Time,* and *The Fat Man*. A Columbia Law School graduate, Stewart was a founder of the American Federation of Radio Artists before he went on to perform in over 50 films. He also directed many radio and TV shows.

Stewart married band singer-radio actress Peg La Centra in 1939.

823. STOESSEL, Albert (conductor; b. Oct. 11, 1884, St. Louis, MO; d. May 12, 1943, New York, NY).

Stoessel conducted the Oratorio Society of New York at the NBC Inaugural broadcast in November 1926. He also led the Chautauqua Symphony for its radio concerts.

At age 15 he studied the violin in Berlin, becoming a member of the Hess String Quartet and a violist in Europe. He divided his time between playing and conducting, and was assisting artist to Caruso on his last U.S. tour. Stoessel established the Music Department at New York University, and in 1930 joined the faculty of Juilliard where he was director of its opera and orchestra.

While conducting a 15-piece orchestra at the annual program of the American Academy of Arts & Letters, he slumped to the floor of the stage and died.

824. STOKOWSKI, Leopold (conductor; b. April 18, 1882, London, England; d. Sept. 13, 1977, Hampshire, England). *NBC Symphony/Symphony of the Air* (1941–44); *New York City Symphony* (1944–45).

A pioneer among conductors in electronic experiments to improve acoustics in radio orchestral performances. Charismatic director of the 110-piece Philadelphia Orchestra, he made his air debut in the fall of 1929 over 52 NBC stations and under the sponsorship of Philco (Philadelphia Storage Battery Company). "The big thing in radio is this, that it permits us to bring our music to all the people, in no matter what station in life, in every part of the world," he said at the time.

Following these concerts, he took a course in radio engineering in order to learn about the broadcasting of music. The outcome was a monitoring system which enabled him both to direct the orchestra and hear the selections as they were heard over the air, rather than in the auditorium. Initially, a glass soundproof booth equipped with a loud speaker was utilized but quickly abandoned in favor of a waist-high table equipped with meters which enabled Stokowski to judge the volume and balance. At one end of the table, was seated an engineer who co-monitored the sound with him during a broadcast. The dials acted as a pair of visual ears, according to press accounts at the time. The aural results were such that CBS signed Stokowski for a half-dozen, full-length symphony concerts for 1931–32.

The pursuit of high quality music-making drove the restless, shrewd maestro to podiums as a master builder of leading U.S. symphonies: Cincinnati (1909–12), Philadelphia (1914–37), New York (1947–50). He championed the phonograph record, and made some of the first electrical discs in 1925. He eagerly undertook transcontinental and Latin American tours and promoted modern music. He premiered noteworthy American performances of Shostakovitch, Stravinsky, Schoenberg and Sibelius, and extended his commanding persona into Walt Disney's *Fantasia* and Deanna Durbin's *100 Men and a Girl.*

When Toscanini walked away from the NBC Symphony over a rife in its "abuse" by guest conductors in the early 1940s, Stokowski stepped in. Toscanini returned a year later, and Stokowski became co-conductor. But few musicians differed more in approach and organization. Stokowski soon left. When the NBC Symphony lost Toscanini in the mid-50s and tried to go it alone as the Symphony of the Air, Stokowski became its director. Active well into his 90s, he made his last recordings in London just a few weeks before his death.

Leopold Stokowski

825. STONE, Ezra (actor; b. Dec. 2, 1918, New Bedford, MA; d. March 3, 1994, Perth Amboy, NJ). *The Aldrich Family* (1939–42, 1945–53).

For a dozen years he answered his mother's call

"Hen-Ree! Henry Aldrich." The lead character on one of the most beloved family situation comedies, Stone became the quintessential teenager with his high-pitched reply: "Coming, Mother." *The Aldrich Family* stemmed from the Clifford Goldsmith play *What a Life* about a misunderstood youngster who was a bit of a trial to his parents and teachers. Excerpts on Vallee's show resulted in weekly dramatizations on the *Kate Smith Hour.* As a full-fledged radio spinoff, it began as a summer replacement for Jack Benny, under the sponsorship of General Foods' Jello. *The Aldrich Family* moved into early "live" television while continuing on radio.

During the war Stone took time out as Henry Aldrich to serve in the Army. As an entertainment specialist, he directed Irving Berlin's GI revue *This Is the Army.* Stone also directed on television and produced training and motivational films.

His broadcasting began at a young age over WCAU Philadelphia, doing recitations (an undertaking he had started to overcome a lisp). He attended the American Academy of Dramatic Arts, before working as casting assistant for George Abbott and winning a part in the 1936 Broadway comedy *Brother Rat.*

826. STORDAHL, Axel (conductor; b. Aug. 8, 1913, Staten Island, NY; d. Aug. 30, 1963, Encino, CA). *Songs by Sinatra/Frank Sinatra Show* (1943–47); *Your Hit Parade* (1947–49); *Coke Time* (1953).

Musical arranger-conductor for Frank Sinatra. They met as part of Tommy Dorsey's band of the early 1940s. Axel began as a trumpet player with Bert Block. When Sinatra starred on his own show and later *Your Hit Parade,* Axel led the orchestra and conducted for most of his Columbia discs. He led a 30-piece group — "well stocked with strings," noted *Variety.* With Paul Weston and Sammy Cahn, he composed the 1946 hit "Day by Day." His wife, vocalist June Hutton, sang with Charlie Spivak and the Pied Pipers.

827. STORM, Gale (actress; b. April 5, 1922, Bloomington, TX). *My Little Margie* (1952–55).

The audio counterpart of her widely popular CBS-TV sitcom *My Little Margie* ran concurrently on radio for three years. In the lead role Storm brought a wholesome appeal as the impulsive, somewhat flighty, daughter of business magnate Charles Farrell. It quickly shot up in the ratings to join *Life with Luigi, Our Miss Brooks* and *My Friend Irma* as a top comedy show of the 1952–53 season. A mainstay among reruns for several decades, the TV version segued into *The Gale Storm Show,* a series of the late '50s.

Storm worked in many low-budget second features as an actress and singer before signing on as Margie. While finishing high school, she had won a Gateway to Hollywood drama contest and a picture contract in 1939. She appeared in radio anthologies

and film adaptations but Margie was her first ongoing starring role.

828. STRATTON, Chester (actor; b. July 31, 1912, Paterson, NJ; d. July 7, 1970, Los Angeles, CA). *The O'Neills* (1934–42); *Against the Storm* (1939–42); *Pepper Young's Family* (1945–46).

Mainstay on soap operas and dramatic shows. In the early 1940s, Stratton played the lead, Monte Kayden, in *The O'Neills;* Mark Scott on *Against the Storm;* Carter Trent in *Pepper Young,* and Hop Harrigan, "Ace of the Airways." His evening shows included *Cavalcade of America* and *First Nighter.*

On Broadway he appeared with Ethel Barrymore (*White Oaks*) and Vivienne Segal (*A Connecticut Yankee*) and with Katharine Cornell in a USO tour of *The Barretts of Wimpole Street.* In early television, he worked in live dramatic presentations, which led to screen assignments (*Advise and Consent*) in the 1960s.

A Rutgers College student, Stratton started at WMCA at five dollars a week. On an episode of one of his ongoing serials, he married after a typically long and eventful courtship. Many joyful listeners actually sent wedding gifts.

829. STUDEBAKER, Hugh (actor; b. May 31, 1900, Ridgeville, IN; d. May 6, 1978, Los Angeles, CA). *Bachelor's Children* (1936–46); *Fibber McGee and Molly* (1937–39); *That Brewster Boy* (1941–43); *Beulah* (1947–54).

Dependable, versatile performer on day and nighttime programs. At KMBC Kansas City in 1929, he announced and supplied organ music. He also played the suave Harry Checkervest in the Happy Hollow series. Settling in Chicago in 1933, he became Silly Watson with Fibber McGee. His soaps included *Road of Life, Midstream, Woman in White,* and *Bachelor's Children* (as the lead, Dr. Bob Graham). On the last voyages of *Show Boat,* he played Cap'n Andy, then Dad on *That Brewster Boy.* From Hollywood by the late 1940s, he played Harry Henderson, Beulah's employer, and supporting roles on *First Nighter.* At one point he faced the bane of every radio performer: a throat illness. His was severe enough to force him off the air for five months in 1940.

Hugh sang in a male quartet in Kansas City in the early 1920s. It led to a song and piano act on an Iowa station and to KMBC in 1929.

830. SULLIVAN, Lee (singer; b. c1911, New York, NY; d. May 29, 1981, Brooklyn, NY). *Vest Pocket Varieties* (1946–47); *Serenade to America* (1947).

NBC singing emcee. A tenor, he performed on a sustainer called *Fashion Show* in 1937 but it took another ten years before he had his own *Vest Pocket* series and a measure of stardom. That year, 1947, he soloed frequently on *Serenade to America* and played Charlie Dalrymple in the original production of *Briga-*

Lee Sullivan

doon. Among his other Broadway shows were *High Kickers* and *Let Freedom Sing.*

He and Ed Herlihy had a daily morning TV show, *Date in Manhattan,* and aired from Tavern on the Green. He later worked as a cruise director for steamship lines.

831. SUNDAY, Billy (preacher; b. Nov. 19, 1863, Ames, IA; d. Nov. 6, 1935, Chicago, IL). *Back Home Hour* (1929–31).

High-pressure evangelist who induced thousands to convert during a career that began in tent tabernacles in the late 19th century and led to urban churches and the radio microphone. CBS aired him for 60 minutes on Sunday nights for several years. Sunday started out as a professional baseball player — an excellent outfielder with the Chicago White Sox and Pittsburgh and Philadelphia National League teams. At 23 he dropped into a Salvation Army meeting and experienced conversion. In 1890 he became a YMCA secretary, and joined the vanguard of evangelistic gospel preachers in the Midwest. Energetic and persuasive, Sunday regularly advocated Prohibition in his sermons.

832. SWARTHOUT, Gladys (singer; b. Dec. 25, 1904, Deepwater, MO; d. July 7, 1969, Florence, Italy). *Palmolive Beauty Box Theatre* (1934–35); *Prudential Family Hour* (1941–45); *Voice of Firestone* (1944–46).

A versatile artist, she called broadcasting "the most demanding and most frightening of all my various performances. In Hollywood, with light and camera they can bring out most of your beauty, hide all of your flaws. In opera you play your part, warmed by a friendly audience. But one mistake over the air goes into the ears of millions of people and can never be taken back."

Her veracious and intelligent musicianship were evident in all her endeavors, from small-town church choirs to world-class opera houses. A mezzo soprano, she made her debut in *La Gioconda* at the Met in 1929. The greatest of her 22 roles there was Carmen. With equally glamorous Lily Pons and Helen Jepson in a take-off of a radio sister act, at a Depression era benefit, she stopped the show with "Minnie the Moocher." To mark the 150th anniversary of the U.S. Congress in 1939 she was invited to sing from the Capitol with John Charles Thomas. Swarthout broadcast on special tributes to the King and Queen of England on their American visit and for the opening of Radio City by NBC. In 1947 she was soloist in the NBC Symphony performance of Berlioz' *Romeo and Juliet,* and a frequent *Telephone Hour* guest. Open heart surgery brought about her retirement at age 52. Her husband, the baritone Frank Chapman, managed her career.

833. SWEENEY, Bob (actor; b. Oct. 19, 1918, San Francisco, CA; d. June 7, 1992, Westlake Village, CA). *Sweeney and March* (1946–48, 1951).

While a San Francisco State undergrad, Sweeney decided on a career as an announcer. He worked an early morning shift as a cab driver in order to be free for auditions. Hired by KSAN San Francisco in the early 1940s, he advanced to chief announcer at KYA. There, in 1942 he met disc jockey Hal March. They teamed up and merged their air time for a comedy format. It led to 26 weeks on Hoagy Carmichael's

Gladys Swarthout, Frank Chapman

Karl Swenson (courtesy of Steve Jelf)

show. When March decided to try for jobs in Hollywood, they broke up but in 1945 were reunited for network guest appearances (Ginny Simms, *Chesterfield Supper Club*) and a CBS comedy series. This show ran 84 consecutive weeks without snagging a sponsor; Sweeney considered it some sort of a CBS sustaining record. Mutual and ABC also offered local and network versions of Sweeney and March.

In the early 1950s the duo again parted, and Hal went on to become quiz master of the *The $64,000 Question*. Sweeney played on *Our Miss Brooks* and teamed with Cathy Lewis for a TV version of *Fibber McGee and Molly*. By the 1970s he was a leading TV producer-director (*Andy Griffith, That Girl, Matlock, Dynasty*).

Sweeney once discussed the movie industry's attitude toward audio performers. "Almost no radio actors could get jobs in feature films. They were regarded as some sort of alien, bastard kind of acting and had no respect from anybody who did any casting or produced or directed." The first radio actor that he recalled having any picture success was Jeff Chandler.

834. SWENSON, Karl (actor; b. July 23, 1908, Brooklyn, NY; d. Oct. 8, 1978, Torrington, CT). *Our Gal Sunday* (1937–c55); *Lorenzo Jones* (1937–55); *Mr. Chameleon* (1948–51).

Lord Henry Brinthrope on *Our Gal Sunday* and the lead on *Lorenzo Jones* and other serials. Swenson made his stage debut with the Berkshire Players summer stock company in 1930; his radio bow came on *The March of Time* in 1935. Swenson successfully ventured onto Broadway with parts in Arthur Miller's first production, *The Man Who Had All the Luck,* and in several musical revues by Leonard Stillman. Television viewers remembered best his role as Mr. Hansen in *Little House on the Prairie*. His films included *The Hanging Tree* and *The Birds*.

In 1940 the onetime medical student joined the cast of *Cavalcade of America* with portrayals of Eli Whitney, Thomas Jefferson and Columbus. In a six-week 1945 production of "Les Miserables" on *World's Great Novels,* Swenson played Jean Valjean and returned a year later for the four-part "Ninety-Three" by Victor Hugo.

835. SWING, Raymond Gram (commentator; b. March 25, 1887, Cortland, NY; d. Dec. 22, 1968, Washington, DC).

His voice as a commentator violated every radio rule — it lacked dramatic appeal and colorful exaggeration. Swing never raised his voice and rather drolled along. But this trained newspaper journalist was listened to by millions who placed him high in radio polls, circa 1939, chiefly because of his sincerity, grasp of world events and desire for impartiality. He had joined the BBC in 1935 to comment on American affairs, and also served as a foreign commentator for Mutual. By 1940 his discourses were aired five or six times a week over 100 stations.

As early as 1931 he broadcast for NBC from Geneva to the United States on an early trans-Atlantic hookup. In the years leading to war, a solid knowledge of German allowed him to translate Hitler's tirades as the Fuhrer spoke. In 1942 he switched to ABC for Socony Oil and later to the Liberty network. Swing's last assignment was with The Voice of America under Ed Murrow. He used a middle name at the insistence of his second wife, Betty Gram, an ardent feminist.

Deems Taylor, Sigmund Romberg, Alexander Woollcott

836. TALLEY, Marion (singer; b. Dec. 20, 1906, Nevada, MO; d. Jan. 3, 1983, Los Angeles, CA). *Ry-Krisp Presents Marion Talley* (1936–38).

Her spectacular debut at the Met in February 1926 signaled a remarkable yet short career. A coloratura soprano, she had the distinction at the time of being the youngest singer ever assigned to a leading role. Nineteen-year-old Talley performed the role of Gilda in *Rigoletto* to an audience of 4,200. A thousand more, unable to gain admission, milled about the opera house. She responded to 20 curtain calls but woke up to lukewarm reviews. She first had auditioned for the Met at age 15 and was well received, but was advised to pursue further studies in New York and Italy to prepare for her debut. Residents of Kansas City helped raise $10,000 to fund her training. Talley made radio guest appearances during four seasons at the Met. In 1929 this country-bred girl announced that she had quit opera to try farming in western Kansas. Talley soon returned for a number of highly successful tours and with Josef Koestner's orchestra on NBC for Ry-Krisp (with a new trim and svelte figure befitting the sponsor). There was a long-term film contract that resulted in single, quickly forgotten musical—*Follow Your Heart* for Republic Pictures. By the end of the 1930s her rare vocal brilliance just fizzled out.

837. TAYLOR, Deems (commentator, composer; b. Dec. 22, 1885, New York, NY; d. July 3, 1966, New York, NY). *Deems Taylor Music Series* (1932); *Kraft Music Hall* (1933–34); *Studio Party at Sigmund*

Romberg's (1935–36); *Prudential Family Hour* (1941–45); *RCA Victor Show* (1945–46).

Narrator, commentator and host on prestigious musical presentations, Taylor worked as an editor (New York *Herald-Tribune*) and music critic (*McCall's*) to "subsidize" his time as composer of such pieces as "Through the Looking Glass" and "The Highwayman." His well-received opera, *The King's Henchman,* had its premiere at the Met in 1927. That year his radio career began when he narrated a one-hour broadcast of his opera to inaugurate the opening of the Columbia network.In 1931, the year his second Met Opera, *Peter Ibbetson,* was presented, he acted as commentator for the first season of Met broadcasts. That led to his own music series, appearances on special concerts, and assignments on NY Philharmonic programs. A polished speaker and outstanding musicologist, Taylor joined the panel of *Information Please* as guest on more than 40 quiz sessions beginning in 1941. His good-humored approach to the broader aspects of music came across as commentator on *Chamber Music Society of Lower Basin Street.*

838. TAYLOR, Frederick Chase (comedian; b. Oct. 4, 1897, Buffalo, NY; d. May 29, 1950, Boston, MA). *Stoopnagle and Budd* (1931–37); *Quizie-Doodle Quiz* (1939–41); *Stooperoos* (1943); *Duffy's Tavern* (1949–50).

At WMAK Buffalo, production man Taylor was pressed into service by announcer Budd Hulick to fill a 15-minute gap when a storm damaged the network transmission line. They ad libbed for two hours with impromptu humor. The outcome was *Stoopnagle and Budd,* one of the earliest top-rated comedy duos, airing on many CBS series during the 1930s. Billed as the Gloom Chasers, they provided all character parts, highlighted "Little Known Interviews with Little-Known People," featured zany inventions and included their "daffynitions." Professionally known as Colonel Lemuel Q. Stoopnagle, he compiled his fictionalized anecdotes in a 1944 book *You Wouldn't Know Me from Adam.* Taylor emceed *Quizie-Doodle Quiz* and *Stooperoos,* and performed on Vaughn Monroe's CBS show for Camel cigarettes and as Clancy the waiter on *Duffy's Tavern.* A World War I Navy veteran, he entered the family lumber company, and in 1929 shifted to a brokerage firm. Some years before he had free-lanced on *Nip and Tuck* over WMAK. The station welcomed him back when the market crash wiped out his securities business.

839. TAYLOR, Henry J. (commentator; b. Sept. 2, 1902, Chicago, IL; d. Feb. 24, 1984, New York, NY). News commentary (1945–56).

Commentator on economic and social issues. A foreign correspondent for Scripps-Howard newspaper chain during World War II, he branched out with twice weekly broadcasts over Mutual in 1945. General Motors sponsored his program, which moved to prime time on ABC and NBC. In the early 1950s, it was called *Your Land and Mine.* He received an Alfred I. duPont award for his radio work. Taylor left the air when President Eisenhower named him Ambassador to Switzerland. In 1961 he returned to journalism as a columnist for United Features Syndicate. He wrote several books, including *Men in Motion* and *An American Speaks His Mind.*

840. TAYLOR, Marion Sayle (advisor [signature song: "My Guiding Star"]; b. Aug. 16, 1888, Louisville, KY; d. Feb. 1, 1942, Hollywood, CA). *The Voice of Experience* (1928–40).

Lecture circuit talks on psychology, juvenile delinquency and fundamentalism (with William Jennings Bryan) led to *The Voice of Experience.* His advice on domestic affairs covered marriage, divorce, child problems — even insomnia and acidosis. As a youngster he accompanied his itinerant Baptist preacher-father to meetings and was coaxed to deliver extemporaneous sermons. It was there he found the voice that would counsel millions. Taylor had considered a medical or musical career but an auto accident injured his hands. He turned to social work gaining insights that would be put to use on radio. While he could no longer play music he could write it. One of his compositions became the theme used on his broadcasts in later years. His own marital life was marked by several rough and tumble divorces. Taylor made his first radio appearance in 1924 in connection with lecturing on psychology. He is believed to have broadcast the first question-and-answer periods and audience-participation programs. His books — *Making Molehills of Mountains, The Male Motor, Life Must Go On* — had sales in excess of three million copies.

841. TEMPLETON, Alec (pianist, satirist; b. July 4, 1910, Cardiff, South Wales; d. March 28, 1963, Greenwich, CT). *You Shall Have Music* (1935–36); *Universal Rhythm* (1937); *Alec Templeton Time* (1939–41, 1946–47).

Blind musician who enjoyed wide popularity as a pianist and composer and "pianologist." His droll "Bach Goes to Town" generated middlebrow interest in longhair music, as did his "St Louis Blues" in Chopin style and "Stompin' at the Savoy" in a Bach fugue. A frequent gimmick was improvising compositions from a half-dozen notes called out by his audience. He composed many piano, full orchestra and chamber pieces, and concertized throughout North America after coming to the United States in 1935 with Jack Hylton's orchestra. Miles Labs, his prime sponsor, showcased his varied and showmanly routines on *National Barn Dance* and *Uncle Ezra.* He had first entered radio at age 12 when he auditioned for the BBC. His wunderkind musical novelties were presented from London almost daily for over ten years.

Alec Templeton

842. TENNYSON, Jean (singer; b. 1905, Chicago, IL; d. March 16, 1991, La Tour-de-Peilz, Switzerland). *Great Moments in Music* (1942–46).

Featured soprano in the CBS *Great Moments* program of serious and light classics, backed by a 75-piece orchestra and a multi-voice chorus. The repertory company series, sponsored by Celanese Corporation (her husband was its chairman), attracted a large listening audience for its condensations of operas and special theme broadcasts. Tennyson, the originator and guiding spirit of the program, chose the material and her guest artists, who from time to time included Jan Peerce, Robert Weede and Mario Lanza. She gave many talented but unknown singers a chance to appear, especially those just beginning to make names for themselves as soloists, and those who had singing experience in choral groups but had never appeared as soloists.

Tennyson studied with Mary Garden and Florence Easton before making her debut as Mimi in *Boheme* in Venice in 1930. Her appearances with La Scala, and the Chicago Civic, San Francisco and San Carlo Opera companies provided a stepping stone to radio. After World War II she founded the Artists' Veterans Hospital Programs to present bedside concerts for patients in veterans hospitals. She also served as vice chairman of New York's Lewisohn Stadium concerts.

843. TETLEY, Walter (actor; b. June 2, 1915, New York, NY; d. Sept. 4, 1975, Encino, CA). *Grouch Club* (1939–40); *The Great Gildersleeve* (1941–58); *Phil Harris–Alice Faye Show* (1947–54).

Child performer who continued playing young teenagers into his forties. His best role — Leroy, the wisecracking nephew of "Unk" Throckmorton P. Gildersleeve — ran for over 16 seasons. As Julius the smartalecky grocery boy, he enjoyed a long run with Phil Harris and Alice Faye. Tetley popped up as a stooge of Fred Allen and regularly faced the mike of Bob Burns and Alan Young.

Starting in vaudeville, then radio, as "Wee Sir Harry Lauder," he had been heard on over 100 different programs by the late 1930s, notably *Coast-to-Coast on a Bus, Buck Rogers, Raising Junior* and *The Cuckoo Hour*. His films as an adolescent included *Lord Jeff* and *Spirit of Culver*.

844. THIBAULT, Conrad (singer; b. Nov. 13, 1906, Northbridge, MA; d. Aug. 1, 1983, Far Rockaway, NY). *Show Boat* (1933–36); *The Gibson Family* (1934–35); *Packard Hour* (1936–37); *If I Had the Chance* (1939); *Manhattan Merry-Go-Round* (1941–43).

A scholarship to Curtis Institute of Music provided the necessary training for this New England choir boy and jazz band vocalist to develop into a concert hall artist. As a student he sang with the Philadelphia Grand Opera Company and on Curtis's very first broadcast. As soon as the program was over, the sta-

tion manager hired him for $5 a week to sing on a 15-minute show. In a matter of months he had several other programs.

A baritone with an even, well-knit and appealing voice and a linguist in five languages with perfect pronunciation, Thibault never lacked a radio sponsor after he was hired for *Show Boat* on a week-to-week basis. He stayed for over three years. *The Gibson Family*, a full-hour comedy drama with both original stories by novelist Courtney Riley Cooper and music by lyrist Howard Dietz and composer Arthur Schwartz, displayed Thibault's fine natural talent to great advantage. For many years he was on the faculty of the Manhattan School of Music and a private vocal coach. In 1978 after establishing a singing school in West Palm Beach, he stated that "teaching is as much a joy to me as singing was."

845. THOMAS, Ann (actress; b. July 8, 1913, Newport, RI; d. April 28, 1989, New Rochelle, NY). *Joe and Mabel* (1941–42); *Abie's Irish Rose* (1942–44); *House of Glass* (1953–54).

Known for her gravelly voice, studied Brooklyn accent and comic demeanor. She frequently portrayed secretaries, switchboard operators and a "stooge for the stars." Whenever a director wanted tough talk from a girl he called upon Ann Thomas. Besides the role of Casey on *Abie's Irish Rose*, she was Sharon O'Shaughnessy opposite Bob Burns, June on *The New Jack Pearl Show* and Miss Thomas on *Easy Aces*. In all, she appeared on over 5,000 broadcasts, beginning in 1938.

A child actress at age four, Thomas worked in 43 Broadway plays and recreated Miss Duffy in the movie version of *Duffy's Tavern*.

846. THOMAS, Danny (comedian; b. Jan. 6, 1912, Deerfield, MI; d. Feb. 6, 1991, Los Angeles, CA). *Danny Thomas Show* (1944–49).

A comedian-storyteller, he started in show business in 1932 on *The Happy Hour Club*, an amateur program on WMBC Detroit. In Chicago he worked as a nightclub emcee and singer in the early 1940s and changed his name from Amos Jacobs so his friends and family would not find out he was making a living in saloons. An engagement at the Chez Paree attracted the networks, and after working with Baby Snooks, he was given his own program. He often appeared on *Welcome, Travelers* when in Chicago.

In 1946 he went into the movies, but television, through *Make Room for Daddy*, made him a household name. Thomas later became a producer with onetime radio actor Sheldon Leonard and Aaron Spelling. They brought Dick Van Dyke and Andy Griffith, among others, to top-rated series.

For his humanitarian achievements in the founding of and raising money for St. Jude Children's Research Hospital, President Reagan gave him a Congressional Medal in 1985. His daughter, actress Marlo Thomas, starred on TV's *That Girl*.

John Charles Thomas

both on TV and radio in December 1957.

848. THOMAS, Lowell (newscaster, commentator [catchphrases: "Good evening, everybody."; "So long until tomorrow"]; b. April 6, 1892, Woodington, OH; d. Aug. 29, 1981, Pawling, NY). *Lowell Thomas and the News* (1930–76).

His nightly 15-minute program was the longest continually operating newscast on radio. The broadcasts lasted 46 years on NBC and CBS, and had been heard by an estimated 70 billion people. His radio career started when the *Literary Digest* was about to drop its sponsorship of the unruly heavy-drinking Floyd Gibbons as its newscaster. Someone at CBS remembered having heard Thomas broadcast and recalled his stentorian yet sonorous voice.

Night after night at the dinner hour, he projected a calm, clear and reassuring air. "I never felt it was my responsibility to destroy the digestive system of the American people," he pointed out. His most embarrassing broadcasting moments came when he referred to "Ambassador Bull Billet," then turned with relief to a dispatch from New Delhi with late news of "Sir Stifford Crapps."

In 1925 he made his first broadcast at KDKA. By then he was an adventurous world traveler, highly successful writer and colorful lecturer. But radio work brought him his greatest fame and fortune. In 1948 he earned more than $400,000 from broadcasting, and he seldom received less in other years. The onetime English literature and oratory professor did not let his programs interfere with travels. The first to broadcast from an airplane and a helicopter, he reached his listeners from Europe, Asia and Africa. He once said that it had cost him $1 million of his own money for such remote hookups.

He broadcast for NBC the first televised news program in 1939. He appeared in several TV series, including the PBS *Lowell Thomas Remembers.* Yet in 1979 he returned to a radio mike with a daily syndicated series, *The Best Years,* about the accomplishments of famous people in their later years.

In 1935 he became the voice of Twentieth Century-Fox Movietone News. In the early 1950s he helped to develop the spectacular three-dimensional film, *This Is Cinerama.* His output of books numbered over 50, including the highly popular *With Lawrence in Arabia* and a two-part autobiography. The se-

847. THOMAS, John Charles (singer [catchphrase: "Good night, Mother"]; b. Sept. 6, 1891, Meyersdale, PA; d. Dec. 13, 1960, Apple Valley, CA). *John Charles Thomas Program* (1934–36); *Westinghouse Program* (1943–46).

One of America's best-loved concert singers. A musical comedy matinee idol, international opera star and popular radio baritone, he was also a great showman. After studies at Peabody Conservatory, the innately musical Thomas appeared in operettas, then opera, chiefly in Europe. His 15 featured roles included Tonio in *Pagliacci.* He scored a triumph in his Met debut in *La Traviata* in 1934.

Each year he gave some 70 concerts. For a time he specialized in foreign songs but became convinced of the merits of American composers and devoted much of his time to them. He sang spirituals and folk songs; "Home on the Range" was a frequent request. He was admired for the deep, rich, effortless quality of his voice.

Westinghouse sponsored his best-produced radio series. During its run as its emcee-soloist, he won a battle with the FCC, which granted him a special dispensation to sign off his programs with a personal "good night" to his mother. From 1948 to 1950 he often sang on *The Telephone Hour.* After his retirement in 1953 he managed a radio station near his Apple Valley home. An avid sportsman, he won many cups for motorboat races. As a golfer, he made an unforgettable hole-in-one at an outing hosted by conductor Gus Haenschen and witnessed by many radio contemporaries.

His last network appearance, as a contestant defending "good music" against a rock 'n' roll teenager, occurred on Groucho Marx's *You Bet Your Life,* aired

CBS Radio president Sam Cook Digges, Lowell Thomas

American Album of Familiar Music (1949–51).

Radio auditions in the early 1930s led to singing in choruses with an occasional brief solo passage. His first featured role was with Jessica Dragonette on *Palmolive Beauty Box Theatre*. In 1937 he joined the cast of *Show Boat*. Appearances on *Chicago Theatre of the Air, Manhattan Merry-Go-Round* and *Highways in Melody* added to his popularity on the concert stage. His voice was the most frequently featured on *Voice of Firestone* on radio and early television.

A winner of the Met Opera radio auditions in 1937, Thomas bowed there in *Pagliacci* before a large contingent of citizens from his hometown of Scranton, Pennsylvania. His voice carried well with a smooth and even tonal texture, but was not particularly voluminous for large opera houses. The Welch-born baritone had little in the way of formal training but learned quickly by on-the-job observation and coaching. He spent his last years as a teacher for voice students in Arizona.

cret of his vigor and activity, he once said, "is that I've usually managed to have a lot of fun."

849.   THOMAS, Thomas L. (singer; b. Feb. 23, 1912, Maesteg, South Wales; d. April 17, 1983, Scottsdale, AZ). *Show Boat* (1937); *Manhattan Merry-Go-Round* (1943–49); *Voice of Firestone* (1947–54);

850.   THOMPSON, Bill (actor; b. July 8, 1913, Terre Haute, IN; d. July 15, 1971, Los Angeles, CA). *Fibber McGee and Molly* (1937–43, 1946–57); *Bill Thompson Show* (1946).

Dialect comedian who created memorable characters—The Old Timer ("That ain't the way I heard it."), Nick DePopolus, Horatio K. Boomer and Wallace Wimple—on the Fibber McGee show. He started with the program in Chicago, where he had won an audition at NBC during the city's Century of Progress expo. He performed a sketch called "An International Broadcast" involving ten languages. The young actor joined the *Breakfast Club, Jamboree* and *National Farm and Home Hour*. He was often called on to reproduce animal noises, and was Snifter, the Talking Dog on *NBC Night Club* and a parrot on *Mary Marlin*. Thompson was the voice of many Disney characters. In 1943 he left the air to serve in the Navy. He rejoined Fibber in 1946, the year ABC gave him his own comedy show with Ken Christy.

His parents were in musical comedy and vaudeville, and at age five he had his own role as a mimic. During World War I he entertained wounded servicemen and sold $2,000,000 worth of Liberty Bonds. When the McGees departed 79 Wistful Vista

Thomas L. Thomas

in 1957, Thompson joined the managerial ranks of Union Oil Company.

851. THOMPSON, Dorothy (commentator; b. July 9, 1894, Lancaster, NY; d. Jan. 30, 1961, Lisbon, Portugal). *Commentary* (1936–38, 1940–45).

A newspaper and magazine writer, she reached over ten million readers with her articles and columns. By radio, she talked to some five million listeners on current events. Her father, a Methodist minister, coached her as a child in recitations of Bible passages and helped make her the effective radio speaker she became in the 1930s.

A dynamic and skillful journalist, Thompson managed to interview many world leaders for her syndicated column "On the Record." She gained wide influence from her fervid opinions and accurate predictions. Familiar with Europe from her free-lance work there as early as 1919, she "stewed publicly about the state of the world" as she observed war developments 20 years later. Her violent attacks upon Hitler and Stalin worried her NBC radio sponsor (Pall Mall cigarettes) to the point where her contract was not renewed. In 1940 she was picked up by MBS. That year, next to Eleanor Roosevelt, Thompson was described as having the "most power and prestige of any woman in America." In 1938 she received a gold medal from the National Institute of Social Sciences for distinguished service to humanity.

852. THOMPSON, Kay (singer; b. Nov. 9, 1909, St. Louis, MO). *Fred Waring Show* (1934–36); *Your Hit Parade* (1935–36); *Rhythm Singers* (1937); *Tune-Up Time* (1939–40).

Thompson came to New York after early 1930s success on *California Melodies*. Not content with passive waiting for proper recognition as a vocalist, she organized and conducted a chorus of 15 girls. Fred Waring liked the idea and made it a companion to his male chorus. By 1939 her own tantalizing voice was spotlighted on CBS programs with Hal Kemp, Lou Holtz, Richard Himber, Andre Kostelanetz and Tony Martin. However, her self-produced show, *Kay Thompson and Company,* proved a flop. A composer-arranger, Kay returned to Hollywood in the early '40s for assignments on MGM musicals; she coached Judy Garland, among others.

In 1947 she entered a new phase of her career with a nightclub act. Lanky, frenetic, witty Kay, backed by the four Williams Brothers (including Andy), proved a top-drawer attraction. She was one of the first women to wear slack suits and pants in public, much less in a nightclub. Thompson turned to writing in 1944 with the first of her books on Eloise, a fiendish six-year-old who lived at New York's Plaza Hotel. Enjoyed by adults as well as children, the fictional escapades of this enfant terrible became perennial bestsellers and spun off dolls, records and TV specials.

Self-described as a "stage-struck kid," she studied dramatics at Washington University and performed Liszt at the piano with the St. Louis Symphony at age 16. She first sang over KMOX, which signed her for an Anheuser-Busch series while an undergrad. Choice West Coast guest spots with Crosby and the Mills Brothers soon resulted.

853. TIBBETT, Lawrence (singer; b. Nov. 16, 1896, Bakersfield, CA; d. July 15, 1960, New York, NY). *Voice of Firestone* (1932–34); *The Circle* (1939); *Your Hit Parade* (1945); *Golden Voices* (1953-54).

A follow-up audition at the Met—at the first his voice cracked on a high note—brought forth a contract for secondary and unheralded parts. But in the 1924–25 season, he stepped in for an ill baritone in the demanding role of Ford in *Falstaff,* singing with a desperation and intensity that stopped the show. The audience stomped and clapped 15 minutes until the young baritone took a solo curtain call. Overnight, the newly discovered singer got new and important assignments as fast as he could master them. As a singing actor, he did leads in the American operas *Peter Ibbetson, Emperor Jones* and *The King's Henchman.* A commanding figure, Tibbett branched into concert, radio and movie work, scoring heavily in each.

He made claim as the first opera singer to appear on a commercial series in 1922 in Los Angeles where he had first appeared on the concert stage in 1917. In 1932 Firestone signed him for its Monday program at $4,000 a week. In demand for other series for Packard

Lawrence Tibbett

Motor and Chesterfield Cigarettes, by 1940 he had severely strained his larynx and had to cancel performances to spend eight months of treatment by physio-therapeutic specialists. Tibbett came back cautiously on a *Ford Symphony* broadcast in January 1941, restraining his mighty voice yet proving it remained basically intact within its two-octave range.

While continuing his opera work, the vigorous and still youthful baritone took over *Your Hit Parade* from bobby-sox idol Frank Sinatra. He proved Met stalwarts could handle pop tunes on a regular basis. His last Met appearance occurred in 1950; his final stage role, in the Broadway musical *Fanny,* in 1956. He was a leader in founding the American Federation of Radio Artists in 1937 and served as president. Among his early vocal teachers in Los Angeles was Basil Ruysdael, later a radio announcer.

854. TILTON, Martha (singer; b. Nov. 14, 1915, Corpus Christi, TX). *Benny Goodman's Swing School/ Camel Caravan* (1937–39); *Fibber McGee and Molly* (1941–42); *Meet Me at Parky's* (1946–47); *Your Hit Parade* (1947); *Curt Massey–Martha Tilton Program* (1949–54).

Popular vocalist with swing-era roots. "Liltin' Miss" Martha Tilton enjoyed big band stints with Hal Grayson and Benny Goodman that she parlayed into solo bookings running into early television. First heard on Los Angeles radio, she became part of Three Hits and a Miss, a singing group. She traveled to the South Pacific with Jack Benny to entertain troops and appeared in several wartime movies. In 1946 Tilton subbed for Jo Stafford on *Chesterfield Supper Club* before moving on to her own programs. Her longest series was with Curt Massey at CBS.

855. TINNEY, Cal (emcee; b. Feb. 2, 1908, Pontotoc County, OK). *Vanity Fair* (1937); *Youth vs. Age* (1939–40); *Sizing Up the News* (1941–44).

Homespun humorist-lecturer in the mode of Will Rogers whom he once portrayed on *Cavalcade of America.* He handled game and panel shows well, and originated the joke-telling contest, *Stop Me If You've Heard This One,* in 1939. Tinney made his first network appearance on *March of Time* in 1932, after producing programs in Kansas and Oklahoma. His slow drawl and folksy way on delivering editorial commentary led to national newscasts presented in a similar dryly humorous vein.

Born on a farm, he left high school for newspaper work that led to Paris and Shanghai. Cal started his own small paper in Oklahoma and advertised it by delivering his own commercials on radio. Listeners liked his voice better that his columns, so he switched to the mike.

856. TODD, Dick (singer; b. Aug. 4, 1914, Montreal, Canada; d. May 1973, New York, NY). *Melody and Madness* (1938–39); *Avalon Time* (1939–

40); *Rinso-Spry Vaudeville Theatre* (1941–42); *Your Hit Parade* (1945–46).

Canadian baritone imported by NBC. Considered a rival of Bing Crosby early in his career, the husky-voiced Todd crossed the border for broadcasts with Larry Clinton in 1938 and stayed for a string of programs, culminating in his own in 1943 with Irving Miller's music. He sang on *Chamber Music Society of Lower Basin Street* and *Your Hit Parade,* and for Victor's Bluebird label. At one point he wrote, cast, produced and directed a half-hour show for NBC in California.

Todd attended McGill University as a music major, and was paid five dollars a sustaining broadcast as a professional vocalist in 1933. He organized a band that traveled most of Canada and the West Indies, and sang on many discs for Canadian distribution.

857. TORME, Mel (singer [Velvet Fog]; b. Sept. 13, 1925, Chicago, IL). *Fitch Bandwagon* (1944–45); *Torme Time* (1947); *New Mel Torme Show* (1948).

Engaging singer and personality whose radio jobs began in 1933 as a child actor in Chicago. He already had been singing on open house nights with the Coon-Sanders band since age four. His juvenile roles in *Jack Armstrong, Lights Out* and *Little Orphan Annie* (as Joe Corntassel) kept him busy until his voice changed. Torme became a rhythm vocalist with the Chico Marx band at 17. Skilled at the drums, as a composer ("Lament for Love," "The Christmas Song") and in script and special material writing, Mel in the mid-1940s was backed by the Mel-Tones, a vocal group, on *Fitch Bandwagon* and Decca recordings.

In 1947 New York disc jockey Fred Robbins dubbed him "the Velvet Fog" because of his "soft, gauzy voice" and sensual way with lyrics. The bobby-sox buildup included a series for Philip Moris on which he played a student working his way through college as a soda jerk. Torme fared better as a sub or guest for Perry Como, Dave Garroway and Dinah Shore. He never reached the level of matinee idol but grew into an elegant and durable artist. A versatile showman, he once made it clear that he liked singing "Live. In Person. Particularly in Manhattan."

858. TOSCANINI, Arturo (conductor; b. March 25, 1867, Parma, Italy; d. Jan. 16, 1957, Riverdale, NY). *NBC Symphony* (1937–54); (aka) *Symphony of the Air* (1943–46).

In his lifetime, he was acknowledged as the world's leading conductor. After his death, he became a legendary high priest of music. Although he had led the NY Philharmonic from 1928 to 1936 to great acclaim, and was heard via its broadcasts over CBS, it was through his association with NBC as its premier musical director and with RCA Victor as its foremost classical recording artist that the charismatic Toscanini achieved unparalleled supremacy.

On Christmas Night 1937 the 70-year-old con-

Arturo Toscanini

ductor inaugurated an era that many people regard as the highest level of orchestral performance yet reached. "The NBC Symphony," wrote Allen Hughes in 1980," was a first-class orchestra and Toscanini made it an instrument acutely responsive to his awesome interpretive powers." He was engaged by David Sarnoff, the head of RCA, to lead this carefully selected aggregation of house musicians who would divide their time between his concerts and other network programs. Music critic and consultant-commentator for NBC, Samuel Chotzinoff, who was a personal friend of the Maestro, helped persuade him to leave retirement and his native Italy to direct a large radio symphony for four or five programs each season from Studio 8H, the biggest broadcasting hall of its time. It later moved to Carnegie Hall where better acoustics prevailed and larger audiences could be accommodated. In 1940 NBC broadcast the orchestra on its South American goodwill tour.

Toscanini's repertoire stressed Wagner, Brahms, Verdi and Beethoven; periodically he scheduled broadcasts of operatic works, chiefly of Puccini and Verdi, with Jan Peerce, Robert Merrill, Nan Merriman, Rose Bampton, Vivian Della Chiesa and the Robert Shaw Chorale.

In 1948 his performances went on television which captured at close range the intensity and stamina of a musician whose conducting roots extended back into the 1880s, and on to La Scala and the Metropolitan Opera at the turn of the century.

Viewed by many players as an uncompromising tyrant, Toscanini believed that his musicians "must give me what I want." This autocrat of the podium combined grace and strength with the baton with a supersensitive ear and remarkable feats of memory. Such attributes gave rise to endless ancedotes of his childlike temper tantrums and tales of his prodigious musical recall. Yet the ultimate beneficiary of this master was the radio listener. With many of his NBC broadcasts recorded by RCA's highly attuned engineers, they remain a widely available legacy of an almost superhuman figure from a brilliant epoch in American music.

859. TOWNSEND, Dallas (newscaster; b. Jan. 17, 1919, New York, NY; d. June 1, 1995, Montclair, NJ). *CBS World News Roundup* (1956–61, 1963–82); *The World Tonight* (1961–63).

News editor and correspondent at CBS for 44 years, beginning in 1941. Townsend presided at the net's *World News Roundup* for which he received an Alfred I. duPont-Columbia University Award in Broadcast Journalism and a Peabody Award. "No other newsman in our day," the duPont jury said in 1983, "has had a broader acquaintance with news nor communicated it with more economy and precision." He covered Democratic and Republican conventions from 1948 until 1984, several Apollo launchings, early atomic tests, and Eisenhower inaugurations.

A graduate of Princeton and Columbia's School of Journalism, he spent World War II assigned to Army signal and communications centers in the Pacific and Japan. Townsend briefly worked as a news editor at WQXR New York before joining CBS.

860. TRACY, Arthur (singer [The Street Singer] [signature song: "Marta"]; b. June 25, 1899, Kaminetz-

Arthur Tracy (courtesy of Arthur Tracy)

Podolsk, Russia). *Street Singer* (1931); *Music That Satisfies* (1931–33).

Listening to the phonograph records of boyhood idol Caruso inspired the robust singing style of Tracy. Born Abbas Tracuvutsky in Russia, he built some local fame with the Philadelphia Operatic Society in the 1920s before touring in *Blossom Time* and entering amateur nights in New York. While working as emcee-singer on a vaudeville bill, he heard about the chance to audition for CBS. Net president Bill Paley gave Tracy six weeks to build an audience and find a sponsor for 15-minute song sessions, five nights a week — a format followed by Crosby, Kate Smith and a host of other young, on-the-rise vocalists.

Billing himself as The Street Singer, he scaled down his voice to the requirements of the sensitive microphone. In the space of a few short months, his inviting presentations of current melodies and traditional ballads brought him national acclaim, and a $3,000-a-week radio contract. He also appeared on theatre stages and in Paramount's *Big Broadcast of 1932.*

Learning of the wide popularity of his recordings in England, Tracy went to London in 1935, performing, recording and making films — and remaining there for nearly six years. Generally overlooked in the 1940s, he sang only briefly on radio — chiefly a daytime series on The Blue Network — and soon devoted his talents to entertaining GIs and wounded veterans. Moving into the business field as a real estate investor, he put aside his career until he was in his 70s. A revival of his old hit "Pennies from Heaven" on TV and theatre screens returned him to the limelight. His commanding voice retained its vibrant charm.

861. TREMAYNE, Les (actor; b. Apr. 16, 1913, London, England). *The First Nighter* (1933–43); *Grand Hotel* (1934–40); *Betty and Bob* (1935–39); *Old Gold Show* (1943–45); *The Falcon* (1946–49).

Tremayne had the kind of radio voice that people accepted as the big leading man-type. In various polls he was voted radio's number one dramatic actor and in the early 1940s was cited as one of the three most famous voices in America along with President Franklin D. Roosevelt and Bing Crosby. Part of Chicago radio's golden era, he replaced Don Ameche as romantic lead on *Betty and Bob, Grand Hotel* and *First Nighter.* On the latter Les played supporting roles until he asked for a chance to audition for Hollywood-bound Ameche. He won the coveted lead. In a 60-year career he estimated that he had worked on more than 30,000 broadcasts, and as many as 45 a week in the 1930s.

In Los Angeles in 1943 he co-starred with Bob Crosby on *Old Gold Show.* When Bob left for wartime service, the program switched to New York where it brought in to replace the singer a relatively unknown comic named Jackie Gleason. Hi Brown hired Les as *The Thin Man* when David Gothard failed to measure up. Tremayne teamed up with his second wife, actress

Les Tremayne (courtesy of Les Tremayne)

Alice Reinhardt for *The Tremaynes,* a WOR breakfast talk show aired six days a week. His other leading ladies included Barbara Lundy, Helen Hayes, Elizabeth Reller and Betty Lou Gerson. At one point he announced the broadcasts of Walter Winchell and Drew Pearson.

Les had entered Chicago radio in 1930 after work in community theatre, vaudeville and amusement parks. Earlier, his first professional job came in silent pictures in England at age three with his mother, Dolly Tremayne, an actress. For the first eight months at the mike, he received no pay — and when he finally did, it ranged from 25 cents to a dollar. His first network show *Fu Manchu* aired from WGN.

While playing *The Thin Man* and *The Falcon,* Tremayne joined the cast of *Detective Story* for its entire 18-month broadway run. He starred in three TV series: *Ellery Queen, One Man's Family* and *Shazam* (as Mr. Mentor), and played a featured role on *General Hospital.* His video exposure began in 1939 on the Zenith experimental channel in Chicago. He played in some 40 motion pictures, including *North By Northwest, A Man Called Peter* and *Goldfinger.*

One of the founders of AFRA's Chicago local in 1937, he has served both on the National Board and Los Angeles local. Treymayne was a founder of Pacific

Pioneer Broadcasters for whom he chaired the Audio History Committee and hosted Nostalgia Nights. "Radio," he points out, "was the one medium that made the actor a home-owning, tax-paying, family-raising, stay-in-one-place person. With regular hours and good working conditions, he became an honest citizen (in the eyes of the community) for the first time."

862. TRENT, Sybil (actress; b. Sept. 22, 1926, Brooklyn, NY). *Let's Pretend* (1935–54); *March of Games* (1939–40); *We Love and Learn* (1950–51).

Show business veteran by age nine. A member of the Warner Bros. Brooklyn studios stock company, as singer, dancer and actress as early as 1930, she bowed as emcee on WHN two years later. Trent was billed as Baby Sybil Elaine and her Kiddie Revue — sponsored by Michael Brothers Furniture Store. She enjoyed a featured role in the 1935 musical extravaganza *Jumbo;* the song "Little Girl Blue" was sung to her. When invited to join *Let's Pretend,* Sybil increasingly focused on dramatic parts, although she later sang the show's musical signature ("Cream of Wheat is so good to eat . . . ") for nine years.

During the 1940s and '50s she had running roles in *We Love and Learn* (the lead as Thelma), *Stella Dallas* (as Countess Marla Darnell) and *Under Arrest* (as the news reporter). Sybil played the Drum Major on the children's quiz, *March of Games* and worked on *David Harum, Front Page Farrell* and *Gangbusters.* After several comedy and dramatic parts on early TV shows, she became a talent agent and ad agency casting director.

Sybil Trent (courtesy of Sybil Trent)

863. TREVOR, Claire (actress; b. March 18, 1908, Brooklyn, NY). *Big Town* (1937–42); *Old Gold Don Ameche Show* (1940); *Results, Incorporated* (1944–45).

Stock, Broadway and film parts, usually as the tough blonde in a second lead, were augmented by a choice radio role. In 1937 Trevor created the glamourous girl reporter Lorelei Kilbourne opposite the crusading, racket-busting managing editor of "The Illustrated Press," Steve Wilson, portrayed by Edward G. Robinson. The widely praised dramatizations were based on authenticated newspaper stories and brought in such colorful characters as Harry the Hack, Willie the Weep and Mozart (a piano player in local "dives"). Trevor's prominence in the weekly stories helped bring her good dramatic roles on screen — the saloon girl opposite John Wayne in *Stagecoach* and the gun moll in *Key Largo* for which she won a Best Supporting Actress Oscar in 1948. From 1938 to 1942 she was married to Clark Andrews, one of *Big Town's* early producers.

In the mid-40s Trevor joined Lloyd Nolan on Mutual's *Results, Incorporated,* a comedy mystery program. She was well cast as his secretary in an agency that specialized in solving problems and finding missing people. On Don Ameche's 1940 Old Gold variety show, Trevor appeared each week as his leading lady in a short dramatic sketch adapted from a story by Mark Hellinger.

864. TRIETSCH, Ken (musician-singer [catchphrase: "Are You Ready, Hezzie?"]; b. Sept. 13, 1903, Arcadia, IN; d. Sept. 17, 1987, Studio City, CA). *National Barn Dance* (1934–46); *Uncle Ezra* (1935–39).

Leader-manager of Hoosier Hot Shots, a foursome of novelty musicians with emphasis on cornball country tunes that grew out of the vaudeville circuit's Buzzington Rube Band. Ken played a handful of instruments, most often the guitar and sousaphone. Brother Paul (Hezzie), a drummer, specialized on the musical wash-board with a woodblock, cymbal, bell and ooga horn attached. Charles Ward (Gabie) handled the clarinet and Frank Kettering, the bass. They first surfaced on radio in 1932 on WOWO Fort Wayne. Within a year, they settled at WLS. One of their assignments was to open the 1933 Chicago World's Fair by broadcasting from an airplane 6,000 feet over the city. The stunt led to weekly *National Barn Dance* appearances, over 100 recordings ("I Like Bananas Because They Have No Bones") and 23 film assignments (*Swing in the Saddle*). When the group signed a Columbia Pictures contract in 1946, they were described as radio's highest-paid novelty musicians.

865. TROTTER, John Scott (conductor; b. June 14, 1908, Charlotte, NC; d. Oct. 29, 1975, Los Angeles, CA). *Kraft Music Hall* (1937–46); *Philco Radio Time* (1946–49).

Arranger and conductor for Bing Crosby for 17 years, including the multi-million-selling recording "White Christmas." In 1936, while vacationing in California, Trotter was signed to orchestrate five songs for Crosby's film *Pennies from Heaven*. A year later he took over as musical director for his radio show. In 1944 *Radio Life* gave him its distinguished achievement award in the category of arranger-conductor.

A pianist, he played with Hal Kemp for eleven years, beginning in his college days at North Carolina in 1925. He helped to create that band's fresh, happy sound on such numbers as "Got a Date with an Angel." In 1959, after the Crosby programs came to an end, Trotter became TV musical director for George Gobel.

866. TROUT, Robert (commentator, announcer; b. Oct. 15, 1908, Wake Country, NC). *Headlines & Bylines* (1936–40); *Robert Trout with the News Till Now* (1946–47, 1952–53); *Who Said That?* (1948–49).

Trout introduced FDR's first fireside chat in 1933, shortly after this news reporter covered the President's inauguration for WTOP and the Columbia network. His cool, unruffled voice became closely linked to Washington events and personalities. In 1935 he transferred to the CBS news and public affairs staff in New York where his polish and stamina and ad-libbing won him the nickname "Iron Man of Radio." His news broadcasts and special remotes stood in contrast to an assignment in 1937 as announcer on *Professor Quiz,* an early game show.

Trout covered the London blitz and shortwaved to home war-related events and talks with ordinary Britishers. In 1943 he presented *Calling America,* a report to the American people about their sons overseas, and a year later announced the Allied invasion of France. In the postwar decade he remained with radio, and occasionally filled in for vacationing CBS newsmen in cities abroad. In 1964 he served as anchorman on a CBS program entitled "Farewell to Studio Nine," presented when CBS News moved to larger quarters in New York. That year he did his first political convention coverage on television to much praise by critics and viewers for his smooth, statesman-like anchoring. He became a special correspondent in Madrid in the mid-60s. On retirement Trout settled there but periodically returned to the States to cover political conventions and related events for ABC.

867. TUBB, Ernest (singer [The Texas Troubador]; b. Feb. 9, 1914, Crisp, TX; d. Sept. 6, 1984, Nashville, TN). *Grand Ole Opry* (1943–84)

Pioneer of country's honky-tonk music. His distinctive, deep baritone was heard on the *Opry* and other country music shows. Influenced by Jimmie Rodgers, he wrote and recorded "I'm Walking the Floor Over You" and "I'll Get Along Somehow." In

1947 he headed the first country show at Carnegie Hall. That year he opened a country music record-book store and commenced his WSM *Midnight Jamboree,* both in Nashville where he had been the second country artist to record.

His early broadcasts in 1934 at KONO San Antonio proved that this 20-year-old guitar player had the makings of an audience-building troubador.

868. TUCKER, Madge (actress; b. 1900, Centralia, IL). *The Lady Next Door* (1929–35).

Originator, writer, director and actress for *The Lady Next Door* and other NBC children's programs. She successfully scouted new child actors for *Coast-to-Coast on a Bus*. It was her theory that if a child read a line wrong twice in rehearsal, it was the line that was wrong and not the child. She rewrote the line to suit the young performers. "I want them to be just what they are supposed to be, a group of children acting naturally."

A graduate of George Washington University with leanings toward the theatre, she substituted as hostess on a children's program on WRC Washington in 1924 and remained to produce one-act plays. Tucker went to NBC New York in 1926 as its first continuity writer. In 1949 she moved into television with children's programs and retired three years later.

869. TUTTLE, Lurene (actress; b. Aug. 29, 1907, Pleasant Lake, IN; d. May 28, 1986, Encino, CA). *The Great Gildersleeve* (1941–44); *Masquerade* (1946–48); *Adventures of Sam Spade* (1946–50); *Red Skelton Show* (1947–49, 1952–53).

Lurene Tuttle (courtesy of Capital Cities/ABC)

Beginning in the CBS series *Hollywood Hotel* in 1936, she turned into one of the busiest supporting character actresses on the West Coast. On thrillers, comedy shows and dramas, Tuttle stood out to the degree that in 1944 *Radio Life* voted her the best supporting feminine player on the basis of her all-round capabilities in such parts as Marjorie on *Gildersleeve,* Dimples on *Blondie,* Judy on *Dr. Christian,* and roles in Arch Oboler programs, *The Whistler* and *Mayor of the Town.* Her most vivid characterization was as Sam Spade's secretary, Effie Perrine.

A gifted dialectician, she did films for Orson Welles and Alfred Hitchcock, and the television sitcoms *Life with Father* and *Julia.* From a show business family, she received professional training from plays produced by her father, ex-minstrel man C.U. Tuttle, and at the Pasadena Playhouse. She was the first woman president of the Los Angeles local of AFRA.

870. VAGUE, Vera (comedienne; b. Sept. 2, 1904, New York, NY; d. Sept. 14, 1974, Santa Barbara, CA). *Chase & Sanborn Hour* (1939–40); *Bob Hope Show* (1942–48); *Jimmy Durante Show* (1949–50).

Barbara Jo Allen adopted the name Vera Vague when she assumed roles as a dizzy, man-chasing old maid. The comedienne first appeared as that character on *Signal Carnival* on the NBC Pacific Coast net. Bergen and McCarthy made her a coast-to-coast name; Bob Hope assured her comic standing. In the late '40s she had her own show, with a comedy and audience-participation format. In a similar vein she emceed early TV game shows: *The Greatest Man on Earth* and *Follow the Leader.* She once played Beth Holly on *One Man's Family.*

Attractive and well-schooled, Allen had started out as a dramatic actress on Broadway.

871. VALENTINE, Lew (quizmaster; b. Aug. 5, 1912, San Benito, TX; d. June 1976, Santa Monica, CA). *Mennen Jury Trials* (1935); *Dr. I.Q.* (1939–41, 1946–50).

Before becoming "The Mental Banker"—*Dr. I.Q.*—Valentine was a radio announcer, singer, dramatic actor, program and production director in San Antonio and Cincinnati. He had no trouble turning himself into a quiz emcee, although in the process was overshadowed by his broadcast moniker. *Dr. I.Q.* moved about the country, broadcasting from theatre stages in various large cities. Initially Chicago was home base but the city police department attempted to stop the quiz on the premise that it was an illegal lottery and a game of chance.

Introduced as "the genial master of wit and information," Valentine worked at a rapid-fire pace with four or five assistants scattered about a theatre with portable microphones used to pick up answers from members of the audience. "I have a lady in the balcony, Doctor," became a stock phrase on every show. Valentine handed over to bright contestants as many

as 100 silver dollars; losers received a box of sponsor Mars Inc.'s Milky Way candy bars.

Valentine sounded older than his 26 years at the program's start in 1939. Not infrequently, fans refused to believe such a young man could be the smart Doctor.

872. VALLEE, Rudy (singer, bandleader, emcee [The Vagabond Lover] [signature song: "My Time Is Your Time"] [catchphrase: "Heigh-ho, everybody."]; b. July 18, 1901, Island Pond, VT; d. July 3, 1986, North Hollywood, CA). *Fleischmann Hour* (1929–39); *Sealtest Show* (1940–43); *Drene Show* (1944–46); *Rudy Vallee Show* (1946–47).

His decade-long variety hour introduced more future stars for the first time than any other series on the air. These Thursday night broadcasts, at first, were made up of Vallee and his 16-piece orchestra; in 1932 they focused more on guest talent, presenting such new and unknown personalities as Bob Hope, Joe Penner, Red Skelton, Victor Borge, Alice Faye, Bob Burns, Frances Langford and Edgar Bergen and Charlie McCarthy, among many.

The show first aired October 24, 1929 from a backroom at the Paramount Theatre where crooner Vallee was the star attraction of four shows a day and did not have the time to travel to the regular NBC New York studios. A singing idol, the boyishly handsome, curly-haired performer drew hordes of young women wherever he appeared, and tickets to his broadcasts were a coveted entry to 60 minutes of top-drawer entertainment, sparked by Rudy's nasal baritone renditions of dreamy love songs.

Rudy Vallee

A self-taught saxophone player, he joined dance bands at Yale and dropped out for a year to play at London's Savoy Hotel. Back in New Haven he formed his Connecticut Yankees about the time he left college. After a vaudeville tour and society dances in Boston, Vallee opened at the Heigh-Ho Club in New York in January 1928. Several times a week WABC and other local stations picked up the band. He sang through a megaphone to amplify his modest resonance. Letters, calls and telegrams began to pour in asking about Vallee. His first sponsor was the Herbert Jewelry Store in Harlem — $100 for his entire band on WMCA Sundays at 2 p.m. for an hour.

"To attract attention to the store," Vallee recalled, "I made what may have been the first too believable commercial in radio history. It began with a clock striking midnight, then some gun shots and a policeman's whistle. The commercial message was contained in some sparkling dialogue between an Irish patrolman (me) and his sergeant (our first violinist) praising Mr. Herbert's jewelry as so dazzling they couldn't blame the thieves for wanting to steal it. . . . Once was enough for the New York police, who complained to our sponsor."

It was Fleischmann's Yeast that launched him nationally and quickly placed this small town, upper New England-born performer in the ranks of superstars. Vallee introduced numerous popular songs over radio, which was the touchstone of his various professional activities: Broadway revues, motion pictures, recordings and club dates. He left the air in August 1942 to join the U.S. Coast Guard as a bandmaster-chief petty officer. He and his military musicians played on Bob Burns and *Fitch Bandwagon* broadcasts before he returned to the microphone for Procter & Gamble in 1944. As his vocal prowess diminished, he turned to character acting and comedy. In 1948 as a sort of high-priced interlocutor he moderated NBC's *Leave It to the Girls.*

Broadway and movie audiences were re-introduced to the Jazz Age crooner in his part as tycoon J. B. Biggley in the musical *How to Succeed in Business Without Really Trying.* The hard-working, never-modest show business legend wrote three autobiographies: *Vagabond Dreams Come True, My Time Is Your Time* and *Let the Chips Fall.* He was working on a third memoir involving the many women in his life when he died in his shrine-like hilltop home watching the Statue of Liberty centennial salute on television. His last words to his wife: "I wish we could be there; you know how I love a big party."

873. VANDERCOOK, John W. (commentator; b. April 22, 1902, London, England; d. Jan. 6, 1963, Delhi, NY). *Newsroom of the Air/News of the World* (1940–46).

Writer and explorer, he got into broadcasting by accident in 1940. While paying a call on a NBC executive, news broke of the United States-British deal of trading ships for Caribbean bases. Vandercook was asked whether he knew anything about the West Indies. It was an area on which he was a specialist and historical researcher. (His book *Black Majesty,* a biography of Henri Christophe of Haiti, had been a best seller in 1928.) He went on the air that night and continued as a news commentator and analyst.

His father was a founder and first president of the United Press, and the son wrote features, editorials and ordinary news for papers in Columbus, Washington, Baltimore and New York. When his employer the New York *Graphic* folded, he began a series of leisurely high adventure journeys without interruption for a dozen years. By 1942 he had explored some 70 different countries. It proved an excellent background to cover world news especially during wartime.

874. VANDEVENTER, Fred (newscaster, panelist; b. Dec. 5, 1903, Tipton, IN; d. Dec. 2, 1971, Colonial Heights, VA). *Twenty Questions* (1946–54); *Vandeventer and the News* (1951–52).

An old-fashioned game played around the Vandeventer dinner table, *Twenty Questions* was taken as a program by Fred's employer WOR. Earlier, station announcer Charles Stark had shown interest in Fred's idea and came up with the suggestion of a panel of experts but never ran with it. Fred, a newscaster, joined his program as panelist as did wife Florence Rinard when Mary Margaret McBride proved unavailable. Their offspring periodically came aboard, too, in the venerable "animal, vegetable, mineral" parlor game. They were Nancy Vandeventer and Bobby McGuire (who used his grandmother's maiden name).

A printer's devil and kid reporter, Fred Lewis VanDevender grew up in Indiana, and by 1925 was in Chicago working for Hearst. The paradigm of the "front page" school of journalism, he, nonetheless, left his newspaper to become a road salesman for King Features Syndicate. With the Depression, he lost his job. For some half dozen years, he survived from hand to mouth, taking whatever he could find. At one point, he and Florence made fudge and sold it at a Muncie hotel. In 1935 he got back into writing and soon landed a job with the AP bureau in Detroit.

Vandeventer successfully auditioned as a newscaster at WJR in early 1942, and quickly gained the highest news ratings in Detroit. (The station manager insisted he broadcast as Van Deventer, dropping his first name and modifying the spelling of his last.) WOR brought him to New York in 1944. Two daily broadcasts at key periods, 6:30 and 11 p.m., placed him among the top newsmen in the city. In 1951 he added a Sunday news analysis show on Mutual but a dispute over content led him to quit all newscasting and concentrate on *Twenty Questions.* When that left the air — it also had been on television — he returned to journalism on a regional scale, dabbled in politics, and began drinking heavily.

In 1960 Mutual recalled him for five-minute news

strips. But he began to lose his voice. Between broadcasts, he would dine and drink. On one occasion, on the air, he gasped for breath. His announcer, Westbrook Van Voorhis, asked if he was all right. "No, I've had a couple of drinks, and . . ." Those were the last words he ever said on the radio.

By the late '60s Vandeventer pursued news reporting and editing jobs in the South. At the home of one of his Virginia political friends, he collapsed during an interview and was briefly hospitalized. In the words of his son: "Bored and thirsty, he went home and died."

875. VAN HARVEY, Art (actor; b. Aug. 23, 1883, Chicago, IL; d. July 7, 1957, Chicago, IL). *Vic and Sade* (1932–44).

After an association with a farmer-oriented ad agency and an earlier stint in vaudeville as a multidialect mimic, Van Harvey at age 45 turned to radio. He was cast as Victor Rodney Gook, the drawling bookkeeper on the quirky serial *Vic and Sade*. He lived with his whiney wife Sade "in the little house halfway up the next block" in "Crooper, Illinois." It was the role that defined his career. He stayed with it — with only a leave of absence in 1940 to recuperate from a heart seizure — until the classic comedy ended after a 12-year run. In the 1950s he picked up an ongoing part on the NBC-TV soap *Hawkins Falls* while continuing with assignments on radio's *Silver Eagle, Mountie.*

As a youngster, Art sneaked off to theatres — to the point where his mother spoke of actors as "emissaries of the devil."

876. VAN STEEDEN, Peter (bandleader [signature song: "Home"]; b. April 3, 1904, Amsterdam, The Netherlands; d. Jan. 3, 1990, New Canaan, CT). *Fred Allen Show* (1935–40); *Dr. District Attorney* (1940–52); *Duffy's Tavern* (1942–45); *Break the Bank* (1946–50).

Orchestra leader — and foil — for Fred Allen on *Town Hall Tonight.* He once arrived at rehearsal with a terrible hair cut. It stuck up and out all over. Fred Allen didn't say a word during rehearsal but that night at the mike, he remarked: "Van Steeden, your hair looks like the elbow on a two-dollar raccoon coat." The audience broke up, so the director ordered Peter to wear his hair in that fashion, thus becoming fodder for Fred's outrageous humor week after week.

Van Steeden organized his first band while studying engineering at New York University. Van and His Collegians played college proms and club dances, and for several summers, resort hotels and restaurants. His undergrads auditioned for Philips Carlin at WEAF in 1923, but everything went wrong. Nevertheless, the station called later and ordered them to report for a broadcast. His aggregation played remotes from many hotels, including the opening of The New Yorker in 1929. They provided music for numerous programs: Ray Perkins' Barbasol broadcasts, *Tim and Irene Ryan*

Peter Van Steeden

Sky Road Show, Stoopnagle and Budd, Jack Pearl and George Jessel. Van Steeden conducted for the Lucky Strike *Hit Parade* and Bristol-Myers *Mr. District Attorney.* One evening while conducting on *Duffy's Tavern,* he fell off the podium into the lap of a woman sitting in the first row. He apologized politely. Whereupon she said, "Think nothing of it . . . now may I have your autograph?" His last major series, *Break the Bank,* took him to television in 1948. Van Steeden co-authored the song "Home," which was introduced across the dial on Thanksgiving eve 1931.

877. VAN VOORHIS, Westbrook (announcer, narrator [catchphrase: "Time marches on!"]; b. Sept. 21, 1903, New Milford, CT; d. July 13, 1968, New Milford, CT). *March of Time* (1937–39, 1942–45).

Authoritative voice of *Time* magazine's radio and movie documentaries for 15 years. His firm, attention-getting manner in describing world-shaking events and major issues of the Depression, World War II, and the aftermath of both, added to the popularity of these dramatized broadcasts and films. Van Voorhis also was a news broadcaster for WOR-Mutual and CBS, and narrated many instructional films for the military service. His colleagues described his distinctive voice as "deep and lyrical"; one said that it was "like the voice of God."

He attended the U.S. Naval Academy and entered broadcasting in the late 1920s. Van Voorhis acted on *March of Time* before becoming its narrator.

878. VENUTA, Benay (singer; b. Jan. 27, 1912, San Francisco, CA; d. Sept. 1, 1995, New York, NY).

Shell Chateau (1935); *Benay Venuta's Program* (1937–40); *Abbott and Costello Show* (1940).

Blues singer-actress. When Mutual started broadcasting in the mid-30s, she wrote, directed, produced, emceed and sang on her own sustaining program for more than three years. Venuta had brief runs with Abbott and Costello, Harry Savoy and Ed Gardner. In 1941 she pitched in as guest captain on the short lived game, *Quizzer Baseball.* On Broadway she appeared to good advantage in *Anything Goes* (replacing Ethel Merman), *Kiss the Boys Goodbye* and *By Jupiter.*

At 13 she began as a singer in vaudeville and entered radio in 1930 at KPO San Francisco. Early credits included *Who Cares Hour* and *Keep Up with the Kids.* Venuta made radio history, of sorts, by opening Mutual's daily lineup from Hollywood and some 20 hours later signing off at night from New York, and reputedly stopping enroute to sing in Cincinnati.

879. VOLA, Vicki (actress; b. Aug. 27, 1916, Denver, CO; d. July 21, 1985, New York, NY). *Death Valley Days* (1938–39); *Mr. District Attorney* (1940–52); *Christopher Wells* (1947–48).

Best known as Miss Miller, secretary to "Chief," *Mr. District Attorney,* played by Jay Jostyn. Her other secretarial role was Stacey McGill in *Christopher Wells,* a newspaper and radio reporter portrayed by Les Damon. As a contract player and busy free-lancer, she was cast in roles from Biblical characters (*Light of the World*) to murderesses (*The Fat Man*). In *Road of Life,* she was a nurse, and obliged to steer that character through a tortuous plot typical of soap operas.

Her own conception of good acting for radio was the ability of a performer to make his presence in a scene felt by the listeners even when he was not delivering lines.

Vola narrated *Woman in Love* and was heard on *Jungle Jim,* a transcribed series. She made her bow over KLZ Denver in 1933 in a series of Bible programs. Moving to Hollywood, she worked on *Lux Radio Theatre,* then in 1938 settled in New York. Vola once played Boris Karloff's leading lady in a broadcast of "Dr. Jekyll and Mr. Hyde."

880. VON ZELL, Harry (announcer, actor; b. July 11, 1906, Indianapolis, IN; d. Nov. 21, 1981, Calabasas, CA). *Old Gold Hour* (1929–30); *Joe and Vi* (1931–34); *Town Hall Tonight* (1935–40); *Time to Smile* (1940–49).

His booming voice and infectious laugh sparked many top-flight shows with Eddie Cantor, Dinah Shore and Fred Allen. As his role as actor-comic grew in this company, his announcing chores gradually diminished.

Von Zell landed his first job as a singer on KMIC Inglewood, California, in 1927. Two years later he was chosen from many contenders as announcer for Paul Whiteman's Old Gold show. He followed the program back East and was taken on staff at CBS for *March of Time* and *Stoopnagle and Budd.* He joined

Vicki Vola (courtesy of Capital Cities/ABC)

Harry Von Zell

Truth or Consequences briefly in 1944 as co-emcee when it was thought host Ralph Edwards would be drafted. Back in California that year, Von Zell began to act in films, then in television as the foil on *Burns and Allen* with whom he had appeared on radio. In a slip of the tongue, he once announced the former U.S. President's name as "Hoobert Heever."

881. VOORHEES, Donald (conductor; b. July 26, 1903, Allentown, PA; d. Jan. 10, 1989, Cape May Court House, NJ). *Show Boat* (1932–33); *Cavalcade of America* (1940–53); *Telephone Hour* (1940–58).

Voorhees conducted every type of radio program, but he is best remembered for directing the orchestra of *The Telephone Hour,* a Monday night institution that mixed classical and popular music performed by outstanding artists, including Heifetz, Pinza, Rubinstein, Crosby, Pons, Segovia and Iturbi. The program won a Peabody Award for outstanding entertainment in music.

A pianist in an Allentown theatre orchestra at 15, he followed a "break in" show to Philadelphia, then Broadway. Soon he was a regular in the pits and on the podiums for revues, particularly the *Scandals* and *Vanities.* In 1925 he conducted experimental concerts over radio from the Earl Carroll Theatre. When CBS was launched in 1927, he became joint house conductor with Howard Barlow. In the 1930s Voorhees was a free-lance leader on *Show Boat, General Motors Hour* and *Fire Chief.* For the duPont historical-dramatic *Cavalcade,* he pored over hundreds of pages of material for the right musical bridge, and sometimes composed the mood music himself.

Called "a musician's musician," he was voted radio's most popular concert and program conductor in *Musical America* reader polls. In 1955 he won the Lowell Mason Award for his "distinguished contributions to music education."

882. WAIN, Bea (singer [The Reverie Girl]; b. April 30, 1917, New York, NY). *Larry Clinton's RCA Victor Campus Club* (1937–38); *Your Hit Parade* (1939–41, (1943–44); *Monday Merry-Go-Round* (1941–42); *Your All-Time Hit Parade* (1943–44).

Although she never studied voice, Bea Wain proved to be a quick-study musician and one of the best all-round singers of popular songs. She made her debut at age six, vocalizing on NBC's *Children's Hour.* Taking up chorus work with the Kate Smith and Fred Waring shows and Kay Thompson's Rhythm Singers, she attracted the attention of Larry Clinton, who was organizing an orchestra. As his vocalist, she made the charts with best-selling records, particularly "My Reverie," an arrangement of a classic Debussy melody.

In 1939 she joined *Your Hit Parade,* co-starring Lanny Ross. She later filled in for Joan Edwards. *Your All-Time Hit Parade* also utilized her talents, as did *Monday Merry-Go-Round.* Just after World War II she and her husband, announcer Andre Baruch, became the first major disc jockey couple, billed as *Mr. & Mrs. Music* over WMCA. A generation later they introduced and spun records of performers on unforgettable tunes in a syndicated version of the old Hit Parade.

883. WALDO, Janet (actress; b. c1920, Grandview, WA). *Meet Corliss Archer* (1943–53); *Young Love* (1949–50).

While attending the University of Washington and working in its Little Theatre, Bing Crosby presented her an award at a campus homecoming. A Paramount scout accompanying him signed her for *The Star Maker,* a Crosby musical, but only small parts followed. Radio better utilized Waldo's charming voice in *The Gallant Heart* over the NBC Pacific chain and *One Man's Family* as Irene, wife of Cliff. In 1943 she assumed the lead as Corliss Archer, teenage scatterbrain.

A serious, diligent actress, she had roles on *Dr. Christian, Silver Theatre, Ozzie and Harriet* and *Railroad Hour.* Those presentations were often adapted or written by her husband Robert Lee. For *People Are Funny,* she was the Raleigh Cigarette Girl.

884. WALL, Lucille (actress; b. Jan. 18, 1899, Chicago, IL; d. July 11, 1986, Reno, NV). *Collier's House* (1927–31); *Island Boat Club* (1932); *Lorenzo Jones* (1940–55); *Portia Faces Life* (1941–52).

As Polly Preston, she began in 1927 at WJZ, playing the "Collier Love Story" girl opposite Frederick March on the *Collier's Hour.* She later utilized her real

Lucille Wall (courtesy of Capital Cities/ABC)

name for leading soap opera roles: Portia and Belle (Lorenzo Jones' wife). When these programs ended after long runs, she retired. But television in 1960 brought her to a new generation in the part of nurse Lucille March on *General Hospital.* The role lasted nearly 17 years, longer than her radio characters.

In 1945 Wall observed that radio had "made citizens out of actors. We used to live out of trunks. Now we can have homes of our own and live like other professional people."

885. WALLENSTEIN, Alfred (conductor; b. Oct. 7, 1898, Chicago, IL; d. Feb. 8, 1983, New York, NY). *Virtuosos* (1931); *Voice of Firestone* (1937–43).

Music director of the Mutual Broadcasting System, he ranked as among the most innovative and prolific conductors on any network staff. He offered programs and interludes for every taste and every preference during his tenure from 1935 to 1945. One series was devoted to all the piano concertos of Mozart; another to that composer's operas, still another to Bach's church cantatas; and others to choral music and modern American compositions. In 1942 he received the Peabody Radio Award for pioneering good music and originating various unique broadcasts. Radio editors applauded his achievements, and in 1940 placed him third among those who made the most eventful musical contributions, the other two being Toscanini and Barbirolli. And his early classical programs were among the first commercially sponsored.

A prodigy on the cello, he assumed a post with the San Francisco Symphony as a teenager. From 1919 to 1922 he played with the Los Angeles Philharmonic, then joined the Chicago Symphony as principal cellist. From that post in 1926, he performed three cello recitals for WGN. In 1929 Toscanini brought him to the NY Philharmonic for the first cello chair, and also encouraged him to move into conducting. He directed a radio concert in 1931, and soon organized his famous Sinfonietta for WOR where he became musical director in 1935. When Toscanini left his Philharmonic post a year later, Wallenstein forsook the cello and devoted himself to radio assignments. He directed the *Voice of Firestone* for six years, and from time to time conducted the NBC Symphony. Among the radio composers and conductors who benefited from his encouragement was Morton Gould.

Wallenstein continued to break new ground in music as director of the Los Angeles Philharmonic from 1943 to 1956 and of the Caramoor Festival from 1958 to 1961.

886. WALLER, Thomas "Fats" (pianist, singer [signature song: "Ain't Misbehavin'"]; b. May 21, 1904, New York, NY; d. Dec. 15, 1943, Kansas City, MO). *Paramount on Parade* (1930–31); *Columbia Variety Hour* (1934); *Saturday Night Swing Club* (1937).

One of the very few black performers to star on a

Fats Waller

country-wide series. CBS brought this genial, highly creative musician to its network in 1934. Waller had already achieved prominence as a jazz pianist on the early morning *Rhythm Club* and as organist of romantic mood music on *Moon River,* both at WLW. During his short career, he was recognized by fellow musicians as a master technician and adored by jazz fans as a master of swing. To the delight of all, he occasionally interpolated his own improvisations, with a garrulous vocal chorus or a half-grunted aside.

At 14 Waller was playing the organ in a Harlem movie theatre. He first broadcast from the stage of the Fox Terminal Theatre in Newark in 1923. In 1925 he toured the country in a vaudeville act with blues singer Bessie Smith and did local programs at WHN and WOR. Among his 360 songs, the best known are "Ain't Misbehavin'," "Honeysuckle Rose" and "I've Got a Feeling I'm Falling." He wrote the music for the Broadway success *Early to Bed* in 1943, and shortly before his death that year in a Pullman berth on his way home from Hollywood, he had appeared in *Stormy Weather,* an all-black musical.

887. WALLINGTON, Jimmy (announcer; b. Sept. 5, 1907, Rochester, NY; d. Dec. 22, 1972, Arlington, VA). *Chase & Sanborn Hour* (1930–35); *Texaco Town/Star Theatre* (1937–40); *Alan Young Show* (1946–47); *Carnation Contended Hour* (1948–49).

His coveted assignments for NBC placed him in the top ranks of announcers. He introduced President Franklin D. Roosevelt's broadcasts, described Lindbergh's flights, and greeted Admiral Byrd from a special NBC tugboat equipped with shortwave transmitters. He was equally at ease on the variety shows of Eddie Cantor, Fred Allen, Dennis Day and Ed Gardner.

In the 1920s Wallington joined WGY in Schenectady where he attended Union College. By 1932 he was one of the highest paid NBC staffers. After a period of freelance commercials, he returned in 1961 to NBC's *Monitor*. His last employment was with the Voice of America.

Singled out for his superb diction, he received the *Radio Stars* magazine award for the best announcing of the year 1934.

888. WANAMAKER, Sam (actor; b. June 14, 1919, Chicago, IL; d. Dec. 18, 1993, London, England). *Road of Life* (1939–40); *Lone Journey* (1940–41, 1946).

Actor-director with roots in radio soaps. Cast member of *Guiding Light, Road of Life* and *Against the Storm* before breaking into classical stage roles in 1942, he starred with Ingrid Bergman in the play, *Joan of Lorraine* and with Madeleine Carroll in *Goodbye, My Fancy*. Blacklisted in the 1950s, he moved to London where he was an active producer, director and actor.

Wanamaker appeared in numerous films (*The Spy Who Came in From the Cold, Private Benjamin*) and the TV miniseries, *Holocaust*. He was instrumental in the campaign to rebuilt Shakespeare's Globe Theatre on the banks of the Thames and to create the New Shakespeare Cultural Center in Liverpool.

889. WARING, Fred (conductor [signature songs: "I Hear Music"; "Sleep"]; b. June 9, 1900, Tyrone, PA; d. July 29, 1984, Danville, PA). *Fred Waring and His Pennsylvanians* (1933–39, 1944–50); *Pleasure Time/Victory Tunes* (1939–44).

Waring mounted a crack stage and recording band in the 1920s but radio success seemed elusive. Even after winning major cigarette sponsor Old Gold for a CBS series, after many auditions, Waring's Pennsylvanians sounded a bit old fashioned. This perplexed Waring who had just completed an unprecedented six-month run at the Roxy Theatre with his 55-piece orchestra. A meticulous craftsman, he sized up the situation and positioned his 18-member choral group as the center piece of the program, with its startling phrasing, sudden changes of volume and tempo, and long hums on traditional and jazz tunes alike. The emphasis on specially arranged vocal numbers turned the program around, inaugurating two decades of exceptional broadcasts.

Waring and his aggregation became an American institution. They moved musically with the times from swing to rock 'n' roll. Perhaps their finest moments drew upon patriotic and devotional songs during the war years. Chesterfield cigarettes changed the show from *Pleasure Time* to *Victory Tunes* to reflect

Fred Waring

the mood of the country. Waring left the selection of many numbers to servicemen. A frequently requested presentation was the stirring "Battle Hymn of the Republic."

In 1945 this showman of high standards moved his richly orchestrated prime-time series into the daytime schedule by signing a NBC contract to broadcast each morning Monday through Friday. A bold step, it stood out as a way to bring quality entertainment to pre-noon programming.

His diversified vocal and instrumental talent at that point included Jane Wilson, Gordon Goodman, Poley McClintock, Livingston Gerhardt, Donna Dae and Virginia Morley (a pianist who became Waring's third wife in 1954). Outstanding was the brisk pacing which made for almost continuous music with Fred's introduction and incidental remarks coming up and under during the first few bars of each new tune.

As a teenager he started a dance band that grew into Waring's Collegians. At Penn State, where he was an undergrad, it played many school parties, then continued on other college campuses and in recording studios, vaudeville and Broadway musicals. His radio debut, a single program over WWJ Detroit, came about in 1921 while playing the Junior Hop at the University of Michigan. Tours of hotels, concert halls and campuses became a staple of the Pennsylvanians. When his popular TV series ended a five-year run in 1954, the upbeat, well-scrubbed group continued to perform extensively on the road and for special occasions, including political campaigns and White House receptions. Meanwhile, the entrepreneurial Waring helped to develop and market the Waring Blendor, owned a Pocono Mountain resort, formed the largest choral and band music publishing company in the world, and ran annual music workshops to teach his choral techniques (they reinforced his reputation for low tolerance for shallowness and inattention). To the end of his 68-year career, he conducted. At his last performance just hours before his death, he led a youth choral group at his alma mater Penn State.

890. WARNER, Gertrude (actress, b. April 2, 1917, West Hartford, CT; d. Jan. 26, 1986, New York, NY). *Against the Storm* (1939–42); *Whispering Streets* (1952–54).

Major player in a dozen radio stock serials, including title roles in *The Man I Married, Joyce Jordan, M.D.* and *Ellen Randolph.* For a time she was the voice of Margot Lane in *The Shadow* and Della Street in *Perry Mason.* Warner began at WTIC Hartford in 1935, and four years later joined NBC's *Against the Storm* and *Valiant Lady.* She later taught acting at Weist-Barron School and Oberlin College.

891. WARNOW, Mark (conductor; b. April 10, 1902, Monastrischt, Russia; d. Oct. 17, 1949, New York, NY). *Chrysler Airshow* (1934); *Evening in Paris* (1935–36); *We, the People* (1937–41); *Your Hit Parade* (1939–47, 1949).

As CBS staff conductor in the early 1930s, he helped present singers Kate Smith, Morton Downey

and Gertrude Neisen, and Helen Hayes' dramatic series. "If it wasn't for radio I'd probably be a starving fiddle player," he said in 1941. "You go along and then something hits you and you suddenly become box office." In his case it was subbing for Morton Downey's conductor when no one in the studio could handle opera.

A violinist, he seesawed between instrumentalist and substitute orchestra leader before directing grand opera companies in Brooklyn and *Music Box Revues* on Broadway. He enjoyed the longest run of any conductor on *Your Hit Parade,* and was starting a new season in 1949 on its podium when he died suddenly. His brother Raymond Scott, also a conductor, replaced him. Warnow had a hand in developing *Stop The Music!* which brought in components of the Hit Parade formula.

892. WARREN, Leonard (singer; b. April 21, 1911, Bronx, NY; d. March 4, 1960, New York, NY).

A pre-eminent opera baritone but one of the least known personalities in show business. A painstaking craftsman, he prepared extensively for his roles, even if he had sung a part for a hundred or more times, as he did Rigoletto. He felt his two-octave range voice (low G to high C) was a great responsibility, a treasured gift.

While working in his father's fur business and studying music as a hobby, Warren found a job in the Radio City Music Hall chorus in 1935. He sang on stage for three years, with no opportunities for a solo turn (Robert Weede was the showplace's baritone star). On a dare he appeared on *Metropolitan Opera Auditions of the Air,* and won over 78 other singers. His unusually resonant voice hit the judges with such impact that one, conductor Wilfred Pelletier, suspected he was hearing a record of some great singer being played as a joke, instead of the young man ostensibly doing the singing in an adjacent radio studio. But Warren only knew the arias he had sung in the auditions. To prepare for his Met debut and seven assigned roles for the 1938–39 season, he left for Italy to study, thanks to a generous check of $5,000 from the president of Sherwin-Williams and the *Auditions* sponsor. Warren bowed in a minor part in Verdi's *Simon Boccanegra,* and gradu-

Mark Warnow

ally moved up to title roles in *Tosca, Aida* and *Falstaff.*

His most frequent appearances were on *Voice of Firestone* and *Telephone Hour,* beginning in 1944. His Met broadcasts numbered two or three each season. At age 48 Warren collapsed and died on the stage of the Met while making his exit in the second act of *La Forza del Destino.* He had just finished the aria "O fatal pages of my destiny" when he passed into operatic history.

893. WARRICK, Ruth (actress; b. June 29, 1915, St. Joseph, MO). *Joyce Jordan* (1938–39, 1955).

Versatile performer who later became synonymous with the character of Phoebe Tyler, the matriarch on the soap world perennial *All My Children.* She began in college plays, then won a contest to publicize a new music center in Kansas City. A trip to New York led to a *Vox Pop* interview, some modeling and showcase productions for the American Theatre Wing. Small parts in NBC's *Great Plays* opened the gates to *Grand Central Station, Joyce Jordan* and *Myrt and Marge,* and led to the major role as Mrs. Charles Foster Kane in Orson Welles' *Citizen Kane.* A substantial film career resulted (*The Iron Major, Guest in the House, Song of the South*).

Warrick returned to radio as *Joyce Jordan, M.D.* in early 1955. She soon became part of the TV soap *As the World Turns,* and a daytime grand dame. Her autobiography, *The Confessions of Phoebe Tyler,* recalls a full life from St. Joe to Pine Valley.

Ruth Warrick (courtesy of Capital Cities/ABC)

894. WATERMAN, Willard (actor; b. Aug. 29, 1914, Madison, WI; d. Feb. 2, 1995, Burlingame, CA). *Girl Alone* (1936–39); *Easy Money* (1946); *Halls of Ivy* (1950–51); *The Great Gildersleeve* (1950–58).

Adept comic lead as the Great Gildersleeve, succeeding the role's originator Hal Peary. Pigeonholed as a Chicago soap opera player beginning in 1934, Waterman had running parts — often as doctors — in *Long Journey, Lonely Women, Road of Life* and *Woman in White.* Before turning to comedy, he played the main character, Mike Trent ("who opens the pages of the racket books") on *Easy Money.* When *Those Web-*

Willard Waterman (courtesy of Anna M. Waterman)

sters moved to Los Angeles in 1946, he (Dad Webster) went with it. Cast member of the shows of Alan Young and Cass Daley in 1949–50, this versatile performer achieved star status as Throckmorton P. Gildersleeve, a role he continued on television.

On film and stage, he played Mr. Babcock in *Auntie Mame/Mame* opposite Rosalind Russell, Angela Lansbury and Eve Arden. Among his screen credits were *Three Coins in the Fountain* and *The Apartment.* For TV he was Mr. Quigley on *Dennis the Menace.* His acting experience began in college theatre at the University of Wisconsin. A charter member of AFTRA, he served its national board and as president of three major locals.

895. WEBB, Jack (actor [catchphrase: "Just the facts, ma'am."]; b. April 2, 1920, Santa Monica, CA; d. Dec. 23, 1982, West Hollywood, CA). *Dragnet* (1949–57); *Pete Kelly's Blues* (1951).

When Webb died the Los Angeles Police Department ordered flags to be flown at half-staff. His highly realistic *Dragnet* was based on actual police files and produced in close collaboration with the Department. Its documentary-like style and Webb's clipped dialogue and no-nonsense approach in portraying Sgt. Joe Friday on the crime drama many awards, including several Emmys after it added a TV version in early 1952. Webb was proud of the fact that he did the show with a minimum of violence.

While working in a clothing store for four years in the late 1930s, he managed to perform on occasion on local Los Angeles radio broadcasts. As an Army Air Corps pilot, he wrote, directed and emceed USO shows. In 1945 he moved to San Francisco where he was hired by KGO to announce news coverage of the UN Charter conference and host a DJ jazz show. A precursor of Friday, *Pat Novak for Hire* ran for 26 weeks at ABC with Webb in the lead. Minor radio and movie parts in Los Angeles followed. On the set of *He Walks By Night,* technical advisor, LAPD Sgt. Marty Wynn, suggested a show based on case history police stories. In June 1949 *Dragnet* made its debut as a summer replacement on NBC. Liggett & Myers Tobacco Company remained the only sponsor for the seven years the program was on the air. Parlaying his show's success to start his own company, Webb produced numerous hard-hitting and realistic TV dramas, and starred in a Dragnet feature film in 1954.

896. WEBBER, Peggy (actress; b. c1925, Laredo, TX). *One Man's Family* (1946–47, 1949); *Dr. Paul* (1949); *Dragnet* (1949–57).

A lead and featured performer on some 8,000 shows, plus 300 TV programs and 21 films. She worked with dramatic actors Basil Rathbone (*Sherlock Holmes*), Vincent Price (*The Saint*) and Herbert Marshall (*The Man Called X*), and comedians William Bendix (*Life of Riley*), Jim Jordan (*Fibber McGee and Molly*) and Harold Lloyd (*Comedy Theatre*). She

created the role of Ma Friday on over 200 *Dragnet* shows, although she was younger than Jack Webb who played her son.

A child performer, Webber became known as the "Girl of 150 Voices" because she took numerous different roles in one single program. Beginning at age 12 at WOAI San Antonio, she acted, wrote and directed for half-hour shows. After graduating from high school, she sold the family car and bought railroad tickets to Los Angeles for herself and her mother. Network radio, however, was closed to outsiders. "There were about 100 working actors in the old days," she remembered, "and of them 75 worked and 30 worked all the time." It was two years before she broke through as a regular on *Dreft Star Playhouse.* One of her roles for that series was Ilsa in an adaptation of "Casablanca." In the mid-1940s she also organized her own stock company on radio, featuring Dan O'Herlihy and Marvin Miller.

897. WEBER, Karl (actor; b. March 17, 1916, Columbus Junction, IA; d. July 30, 1990, Boston, MA). *Story of Mary Marlin* (1937–45); *Don Winslow of the Navy* (1938–39); *Woman in White* (1939–42); *Cloak and Dagger* (1950).

Ongoing character in many soaps. Weber started in 1937 in Chicago. His portrayal of Dr. Kirk Harding on *Woman in White* and *Road of Life* brought him to New York and roles in *The Guiding Light, David Harum* and *Lora Lawton.* He both announced and acted for the anthology *Cloak and Dagger.*

On Broadway the tall Midwesterner played key parts in *Tea and Sympathy* and *The Best Man* and had featured roles on TV's *Perry Mason* and *Search for Tomorrow.* A graduate of the University of Iowa, he first acted with Shakespearean troupes. Later Weber helped to start New Stages, an Off-Broadway theatre. Weber was also one of the country's top voiceover announcers.

898. WEBSTER, Charles (actor; b. Nov. 19, 1901, England; d. Feb. 1965, Los Angeles, CA). *Roses and Drums* (1933–36); *Life Can Be Beautiful* (1940–54); *Light of the World* (1942–43, 1947); *Backstage Wife* (1945–59); *The Falcon* (1951–52).

Until pre-empted in the role of Abraham Lincoln by Raymond Massey, Webster had played the martyred President more than 300 times on radio, beginning in 1926. He appeared in Lincoln sketches on a variety of shows, ranging from *Believe It or Not* and *Roses and Drums* to those of Floyd Gibbons and Joe Cook. On Broadway he portrayed the 16th President in John Drinkwater's *Abraham Lincoln.*

By 1940 he had switched to soaps, often into parts as a stalwart physician on *Pretty Kitty Kelly, Linda Dale, Rosemary, Mary Marlin* and *Young Dr. Malone* (as Dr. Markham). On summer primetime, 1945–47, he co-starred with Julie Stevens on the light-veined *Abbott Mysteries* at Mutual. In the early 1950s he added Sarge Corbett, a *Falcon* character, to his credits.

Raised in Montreal, Webster worked as a telegraph operator before turning to acting.

899. WEEDE, Robert (singer; b. Feb. 22, 1905, Baltimore, MD; d. July 9, 1972, Walnut Creek, CA). *Great Moments in Music* (1942–46).

A discovery of S. L. (Roxy) Rothafel who brought him to the air and Radio City Music Hall. A leading baritone at the Met from 1937 to 1945 and at the San Francisco Opera for some 20 years, he appeared on *Manhattan Merry-Go-Round* and *For America We Sing*. He sang in the first performance of Menotti's radio opera *The Old Maid and the Thief* in 1939. When he left *Great Moments in Music* after a run of 4½ years, he didn't get any offers for a while because "everybody imagined I was 'on the air' even a year after it ended." In the 1950s he moved to Broadway as the star of the long-running musicals *The Most Happy Fella* and *Milk and Honey*.

As a boy he sang in church choirs and at WBAL. In 1927 Weede won a National Federation of Music Clubs singing contest, which led to vocal studies in Milan and recitals in all 48 states.

900. WEEMS, Ted (bandleader [signature song: "Out of the Night"]; b. Sept. 26, 1901, Pitcairn, PA; d. May 6, 1963, Tulsa, OK). *Fibber McGee and Molly* (1936–38); *Sunday Matinee* (1938); *Beat the Band* (1940–41).

Leadership of high school and college musical aggregations in Pennsylvania influenced Ted and brother Art Weems to organize their own All-American Band, for which they recruited the best collegiate musicians. They made a tour of the country playing at hotels in many large cities. Eventually the Weems band settled in New York for engagements at the Waldorf-Astoria and Pennsylvania Hotel, and appearances over the air from a number of stations. From 1931 to 1933 they regularly broadcast over the Lucky Strike Dance Orchestra series. *Beat the Band,* a musical quiz among his musicians, with questions sent in by listeners, featured his vocalists Perry Como and Marilyn Maxwell. When the war came, the band broke up, and Weems himself enlisted with the Merchant Marines in 1942.

The band waxed frequently for Victor. Their 1932 disc "Heartaches" with a whistling interlude by Elmo Tanner made little impression. Likewise, a 1937 version for Decca passed unnoticed. A decade later disc jockey Kurt Webster, the "Night Mayor" at WBT Charlotte, North Carolina, reached into a pile of old records and picked up the Weems disc. As he spun the record, the studio telephone rang with requests for replays and for information on where to buy the catchy disc. The craze for "Heartaches" spread until it swept the nation and made the No. 1 spot on *Your Hit Parade.* A re-issue sold over three million copies and revived the Weems orchestra in the waning days of the big bands.

Dwight Weist (courtesy of Weist-Barron School of Television Commercial Acting)

901. WEIST, Dwight (actor, announcer; b. Jan. 16, 1910, Palo Alto, CA; d. July 16, 1991, Block Island, NY). *March of Time* (1932–39); *Cavalcade of America* (1936–39); *We, the People* (1938, 1948–49); *Mr. District Attorney* (1939–40).

Known as "the man of 1,000 voices" for his impersonations on *March of Time* which re-enacted news events using actors to play the international newsmakers. Weist portrayed Hitler, Mussolini, Roosevelt and George Bernard Shaw, among many others. "My characters keep dying under me," he once complained. His ability to imitate a broad range of accents and ages made him a busy performer on dramas. He was the first to play the title role in *Mr. District Attorney.* He also was Police Commissioner Weston on *The Shadow.* As an announcer, he worked on *The Aldrich Family, Big Town* and *Andy Hardy.* He emceed *We, the People* and assisted Irene Beasley on the daily *Grand Slam* giveaway. His voice was heard on Pathe Newsreels in theatres and on many commercials.

While attending Ohio Wesleyan, Weist wrote for the local station, read his own lines now and then, and took a job as staff announcer. He acted at the Cleveland Playhouse before moving to New York. Weist co-founded the Weist-Barron School of Television and Commercial Acting, where he taught for 35 years.

902. WELK, Lawrence (bandleader [signature song: "Bubbles in the Wine"] [catchphrase: "Wunderful, wunderful."]; b. March 11, 1903, Strasburg,

ND; d. May 17, 1992, Santa Monica, CA). *Lawrence Welk Orchestra* (1949–56).

"Champagne music" maestro entertainer. His greatest success came after the decline in the big bands. Although thought well of across the country through radio, he built his largest following when he entered national television in 1955 with a weekly show. Welk's danceable mix of swing, country, polkas, waltzes and pop vocals remained visible and well received into the 1990s.

Raised in a German-speaking immigrant family, he learned to play an accordion, and from age 13 earned money at social gatherings. In 1920 he formed the three-piece Biggest Little Band in America to help inaugurate WNAX in Yankton, South Dakota. It grew into six pieces, adopted the name The Hotsy Totsy Boys, traveled the ballroom and dance hall circuit, and picked up radio remotes. At one brief point Welk also manufactured chewing gum and became his own sponsor. In the late 1940s he intermittently broadcast as the Roosevelt Grill Orchestra before beginning a long association with ABC. His effervescent sort of style took hold in southern California where frequent KLTA telecasts broadened his popularity. Welk gathered a stable of wholesome, clean-cut talent, including the Lennon Sisters, a youthful vocal quartet.

903. WELLES, Orson (actor; b. May 6, 1915, Kenosha, WI; d. Oct. 10, 1985, Los Angeles, CA). *The Shadow* (1937–38); *Mercury Theatre on the Air* (1938); *Campbell Playhouse* (1938–40).

Welles' career in Hollywood might never had taken the dimensions it assumed if it had not been for radio and, in particular, one singular broadcast. His phenomenal overnight acclaim resulted from a dramatization of H. G. Wells' "War of the Worlds" on his CBS Mercury Theatre, October 30, 1938. Welles' Halloween eve prank used realistic news bulletin techniques and field reporting and inventive sound effects in the well-crafted production. Many listeners panicked upon hearing "coverage" of the invasion by Martians in New Jersey. Their frantic calls tied up police switchboards around the country. A million or more terrified people believed it was the end of the world, and hundreds actually made preparations for that calamity.

Perhaps the most famous broadcast of all time, it made Welles a household name. He called it his version of "dressing up in a sheet and jumping out of a bush and saying 'boo.'" The FCC thought otherwise, and demanded an apology. Ever since, no broadcaster has been allowed to take such a cavalier approach of combining newsroom bulletins with dramatic entertainment. Actually Welles' radio play was a last-minute choice; the novel *Lorna Doone* had been adapted for his 60-minute series but was shelved for more thrilling fare. The Martian broadcast led to his screen colossus *Citizen Kane,* the first of a handful of innovative and often controversial films.

Orson Welles

Before Welles' assault on the airwaves, he had made an impression as an actor on Broadway in *Romeo and Juliet* with Katharine Cornell and as *The Shadow* on radio. His trailblazing *Mercury Theatre*—which had failed to pick up a radio sponsor until "War of the Worlds" made him a commercial property—paid him well when it became the Campbell Playhouse. The film maker-actor later hosted a variety show called *Orson Welles Almanac,* occasionally played leads on *This is My Best,* a dramatic anthology, and subbed for an ill Jack Benny in 1943. In the 1950s he re-created his role of Harry Lime from the movie *The Third Man,* on *The Adventures of the Third Man.*

On a special Pan American Day program in April 1942, Welles, while filming in Brazil, broadcast from Rio de Janeiro. He described Brazil and its people as seen through the eyes of an average American. The hookup promoted Roosevelt's Good Neighbor Policy.

904. WESTON, Paul (conductor; b. March 12, 1912, Springfield, MA). *Chesterfield Music Shop* (1944); *Chesterfield Supper Club* (1946–49); *Paul Weston Orchestra* (1951–52).

Sought-after arranger-conductor with high musical standards. Best remembered for his Chesterfield series, he broke into radio as musical director for *Johnny Mercer's Music Shop* in 1943. Earlier, he arranged for Rudy Vallee, Tommy Dorsey and Bob Crosby. Weston joined Capitol Records at its start and became A&R chief, and in the 1950s held a similar post for Columbia. In 1952 he married Jo Stafford for whom he had conducted on *Supper Club* segments from Hollywood.

Weston once explained his version of arranging. "You let some of the instruments carry the tune. You have others dancing around it — cutting up, clowning, crying a little, playing counter stuff . . . You write a little introduction of your own, an orchestral buildup before the vocalist takes off with that first note. It comes down to this. An arrangement for a band, say of 20 pieces, means writing almost 15 different versions of the same song."

As a composer, Weston did well with "Day by Day," "I Should Care" and "Shrimp Boats."

905. WEVER, Ned (actor; b. April 27, 1902, New York, NY; d. May 6, 1984, Laguna Hills, CA). *Dick Tracy* (1935–44); *Grand Central Station* (1937–38); *Young Widder Brown* (1938–56).

On many sponsored serials, Wever, a stage veteran, played heavies and detectives. He was best cast as Dick Tracy, the stentorian-voiced hero of comic strip readers. He also played *Bulldog Drummond* at Mutual; Dr. Loring, the emotionally-drained suitor of *Young Widder Brown,* and Peter Carver, industrialist-husband of *Lora Lawton.*

He had joined CBS in 1929 for leads in *True Detective* and *True Story.* A frequent radio leading man of Helen Hayes and Irene Rich, he had appeared on Broadway in *The Great Gatsby* and *Lady, Be Good.* As a Princeton student, he wrote songs and skits for Triangle Club shows. He went on to contribute tunes for the Broadway shows of Billy Rose and Ed Wynn. For television he had some 70 credits, ranging from *Bonanza* to *Get Smart.* His movie work included *Some Came Running* and *The Prize.*

906. WHITE, Francia (singer; b. Oct. 30, 1910, Greenville, TX; d. Oct. 22, 1984, Van Nuys, CA). *Palmolive Beauty Box Theatre* (1935); *Fred Astaire Show* (1936–37); *Telephone Hour* (1940–42).

Soprano star of the *Telephone Hour* at the beginning of this weekly series in 1940 (with James Melton). In the 1930s she appeared in grand opera, light opera and concerts with Los Angeles and San Francisco orchestras and opera companies. In 1938 she helped to launch the Los Angeles Civic Light Opera and became its leading lady. The petite brunette made a number of appearances on *Palmolive Beauty Box Theatre,* notably with Jan Peerce, John Barclay and James Melton. At 36 an arthritic condition brought an end to her short career.

907. WHITE, Joseph M. (singer [The Silver-Masked Tenor]; b. Oct. 14, 1891, New York, NY; d. Feb. 28, 1959, Bronx, NY). *Goodrich Silvertown Orchestra* (1923–27).

Soloist with a trailblazing commercial music series sponsored by B. F. Goodrich Rubber Company. His identity was carefully guarded once the publicity

value of keeping him a man of mystery was established. On national tours with the orchestra, White wore a sterling silver mask.

The mask was an accident. At WEAF he had just finished a program and was on his way home when a frantic director rushed out of another studio. The star of his show hadn't appeared. He grabbed White's arm and pushed him to the mike. "Sing, Joe, sing" was the only instruction. The producer apparently had neglected to tell the announcer, Phillips Carlin, Joe's name. Carlin came up with some fast thinking. A movie current then was *The Man in the Iron Mask.* The sponsor of the show was Silvertown tires. He put these two ideas together and in a split second created Joe's trademark. "The tenor you have just heard is a man of mystery. No one knows his name. He is the man in the Silver Mask." Such was the spontaneity of early radio.*

Prior to his series with Goodrich, White sang at WJZ Newark, and from there was the first singer to broadcast from the United States to England (July 4, 1922). In 1929 White signed an exclusive contract with NBC, and was heard periodically as a sustaining artist on its two New York stations. A walking encyclopedia of popular music, he was hired by the network to work in its music library. He also composed and recorded songs for Columbia and Victor, and taught his youngest son to sing. Boy-soprano Robert White began singing professionally on prime time with Fred Allen in the late '40s and developed into a leading Irish tenor of his generation.

908. WHITE, Lew (organist; b. c1895, Philadelphia, PA; d. March 4, 1955, New York, NY). *Lucky Strike Dance Orchestra* (1928–31); *Cook's Travelogue* (1934–39); *Betty Moore* (1936–39); *Break the Bank* (1950–51).

Premier organist in theatres and radio and on recordings. A graduate of the Philadelphia Conservatory of Music, he accompanied cellist Hans Kindler before turning to the pipe organ. White provided background music for films as well as mood music for *Grand Central Station, Mary Marlin* and *Inner Sanctum.* He served as musical director for the daytime version of *Break the Bank.* A number of his recordings, circa 1930, were made at the console of the Roxy Theatre organ.

909. WHITEMAN, Paul (conductor [Pops] [signature song: "Rhapsody in Blue"]; b. March 28, 1890, Denver, CO; d. Dec. 29, 1967, Doyestown,

*Ward Byron of the then-newly organized NBC staff at 195 Broadway believes White had dallied at a nearby bistro and missed his program. To fill air time between orchestral numbers, Carlin painted a word picture of musicians in silver garb playing silver instruments — all waiting for the arrival in a silver limousine of the mysterious singer in a silver mask. According to this account, the unidentified White did appear to sing before the show ended — as the Silver-Masked Tenor.

Paul Whiteman

PA). *Old Gold Hour* (1929–30); *Kraft Music Hall* (1933–35); *Woodbury Musical Varieties* (1936); *Chesterfield Presents* (1937–39); *Burns and Allen* (1941–42); *Philco Radio Hall of Fame* (1943–46); *Paul Whiteman Club* (1947–48).

Widely proclaimed as the Dean of Modern American Music. His Victor records, beginning with "Whispering" in 1920, enthralled youth of the emerging Jazz Age. A string of top-drawer nightclub and theatre engagements brought his crisp well-crafted arrangements to more and more people as did the million-plus sales of his discs. The commission of George Gershwin's "Rhapsody in Blue," first performed in 1924 at New York's Aeolian Hall before a distinguished audience of music connoisseurs, placed the classically-trained former symphony violist at the apex of show business and led to the birth of the big bands with their extensive cross-country tours, frequent radio remotes and prolific dance disc releases.

Constant travel ruled out a regular radio series until the end of the decade. Whiteman, however, worked on special broadcasts as early as February 12, 1922. That evening he played from WJZ Newark for his mother's birthday. The program was picked up by her at the Whiteman home in Denver. A year later Paul was persuaded to transmit jazz tunes to Japan. Nightly for two weeks, his band played from WOR. The final program brought an acknowledgement from a Tokyo fan saying that he had heard the music. In his book *Jazz,* Whiteman states that he was the first to perform "The Star-Spangled Banner" on radio. Whiteman's large aggregation also joined several all-star hookups

to promote the new Dodge Victory and Standard Six automobiles in 1928.

His full-hour *Old Gold* show for CBS in 1929–30 proved a trailblazer of outstanding orchestral selections, performed by the Rhythm Boys (with Bing Crosby's first radio solos) and the instrumental brilliance of Bix Beiderbecke, Frank Trumbauer, Lennie Hayton and Matty Malneck. When the 33-piece troupe headed west for its film debut, the sponsor hired a special railroad train. Network stations along the route picked up the weekly program. From then on, Whiteman viewed broadcasting as a necessary and ongoing part of his music making.

In mid-1932, in a response to writer Ring Lardner, he outlined his broadcast schedule: "We do a rythmic (sp) concert every Sunday night from 6:00 to 7:00 featuring the works of Grofe, Gershwin or some new modern composition by some new modern composer. . . .We also feature classical vocalists at these concerts such as Jimmy Melton, Gladys Rice, and in the future such artists as Virginia Rea — Olive Palmer to you — will be featured. Then I have my regular sponsored broadcasts (Allah be praised) each Friday night from 10:00 to 10:30 — Buick-Olds-Pontiac. The Rhythm Boys broadcast thrice weekly from 5:15 to 5:30, and then we are on the air every night from the Cascades at the Biltmore at any old time when the N.B.C. happens to run out of funds for more artists."

In 1933 he began *Kraft Music Hall;* in 1936 he segued into a similar variety show. When swing took hold, he revamped his bandstand, bringing in vocalists: Joan Edwards and The Modernaires, and Swingin' Strings. When he broke up his original band for "semi-retirement," he became musical director for the new ABC network. A bold innovator, he commissioned many serious works from contemporary composers for radio premieres. In 1947 he came up with the idea of a disc jockey on a nation-wide network. His daily sessions outshone all other turntable spinners. ABC's sales of the program to four sponsors was the biggest time sale in the history of radio — $5,900,000 a year for an hour a day on ABC's 228 stations. Of this, $4,000 a week went to Whiteman.

By the late 1940s the sartorially resplendent Pops had expanded into television, first with *TV Teen Club,* and then with a full-blown musical presentation for Goodyear. On the podium and off, the larger-than-life Whiteman never did anything in a small way, be it in the role of conductor, song plugger, impresario or sportsman.

910. WHITING, Margaret (singer; b. July 22, 1924, Detroit, MI). *Philip Morris Frolics* (1946); *Barry Wood Show* (1946–47); *Bob Hope Show* (1953–58).

Pop standard performer favored by mainstream composers. Daughter of songwriter Richard Whiting, she was musically guided by family friend and collaborator Johnny Mercer and sang on his broadcasts in 1941. She briefly appeared on Lucky Strike's *Hit Pa-*

rade from which she was fired for singing too slowly. Philip Morris, however, liked her tempo and style, which she claims was greatly influenced by jazz pianist Art Tatum.

In 1943 the Hollywood-raised artist became one of the first performers signed to the new Capitol label. She recorded "Moonlight in Vermont," "That Old Black Magic" and "My Ideal," and numerous perennials during a 17-year association. Few vocalists of the '40s had a greater choice of guest spots — with Fred Waring, Eddie Cantor and Mario Lanza, and on *Grand Ole Opry* (where with Jimmy Wakely she brought down the house with "Slippin' Around"). Whiting sang and took part in skits with Bob Hope in the 1950s.

911. WICKER, Ireene (actress; b. Nov. 24, 1900, Quincy, IL*; d. Nov. 17, 1987, West Palm Beach, FL). *The Singing Lady* (1931–38, 1940–41); *Song of the City* (1934–35); *Deadline Dramas* (1940–41).

At the beginning of her storytelling over radio Wicker wove in so much singing that her sponsor called the program *The Singing Lady.* Music stood as an important ingredient and made her fairy tales, nursery rhymes, folktales and historical biographies highly appealing. Trained as a dramatic actress, she virtually did all the voices of her characters, from little children to gruff old men, earning the sobriquet, "The Lady with a Thousand Voices." Adults, too, listened in to this entertaining and educational program.

Petite with one of the brightest smiles in radio and chummy ingratiating personality, Ireene made her debut over CBS Chicago in 1930, and played as many as 13 parts in a single series. Her soap opera roles on *Painted Dreams, Judy and Jane* and *Today's Children* prepared her well for children's shows, and in 1948 for *Singing Lady* telecasts that used marionettes to act out her stories while she supplied the voices. For much of its run, Kellogg cereals sponsored her late afternoon story times where frequent premium giveaways drew tons of mail from eager fans.

Her 1958 Peabody Award for lifetime achievement bore the inscription: "For the literate taste, the tender understanding, the wit, gaiety, and style which Miss Wicker brings to her program, *The Singing Lady.* A benign sorceress as well as an artist of consummate skill, Miss Wicker has been a steadfast foe of violence and brutality and a true friend to children everywhere." She also wrote children's books, made recordings and produced a weekly series *Ireene Wicker Musical Plays,* dramatizing opera and folk legends.

During the McCarthy era, she was blacklisted as a possible communist after she was falsely accused of backing a left-wing politician. The controversy caused ABC to drop her show; it later ran periodically on WNYC and PBS until 1975. The recipient of some 30 citations by Parent-Teacher Associations and edu-

Other sources give 1906.

Ireene Wicker

cational groups, she was awarded a medal by *Radio Stars* magazine for Distinguished Service to Radio.

During her first year at the University of Illinois, she met and married radio actor-writer Walter Wicker. Her second husband was art dealer Victor Hammer.

912. WIDMARK, Richard (actor; b. Dec. 26, 1914, Sunrise, MN). *Home of the Brave* (1941); *Helpmate* (1941–42); *Front Page Farrell* (1942–45).

Radio gave him his start in acting. He starred in many popular programs from 1938 to the late 1940s, including *Suspense, Cavalcade of America, March of Time* and *Gangbusters.* He was the original Albert of *Ethel and Albert* and played a reporter trying to track down petty racketeers on *Front Page Farrell,* a daily pulp magazine serial. Widmark expressed a special fondness for that period. "That was the best time of my life," he said in a 1977 *NY Times* interview. "It was a very nice living, and completely anonymous. I worked with some marvelous people — Joe Cotton, Arlene Francis, Agnes Morehead, Orson Welles, Art Carney. It took me the longest time to realize that Art Carney was funny, because we were always doing 'Gangbusters' together on Saturday night."

Widmark's movie work began with an Academy Award-nominated performance as the depraved gangster in the 1947 release, *Kiss of Death,* and he was type-cast as a villain or spoilsport for numerous cinema roles.

On television he starred in the Madigan series, and returned to radio in the late 1970s as host and occa-

Richard Widmark

sional star of *Sears Radio Theatre,* an adventure story series on CBS.

913. WILCOX, Harlow (announcer; b. March 12, 1900, Omaha, NE; d. Sept. 24, 1960, Hollywood, CA). *Fibber McGee and Molly* (1937–53); *Amos 'n' Andy* (1943–48); *Truth or Consequences* (1946–54).

Tagged as "Waxey" because of his integrated commercials about Johnson's Wax week after week into the storyline of Fibber McGee. His first radio appearance in 1929 came at the small Chicago station WGES. Two years later he was on staff at CBS, handling *Myrt and Marge* and *Pennzoil Parade.* NBC added him to its Chicago announcers for work with *Betty and Bob,* Phil Baker and Tony Wons. When McGee headed to Hollywood, he followed, playing a comic part opposite Fibber, straight man to Victor Borge and assistant emcee on The King's Men 1949 summer show.

In his teens, Wilcox studied voice and acted in and directed amateur theatricals. He sold electrical equipment, and after five years on the road became the company's sales manager. That experience taught him to put a product over to listeners. A top commercial spokesman, he had loyal clients who invariably renewed his contract for what formed long and mutually rewarding associations.

914. WILE, Frederic William (commentator; b. Nov. 30, 1873, La Porte, IN; d. April 7, 1941, Washington, DC). *The Political Situation in Washington* (1926–38).

One of the microphone's first political analysts. A foreign correspondent and an authority on German politics, he wrote columns, editorials and books, and served with the Army Intelligence Service. Post-World War I, Wile was head of the Washington bureau for *The Philadelphia Public Ledger,* founded his own news service and wrote a column entitled "Washington Observations."

He went to the microphone in the fall of 1923, at the invitation of WRC, to speak on "The Political Situation in Washington Tonight." It inaugurated a weekly 15-minute talk on national politics that NBC later picked up. At the inauguration of Coolidge, he spoke over the air on "The Presidency"—the only time on record that a private citizen had been privileged to stand at the podium and speak just prior to the address of the incoming President. At the time of the inaugural of President Hoover in March 1929, Wile joined CBS. For the first time, he was paid for his broadcasts. In 1930 he covered the London naval armaments limitation conference, broadcasting his biweekly summaries and introducing international leaders to audiences. Wile entitled his memoirs, *News Is Where You Find It.*

915. WILLIAMSON, Dudley (emcee; b. c1903, 32-Above Discovery, AK; d. May 2, 1948, Lido Beach, CA). *What's the Name of That Song?* (1944–48); *Queen for a Day* (1945).

Announcer, director, producer and actor at regional stations, including KOL Seattle, until he got the idea for his musical quiz in the early 1940s. The brisk, lighthearted song-guessing sessions caught on over Mutual with Knox Gelatin as sponsor. The stage show proceedings moved from a Sunday afternoon slot to prime time after a season, yet it soon struggled against the flood of post-war big money giveaways. When Dud Williamson died suddenly in 1948, it faded from the air the next season.

Born in the Klondike where his father was a gold prospector, Dud grew up in Seattle. He entered show business as a singer with a local theatre chain. In San Francisco he worked as an announcer and had a network comedy show for three years, then went to Chicago. Dud suggested the format for *Queen for a Day,* an audience-participation show for women contestants with special wishes. He emceed at its startup but relinquished host chores to Jack Bailey within a year.

916. WILLSON, Meredith (conductor, composer [signature song: "Thoughts While Strolling"]; b. May 18, 1902, Mason City, IA; d. June 15, 1984, Santa Monica, CA). *Ship of Joy* (1933–34); *Good News of 1938–41* (1937–41); *Maxwell House Coffee Time* (1941–42, 1945–48); *Meredith Willson/Music Room* (1948–49, 1951–53); *The Big Show* (1950–52).

A busy conductor on radio long before his brilliant success as the composer, librettist and lyricist of *The Music Man* in 1957. He left his small-town roots to

headed the music division of the Armed Forces Radio Service.

On one of radio's last all-star series, *The Big Show,* he also enjoyed a speaking role. He began his responses to the deep-voiced declamations of hostess Tallulah Bankhead with "Well, Sir, Miss Bankhead." He wrote the program's hymnlike closing "May the Good Lord Bless and Keep You."

917. WILSON, Don (announcer; b. Sept. 1, 1900, Lincoln, NE; d. April 25, 1982, Palm Springs, CA). *Jack Benny Program* (1933–55); *Good News of 1941* (1940–41); *Victor Borge Show Starring Benny Goodman* (1946–47).

The rotund announcer and lovable foil for Jack Benny. He regularly tried to get the commercial into the program and Benny would try to thwart him. At rehearsals, if a gag didn't tickle Don, Benny usually tossed it out. Originally a sportscaster for NBC, which built him up as "the fastest eye-to-microphone in existence," he joined Benny in New York in 1933. He was also commercial announcer for *Light Up Time, Baby Snooks* and *Starlight Concert.* His last engagement was in the nostalgic *Big Broadcast of 1944,* a touring show with another Benny character, singer Dennis Day.

After graduation from the University of Colorado, Wilson had entered radio in San Francisco, then moved to KFI Los Angeles where he became chief announcer. His fourth wife was actress Lois Corbet who specialized in mommy roles on *Baby Snooks, A Date With Judy* and *Corliss Archer.*

Don Wilson

study at the Institute of Musical Art (Juilliard). He toured with the Sousa band, played flute with the NY Philharmonic, under Toscanini, and conducted the Seattle Symphony. Becoming musical director at NBC Hollywood in 1932, he contributed to many programs. His 1941 song "You and I" received extensive radio play. In 1942 he joined the U.S. Army and

918. WILSON, Marie (actress; b. Dec. 30, 1917, Anaheim, CA; d. Nov. 23, 1972, Hollywood, CA). *My Friend Irma* (1947–54).

Archetypical good-looking dumb blonde. On that basis, Wilson signed a contract at Warner Brothers when age 15. But off screen she was actually "smart, witty and kindhearted." When comedian Ken Murray started his *Blackouts* in Hollywood in 1942, he hired her to do a satirical strip-tease act. The long-running revue led to guest appearances on radio, and an offer to play Irma at CBS. She reportedly turned down producer Cy Howard, saying he would not like the way she performed the character. He persisted, and she became one of the country's most popular radio come-

Marie Wilson, Ken Murray, Jack Oakie, Olivia de Havilland

diennes. The series moved to television, led to two Irma films and the nightclub circuit, where she usually did a version of the wide-eyed, spacey bosom friend.

919. WILSON, Ward (actor, announcer; b. May 22, 1903, Trenton, NJ; d. March 21, 1966, West Palm Beach, FL). *Royal Vagabonds* (1932); *Phil Baker Show* (1934–39); *Can You Top This?* (1945–54); *The Aldrich Family* (1946–51).

NBC field engineer with a flair as an impersonator. His switch to performing came about after several years of testing lines and mikes at rehearsals. He developed over 80 characters. His most famous was the off-stage heckling voice, "Bettle," who trailed Phil Baker in the 1930s. His character and comedy parts added to the mayhem of *Cuckoo Hour* and the shows of Burns and Allen, Fred Allen and Judy Canova. As an announcer, he handled the newscast intros of Raymond Gram Swing, Van Deventer and Winchell (whom he impersonated in "The Case of the Cornered Cat" on a 1947 broadcast of *The Big Story*). Wilson enjoyed a long run as moderator/emcee on *Can You Top This?*, and held the reins on a similar gagfest, *Stop Me If You've Heard This One,* and the quiz series, *Winner Take All.* At WHN he initiated *Gloom Dodgers* and *Itty Bitty Kitty Hour.*

This electrical engineer-turned-broadcaster once hosted *Tower Health Setting Up Exercises.* In the 1960s he worked as sports director for WEAT Radio-TV in West Palm Beach.

920. WINCHELL, Walter (news-gossip caster [catchphrase: "Good evening, Mr. & Mrs. America — and all the ships at sea."]; b. April 7, 1897, New York,

Walter Winchell (courtesy of Capital Cities/ABC)

NY; d. Feb. 20, 1972, Los Angeles, CA). *Lucky Strike Dance Hour* (1931–32); *Jergens Journal* (1932–48).

Daily columnist of the Broadway scene, he broadcast a weekly potpourri about personalities in show business and politics and "inside" bits and pieces about business, government and the underworld. His breathless, staccato delivery had a compelling allure for millions of Americans who tuned in Sunday evenings for 15 minutes of high-powered Winchellized items, gossip and innuendoes. Often thought lacking in taste, he cultivated friends in high places — not to overlook an army of press agents — who fed him submissions. Powerful and influential, the freewheeling Winchell could make or break a Broadway play, political candidate or stock offering.

He earned his first money as a street-corner newsboy, quit school in the sixth grade and sang in Gus Edwards' kid revue in vaudeville. In 1920, while part of a struggling song-and-dance act, he collected road show gossip for backstage bulletin boards and submitted items to the trade journals. New York tabloids picked up his copy, and the *Graphic* added him to staff. In 1929 he joined Hearst's *Mirror* at a hefty $500 a week. His "town gossip" coverage for Lucky Strike began at NBC in 1931, although he had already been "Peek's Blab Boy" on CBS programs for Saks & Co., Wise Shoes and La Geradine.

When ABC was spun off, he became one of its greatest single attractions. His ratings outpaced most of this network's weekend offerings, and he often reminded ABC that this was achieved in spite of lead-ins of "funereal music" and similar drab fare. In the late '50s he ended his 25-year melange of news via Mutual. Television versions of his brash hyperbole never caught the public fancy. The decline of Broadway diluted his columns, and they, too, faded in the mid-1960s. In 1946 Winchell established a cancer research fund as a memorial to his close friend and popular writer Damon Runyon. By 1970 it had collected and disbursed $32 million.

921. WINKLER, Betty (actress; b. April 19, 1914, Berwick, PA). *Grand Hotel* (1933–37); *Girl Alone* (1935–41); *Joyce Jordan, M.D.* (1944–47); *Rosemary* (1944–55).

Lead dramatic actress in many Chicago series. Beginning in 1933, Winkler was singled out for exceptional performances in *Girls Alone, Betty and Bob, Chicago Theatre of the Air* and *Don Winslow of the Navy.* In the early 1940s she settled in New York for *The O'Neills, Just Plain Bill* and the lead in *Joyce Jordan, M.D.* Versatile and adaptable, she played 80-year-old women as well as babies, and even meowed like a cat in "The Cat Wife" on *Inner Sanctum Mysteries* with Boris Karloff. She was a regular on P&G's *Knickerbocker Playhouse* and *Abie's Irish Rose.* She reportedly wore gloves to keep her fingers from sticking to the pages of her scripts.

A student at Western Reserve, Winkler appeared

at the Cleveland Playhouse prior to a WTAM audition for *Vivian Ware*. In retirement, she taught sensory awareness classes at The New School in Manhattan. Husband George Keane co-starred with her as Bill, a shell-shocked war veteran, on *Rosemary*.

922. WINNINGER, Charles (actor; b. May 26, 1884, Athens, WI; d. Jan. 19, 1969, Palm Springs, CA). *Show Boat* (1932–37).

Stage favorite in revues and musical comedy. His memorable portrayal of Cap'n Andy, jovial master of the Cotton Blossom, in *Show Boat* cast him in that role in two movie versions of the Jerome Kern classic, and radio's carryover of the riverboat saga. The beloved central character of the NBC series, he had begun his career as a drummer-singer with the Winninger Family Concert Company in the 1890s, then learned acrobatics to join a circus. He made it to Broadway in 1910 in *The Yankee Girl* and on to the *Ziegfeld Follies* in 1921.

His genial old gentleman parts were repeated on screen as the father of Deanna Durbin (*Three Smart Girls*) and Judy Garland (*Little Nellie Kelly*). His broad show business background came across in the short-lived *Uncle Charlie's Tent Show,* a NBC series built around his appeal as emcee.

923. WINTERS, Roland (actor; b. Nov. 22, 1904, Boston, MA; d. Oct. 22, 1989, Englewood, NJ). *Highways in Melody* (1944–45); *Just Plain Bill* (1945–46); *Milton Berle Show* (1947).

The one-time Ruppert Sports Reporter on *Football Scores* in the early 1940s, Winters moved on to actor and narrator on *Gaslight Gayeties, Lora Lawton* and *Backstage Wife*. He succeeded Sidney Toler as Chinese detective Charlie Chan on screen and appeared in *The Country Girl* on Broadway. He played Mr. Boone in the sitcom *Meet Millie* on TV. He served as president of New York's Players Club from 1978 to 1983.

A native of Boston, Winters started on New England's Colonial network and WAAB. In 1939 he switched to WJZ, beginning as a street-side interviewer. At one point his resonant, dramatic voice introduced John J. Anthony on *The Original Good Will Hour.*

924. WIRGES, William (conductor; b. June 26, 1894, Buffalo, NY; d. Sept. 28, 1971, Syosset, NY). *Club Valspar* (1931–32).

Starting at the mike in 1923, he led orchestras for *Arabesque, Colonial Minute Men* and *Club Valspar*. Wirges appeared as a piano soloist with the *Cliquot Club Eskimos,* as guest artist on *Goodrich Hour* and as instrumentalist with the *Gold Dust Twins*. He was active as musical director at Brunswick Records in the 1920s, making arrangements and directing accompaniments for Al Jolson, Belle Baker, Harry Richman, Frank Munn, Jessica Dragonette and John Charles

William Wirges

Thomas. The company's popular waltzes were waxed by his Regent Club Orchestra.

Wirges made his debut with theatre and hotel bands in Buffalo while teaching piano, theory and harmony. An early performer in television, he wrote "Dear Friends and Gentle Hearts," the jingle "Chiquita Banana" and many religious songs.

925. WISE, Dr. Jonah B. (preacher; b. Feb. 21, 1881, Cincinnati, OH; d. Feb. 1, 1959, New York, NY). *Message of Israel* (1935–59).

Pioneer in Jewish religious broadcasting. Dr. Wise founded the *Message of Israel* program and conducted it for nearly 25 years. It began on the Blue network as a Saturday evening presentation and moved to Sunday morning in 1948.

Dr. Wise was rabbi of the Central Synagogue, New York and a leader of Reform Judaism. He helped to found the United Jewish Appeal and served as chairman from 1939–58. President Franklin D. Roosevelt chose him as delegate to the International Refugee Conference in 1938. A graduate of Hebrew Union College and the University of Cincinnati, he long advocated interfaith relationships and cooperation.

926. WISEMAN, Scotty (singer; b. Nov. 8, 1909, Ingalls, NC; d. Jan. 31, 1981, Ingalls, NC). *National Barn Dance* (1934–38, 1941–46); *Boone County Jamboree* (1938–41).

Country music singer-banjoist. With his wife Myrtle Cooper, a singer and guitarist, the duo were known as Lulu Belle and Scotty, starting on *National Barn Dance*. They had met in Chicago on the program; their courtship and wedding was a high point of the Saturday night hoedown in the mid-1930s.

His first broadcast via WBT Charlotte was in 1927 when he did specialty songs with a high school glee club. Professional work as Skyland Scotty followed six years later after an audition at WLS. Wiseman composed some 70 songs, among them, "Have I Told You Lately That I Love You?" He held A.B. and Masters degrees in education; as an undergrad in 1932, he was named outstanding student at Fairmont (West Virginia) Teachers College.

927. WOLFE, Miriam (actress; b. Feb. 1, 1922, Brooklyn, NY). *Let's Pretend* (1934–54); *The Witch's Tale* (1934–38); *Studio One* (1947–48).

Specialist in character leads, dialects and trick voices. Even at the young age of 12, she played old crones, including Old Nancy in the prologue and epilogue of Mutual's *Witch's Tale* and Olive Oyl on *Popeye the Sailor*. Wolfe branched out into soaps (*Portia Faces Life*) and prime-time dramas (*Ford Theatre*). For WMCA's *Five Star Final,* she played the signature newsboy as well as varied character roles.

Her first experience in radio was in the Gimbel Bros. WGBS feature, *Uncle Gee Bee Kiddie Hour,* at age four. She appeared on the *Children's Hour* before joining *Let's Pretend* on a regular basis. In 1940 Wolfe began directing dramas on WNYC, then became an actress-writer-director-DJ at WKBW and WGR Buf-

falo, all for $50 a week. During World War II she directed overseas multilingual broadcasts for the OWI. In 1957 she originated a children's series (*Miss Switch*) at CBC Toronto where she appeared with its repertory company. She also made over 150 TV appearances, dubbed many films for UPA Studios, worked in Off-Broadway theatre and stock, and recorded more than 50 record albums for children. For 20 years, beginning in 1960, she lived in France before returning to Canada to work with the Young People's Theatre and Ontario Gifted Children's Program as a teacher and writer.

928. WONS, Tony (host [catchphrase: "Are yuh listenin'?"]; b. Dec. 25, 1891, Menasha, WI; d. July 1, 1965, Iron Mt., MI). *Tony Wons' Scrapbook* (1930–43); *Camel Quarter-Hour* (1931–32); *House by the Side of the Road* (1934–35).

His poetry readings, romantic dialogue and picturesque commentary gave clear proof that early radio offered a variety of subject matter. His diverse background — cow puncher, college student, soldier, factory worker — shaped his kindly, homespun philosophy. The thin, shy broadcaster collected writings of authors and also solicited poems from fans. Wons read them with a slow, full-toned and low-pitched voice. At one point he felt the pace of radio was asking too much of him. He left the air and spent a year in his backwoods barn-studio in Wisconsin, and according

Miriam Wolfe (courtesy of Miriam Wolfe)

Tony Wons (courtesy of Photofest)

to all accounts, making violins and furniture. He returned in October 1937 for a CBS morning show with organist Ann Leaf.

Wons started out at WLS with hopes of bringing Shakespeare to the air. The station gave him a series on the Bard; it ran for three years in the 1920s.

929. WOOD, Barry (singer; b. Feb. 20, 1909, New Haven, CT; d. July 19, 1970, Miami Beach, FL). *Lyn Murray's Musical Gazette* (1938); *Your Hit Parade* (1939–43); *Million Dollar Band/Palmolive Party* (1943–44).

Co-star of *Your Hit Parade,* baritone Barry Wood played saxophone and sang with Buddy Rogers and Vincent Lopez before concentrating on his voice. CBS provided an early sustaining platform until Lucky Strike signed him to replace Lanny Ross on *Your Hit Parade.* In 1950 he switched to producing and at NBC handled the *Kate Smith Show* and *Wide Wide World.* Wood also was director of special events before joining the Bell Telephone series as executive producer.

A brother of bandleader Barney Rapp, Wood was a top swimmer while pre med at Yale.

930. WOODS, Donald (actor; b. Dec. 2, 1906, Brandon, Manitoba, Canada). *Those We Love* (1938–45); *Woolworth Hour* (1955–57).

Studio contract player, beginning at Warner Brothers with *As the Earth Turns* in 1935. Cast in clean-cut, nice-guy roles for *Anthony Adverse, Watch on the Rhine* and *Night and Day,* he co-starred with Nan Grey in the 1938 film *Danger on the Air.* It led to a running part as Dr. Leslie Foster opposite Grey in the serial *Those We Love.* Woods appeared on *My Friend Irma* and narrated daily stories on *True Confessions.* He hosted the *Woolworth Hour,* a musical show starring Percy Faith. His TV credits included *Ironside* and *Bonanza,* and leads in GE, Philco and Lucky Strike anthologies.

A drama major at the University of California, Berkeley, Woods played with the Long Beach Stock Company and on Broadway. His network initiation came on *Roses and Drums* at CBS.

931. WOOLLCOTT, Alexander (commentator; b. Jan. 19, 1887, Phalanx, NJ; d. Jan. 23, 1943, New York, NY). *The Early Bookworm* (1930–31); *The Town Crier* (1930–37).

Woollcott added radio commentary to his accomplishments as author, lecturer and drama critic when the stock market crash upset his comfortable lifestyle, and he sought additional income. The erudite *Town Crier* attracted listeners with anecdotes and observations of the cultural scene, and particularly of his confreres of the witty and literary Algonquin Roundtable. He was described as the "most influential salesman of books in the United States." Among the titles he lifted to best-seller lists were James Hilton's *Lost Horizon* and his own *While Rome Burns.*

The comings and goings of the cantankerous, owlish-looking Woollcott inspired the wheelchair-ensconced central character of the classic comedy *The Man Who Came to Dinner*—"radio speaker, writer and friend of the great." An occasional actor, he impersonated himself in a road company of this play. In 1941 he journeyed to England where he broadcast as the Town Crier in a series of inspirational addresses on the resistance of the British people to Nazi aggression. Woollcott had seen service in World War I as a Medical Corps private and a reporter for *The Stars and Stripes.* He visited the front lines and came through some action, as he observed, "unperforated."

During a round-table discussion on Nazism in Germany on CBS's *People's Platform,* Woollcott passed a note to the moderator that he was feeling ill. Before he could leave the studio, he was fatally stricken with a heart attack. Listeners were only vaguely aware that anything out of the ordinary occurred—only that the usually verbose raconteur was participating less in the broadcast.

932. WOOLLEY, Monty (actor; b. Aug. 17, 1888, New York, NY; d. May 6, 1963, Saratoga Springs, NY). *Monte Woolley Program* (1943–44); *Drene Show* (1944–45); *The Magnificent Montague* (1950–51).

Until his casting as *The Man Who Came to Dinner* on Broadway in 1939, Woolley chiefly had taught English and coached dramatic productions at Yale, directed musical comedies and played a few small parts in films. His career-making role as the bombastic, self-centered house guest immobilized with a broken leg in a small Ohio town opened up a raft of movie opportunities, including the screen version as Sheridan Whiteside. The outspoken, erudite Woolley, whose smartly trimmed, snowy-white beard was a conversation piece as much as a trademark, exchanged comic barbs with Fred Allen, Joan Davis, Victor Borge and Charlie McCarthy. For one season he played a foil to Rudy Vallee. He starred on his own series in the early 1940s and 1950s, and portrayed himself in *Night and Day,* the film bio of Yale classmate Cole Porter.

933. WRAGGE, Betty (actress; b. Sept. 22, 1918, New York, NY). *Red Davis* (1933–35); *Pepper Young's Family* (1936–60).

Wragge crashed the audition for a new show called *Red Davis* and got the part of Betty, the daughter of Red (played by Burgess Meredith). When Proctor and Gamble assumed sponsorship from Beechnut gum, the soap opera became *Pepper Young's Family,* and Wragge stayed on for a total of 27 years and nearly 7,000 episodes.

Her radio work began at NBC in 1927 in a series called *Gold Spot Pals,* believed to be the first commercial series with child actors. Madge Tucker's children shows, including *Our Barn,* followed. Once established, she appeared on NBC's *Home Is What You Make*

Earl Wrightson

It and in the Broadway production of *Dead End*. When *Pepper Young* ended, she worked in industrial and training films, and TV commercials, dubbed Italian films into English, and toured in musicals.

Her brother, Eddie Wragge, also pursued a radio career, and appeared on *Show Boat, When a Girl Marries* and *Paul Whiteman's Varieties*.

934. WRIGHTSON, Earl (singer; b. Jan. 1, 1916, Baltimore, MD; d. March 7, 1993, East Norwich, NY). *Highways in Melody* (1945–46).

A leading baritone on 1940s musical series. A student of Met Opera singer Robert Weede while working as a Radio City page, he became a regular performer on *Getting the Most Out of Life* and *Highways in Melody*.

Television utilized his imposing stage presence on such vehicles as Paul Whiteman's *Goodyear Revue* and the Emmy Award-winning *American Musical Theatre*. He starred on tour and in summer stock in many popular musicals, and often performed show tunes in concert with Lois Hunt.

935. WYNN, Ed (comedian [The Perfect Fool] [catchphrase: "So-o-o-o."]; b. Nov. 9, 1886, Philadelphia, PA; d. June 19, 1966, Beverly Hills, CA). *Texaco Fire Chief* (1932–35); *Gulliver the Traveler* (1935–36); *Ed Wynn Program* (1944–45).

Giggling and befuddled, he joked, danced and sang for more than 60 years. Often dressed in outlandish clothes and hats, and carrying zany inventions, Wynn produced some of the biggest laughs in Broadway history. A *Ziegfeld Follies* star, he performed acts as the hardpressed King's Jester, with trick headpieces, and on a small piano mounted on a three-wheel pedal bike.

His unusually funny voice made him a distinctive comic in radio as early as 1922. In 1932 Wynn starred as The Texaco Fire Chief. During this period he introduced the technique of spoofing commercials, and would break in on Graham McNamee's praises of the value of Texaco gas for automobile driving. "I'll stick to my horse," Wynn might quib, "he doesn't have to be repainted every year."

With his sizable income, he invested in a proposed network, Amalgamated Broadcasting System. The only vestige of the project that never came to pass was WNEW. His name is honored in the last two letters of the New York station. Radio stardom ended by 1945 but renewed success came on Broadway and in the 1950s as a dramatic actor in films and television, occasionally with his son Keenan Wynn.

936. YARBOROUGH, Barton (actor; b. 1900, Goldthwaite, TX; d. Dec. 19, 1951, Hollywood, CA). *One Man's Family* (1932–51); *I Love a Mystery* (1939–44, 1948); *Dragnet* (1949–51).

Sure-fire actor in key co-starring or supporting roles. Yarborough portrayed well-scripted characters: Clifford (*One Man's Family*), Doc Long (*I Love a Mystery*) and Sgt. Ben Romero (*Dragnet*). He also played Rusty on the soap, *Today's Children*. When *Dragnet*

Barton Yarborough (courtesy of Steve Jelf)

added a video version, he continued his Los Angeles police officer role. In 1951 he became Gabby Calhoun on *The Halls of Ivy,* his last featured part. That December he died at age 51. *Dragnet* carried the news of his death into the regular story line of the script.

Educated at the Universities of Texas and California, Yarborough acted in Eva Le Gallienne's rep company. His 1942 Universal film, *Ghost of Frankenstein,* became a cult classic.

937. YORK, Dick (actor; b. Sept. 4, 1928, Fort Wayne, IN; d. Feb. 20, 1992, Grand Rapids, MI). *Jack Armstrong* (1946–50).

Chicago radio provided opportunities for York's acting career as a child. His best juvenile role was on Jack Armstrong, "the All-American Boy," as Billy Fairfield. He also played the lead on *That Brewster Boy.* Moving to New York, the networks provided mature roles on soaps and a part on *Michael Shayne, Private Eye.* Then came *Tea and Sympathy* on Broadway, *Inherit the Wind* and several other films, and the television series *Bewitched.* He played the befuddled husband of Samantha, a witch with supernatural powers. Beginning in 1964 for five years, it remained in the top ten. A painful physical condition resulting from an old back injury brought about York's complete retirement by the early 1980s. His last years were spent raising funds for the homeless, working by telephone from his sickbed.

938. YOUNG, Alan (comedian [catchphrase: "Oooh, I could give you such a pinch."]; b. Nov. 19, 1919, North Shields, Northumberland, England).

Alan Young (courtesy of Capital Cities/ABC)

Alan Young Show (1944–47, 1949); *Tony Martin Show* (1947–48); *Jimmy Durante Show* (1948–49).

A star of Canada's CBC out of Toronto, he was brought to New York by NBC. Bristol-Myers signed him as Eddie Cantor's summer replacement in 1944. That October he had a situation-gag comedy show at ABC. He often had to wrestle with bad scripts but his character — a shy, naive, blundering boy — overcame some weak writing. Young appeared as comedian with Tony Martin and Jimmy Durante in the late '40s, then returned for a short run with his own show just before moving it into television. The personable sitcom pioneer won a Best Actor Emmy during his first season. Young also had film roles during his radio days (*Margie, Mr. Belvedere Goes to College*).

A teenage monologist and stand-up comic over CJOR in his hometown of Vancouver, he specialized in dialect bits. His TV role opposite a talking horse, *Mr. Ed,* in the 1960s proved to be his most widely seen and best-remembered work; the series played in syndication around the world. During a break in his career he settled briefly in Boston where he helped to organize a broadcasting division for the Christian Science Church.

939. YOUNG, John S. (announcer; b. Aug. 3, 1903, Springfield, MA; d. Jan. 12, 1976, New York, NY).

A would-be actor and playwright — he studied under George Pierce Baker at Yale where Rudy Vallee was a classmate — Young tried announcing at WBZ Boston. He found his calling on the 50-yard line in New Haven with a mike in one hand and the football line-up in the other. He came to NBC in New York, specializing in foreign news until 1936. That year he joined CBS.

In 1937 Young became director of radio for the emerging New York World's Fair, and also played a part in bringing about early television transmission from the fairgrounds.

940. YOUNG, Robert (actor; b. Feb. 22, 1907, Chicago, IL). *Good News of 1938/1939* (1938–39); *Maxwell House Coffee Time* (1944–45); *Father Knows Best* (1949–54).

Many-sided actor whose radio work ran parallel with his motion picture work. A talent scout lined up a contract at MGM in 1931 after Young had studied and acted at night for four years at the Pasadena Playhouse. By 1935 he had appeared in serious roles in 24 films. Then, with *Vagabond Lady,* came the first of his charming comedy parts.

His broadcast bow was on *Kraft Music Hall* in 1936. After several guest appearances on *Good News of 1938,* he became the show's emcee. He recreated his movie role in *Western Union* on the *Kate Smith Hour* and introduced *One Man's Family* on President Roosevelt's 1940 Birthday Ball broadcast. In 1944 he joined Frank Morgan's comedy series as emcee and

Robert Young

straight man. His well-honed historical portrayals on *Cavalcade of America* ranged from George Pullman and Peter Cooper to George Rogers Clark and Abraham Lincoln.

Young's definitive role was as Jim Anderson in the family comedy, *Father Knows Best,* first aired in 1949. The story of an average household in suburban America, the series was called by *Variety,* a "honey of a package" with "hilarious situations and unforced punchy lines." The program moved easily into television in the mid-50s. By then, the affable actor devoted his career to the weekly adventures of the Andersons. A dozen years later he placed the medical profession in the best light as Dr. Welby in the long-running episodes of that genial family physician.

Shortly after *Father Knows Best* came to radio, Young launched the Good Driver Club movement into the scripts. A safe driving campaign among teenage drivers, it distributed several million safe-driving "agreements" among young people and their parents. Young's father had been killed a decade or so earlier in an accident involving two teenage drivers. So when approached by the Inter-Industry Highway Safety Committee, he readily agreed to discuss auto safety on his program and speak before groups of teenagers and civic and safety organizations. In 1950 he was honored as a "Father of the Year" by the National Father's Day Committee.

941. YOUNG, Victor (conductor, composer; b. Aug. 8, 1900, Chicago, IL; d. Nov. 11, 1956, Palm Springs, CA). *Shell Chateau* (1935–36); *Old Gold Don Ameche Show* (1940).

One of the best known and most assiduous conductors on the air and on recordings in the early 1930s. A child prodigy on the violin, Young studied abroad. While in Russia during the Bolshevist revolution he faced a death sentence because the government insisted he was a citizen and subject to Army duty. He escaped to Germany, only to be taken as a prisoner of war. In 1919 he returned to America and work on the Orpheum circuit. Young soon gave it up to become concertmaster in theatres and arranger for Ted Fio Rito and others. In 1929 he was in charge of the *Atwater Kent Hour* and later directed the Studebaker Champions. He conducted for James Melton, the Mills Brothers, Bing Crosby and Tony Martin. As musical director for Brunswick records, Young turned out the first Broadway musical cast album, *Show Boat,* and dozens of finely arranged singles of such tunes as "My Moonlight Madonna" and "Goodnight Sweetheart." He was also associated with over 300 motion pictures, chiefly at Paramount. His own compositions ranged from "Sweet Sue" and "Ghost of a Chance" to film scores to *Samson and Delilah* and *Around the World in 80 Days.*

Select Bibliography

Amory, Cleveland (ed. in chief). *International Celebrity Register,* New York: Celebrity Register Ltd., 1959.

Anderson, Arthur. *Let's Pretend: A History of Radio's Best Loved Children's Show by a Longtime Cast Member.* Jefferson, NC: McFarland & Co., 1994.

Brooks, Tim. *The Complete Directory to Prime Time TV Stars, 1946–Present.* New York: Ballantine Books, 1987.

Buxton, Frank, and Bill Owen. *The Big Broadcast: 1920–1950.* New York: Viking Press, 1972.

Cackett, Alan. *The Harmony Illustrated Encyclopedia of Country Music.* New York: Crown Trade Paperbacks, 1994.

DeLong, Thomas A. *The Mighty Music Box: The Golden Age of Musical Radio.* Los Angeles: Amber Crest Books, 1980.

—— *Quiz Craze: America's Infatuation with Game Shows.* New York: Praeger, 1991.

—— *POPS: Paul Whiteman, King of Jazz.* Piscataway, NJ: New Century, 1983.

Dunning, John. *Tune in Yesterday: The Ultimate Encyclopedia of Old-Time Radio, 1927–1976.* Englewood Cliffs, NJ: Prentice-Hall, 1976.

Grunwald, Edgar A. (ed.). *Variety Radio Directory: 1940–1941.* New York: Variety, Inc., 1940.

Harmon, Jim. *Radio Mystery and Adventure and Its Appearances in Film, Television and Other Media.* Jefferson, NC: McFarland & Co., 1992.

Higby, Mary Jane. *Tune in Tomorrow.* New York: Cowles, 1968.

Jackson, Paul. *Saturday Afternoons at the Old Met: The Metropolitan Opera Broadcasts, 1931–1950.* Portland, OR: Amadeus Press, 1992.

Kinkle, Roger D. *The Complete Encyclopedia of Popular Music and Jazz, 1900–1950,* Volumes 1–4. New Rochelle, NY: Arlington House, 1974.

LaGuardia, Robert. *From Ma Perkins to Mary Hartman: The Illustrated History of Soap Operas.* New York: Ballantine Books, 1977.

Lamparski, Richard. *Whatever Became of . . .* First, Second, Third, Fourth, Fifth, Sixth, Seventh, Eighth, Ninth, Tenth, Eleventh Series. New York: Crown, 1967, 1968, 1970, 1973, 1974, 1976, 1977, 1982, 1985, 1986, 1989.

Poindexter, Ray. *Golden Throats & Silver Tongues: The Radio Announcers.* Conway, AR: River Road Press, 1978.

Simon, George T. *The Big Bands,* New York: Macmillan, 1967.

Slide, Anthony. *Great Radio Personalities in Historic Photographs.* New York: Dover, 1982.

Stedman, Raymond William. *The Serials: Suspense and Drama By Installment.* Norman: University of Oklahoma Press, 1971.

Steiner, Rodney and Thomas A. DeLong. *Frank Munn: A Biodiscography of the Golden Voice of Radio.* Southport, CT: Sasco Associates, 1993.

Summers, Harrison B. (ed.). *A Thirty-Year History of Programs Carried on National Radio Networks in the United States, 1926–1956.* New York: Arno Press and The New York Times, 1971.

Swartz, Jon D. and Robert C. Reinehr. *Handbook of Old-Time Radio: A Comprehensive Guide to Golden Age Radio Listening and Collecting.* Metuchen, NJ: Scarecrow Press, 1993.

Walker, Leo. *The Big Band Almanac.* Pasadena, CA: Ward Ritchie Press, 1978.

Wertheim, Arthur Frank. *Radio Comedy.* New York: Oxford University Press, 1979.

Who's Who in Radio: A Quarterly Review of American Broadcasting Personalities. New York: Radio Publications, July 1935.

Periodicals

Bridgeport (CT) Post   *New York Post*   *Radio-TV Mirror*
Collier's   *New York Times*   SPERDVAC *Radiogram*
Current Biography   *New York World-Telegram*   *Sponsor*
Etude   *The New Yorker*   *Tune-In*
Los Angeles Times   *Radio Guide*   *Variety*
New York Daily News   *Radio Life*   *Wireless Age*
New York Herald-Tribune   *Radio Stars*

Index